International Debt
and the
Developing Countries

A World Bank Symposium

International Debt
and the
Developing Countries

edited by
Gordon W. Smith
John T. Cuddington

The World Bank
Washington, D.C., U.S.A.

Manufactured in the United States of America
First printing March 1985

Library of Congress Cataloging in Publication Data
Main entry under title:

International debt and the developing countries.

(A World Bank symposium)
Bibliography: p.
1. Debts, External—Developing countries—Addresses, essays, lectures. I. Smith, Gordon Whitford, 1934– . II. Cuddington, John T. III. Series.
HJ8899.I575 1985 332.1'5 84-29946
ISBN 0-8213-0457-7

Contents

Contributors

The affiliations shown are those at the time of the seminar, April 18–20, 1984.

Richard N. Cooper
The Center for International Affairs
Harvard University

John T. Cuddington
Department of Economics
Stanford University

Rudiger Dornbusch
Department of Economics
Massachusetts Institute of Technology

Richard Eckaus
Department of Economics
Massachusetts Institute of Technology

Gershon Feder
Agriculture and Rural Development Department
The World Bank

Mark Gersovitz
Woodrow Wilson School of Public and International Affairs
Princeton University

Jack M. Guttentag
Department of Finance
The Wharton School
University of Pennsylvania

Vassilis Hajivassiliou
Department of Economics
Massachusetts Institute of Technology

Arnold Harberger
Department of Economics
University of Chicago

Richard J. Herring
Department of Finance
The Wharton School
University of Pennsylvania

Anne O. Krueger
Economics and Research Staff
The World Bank

Paul R. Krugman
Sloan School of Management and Department of Economics
Massachusetts Institute of Technology

Daniel McFadden
Department of Economics
Massachusetts Institute of Technology

Stephen O'Connell
Department of Economics
University of Pennsylvania

Yung Chul Park
The Institute of Economic Development
Korea University

Jeffrey Sachs
Department of Economics
Harvard University

Mario H. Simonsen
Graduate School of Economics
Fundação Getulio Vargas
Rio de Janeiro, Brazil

Gordon W. Smith
Department of Economics
Rice University

Leopoldo Solís
Bank of Mexico

Alexander Swoboda
Graduate Institute of International Studies
Geneva, Switzerland

D. J. Wood
Financial Policy, Planning, and Budgeting
The World Bank

Ernesto Zedillo
Bank of Mexico

Preface

The papers published in this volume were presented and discussed at the World Bank on April 18–20, 1984. This symposium was part of a continuing program to have Bank research staff interact with other researchers to consider the latest thinking and most recent research results on topics relevant to the economic prospects of developing countries. With the emergence of debt as an issue of major importance for developing countries, it seemed natural that Bank staff should assemble a conference of many who are active in research on this topic.

The contribution the symposium made to understanding of debt in its relationship to trade, macroeconomic policy, and development is only partly reflected in these papers. Many people whose names did not appear on the program made significant contributions from the floor. Were it possible, we would like to mention each one of them. Space and information constraints limit us to naming here only the participants who took on the formal responsibility of chairperson or discussant. They were Robert Aliber, Jean Baneth, Bela Balassa, Frederick Berger, Jayati Datta-Mitra, Barend de Vries, Chandra Hardy, Robert Heller, John Holsen, Basil Kavalsky, Homi Kharas, Guy Pfeffermann, and Marcelo Selowsky.

The symposium was planned by J. Michael Finger, Nicholas Hope, and Gordon W. Smith, organized by Finger and Smith, and skillfully managed by Paula E. Holmes. John T. Cuddington of the Economics and Research Staff and members of the Bank's Publications Department kept us on a tight publication schedule. The end result—the joint product of the authors, the discussants, the planners, and the managers—is, we believe, an unusually good collection of essays made available in an unusually short time. We are confident that discussion of the debt issue has been significantly advanced by their efforts.

Anne O. Krueger
Vice President
Economics and Research Staff
The World Bank

December 1984

Overview

International Borrowing and Lending: What Have We Learned from Theory and Experience?

John T. Cuddington and Gordon W. Smith

During the decade ending in 1983, developing countries' outstanding international debt increased fivefold to $810 billion.[1] In some ways this massive flow of capital represents a remarkable success, unimaginable only twenty years ago. Equally unexpected was the prime role played by commercial banks in the whole process. The World Debt Tables (World Bank 1984) indicate that fully two-thirds of net flows from all private and official sources were intermediated by the international banking system.

Events of the last three years, however, have raised serious questions about the mechanisms that evolved in the 1970s for transferring resources. More than eighty reschedulings in the 1975–83 period, numerous arrears, moratoriums, and a rising number of nonperforming loans demonstrate the inability of many countries to service their debts according to the terms originally contracted. Restoring creditworthiness following repayment difficulties has usually implied a period of rather severe economic austerity in the borrowing country. In some cases, the political and social costs, as well as the economic costs, of such austerity measures have been high.

In the wake of the recent crises, the prospects are dim for the immediate resumption of net resource transfers from rich to poor countries through traditional means. Indeed, for some countries negative resource flows over the next few years are a distinct possibility. A severe reduction in net capital inflows, let alone the imposition of a net capital outflow over an extended period, could have profound consequences for the economic development prospects of debtor countries.

In light of recent debt-servicing difficulties and the importance of international capital flows in the economic development process, several broad questions must be addressed:

- What are the potential benefits of international capital flows? How much should countries borrow and in what form? How can policymakers ensure that the potential benefits of international capital flows are realized?
- How can we explain the dominant role of the international banking system as a conduit for capital flows in the past decade? Would alternative mechanisms be mutually beneficial for debtors and creditors? If so, why have they not emerged?
- To what extent have banking practices led to excessive loan exposure in developing countries? What role did existing banking regulation or the lack of appropriate regulation play in these developments?
- Is it possible to estimate econometrically the precursors of debt repayment problems? Can an "early warning system" be devised to forecast such problems in time to take preventive policy action?
- To what extent have ineffective macroeconomic policies in either debtor or creditor countries contributed to debt-servicing problems? What are the interactions between macroeconomic management—including interest rate, exchange rate, and budget policies—and external debt?
- Given the present accumulation of debt, what institutional and policy changes in the financial markets and in developing countries would permit the latter efficient

adjustment and restoration of growth, while at the same time reduce the likelihood that the present problems will recur?

In an effort to shed light on these and other related issues, the Economic Research Staff of the World Bank held a conference entitled "International Debt and the Developing Countries" in April 1984. A number of experts were brought together to discuss relevant theoretical and empirical economic research. One important objective of the conference was to determine what insights recent research on various aspects of international borrowing and lending can contribute to our understanding of the current debt-servicing problems. A second objective was to distill valuable lessons for economic management from empirical and case studies of individual debtor countries. It is hoped that the present collection of papers will help policymakers deal with the current debt problems and will indicate important directions for future research.

We have organized the conference papers into four sections. In the first, microeconomic theories of international borrowing and lending are developed and applied to the current situation. Sovereign risk—the possibility that governments will elect either not to adhere to their past commitments with foreign creditors or to change domestic policies or laws in a way that severely reduces the real value of foreign loans to creditors—is an important feature in these analyses. Part II deals in greater depth with bank behavior, the structure of financial markets, and recent suggestions for structural reform of these markets. Part III contains an econometric analysis of the precursors of debt repayment problems and asks whether they can be predicted in advance with the use of available macroeconomic information. A number of developing countries are studied in Part IV to determine how and why they experienced debt-servicing problems in 1982–84. The roles of domestic macroeconomic policies as well as of external shocks are carefully considered.

THEORETICAL ANALYSES OF SOVEREIGN BORROWING

Determining the optimal amount of external borrowing is a difficult task, as the recent experience of debtor countries makes clear. Chapter 1 by Richard N. Cooper and Jeffrey D. Sachs begins by discussing optimal borrowing from the point of view of a central planner charged with maximizing national welfare by choosing appropriate levels of consumption and investment each period. The optimal amount of external borrowing is then determined residually as the capital inflow which, when added to domestic saving, enables the optimal level of investment to be undertaken. Using this model, which ignores monetary or macroeconomic considerations, the well-known conclusion emerges that capital investment should be undertaken as long as the marginal return on investment exceeds the marginal cost of funds in world capital markets. Furthermore, borrowing should be used to partially shield consumption from temporary adverse shocks to national income caused by commodity price movements, crop failures, worldwide recessions, and the like. In cases where the change in income is perceived to be permanent, however, much less reliance on world capital markets is justified.

In practice, of course, a country's external borrowing may not be the result of optimizing decisions by a central authority. Instead it may reflect the behavior of an amorphous group of households, firms, banks, and government agencies. Under certain idealized assumptions enumerated by Cooper and Sachs, optimal levels of saving, investment, and external borrowing can be attained in a free-market system where interest rates adjust to equate the worldwide supply of and demand for loanable funds. They go on to stress the difficulties in achieving the optimal amount of borrowing by adopting a laissez-faire attitude toward capital inflows and outflows. In decentralized economies, for example, price distortions caused by inappropriate domestic policies (such as those leading to exchange rate overvaluation) can easily result in overborrowing or underborrowing in the absence of direct government intervention in credit allocation and external borrowing. Narrower concerns of policymakers (prompted by special interest groups or political corruption, for example) may also cause the extent and character of borrowing to be suboptimal with regard to national welfare. In sum, treating the country as a single rational actor, as many of the theoretical analyses do, is useful for describing how much external borrowing ought to be undertaken in order to maximize national welfare. Explaining actual levels of borrowing, however, requires analyses of the interaction between government behavior and that of its constituents, as the case studies by Arnold Harberger and Leopoldo Solís and Ernesto Zedillo in Part IV illustrate.

In the absence of any uncertainty (concerning future income or interest rates, for example), the traditional model of international borrowing indicates that the only limit on a country's access to international capital markets is given by the present value of its future income. As long as this present value, which is the economic definition of national wealth, exceeds a country's external indebtedness, the country is solvent. Cooper and Sachs note several qualifications. First, one could argue that a subsistence level of consumption should be subtracted from national income before making the above-mentioned present-value calculation. Second, it could be argued that only the present value of tradables output, rather than total national income (minus subsistence consumption), is relevant because external debt must ultimately be serviced by selling tradables in the world market.

Cooper and Sachs, as well as some of the other authors, note that although the traditional model of borrowing and lending based on the economist's "competitive market" paradigm yields important insights, it is inadequate for describing the behavior in either domestic or international credit markets.[2] Mark Gersovitz (chapter 2) points out: "For many markets, it is sensible to analyze the behavior of demanders and suppliers separately. The two groups interact only through the single variable of price. But in credit markets, where the debtors' adherence to contracts is in question, the creditor must be concerned with the many attributes of the debtor in order to understand if and when a breakdown [in the loan contract] will occur."

The papers in Part I point out that, in most cases, it is unrealistic to view current debt crises as situations in which a debtor country's foreign loans have become so burdensome that they exceed the total value of the economy's future stream of national output. Gersovitz stresses that the country's willingness to pay, not its ability to pay, is the key consideration when sovereign risks are involved.

Willingness to pay is particularly important in the context of international loans to sovereign governments, because there is no supranational legal system governing international loans. Foreign debtors therefore have the option, albeit a costly one, of repudiating their debt obligations if they become too onerous. In the context of domestic loans, in contrast, there are well-defined rules that give creditors title to the residual assets of a corporation that defaults on its debt.

Recognizing the existence of repudiation risk is central to an understanding of the functioning of the international credit market. The amount of capital that creditors are willing to supply is affected by the perceived risk of debtor repudiation. Furthermore, during repayment crises in the international credit markets, the negotiating position of heavily indebted countries is influenced by their option to repudiate. This undoubtedly affects the terms under which rescheduling occurs.

An important implication of the analysis of sovereign risk is that, even in normal times (as opposed to times of debt crisis), countries may face credit rationing. That is, lenders may set a credit limit as well as the interest rate for the borrowing country in order to reduce the probability that the borrower will face repayment difficulties and elect to default. Even in instances where lenders do not impose a credit limit, they may charge higher interest rates as the amount of borrowing rises, if they believe that the probability of repayment problems increases with the amount borrowed.

From the borrower's standpoint, the existence of an upward-sloping supply schedule of external funds (which may become vertical after some point because of a credit ceiling) means that the shadow value of external funds for the country as a whole may be considerably higher than the interest rate charged to individual borrowers. To avoid a misallocation of foreign capital inflows and the possibility of overborrowing, it is optimal for the government to impose a tax on external borrowing to remove this discrepancy between private and social costs.

The theoretical analyses of repudiation risk assume that creditors set country credit limits and the level, not the spread, of the borrowing rate of interest. The gradual shift toward floating rate loans by both commercial banks and official lending institutions such as the World Bank has not yet been studied in the theoretical literature. Yet this institutional development would seem to have important implications for an efficient and equitable sharing of interest rate risk between borrowers and lenders. Furthermore, the degree of interest variability in loan contracts where the lending rate is a markup over the London interbank offered rate (LIBOR) has an important effect on the probability that the borrower will experience repayment difficulties. In fact, the unprecedented and unanticipated rise in interest rates has undoubtedly been an important cause of the recent rash of reschedulings.

A second implication of analyses incorporating sovereign risk is that debtor countries may be able to change macroeconomic policies, investment and development strategies, and so on, in a way that will improve their creditworthiness and thereby increase their access to foreign capital. The magnitude of the latter effect will, of course, depend to a considerable extent on whether the debtor can credibly promise to maintain a preannounced policy stance after foreign capital has been obtained. The adoption of an International Monetary Fund (IMF) stabilization program is potentially important in this regard. Apart from these reassurances, lenders must rely on the threat of severely reduced access to international capital markets and normal trade credit to prevent debtors from defaulting.

In discussions of developing-country debt, the analytical distinction between insolvency and illiquidity, which is well known from the corporate finance literature, is often employed. The presence of repudiation risk, however, suggests that the insolvency-illiquidity distinction must be extended in order to understand the international debt crisis. All four chapters in Part I elaborate on this point. As mentioned above, they tend to dismiss the likelihood that debtor countries—with the possible exception of some sub-Saharan African countries—are insolvent. Cooper and Sachs (chapter 1), for example, maintain: "Debt crises almost never involve the strict solvency constraint in foreign borrowing. Well before consumption levels are driven to subsistence, countries typically repudiate their foreign debt or succeed in gaining debt relief. Often a debt crisis has little to do with fundamental solvency considerations but, rather, turns on the short-run difficulties of debt servicing."

Paul Krugman (chapter 3) goes further by claiming that in an uncertain world where future income, export earnings, interest rates, and the costs incurred by a country that repudiates its debt are unknown, it is difficult to determine whether a country is insolvent or not. Whether a country is solvent depends to a considerable extent on the future state of the world economy and on the macroeconomic policy stance adopted by the country itself, as well as on the policies of other countries. In short, Krugman maintains that the solvency-insolvency distinction is impossible to operationalize when deciding how to respond to specific debt crises. From the point of view of debtor countries, this analysis implies that maintaining sound macroeconomic policies and good management of public investment projects is important, not only in and of itself, but also because it will relax the credit-rationing constraint imposed by creditors.

Krugman also notes the rather unsatisfactory nature of the diagnosis that a country is "only illiquid, not insolvent." If this were the case, it is unclear why individual banks or groups of banks would not voluntarily provide the necessary bridge loans needed to tide the country over until normal debt servicing could resume. In fact, they frequently do so, but sometimes only after protracted negotiations. One possible reason that individual lenders may try to reduce their country exposure during a liquidity crisis, even if they believe the country is willing and able to service its debts in the long run, is that the size of the loan they can extend to a particular country is limited. For either portfolio diversification or regulatory reasons, they may be unable to provide a bridge loan that is large enough to forestall a liquidity problem—even for an otherwise well-managed borrowing country—if other lenders decide to pull out.

Cooper and Sachs, Krugman, and Gersovitz stress the importance of creditors' confidence in preventing liquidity crises. There are, they claim, two possible equilibriums in the credit market: a low-level equilibrium when lenders lose confidence and pull out, causing a liquidity crisis for the debtor country, and a high-level equilibrium when confidence is maintained so that developing countries can roll over their short-term debt without difficulty. Krugman stresses a point made earlier by William Cline: for creditors that already have loans outstanding in debtor countries, continued lending has a "public good" aspect. That is, the collective welfare of existing creditors may be increased by continuing to lend even in situations where new lenders would not be willing to commit funds. Given the uncertainty about whether or not a high-level equilibrium will in fact be sustained, individual creditors will have incentives to opt out before other creditors do. Hence, there may be an important role for official intervention to ensure the necessary coordination among creditors so that continued lending results, and periodic crises of confidence are prevented from causing a collapse of the international banking system.

In the case of sovereign loans, "liquidating" the country in order to repay external loans is not a remedy available to lenders regardless of their assessment of whether problem debtors are insolvent, illiquid, or unwilling to pay. There may be situations in which a heavily indebted country can improve the welfare of its constituents by electing not to service its debts according to the terms specified in the contract. Recent theoretical work exemplified in the chapters by Cooper and Sachs, Gersovitz, and Krugman focuses on the strategic decision faced by debtor countries when the option to repudiate their debt is available.

The difficult task facing lenders in such an environment is to structure lending contracts in a way that not only correctly recognizes the possibility that debtors may wish to restructure the terms under some circumstances, but also prevents them from doing so when this is inefficient—inefficient in the sense that it misallocates scarce loanable funds or creates incentives for perverse behavior by either borrowers or lenders in the future. The presumption of the analytical models is that, in the vast majority of debt crises, both creditors and debtors will be better off by avoiding defaults through negotiation. Thus, by providing renewed lending to prevent immediate outright default, creditors ensure that the debtor does not face an insurmountable liquidity crisis.

A number of other considerations besides sovereign risk are given specific attention in Part I. First, to understand better the developing countries' debt problems at present, it is essential to analyze the effect of uncertainty on borrowing and lending decisions (see especially Krugman). It is abundantly clear that unanticipated changes in interest rates, world economic activity, and export prices have contributed greatly to the current problems faced by developing countries and have affected their ability to service external debt. Second, governments have virtually always granted explicit or implicit loan guarantees on behalf of their constituent borrowers in times of debt crises. This may in fact be quite defensible to the extent that macroeconomic management influences the viability of all investment projects within the economy. Third, the ultimate servicing of debt denominated in foreign currency depends critically on appropriate fiscal, commercial, and exchange rate policies, both domestically and in the rest of the world. This, too, contributes to a type of countrywide risk, transfer risk, which arises when debtors are unable to obtain foreign exchange for local currency in order to make debt payments. Cooper and Sachs, in their analysis, stress the importance of generating domestic excess supplies of tradable goods, not nontradables (which include much of the output of the public sector), in order to service external debt. These sectoral considerations have sometimes been ignored by countries that borrow extensively abroad for infrastructure projects that do not directly generate foreign exchange.

Cooper and Sachs also develop a point made elsewhere by Homi Kharas: the minimum acceptable rate of return for public investment projects should be higher than the country's borrowing rate in world capital markets if the government faces binding constraints on the level of taxes that can be levied on domestic residents to repay foreign loans to the public sector. This so-called public finance aspect of external debt servicing by the public sector seems to be of considerable practical importance in a number of heavily indebted developing countries—for example, countries such as Argentina and Venezuela whose rapid growth in official debt, in part, reflects capital flight by the private sector. If the government could effectively tax the overseas assets of the private sector, it would have little difficulty meeting the external debt-servicing requirements of the public sector. The impossibility of levying such taxes is indicative of the public finance aspect of debt servicing. Furthermore, it reemphasizes the shortcoming, highlighted above, of treating capital flows as the result of a single optimizing agent's decision.

BANK BEHAVIOR AND FINANCIAL MARKETS

It is often said that banks should have acted more prudently—regarding their overall level of lending as well as the thoroughness of their project evaluation procedures—in countries such as Mexico, Chile, Brazil, and Argentina. The theoretical chapters in Part I, however, provide little insight into the factors that could have generated ex ante overexposure and overconcentration of loan portfolios. In fact, they generally assume that debtors and creditors have the same information regarding the viability of various investment projects and the same ability to process and interpret this information. As the Harberger and Solís-Zedillo chapters in Part IV make clear, such assumptions rule out many of the reasons for overborrowing in Latin America in the late 1970s.

Ex ante overexposure by commercial banks in developing countries can result from distorted incentives that banks face. Both chapter 5 by Jack M. Guttentag and Richard Herring and chapter 6 by Alexander K. Swoboda suggest that profit-maximizing banks will overinvest in external loans and downplay the associated risks if they have government guarantees of support, either explicit or implicit, in times of trouble. (This is the so-called moral hazard problem: insurance alters the behavior of the insured party in perverse, risk-increasing ways.) Deposit insurance, as well as the beliefs that debtor countries would be bailed out by official loans and that large banks would not be allowed to fail, all allegedly play some role in causing banks to discount heavily the risks of large and concentrated exposures.

Parenthetically, government guarantees also help to explain the predominance of commercial bank loans, rather than equity commitments or foreign bond issues, as mechanisms for transferring capital to developing countries. The predominance of commercial banks, in turn, may make it easier to achieve cooperative behavior among creditors in times of debt repayment crises. This facilitates negotiation between overburdened debtors and creditors, thereby reducing the frequency of outright debt repudiation.

Inadequate data may also have been an important factor explaining overlending in some cases. According to Leopoldo Solís and Ernesto Zedillo, for example, banks probably continued to lend aggressively in Mexico after it was prudent to do so, because individually they were unaware of how large their collective exposure actually was. The best available information was not good enough!

Guttentag and Herring provide a more controversial explanation for overlending by banks, which is rooted in results established in cognitive psychology. According to their hypothesis, bankers (like all human beings) suffer from "disaster myopia"; that is, they greatly discount or ignore altogether the possibility of very infrequent but extremely costly events. The longer the system operated without the generalized defaults of the 1930s, the more confident bankers became that such disasters would not occur again. Indeed, such disastrous events became so unlikely in the bankers' view that they were treated as if their probability were effectively zero. Consequently, little attention was paid to the correlation between the returns on different developing-country loans created by the vulnerability of all borrowers to high interest rates and worldwide economic downturns. When, in the early 1980s, troubles began unfolding in many countries, banks continued to lend for some time as if they did not believe the new evidence. Guttentag and Herring attribute this in part to "cognitive dissonance." Some of the participants at the World Bank conference on international debt, including Robert Heller, found this recourse to psychological explanation unconvincing, but others were not so sure.

ECONOMETRIC ANALYSIS OF BALANCE OF PAYMENTS PROBLEMS

In Part III of the volume, Daniel McFadden et al. (chapter 7) carry out an econometric analysis of the precursors of debt-servicing problems and estimate crisis probabilities using data on ninety-three countries over the 1970–82 period. They consider a number of indicators of repayment problems, including arrears in debt servicing, the existence of an IMF upper credit tranche facility, and current negotiation to reschedule private or official debt for the country under consideration. Using various probit and logit specifications, which have been employed in earlier writings in this area, the authors estimate the probability of a country experiencing debt repayment problems in the following year as a function of an indicator of debt problems in the previous period and of a number of macroeconomic ratios such as debt service/exports, nondebt inflows/debt service, foreign exchange reserves/imports, exports/GDP, and real GDP/population.

Although econometric models help explain—after the fact—the occurrence of debt-servicing problems, it is extremely difficult to develop an early warning system that will predict repayment crises in advance. Conference participants echoed the authors' caveat that "there are questions as to whether these studies identify leading rather than coincident indicators of repayment problems." In many instances, because of lags in data availability, it is necessary to forecast the macroeconomic variables on the right-hand side of the probit or logit specification that is used to estimate the probability of repayment problems. McFadden et al. find evidence that country-specific and repayment history effects on probabilities of repayment problems are especially important. Thus, once a debt repayment problem has developed, as indicated by a lagged dependent variable in the probit or logit equations, we have good reason to believe that it will still exist in the next period. Unfortunately, the importance of the lagged dependent variable in the above models is of little help in forecasting repayment problems in time to take preventive action. Part of the explanation for this persistence effect is undoubtedly that under present procedures both commercial banks and foreign governments (via the Paris Club) typically insist on rescheduling for only a year or two at a time. If there were medium-term rescheduling, debt-servicing problems would presumably not be observed period after period; hence, the lagged dependent variable would be less significant.

Splitting their sample period into two subperiods, 1971–75 and 1976–82, the authors discover that the estimated coefficients of their cross-section/time-series model are "definitely not stable over time." This finding causes skeptics to hark back to the authors' introductory remark: "Before beginning an econometric analysis of repayment problems, one must ask whether it is reasonable to expect a macroeconomic pattern that is stable over countries and over time. Case studies make clear that the circumstances of different developing countries vary considerably, and the apparent origins of repayment problems are quite heterogeneous."

If one takes the split sample results for the two subperiods at face value (in particular, if one assumes the coefficients are stable within each subperiod), two interesting conclusions can be drawn. First, there is evidence of a signficant shift in the structure of debt problems after 1976, with "liquidity" variables such as reserves and debt service due becoming much more significant factors in repayment problems. Second, real exchange rate misalignment becomes highly significant as a precursor of repayment problems in the later period, whereas it was not statistically significant in the earlier period.

In addition to reestimating and extending various probit and logit models that have appeared in the literature, McFadden et al. make a major advance beyond the earlier work of Eaton and Gersovitz (1981) by specifying and estimating a structural model, which separately identifies the supply of and demand for new loans as well as the limit on arrears that will be permitted before debt must be rescheduled or restructured. The estimates of this model suggest the following conclusions: demand for new loans is extremely sensitive to debt service due, indicating either a strong rollover component in demand, a strong demand component to smooth export fluctuations, or strong cross-country variations in willingness to borrow. Openness of the economy, as reflected by the import ratio, increases demand. The supply of new loans is affected by past repayment problems, is insensitive to principal due (which indicates that lenders are unwilling to accommodate rollovers), and is notably insensitive to standard indicators of country performance such as the growth rate of GNP or the reserve ratio. There is no evidence that worldwide lender behavior, measured by overall indices of availability of credit or cost of capital, has influenced repayment problems beyond its direct impact on debt service due.

Finally, the authors calculate probabilities of repayment problems for Argentina, Brazil, Chile, Korea, Mexico, Peru, the Philippines, and Venezuela, including forecasts through 1985. The estimated probabilities of repayment problems in these countries were quite high, and remain so through 1985 even though they are below their peaks of 1982–83. On the basis of simplified specification of the historical development of energy prices and the world business cycle, the authors conclude that the recent problems of oil importers were primarily attributable to the real increase in the price of fuels. The effects of world recession and other impediments to GNP growth are significant for Argentina, Chile, and Peru in the 1982–83 period. Unfortunately, the analysis does not account for domestic macroeconomic mismanagement, which, according to case studies in Part IV, played a key role.

All in all, the empirical results seem to indicate that getting operational models from cross-country statistical analysis for assessing creditworthiness and isolating the precursors of debt-servicing problems is an extremely difficult task. This should make one skeptical about the possibility of developing a generally applicable early warning system for detecting rising probabilities of debt-servicing problems. Nevertheless, econometric analysis may be important in explaining the causes of debt-servicing problems after the fact, thereby preventing some mistakes from being repeated. This in itself undoubtedly justifies further research in this area.

MACROECONOMIC MANAGEMENT

The oil price shocks, rising interest rates, and worldwide recessions of the 1970s and early 1980s are often cited as the chief causes of the current debt crisis. Rudiger Dornbusch (chapter 8), however, stresses that overvalued exchange rates and large budget deficits in developing countries, themselves related phenomena, were often important causes of excessive foreign borrowing. Countries with these inappropriate domestic policy stances in the 1970s found themselves vulnerable during worldwide slowdowns, particularly if much of their debt was floating rate debt with short maturity. (McFadden et al. do not consider budget deficits as contributors to debt difficulties in their econometric model, but their analysis does confirm the importance of real exchange rate overvaluation—at least for the 1976–82 period.)

With the help of a simple accounting framework, Dornbusch attributes gross increases in a country's external debt to either (1) current account deficits (that is, net merchandise imports and interest payments on existing foreign debt) minus any long-term non-debt-creating capital inflows, including direct foreign investment, (2) gross private capital outflows, or (3) net accumulation of official foreign exchange reserves. He then analyzes three countries (Argentina, Brazil, and Chile) during the 1978–82 period to determine which factors contributed most significantly to the growth in their external debts.

A massive deterioration of the current account was in his view the major source of Brazil's increase in external debt. This deterioration, in turn, was a consequence of loose fiscal policy and a large increase in interest payments to foreigners. According to Dornbusch, "The deterioration of the Brazilian external indebtedness is largely attributable to failure to adjust the [government] budget to the combined external shocks of higher world interest rates and increased real oil prices."

In contrast to the Brazilian case, Dornbusch feels that private capital flight (facilitated by the absence of capital account restrictions) was the major contributor to Argentina's foreign debt. The openness of the Argentinian capital market, in contrast to that of Brazil, facilitated massive private outflows as the real exchange rate became increasingly overvalued. Dornbusch discusses how misalignment of the exchange rate affects not only capital flows but also various components of domestic expenditure, including private consumption and investment, and the government budget. The negative effects that large fiscal deficits are likely to have on private saving and investment, and hence on the current account, are also stressed.

What this study makes clear is that sensible macroeconomic management—in addition to sound cost-benefit analysis and feasibility studies of major investment projects—is necessary, if countries are to avoid external debt difficulties. As Mario H. Simonsen emphasizes in chapter 4, the distinction between project loans and balance of payments financing is meaningful only if a country maintains its exchange rate near an equilibrium level. The links between a country's internal capital market structure and its macroeconomic policy, investment decisions, and external debt must also be considered. This is clearly an important area for future research.

Arnold C. Harberger's central point—and presumably the main lesson that he would draw for policymakers—is that developing-country governments should not allow capital inflows to exceed longer-run sustainable levels for any appreciable period of time (see chapter 9). Unsustainable borrowing leads inevitably to rather sudden counterbalancing outflows or cutoffs. It first generates a real exchange rate appreciation and then a depreciation. This sets in motion a cycle in production and employment, the down side of which will be extremely painful in terms of unemployment and lost output.

Harberger examines the experiences of Chile, Argentina, and three oil exporters from this perspective. The bulk of his chapter deals with Chile. He rejects the explanation suggested by Dornbusch that the pegging of the exchange rate from July 1979 to October 1982 was, in the face of substantial domestic inflation, the main source of Chile's ultimate collapse in 1982–83. Signs of overvaluation—such as low prices of tradables in relation to nontradables, a loss of reserves, high real wages, and a decline in industrial production—appeared only in mid-1981, two years after the exchange rate was pegged. The immediate cause of Chile's crisis was rather the massive swing in net capital transfers from 2 percent of GDP in 1979, to 10 percent in 1981, to 1.7 percent in 1982. Unsustainable inflows in 1981 brought a real exchange rate appreciation, while their cessation in 1982 set the stage for real depreciation in 1982. Indexation of wages postponed the required real depreciation until late 1982, by which time a severe depression had begun.

Why were international banks willing to lend to Chile at such unsustainable rates and at extremely low spreads? A large portion of the external loans went to Chilean banks. These banks were earning 3–4 percent a month while the exchange rate was pegged. Seeing these returns, the international banks concluded that their Chilean counterparts would have little trouble repaying. Unfortunately, Chilean bank portfolios included bad loans still carried as if they were good. The international banks were not sufficiently prudent in scrutinizing the balance sheets of the Chilean banks to which they were lending.

In Harberger's view, the chief mistakes of Chilean policymakers were, first, that they relaxed controls over capital inflows too much in 1980; and, second, that they should have kept the banking system under stricter discipline.

Argentina's capital markets were completely opened in the late 1970s. This was a mistake, according to Harberger. But the country's biggest mistake was fixing a "tablita" of future exchange rate devaluations which, in combination with a very inflationary fiscal policy, guaranteed excessive increases in the real value of the peso. Internal interest rates were high, reflecting expected inflation. Foreigners could earn 3.5 to 4 percent a month by moving funds into Argentina and later reconverting the funds into U.S. dollars at the tablita's 1979 exchange rates. For a time, funds flowed in. By late 1980, however, it was clear that the situation was unsustainable and capital flight began to accelerate.

Finally, Harberger compares the responses of Mexico, Venezuela, and Indonesia to the oil boom. The first two countries borrowed heavily against projected future increases in oil revenues. These loans were funneled into investment projects with low and even negative returns, as well as into consumption by the private and public sectors. In Mexico, the capital inflows brought substantial real exchange appreciation which had to be reversed by a devaluation in 1982. Indonesia avoided this pattern in the second oil boom because, according to Harberger, it had already been seriously burnt by the excesses of Pertamina, the national oil company, following the first oil boom.

Mexico is examined in more detail by Leopoldo Solís and Ernesto Zedillo (chapter 10). In spite of the surge in its oil export volume and prices in the late 1970s and its easy access to international capital markets, Mexico faced a more serious economic crisis by the end of 1982 than it had at the end of the discredited Echeverría administration six years before. The ingredients of the crisis were a mixture of those that befell Chile, Argentina, and Brazil. Extraordinary debt accumulation occurred in 1979–81, but especially in 1981, the climax year. There was a dramatic real appreciation of the peso, which had been virtually pegged in nominal terms for five years (1977–81) even though inflation averaged more than 20 percent. Massive increases in public expenditure and fiscal deficits reached 17.9 percent of GDP in 1981. These factors led to a big import bulge and, ultimately, flight from the peso. Estimates by the authors using an ex post accounting decomposition suggest that during the critical three years, 1979–81, Mexico borrowed some $31 billion more than would have been expected on the basis of past trends. Of this total, capital flight and smuggling accounted for $16.3 billion; higher import propensities, $13.2 billion; and higher international interest rates, $6.7 billion. The critical year was 1981 when the big public sector deficit spilled over into the balance of payments. The availability of foreign finance (the net inflow to public entities reached 10 percent of GDP) postponed immediate adjustment and allowed the government to pursue halfhearted measures through much of 1982. As the framework laid out by Harberger would clearly suggest, the capital inflow was unsustainable, and its reversal would bring much greater adjustment costs in late 1982–84.

Solís and Zedillo believe that the immediate debt crisis of 1982 has been overcome. They explained the de facto debt moratorium of late 1982 and the arrangement of the "mammoth" $5 billion loan that was facilitated by IMF insistence that all banks contribute to it in proportion to their exposure in Mexico. This pressure resolved the potential free-rider problem, which was emphasized in the theoretical chapters of Part I. Debt due to private institutions between August

1982 and December 1984 was rescheduled. The government did not assume private debts, but it did in effect guarantee foreign exchange cover for private institutions that managed to reschedule their dollar debts.

At present, the Mexican stabilization program seems to be working more or less as planned. The public deficit was reduced to 8.7 percent of GDP in 1983 and the current account moved into surplus, mostly because of a compression in imports. Mexico's creditworthiness is again improving, and the new mammoth loan for 1984 has significantly lower spreads and longer maturity.

On the negative side, however, inflation has not been reduced as originally expected, GDP has fallen by 4.7 percent, and employment and the real wage have also fallen considerably. Therefore, Mexico is not out of the woods yet, according to Solís and Zedillo. First, the debt amortization profile facing Mexico is ominous: $50 billion, more than half the debt, is due to be repaid during the period 1985–88. Further reschedulings are necessary, with perhaps as much as all of the principal due over the next five to six years.[3] Second, there is a distinct possibility that Mexico will have to make do with zero or perhaps even negative real capital inflows over the next few years.

Using a simple growth-debt simulation model with fixed coefficients, Solís and Zedillo find that with no real growth in debt, a 2.5 capital/output ratio, and a 5 percent annual real growth in exports, Mexico can grow 5.1 to 5.3 percent from 1985 to 1990, even with real interest rates as high as 8 percent. Unfortunately, zero real growth in debt would still require a net nominal inflow of $4.6 billion to $6.0 billion, depending on inflation, and would imply a "deterioration in the unemployment situation." New inflows of $9 billion to $11 billion would be necessary to stabilize unemployment at reasonable levels.

Necessary conditions, the authors conclude, for Mexico's long-run solvency are: the success of the current stabilization program, orderly rescheduling of future principal repayments, a modest increase in the real stock of debt, and an expansion of international trade.

In the final case study (chapter 11), Yung Chul Park examines the Republic of Korea, one of the very few big borrowers that has managed to avoid reschedulings, persistent arrears, and moratoriums of debt service payments. He traces Korea's development and economic policies from 1965 to 1984, highlighting the substantial role of foreign loans in that process, and concludes that, by most traditional indicators, Korea remained very creditworthy even in the tightest days of 1982–83. Korean policymakers have normally treated foreign borrowing as filling the gap between the investment required for the target rate of growth and expected savings. The government has exercised considerable control over the magnitude and allocation of foreign funds, giving high priority to export industries in the 1960s and early 1970s and to heavy and chemical industries in the latter half of the 1970s. Free capital inflows and outflows were never permitted. Consequently, according to Park, foreign capital inflows were used to finance either current account deficits or reserve accumulation, but very little acquisition of foreign assets by Koren residents (capital flight). Furthermore, Park claims that there is no evidence that Korean savings were on balance reduced by the inflow of foreign capital.

This is not to say that Korea avoided all problems. It has faced three balance of payments "crises" in the past twenty years, one in 1971–72 and the others following the two oil shocks in the 1970s. The first crisis resulted in part from the heavy foreign borrowing of 1966–70, which raised debt service requirements substantially. This crisis was resolved quickly by a cutback in borrowing, real devaluation, and a surge in exports.

After the first oil crisis, Korea opted for growth, another real devaluation, and a concerted export drive. The country borrowed heavily to maintain growth and permit a more gradual adjustment to the oil shock. Park contends that this approach may have only postponed (and aggravated) the adjustment problem until 1977–78.

The Korean response to the second oil shock was more conventional in that monetary and fiscal restrictions accompanied increased borrowing and further export promotion. In the remainder of the decade Korea intends to reduce its dependence on foreign loans by increasing its internal savings rate. It apparently considers the 50 percent debt/GNP ratio to be too high for the long haul.

Several other points distinguish Korea from other indebted countries. First, Korean groups (such as exporters and public corporations) with access to foreign capital benefited from negative real interest rates in most years because of a gradual real appreciation of the won, the Korean currency. Without controls, foreign borrowing would have been much larger. Second, the impact of the periodic real appreciations of the won (which were due to the adjustable peg and internal inflation) was greatly softened by compensating increases in financial subsidies. Third, the real exchange rate in Korea never appreciated to anything approaching the magnitudes registered in Chile, Mexico, and Argentina.

Park argues that Korea has, on balance, used borrowed funds efficiently. There have been some distortions, however. In the late 1960s, for example, nontradables were squeezed under a tight credit policy designed to mop up the excess liquidity that had been created by external borrowing in excess of current account needs. Second, the policy emphasis on capital-intensive heavy industry and chemicals in the 1970s, with a large component of foreign finance, caused many plants to be built which, according to Park, are not competitive internationally and which have little prospect for becoming so in the near future.

Several generalizations can be made from the case studies presented in this volume:

- There are many paths to a debt crisis, but overvaluation of the real exchange rate lies along all of them. It is significant that Korea, the only major debtor without debt-rescheduling problems, has managed to avoid large and persistent overvaluations. Any tendency toward overvaluation has not been allowed to affect the international competitiveness of Korea's export industries.
- In its latter-day incarnation, overvaluation is often caused or supported by extensive overseas borrowing from private sources. Before the late 1960s, exchange or trade interventions were often the cause of overvalued rates or served to maintain them once they had occurred.
- Large government deficits typically contribute to debt difficulties—but this is not always the case. At the time Chile began experiencing debt-servicing problems, its budget was near balance. Deficits in Korea, however, have often been large, but that country has avoided major debt-servicing difficulties. In Mexico and Brazil, public deficits absorbed a large portion of the foreign capital inflows, and debt servicing has been a heavy burden in recent years.
- The worst of all scenarios seems to include large public deficits, relatively free capital inflows, ineffective control over private capital outflows, and real overvaluation of the exchange rate followed by precipitous depreciation as difficulties materialize.
- The countries studied here used foreign funds in the late 1970s and early 1980s in contrasting fashions: Argentina, primarily to finance capital flight and unrecorded military imports; Brazil, to increase private and public sector consumption; Chile, to finance a boom in consumption and investment; Mexico, to encourage somewhat greater imports than otherwise would have been possible, but mainly to offset private capital flight. Only Korea seems to have borrowed almost entirely to raise investment.
- The case studies suggest that a laissez-faire policy toward capital inflows is probably a bad idea for most developing countries, particularly those suffering from substantial macroeconomic, capital market, and exchange rate distortions. For more definitive conclusions, further research will be required: first, on the macroeconomic links between internal capital markets, macroeconomic policy, investment decisions, and external debt; second, as suggested by Harberger, on the optimal welfare-efficiency stance toward foreign borrowing when the creditworthiness of a country depends upon the level of debt and an uncertain future.

DEALING WITH THE PRESENT SITUATION AND BEYOND

The present handling of repayment problems involving debtor countries and commercial banks is characterized in the chapters of Part I as a bilateral bargaining game in which both debtors and creditors recognize that they may be better off if default can be avoided—or at least postponed—by negotiation. Although this is in the interest of each party, the instability of ad hoc arrangements because of the so-called free-rider problem is emphasized: each bank has an incentive to cut its losses by refusing to renew its debtor-country loans. By attempting to do so, however, a bank increases the likelihood that a debtor will be unable to obtain an aggregate amount of funds sufficient to meet its debt-servicing obligations. As Simonsen emphasizes, the value of existing bank loans to developing countries is much greater if banks can act cooperatively and prevent individual banks from futile attempts to opt out.

Official institutions such as the IMF and the World Bank play an important role in helping to coordinate the behavior of lenders so that a cooperative, nondestructive outcome prevails. Furthermore, official institutions can perform an important function in establishing conditions to which debtors must adhere in order to obtain official debt rescheduling. This may create sufficient confidence among private creditors to prevent an immediate withdrawal of funds and refusal of vital additional funding during a transitional period.

Several suggestions are made herein about how the existing procedure might be improved and rendered less volatile. There is a widespread belief among conference participants that a move to multiyear rescheduling is essential. The year-by-year approach leaves the international financial system in a precarious state, since a return to normalcy in debt servicing will take a number of years even under the most optimistic macroeconomic and policy scenarios. The needs to cap interest rates on developing-country debt and to allow negative amortization once interest payments rise beyond manageable levels are also discussed. Krugman stresses that in a debt crisis situation where the debtor's and creditors' fates are inextricably linked, the distinction between principal repayments and interest is artificial. In their monitoring operations, bank regulators should recognize this reality.

The two most ambitious plans for improving the situation of debtors and creditors alike, the Kenen and Rohatyn plans, received little support at the conference. Both envisage an exchange of assets between the banks and an official institution patterned after New York's Municipal Assistance Commission. This would be followed by a restructuring of the acquired external debt by the official entity. Aside from many technical and political problems, the most serious objection raised to both plans is that they remove the incentive that creditors now have to continue lending to developing countries.

Several proposals designed to improve the longer-run efficiency of lending to developing countries are discussed. Guttentag and Herring favor the establishment of a conduit for these loans similar in intent and structure to the Federal Home Loan Mortgage Corporation in the United States. The conduit would buy primary debt instruments, pool them into closed-end funds, and sell participation certificates in them. Initially, official guarantees for the certificates would be required to assure their acceptance in the market. A restructuring of existing debts is not an activity envisaged for the conduit, but rather one "designed to improve the normal functioning of the market for loans to developing countries and prevent debt crises from occurring." Nevertheless, the extent to which the conduit would increase flows to developing countries instead of merely reducing banks' overexposure à la Rohatyn and Kenen is unclear. The authors give no indication of the scale they foresee for the operation.

Some participants (Guttentag and Herring, Swoboda, and, to a lesser extent, Gersovitz) would like to see the establishment of an active secondary market in external debt instruments. Several advantages are claimed for this market. It would spread risk more broadly, would generate information on the value of loans as perceived by market participants, and, by rendering developing-country loans more liquid, would reduce somewhat the returns required by lenders. Through its pricing of individual country debt the market should also provide a more effective means of disciplining borrowers and lenders. Along this line, Guttentag and Herring and Swoboda favor mark-to-market accounting for banks. The relevant prices would be those in the secondary market, were it to exist.

The existence of a large secondary market, however, may be a mixed blessing. Mario Simonsen (chapter 4) points out that the value of loans in the secondary markets would depend, among other things, on the likelihood that future potential default situations could be resolved in a cooperative manner with benefits to both creditors and debtors. Other things being equal, the larger the number of participants in the market, the more likely it is that free-rider problems would prevent a cooperative solution from being attained. Consequently, developing-country loans would be worth less in a competitive secondary market than they would be in a market where, for example, a single central lender could achieve the cooperative outcome without having to deal with numerous free riders. The differences in values could be dramatic in times of debt-servicing difficulties. Simonsen's point is most telling as a critique of totally laissez-faire solutions to the current debt situation espoused, for example, by Milton Friedman. The authors in this volume who would like to see a secondary market for external debt do not advocate laissez-faire. They see the need for considerable official presence in order to overcome the free-rider problem.

Simonsen's chapter also makes an innovative suggestion for reducing the interest rates paid by developing countries. He advocates making the interest income on these loans exempt from creditor countries' income taxation. Such tax treatment, which is similar to that given to municipal and state bonds in the United States, would eliminate the tax wedge that is currently built into the borrowing rates paid by developing countries.

Many of the conference participants emphasized the need for a more efficient, and some would argue "fairer," sharing of interest rate risks than that inherent in the current variable-rate, fixed-principal loans offered by commercial banks. Capping interest rates and capitalizing any excess is one of many modifications that can be envisaged. The problem, as Guttentag and Herring point out, is that in a decentralized market there is little incentive for individual lenders to make such loan modifications. Those who do not will find their prospects for prompt payment enhanced at no cost to themselves, but at a cost to other lenders—a classic "prisoners' dilemma" situation. The same lack of incentives to individual lenders is an impediment to the development of financial instruments (such as commodity-price-indexed securities and exchange participation loans) designed to reduce the instability in borrowers' debt-servicing obligations. Such changes would probably require a coordinated effort by lenders.

CONCLUDING COMMENTS

The conference on "International Debt and the Developing Countries" was a sobering one. While it would be an exaggeration to characterize the mood as "gloom and doom," it was nevertheless clear at the end of the conference that many serious problems that had been extensively analyzed remained unresolved.

The sheer magnitude of the debt-servicing burden facing several countries over the next decade was highlighted by many participants. There was also fairly general agreement that the outlook for voluntary net lending through banks to developing countries is bleak indeed for the next three to five years. The current IMF scheme of sustaining involuntary bank lending via a sequence of annual rescheduling operations conducted on a country-by-country basis has thus far averted defaults by major debtors. The possibility that the whole procedure, when it must be repeated so frequently, could ultimately break down was agreed to be a very real one.

The individual country analyses, with the exception of Korea, highlighted avoidable errors in exchange rate management, budgetary finance, or debt management. Overlending by commercial banks compounded these errors.

The proposals for reform presented at the conference, while meritorious in some respects, seemed somehow inadequate for the problems they addressed. It is interesting to note, however, that many participants agreed with the notion that some form of debt relief (in effect, forgiveness) may now be necessary. This viewpoint is rather new for market-oriented professional economists. Some authors (for example, Krugman and Simonsen) see partial debt relief as a plausible outcome of a cooperative game involving borrowers and lenders. Furthermore, it might well improve the welfare of both parties in the highly unstable situation in which several debtor nations find themselves today.

The conference participants did not come to any agreement on the best ways to achieve debt relief, although the Rohatyn and Kenen plans were generally rejected. The conference thus closed with a certain sense of urgency but with an uneasiness that what is currently being done will not suffice.

NOTES

1. Dollar figures throughout the present volume are in U.S. dollars; billion refers to thousand million.

2. The competitive paradigm may work quite well for describing aggressive commercial bank lending abroad in the 1970s, when exposure levels were low and loan expansion was rapid.

3. Since the conference, the Mexican government and a commercial bank steering committee have negotiated a $49 billion multiyear rescheduling of external commercial bank debt, the largest rescheduling in history. The agreement, which is pending ratification by the 550 commercial banks involved, would reschedule the commercial debt over a fourteen-year period.

REFERENCES

Eaton, Jonathan, and Mark Gersovitz. 1981. "Debt with potential repudiation: Theoretical and empirical analysis." Review of Economic Studies 48 (February): 289–309.

World Bank. 1984. World debt tables, 1983–84 ed. Washington, D.C.

Part I

The Conceptual Framework

1

Borrowing Abroad: The Debtor's Perspective

Richard N. Cooper and Jeffrey D. Sachs

External debt has risen to the top of the agenda of international monetary economics in recent years. This is partly because developing countries have become much more dependent on external funding for their economic development during the past decade than they were previously and partly because a growing number of countries have experienced difficulties in servicing their external debts since 1981. This chapter explores the question of external borrowing from the perspective of the borrowing country, with a view to discovering principles or guidelines that might be helpful to such countries in managing both the level and the character of their external debt.

The structure of the chapter is as follows. The first section sketches a formal framework, from a planner's point of view, for optimal borrowing by a developing country. In the next three sections this framework is used for the development of three important considerations in external borrowing: solvency, liquidity, and the possibility of repudiation. The fifth section outlines the relationship of external borrowing to the macroeconomic management of the borrowing country, and the sixth summarizes the many factors that suggest that the external debt of a country should be subject to central management or at least surveillance. Following that are some guidelines for limits to the magnitude of external debt and a discussion of the composition of the debt. A brief concluding section pulls some of the strands together.

The first four sections are more formal and algebraic in their approach to the subject. This treatment will appeal to some readers and offend others. It is offered not merely to appeal to those who prefer a formal approach to a subject that lends itself to formal analysis, but also to suggest a format that can be adapted to the formal planning models used by many developing countries. An appendix offers a numerical illustration of how the framework can be used. The final four sections are written to be accessible to a wider audience and to present some observations on issues that are not fully covered in the more formal treatment. Our discussion throughout on the links between borrowing and monetary policies is necessarily brief; we refer the reader to Dornbusch's detailed contribution in this volume (see chapter 8).

STRATEGIES FOR INTERNATIONAL BORROWING

We approach the management of international borrowing as a formal problem of dynamic resource allocation. (The formal approach taken here follows closely the treatment in Sachs 1982a and 1984, wherein further details may be found.) Admittedly, a formal approach may neglect some aspects of the borrowing decision; we take up some of these in later sections. The formal approach, however, has the advantage of showing how a quantitative assessment of borrowing may be made by using standard models of development planning. This section illustrates how such development models can be used.

All models of optimal borrowing have two features. The first is a dynamic budget constraint, which determines the country's long-term options with respect to foreign borrowing. The second feature is a planning function or social welfare function, which describes in a dynamic setting the desirability of various possible paths for consumption and output over time. The borrowing problem is solved in a formal way by maximizing the social welfare function subject to the dynamic budget constraint.

We add a third feature, which is sometimes missing in borrowing models—optimal implementation of a borrowing strategy. The solution of a borrowing model typically yields a path of investment, consumption, and foreign indebtedness that maximizes the social welfare function. What it may not yield, however, are the policies needed to achieve that path. Will the path result from decentralized market forces, with direct private sector access to foreign capital? Or does the path require active government intervention in the borrowing process? In other words, in addition to studying the correct path for borrowing, we must ask how that path may in fact be reached.

This section outlines the three key elements of the formal borrowing problem: the budget constraint, the welfare function, and the instruments for policy implementation. (Later sections are devoted to a more refined treatment of these elements and address special features of the actual borrowing process.)

The Dynamic Budget Constraint

Many features in the economy of the country determine how much and on what terms it may borrow from the rest of the world. Potential lenders as well as equity investors must assess the country's future ability and willingness to service its external obligations. New credit may be limited because creditors doubt that the economy can ever earn sufficient foreign exchange to repay a new loan. In this case, the country is said to be under a solvency constraint. Under another scenario, the country may be deemed unsuitable for additional loans because of short-run difficulties, even though its long-run prospects are bright. Here, the lending is bound by a liquidity constraint. Finally, the country may have foreign exchange earnings sufficient to honor its obligations, but may be judged unwilling to do so, either because current debt repayment is too onerous or because it is holding out for some sort of debt relief. New lending may therefore be constrained by repudiation risk.

The country's capacity to borrow will thus reflect creditors' concerns about solvency, liquidity, and repudiation risk. The interaction of these constraints determines the dynamic budget constraint facing an economy. For the purposes of analytical simplicity, we will consider each of these factors in turn. In truth, a full model of optimal borrowing must incorporate all of them.

The Solvency Constraint. If there were no liquidity or repudiation risks, country borrowing would still be bound by the country's long-run capacity to service its debt. From a creditor's point of view, long-run solvency does not mean that the debtor nation must have the prospect to become a creditor nation in the long run (that is, actually repay its debt). The only requirement is that the debtor have the future resources to service its debt, without the need to borrow forever in order to make interest payments. As an extreme example, a $1 million loan typically has a market value of zero if the debtor always has to borrow all the money needed to service the loan, while the loan is worth $1 million if the country always services the debt out of its own earnings, even though it never repays the principal. (There are exceptions to this case, as described later in the text and in Note 2.).

The country's resources for external debt servicing during each period may be measured by its trade surplus, TB_t (when $TB_t < 0$, the country is running a trade deficit). If the maximum discounted sum of current and future trade balances, $\max \Sigma_{i=t}^{\infty} (1 + r)^{-(i-t)} TB_t$, is less than the current debt, the country can never service the debt out of its own resources (r is the real interest rate; it is assumed to be constant unless otherwise specified). It will have to borrow forever, and in an amount growing at the real interest rate, in order to continue debt servicing. Let D_t be the stock of debt at the end of period $t - 1$, so that $(1 + r)D_t$ is the debt due as of period t. The solvency constraint can be stated simply as the requirement that:

$$(1.1) \qquad (1 + r)D_t \leq \max \sum_{i=t}^{\infty} (1 + r)^{-(i-t)} TB_i.$$

To gain some insight to (1.1), let us turn to the goods market. Suppose, as the first illustration, that the country produces a single tradable good, with real GDP given by Q_t. Output is a function of the capital stock K_t, with $Q_t = F(K_t)$. K_t evolves according to the path of investment, with $K_{t+1} = (1 - d)K_t + I_t$, where d is the rate of depreciation and I_t is gross capital formation (public plus private). The trade balance is $TB_t = Q_t - I_t - C_t$, where C_t is gross domestic consumption (public plus private). Let $\overline{C}_t$ be the subsistence or minimal level of consumption possible in period t, so that TB_t is maximized with $C_t = \overline{C}_t$.[1] Then, from (1.1),

$$(1.2) \qquad (1 + r)D_t \leq \max \sum_{i=t}^{\infty} (1 + r)^{-(i-t)}(Q_i - I_i) - \sum_{i=t}^{\infty} (1 + r)^{-(i-t)} \overline{C}_i.$$

The first term on the right-hand side of (1.2) is the maximum discounted sum of $Q_i - I_i$ and may be considered the productive wealth of the economy, in dynamic terms. The second expression is the discounted sum of minimum consumption expenditure. In words, the solvency constraint is that the economy's debt D_t must be less than or equal to the productive wealth net of minimum consumption expenditure. For the sake of simplicity in the discussion that follows, we set $\overline{C}_t = 0$ in (1.2) and simply compare the external debt with the economy's productive wealth. Reintroducing $\overline{C}_t$ in the later discussion is straightforward.

If the country is always willing to repay its debt as long as it can repay it, and if it can always borrow freely subject to the condition that it remain solvent, then (1.1) or (1.2) defines the loan supply schedule to the country. In particular, it can borrow to the point where $(1 + r)D_t$ just equals $\Sigma_{i=t}^{\infty}(1 + r)^{-(i-t)}(Q_i - I_i)$ (ignoring $\overline{C}_i$). This loan supply schedule is shown in figure 1-1. We will return later to more refined measures of solvency that take into account traded versus nontraded goods, and the public versus private sectors.

There are two important qualifications that must be added to equation (1.2) and figure 1-1. Note that if $Q_i - I_i$ grows in the steady state at a rate n greater than r, then the economy faces no solvency constraint. The sum $\Sigma_{i=t}^{\infty}(1 + r)^{-(i-t)}(Q_i - I_i)$ is infinite (that is, the economy's productive wealth is infinite). Starting from any level of debt D_t, the economy has the future resources to repay the debt! A curious fact is that even if the borrowing country is not growing at a rate n greater than r, there may be no solvency constraint as long as lender countries are growing at n greater than r. This situation can arise if creditors are always willing to make new loans to debtors so that the debtors can service their debts. In such a Ponzi scheme, the borrower's debt grows at the rate of interest (and becomes infinite), but since the lenders' economies are growing even faster, the debt remains a small (and even decreasing) fraction of the creditors' wealth. If the creditors' economies are always growing at $n > r$, such a Ponzi scheme is viable forever. The debtor cannot repay its debt but never has to! Creditors do not call in their loans—they assume that future lenders will keep the debtor afloat.[2]

Note, therefore, that a rise in the real interest rate r above the growth rates of debtor and creditor countries can have a profound effect on the debtor's solvency constraint. When r is low, there may be no solvency constraint on borrowing, while when r is high there surely is. Thus, the rise in real interest rates after 1979 may have severely jolted long-term expectations about the debtor country's capacity to repay.

The Liquidity Constraint. According to some theories, solvent countries can always borrow up to the point of the solvency constraint. We suspect, however, that a borrowing limit may be

Figure 1-1. Loan Supply with No Liquidity or Repudiation Risk

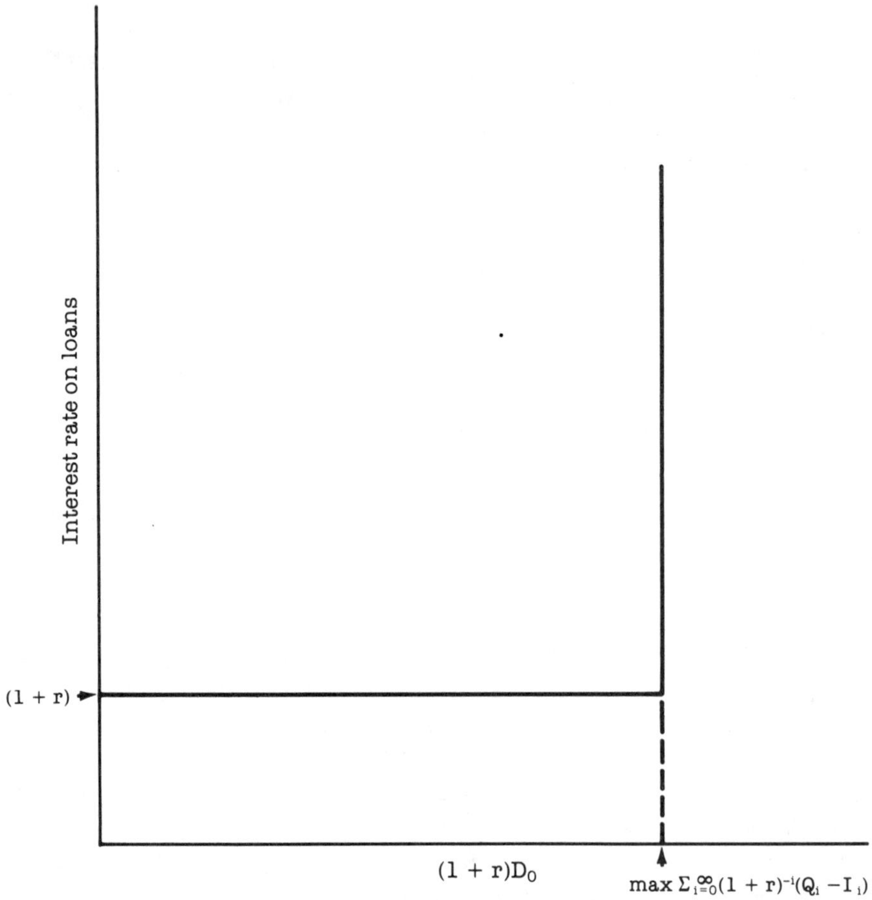

reached far below the solvency limit: creditors fear both the liquidity problems and the possibility of debt repudiation that are associated with heavily indebted countries. A liquidity constraint may (but need not always) occur when a country owes more in a given period than it can service in the absence of new loans. In specific terms, if a percentage of outstanding debt is coming due in period t, amortization payments are αD_t and interest payments are rD_t, so that total debt servicing is $(r + \alpha)D_t$. It may well happen that $(r + \alpha)D_t$ exceeds Q_t (especially when Q_t represents tradable goods alone rather than total GDP), even though $(1 + r)D_t \leqslant \max \Sigma_{i=t}^{\infty} (1 + r)^{-(i-t)}(Q_i - I_i)$. In other words, the country faces a cash flow problem, although it is solvent by long-run criteria.

During normal periods, such a country will be able to borrow $(r + \alpha)D_t - Q_t$ in order to honor its current debt service obligations. However, the loan markets may not function well under certain circumstances, and the country may find itself unable to borrow. Rationing may result when the lending decisions of each bank are affected significantly by the actions of other banks. For example, regulations governing bank capital may dictate that each bank make loans to the country in amounts L less than $\bar{L}$, where $\bar{L} < (r + \alpha)D_t - Q_t$. In this event, no single bank can lend enough to the country for that country to honor its current debt servicing. One of two situations can then develop. On the one hand, n banks may each make loans L such that $nL \geqslant (r + \alpha)D_t - Q_t$. They should be quite willing to do so, because the country is fundamentally healthy (that is, solvent).

On the other hand, if each bank suspects that other banks are not going to make new loans, a panic may ensue. When it appears that no other banks are extending loans, it is rational for each individual bank to stop as well since its loan of size $\bar{L}$ is not big enough to keep the country solvent. Thus, two equilibria are possible, one in which the country is able to refinance its debt and the other in which it is forced into arrears by its inability to obtain new lending. Once the arrears appear, the banks may feel vindicated in their decisions to pull out of new lending. It may become ever more difficult for the country to attract new loans, and a debt rescheduling or moratorium, injurious to creditor and debtor alike, may eventually be necessary.

In addition to restrictions on bank capital, there are several other reasons why a panic might arise (some of these have been spelled out in other studies; see, for example, Sachs 1984). An individual bank may be willing to loan the requisite amount $(r + \alpha)D_t - Q_t$, but only at a new interest rate $\tilde{r}$ much above the existing rate r. The spread $\tilde{r} - r$ would be necessary to compensate a new lender for tying up a large fraction of bank capital. Therefore, the rate $\tilde{r}$ might be so high that a new loan at rate $\tilde{r}$ would push the country over the brink of insolvency. In other words, with a new loan $L_t = (r + \alpha)D_t - Q_t$ at rate $\tilde{r}$, indebtedness might rapidly rise above productive wealth. Once again, the individual bank would be unwilling to lend if it saw that the other banks had also stopped making loans.

There are many situations in which banks might make small loans readily as part of a group but hesitate to make large loans when standing alone. For example, a syndicate may have a stronger bargaining position than a single bank vis-à-vis a debtor country. A bank may therefore fear to be the only lender because its realizes that its future bargaining position with the debtor may be weak. In addition, banks may feel that a central bank is more likely to protect them from default risk if other banks are also involved in loans to a defaulting country. The central bank might be content to let a single irresponsible bank fail, as an example to the others, but it would not jeopardize the banking system by letting several banks fail.

The upshot of liquidity risk is that credit rationing may be far more restrictive than the limits reflected in figure 1-1. Healthy countries with heavy debt-servicing obligations may suddenly find that they have no new avenues for credit and that they have to make rather drastic short-run adjustments.

Repudiation Risk. A country may be unable to obtain new loans because there is little confidence that it will choose to repay the debt. Let us assume that the debtor country owes D_t, and has productive wealth $W_t > D_t$. If the country defaults, the creditors receive a fraction γ of W_t, perhaps by direct confiscation of the debtor country's assets. Moreover, the creditors can impose sanctions on the defaulting country in the amount θW_t. These sanctions include the direct seizure of assets, γW_t, and other penalties that may be costly to the debtor without yielding direct benefits to the creditors. In general, then, we may assume that the sanctions exceed the payments to the creditors $(\theta > \gamma)$.

Consider the default decision. A repudiation of debt yields a gain of D_t and a loss of θW_t to the debtor, and a net loss to the creditor of $D_t(1 - \gamma)$. For debtors and creditors within a closed economy, θ is generally near 1.0, since creditors can use the legal system to seize much of their debtors' assets in the event of a repudiation. When $\theta = 1$, debt repudiation will make sense only when $D_t > W_t$, that is, when the debtor is insolvent. In the international setting, the seizure of assets on a large scale is very difficult, and sanctions such as trade embargoes against a defaulting country may have only limited effect. Thus, θ is usually much smaller than 1.0, so that it may be true that $D_t > \theta W_t$ even when D_t is much less than W_t.

The penalty function and the institutional setting together determine the loan supply schedule for a debtor country. In one extreme case, closer to nineteenth-century bond financing than to the twentieth-century bank financing of loans to developing countries, there is little negotiation between creditors and debtors before a loan is defaulted. Debtors simply compare

D_t and θW_t, and repudiate when $D_t > \theta W_t$. Farsighted creditors therefore restrict loans to assure that $D_t < \theta W_t$, and therefore shrink the loan supply relative to that of figure 1-1.

When active negotiation is possible between creditors and debtors, the situation is far more complicated. Suppose that $D_t > \theta W_t$, so that the debtor has an incentive to repudiate the debt. Both creditors and the debtor also have an incentive to agree to debt relief in lieu of a complete debt repudiation, since both sides can be left better off with debt relief than with default. In the event of default, the creditors receive γW_t and the debtor loses θW_t, with $\theta > \gamma$. If, instead of default, an agreement is reached by which the debtor pays θW_t of the debt while the creditors agree to forego retaliation, the creditors are better off by $(\theta - \gamma)W_t$, and the debtor is left as well off. Alternatively, if the debtor agrees to pay γW_t to the creditors in exchange for no retaliation, the creditors are as well off as with repudiation, while the debtor's situation improves by the amount $(\theta - \gamma)W_t$. Therefore, as long as the creditors impose no sanctions, any payoff from debtor to creditors between γW_t and θW_t would benefit both sides more than would an outright repudiation.

Inevitably, then, in the event that indebtness approaches or exceeds the repudiation threshold θW_t, there will be a strong incentive to negotiate. In general, economic theory cannot predict precisely the outcome of these negotiations, but standard models of bargaining can give us some indication of likely results. In the Nash bargaining solution, for example, there exists a so-called threat point, which is the outcome when negotiations break down. Let us assume that, for a single debtor and creditor, debt repudiation occurs in the absence of successful negotiation, so that the creditor gets γW_t, and the debtor ends up with $(1 - \theta)W_t$. A successful bargaining outcome is a payoff P, which leaves the creditor with P and the debtor with $W_t - P$, and under which the creditor agrees to impose no sanctions on the debtor. Let U be the utility level of the creditor, and V be the utility level of the debtor. The creditor's gain in utility from a successful negotiation is $U(P) - U(\gamma W_t)$, and the debtor's gain is $V(W_t - P) - V[(1 - \theta)W_t]$. In the Nash bargaining solution, the product of the gains to the debtor and creditor is maximized, subject to $P \leqslant D_t$. In other words:

$$\text{(1.3)} \qquad P \text{ maximizes } [U(P) - U(\gamma W_t)] \cdot \{V(W_t - P) - V[(1 - \theta)W_t]\}.$$

Let us suppose, for example, that both creditor and debtor are risk neutral, so that $U(P) = P$, $V(W_t - P) = W_t - P$, and so on. We then maximize $(P - \gamma W_t)(\theta W_t - P)$ subject to $P \leqslant D_t$. The payoff schedule is thus:

$$\text{(1.4)} \qquad P = D_t \qquad \text{for } D_t \leqslant (\theta + \gamma)W_t/2$$

$$P = (\theta + \gamma)W_t/2 \qquad \text{for } D_t > (\theta + \gamma)W_t/2.$$

Therefore, for small levels of debt, the country has no bargaining power, and the payoff equals the entire debt due. However, as D_t rises above $(\theta + \gamma)W_t/2$, the country ends up paying only $(\theta + \gamma)W_t/2$. Note that the payoff rises with θ and γ. Thus, as the creditor is able to impose large penalties on the debtor (high θ) and to seize a large amount of assets (high γ), the creditor's bargaining power—and ultimate payoff—are raised.

It is reasonable to suppose that a potential creditor understands its prospects in the event of negotiations, so that it limits its debt exposure to levels that the country will choose to repay. In this case, the required debt servicing will be kept below $(\theta + \gamma)W_t/2$. Note that the lower is the creditor's ability to retaliate in the event of repudiation, as measured by θ and γ, the tighter is the lending limit that creditors will impose. At least in the absence of uncertainty, borrowers are better off with high θ and γ, since the existence of large penalties for repudiation frees up capital inflows.

The Planner's Problem

We have so far discussed three aspects of loan supply to a borrowing country. While a country's ability to repay debt is most likely a necessary condition for attracting new loans, its willingness to repay—and ability to do so on a short-term basis—are probably even more important. Our next task is to study the optimal borrowing choice in light of these constraints.

Let us suppose that the goal of debt policy is to maximize a social welfare function that depends on the consumption flow over time. We will write debtor utility V as:

$$V = \sum_{i=0}^{\infty}(1 + \delta)^{-i}U(C_i). \tag{1.5}$$

C_i is real consumption (either per capita or aggregate) in period i, and $U(C_i)$ is an instantaneous utility in period i, with $U' > 0$ and $U'' \leq 0$. Intertemporal utility is given by a discounted sum of instantaneous utilities, where δ measures the rate of subjective time discount. A function like (1.5) is really an economist's presumption about what borrowing policy should be about, and much less a statement about the actual determinants of borrowing policies. The goals of planners or economic authorities might be much more concerned with the growth of GDP, the use of debt to stabilize a political regime, or even nationalist sentiments against foreign indebtedness, rather than a careful calculation of intertemporal consumption possibilities. Since our topic is an analysis of appropriate borrowing strategies and not an empirical account of actual borrowing behavior, we choose to proceed with (1.5).

Under certainty, and with no illiquidity or repudiation risk, the optimal borrowing problem is:

$$\max V = \sum_{i=0}^{\infty}(1 + \delta)^{-i}U(C_i) \tag{1.6}$$

subject to:

$$\text{(a) } K_{t+1} = K_t(1 - d) + I_t$$

$$\text{(b) } Q_t = F(K_t)$$

$$\text{(c) } D_{t+1} = (1 + r)D_t + (I_t + C_t) - Q_t$$

$$\text{(d) } \lim_{t\to\infty} (1 + r)^{-t} D_t = 0$$

$$\text{(e) } K_0, D_0 \text{ given.}$$

Condition (d) is a convenient way to impose the solvency constraint on borrowing. Implicitly, we are taking the case in which $n < r$, so that foreign borrowing is limited by the future capacity to repay debt. In that case, (d) is equivalent to the condition (1.2) described earlier. Rather than proceeding to a complete solution of (1.6), we shall simplify the problem further. (The complete solution is found numerically in the appendix.) Under optimal policies, the maximum value V is implicitly a function of K_0 and D_0. We write this value at time zero as $V = V(K_0,D_0)$. In a similar way, if the economy enters any period t with an inherited capital stock K_t and debt D_t, optimal policies from that period on will yield intertemporal utility of $V(K_t,D_t)$. Now we will consider the planner's problem at time zero. He will choose values of C_0 and I_0, which then yield K_1 and D_1 via (1.6) (a)–(c). Thereafter, he will continue to borrow optimally, so that from period 1 onward, the economy achieves $V(K_1,D_1)$. From the perspective of period zero, utility is therefore $V(K_0,D_0) = U(C_0) + V(K_1,D_1)/(1 + \delta)$. The infinite horizon problem becomes a one-period problem as long as $V(K_1,D_1)$ is known.

Since it will be more useful to work with a two-period variant of the problem in (1.6), we will rewrite the planner's problem as:

(1.7) $$\max V(K_0,D_0) = U(C_0) + U(C_1)/(1 + \delta) + V(K_2,D_2)/(1 + \delta)^2$$

subject ' :

$$\text{(a) } K_{t+1} = K_t(1 - d) + I_t \qquad t = 0,1$$

$$\text{(b) } Q_t = F(K_t)$$

$$\text{(c) } D_{t+1} = (1 + r)D_t + (I_t + C_t) - Q_t$$

(d) K_0,D_0 given.

We shall assume that the function $V(K_2,D_2)$ is known, and study the optimal choices in periods zero and 1. In fact, for many of our results we will not need to know $V(K_2,D_2)$. In general, $V(K_2,D_2)$ may be found by more powerful methods of optimal control or dynamic programming, or the infinite horizon problem in (1.9) may be approached more directly, as in the appendix.

OPTIMAL BORROWING WITHOUT ILLIQUIDITY OR REPUDIATION RISKS

In this section we study the optimal borrowing decision when borrowing is limited only by a solvency constraint. The solvency constraint is implicitly built into the $V(K_2,D_2)$ function. Let $W_2 = \max \Sigma_{i=2}^{\infty}(1 + r)^{-(i-2)}(Q_i - I_i)$. W_2 is implicitly a function of K_2, so that the solvency constraint $(1 + r)D_2 \leq W_2(K_2)$ is a constraint on debt relative to the capital stock. When $(1 + r)D_2 = W_2(K_2)$, consumption must be zero forever into the future in order to service the debt, so that $V[K_2,W_2(K_2)] = \Sigma_{i=2}^{\infty}(1 + \delta)^{-(i-2)}U(0)$, which is obviously a lower limit for V.

The optimal borrowing strategy is found by direct optimization of (1.7). The first-order conditions are:

(1.8)

$$\text{(a) } U_0(C_0) = \lambda$$

$$\text{(b) } U_1(C_1)/(1 + \delta) = \lambda/(1 + r)$$

$$\text{(c) } F_K(K_1) = (r + d)$$

(d) λ is the marginal utility of wealth.

The results of the optimization are straightforward and well known. With a perfect world capital market, borrowing and lending should be undertaken to smooth the marginal utility of consumption over time. The marginal utility of consumption in period i (MUC_i) is given by $U_i(C_i)/(1 + \delta)^i$, where $U_i(C_i)$ denotes $\partial U(C_i)/\partial C_i$. The present-value price of output in period i is $\pi_i = (1 + r)^{-i}$, where π_i is the number of units of output that must be saved at time zero in order to yield one unit of the good in period i. The consumption smoothing rule is then:

(1.9) $$MUC_i/\pi_i = \lambda \text{ for all periods i.}$$

The major implication of (1.9) has been described in earlier works (Sachs 1982b, 1984). Basically, it reflects the old dictum, "Finance a temporary shock, adjust to a permanent shock." When output is temporarily depressed, λ does not change much, and, according to (1.9), the MUC should also remain unchanged. This involves maintaining a high rate of consumption, in spite of temporarily low output, by accumulating debt. When output is permanently reduced, λ rises, so that MUC in every period should also rise. In effect, consumption is reduced in line with lower permanent income, and the country should not borrow in order to maintain a high rate of consumption.

(1.8)(c) expresses the second half of the standard borrowing strategy. Investments should be undertaken to the point where the marginal product of capital equals the world cost of capital, where the latter is measured as a world real interest plus the rate of depreciation. In more complex investment environments, this rule would be restated as a rule to undertake all investment projects with positive present value at the world interest rate.

Let us suppose that these guidelines are to be adopted. By what set of policy rules can they be implemented? Under a set of restrictive conditions, the guidelines are those that would be adopted, in a fully decentralized economy, by firms that maximize value and by households that maximize utility. The necessary assumptions are:

- perfect foresight (or rational expectations under uncertainty)
- the social welfare function V as the representative household's utility function
- unrestricted access of households and firms to the world capital market
- no taxes on other distortions that cause the private marginal product of capital to diverge from the social marginal product of capital (F_K)
- no taxes or other distortions that cause the posttax real interest rate to diverge from the world real interest rate.

If these conditions hold, then the laissez-faire approach to foreign borrowing will yield an optimal path of external indebtedness. When any of these conditions is violated, the case for laissez-faire is substantially weakened. Although much of the rest of the chapter involves relaxing the assumptions needed to justify laissez-faire, it is useful to mention a few examples of how these assumptions may be violated. Some illustrative cases are described in table 1-1.

We now turn to some key extensions of the basic model, still assuming the absence of liquidity and repudiation risk.

Traded versus Nontraded Goods

Let us suppose that the economy produces nontraded as well as traded goods. Sectoral output is written as a function of sectoral capital stocks (labor input is suppressed, but could be added easily): $Q^T = F^T(K^T)$ and $Q^N = F^N(K^N)$. Let P_t^N signify the relative price of nontradables in terms of tradables in period t. Consumption is divided between N and T subject to an intertemporal

Table 1-1. Assumptions Underlying the Case for Laissez-faire

Assumption	Examples of violation
Perfect foresight or rational expectations	Households or firms may incorrectly extrapolate current exchange rates and interest rates into the future, particularly since governments tend to promise that there will be no exchange rate changes.
Social welfare function	The government's planning horizon and rate of time preference may differ from that of a "typical household." Ideally, governments may represent future generations that are underrepresented in the interests of current households.
Access to world capital markets	Most capital markets in developing countries are highly segmented, so that "free" access to the world market may imply a sharply different degree of access for different groups within the economy, and may therefore have perverse effects on resource allocation.
Equality of social and private marginal products of capital	This assumption will be violated for public goods (for example, physical infrastructure)—a crucial reason for direct government intervention in the investment process. Similarly, tariffs and domestic taxes may drive a wedge between market and shadow prices.
Equality of domestic and world interest rates	Taxes and subsidies on capital, market segmentation, and a noncompetitive financial sector may all contribute to a major divergence between the world cost of capital and the domestic interest rate. In addition, externalities in the borrowing process may lead individual borrowers to drive up the external cost of funds for others. In this case, interest rates will not equal the marginal cost of funds to the country as a whole.

social welfare function of the form $V = \Sigma_{i=0}^{\infty}(1 + \delta)^{-i}U(C_i^T,C_i^N)$. For the sake of simplicity, all investment is assumed to use the traded good (here, too, extension to the general case is straightforward). Let I^N be investment made in the non-traded-goods sector (using tradable output) and I^T be investment in tradable goods production, so that $K_{t+1}^T = K_t^T(1 - d) + I_t^T$ and $K_{t+1}^N = K_t^N(1 - d) + I_t^N$. The trade balance is $Q^T - C^T - (I^T + I^N)$ and non-traded-good equilibrium is $Q^N = C^N$.

With regard to the solvency condition, productive wealth must be redefined as productive tradables wealth, max $\Sigma_{i=0}^{\infty} (1 + r)^{-i}(Q_i^T - I_i^T - I_i^N)$. External debt cannot exceed the present discounted value of net tradables production, since by definition only tradable goods can be used for exports to service the external debt.

Let us now consider the two-period borrowing problem with tradables and nontradables:

$$\max U(C_0^T,C_0^N) + U(C_1^T,C_1^N)/(1 + \delta) + V(K_2^N,K_2^T,D_2)(1 + \delta)^2 \tag{1.10}$$

subject to:

$$\begin{aligned}
D_{t+1} &= (1 + r)D_t + Q_t^T - C_t^T - (I_t^T + I_t^N)\\
Q_t^N &= C_t^N\\
K_{t+1}^T &= K_t^T(1 - d) + I_t^T\\
K_{t+1}^N &= K_t^N(1 - d) + I_t^N\\
Q_t^T &= F^T(K_t^T)\\
Q_t^N &= F^N(K_t^N).
\end{aligned}$$

The solution to this problem is easily shown to be:

$$\begin{aligned}
&\text{(a) } U_{OT} = \lambda\\
&U_{ON} = \lambda P_O^N\\
&U_{1T} = \lambda(1 + \delta)/(1 + r)\\
&U_{1N} = \lambda P_1^N(1 + \delta)/(1 + r)\\
&\text{(b) } F_K^T(K_1^T) = (r + d)\\
&P_1^N F_K^N(K_1^N) = (r + d).
\end{aligned} \tag{1.11}$$

The main insight from this optimization is that current decisions regarding consumption and investment must involve forecasts of the future relative price of nontradables. At time zero, for example, the investment in nontraded goods should equate $P_1^N F_K^N(K_1^N)$ with $(r + d)$. It will likely be the case that P_1^N will not equal P_O^N, so that unrealistic expectations regarding P^N will result in a misallocation of investment expenditure. We provide a quantitative illustration of this point in the appendix.

Official Borrowing To Augment Private Savings

In many countries, private investment may be insufficient for generating desired growth rates in the economy. The public sector is often regarded as an "engine of growth" in augmenting the rate of capital accumulation. Underdeveloped domestic capital markets may cause private savings, and hence private investment, to remain low. Fiscal expenditures on investment goods may then form a significant share of total capital formation, with foreign official borrowing playing an important role in the finance of government investment, and taxes playing a crucial role in generating official resources for debt servicing. It is not surprising that the optimal borrowing strategy must be recomputed under these circumstances, for debt-servicing capacity depends not only on national wealth but also on the public sector's ability to tax that wealth. When there are weaknesses (either political or economic) in the government's authority to raise taxes, governments must be especially cautious in their foreign borrowing. The following illustration underlines this need for caution. (This section relies heavily on Sachs 1984.)

Let us suppose that, because of an underdeveloped capital market, the private sector in the developing country saves a fixed fraction of posttax income, rather than optimizing intertemporally. The government uses its taxing and borrowing authority to supplement private savings. (See Arrow and Kurz 1970, chap. 6, for a similar model of imperfect capital markets.) Private investors have no direct access to the international loan market. The government taxes domestic output at rate τ_t, which may change over time. This rate must be less than 1.0, and may be less than zero if the government is making net income transfers to the private sector. There is no public consumption.

With domestic output given by Q_t, tax revenues are $\tau_t Q_t$, and private sector savings are $s(1 - \tau_t)Q_t$. Private consumption is given by $C_t = (1 - s)(1 - \tau_t)Q_t$. In any period, the government borrows D_{t+1} and repays $(1 + r)D_t$. Total investment in the economy is given by:

$$I_t = \underset{\text{(private savings)}}{s(1 - \tau_t)Q_t} + \underset{\text{(tax revenue)}}{\tau_t Q_t} + \underset{\text{(net foreign resource inflow)}}{[D_{t+1} - (1 + r)D_t]}. \tag{1.12}$$

As written, it appears that all foreign borrowing is used for investment rather than consumption, but this is true only as an accounting matter. For example, the government may want to raise private consumption while holding investment levels fixed. It merely raises D_{t+1} while reducing τ_t sufficiently to keep I_t constant; in that case the borrowing finances consumption 100 percent on the margin.

Let us now calculate the optimal financial policy of the government, assuming again that it tries to maximize an intertemporal utility function of the form $U(C_0) + U(C_1)/(1 + \delta) + V(K_2,D_2)/(1 + \delta)^2$.

(1.13) The Basic Public Finance Problem with International Borrowing

$$\max_{I_0,I_1,\tau_0,\tau_1} U(C_0) + U(C_1)/(1 + \delta) + V(K_2,D_2)/(1 + \delta)^2$$

subject to:

$$Q_t = F(K_t)$$

$$K_{t+1} = K_t(1 - d) + I_t$$

$$C_t = (1 - s)(1 - \tau_t)Q_t$$

$$I_t = s(1 - \tau_t)Q_t + \tau_t Q_t + D_{t+1} - (1 + r)D_t.$$

As long as tax rates are completely flexible, the solution to this problem is identical to the solution to (1.7), since the dynamic budget constraint facing the government is no different whether it chooses C_t and I_t, as before, or τ_t and I_t, as here.

To find the tax rates corresponding to this optimal plan, note that $C_1 = (1 - s)(1 - \tau_1)F(K_1)$, so that $\tau_1 = 1 - [C_1/F(K_1)][1/(1 - s)]$. Assuming that s is fixed, a typical optimal growth path will involve a rising τ. Low tax rates in the early period allow households to benefit early on from the growth that will be achieved in periods 1 and 2. Higher taxes later on are necessary to service the international debt.

Now let us introduce a simple yet crucial hitch into the model. The government can only raise tax rates to a limit $\bar{\tau} < 1$, and the constraint is binding in the sense that the optimal τ_0 or τ_1, or both, exceeds $\bar{\tau}$. The first effect of the tax ceiling is a significant tightening of the solvency constraint in (1.2). Debt repayment now depends on taxing authority as well as national wealth. The new constraint is that $D_t(1 + r)$ must be less than or equal to the maximum level of tax revenues net of government investment. Government investment is I_t minus private investment, $s(1 - \tau_t)Q_t$. Thus,

$$D_t(1 + r) \leq \max_{\tau, I} \sum_{i=t}^{\infty} (1 + r)^{-(i-t)} [\tau_t Q_t - I_t + s(1 - \tau_t)Q_t]. \tag{1.14}$$

It is more likely that (1.14) rather than (1.2) holds as a binding constraint, since (1.14) does <u>not</u> imply that future consumption must equal zero when the constraint binds. Nonetheless, in the examples that follow, we do not consider the case in which (1.14) binds. We focus rather on the constraint $\tau = \bar{\tau}$, assuming D_t remains below the maximum level in (1.14).

Since the optimal tax path tends to involve rising τ, a natural case to consider is one in which the tax constraint does not bind in period zero while it does bind in period 1. Thus, we assume $\tau_0 < \bar{\tau}$ and $\tau_1 = \bar{\tau}$. What are the implications of the tax constraint? Basically, first-period consumption C_1 remains "too high" relative to the plan that an unconstrained government would choose, since the fiscal authority would like to raise taxes in the first period but cannot do so. Therefore, the marginal utility of income in the first period is <u>too low</u>, and the returns to investment in period 1, namely, $F_K(K_1)$, should be given a weight less than 1.0 in project analysis. After some algebraic computations, we can prove:

$$F_K(K_1) = (r + d) \cdot \varepsilon \text{ where } \varepsilon > 1. \tag{1.15}$$

We have the key result:

> Under a regime of constrained tax levies, the marginal product of capital should no longer be equated with the world market cost of capital but rather should be kept <u>higher</u>, to reflect a lower shadow value of first-period output.

If the government follows the standard rule $F_K(K_1) = r + d$, the country is led to <u>overborrow</u>, with the result that social welfare is reduced.

Let us consider a graphic case of this issue that follows the analysis in Kharas (1981). A government cares only about <u>growth</u>, in the sense that $u(C_0) \equiv (C_1) \equiv 0$, and $V(K_2,D_2) = F(K_2) - (1 + r)D_2$. The government is trying to maximize national income (net of international indebtedness) in the second period. If τ_t is not constrained, τ_0 and τ_1 should be set at 1.0, with government revenue plus net foreign borrowing used to equate $F_K(K_1)$ with $r + d$, according to the classical policy prescription.

Now let us suppose that $\tau_0, \tau_1 \leq \bar{\tau} < 1$. Since consumption has no weight in utility, it is optimal to set taxes at their maximum rate: $\tau_0 = \tau_1 = \bar{\tau}$. Then, D_2 and K_2 are given by:

$$D_2 = (1 + r)\{I_0 - [s(1 - \bar{\tau}) + \bar{\tau}]F(K_0)\} + \{I_1 - [s(1 - \bar{\tau}) + \bar{\tau}]\,F[K_0(1 - d) + I_0]\}$$

$$K_2 = K_0(1 - d)^2 + I_0(1 - d) + I_1.$$

By setting $\partial V/\partial I_0 = \partial V/\partial I_1 = 0$, we find the optimal investment policy. Using algebra, we find:

$$\begin{aligned} F_K(K_1) &= \frac{(r + d)}{s(1 - \bar{\tau}) + \bar{\tau}} > r + d \\ F_K(K_2) &= (1 + r). \end{aligned} \tag{1.16}$$

Once again, the country should not invest enough to equate $F_K(K_1)$ and $r + d$.

This model provides a powerful indictment against foreign borrowing—even for productive

Figure 1-2. Foreign Borrowing and Growth in a Tax-Constrained Regime

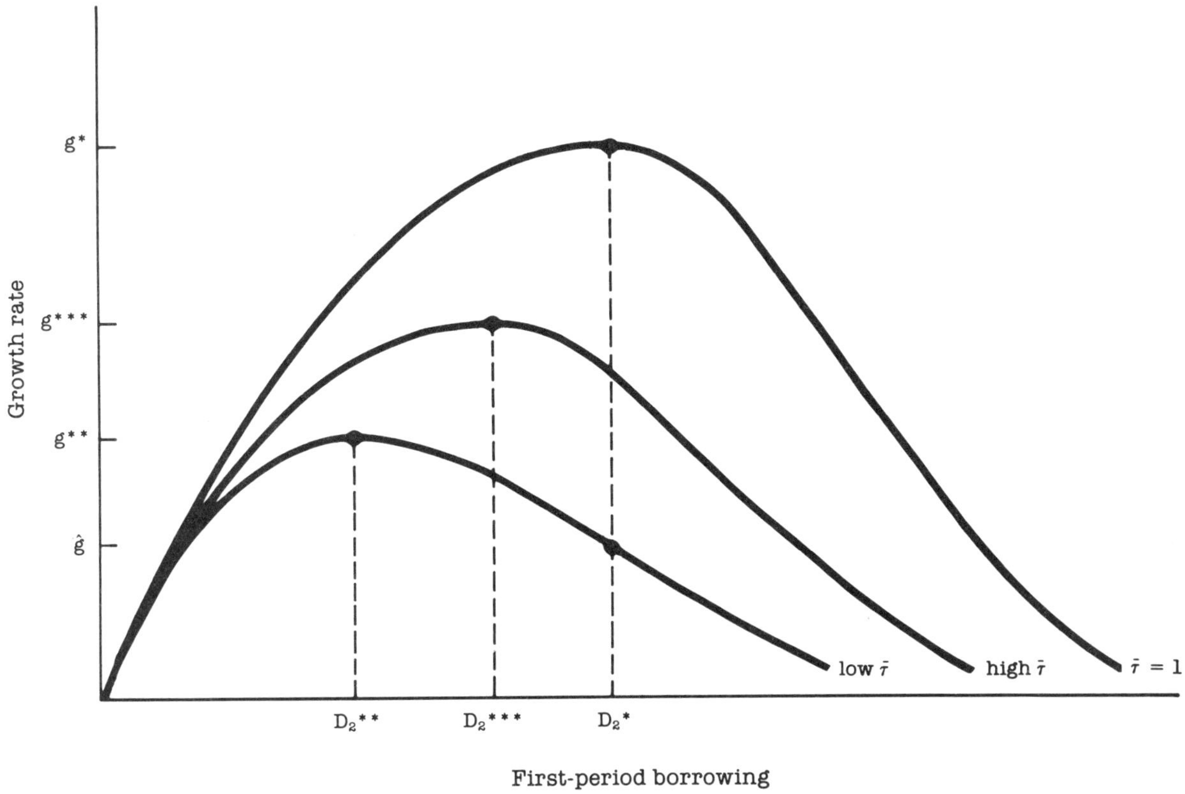

Note: Growth is measured by $F(K_3) - (1 + r)D_3$, as in text.

investment projects—if the domestic fiscal system is not equipped to handle rising debt-service ratios. Figure 1-2 illustrates how aggregate growth is slowed, for specific parameter values of the model, by excessive borrowing in a tax-constrained regime. In the unconstrained regime, optimal borrowing is at D_2^*, with growth g^*. In the constrained case, with a low $\bar{\tau}$, the optimum is at $D_2^{**} < D_2^*$, with growth at $g^{**} < g^*$; and in the constrained case with a high $\bar{\tau}$, the optimum is at D_2^{***}, with growth at g^{***}. If the borrower with low $\bar{\tau}$ equates $F_K(K_1)$ with $r + d$, in spite of the tax constraint, the growth rate ends up at $\hat{g}$ (corresponding to D_2^*), which is lower than can be achieved with less foreign borrowing, g^{**}.

OPTIMAL BORROWING WITH LIQUIDITY CONSTRAINTS

Debt crises almost never involve the strict solvency constraint in foreign borrowing. Well before consumption levels are driven to subsistence, countries typically repudiate their foreign debt or succeed in gaining debt relief. Often a debt crisis has little to do with fundamental solvency considerations but, rather, turns on the short-run difficulties of debt servicing. In this section, we explore how borrowing strategies should be modified when short-run liquidity risks are present. We establish two principal results. First, the optimal level of borrowing depends importantly on the probability of a cutoff in lending. Second, the possibility of a lending cutoff increases the importance of the maturity structure of the debt. The standard prescription that long-term projects should be financed with long-term loans grows in importance as the probability of a lending cutoff rises.

We begin with an extremely simple version of the two-period model, without considering physical investment. The goal of borrowing is to maximize expected utility.

$$\max E(V) = E[U(C_0) + U(C_1)/(1+\delta) + V(D_2)/(1+\delta)^2] \tag{1.17}$$

subject to:

$$C_0 = Q_0 + D_1$$

$$C_1 = Q_1 + D_2 - (1+r)D_1$$

Borrowing constraint:

with probability π, $D_2 \leq 0$ (that is, no foreign borrowing)

with probability $(1-\pi)$, D_2 not restricted

With probability π, the country is unable to obtain new finance D_2 in period 1, and the country must borrow D_1 without knowing whether D_2 will in fact be available. At this point, we assume that π is independent of the level of debt. Below, we introduce the more realistic assumption that π rises with D_1, that is, that high debt levels make potential creditors less likely to extend new debt.

Let us first consider the case when $\pi = 0$. From our earlier results we know that $U_0(C_0) = U_1(C_1)(1+r)/(1+\delta)$ and that $U_1(C_1) = -V_D/(1+\delta)$. When $\pi > 0$, there may be two outcomes: either the economy is liquidity-constrained (denoted by superscript L) or it is not (denoted by superscript N). D_1 is borrowed before the outcome in the next period is known. Consumption turns out to be $C_1^L = Q_1 - (1+r)D_1$ if the borrowing constraint holds, and $C_1^N = Q_1 - (1+r)D_1 + D_2^N$ if it does not.[3] Clearly $C_1^N > C_1^L$. In case N, D_2^N is selected according to the standard criterion $U_1^N(C_1^N) = -V_D(D_2^N)/(1+\delta)$. In case L, we have $U_1^L(C_1^L) > -V_D(0)/(1+\delta)$. Parenthetically, D_2^N is an increasing function of D_1.[4]

By writing $E(V)$ as $U(C_0) + \pi[U(C_1^L)/(1+\delta) + V(0)/(1+\delta)^2] + (1-\pi)[U(C_1^N)/(1+\delta) + V(D_2^N)/(1+\delta)^2]$, we find the optimal borrowing level D_1 as the solution to $d(EV)/dD_1 = 0$:

$$d(EV)/dD_1 = 0 \Rightarrow U_0 = [(1+r)/(1+\delta)][\pi U_1^L + (1-\pi)U_1^N] \tag{1.18}$$

By totally differentiating this equation with respect to D_1, D_2^N, and π, we can find the dependence of D_1 on π. With the help of some algebra, we can show[5]

$$dD_1/d\pi < 0 \tag{1.19}$$

Thus, as the probability of a second-period lending cutoff rises, optimum first-period borrowing should decline.

Liquidity Crises and Borrowing Externalities

Should governments regulate foreign borrowing if liquidity crises are possible? Under special circumstances, the answer would be no. In general, however, this form of market failure does provide a case for intervention. The model we have just explored can justify laissez-faire, if the following assumptions hold:

- The private sector has rational expectations of a liquidity crisis.
- The probability π is not a function of the overall level of borrowing.
- The government can credibly commit itself to refuse to bail out private agents who find their credit cut off.
- The liquidity crisis causes no widespread bankruptcies; or, if bankruptcies occur, they are handled efficiently, without social cost.

If these assumptions are maintained, then individual agents will choose their intertemporal plans so that $U_0 = E(U_1)[(1 + \delta)/(1 + r)]$, where $E(U_1) = \pi U_1^L + (1 - \pi)U_1^N$. This is precisely the first-order condition found in (1.18).

All of these assumptions are highly suspect. As far as the first assumption is concerned, borrowers probably do not have a good understanding of financial crises (neither, it would seem, do many economists or governments), much less an ability to predict their occurrence. With regard to the second, although π is hard to forecast, it is likely that the frequency of a loan cutoff increases with the amount of debt outstanding. We have already argued that such a crisis arises when no single lender is willing to lend the country as much as it needs to remain current on debt servicing. That possibility cannot arise when D_1 is very low.

The third assumption is doubtful because, when liquidity crises arise, governments are almost inevitably called upon to bail out debt-ridden firms. As Diaz-Alejandro has recently argued (1984, pp. 19, 22), based on the experience of Argentina, Uruguay, and Chile:

> Whether or not deposits are explicitly insured, the public expects governments to intervene to save most depositors from losses when financial intermediaries run into trouble. Warnings that intervention will not be forthcoming appear to be simply not believable. . . .
>
> Foreign lenders take government announcements that it will not rescue local private debtors, especially banks, with non-guaranteed external (or domestic) liabilities even less seriously than depositors take the threat of a loss of their money. . . . Foreign bank lending to both the public and private sectors of a country have considerable leverage to convince governments to take over ex-post bad private debts, especially those of financial intermediaries.

If the government is always expected to bail out bad debts, moral hazard problems will be rife. Debtors will no longer expect to feel the full brunt of the crisis, since losses will be socialized (that is, spread among borrowers and nonborrowers throughout the economy). Obviously, overborrowing may then arise.

The fourth assumption, that bankruptcies impose no social costs, is also unlikely. In an ideal legal system, overextended debtors would simply transfer their equity claims to creditors without a loss of production in those firms still covering variable costs. In practice, when firms go bankrupt, they often cease operations in the short or long run, which leads to unemployment of resources. Indeed, it is often because bankruptcies impose heavy social costs that governments are obliged to extend debt relief.

It is not very easy to specify the appropriate borrowing strategy when the above complexities exist. It is, however, worthwhile to take just one of the issues and develop its implications analytically. Let us suppose that the model remains as in (1.17), but now with π an increasing function of D_1. When we recalculate the optimal borrowing level by setting $d(EV)/dD_1 = 0$, we find:

$$U_0 = [(1 + r)/(1 + \delta)][\pi U_1^L + (1 - \pi)U_1^N] + (d\pi/dD_1)[V_1^N - V_1^L]/(1 + \delta) \tag{1.20}$$

where

$$V_1^N = U(C_1^N) + V(D_2^N)/(1 + \delta)$$

$$V_1^L = U(C_1^L) + V(0)/(1 + \delta)$$

and

$$V_1^N - V_1^L > 0.$$

Compare the expressions for U_0 in (1.18) and (1.20). We see in (1.20) that U_0 is greater than $[(1 + r)/(1 + \delta)][\pi U_1^L + (1 - \pi)U_1^N]$ by a term that reflects the effect of D_1 on π. Basically, (1.20) holds that r does not reflect the marginal cost of external funds, since an increase in D_1 also makes more likely a liquidity crisis that reduces welfare.

If the marginal borrower behaves as if π is given, the private marginal cost of funds (r) will fall short of the social cost, and overborrowing will occur. Laissez-faire is no longer the best policy, even if all of the other necessary assumptions hold true. The optimal borrowing strategy is then to tax foreign borrowing, so that private and social costs are aligned. The situation is formally equivalent to the Bhagwati and Srinivasan (1975) argument for a disruption tariff when high export levels raise the possibility of foreign trade retaliation.

Liquidity Crises and Debt Maturities

The possibility of a cutoff of the loan supply provides an important reason for matching the maturity structure of the debt with the gestation period of physical capital investment. Let us suppose that an incremental investment opportunity dI_1 becomes available in the problem in (1.20). We call the investment "short-term" if it pays off in the next period and "long-term" if it pays off in two periods. For the short-term case, we assume that the yield is $(1 + \theta)dI_1$, with $\theta > r$. For the long-term case, the yield after two periods is $(1 + \theta)^2 dI_1$, again with $\theta > r$. We also assume the existence of short- and long-term loans, with the same interest rate per period. A short-term loan D_1^S requires repayment $(1 + r)D_1^S$ in the next period. A long-term loan D_1^L requires repayment $(1 + r)^2 D_1^L$ in two periods.

It is easy to prove the following results:

- For any π, the short-term project should be undertaken with short-term finance.
- For any π, the long-term project should be undertaken with long-term finance.
- The long-term project should not necessarily be undertaken with short-term finance. This is true even though the project has positive present value at the world interest. The project becomes more desirable the lower is π and the greater is θ relative to r.

The proof of these propositions is simple. Let us start at an equilibrium with no investment. When maturities of I and D are matched, it is easy to show that consumption plans can be left unchanged, and final indebtedness D_2 can be lowered, by undertaking the investment project. In the case of short-term finance for a long-term project, the demonstration is a little more involved. Basically, a liquidity crisis is more severe the larger is D_1. If $\theta = r$, then undertaking the investment yields no net benefits, but it does impose a cost by raising D_1 (and therefore raising the welfare loss in the event of a liquidity crisis). Therefore, θ must be sufficiently above r to justify new borrowing.[6]

Generally, long-term debt reduces the costs of a possible lending cutoff. This is true for two reasons. First, and most obvious, for a given external debt, the shorter is the maturity structure, the greater on average is the amount of principal repayment in a given period. Therefore, the larger is the required short-run cut in domestic spending if new lending suddenly ceases. Second, and perhaps more important, a judicious use of long-term borrowing with short-term lending (that is, reserve accumulation) can help to obviate liquidity crises by reducing the need to borrow in a given period. Let us suppose that without fear of a debt cutoff the optimal path of short-term borrowing would be D_1 in the first period and D_2 in the next. With long-term loans, this pattern can be replicated without any second-period borrowing (if, as we have assumed, both short-term and long-term loans have the same interest rate per period). The economy simply borrows $[D_1 + D_2/(1 + r)]$ in long-term funds, and puts $D_2/(1 + r)$ into reserves. The reserves have value D_2 in the next period, and these reserves are then drawn down to zero in the following period. Thus, it becomes irrelevant whether new lending is or is not available in that period!

The fact that countries hold substantial reserves provides good evidence that liquidity can be a serious concern. Governments borrow long term to hold reserves even though the cost of long-term finance is higher than the returns to official reserves. This behavior makes sense if governments are willing to pay a premium to assure the availability of foreign exchange in a given period. Other evidence in this regard shows that countries often pay commitment fees to guarantee the availability of loans at a future date.

BORROWING STRATEGIES WHEN DEBT REPUDIATION IS FEASIBLE

Now we examine the case in which countries can repay debt in both the short term and long term, but may be unwilling to do so (this section relies heavily on Sachs and Cohen 1982). The key to modeling debt repudiation is an explicit assumption regarding its benefits and costs. The benefits are straightforward: the borrower saves the real value of the outstanding debt, which it no longer services. The costs are far more difficult to specify (see Sachs 1982b, for a discussion of the historical experience). One aspect of the costs may be a partial or complete inability to obtain new loans in the world capital markets, at least for some time after the repudiation occurs. Another aspect of the costs may be a direct seizure of the country's overseas assets, including bank accounts, foreign direct investments, ships, and aircraft. A third, and even more important, cost may be a dramatic decline in the country's capacity to engage in trade, even if no net new borrowing is involved. Modern trade is built on a sophisticated system of revolving trade credits. Even if a country's net debt is zero, its gross stocks of financial assets and liabilities related to trade are likely to be large. Because a borrower would have difficulty arranging trade credits after a repudiation, the mechanics of trade would be made onerous. Moreover, merchandise at ports ready to be dispatched to the debtor country could be subject to seizure by creditors.

To introduce these elements, we assume that when a debt is repudiated the creditors retaliate by imposing two costs: in all future periods, the borrower's production is reduced, for given K, by a fixed fraction θ; and, second, the borrower is excluded from all further borrowing. We now assume that this retaliation yields neither costs nor benefits to the creditors (or that the costs and benefits cancel). In terms of the discussion in the first section, we set $\gamma = 0$.

We begin with a simplified version of the international borrowing model (we simply drop $V[K_2,D_2]$). The tax considerations are ignored, so that we implicitly assume that domestic tax levies are not constrained. Loans are made to the sovereign borrower in period zero. If they are not repaid in period 1, the penalty is enforced and output is reduced by θQ_1. The borrower makes the repudiation decision in period 1; there is no way that it can "precommit" itself, that is, commit itself to a decision before the period arrives. Moreover, for the purposes of this section, the possibility of a negotiated settlement is put aside. (The general principles of credit rationing are the same when ex post facto negotiations are allowed.) Since second-period utility is simply $u(C_1)$, the borrower compares consumption levels with and without repudiation. With repudiation, C_1 equals $Q_1 - \theta Q_1 = (1 - \theta)Q_1$. (We denote this level as C_1^R.) With no repudiation, C_1 equals $Q_1 - (1 + r)D_1$, which we term C_1^N. The borrower defaults whenever C_1^R exceeds C_1^N, and thus whenever $(1 + r)D_1 > \theta\, Q_1$.

There are two choices with respect to the timing of loans. The level of credit D_1 may be extended before or after the investment decision I_0 is made. We shall see shortly that it is a great advantage to the country to be able to choose I_0 before going to the capital markets. I_0 may then be chosen to make the credit terms on a given loan more favorable, or to increase the total amount that the country can borrow. A more natural assumption, however, is that loans are arranged first and the government then allocates them to consumption and investment. In this case, the government will generally have an incentive to renege on a promised level of I_0 once a loan has been arranged, even if ex ante it would be better off to fix I_0. Thus, promises concerning I_0 will be unconvincing. We term the example in which I_1 is set first the "precommitment" equilibrium, and regard the other case as the "standard" assumption.

A linear model offers a vivid illustration of the effects of repudiation risk and of investment precommitment. Let

$$
\begin{aligned}
(1.21)\qquad Q_0 &= \overline{Q} \\
Q_1 &= \overline{Q} + (1+\gamma)I_0, \qquad I_0 \leq \overline{I} \\
V &= C_0 + C_1/(1+\delta) \\
\delta &> \gamma > r.
\end{aligned}
$$

According to (1.21), there is a quantity $\overline{I}$ of investment projects with a rate of return γ exceeding the world interest rate r. The rate of time discount δ is assumed to be greater than the world interest rate. In the no-repudiation model, utility V is maximized by setting $I_0 = \overline{I}$ (all investment projects are undertaken). Consumption is shifted entirely to the first period with no consumption in the second (since $\delta > r$ and utility is linear). In sum:

(1.22) The Case of No Repudiation

$$
\begin{aligned}
C_0 &= \overline{Q} + [\overline{Q} + (1+\gamma)\overline{I}]/(1+r) \\
I_0 &= \overline{I} \\
C_1 &= 0 \\
D_1 &= C_0 + I_0 - \overline{Q}
\end{aligned}
$$

We now turn to the "standard" case of the repudiation model. Once a loan D_1 is arranged, the borrower will choose to set $I_0 = 0$, since $\delta > \gamma$. Therefore, $Q_1 = \overline{Q}$, and the debt ceiling is given by $\overline{D}_1 = \theta\overline{Q}/(1+r)$. The complete solution is:

(1.23) The Standard Repudiation Case

$$
\begin{aligned}
C_0 &= \overline{Q} + \theta\overline{Q}(1+r) \\
I_0 &= 0 \\
C_1 &= \overline{Q} - \theta\overline{Q} \\
D_1 &= \theta\overline{Q}/(1+r)
\end{aligned}
$$

Therefore, the presence of repudiation risk results in rationing for the borrower (note that D_1 is lower in [1.23] than in the previous equation). Investment is reduced (all the way to zero in this example) and consumption is pushed to the second period. The presence of repudiation risk reduces the borrower's welfare by restricting capital inflows.

Finally, we turn to the precommitment case. The borrower may be able to raise its welfare by promising a high level of investment I_0. Higher I_0 raises Q_1 and thus raises the penalty for repudiation, which equals θQ_1. When I_0 is high, creditors are therefore more willing to lend, and the credit constraint is eased. In this version, the borrowing country will choose to precommit to $I_0 = \overline{I}$ when γ is close to δ, and when δ is much greater than r. Specifically, we find:

(1.24) The Precommitment Repudiation Case

$$
\begin{aligned}
C_0 &= \overline{Q} + D_1 - I_0 \\
I_0 &= 0 \text{ for } (\delta - r)\theta(1+\gamma) < (\delta - \gamma)(1+r) \\
I_0 &= \overline{I} \text{ for } (\delta - r)\theta(1+\gamma) > (\delta - \gamma)(1+r) \\
C_1 &= Q_1 - \lambda Q_1 \\
D_1 &= \theta Q_1/(1+r)
\end{aligned}
$$

Thus, the precommitment case may be the same as the no-precommitment case, but might (and generally will) result in an equilibrium somewhere between the textbook model and the standard repudiation model. Precommitment makes sense when $\delta \approx r$ (that is, the rate of time discount is not too high), and when $\gamma >> r$ (that is, investment is quite profitable). Precommitment allows greater borrowing, greater investment in profitable projects, and higher consumption in the first period.

Repudiation Risk with Uncertainty

So far, an actual default never occurs in the model, although the threat of default has a profound effect on economic welfare and the nature of macroeconomic equilibrium. Once uncertainty is introduced into the model, debt repudiations will actually occur as random events. The presence of uncertainty has several effects. First, the loan supply schedule slopes upward, rather than being perfectly elastic, to a maximum debt level $\bar{D}$. Second, and even more important, the incentive structure for macroeconomic management may become perverse in ways now described. A more complete treatment of debt repudiation under uncertainty may be found in Sachs and Cohen (1982) and Sachs (1984).

A recent theme of financial economics is that the various claimants on a firm's income stream (for example, the shareholders, bondholders, and workers) have differing interests in the firm's policies because alternative policies affect the relative valuation of the different claims. Thus, the shareholders may urge policies that raise shareholder wealth at the expense of bondholder wealth, as described by Jensen and Meckling (1976). Coalitions of the shareholders and banks may engage in policies at the expense of bondholders, especially in the context of bankruptcy actions (see Bulow and Shoven 1978). A notable feature of these examples is that, in order to benefit some groups, the firm may pursue inefficent policies that not only hurt other groups but also reduce the overall value of the firm. A related theme is that all groups are generally left better off, ex ante, if the firm can be constrained from pursuing such inefficient policies.

Several direct analogies can be made from the above example to macroeconomic behavior by the borrowing country. As is the case with a firm, a country also has various claimants on the income stream, including the government, domestic citizens, and international creditors. The country may also be led to select inefficient policies to transfer income from the creditors to the "shareholders" (the government and domestic private sector). In general, the country would like to foreswear these policies ex ante but may find it difficult to do so.

There are several areas of behavior in which timing and default risk interact to produce bad microeconomic choices. The earlier discussion of investment precommitment can be thought of precisely in these terms. From an ex ante point of view, it is best for the country to choose a high level of investment, because high investment relaxes borrowing constraints. However, once a loan package is arranged, the country prefers to raise first-period consumption at the expense of investment. Since creditors understand this, they will tend to discount initial promises of high investment plans, and indeed they will be right.

A similar phenomenon occurs when countries borrow with long-term debt. When a country owes long-term debt, each new amount of borrowing tends to reduce the expected value of the original debt by making its eventual repudiation more likely. In many cases, the borrowing country would like to be able to promise a potential long-term creditor that it will not overborrow once the long-term debt is arranged. Such a promise would reduce the risk premium on the long-term debt. However, there will generally be strong incentives, ex post, to do precisely the contrary. The result is, in general, that long-term debt will command a high risk premium and that, as expected, overborrowing will occur.

Market participants search for ways to reduce these deleterious incentives. It may be the case that countries can establish reputations for maintaining macroeconomic policies in line with announced plans. There is a growing economics literature on establishing a reputation which may well give some insights in this direction. Other specific actions, such as relying on short-term borrowing rather than long-term borrowing, may reduce some of the incentive problems. In domestic capital markets, and to a much smaller extent in international lending, bond covenants can be used to precommit the borrower to a future line of action. Smith and Warner (1979) provide an excellent survey of such covenants, indicating how they help to enforce an efficient borrowing and investment plan by corporate borrowers. For example, covenants often directly restrict dividend payments, which may be tantamount to requiring the shareholders to invest rather than "consume" their loans. Other types of provisions include restrictions on new borrowing, maintenance of the firm's existing assets, financial disclosure requirements, and restrictions on merger activity. Such provisions are typically unenforceable when foreign sovereign borrowers are involved and thus are not part of most (international) syndicated loan agreeements.

Further Aspects of Managing Repudiation Risk

So far, we have deduced the optimal borrowing behavior for an economy that has the option of repudiating its debt. As in earlier sections, we should now ask how these optimal borrowing policies can be implemented. What is the role of the government in managing repudiation risk?

Under repudiation risk, there is a profound externality in the borrowing process that leads governments into a central policy role. In many cases, a default or debt repudiation by an individual agent affects market judgments regarding creditworthiness of the country as a whole. Most potential creditors are unable to discern the ultimate causes of a default, and in particular whether the action reflects a weakness of a particular debtor or is instead a signal about government policy and economic health in the whole debtor economy. An individual default raises subjective probabilities of structural weaknesses or widespread mismanagement in an economy, and so causes credit to tighten for all borrowers.

The implications of this spillover are immediate. First, governments—even the most laissez-faire—must assume some responsibility for honoring the external obligations of bankrupt firms in the private sector. Second, creditors act on the expectation of such actions, and indeed may withdraw credits from countries when such actions are not forthcoming. Naturally, therefore, governments must at the minimum undertake the prudential supervision of foreign borrowing by the private sector in order to safeguard the economy's international creditworthiness. In some cases, it may be necessary to make government backing explicit to facilitate the appropriate levels of inflow.

Even when all lending is to the private sector of an economy, creditors will still be correct to aggregate the country's debt in assessing an economy's incentive to repudiate. This is because a government always has ability to nationalize a substantial part of the external debt, and bargain for the country as a whole vis-à-vis the foreign creditors. This has been the experience of several Latin American countries in recent years.

Since the risk of repudiation puts a limit on overall borrowing, the interest rate on international loans may be a poor measure of the marginal cost of funds to a borrowing country. Let us suppose that total lending is rationed at the point $D = \theta Q/(1 + r)$. Those fortunate enough to borrow at the world market rate will pay a price r, while borrowers on the domestic market will be forced to pay a higher price. The shadow price of capital appropriate for the marginal investment decision will be the higher rate. Note that an interest equalization tax on foreign borrowing, raising costs to domestic levels, would improve the microeconomic allocation of investment funds without necessarily increasing the overall supply of external credits.

We have already observed that there may be additional scope for active policies. Governments may have an incentive to spur investment projects for the purpose of enhancing creditworthiness. Another possibility is that governments act to change λ, the cost of repudiation. Trade policies that are geared toward exports probably raise the costs of repudiation by making the country more vulnerable to such penalties as trade embargoes and credit cutoffs. Thus, a bonus for such policies may well be an enhanced access to world credit markets. To a limited extent, governments may also be able to raise θ by offering to collateralize loans. There are cases in which planes and ships have been offered as collateral on trade financing.

It is not easy to discern the welfare effects of changes in θ that are induced by policy. On the one hand, higher θ stimulates the inflow of capital by reducing the likelihood of repudiation. On the other hand, if an economy runs into severe macroeconomic difficulties, the benefit of default is compromised by a high value of θ. Analytical work suggests that there is likely to be an intermediate value $0 < \theta^* < 1$ that maximizes the debtor's expected utility under repudiation risk.

EXTERNAL DEBT AND MACROECONOMIC POLICY

This topic is covered in detail by Dornbusch in chapter 8 of this volume. Here we will focus on the possible complications for macroeconomic policy that are created by (1) the buildup of external debt, and (2) the presence of large external debt.

Despite the fact that countries are free to float their currencies under present international arrangements, most borrowing countries in fact fix their exchange rates—either to another currency or to a weighted average of other currencies. Often, there are periodic adjustments of the central rate, but, in the short run, the exchange rate is fixed by the central bank.

Under these circumstances, external borrowing for local expenditure will lead to monetary expansion. If undertaken freely and extensively, either by the government or by private economic agents, this borrowing interferes with monetary control. Borrowing countries typically have little opportunity to "sterilize" inflows of foreign exchange through the domestic sales of securities or by other means. Thus, new external borrowing more or less directly increases the money supply. External debt that is acquired to cover directly the import of foreign goods or services does not have these internal monetary effects. It is the conversion to local currency at a fixed exchange rate that creates the complication.

Of course, in the short run, the counterpart to external borrowing for local expenditure is an increase in international reserves, and these reserves are available to finance imports. As monetary and income effects work their way through the economy, the demand for imports will increase and reserves will be drawn down; thus, the initial monetary expansion will eventually be reversed. But this corrective process is brought about by the monetary expansion itself. Under some circumstances, therefore, it might be advisable to avoid such expansion. For this reason, many developing countries operating under fixed exchange rates have found it desirable to limit the inflow of foreign capital, especially that which comes through the banking system. Unless their access to international credit is restricted, banks and private firms with access to the international market can escape the rigors of a tight domestic monetary policy. For example, a multinational corporation that is denied credit at the local bank because of monetary restriction can resort to borrowing from its head office or directly from the international market and thereby bypass the local restrictions. In sum, a commitment to a fixed exchange rate under this scenario weakens monetary control; its restoration may require limitations on capital flows.

A high level of debt, not just its rate of change, can also create problems for monetary policy. This is especially true when it comes to rolling over a large external debt or correcting a misalignment in the exchange rate. When such factors are present, changes in the exchange rate can have important effects on the balance sheets of business and financial firms. In particular, a currency devaluation can transmute a solvent firm overnight into a technically insolvent one as the local currency value of external debt is raised.

This process is sometimes necessary and even useful. Firms may have overextended themselves with foreign credit on the basis of an overvalued currency. Their operating costs may have been artificially reduced, insofar as they have imported inputs, by the overvalued currency. Currency devaluation puts a halt to the process and introduces some useful economic disciplines. This affects both the debtors and the foreign creditors, who, under bankruptcy proceedings, would normally share in some of the losses.

Governments are typically reluctant, however, to take steps that will throw firms, especially major firms, into bankruptcy. The presence of extensive external debt may therefore inhibit or force changes in exchange rates in order to limit the financial difficulties of large firms. In 1967, for instance, following the devaluation of sterling, Hong Kong at first devalued the Hong Kong dollar. Not to have done so would have badly weakened the balance sheets of some leading banks, which had assets in sterling, even though on other economic grounds the devaluation was not justified. (Indeed, the action was reversed after a few days when alternative methods for protecting the banks were devised.) In a similar way, some countries put their local development banks into technical insolvency by devaluing the currency. Here, too, the presence of external debt serves to limit macroeconomic policy.

In addition, a large external debt owed by the government itself reduces the flexibility of fiscal policy. Large interest payments cannot be cut if the government desires to retrench. A government may make total budget expenditures, or the total budget deficit, a target of economic policy. The larger is the external debt service, the more pressure must the government bring to bear on domestic expenditures. This is especially true following a currency devaluation—the local currency counterpart of an external debt that is denominated in foreign currency will then rise in proportion to the devaluation. When framing national stabilization programs, however, governments must recognize that interest payments to foreigners do not stimulate the domestic economy. Thus, interest on foreign debt should be treated differently from normal government expenditures.

IS LAISSEZ-FAIRE A DESIRABLE BORROWING STRATEGY?

In an evaluation of the debtor's policies toward external borrowing, a useful reference point is the system whereby all economic agents are completely free to borrow abroad without restriction by the borrowing country. This regime generally existed in the nineteenth century and continues to exist in some advanced countries today (Canada and the United States, for example). Under these circumstances, creditors must assess and take the risks of each borrower separately, just as they do with domestic loans. If a particular loan cannot be repaid, the external creditors share the lose through bankruptcy, without (in principle) affecting the creditworthiness of other (independent) borrowers in the same country.

There are a number of reasons why, at present, the laissez-faire approach is not likely to be suitable for most developing countries. First, their governments have almost universally taken a strong hand in economic management, including economic development. Government influence not only on the macroeconomic environment but also on resource allocation is so pervasive that it is often difficult to say whether a firm's insolvency is attributable to bad management or to government actions. In this situation, creditors will not view the individual projects as independent and will attach great significance to the "country factor."

Second, even under true laissez-faire, creditors may find it prudent to ration credit to an individual borrower when they fear that their information may be imperfect (Stiglitz and Weiss 1981). If the borrowing is truly and persuasively decentralized, the rationing will be by individual borrower, not (in general) by country, except when the risk is identifiable as countrywide. It is common for a country to be at risk, however, because of the usual strong government involvement. In this case, prospective debtors can enlarge their access to credit by taking steps to reduce the perception of country risk. One step, paradoxically, may be to exert closer control over the external borrowing of economic agents.

Furthermore, many of the potential foreign borrowers in a country may be so vital to the maintenance of the national economy that bankruptcy—involving a write-down of the foreign debt—cannot be effected. As we have already seen, this is especially true of banks and of some other financial intermediaries. Both the external reputation of the country and the internal confidence in its institutions may be so closely tied to particular firms that in practice the government must guarantee their external debt or at least avoid any actions that would bring debt servicing into question. Thus, the national government provides guarantees—formal or informal—to the external creditors of the leading banks, and the expectations of the foreign lenders reflect this fact. This may also be true of other important commercial enterprises, especially those that are government-owned. In short, the bankruptcy of certain institutions would have extremely negative repercussions on the external reputation of the debtor country. With this knowledge, the government should monitor closely and perhaps even limit the external indebtedness of these institutions.

The general point is that countries acquire reputations—for prudence or foolhardiness, for caution or boldness in economic planning, for market orientation or "dirigisme," and so on—that are important to creditors in their assessment of creditworthiness. Difficulties experienced by certain borrowers affect the supply-of-funds schedule for the entire country (and, in periods of rapidly moving crises, fraught by exceptional uncertainty, for neighboring countries as well). In short, an informational or reputational externality arises from the inability or unwillingness of lenders to make fine distinctions among borrowers. This occurs in domestic markets as well. For example, virtually all utility stocks are depressed in the United States, in part because of the difficulties of those relatively few utilities with nuclear power plants under construction. Such "pigeonhole effects" dissipate over time as more information becomes available. This may happen, however, only after a liquidity crisis (discussed above) has occurred and much damage has been done—which in turn can lead to the self-fulfillment of pessimistic prophesies.

Direct Responsibility

There are three circumstances in particular under which the government cannot really escape responsibility for external borrowing and therefore must make decisions on both the level and the character of external borrowing.

The first concerns borrowing by the government itself for the provision of public goods and services. Much traditional external borrowing has been for such purposes (indeed, one of the functions of the World Bank as a mediating lender is to help fund public investments).

Some public infrastructure, such as railroads, is potentially revenue-producing, but much of it is not. The government must raise the debt service through general taxation, with all the implications discussed above. While the old borrower's guideline—matching the maturity of the loan to the life of the project—is not strictly pertinent when the project does not produce revenue, it is a good rule nonetheless. According to this principle, long-term projects, whose contribution to the GNP and hence to taxable income is spread over many years, should, if possible, be financed by long-term borrowing. Not doing so would place more pressure on the internal terms of trade to generate the trade surplus necessary for rapid amortization of the debt.

The main point here is that governments of developing countries may well be borrowing abroad to finance public infrastructure, and they must take a position on the amount and character of their external debt.

The second reason that a government cannot avoid responsibility for external debt is the widespread government ownership of commercial enterprises that generate revenue—the so-called parastatals. Rare is the country that does not have some parastatals, and in many countries they generate over half the output of the modern sectors of the economy. The government, as chief or sole stockholder, cannot ultimately dissociate itself from the parastatals, although varying degrees of association are possible. Some parastatals can be chartered with a high degree of independence regarding all business decisions and an independent top management that is compensated in relation to the profitability of the enterprise. (Some British firms approach this model.) Such arrangements make as clear as possible to lenders that it is a commercial enterprise with all the attendant risks, and that it does not have the full credit backing of the government. Even in such extreme circumstances, it is unlikely that a government-owner could allow such a business to go into bankruptcy—at some loss to its foreign creditors—lest the reputation of the country, and especially the government as a borrower, be damaged. This kind of linkage is not limited to enterprises owned by the government. In the mid-1970s, several U.S. banks expended considerable funds to bail out insolvent or weak real estate investment trusts under their sponsorship—trusts that were legally separate and could have been allowed to fail (as many did). The banks intervened to perserve their overall reputation with both creditors and customers.

In most cases, parastatals are not put at arm's length from the government that owns them; managers are not given full autonomy, nor are they typically compensated on the basis of the firm's profitability. These factors make it all the more difficult for a government to dissociate fully from the economic performance of its state enterprises.

One reason is that government often uses parastatals to pursue social goals other than profitability. Therefore, it would be inappropriate to hold management responsible for profitability, as would be the case with a privately owned firm. Major investment plans must typically be approved by the relevant ministry, and employment levels and practices are subject to government guidance (as is also true, to a lesser degree, of privately owned firms in many countries). In addition, management is usually on salary—often very low compared with compensation in privately owned enterprises of similar size. While salaries are occasionally augmented by incentive bonuses, the bonuses are generally not related to profitability. For these reasons, managers have no direct incentive to gauge their borrowing to the requirements of profitability. Indeed, since, in many countries, the main motivation of parastatal managers is some combination of personal enrichment (other than through direct compensation) and political advancement, the principal incentive is toward enlargement of scale rather than profitability. Yet if enlargement of scale is not limited, it is likely to lead to excessive external borrowing by the enterprise. The now classic case is the rapid expansion and diversification of the Indonesian national oil firm Pertamina in the wake of its enhanced borrowing power following the 1974 oil price increase (Wellons 1977).

The divergence of interest between managers and owners is not limited, of course, to state-owned enterprises and can be found in large privately owned firms as well. One study has shown that U.S. firms managed by owners, or under close control of owners, tend to be more profitable than those in which the role of owners is more remote (McEachern 1975).

For this reason, too, governments will want to monitor closely, and perhaps even control directly, the external borrowings of their parastatals. Under prevalent arrangements, their managers cannot be assumed to borrow abroad to the socially optimal degree; in general, they will tend to overborrow if left unrestrained.

A third reason that the government cannot in practice escape responsibility for the level and character of external borrowing concerns the local banks, and perhaps other similar financial institutions. Banks are typically under heavy regulation, usually for the protection of the public. They are, furthermore, the repositories of public confidence in the functioning of an economic system. If a major bank fails, the potential ramifications go far beyond the failure of one enterprise. Both borrowers and lenders become much more cautious, a development that on occasion is welcome but generally results in economic recession and economic hardship. For this reason, governments must take an active interest in the smooth functioning of the major banks under their jurisdiction. This does not mean that they must protect bank managers against their mistaken judgments; management can be dismissed. It does mean that poor judgments by bank management cannot be allowed to weaken the institution at the expense of depositors and creditors, except at a cost that may go far beyond the institution in question. We are speaking here of both the financial system as a whole and its major components. Minor banks whose fate can be separated clearly from the greater financial system may be allowed to fail.

The reputation and fate of the banks can influence a country's reputation with foreign creditors as well. In the late seventies, Chile was widely applauded in some circles for its return to a relatively unregulated, free enterprise system. Chilean banks had borrowed heavily in international markets for relending in the local economy. When a private bank became insolvent in 1982, the government let it be known that the bank was private and that creditors had lent to it at their own risk. External credits to Chile immediately dried up. Within a short interval, the government felt obliged to reverse itself and guarantee the external liabilities of the bank. Despite their broad support for Chilean policy, creditors did not accept the dissociation of the government from the banks. Consequently, government must perforce be concerned with both the internal and the external exposure of the banks. (Even a country as averse to government interference as Switzerland has let it be known that the country's three largest banks cannot be allowed to fail.)

GUIDELINES FOR EXTERNAL BORROWING

If it is in fact advisable for a government to take a strong interest in the total level and character of external indebtedness, what guiding principles should it follow? Unfortunately, it is difficult to lay down quantitative guidelines for external debt that are universally applicable. Because reputation so heavily influences the possibilities and difficulties that a country will face in international financial markets, and because that reputation is based on the history, experience, and prevailing ideological views of the borrowing country, each nation confronts a distinctive set of issues and problems.

Indicators such as the debt/GDP ratio or the debt-servicing ratio are often used as signals when the external debt is reaching dangerous levels. As long as these indicators are widely used, they, of course, become important in establishing creditworthiness. These types of signals have little objective basis, however, because they can vary substantially with safety, depending on the circumstances. For instance, table 1-2 sets out a series of debt/GDP ratios and their implied debt-servicing requirements, all on the assumption that the (constant) rate of return on investment is 15 percent and the (constant) cost of borrowing in world capital markets is 10 percent. These numbers were plausible, and even conservative, for many countries in the late 1970s.

The advantages of external borrowing, as long as the return to investment exceeds servicing requirements, are quite dramatic. For example, let us assume that the yield on investment is 15 percent and the cost of borrowing is 10 percent a year, with external borrowing the sole source of growth in output. By borrowing an amount equal to 4 times its postborrowing GDP, a country can increase its output to 2.5 times its initial level in steady-state equilibrium (where the debt remains outstanding but does not grow further). Of course, under these circumstances, interest payments on outstanding debt will be very high—40 percent of total output. Moreover, if import requirements are 20 percent of GDP, the interest-servicing ratio (interest payments/ total exports) will be two-thirds. Even after these large interest payments to foreigners, however, output available for the residents of the borrowing country (GNP) will be 1.5 times the initial, predebt level of GNP. This represents the net gains from borrowing abroad, which, as indicated,

Table 1-2. Debt, GDP, GNP, and Debt Service in a Steady State

Debt/GDP	Exports/GDP	Debt service exports	Relative to predebt GDP: GDP	GNP	Debt
0	0.2	0	1.0	1.0	0
0.5	0.25	0.2	1.08	1.03	0.54
1	0.3	0.33	1.18	1.06	1.18
2	0.4	0.5	1.43	1.14	2.86
3	0.5	0.6	1.82	1.25	5.46
4	0.6	0.67	2.50	1.50	10.0

Quantitative assumptions: Return on investment = 0.15; interest on debt = 0.1

can be dramatic. In this example, while the final debt to GDP ratio is 4, total borrowings will be ten times the initial level of GDP. Lower levels of borrowing will of course result in lower debt/GDP ratios and lower debt-servicing ratios (see table 1-2). In other words, debt ratios that are quite high are sustainable in long-run equilibrium, provided the country is not subjected to large uncertainty in output or exports.

A debt/GDP ratio of 4, although sustainable on the assumptions given, is far higher than anything we actually observe. Actual debt/GDP ratios, even of countries heavily in debt, are in the vicinity of 0.6, well under unity. Israel has the highest observed debt/GDP ratio, 1.6, and much of Israel's external debt is on concessional terms. Interest-service ratios as high as 50 percent can be observed but are still well below the two-thirds given in the illustration.

We may well ask why countries do not borrow even more than they have, for the illustration suggests much higher sustainable debt than we observe. One explanation might be that debt on a much larger scale would depress returns to investment, so that the assumption made here of a constant return is unrealistic. In fact, however, we have observed roughly constant returns to investment (abstracting from economic cycles) over a long period of time. If the debt is acquired quickly, returns are indeed likely to diminish. But that is less apt to be true of investments made over several decades, unless the investment itself depresses the external terms of trade of the borrowing country.

A second possibility is that the cost of borrowing will rise with the amount of outstanding indebtedness, or, more generally, that countries are rationed in their total borrowing well before the solvency constraint is reached. This is particularly true if repudiation risk is a major concern of the creditors. Again, the pace of borrowing is important; a rapid increase in debt is very likely to increase the cost to the borrowing country, but a slower, more gradual increase is less likely to do so. Nonetheless, for debt/GDP ratios much higher than are normal, a risk premium is likely to be added to interest rates, even if the buildup is gradual. After a relatively high debt/GDP ratio is reached, the borrower may be frozen out of further borrowing.

A third possible reason is that debt must be serviced in tradables, but debt is often acquired to finance investment in nontradables (although some infrastructure investments—such as feeder roads or port facilities—are indirectly in tradables, because they help to lower the domestic cost of getting exportables to market). Several factors are important in determining a sustainable amount of investment of external debt in nontradables: the return on investment in tradables relative to the cost of investment, the share of investment in tradables as opposed to nontradables, and the ability of the government to raise revenues in tradables in order to service debt acquired to invest in nontradables. If, as is likely, the investment in nontradables will require a decline in the domestic prices of nontradables relative to tradables, the extent of decline that is tolerable may also influence the amount of debt that can be acquired for this kind of investment.

These points can be illustrated with a numerical example. Let us assume, as was the case in table 1.2, that the yield on investment is 15 percent in both the tradable sector and the nontrad-

Table 1-3. Relative Price Changes Required by Investment of External Funds in Nontradables

Share of investment in nontradables (percent)	Required fall in relative price of tradables (percent)
0	−7
20	2
40	8
60	13
80	18
100	22

Note: See text and note 7 for assumptions.

able sector of the economy, and that the cost of foreign borrowing is 10 percent a year. Let us also suppose that import requirements are 20 percent of GDP and that domestic expenditure out of disposable income is at first evenly divided between tradables and nontradables. A further assumption is that the price elasticity of substitution between tradables and nontradables in domestic demand is −2, but that the structure of production is not influenced by relative prices. The government must raise revenues to service the external debt invested in nontradables, and it does so through lump sum taxation. On these assumptions, and for the case in which external debt is twice GDP, table 1-3 shows the fall in the relative domestic price of nontradables that must occur in order to service the external debt (the overall debt-service ratio is 0.5, from table 1-2), given different shares of investment that is made in nontradables.[7] For instance, if 60 percent of the external funds is used for investment in nontradables, the relative price of tradables will have to rise by 13 percent so that enough tradables are released from domestic consumption to pay interest on the external debt. (An illustration of the time profile of the relative price of nontradables in an optimizing model is given in the appendix.)

If there are political limits to the permissible change in relative prices, they may in turn limit the amount of external debt that can be invested in nontradables. On the assumptions made here the world price of exports and imports is unchanged. Therefore, alteration of the internal terms of trade will require either a currency devaluation, which will raise the local currency prices of tradable goods, or a decline in the local prices of nontradables. Either course poses difficulties of its own.

The above illustration has used a debt/GDP ratio of 20. A lower debt ratio will reduce the required change in relative prices simply because it requires a smaller increase in exports. This may be another reason for limiting external borrowing for investment in nontradables even when it augments GNP. A lower elasticity of substitution in demand will call for a larger change in relative prices, while allowing the composition of output to respond to relative prices will work in the other direction.

Finally, any practical limit to the taxing powers of government may in turn limit the amount of investment in nontradables. For instance, if 100 percent of investment is in nontradables in the example offered in table 1-3, the government must tax 20 percent of GDP (and 25 percent of GNP), valued at predebt prices, in order to service the debt. If the practical limits on taxation are 10 percent of GDP, the country will be unable to service external debt if more than 50 percent is invested in the nontradable sector.

A fourth response to the question of why actual debt/GDP ratios are not higher than they are might be that countries face uncertainty in their output and export receipts. If debt service takes priority and the country has exhausted its reserves and lines of credit, any shortfall in exports must be met by squeezing imports. In many developing countries, this can be accomplished in the short run only by cutting production. The necessity of cutting production from time to time in response to unforeseen shortfalls in net exports will, in turn, reduce the optimal level of foreign indebtedness. Usually, a less costly way of absorbing these shocks is to hold sufficient reserves to cover normal and even some extraordinary variations in net exports. Such reserves typically will earn a lower rate of return than could real investment under stable conditions, but they will protect the country from large losses when conditions are not stable.

One method for hedging against uncertainty in output and export receipts is to have foreign creditors share the risks directly, as they would with equity investments. We believe that most developing countries have paid too little attention to the advantages of foreign direct investment—not only for risk sharing, but also for the technology transfer that would normally occur. It might be more accurate to say that many countries have been equivocal in their official stance toward direct investment. Ambivalence—which is often understandable in historic terms—does not provide the stable business environment in which foreign investment thrives. Political ambivalence is a reality in many countries, however; and, as long as it is there, the scope for proportionately large inflows of direct investment will be limited.

This brings us to the final section, a discussion of the appropriate combination of foreign obligations.

THE MIX OF EXTERNAL OBLIGATIONS

The discussion so far has been in terms of external debt in conventional form: interest-bearing debt with a fixed foreign-currency value at maturity. In practice, a borrower may face several different kinds of opportunity for drawing capital from the rest of the world: (1) concessional aid, including grants; (2) equity investment by foreigners, which may involve some managerial control by foreigners (direct investment) or simply minority foreign shareholders; and (3) interest-bearing obligations of fixed value, which in turn may be directly linked with imports (trade credits), may involve shorter or longer maturities, and may be denominated in local or foreign currency. We offer some observations on each of these forms of obligation, and on their "mix."

As long as domestic investment opportunities are available, with expected rates of return exceeding the cost of foreign capital, a country can always raise its expected level of income by borrowing abroad. It should be cognizant, however, of the constraints that we have discussed in previous sections. In particular, it should take as much concessional aid as possible, provided that certain conditions are met (the question of political overtones that often pervade bilateral aid will not be considered). The first condition is that the country should be able to service the debt adequately from tax and other government revenues. Second, supplementary domestic financing of the aid-supported projects should not draw domestic savings away from investments that offer far greater returns to the country. Third, the aid should not be so tied up with procurement and other conditions that it turns out to be much less concessional than it seemed at first glance. Many governments seem to give much greater weight to obtaining low interest rates, if necessary at the expense of higher purchase prices or lower quality products, than is economically warranted. This can be a serious mistake, one which arises from the accepting of medium-term trade credits as well as aid-financed projects.

Foreign equity investments have the obvious advantage over interest-bearing obligations in that they do not have to be amortized and in that earnings are likely to be positively correlated with the general economic performance of the country. We believe that countries would be well advised to encourage direct foreign investment as long as the attraction to foreign investors is not attributable mainly to price distortions in the economy. In the presence of severe price distortions, however, foreign investments can actually worsen the country's condition (Brecher and Diaz-Alejandro 1977). With the high, selective import tariffs and other price distortions prevalent in many developing countries, evaluating all projects, not merely those undertaken by foreign investors, becomes a serious problem.

In general, direct investment has advantages that go beyond the provision of foreign capital. It introduces technical know-how and useful managerial and marketing skills; it may also, in a world of imperfect capital markets, provide access to additional debt capital for the country. The final advantage is that, if the activity fails economically, there is no need to repay the capital, since the foreign investor bears the commercial risk.

Equity investments also have some disadvantages. First, while earnings will generally be high when the economy is doing well, remittances of earnings may not be so strongly correlated with domestic or export performance. They may actually be somewhat perverse, since earnings tend to be reinvested more readily when the economy is going well. As can be the case with domestic firms engaged in foreign trade, foreign investors may aggravate a liquidity crisis by exporting capital if a devaluation of the currency (or the introduction of exchange controls) is thought to be imminent. This can be done either directly or by manipulating the timing of receipts and payments associated with exporting and importing. These swings can often be large relative to the equity stake of the foreign investor. The host country then faces a dilemma. Absence of exchange controls invites the speculative movement of capital, but the imposition of exchange controls damages the country's reputation as a debtor. If exchange controls are in place, they can be used to discourage speculative withdrawals of capital, but it is difficult to control firms that are heavily engaged in foreign trade.

Finally, it is a fact of life that foreign direct investment, involving management control and foreign ownership of land, is a politically sensitive issue in many countries. Too much foreign investment may result in a political reaction that damages the country's overall reputation as a borrower. In some countries, fear of arousing political sensibilities may be the most significant restraint on direct investment. And, of course, fear of expropriation is one of the factors inhibiting investment by prospective foreign investors.

Foreign purchases of noncontrolling equity interests in indigenous firms carries some but not all of the disadvantages of foreign direct investment, and joint ventures are actively encouraged by many countries. But, for a variety of reasons, including the lack of well-developed equity markets, the scope for equity investment in developing countries that does not involve some foreign influence on management is quite limited.

Our principal focus above has been on interest-bearing obligations, and there is little more to be said here. Trade credits, whether officially guaranteed by the government of the exporting country or not, are often considered separate and distinct from bank term loans or other forms of interest-bearing investment. They represent, as it were, a somewhat separate "pool" from which borrowing can take place. Because they tend to be less centralized in the borrowing country, however, they can offer a troublesome surprise when they begin to dry up during a liquidity crisis. The country then senses, perhaps for the first time, how large the total of trade credit is and how difficult it would be for the economy to function if such credits should suddenly disappear. For this reason, countries that have heavy debt obligations should monitor their trade credits closely.

When it comes to debt maturity, we observed earlier that a serious mismatch between the maturity of credits and the maturity of the projects they are financing increases the exposure of a country to liquidity crisis. Having to repay a debt before the returns to the project are fully realized can be costly. For this reason, the old banker's rule of thumb, that debt maturity should be matched to maturity of the underlying investment, is a sound one.

In principle, countries have the choice of borrowing in their own currency or in some foreign currency. Borrowing in the home currency shifts to the lender not only convertibility risk but also exchange risk, and he will extract a price for that. In reality, without exchange rate guarantees, few developing countries have a practical possibility of borrowing abroad in their home currency on any scale. Indeed, even most developed countries are limited to borrowing abroad in one of the four or five leading currencies rather than their own.

CONCLUDING REMARKS

Actual levels of external borrowing by developing countries are considerably less than could in principle be serviced from productive investments. This may reflect restraint on the part of borrowers arising from concerns about their ability to raise the funds required for debt servicing when the projects are government-sponsored or are in sectors of the economy that do not directly save or generate foreign exchange. It may also reflect concern about taking on fixed external obligations in an uncertain world when the capacity of the domestic economy to absorb shocks at low cost is limited.

But much of the reason for lower-than-sustainable external borrowing is no doubt due to constraints imposed by lenders who fear that (1) mismanagement of the borrowing economy may reduce returns on investments; (2) future difficulties may lead the authorities to repudiate the debt, in whole or in part, openly or (more likely) tacitly; or (3) waves of sentiment in world financial markets may lead to periodic liquidity crises that prevent an otherwise viable economy from servicing its debt. All these factors lead to a supply-of-funds schedule for each borrower that reflects borrowing costs which increase as a function of outstanding debt and current borrowing levels. Beyond some (according to our calculation, modest) level, higher interest rates elicit no new lending at all.

From the perspective of debtors, when there are many productive investment opportunities, the task is to lower and flatten the supply of the external fund schedule the debtor faces. It can thereby increase its gross national product and per capita income after servicing external debt. How can the debtor accomplish this?

Since the main restraints on further borrowing seem to be concerns by lenders, borrowers must pay attention to these concerns. We offer some observations which flow from our earlier analysis of external debt.

First, the debtor can improve the lender's perceptions of its ability to pay by concentrating external borrowing on productive investments, especially investments that will generate foreign exchange. (Borrowing for investment purposes is more desirable here than borrowing for consumption—even though, as we have seen, consumption loans are sometimes perfectly sensible.) If foreign currency is to be produced, the pricing structure of the economy cannot be too far out of line with that prevailing in world markets. Where possible, the debtor should become thoroughly committed to the investments in question so that there is a limited scope for diversion of funds away from the project. From this point of view, World Bank or regional development bank loans, and even medium-term trade credits, are seen as being in a different and (to the lender) more comforting category than are straight term bank loans that are not linked to projects or to procurement of project-related equipment.

A second way in which the debtor can allay the lender's concerns about repayment is for the debtor to raise the visible costs to itself that would be incurred on nonpayment. That could involve such traditional steps as offering central government guarantees, posting collateral (such as reserves), pledging particular export revenues, and agreeing to third party arbitration or even to jurisdiction of courts in the lending countries.

Receptivity to foreign direct investment is taken as a positive general attitude toward foreign capital even when direct investment flows themselves are small. Over time, the country can establish a reputation for punctiliousness in servicing its debts. Since good reputation is itself an important asset, especially in the world of finance, loss of reputation is one of the visible costs associated with nonpayment. The cooperation of international institutions, such as the World Bank and the regional development banks, in the investment planning and financing can also improve perceived willingness to pay. Each country's relationships with these institutions is a continuing one, and no government likes to be a pariah in organizations with which they must deal on a regular basis.

Finally, to reduce the harm from liquidity crises, and hence also the probability of such a crisis, the country should recognize the advantage of longer maturities of debt, and balance these advantages against the higher costs of long-term debt. Similarly, the debtor should recognize the gains from diversifying as much as possible the sources and character of its external financial support. Although trade credits and direct investment are not immune to the forces involved in a liquidity crisis, as we have seen, they are influenced by somewhat different factors. They may thus help to forestall this type of crisis.

In the case of bank term lending, however, the presence of a strong lead bank whose leadership is accepted by other banks might offer better assurance against a liquidity crisis than would the existence of a large number of unrelated banks. To some extent, the former arrangements internalizes the external pressures that generate liquidity crises.

The conventional indicators of capacity to handle external debt, such as the debt-servicing ratio or the debt/GDP ratio, have little theoretical basis, at least in the vicinity where they are generally observed. Nonetheless, they have become important indicators in the eyes of lenders, with each borrowing country measured both against other countries and against the borrowing country's own past. This, in effect, makes them important to borrowers. A sharp increase in these indicators is taken as a warning signal even when they are relatively low. Expectations concerning appropriate levels can be altered only gradually, and in the context of other actions that persuade lenders of the soundness of the borrowing.

APPENDIX: SIMULATION MODELS FOR OPTIMAL BORROWING

This appendix illustrates the use of simulation techniques to calculate optimal borrowing paths. While we rely on fairly simple dynamic models, the methods may be directly extended to more complicated, multisector models. Earlier studies using the techniques in this appendix include: Blanchard (1983), Sachs (1983), Bruno and Sachs (1983), Lipton and Sachs (1983).

We illustrate three models from the text: (1) the one-sector optimal borrowing model; (2) the two-sector optimal borrowing model (for traded and nontraded goods); and (3) the one-sector model with a public sector facing tax constraints.

We make only one amendment to the models in the text, namely, that investment imposes adjustment costs on the economy, so that the marginal product of capital F_K should adjust slowly rather than instantaneously to equal the world cost of capital. In particular, following Hayashi (1982), we distinguish between gross capital formation J_t and total investment expenditure I_t, which includes adjustment costs as well as the direct cost of capital goods. In specific terms, let ψ be the per-unit adjustment cost, so that $I_t = J_t + \psi J_t$. We now assume that ψ is not constant but rather a linear function of the rate of capital formation, $\psi = (\phi/2)(J/K)$. Thus, rapid investment rates impose higher per-unit costs of adjustment than slow investment rates. The accumulation equation is: $K_{t+1} = K_t(1 - d) + J_t$, where d is the rate of geometric depreciation. Since $I_t = J[1 + (\phi/2)(J/K)]$, we may derive that $J_t = -(K_t/\phi) + (K/\phi)\sqrt{1 + 2\phi(I_t/K_t)}$. Plugging this into the accumulation equation yields:

$$K_{t+1} = K_t(1 - d) + f(I_t,K_t) \tag{1.25}$$

where $f_t = -(K_t/\phi) + (K/\phi)\sqrt{1 + 2\phi(I_t/K_t)}$. For later reference, we note that $f_{K_t} = -(1/\phi) + (1/\phi)\sqrt{1 + 2\phi(I_t/K_t)} - (I_t/K_t)/\sqrt{1 + 2\phi(I_t/K_t)}$. When I_t/K_t is small, $f_{K_t} \approx' 0$.

Table 1-4. The One-Sector Model

I. Problem

$$\max_{G_t,C_t,I_t} \sum_{0}^{\infty}(1+\delta)^{-t}U(C_t,G_t)$$

such that:

$$\text{(a) } D_{t+1} = D_t(1+r) + I_t + G_t + C_t - Q_t(K_t)$$
$$\text{(b) } K_{t+1} = K_t(1-d) + f(I_t,K_t)$$
$$\text{(c) } \lim D_t(1+r)^{-t} = 0$$
$$\text{(d) } K_0, D_0 \text{ given}$$

II. Lagrangian

$$\mathcal{L} = \sum_{0}^{\infty}(1+\delta)^{-t}\{U(C_t,G_t) + \mu_t[D_{t+1} - D_t(1+r) - I_t - G_t - C_t + Q_t(K_t)] + \lambda_t[K_{t+1} - K_t(1-d) - f(I_t,K_t)]\}$$

III. First-Order Conditions

$$\text{(a) } \partial\mathcal{L}/\partial C_t = 0 \Rightarrow U_C = \mu_t$$
$$\text{(b) } \partial\mathcal{L}/\partial D_t = 0 \Rightarrow (1+r)\mu_t = (1+\delta)\mu_{t-1}$$
$$\text{(c) } \partial\mathcal{L}/\partial I_t = 0 \Rightarrow \lambda_t f_{I_t}(I_t,K_t) = -\mu_t$$
$$\text{(d) } \partial\mathcal{L}/\partial K_t = 0 \Rightarrow \lambda_t[1-d + f_{K_t}(I_t,K_t)] = \lambda_{t-1}(1+\delta) + M_t Q_{K_t}$$
$$\text{(e) } \partial\mathcal{L}/\partial G_t = 0 \Rightarrow U_G = \mu_t$$

The infinite-horizon, one-sector borrowing problem is shown in table 1-4. The aggregate production function is $Q_t(K_t)$. It is implicit that labor is held fixed at $L_t = 1$. Note that, for completeness, government expenditure has been placed in the utility function. The entire system is set up as a Lagrangian and the first-order conditions are solved in part III of the table. μ_t is the co-state variable (or dynamic Lagrange multiplier) attached to D_t, so it represents the marginal utility of wealth. λ_t is the shadow value of installed capital. In all, the system is a four-dimensional, nonlinear difference equation system in λ_t, u_t, K_t, and D_t. We solve the system below, for particular numerical values.

It is easy to extend the model to include nontraded goods, with sector-specific capital and freely mobile labor. Thus, we introduce production functions $Q^T = F^T(K^T,L^T)$ and $Q^N = F^N(K^N, L^N)$. Full employment of labor requires $\bar{L} = L^T + L^N$. Capital in each sector is governed by an accumulation equation of the form $K^i_{t+1} = K^i_t(1 - d) + f(I^i_t,K^i_t)$, where $i = T,N$. For simplicity, we treat all investment expenditure as drawing on the traded good (this can easily be modified). Thus, the market-clearing condition for nontraded goods is $Q^N = C^N + G^N$, where C^N and G^N are real consumption expenditures falling on N. The debt accumulation equation is $D_{t+1} = D_t(1 + r) + C^T_t + G^T_t + (I^T_t + I^N_t) - Q^T_t(K^T_t,L^T_t)$. The entire model, including Lagrangian and first-order conditions, is shown in table 1-5.

Note that θ_t is the co-state variable for the constraint that the non-traded-goods sector clears. It is easy to show that (θ_t/μ_t) is the shadow price of nontraded goods relative to traded goods in the model. If the optimal solution is to be decentralized via market forces, θ_t/μ_t will be the ratio P^N_t/P^T_t. The entire system is now implicitly a six-dimensional nonlinear difference equation system in the variables K^N_t, K^T_t, D_t, λ^N_t, λ^T_t, and μ_t. All of the other variables may be expressed in terms of these six variables.

The final model we consider is the one-sector, tax-constrained economy, in which official borrowing is used to augment (suboptimal) private savings, but in which the maximum tax rate is constrained to be below some rate $\bar{\tau}$. As it is explained in the text, private saving is assumed to be a constant fraction s of after-tax income $(1 - \tau)Q_t$, so that private consumption expenditure is $C_t = (1 - s)(1 - \tau)Q_t$. Total investment expenditure is equal to private savings, $s(1 - \tau)Q_t$, plus public savings, $\tau Q_t - G_t - rD_t$, plus new borrowing $D_{t+1} - D_t$ (in the text, government consumption expenditure was ignored). Thus, $I_t = s(1 - \tau)Q_t + (\tau Q_t - G_t - rD_t) + (D_{t+1} - D_t)$. Since $s(1 - \tau)Q_t = Q_t(1 - \tau) - C_t$, we have $I_t = [Q_t(1 - \tau) - C_t] + (\tau Q_t - G_t - rD_t) + (D_{t+1} - D_t)$, which, after rearrangement, yields the standard balance of payments identity $D_{t+1} = (1 + r)D_t + C_t + I_t + G_t - Q_t$.

Table 1-5. The Two-Sector Model

I. Problem

$$\max_{G_t^N, G_t^T, C_t^N, C_t^T, I_t^N, I_t^T} \quad \textstyle\sum_0^\infty (1+\delta)^{-t} U(C_t^N, C_t^T, G_t^N, G_t^T)$$

such that:

(a) $D_{t+1} = D_t(1+r) + (I_t^N + I_t^T) + G_t^T + C_t^T - Q_t^T(K_t, L_t^T)$

(b) $Q_t^N(K_t^N, 1 - L_t^T) = C_t^N + G_t^N$

(c) $K_{t+1}^i = K_t^i(1-d) + f(I_t^i, K_t^i) \quad i = N,T$

(c) $\lim D_t(1+r)^{-t} = 0$

(d) D_0, K_0^T, K_0^N given

II. Lagrangian

$$\pounds = \textstyle\sum_0^\infty (1+\delta)^{-t}\{U(C_t^N, C_t^T, G_t^N, G_t^T)$$
$$+ \mu_t[D_{t+1} - D_t(1+r) - (I_t^N + I_t^T) - G_t^T - C_t^T + Q_t^T(K_t^T, L_t^T)]$$
$$+ \theta_t[Q_t^N(K_t^T, 1 - L_t^T) - C_t^N - G_t^N] + \lambda_t^T[K_{t+1}^T - K_t^T(1-d) - f(I_t^T, K_t^T)]$$
$$+ \lambda_t^N[K_{t+1}^N - K_t^N(1-d) - f(I_t^N, K_t^N)]\}$$

III. First-Order Conditions

(a) $\partial\pounds/\partial C_t^N = 0 \Rightarrow U_{C^N} = \theta_t$

(b) $\partial\pounds/\partial C_t^T = 0 \Rightarrow U_{C^T} = \mu_t$

(c) $\partial\pounds/\partial G_t^N = 0 \Rightarrow U_{G^N} = \theta_t$

(d) $\partial\pounds/\partial G_t^T = 0 \Rightarrow U_{G^T} = \mu_t$

(e) $\partial\pounds/\partial D_t = 0 \Rightarrow (1+r)\mu_t = (1+\delta)\mu_{t-1}$

(f) $\partial\pounds/\partial K_t^T = 0 \Rightarrow \lambda_t^T[1 - d + f_{K_t}(I_t^T, K_t^T)] = \lambda_{t-1}^T(1+\delta) + \mu_t Q_{K_t}^T \; i = T,N$

(g) $\partial\pounds/\partial I_t^i = 0 \Rightarrow \lambda_t^i f_I(I_t^i, K_t^i) = -\mu_t \quad i = T,N$

(h) $\partial\pounds/\partial L_t^T = 0 \Rightarrow \mu_t Q_{L^T}(K_t^T, L_t^T) = \theta_t Q_{L^N}(K_t^N, L_t^N)$

(i) $\partial\pounds/\partial K_t^N = 0 \Rightarrow \lambda_t^N[1 - d + f_{K_t}(I_t^N, K_t^N)] = \lambda_{t-1}^N(1+\delta) + \theta_t Q_{K_t}^N$

It is easy to demonstrate that if $\bar{\tau} = 1$, in other words, tax rates are unconstrained. The optimization problem in which the government controls τ_t, G_t and $D_{t+1} - D_t$ amounts to precisely the same problem as in table 1-4, where the government controls C, I, and G. In other words, when taxes are unconstrained, the economy can reach the first-best optimum of table 1-4, even though private savings are set in an ad hoc way as a fixed fraction of disposable income.

The more interesting case occurs when the tax constraint $\bar{\tau}$ is binding. Let C_t^* and Q_t^* be optimal in the solution to the problem in table 1-4. If C is controlled directly, C_t is simply set at C_t^*. If C is to be controlled via taxes, the authority should set $\tau_t^* = 1 - [C_t^*/(1 - s)Q_t^*]$. If $\tau_t^* > \tau$, the first-best solution is no longer feasible when taxes are the control instrument. We now assume that for some period t, $\tau_t^* > \bar{\tau}$. Thus, we must find a second-best solution.

The tax management problem is shown in table 1-6. It is convenient to rewrite the tax

Table 1-6. Optimal Borrowing with Tax Constraints

I. Problem

$$\max_{G_t, \tau_t, D_t} \Sigma_0^\infty (1+\delta)^{-t} U(C_t, G_t)$$

such that:

(a) $D_{t+1} = (1+r)D_t + I_t + G_t + C_t - Q(K_t)$

(b) $C_t > \bar{C}$

(c) $\bar{C}_t = (1-s)(1-\bar{\tau})Q_t$

(d) $K_{t+1} = K_t(1-d) + f(I_t, K_t)$

(e) D_0, K_0 given

II. Lagrangian

$$\pounds = \sum_0^\infty (1+\delta)^{-t}\{U(C_t, G_t) + \mu_t[D_{t+1} - (1+r)D_t - I_t - G_t - C_t + Q(K_t)]$$
$$+ \lambda_t[K_{t+1} - K_t(1-d) - f(I_t, K_t)] + \gamma_t[C_t - (1-s)(1-\bar{\tau})Q(K_t)]\}$$

III. First-Order Conditions

(a) $\partial\pounds/\partial C_t = 0 \Rightarrow U_C(C_t, G_t) = \mu_t - \gamma_t$

(b) $\partial\pounds/\partial G_t = 0 \Rightarrow U_G(C_t, G_t) = \mu_t$

(c) $\partial\pounds/\partial D_t = 0 \Rightarrow (1+r)\mu_t = (1+\delta)\mu_{t-1}$

(d) $\partial\pounds/\partial K_t = 0 \Rightarrow \lambda_t[1 - d + F_{K_t}(I_t, K_t)] = \lambda_{t-1}(1+\delta) + \mu_t Q_{K_t} - \gamma_t(1-s)(1-\bar{\tau})Q_{K_t}$

(e) $\gamma_t = 0$ when $C_t < \bar{C}_t$ and $\gamma_t > 0$ when $C_t = \bar{C}_t$

constraint as a constraint on consumption, $C_t \geqslant \overline{C}_t$ where $\overline{C}_t = (1 - s)(1 - \overline{\tau})Q_t$. Then we rewrite the first-order conditions (a) and (e) and define a "notional" demand C^D such that $U_C(C_t^D, G_t) = \mu_t$. C_t^D is the level of consumption that would be chosen on the assumption that the tax constraint is not binding in the current period. Actual consumption is given by $C_t = \min(C_t^D, \overline{C}_t)$.

The problem in table 1-6 presents a highly nonlinear difference equation system in four variables: D_t, K_t, μ_t, λ_t. The other variables can all be expressed as functions of these four variables.

We now proceed to numerical simulations of these optimal borrowing models. For purposes of the simulations, we assume the following:

In the one-sector model:

$$Q_t = K_t^{\alpha}$$

$$U(C_t, G_t) = \log [C_t^{\beta} G_t^{(1-\beta)}]$$

$$\alpha = 0.5 \qquad r = 0.12$$

$$\beta = 0.67 \qquad \delta = 0.12$$

$$\phi = 10.0 \qquad \overline{\tau} = 0.45$$

$$d = 0.10$$

In the two-sector model:

$$Q_t^T = (K_t^T)^{\alpha}(L_t^T)^{(1-\alpha)}$$

$$Q_t^N = (K_t^N)^{\alpha}(L_t^N)^{(1-\alpha)}$$

$$1 = L_t^T + L_t^N$$

$$U(C_t^T, C_t^N, G_t^T, G_t^N) = \log [(C_t^T)^{a_1}(C_t^N)^{a_2}(G_t^T)^{a_3}(G_t^N)^{1-a_1-a_2-a_3}]$$

$$\alpha = 0.5 \qquad \delta = 0.12 \qquad a_2 = 0.41$$

$$\phi = 10.0 \qquad d = 0.10 \qquad a_3 = 0.13$$

$$r = .12 \qquad a_1 = 0.25 \qquad a_4 = 0.21$$

Two simulations are performed. In the first, we begin with K_0 below the steady-state level in the one-sector model and compare the adjustment costs in the tax-constrained ($\overline{\tau} = 0.45$) and tax-unconstrained model ($\overline{\tau} = 1.0$). Remember that the case $\overline{\tau} = 1.0$ in the model of table 1-6 will give exactly the same outcome as the solution to the model of table 1-4. In the second simulation, the process of capital accumulation in the trade/non-traded-goods model is studied.

Figure 1-3 illustrates the basic proposition with respect to the fiscal constraint: with low $\overline{\tau}$, the country should not borrow as rapidly as on the unconstrained path. The solid line is the debt/GDP ratio for the unconstrained case, and the dotted line is the optimum path in the constrained case (the economy is assumed to begin in 1970 with D/Q equal to 0.38). When taxes are unconstrained, foreign borrowing is more rapid and stabilizes at a much higher level of debt than in the tax-constrained case. Note that the optimal path in the unconstrained case involves a very high D/Q ratio, a point we made in the text in a static context. Figure 1-4 illustrates the path of physical capital in the two economies. The counterpart of the larger foreign borrowing in the unconstrained economy is more rapid capital formation and a higher steady-state capital stock.

Figure 1-3. A Comparison of Optimal Foreign Debt Accumulation in the Tax-Constrained and Unconstrained Models

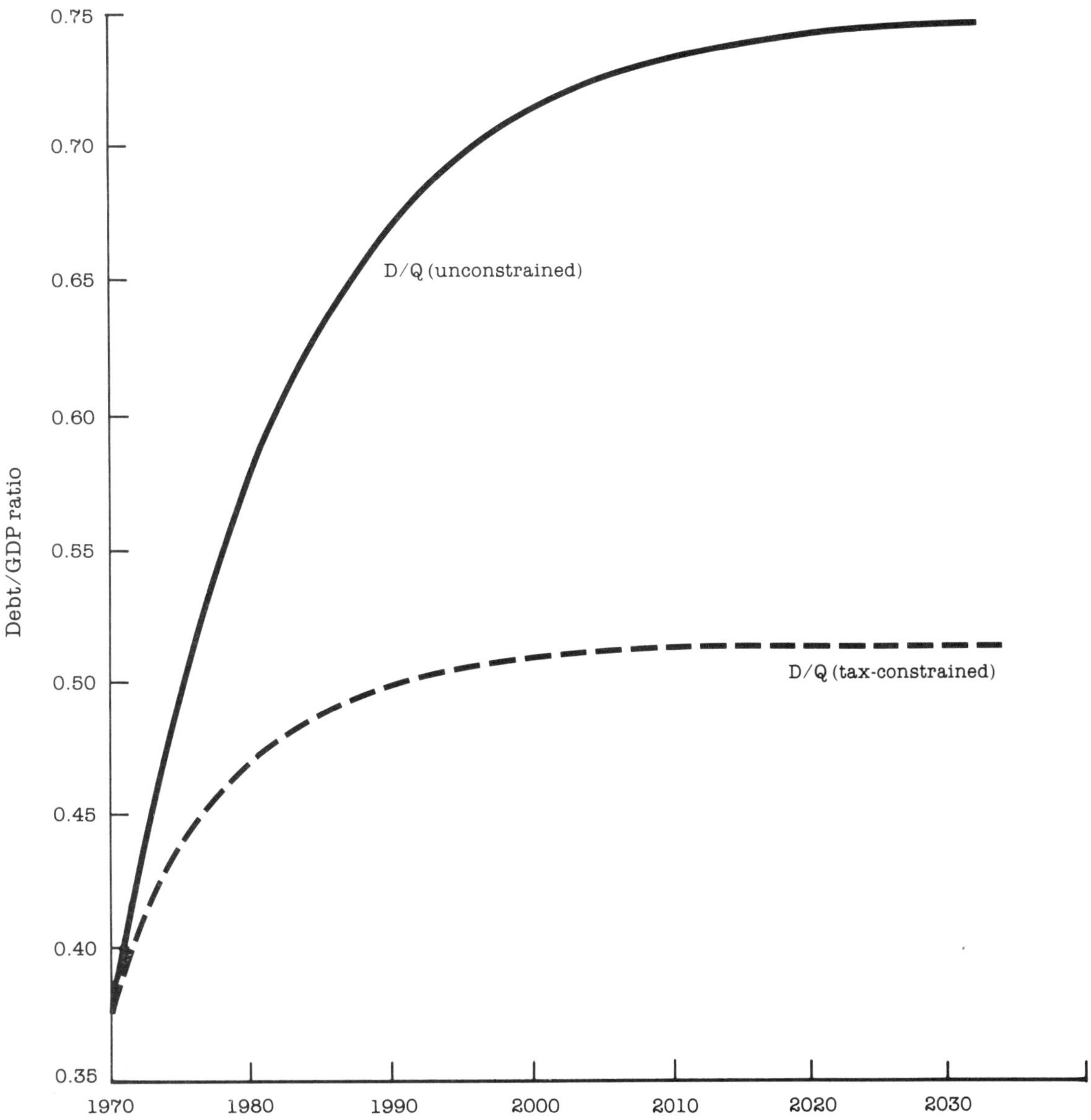

The two-sector model simulation is illustrated in part in figure 1-5. Once again, we assume that capital stocks (in this case both K_0^T and K_0^N) are sufficiently low so that rapid accumulation of capital should take place in both sectors. As shown in figure 1-5, the relative price of nontraded goods declines over time, as the initial current account turns into eventual balance and the initial trade deficit turns into long-run surplus. Figure 1-6 shows the paths of K^N and K^T. In the simulation shown, the optimal planner (or the market, in its decentralized interpretation) has perfect foresight of the long-run changes in P^N/P^T. In practice, however, it is likely that many agents will underestimate the necessary long-run decline in P^N/P^T, and thereby overinvest in the non-traded-goods sector in the initial phase of adjustment. Such overinvestment would

(Text continues p. 58.)

Figure 1-4. A Comparison of Capital Accumulation in the Tax-Constrained and Unconstrained Models

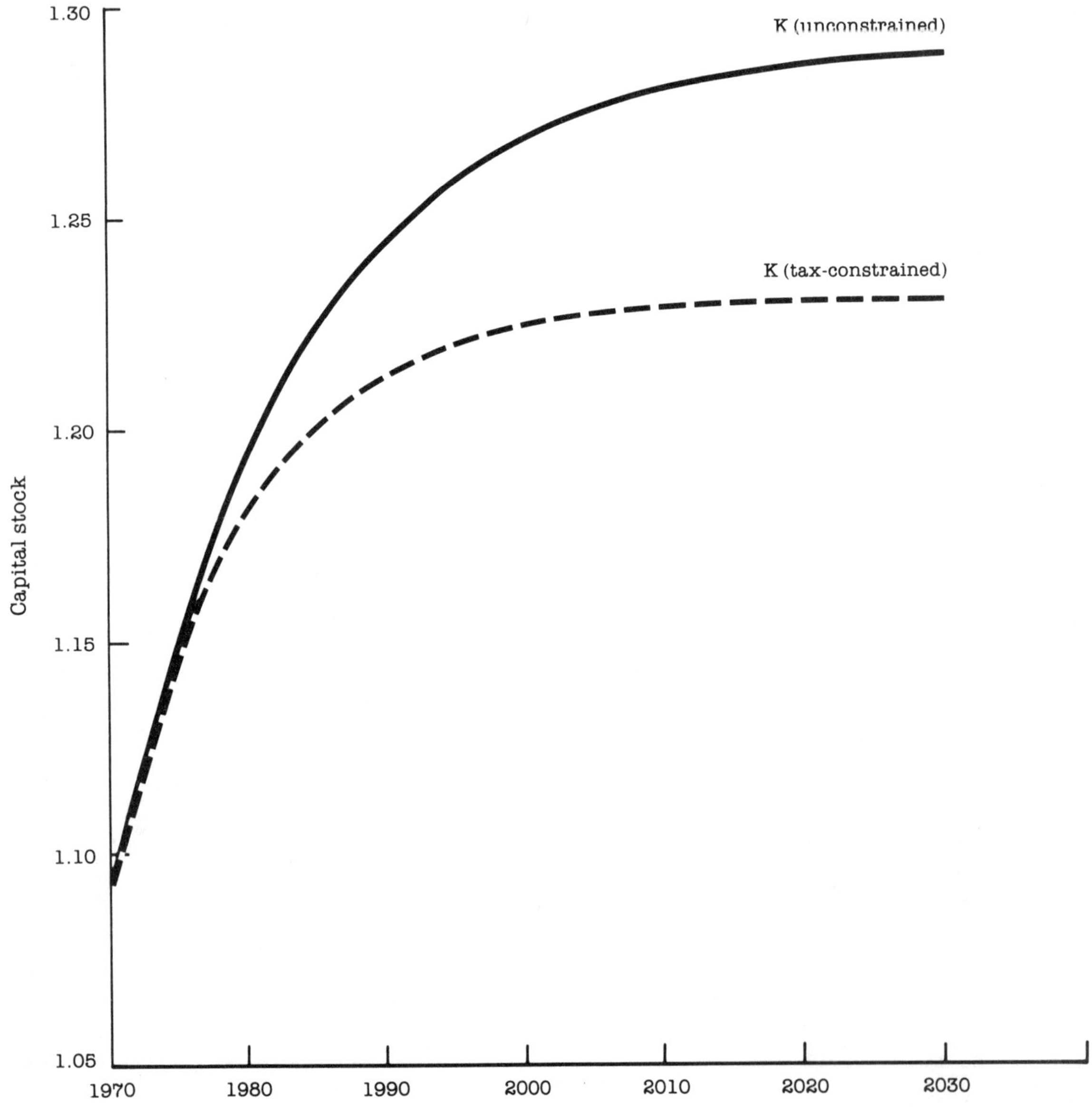

Figure 1-5. Paths of the Current Account/GDP Ratio and P^N/P^T
(percentage deviations from a constant baseline)

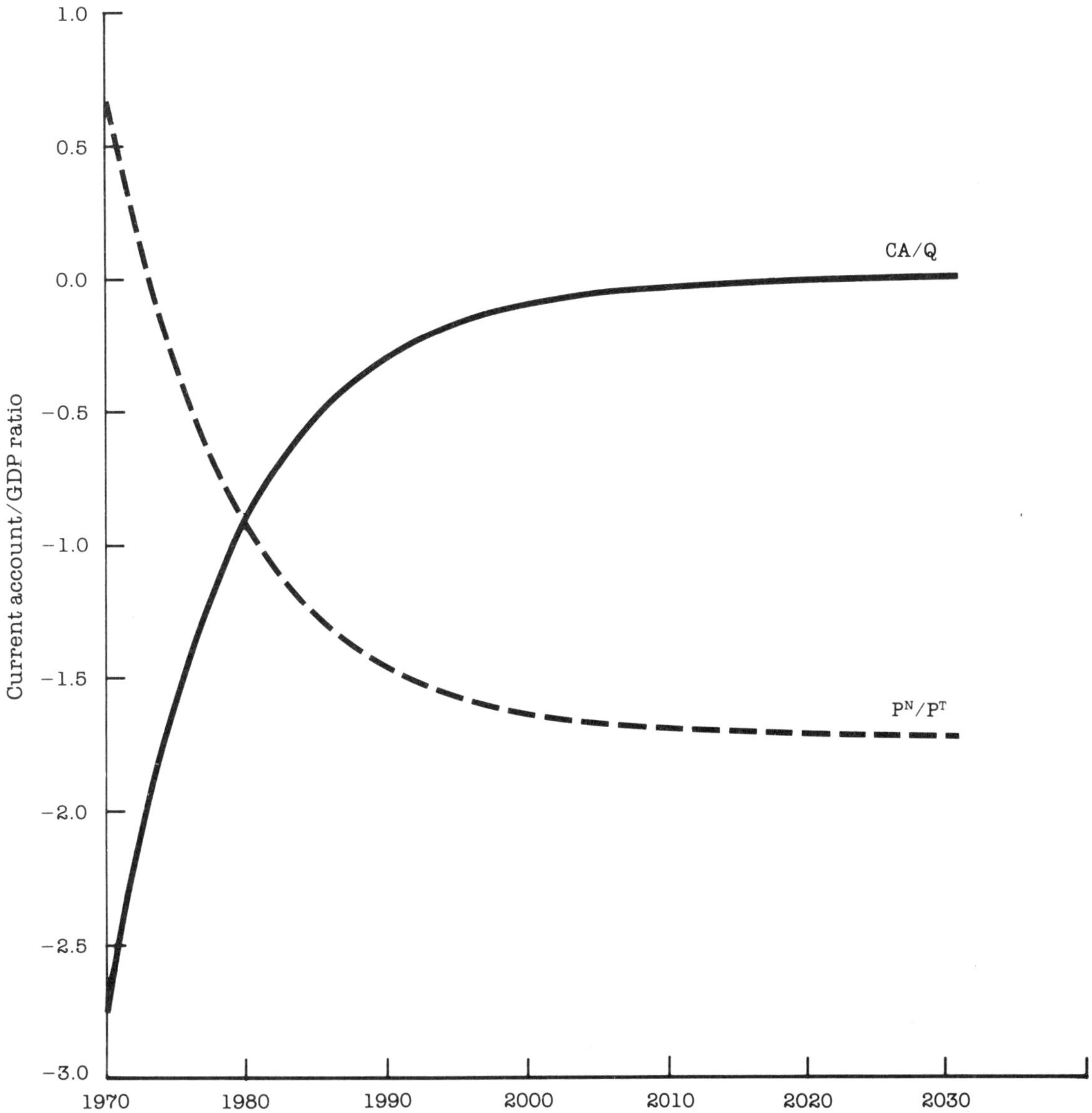

Figure 1-6. Paths of Capital Accumulation for K^T and K^N
(percentage deviations from a constant baseline)

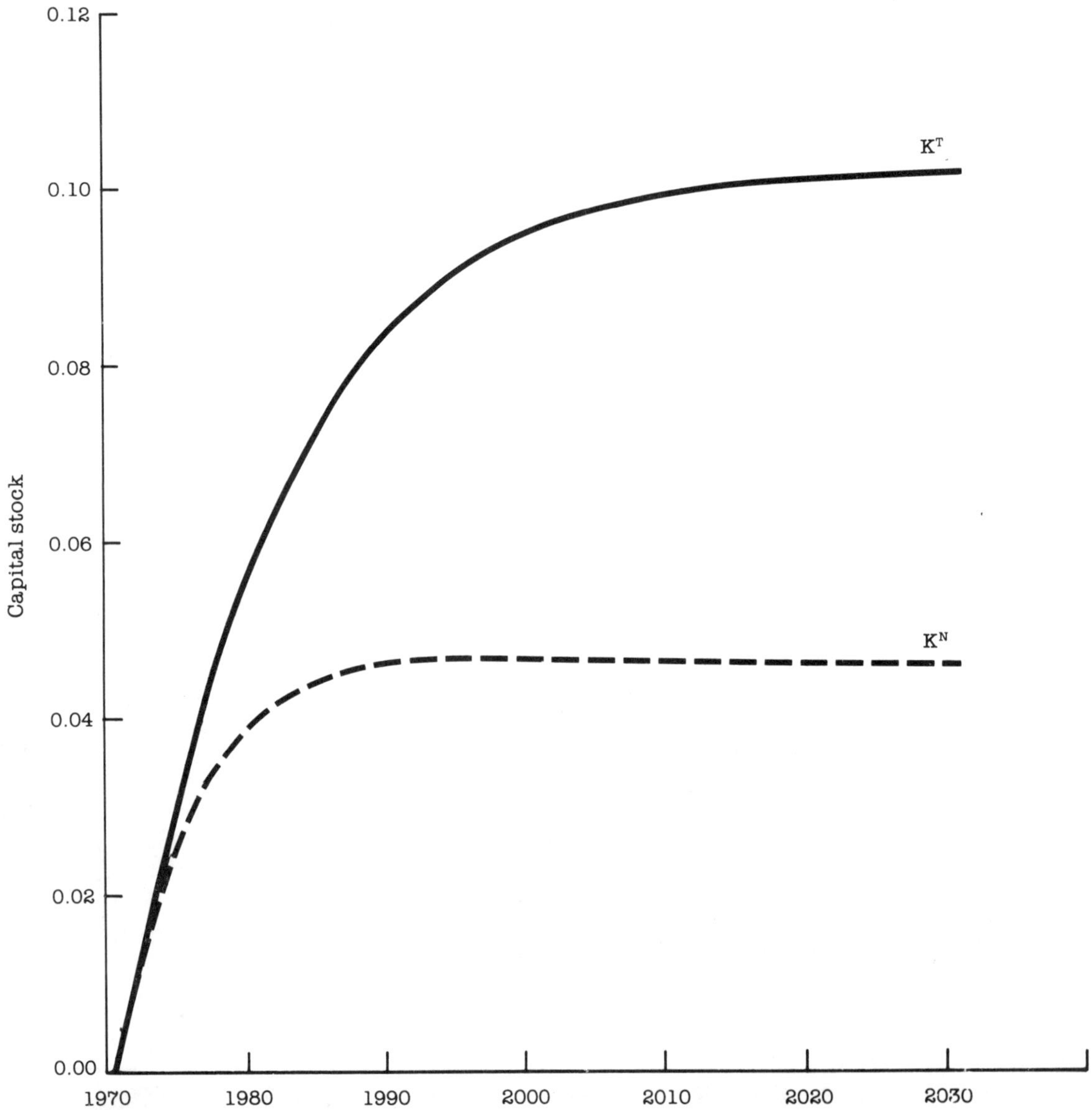

eventually necessitate even larger declines in P^N/P^T along the adjustment path, in order to move capital and labor back to the traded-goods sector.

The simulation techniques outlined here can be extended to larger and more realistic models that include Keynesian and monetary features not explored in this chapter (see Blanchard and Sachs 1982 for an example). Such models should prove fruitful in improving medium-term assessments of an economy's debt-servicing capacity and creditworthiness.

NOTES

1. Equation (1.2) implicitly assumes that Q_t is independent of C_t each period, which is correct under the assumptions made. In more general models, with a variable labor supply or with work effort a function of C_t, we cannot simply maximize TB_t each period by setting $C_t = \overline{C}_t$.

2. Such a Ponzi scheme is called a "rational speculative bubble" in the finance literature, where it is shown that with $n > r$ the bubble can last forever. In a sense, the debt is an "unbacked asset" that maintains value because each creditor believes that future creditors will make the necessary loans to the debtor country.

3. Note that by writing $C_1^L = Q_1 - (1 + r)D_1$, we are assuming that the borrower always repays D_1 and never opts to repudiate if credit rationing on D_2 in fact occurs.

4. By totally differentiating $U_1^N = -V_D^N/(1+\delta)$, we have $dD_2^N/dD_1 = (1 + r)U_{11}^N/[U_{11}^N + V_{DD}/(1 + \delta)]$. Since U_{11}^N and $V_{DD} < 0$, $0 < dD_2^N/dD_1 < (1 + r)$.

5. In specific terms,

$$dD_1/d\pi = [(1 + r)/(1 + \delta)](U_1^L - U_1^N)/[U_{00} + \pi(1 + r)^2U_{11}^L/(1 + \delta) + (1 - \pi)(1 + r)\gamma U_{11}^N/(1 + \delta)]$$

where $\gamma = (1 + r) - dD_2^N/dD_1 > 0$.

6. The proof is as follows. We start at an equilibrium with $U_1(C_1^N) = -(1 + r)V_D(D_2^N)/(1 + \delta)$ and $U_1(C_1^L) > -(1 + r)V_D(0)/(1 + \delta)$. Utility is given by $V_0 = U(C_0) + \pi\{U(C_1^L)/(1 + \delta) + V(0)/(1 + \delta)^2\} + (1 - \pi)\{U(C_1^N))/(1 + \delta) + V(D_2^N)/(1 + \delta)^2\}$. The investment project has an income stream of $-dI_1$, 0, $(1 + \theta)^2dI$, over the three periods, so that $dV = -U_0dI_1 - [\pi V_D(0)/(1 + \delta)^2](1 + \theta)^2dI_1 - [(1 - \pi)V_D(D_2^N)/(1 + \delta)^2](1 + \theta)^2dI_1$. Now, by the conditions of optimality, $U_0 = (1 + r)\pi U_1(C_1^L)/(1 + \delta) + (1 + r)(1 - \pi)U_1(C_1^N)/(1 + \delta)$. Substituting in the dV equation, we find $dV/dI_1 = -\pi[(1 + r)U_1^L/(1 + \delta) + (1 + \theta)^2V_D(0)/(1 + \delta)^2] - (1 + \pi)[(1 + r)U_1^N/(1 + \delta) + (1 + \theta)^2V_D(D^N)/(1 + \delta)^2]$. Let $\gamma = U_1^L + (1 + r)V_D(0)/(1 + \delta)$. Then, by substituting in dV the relationships between U_1 and V_D, we get $dV/dI_1 = [\pi V_D(0)/(1 + \delta)^2][(1 + r)^2 - (1 + \theta)^2] + [(1 + \pi)V_D(D_2^N)/(1 + \delta)^2][(1 + r)^2 - (1+\theta)^2] - \pi(1 + r)\gamma/(1 + \delta)$.
For $r = \theta$, $dV/dI_1 = -\pi(1 + r)\gamma/(1 + \delta) < 0$. For $\theta >> r$, $dV/dI_1 > 0$.

7. Table 1-3 is calculated from the following model, using the notation of appendix:

$$\begin{aligned} Q^T &= Q_O^t + \rho K^T \qquad & C^N &= .5(P_N/P_T)^\varepsilon(Q - rD) \\ Q^N &= Q_O^N + \rho K^N \qquad & Q^N &= C^N \\ Q &= Q^T + Q^N & & \\ K^N &= \gamma D & K^T &= (1 - \gamma)D \end{aligned}$$

where $\rho = .15$, $r = .10$, $\varepsilon = -2.0$, and γ is shown parametrically as the first column of table 1-3.

REFERENCES

Arrow, K., and M. Kurz. 1970. Public investment, the rate of return, and optimal fiscal policy. Baltimore, Md.: Johns Hopkins University Press.

Bhagwati, J., and T. N. Srinivasan. 1975. "Optimal trade policy and compensation under endogenous uncertainty: The phenomenon of market disruption." Journal of International Economics 6:317–36.

Blanchard, O. 1983. "Debt and the current account deficit in Brazil." In Financial policies and the world capital market: The problem of Latin American countries, edited by Pedro Armella et al. Chicago: University of Chicago Press.

Blanchard, O., and J. Sachs. 1982. "Anticipations, recessions, and policy: An intertemporal disequilibrium model." Annales de L'Insee (July-December):47–48.

Brecher, R. A., and C. F. Diaz-Alejandro. 1977. "Tariffs, foreign capital and immiserying growth." Journal of International Economics 7 (November):317–22.

Bruno, M., and J. Sachs. 1982. "Input price shocks and the slowdown in economic growth." Review of Economic Studies 49:679–705.

Bulow, J. and J. B. Shoven. 1978. "The bankruptcy decision." Bell Journal of Economics 9(2):437–56.

Diaz-Alejandro, C. 1984. "Good-bye financial repression, hello financial crash." Columbia University. Processed.

Eaton, J., and M. Gersovitz. 1981. "Debt with potential repudiation: Theoretical and empirical analysis." Review of Economic Studies 48:289–309.

Hayashi, F. 1982. "Tobin's marginal q and average q: A neoclassical interpretation." Econometrica 50 (January):213–24.

Jensen, M., and W. Meckling. 1976. "Theory of the firm: Managerial behavior, agency costs, and capital structure." Journal of Financial Economics 3:305–60.

Kharas, H. J. 1981. "Constrained optimal foreign borrowing by less developed countries." Development Policy Staff, World Bank, August. Processed.

Lipton, D., and J. Sachs. 1983. "Accumulation and growth in a two-country model." Journal of International Economics 15:135–59.

McEachern, W. A. 1975. Managerial control and performance. Lexington, Mass.: Lexington Books.

Sachs, J. 1981. "The current account and macroeconomic adjustment in the 1970's." Brookings Papers on Economic Activity no. 1:201–68.

———. 1982a. "The current account in the macroeconomic adjustment process." Scandinavian Journal of Economics 84, no. 2.

———. 1982b. "LDC debt: Problems and prospects." In Crises in the economic and financial structure, edited by P. Wachtel. Lexington, Mass.: Lexington Books.

———. 1983. "Energy and growth under flexible exchange rates." In J. Bhandari and B. Putnam, The international transmission of economic disturbances. Cambridge, Mass.: MIT Press.

———. 1984. "Theoretical issues in international borrowing." Princeton Studies in International Finance 54. Forthcoming.

Sachs, J., and D. Cohen. 1982. "LDC borrowing with default risk." NBER Working Paper no. 925.

Smith, Clifford, and J. Warner. 1979. "On financial contracting: An analysis of bond covenants." Journal of Financial Economics 7:117–61.

Stiglitz, J. E., and A. Weiss. 1981. "Credit rationing in markets with imperfect information: I." American Economic Review 71(3):393–410.

Wellons, P. A. 1977. Borrowing by developing countries in the Euro-currency market. Paris: OECD Development Centre.

2

Banks' International Lending Decisions: What We Know and Implications for Future Research

Mark Gersovitz

In 1982 and 1983, many observers feared that the debt situation of developing countries would lead to a serious impairment of financial markets within the Organisation for Economic Co-operation and Development (OECD) if major banks became insolvent. Since this scenario has not occurred, there has been a loss of interest in the subject of developing-country debt among individuals concerned primarily with the fate of the OECD. It is clear, however, that there should be no parallel loss of interest among bank shareholders or among individuals concerned with the economic prospects of these debtor countries. In this chapter, I will discuss how banks act in their role as creditors for developing nations, and what the implications of these actions are for importers of capital.

For many markets, it is sensible to analyze the behavior of demanders and suppliers separately. The two groups interact only through the single variable of price. But in credit markets where debtors' adherence to contracts is in question, the creditor may give attention to many attributes of the debtor in order to understand if and when a breakdown will occur.

The structure of the chapter reflects these considerations. First, I discuss the reasons developing countries borrow and the situations in which repayment may be called into doubt. These analyses lead naturally to a discussion of the behavior of lenders—both in their attempts to avoid debt-servicing problems and in their responses to the problems that occur. A subsequent section deals with the impact on the creditworthiness of developing nations of their decision to invest or consume from borrowed funds. Following that is evidence from country experience, prospects for econometric evidence on behavior in these markets, and scenarios for international lending in the near term.

Throughout the chapter, I try to delineate two levels of abstraction. On the one hand are the fundamental questions: Under what circumstances will bankers regret having made loans to developing countries? Will these nations be constrained in the amount of loans they can obtain as a consequence, how badly, and in what ways? What other outcomes (such as sanctions) will follow a rupture between creditors and debtors?

On the other hand, there are questions about the process of renegotiation among creditors, debtors, and third parties such as the International Monetary Fund (IMF). These issues range from the determination of the exact amounts owed to individual creditors in situations of chaotic record keeping to the legally appropriate drafting of rescheduling agreements. Questions of this type may have great significance to the frantic participants involved in the resolution of problem cases, but are of much less fundamental importance. A failure to distinguish between these two categories—fundamentals and process—is responsible, to some extent, for confusion about developing-country debt. That the process of renegotiation evolves in an atmosphere of crisis for various institutional reasons should not prejudice answers to the more fundamental questions or determine public policy.

A CONCEPTUAL APPROACH

Eaton and Gersovitz (1981b) emphasize four reasons why countries may wish to borrow in international financial markets. First, borrowing allows a country to divorce its level of consumption from short-run fluctuations in its income. A second reason for borrowing arises when the domestic marginal product of capital exceeds the world cost of capital. Provided this condition is satisfied, borrowing to increase the capital stock will raise income above the level of debt-servicing obligations. Third, a country experiencing a permanent shock, for example to income, may wish to adjust its level of absorption slowly toward its new sustainable level. A smoother transition is likely to be a less costly one. Finally, borrowing can provide liquidity to facilitate international transactions, for instance, via suppliers credits.

If a developing nation becomes indebted for any of these reasons, when will problems arise in the servicing of the debt? There are three broad explanations for the occurrence of problems, which I label cannot-pay, liquidity, and willingness-to-pay. Each of these contending hypotheses has logical validity. While they share some qualitative implications, on balance they point to very different strategies for developing countries, banks, and policymakers.

One variant of the cannot-pay position is that problems arise when the present value of debt service exceeds the present value of the debtor nation's resources, so that the intertemporal budget constraint cannot be satisfied. An analogy would be corporate insolvency, when net worth becomes negative. Another variant of the cannot-pay hypothesis is focused on the present discounted value of the balance of trade. This case differs from the intertemporal budget constraint to the extent that the full present value of income cannot be made available to foreigners, perhaps because there are nontradables or because the country's terms of trade will deteriorate as a consequence of the transfer. The last variant of the cannot-pay explanation centers on the fact that country debt is largely owed by governments. Servicing debt therefore depends on the government's ability to raise revenues. Kharas (1981) develops models based on a fixed tax rate. His assumption could be justified by the expectation that the elasticity of revenue with respect to the tax rate will become negative long before the government can gain control of total national income or wealth in order to service foreign debt.

The three cannot-pay approaches present sufficient conditions for debt problems to arise. But one can doubt their practical relevance, especially to the current situation. Present levels of indebtedness do not seem so high as to exceed these cannot-pay thresholds when calculated on the basis of present value. There may be some exceptions among the African countries, most likely concerning a government's ability to raise revenue. In the case of Mexico, however, the country could surely wipe out its debts if it could credibly pledge its oil reserves, an exportable commodity that is almost completely controlled by the government. Even if the cannot-pay condition were extended here to allow for some minimum subsistence for the country's population, however arbitrarily defined, this constraint was clearly met before Mexico developed its oil reserves, and would be met if the oil reserves were surrendered. This is a logical test of the applicability of a solvency approach, and it indicates that this approach does not make much sense in the current situation. A more general explanation of why it does not pertain is the suspicion that, long before a developing country is unable to service its debts, it will choose not to do so. I will turn to this view of debt crises after considering the liquidity view.

Corresponding to three versions of the cannot-pay hypotheses are three analogous liquidity hypotheses based on current-value rather than present-discounted-value interpretations of the three budget constraints. For instance, it may be that current income is inadequate to meet current debt service. If there is no reason for this problem to persist indefinitely, however, it is tempting to argue that the problem will be resolved by the creditors' recognition of its temporary nature and their consequent willingness to provide additional loans. In practice, such a process is likely to be cumbersome. The mechanics of establishing what each creditor is owed, under what terms, how much debt service should be postponed or additional loans made are complicated. This is especially so because there is a need to adopt appropriate legal formulations and to comply with banking regulations at minimum cost. As a result, participants in, and observers of, the process will feel that a crisis is in progress. A liquidity theory suggests that there need not be any serious long-run problems in servicing debts.

In a more pessimistic variant of the liquidity hypothesis, banks may be incapable of the coordination necessary to overcome a liquidity problem. Sachs (1983) and Krugman [see chapter 3 in this volume] argue that this type of problem may occur if an individual bank expects all the other banks to stop lending. Each bank is assumed to face a rising cost of lending to developing countries, and a loan from a single bank, therefore, is more expensive than the same size loan from many banks. Thus situations may arise in which no one bank can profitably protect its loans by lending to the country until that country resumes debt service, but all banks acting together may find it profitable to do so. The problem is to coordinate lending when an individual bank does not affect the size and success of the loan but benefits from it. In other words, proponents of a liquidity view must believe that there would be no problem with debt service at present if there were only one bank instead of many.

Several objections can be raised to this scenario. It is unclear why banks should develop the expectation that others will not lend, unless there is a fundamental reason why lending is unprofitable. Further, the debtor country has the opportunity to insist on the prorated participation of each of its creditors in the bailout loan, which would overcome the free-rider problem. Under this rule, nonparticipants could be discriminated against if the loan succeeded. This debtor-initiated solution is particularly plausible when the question is one of postponing debt service rather than providing new net flows. In fact, the current situation provides examples of debtors pursuing just such a strategy.

The theory offered by Sachs and Krugman thus explains why prorated reschedulings ("involuntary lending") occur rather than loans from an arbitrary configuration of lenders. The success of the involuntary lending strategy, however, depends on the assumption that debt service will probably be resumed. For reasons discussed above, a solvency problem seems unlikely to explain why new lending would be unsound at present. But there is another factor that must be considered before one can dismiss the existence of a fundamental problem: countries, while able to service their debts, may choose not to do so.

In the willingness-to-pay approach, the essence of the creditor's problem is the absence of any institution ensuring that a sovereign borrower able to service its debts will choose to do so. A borrower may wish to make a binding promise to foreign lenders that it will service its debts. But such promises are not generally feasible since there is no international forum in which this type of contract can be enforced. Once loans have been made, servicing the debt may no longer be optimal; the government may prefer to renege on its promise.

On the assumption that governments weigh costs and benefits in taking these steps, the nature and extent of the sanctions that creditors can use to increase the costs of breaking loan contracts would be critical to the lending decision. Therefore, it would be the identification of these sanctions, and of the characteristics of individual countries that make them vulnerable to sanctions, that would comprise the goals of so-called country risk analysis. These are the factors that determine capital mobility. Eaton and Gersovitz (1981a, 1981b, 1983, and 1984) and Gersovitz (1983) emphasize that the sanctions available to aggrieved creditors are rather indirect and their implications must therefore be carefully modeled.

Among the principal sanctions are (1) an embargo of future borrowing with a consequent loss of the ability to smooth consumption, and (2) various forms of interference with the debtors' international transactions and transfers. Because these sanctions are not necessarily effective, the amount of credit that can be safely extended may be quite low. It is therefore plausible that current debt levels are in excess of those for which debt service can be ensured by these sanctions. When the threshold for safe loans has not yet been reached, creditors can contemplate accommodating their debtors with reschedulings and even additional loans. Indeed, creditors may even provoke a crisis that need not otherwise have occurred by imposing an embargo regardless of the debtor's intention with regard to ultimate repayment; an incentive for debt service is thereby removed. But if the threshold has been passed, lenders must look to salvaging what they can by threatening sanctions, and will certainly not wish to exacerbate their problem by increased lending.

Rarely does a quantitative judgment (on the amount of debt relative to the threshold) translate into such divergent qualitative behavior—to increase exposure or draw back. It is because quantitative estimates are difficult to make that it is hard to predict how the problems of individual debtors will be resolved. But this does not mean that the theory is without operational implications. For example, it is easy to see that the Republic of Korea is a better credit risk than Argentina because of the relative vulnerabilities of their trading positions, and similar distinctions could be drawn with more analysis of individual country situations. The conundrum facing the banks and other analysts is to decide whether the debt problem is one of process (liquidity) or of fundamentals (willingness to pay).

THE IMPORTANCE TO CREDITORS OF HOW BORROWERS USE FUNDS

Loans can be categorized by how borrowers spend the proceeds: project loans versus balance of payments loans, and investment versus consumption. The three theories of creditworthiness discussed above have different implications for the importance of these distinctions to creditors. And within the general willingness-to-pay category, there are also important differences depending on the nature of the specified sanctions. An analysis of these issues from the perspectives of the different theories helps to understand both the behavior of creditors and the nature of the theories themselves.

A solvency approach addresses in a relatively straightforward way the importance of how debtors use funds. Anything that increases the resources available for debt service enhances the borrower's creditworthiness. From the creditor's viewpoint, projects should be efficiently designed to yield large returns—that accrue specifically to the debtor rather than society at large—in the form of exportable goods. The solvency theory suggests the possibility of tying debt service to specific projects. In this case, if the project yields adequate returns, the loans can be serviced as long as the returns can be transferred to foreign creditors. The possibility of any obstacles to a linkage between project returns and debt service, however, is not addressed. Implicit in the solvency approach is the suggestion that a project can be insulated from the rest of the economy and that tying loans to projects can increase the flow of loans. In general, investment rather than consumption ensures that the debtors maximize the resources available for debt service.

These same concerns carry over to the liquidity view of the determinants of creditworthiness. In this case, the timing of project returns vis-à-vis debt service payments is also important. If creditors such as banks deal in short- to medium-term finance, these creditors can be attracted by projects of shorter gestation. When loans are not linked to specific projects, there may be scope for undertaking projects with longer horizons. Individual projects could be phased to yield a fairly smooth stream of income when taken together. This, in turn, suggests that it may be beneficial for these different projects to have a common owner—the government, for example—that can ensure the necessary coordination of project returns and debt payments.

In contrast to the solvency and liquidity theories, the willingness-to-pay approach predicts that it may be meaningless to tie loans to projects. In addition, investing rather than consuming the proceeds may actually <u>lessen</u> creditworthiness. The supposition is that governments cannot credibly promise to dedicate the proceeds of projects to debt service. This agnostic approach toward the positive effect of investment (as opposed to consumption) on creditworthiness is a touchstone of the willingness-to-pay theory.

Tying loans to projects does little to enhance the sanctions that aggrieved creditors have available if the debtor chooses not to pay. An exception occurs if such tying increases the creditor's prospects in foreign law courts when the debtor has assets abroad that can be attached. Holders of tied loans may have a preferred position relative to other creditors (Wood 1982, p. 6). But this is only true for an individual creditor; the tying of loans to projects primarily affects the priority of repayment among creditors and not the amount of funds available to creditors as a whole.

The strength of the creditor's position usually depends much more on the debtor's overall situation. In this sense, all loans are, or might as well be, general loans. It is not useful for creditors to focus on the attributes of individual projects unless they are very large; the formalities of making project loans may hardly be worth the effort. Exceptions do arise, such as Zaire's ill-designed Inga-Shaba hydroelectric scheme, which was allocated one-quarter of all funds borrowed between 1970 and 1977 (World Bank 1980b, p. 39). It must be emphasized, however, that the willingness-to-pay approach implies that evaluation of this type of project is equally relevant to all creditors, not just to those who appear to be financing it.

The view that investment necessarily enhances creditworthiness is widely held. But a willingness-to-pay theory provides little support for this conclusion. In Gersovitz (1983), the role of the investment–consumption decision is examined in a model where repudiation is deterred by the loss of access to trade. This is a realistic sanction based on the fact that banks provide trade finance, facilitate international transactions through payments transfers, and can take action under the sovereign immunity laws that disrupt trade. Since an increase in its capital stock can increase or decrease the value of trade to a country, investment may raise or lower creditworthiness. A country like Nigeria, for which investment means import substitution, may become less creditworthy with increases in investment. A country poor in resources like Korea, however, increases its gains from trade with increased investment.

In the model of Eaton and Gersovitz (1981a), exclusion from the insurance that is implicit in the option of future borrowing provides another realistic penalty if the borrower is risk-averse and faces uncertainty. Although the role of investment is not analyzed in this model, some implications are clear (Eaton and Gersovitz 1981b). If the borrower undertakes risk-reducing investments, it can diminish the value of this sanction and hence its creditworthiness. Further, if a given amount of risk becomes subjectively less important at the higher average income levels reached by investment, then creditworthiness will be impaired by investment.

By contrast, Sachs (1983) argues, also within a willingness-to-pay framework, that investment does increase creditworthiness. He assumes that the penalty faced by repudiators is a loss of a fixed proportion of their future incomes. Since investment increases future income, it clearly increases the sanction. But the assumed form of the penalty is not a realistic one since creditors cannot confiscate a proportion of the debtor's income. As a consequence, there can be little confidence in the predicted relationship between investment and creditworthiness. Indeed, setting the proportion equal to 1 would return the argument to a pure solvency approach.

A similar contrast can be drawn with respect to the effect of international reserves on creditworthiness as predicted by the solvency, liquidity, and willingness-to-pay theories. Both the solvency and liquidity approaches imply a positive relation between reserves and creditworthiness. A liquidity theorist would stress that reserves are among the most liquid of assets.

In a willingness-to-pay approach, a country can choose not to use reserves for debt service, if it can protect them from seizure. The very liquidity of resources in the form of reserves may make them ideal for surviving sanctions after default (Eaton and Gersovitz 1981b, p. 29). The first period after a repudiation may find the country most vulnerable since it will take time to set up alternatives to the banks for facilitating international trade. A foreign exchange war chest can be especially important in this transition period. Recent rumors that developing countries are choosing to rebuild reserves rather than to service debts must be viewed as particularly ominous in this context. Argentina, for instance, appears prepared to threaten its creditors with having to classify its loans as nonperforming rather than use its increased reserves for debt service.

RECENT EXPERIENCE OF DEBTORS AND THEIR CREDITORS

The section on conceptual approaches sketched theories of both the motives for borrowing and the prospects that debts will be serviced. This section considers evidence on various aspects of the debtor-creditor relationship: the effect of shocks on debt outstanding, the nature of past problem cases, the dimensions and extent of bank cohesion in dealing with problems, and the rehabilitation of developing countries as borrowers after problem periods. At this point, difficulties in operationalizing definitions and documenting experience arise. What exactly is it that the different participants fear, what do they do to avert it, and how does an outside observer know that what is feared has actually happened?

When lenders and debtors act voluntarily and when new loans are being made, the quantity of debt outstanding (D) will be the minimum of what countries wish to borrow (D^*) and what their creditors wish to lend ($\bar{D}$), the credit ceiling. Thus $D = \min(D^*, \bar{D})$. The expectation is that countries will wish to increase their indebtedness proportionately more when shocks are negative, such as when income falls below anticipations or when the London interbank offered rate (LIBOR) is unexpectedly high (on the assumption that the income effect dominates in the short run). This borrowing strategy allows them to smooth their absorption, and I term it countershock. Creditors also want loans to take this pattern since it maximizes the value of consumption smoothing to the debtor countries, the denial of which is a penalty. Without econometric estimation, it is difficult to say whether the theoretical expectation—that lending will offset negative shocks—has prevailed in practice. My belief is that it has not.

Changes in the terms of trade can be one important example of a shock. Debt outstanding seems to increase for most countries as the terms of trade improve, while debt accumulation slows when the terms of trade deteriorate. This pattern seems to be typical for oil exporters, where improvements in the terms of trade may have been thought to be permanent, and for beverage exporters and copper exporters, where improvements in the terms of trade should have been seen as clearly transitory. Among the copper exporters are the earliest large borrowers and the earliest problem cases. The experience of this last group suggests that the pro-shock pattern is, for many countries, not merely a consequence of the simultaneity of improved terms of trade, low real interest rates, and abundant Organization of Petroleum Exporters (OPEC) dollars. Two typical cases, Algeria and the Sudan, are illustrated in figures 2-1 and 2-2.

Why countries choose to lever themselves at the time of favorable shocks, and why their creditors cooperate, is unclear. It obviously means that the country's credit ceiling will be easily exhausted by negative shocks. As a consequence, debt service problems will arise almost immediately, rather than only after poor terms of trade have persisted and debt has built up.

Nigeria (figure 2-3) provides one of the few counterexamples I know to this pro-shock pattern. Prior to 1974, Nigeria's long-term debt exceeded its international reserves and was more than half owed to official lenders. From 1974 to 1977, Nigeria benefited from the first oil price increase, its reserves increased dramatically, and it actually repaid most of its long-term debt to private creditors. Faced by unfavorable conditions in world oil markets in 1978–79, Nigeria expanded its debt markedly. With the second oil price increase, Nigeria's foreign exchange reserves rose so that its debt net of reserves fell. The debt itself was not repaid, however, and instead grew by about the same absolute amount as previously. When oil markets once again became unfavorable, Nigeria increased its debts. It was one of the few countries to register large

(Text continues p. 70.)

Figure 2-1. Algeria: Terms of Trade and Export Quantum and Disbursed Debt Owed to Private Creditors

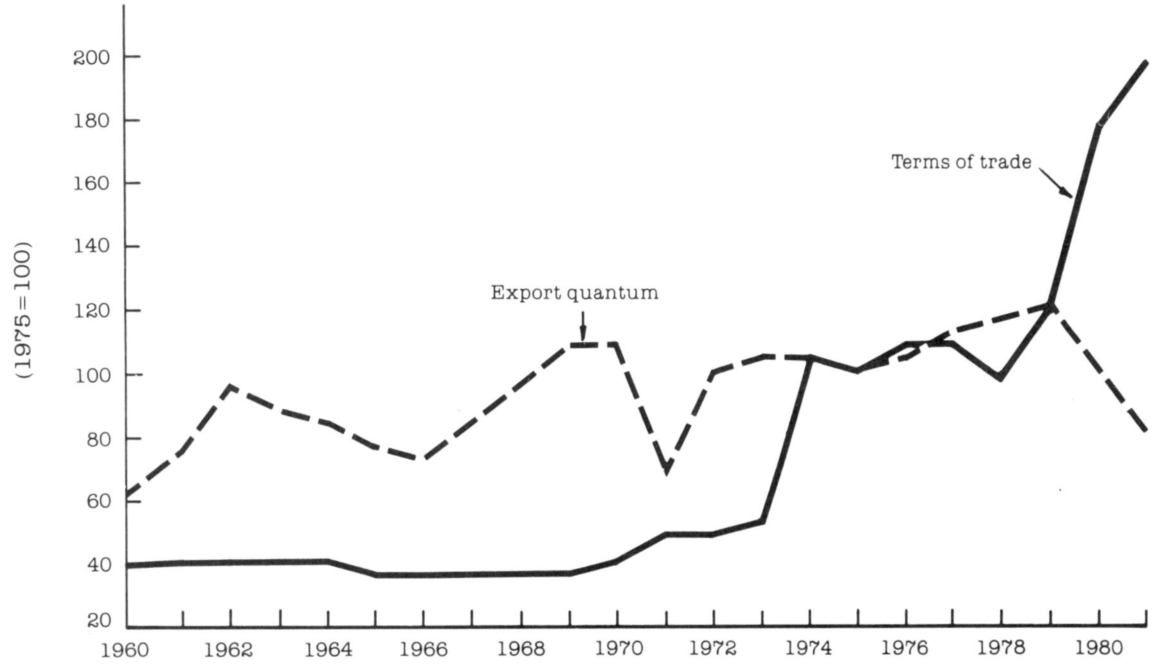

Source: UNCTAD, Handbook of International Trade and Development Statistics, computer tape.

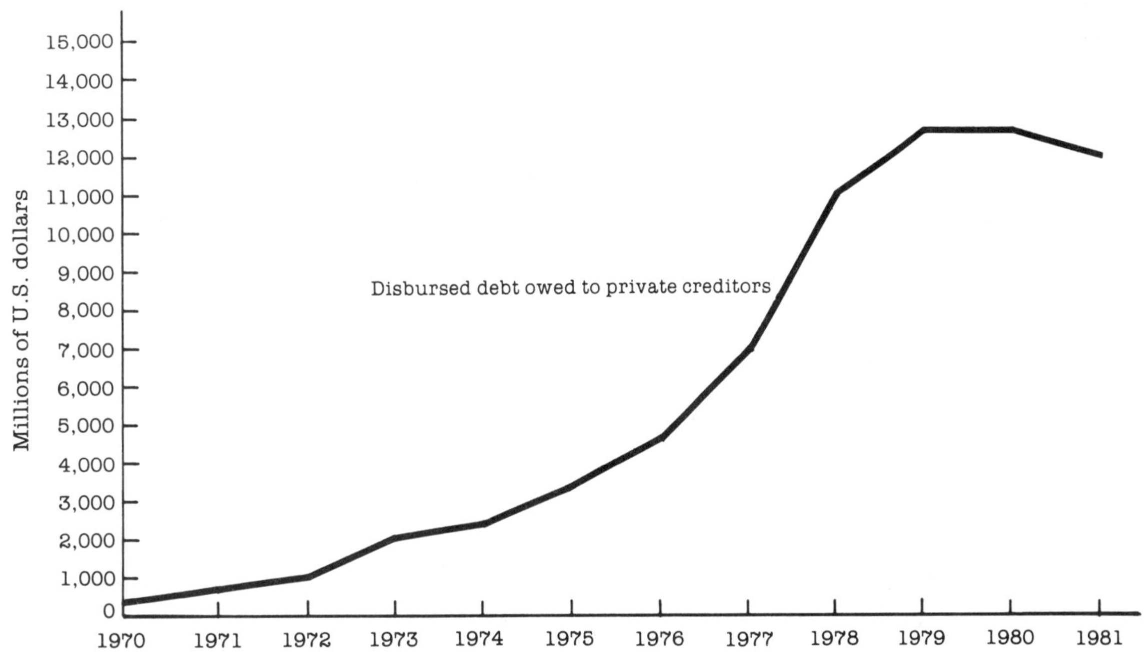

Source: World Bank, World Debt Tables, computer tape.

Figure 2-2. Sudan: Terms of Trade and Export Quantum and Disbursed Debt Owed to Private Creditors

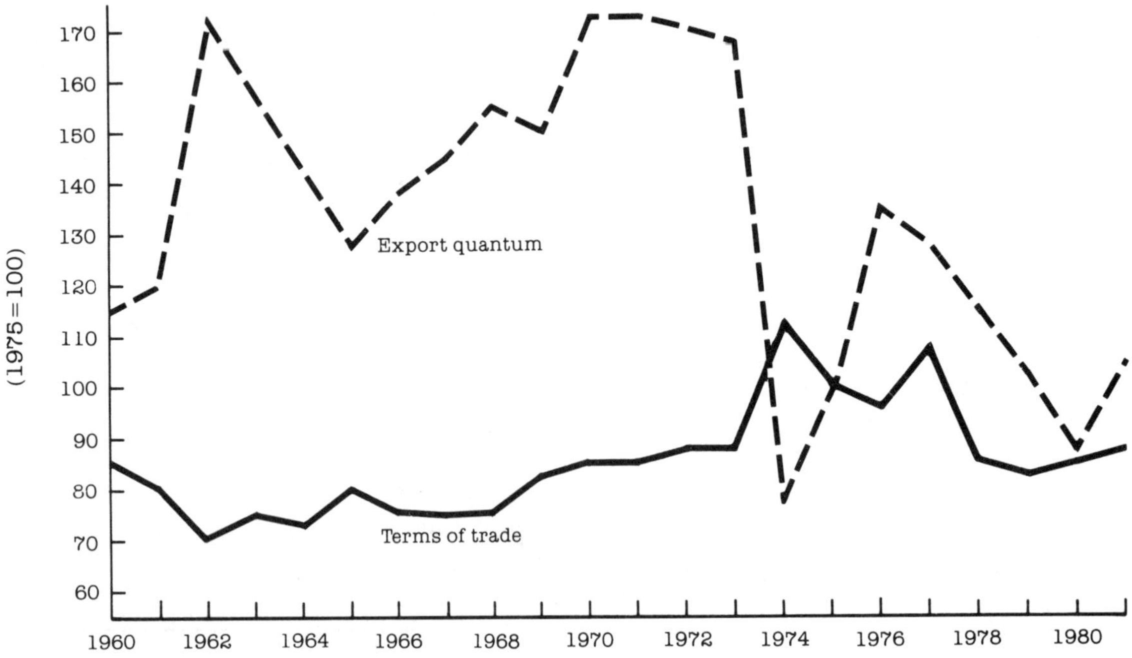

Source: See figure 2-1, top.

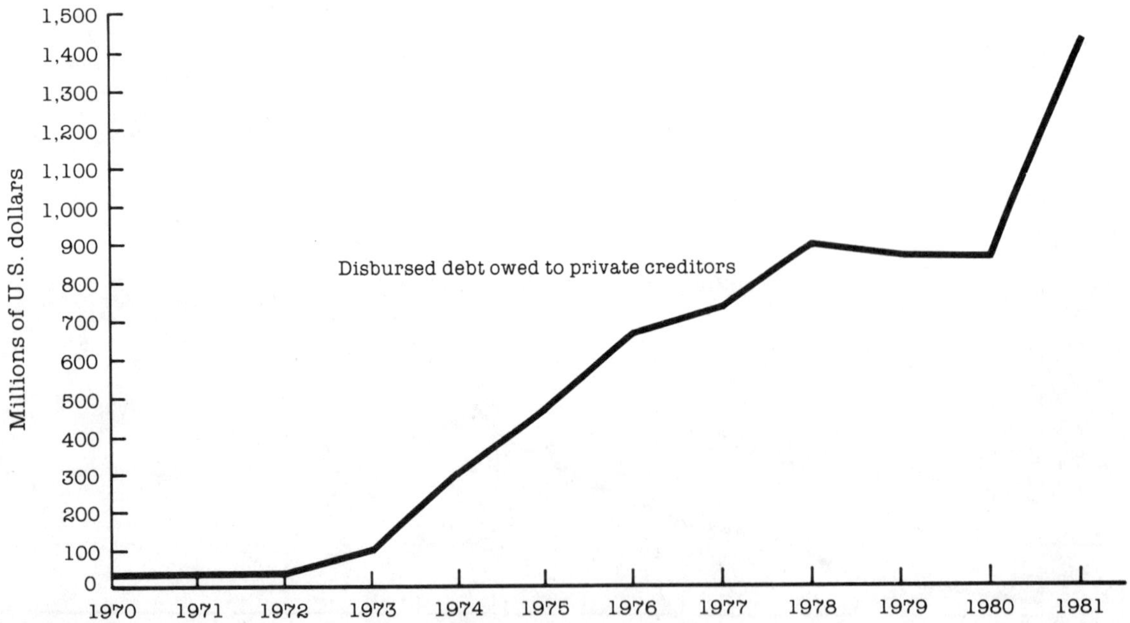

Source: See figure 2-1, bottom.

Figure 2-3. Nigeria: Terms of Trade and Export Quantum and Disbursed Debt Owed to Private Creditors

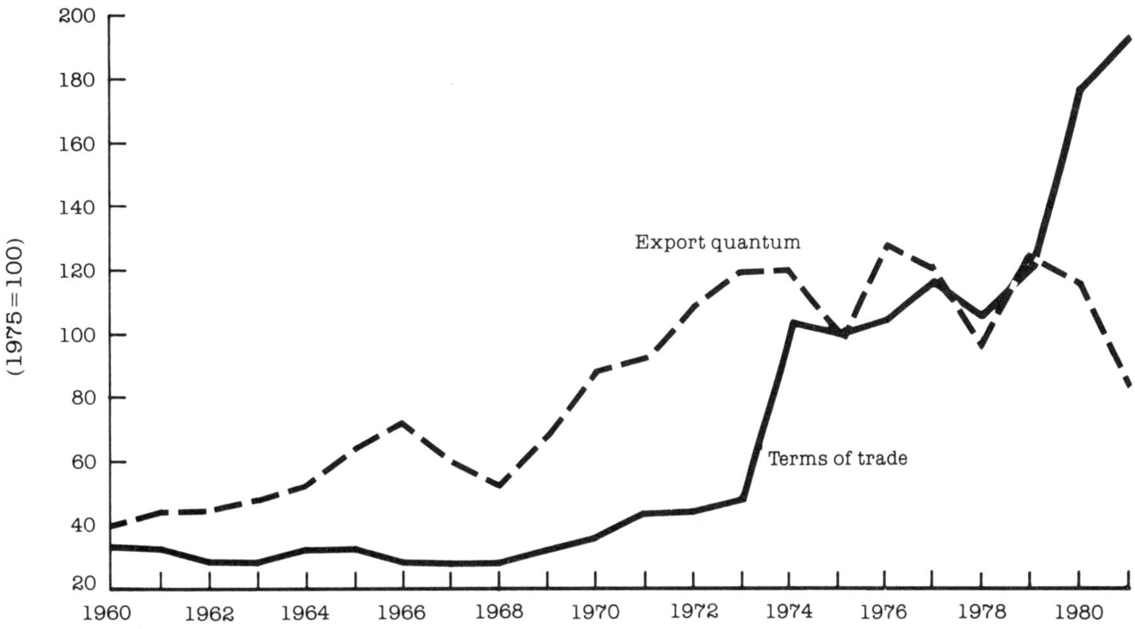

Source: See figure 2-1, top.

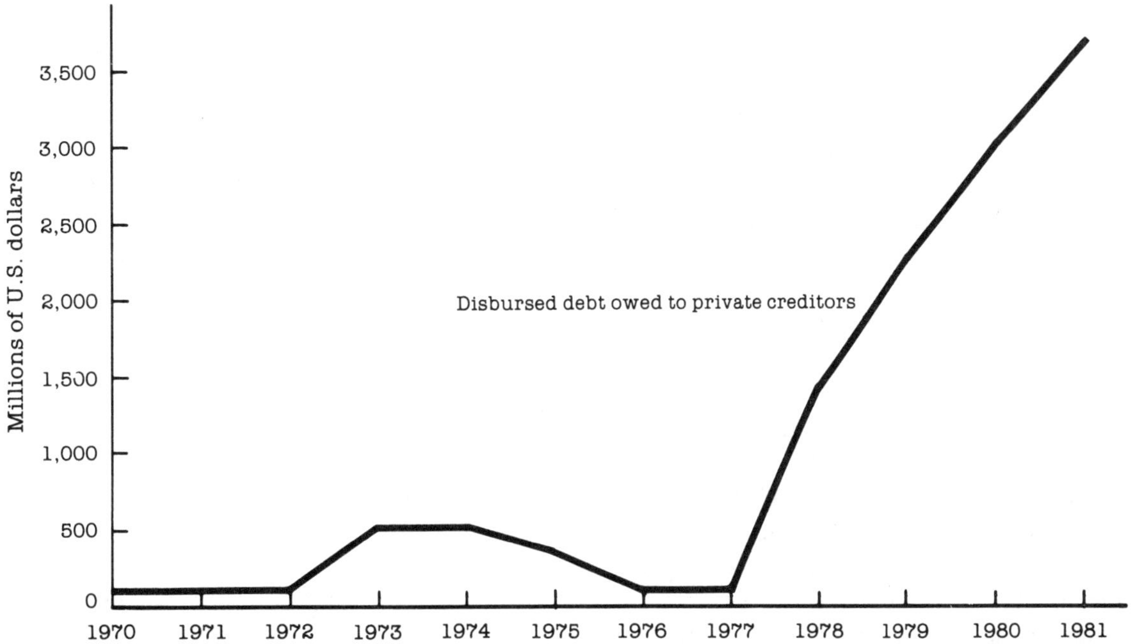

Source: See figure 2-1, bottom.

Table 2-1. Private Bank Reschedulings for World Bank Members

1975–82	1982
New World	
Argentina	Argentina
Bolivia	Bolivia
Guyana	Brazil
Jamaica	Chile
Nicaragua	Costa Rica
Peru	Dominican Republic
	Ecuador
	Honduras
	Jamaica
	Mexico
	Uruguay
Old World	
Liberia	Madagascar
Sudan	Malawi
Togo	Nigeria
Turkey	Senegal
Zaire	Romania
	Togo

Source: World Bank, World Debt Tables (Washington, D.C., 1983).

increases in so-called voluntarily provided private credits over the past two years. Thus Nigeria's bank debt as recorded by the Bank for International Settlements (BIS 1984) was \$4.7 billion as of December 1981 and \$7.5 billion in March 1983. Nigeria is now a problem debtor, whose BIS debt has stagnated over the last year, but its borrowing history can be termed countershock.

Table 2-1 lists World Bank member countries that have rescheduled bank debt between 1975 and 1982. This list of reschedulings is somewhat incomplete since it excludes reschedulings for non-Bank members for which I have not yet established dates. A rescheduling is, however, a rather indistinct form of debt problem. Often problems such as arrears arise years before a rescheduling. Thus, a list of reschedulings and their dates does not reflect the timing for the onset of troubles, a rather more subjective notion. Further, there are some cases so bad that reschedulings are never even attempted. These are obviously the most serious cases, yet they will not appear in any econometric analysis that is focused on predicting reschedulings. (The Democratic Republic of Korea, or North Korea, is an example of a really serious breakdown between debtor and creditors that has persisted for years.) What lenders fear is a loss of the present value of their loans. Outside observers, however, cannot easily know all the terms of these reschedulings. In addition, no one can now know whether it is reasonable to expect that these terms will be respected, and what present value can be expected to be realized.

When a problem arises and lending is suspended, the relation $D = \min(D^*, \bar{D})$ need no longer hold. The very definition of a problem is that outstanding debt exceeds the credit ceiling desired by lenders. In this case, if one looks at countries of all types, actual debt outstanding will equal either $\min(D^*, \bar{D})$, or, if it is a problem case, D_{-1}, debt previously outstanding, adjusted by capitalized interest, arrears, or involuntary lending.

Have banks actually written down the present value of their loans in any of these reschedulings, on the assumption that all the terms will be adhered to in the future? In the case of Nicaragua, the answer seems to be yes (Weinert 1981)—but by how much is difficult to calculate. On most other reschedulings, the answer seems to be no. For instance, many of the spreads above the LIBOR charged on reschedulings exceed those customary in the 1970s, and now range from just below 2 percent to 2.5 percent (IMF 1983). There has, however, been a reversal in these terms. Several debtors have obtained lower rates on the most recent reschedulings: Brazil (by 0.125 percent), Mexico (by 0.75 percent), and Peru (by 0.5 percent) (Montagnon 1984). These concessions seem to accord roughly with the countries' recent performance with respect to arrears and IMF conditions. As with the earlier Nicaraguan case, in April 1984, Argentina, which had sought large concessions but had large arrears and had not complied with the IMF, has shown that these concessions can also reflect the potential for brinkmanship by the debtors. The rate on the Argentinian rescheduling loan of April, 0.125 percent over LIBOR, is one of the lowest ever recorded in country lending, including those made in the period of voluntary lending.

An area where banks have been successful in getting countries to adopt policies favorable to their interests is in the treatment of debt owed by private debtors and not guaranteed by governments of developing countries. In most cases, countries have assumed some responsibility for these debts. Chile is an extreme example. Much of the country's public debt to foreign banks has arisen from the takeover of previously unguaranteed debts of Chilean private banks in January and February of 1983. Of course, some of the failure by private borrowers to service debts may result from government rationing of foreign exchange and other policies. Therefore, these loans are definitely subject to sovereign risk.

Have creditors taken sanctions against debtors? Certainly, problem debtors have lost access to loans, including trade credit. North Korea is notable for being reduced to trade on a cash-only basis (FEER 1982, p. 180). Even in this case, however, the country has not had to resort to barter; when it makes payments, no attempt is made to seize them in the process of transfer. Nor does North Korea have to balance its trade on a country-by-country basis. Turkey in the late 1970s was also having trouble effecting international transactions (World Bank 1980a, p. 34).

Only in the case of Iran in 1979 and 1980 have banks actively pursued large-scale legal action to seize assets abroad, and this episode involved special political factors. With this exception, banks have been generally concerned not to call debtors in default. There have, however, been some isolated instances of legal action. At least one relatively small Venezuelan loan was paid in full after banks obtained attachments of the debtor's assets through New York's courts (Brown 1983). A Geneva court, however, ruled that a bank could not declare Costa Rica in default on bonds held for a client; instead, the client would have to sue (Montagnon 1983). The technicalities of the law in different jurisdictions can lead to quite diverse outcomes for market participants. There is clearly the potential for much greater confrontation—conflict which the Iranian case only weakly foreshadows since, in that case, activity was restricted to American banks.

In general, the 1970s saw legislation that appears to have weakened sovereign immunity in most OECD jurisdictions; there is now the potential for more legal action on the part of aggrieved creditors than ever before (Delaume 1977 and Higgins 1977). But a recent loss by a U.S. bank in a New York court case casts doubt on the strength of the creditor's legal position (Witcher 1984). Systematic research by legal scholars is needed on the nature of these cases to establish the prospects for success by creditors in the courts.

What other evidence is there on private bank cohesion? The early fears that individual banks—especially smaller ones without a potential long-term commitment to overseas business—would refuse to participate in reschedulings and call defaults have proved almost entirely groundless. From the point of view of these banks, such action would be of benefit only to the extent that the debtor had some assets abroad that could be attached. Even in this case, so-called sharing clauses in syndicated loans (Cates and Isern-Feliu 1982) would often mean that any funds obtained would have to be shared with other syndicate members. In the absence of a sharing clause, any bank undertaking legal action could expect to be joined quickly by other creditors suing to get their share. Finally, small banks have felt that their corresponding and other long-term relationships with large banks would be threatened by a refusal to participate in reschedulings (Witcher 1983).

For all these reasons, attempts by small banks to avoid participation in reschedulings have been extremely rare. A notable exception is the 1983 action by Michigan National Bank to sue Citibank as syndicate manager for renewing its participation in a Pemex loan (Hall 1983b). Nonetheless, small U.S. banks have managed to reduce their loans to developing-country debtors (by 5.7 percent to Latin America in the second half of 1982), while large banks have been increasing their exposure (Hall 1983a). Moreover, having to deal with many small banks undoubtedly increases the costs and time involved in reschedulings, thereby heightening the atmosphere of crisis.

One bank's (A's) calling of a default would activate the so-called cross-default clause whereby other lenders could then call their loans in default. This right, however, is typically given to these other lenders by the cross-default clauses in their contracts—regardless of whether A actually calls a default—so long as an event of default has occurred according to the terms of A's loan contract (Clark and Taylor 1982). In any event, the cross-default clause does not force other lenders to call defaults or to take sanctions in support of a lender calling a default; it merely provides the option of doing so. Further, most lenders have the option of calling defaults on the major problem borrowers based on what has happened to their own loans in isolation from the fate of any other loans. Under current conditions, therefore, the cross-default clause would appear to have very little influence on events, whether one creditor calls a default or not.

While the small banks have not precipitated a breakdown in the rescheduling process, there have been some other intrabank cleavages which possibly have provided greater difficulties. In the Costa Rican rescheduling, banks that held bonds (and the Costa Rican government) tried to avoid having the relatively small number of bonds included in the rescheduling. These banks failed, although nonbank (natural) bondholders were exempted (Euromoney 1982). It may be that there are even more important cleavages among banks that will surface in future reschedulings and lead to actual breakdowns. One potential division is among banks resident in different national jurisdictions. In these situations, governments may see different political costs to various bank strategies, bank regulations or tax laws may be different, or banks may have different prospects of being compensated by their governments. U.S. banks and European banks may be affected in rather different ways for these reasons in, for example, Poland or Latin America.

Very early on, private banks attempted to impose their own conditionality on problem debtors. By far the most notable case was Peru in 1976. Banks, however, lacked the information and expertise to develop such plans. They could not decide on what was important. Monitoring of compliance proved difficult, and, when the terms were not met, banks could not agree on what to do. They feared becoming a focus of political discontent within the debtor country and did not want to be seen as interfering with a debtor's political sovereignty (Belliveau 1976). Legislators in the United States expressed concern about banks' involvement in the policy decisions of a debtor country (Shapiro 1976). These efforts to operationalize conditionality clauses broke down, were eventually abandoned, and are now widely considered within the private banking community to have been failures. The private banks then came to rely on the International Monetary Fund (IMF) to design economic programs that they believed would facilitate debt service, often making agreement between the debtor and the IMF a condition for rescheduling.

The perception that the IMF is equipped to handle many of these roles, which the banks could not fulfill, gives it great leverage with the banks. But while the IMF certainly can successfully undertake some of these roles, it is an open question whether the IMF can ensure adherence to its own conditionality. In the case of Zaire, the arrears problem remained unsolved even after the IMF and other foreign personnel undertook high-level line positions in the government. It is unclear what the IMF's own arsenal of sanctions contains beyond those implicitly put at its disposal by the banks.

Until recently, there have been no resales of the developing-country debt that is owed to banks.

Therefore, there has been no direct market-based way to gauge creditors' expectations about prospects for debt service. Quotations on bank shares do provide evidence of the market's view about the value of bank portfolios. Knowledge of the composition of individual bank portfolios is, however, not public, and it is difficult to infer the discount on the debt of individual countries that is implied by the stock market value of banks with differing portfolios. In the last year or so, there have been a limited number of resales of the bank debt of developing countries at discounts ranging up to 25 percent for major debtors (Business Week 1983). While these trades provide evidence that not all debts are valued at par, there is no established market, and prices may reflect idiosyncratic circumstances or provisions of original loan contracts particularly unfavorable to creditors. Still, such transactions support arguments that debtor nation debts should not be carried on bank balance sheets at original value and that loan loss provisions should be made.

The development of an active secondary market in bank loans would have advantages beyond these informational benefits. It would allow small banks to exit from the market, thereby streamlining the rescheduling process. Individual banks with a desire for liquidity relative to other banks could sell loans. Concentrating the holding of debt may increase sanctions if banks that leave the market intend to do no future business with the developing countries, while the remaining banks can coordinate more easily to threaten problem debtors. However, if banks that sell their loans lose interest in imposing sanctions and are willing to help debtor nations effect transactions, sanctions will be lessened and the value of loans to the remaining banks will fall. It has often been felt that the participation of many banks in syndicates means that a potential repudiator would be deterred by having few alternatives. For similar reasons, it is unlikely that nonbank investors will desire to purchase bank loans on a large scale. In general, dispersing the ownership of debt is likely to weaken sanctions, and, in particular, banks would seem to have a comparative advantage in imposing sanctions since they are the primary facilitators of international transactions.

While banks are the major private creditors of the developing countries at present, bondholders were the major creditors in the last great episode of defaults and debt moratoriums in the 1930s. Nevertheless, there are currently some bondholders, grantors of trade credit, and depositors in developing-country banks who are creditors in addition to the banks. What can be learned from the experience of such nonbank creditors as bondholders? Eaton and Gersovitz (1981b) discuss the differing attributes of banks and bondholders.

Publicly traded bonds provide information on the expectations of market participants about debt service. Increases in relative yields on bonds for developing countries suggest a mild write-down in the value of these issues (see table 2-2). This evidence, however, must be treated with caution since the theories of debt payment problems suggest that different creditors may have quite varied prospects of being repaid. This is clearly the case where enforceable contracts tie debt service to the returns from different projects or where certain debts are senior to others.

Table 2-2. Comparative Bond Yields

Issue	Percentage of yields as of: January 1981	July 1983
Brazil, 1987	n.a.	16.36
Mexico, 1997	16.02	16.23
Venzuela, 1992	16.02	16.19
United States, 1992	12.05	11.11
Moody's Baa average	15.03	13.39

n.a. Not available.
Source: Moody's Bond Record, various issues.

But what I want to emphasize is that a willingness-to-pay framework implies that attention must be given to the different costs faced when debtors fail to service different classes of debt. With the relatively low amounts of developing-nation bonds currently outstanding, and the difficulty involved in rescheduling them when there are many dispersed bondholders, it may be in the interests of these countries to accord the debtors generous treatment relative to banks. In this way, the explicit rupture involved in a bond default would be avoided. If bonds go into default, it may be much more difficult for banks to avoid classifying loans as nonperforming; this in turn might have costs for the debtor. Bondholders may find it harder to impose sanctions, however—unlike banks, they are not involved in international transfers. If this factor were dominant, the discounts on bonds might overstate potential bank write-downs.

The current fate of these nonbank creditors also reveals information about the functioning of these markets. In the case of mexdollars, dollar deposits held by non-Mexicans (and Mexicans) in Mexican banks, the Mexican government forced conversion of these deposits into inconvertible pesos at an unfavorable rate. This illustrates the lack of compunction felt by debtors facing weak lenders. Suits brought by these small creditors in U.S. courts will provide a keen test of the usefulness to creditors of legal recourse (Rout 1982).

Finally, what can be said about debtor prospects after a rescheduling? The cases prior to 1983 that are listed in table 2-1 provide some evidence on this question. I have not yet been able to document Argentina, Bolivia, Guyana, and Jamaica. Nicaragua and the African countries give no evidence of having been able to reenter the markets, and there seems to be little hope of acceptance by lenders over the medium term. Peru did manage modest borrowing after its 1976–78 crisis, but total BIS debt rose only from $3.4 billion in 1978 to $5.2 billion in 1982. Despite a fairly successful economic recovery and the backing of OECD governments, Turkey has had limited success in attracting private creditors since its crisis in the late 1970s. Its BIS debt has stagnated since 1978 at roughly $3 billion. It may be that banks are waiting to see what will become of the debt rescheduled by Turkey in 1979 (and again in 1982) with a grace period running into 1984 (IMF 1983, p. 39). Nonetheless, Turkey has received some apparently voluntary loans since 1982 (Tonge 1983) and is in the process of completing a further deal of $250 million at 1.5 percent above LIBOR (Truell 1984). These cases suggest that problem debtors cannot expect to resume borrowing very easily.

ECONOMETRIC ESTIMATION

Estimating the determinants of debt outstanding is quite difficult. Even in the absence of problem cases, it is necessary to allow for the possibility that observed debt is the minimum of the credit ceiling and desired debt. This implies two regimes. An appropriate econometric technique produces not only coefficient values but also a probabilistic separation of the sample into the two regimes. The existence of problem debtors whose debt exceeds the level desired by creditors means that a third regime is required in empirical work.

At present, only the two-regime model has been estimated (Eaton and Gersovitz 1980, 1981a). In these studies, the observations on individual countries were from 1970 and 1974, so that there was no need to account for problem debtors. By the same token, however, these results apply to only a very early period in the evolution of lending to developing countries. Bank lending was much less important before 1973–74. The results of these studies indicate that two regimes rather than only one are justified; the credit-constrained regime was relatively more prevalent. In 1974 relatively more countries were credit-constrained. Some of the oil exporters that were included in the sample for both years moved against this trend, however. The analysis of Eaton and Gersovitz (1980), which considers determinants of foreign reserve holdings as well as international indebtedness, suggests that debt was a substitute for reserves in these years. Other estimated parameters are consistent with a view that the vulnerability of countries to penalties influences credit ceilings.

While I would like to feel that these two studies are of interest both for their methodology and for their results, additional research is needed. The following suggestions derive from my own further reflection on how to improve the specification of these models so as to take account of new phenomena that have appeared since the studies were undertaken, such as the emergence of problem debtors (which necessitated an extension to three regimes). Newly available data make possible the use of variables more closely approximating theoretical constructs.

In all empirical work where the unit of observation is the country, a serious problem is that few variables can be considered exogenous. In the case of sovereign debt, the country is unavoidably the unit of analysis, and interest focuses on the determinants of differences in country behavior. If the consequent difficulties are faced squarely, however, it should be possible to mitigate them substantially. For instance, in dealing with external shocks, care should be taken to use the terms of trade as an explanatory variable, rather than other variables, such as the value of exports, that involve country responses as well as external influences. Most developing countries are sufficiently small in the world economy that their terms of trade are approximately exogenous. Although tedious to implement, it may also be possible to use weather variables to capture other sources of exogenous shocks, especially in a time-series analysis of particular countries. Weather shocks are often cited as an important precipitant of debt problems in such countries as Sudan and Peru.

In the analysis of debt levels and debt problems, an important distinction is between the long-run characteristics of countries (for instance, the standard deviation of the terms of trade about trend) and transitory shocks they may experience (the deviation of the terms of trade from trend in any one year). For instance, Eaton and Gersovitz (1981a) present a model in which an increase in the permanent variability of a debtor's income can increase the debt ceiling it faces, although a failure to repay, if it occurs at all, will occur in a period of relatively low income. Existing studies use some constructed measures for long-run country characteristics such as the variability of exports. They do not, however, incorporate variables capturing transitory factors into the estimation. Under reasonable distributional assumptions, the omission of these variables (and their implicit inclusion in the error term) need not bias the estimated coefficients. Of course, their omission does mean that these models do not reflect the role of shocks in determining indebtedness. It may be that, when these variables are included, the pro-shock pattern apparent from a graphical examination of the data alluded to above will be seen instead to be one of countershock. If the pro-shock pattern persists, however, it will be possible to see whether it derives from the behavior of borrowers or lenders, or both.

Finally, there is scope for improving these models by using data available since the earlier studies and variables that could be constructed from unpublished data sources. The Eaton-Gersovitz studies use the World Bank World Debt Tables series on debt to private creditors. It is important to add short-term debt guaranteed by the debtor country to the World Bank figures to produce a dependent variable that is more comprehensive. It is also necessary to integrate debt owed by the private sector that is not guaranteed by the debtor's government, although this leads to questions of model specification as well as data. At the same time, a significant part of debt owed to private creditors is guaranteed by the governments of these creditors, and these debts must be treated more like debt to public creditors.

CONCLUSIONS

This chapter has described a set of theories about how sovereign debtors and their creditors interact, and has assessed these theories for logical consistency and for their conformity with recent experience. The questions before participants in international financial markets and policymakers are: Will banks regret having made these loans? Will banks be prepared to extend further loans to the developing countries? Will ruptures between lenders and creditors lead to sanctions? What can public policy authorities do to mitigate problems in these markets? In concluding, I offer a scenario for the future evolution of debtor-creditor relations to show how the theoretical notions can be used to approach these questions. Although informed by the material in this chapter, there is no way to say that the scenario can be formally deduced from the preceding discussion, particularly because of the uncertainties in establishing willingness-to-pay thresholds.

The loans to many countries that are at present rescheduling debts will eventually be serviced in a way that preserves their present values. But there is a reasonable probability that several large debtors will choose not to service their debts in this way. This decision need not mean an explicit repudiation. Instead, there could be repeated rescheduling of debts with partial but distinctly incomplete debt service that will roughly equal the cost to the country of the sanctions that banks would otherwise impose. To the extent that countries are credibly able to threaten not to pay at all, payments may even fall below the costs to them of these sanctions. This compromise seems consistent with the experience of chronic problem borrowers: Zaire, Sudan, and North Korea. For this group of countries, there is no prospect for new loans, since any marginal loans will not be serviced at all.

But explicit repudiations are not ruled out. Such an act seems most likely if the political opposition within a country attempts to undermine the government's power base by raising the repudiation issue. In this case, it may be difficult for the government to explain adequately that it is more beneficial to participate in negotiations that maintain the pretense of ultimate repayment with the intention of paying only enough to avoid sanctions. There will be other developing countries, however, for which potential sanctions are so costly that banks will still feel confident in lending to them. Thus, the experience of developing-country borrowers will become much more diverse than in the past.

Whether the level of debt service will be adequate to maintain the solvency of all bank lenders is an open question. For many large banks, the amounts at stake are several times their capital, although some parts of these loans are guaranteed by the banks' own governments. Even a 10 percent write-off of their total developing-nation portfolio would cripple many of these banks. Such a write-off is not inconsistent with recent movements in yields on the publicly traded bonds issued by these countries, although for reasons mentioned this is only an approximate guide to the fate of banks. Current trends to lower interest rate spreads and rescheduling fees suggest that there may be little upside possibilities for the banks—contrary to speculation based on the terms established for the initial rescheduling of the large Latin American borrowers. It would be a serious mistake to believe that a major restructuring of, for example, the American money center banks could occur only during a crisis so large that the governments of the OECD would have to prevent it. (Continental Illinois is a possible case in point.) Whatever their exact condition, these banks are likely to hesitate to resume lending to developing countries near their willingness-to-pay threshold now that experience has made clearer the risks of sovereign lending. Tightened bank regulations may also leave less scope for bank lending abroad.

There is little opportunity for policymakers to affect this scenario, short of subsidizing loans to developing nations or paying off their debts. The IMF has played an important role in the process of rescheduling. By functioning in ways the banks find difficult to duplicate, it has helped to avert a breakdown stemming from the multiplicity of lenders, that is, a liquidity crisis. In other dimensions affecting their interests, the banks have displayed considerable cohesion without assistance. The IMF does not, however, have any special powers by which it can assure anxious creditors that the willingness-to-pay thresholds can be significantly increased. Better project evaluation can benefit the developing countries by increasing the efficiency of their use of resources, but it is unlikely to improve their access to credit as a group.

In some absolute sense, this is a pessimistic scenario. It says that the institution of the sovereign state makes it impossible to realize the gains from an international allocation of capital based solely on efficiency considerations. But from the perspective of the fearful commentary of 1982 and 1983, it is an optimistic scenario for the OECD, for debt-ridden developing countries, and possibly even for the banks.

REFERENCES

BIS. 1984. International banking statistics 1973–1983. Basel: Bank for International Settlements.

Belliveau, Nancy. 1976. "What the Peru experiment means." Institutional Investor (October):145–148.

Brown, Christopher R. 1983. "How to be paid on a defaulting loan." International Financial Law Review 2 (April):10–12.

Business Week. 1983. "A hot new market in swapping high-risk debt." (December 5):144.

Cates, Armel C., and Santiago Isern-Feliu. 1982. "The real purpose of the sharing clause." Euromoney (November):139–44.

Clark, Keith, and Andrew Taylor. 1982. "Events of default in Eurocurrency loan agreements." International Financial Law Review 1 (September):12–15.

Delaume, Georges R. 1977. "Public debt and sovereign immunity: The Foreign Sovereign Immunities Act of 1976." American Journal of International Law 71:399–422.

Eaton, Jonathan, and Mark Gersovitz. 1980. "LDC participation in international financial markets: Debt and reserves." Journal of Development Economics 7 (no. 1):3–21.

———. 1981a. "Debt with potential repudiation: Theoretical and empirical analysis." Review of Economic Studies 48 (no. 152):289–309.

———. 1981b. Poor country borrowing in private financial markets and the repudiation issue. Princeton Studies in International Finance no. 47. Princeton, N.J.: International Finance Section, Princeton University.

———. 1983. "Country risk: Economic aspects." In Managing international risk, edited by R. J. Herring. New York: Cambridge University Press, pp. 74–107.

———. 1984. "A theory of expropriation and deviations from perfect capital mobility." Economic Journal 94 (no. 373):16–40.

Euromoney. 1982. "Step by step through the Costa Rica saga." (August):33–45.

FEER. 1982. "Korea-North." Asia 1982 yearbook. Hong Kong: Far Eastern Economic Review.

Gersovitz, Mark. 1983. "Trade, capital mobility and sovereign immunity." Research Program in Development Studies Discussion Paper no. 108. Princeton, N.J.: Princeton University.

Hall, William. 1983a. "Small US banks cut Latin American loans." Financial Times (June 6):1.

———. 1983b. "Challenge to Citibank rocks world banking boat." Financial Times (December 6): 21.

Higgins, Rosalyn. 1977. "Recent developments in the law of sovereign immunity in the United Kingdom." American Journal of International Law 71:423–37.

IMF. 1983. Recent multilateral debt restructurings with official and bank creditors. Washington, D.C.: International Monetary Fund.

Kharas, Homi J. 1981. "Constrained optimal foreign borrowing by less developed countries." Washington, D.C.: Development Policy Staff, World Bank. Processed.

Montagnon, Peter. 1983. "Dow banking loses Costa Rica suit." Financial Times (February 11):1.

———. 1984. "Peru debt concession confirms trend to lower margins." Financial Times (February 13):21.

Rout, Lawrence. 1982. "Americans with dollars in Mexico hope suit will recoup big losses." Wall Street Journal (October 8):1.

Sachs, Jeffrey. 1983. "Theoretical issues in international borrowing." NBER Working Paper no. 1189. Cambridge, Mass.: National Bureau of Economic Research. August.

Shapiro, Harvey D. 1976. "Monitoring: Are the banks biting off more than they can chew?" Institutional Investor (October):140–42.

Tonge, David. 1983. "Bad debtor who made good." Financial Times (May 17): VII.

Truell, Peter. 1984. "Turkey seeking bank borrowing of $250 million." Wall Street Journal (January 24):36.

Weinert, Richard S. 1981. "Nicaragua's debt renegotiation." Cambridge Journal of Economics 5, (no. 1):195–200.

Witcher, S. Karenne. 1983. "Little fish: Small bank in the South comes to regret entry into foreign lending." Wall Street Journal (March 25):1.

———. 1984. "Appeals court rule may allow nations to renege on some debts to U.S. banks." Wall Street Journal (April 27):2.

Wood, Philip R. 1982. "Debt priorities in sovereign insolvency." International Financial Law Review 1 (November):4–11.

World Bank. 1980a. Turkey: Policies and prospects for growth. Washington, D.C.

———. 1980b. Zaire: Current economic situation and constraints. Washington, D.C.

3

International Debt Strategies in an Uncertain World

Paul Krugman

It is now more than a year and a half since a balance of payments crisis forced Mexico into a suspension of debt service, setting off what we now regard as a global debt crisis. From the earliest stages of the crisis, there have been two opposing views about the appropriate response of creditors and creditor governments. One view—the view that has prevailed so far—holds that the crisis is a temporary one and should be met by ad hoc financing arrangements designed to buy time until the situation improves. The other belief is that the debt of many developing nations is too large ever to be serviced, and that the only thing that makes sense is to restructure comprehensively and perhaps heavily write down external claims on these countries.

How are we to evaluate these views? The issue is often posed as a simple factual one. Proponents of temporary financing often assert that the problem is one of liquidity but not of solvency. In other words, debtor countries may be short of cash now, but they will eventually be able to service their debts once recovery in the industrial countries, declining interest rates, and the increasing effectiveness of new incentives for exporting and import substitution take hold. The other side agrees that the issue is factual, but disagrees about the facts: the OECD recovery will not be sustained enough, real interest rates will remain high, increased developing-country exports will encounter protectionist obstacles. If the debate is phrased in these terms, it ought to be settled on the basis of statistics and simulation models.

The idea of a simple factual distinction between liquidity and solvency, however, while a useful organizing principle, does not stand up well under careful examination. It has two major problems in the current context. First, it is difficult to explain the behavior of creditors in terms of any simple liquidity–solvency dichotomy. If the debtor nations are truly only illiquid, why are they not able to borrow freely to cover their temporary shortfall? Bankers might be irrational in refusing to lend, but such a hypothesis would not seem to pertain to a crisis that has persisted this long. The point is that it is difficult to explain a liquidity crisis unless there is a real possibility that the debtor is truly insolvent. If the debtors are truly insolvent, however, why have their creditors been willing to continue increasing their exposure? Banks might be irrational or might be waiting for governments to bail them out, but this is again an unsatisfactory explanation. It is much more plausible to suppose that creditors are willing to play for time because there is a real possibility that normal debt service can eventually be resumed.

Closely related to the problem of explaining creditor behavior is the observation that we do not in fact know whether the problem is one of liquidity or solvency. We do not know—nor do the debtor countries and their creditors know—how durable recovery in the OECD will be, what will happen to interest rates and inflation, how trade policy in OECD countries will respond to increased exports by developing countries, or how the political stability of developing countries will respond to squeezed imports.

In other words, the key both to understanding what has happened so far and to formulating an international debt strategy is to allow for the reality of uncertainty.

This chapter has two purposes. The first is to lay out a framework for exploring the international debt crisis that explicitly acknowledges the role of uncertainty. The second, more difficult purpose is to assess the implications of this framework for policy; in particular, to ask whether the current debt strategy should be replaced with a more comprehensive approach, and what this approach should look like.

There are four parts to the chapter. The first is a review of that area in the recent theoretical and practical discussion of international lending with the risk of default which seems relevant to the issue of international debt strategy. The second part attempts to sharpen the discussion by presenting a simple theoretical model of international debt and default. In the third part, several alternatives strategies for dealing with a debt crisis are discussed. Finally, the fourth part of the chapter attempts to evaluate the scope for large-scale schemes of debt restructuring.

THE ANALYSIS OF DEBT AND DEFAULT

In the past few years, considerable effort has gone into the development of a theory of international lending with default risk. The seminal contribution by Eaton and Gersovitz (1981) poses the issue clearly: how is international lending possible when debtor nations have the option of repudiating their debt? Unlike a domestic debtor, a country cannot have its income attached or, with minor exceptions, its assets seized. Why, then, should a country ever repay its debts? And if countries do not have an incentive to repay, why would rational lenders lend to them in the first place?

The answer proposed by Eaton and Gersovitz and elaborated by later authors is that, for the system to work, a failure to repay debt must impose costs on the defaulting country. A country will not default if these costs are believed to be larger than the benefit of not repaying. Since this benefit depends on the size of a country's debt, however, lenders will try to ration credit so as not to lend so much as to provide an incentive for default.

There are two main themes in the recent literature generated by this insight. The first is concerned with the question of defining the costs of default—a critical issue, yet a source of great uncertainty. The second attempts to assess the implications for international lending of uncertain costs of default, and hence the possibility of a failure of default deterrence. Both themes are important for a debt strategy, and we discuss each in turn.

The Costs of Default

If a country fails to pay its debts, its creditors can of course seize whatever assets they can lay their hands on. For heavily indebted nations, however, the seizable external assets are generally small relative to their debt. Thus the threat of seizure per se is not a major deterrent to default. Rather, the crucial deterrent is the likely consequences as creditors try to get what they can. At minimum, an outright default would cause a country to be excluded from international capital markets, at least for a time. More than this, an outright repudiation of debt might lead to a country's exclusion from much ordinary trade as well.

But need debt repudiation be outright? One important possibility is that a debtor country might, when the time for repayment comes, be able to use the threat of repudiation to induce its creditors to renegotiate their terms in its favor. Thus, key to any analysis of the debt problem is not only the question of the possible sanctions against a defaulter but an explanation of why these sanctions might actually be invoked.

Access to capital markets. The most basic effect of a national default is the inability of a country to borrow again. It seems unlikely that new lenders would be willing to provide money soon to a country that has failed to pay previous debts. Even if they were willing, existing creditors would try to seize the funds. Therefore, a failure to pay would presumably force a country to operate its international transactions on the basis of balanced trade thereafter.

On first examination, this may seem an unimportant sanction. A country that is considering default must, if it is at all rational, be considering this action because it is being forced to run a trade surplus to service its debt. An exclusion from capital markets cannot be a current cost.

However, even a country that is currently running a trade surplus may anticipate the possibility that it may want to run a deficit in the future. The loss of this flexibility is a real cost, and it is certainly a part of the cost of default which makes international lending possible.

It is difficult, however, to explain the willingness of debtor countries to undertake austerity programs on the basis of their fear of losing access to capital markets alone. Far more important is the concern that a defaulting country might find itself largely excluded from international trade.

Access to trade. It is widely believed that a country that repudiates its debt will find itself excluded from most international trade. What seems fairly certain is that such a country would find itself excluded from the usual way of doing business. It is less clear whether alternative ways of conducting trade could be developed or whether they would prove prohibitively costly.

Under normal conditions, most trade is financed by trade credit. A country that repudiated its debt would of course be excluded from this usual procedure. At least in the short run, this would probably produce a serious interruption of trade. In fact, unavailability of trade credit has probably played a key role in the dramatic decline of Mexican imports since 1981.

It might seem at first that a country could get around the problem of lack of trade credit, albeit at a cost, by paying cash for its imports. Saying that one pays "cash," however, usually means that one pays from a bank account rather than literally with currency. A defaulting debtor country would be unable to maintain an external bank account without having its contents seized. While some limited trade could be conducted on a "brown paper bag" basis, the costs would be high.

A third alternative might be barter trade. Barter with individuals or firms may or may not be possible. In principle, creditors could put liens on cargoes, either export or import, whenever they entered a port in the jurisdiction of courts honoring the debt. Enforcing such a blockade would be costly, and there would doubtless be leakage, but the scope for barter transactions would certainly be limited—with one major exception.

The exception is government-to-government barter arrangements. There does not seem to be any way in which creditors could prevent debtor nations from managing at least some trade in this way. This possibility is a significant loophole in the sanctions against defaulting debtors.

The most significant loophole, however, is the lack of any certainty that the available sanctions would in fact be applied.

Will Defaulters Be Punished?

Let us suppose a debtor country offers to pay part of its debts provided that its creditors refrain from declaring the country in default and invoking their sanctions. Ex ante, creditors would like to commit themselves to imposing sanctions when a country attempts to evade its obligations; but ex post, the creditors might prefer to renegotiate terms rather than lose all their claims. Therefore, creditors, although they can impose serious costs on defaulting nations, may have a problem making credible the threat that they will actually impose these costs.

Why, then, don't countries freely seek to renegotiate the terms of their debt? Creditors might impose sanctions, even when they might receive partial payment if they refrained, for at least two reasons. The first is that creditors may view themselves as playing a "repeated game" in which reputation is important. The second is that creditors are not perfectly collusive and may have an individual interest in invoking sanctions even if collectively they would be better off not doing so.

The repeated game argument is one that comes from pure theory, but it does seem quite realistic. If creditors believe that leniency with one debtor will result in demands from others for renegotiation, the additional cost may make creditors unwilling to be lenient. Recognition of this unwillingness may make debtors pay; and the result will be a self-sustaining set of beliefs.

An interesting fact about this explanation is that it might provide an incentive for debtors to form a cartel. Creditors who are willing to discipline one debtor as an example to others might not be able to make credible the threat to discipline several at once. We know that a debtor's cartel was proposed in 1982. The incentive to form one still exists.

While a debtor's cartel might make it in the collective interest of creditors to renegotiate the terms of loans, creditors may not themselves be perfectly collusive. An individual creditor might have an incentive to seize whatever assets of a defaulting country it can, even though in the aggregate such a move would not be in creditors' ex post interest. The consequences of such a move for the debtor country's trade might be nearly as serious as a deliberate invoking of sanctions.

The end result of the discussion, then, is that a defaulting country faces at least the possibility of serious penalties. The expected cost of these penalties is enough to induce countries to service their debt if it is not too large. But the cost of default does not appear to be so large as to insure that default will never happen.

The expectation that costs will be imposed on defaulting countries and provide them with incentive to repay makes international lending possible. It does not, however, ensure that lending proceeds freely. The possibility of nonpayment leads to credit rationing or, more generally, to upward-sloping supply curves for funds to borrowing nations. A formal model of the lending and borrowing decisions will be developed in the next section. Several general points can be made, however, before setting out a formal model.

For an analysis of international borrowing and lending, it would be useful to state the problem in terms of two periods: a borrowing period and a repayment period. The actual discussion of the debt crisis, however, is difficult to interpret in a two-period framework, since it involves not so much the amount of repayment as the rate at which repayment takes place. I will attempt a brief treatment of this issue, reserving a more thorough treatment for the formal model of the next section.

Two-Period Analysis

Suppose that the problem of international borrowing could be adequately understood in a two-period world, comprising a present in which countries borrow and a future in which they either repay or default. Another initial assumption would be that the costs of default are known with certainty by both lenders and borrowers. The description of financial equilibrium in this world would be straightforward: lenders would ration borrowers to an amount of credit slightly below what would make default worthwhile. In a world of certainty, this means that there would be no defaults and thus that borrowing countries would be charged the riskless interest rate. Therefore, if the costs of default were known with certainty, we would simply have credit rationing, with the credit limit determined by these costs.

In the real world, however, the costs of default are not known with any degree of certainty. More significant is the fact that estimates of these costs are likely to change over time. We have argued that the most important sanction against a defaulting debtor is likely to be disruption of trade. This means that the costs of default depend on gains from trade. If a country has slower growth than expected or suffers a deterioration in its terms of trade, the cost of losing trade access may be lower than the forecast when the country borrowed. As a result, the advantages of default may look larger than anticipated; in the presence of uncertainty, it is no longer possible to set a credit limit that assures repayment.

How would markets react to this uncertainty? Lenders would recognize that the larger is a country's indebtedness, the larger is the probability of a default. Thus they would charge a borrowing country a premium, which would increase the country's expected future debt burden. The country would then face not a simple cost of funds but a supply schedule, off which it would choose its preferred point. The result is illustrated in figure 3-1 (which will be further discussed

Figure 3-1. Equilibrium Lending to a Sovereign Borrower

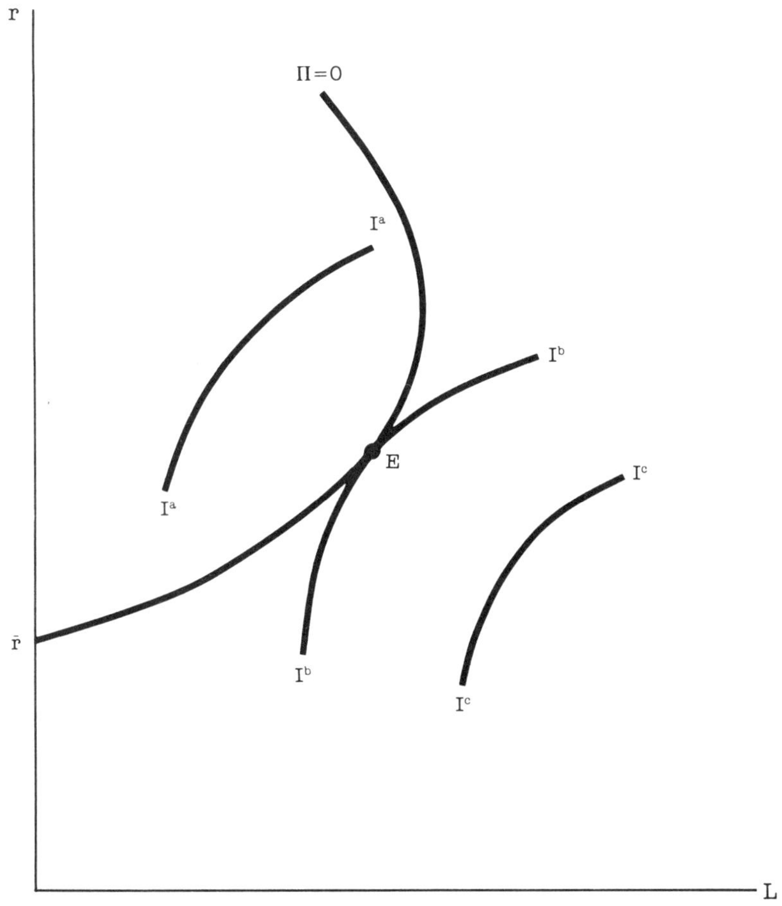

below). On the horizontal axis is the volume of credit extended to a country; on the vertical axis the interest rate it agrees to pay ex ante. The schedule $\Pi = 0$ represents points of zero expected profit to lenders, that is, where the probability of default just offsets the premium of the interest rate over the riskless rate $\bar{r}$. The country's preferences are represented by indifference curves: the country would like to borrow more and pay lower interest. The equilibrium at E will involve both credit rationing and at least some risk premium.

Multiple-Period Analysis: Confidence and Liquidity

While simple two-period analyses of borrowing and lending can lead to useful insights, they miss one of the crucial aspects of recent debt problems. None of these problem debtors was, at the time of crisis, in a period of pure borrowing or pure repayment. They were instead in a situation of both repayment of old loans and new borrowing. The key element of the crisis was an unwillingness of banks to continue lending; this presumably reflected their perception of an increased probability of future default. The problem created by this "drying up" of lending was, of course, that it created an incentive for immediate default.

The debt strategy adopted by creditor nations and the International Monetary Fund (IMF) is based on the belief that a loss of lender confidence can provoke an unnecessary default. In other words, countries could be led to default in a situation where it would be reasonable to expect that, given time to adjust, they could return to normal debt servicing. This provides a justification for a period of forced lending by creditors or perhaps official lending to bridge the crisis period.

Does this view make sense? Despite the recent flowering of theoretical analyses of international lending, the problem of confidence and liquidity has not yet been the subject of much formal modeling. (See, however, Sachs 1983, whose analysis somewhat resembles that in the next section.) The best available discussion of the theoretical basis for the current strategy is by Cline (1983), who stops short of a full model but presents an extremely useful analysis.

Cline's analysis stresses the role played by the already outstanding exposure of creditors. A failure to continue lending may provoke a default and thus the loss of existing claims. What this means is that, from the point of view of creditors, new lending takes on the character of a public good. This, in turn, has several implications. First, it is in the interest of existing creditors to lend even when the risks of future default are enough to make new loans unprofitable when viewed in isolation. Second, this is nonetheless a collective interest, not an individual interest, and creditors may suffer from a free-rider problem. Third—a point not made by Cline, but implicit in his discussion—there is a case for official provision of at least part of the public good, through an official role in crisis lending.

The problem with Cline's analysis is that it is conducted entirely from the point of view of the creditors. There is no explicit discussion of the motives of the debtor. In particular, the presumed connection between the rate of new lending and the probability of default is entirely ad hoc. To check the validity of this analysis, one must be explicit about the motives of both sides.

In the next section we develop a simple formal model designed to accomplish this; the model confirms the basic argument made by Cline. However, it also suggests some other issues bearing on the question of debt strategy.

A SIMPLE MODEL OF DEBT, DEFAULT, AND RESCHEDULING

As sketched in the previous section, some basic elements of an analysis of international debt problems include the reasons for, and the nature of, the costs of default, and the behavior of lenders and borrowers in a world where these costs are uncertain. The existing theory, however, seems to be weak in one crucial area: understanding the role of confidence and liquidity in provoking "unnecessary" defaults, and assessing appropriate policy responses.

The purpose of the following discussion is to help remedy this weakness by presenting a simple formal model of debt and default which allows for confidence and liquidity issues in at least a rudimentary way. The main purpose of this exercise is to provide a firmer basis for the insight of Cline (1983) and others that the maintenance of lending in a debt crisis can be perceived as a sort of public good.

Assumptions of the Model

Consider a country attempting to borrow on the international capital market. The assumption is that the country's decision problem can be adequately represented by looking at two periods: a current period in which the country borrows, and a future period in which the country either repays or defaults. As we know from the last section, however, a pure two-period model cannot capture the key problems of confidence and liquidity. To introduce these, we add one additional feature: an allowance for the possibility that the country has "inherited" a debt from the past, which obliges it (if it does not default) to pay debt service even if it does no further borrowing. This inherited debt plays a crucial role, possibly leading the country to default immediately and offering a rationale for "forced" lending by creditors.

The country is assumed to be acting as a single rational agent. Creditors and new lenders are assumed to be rational and risk-neutral, and we will also assume initially that they behave in a competitive, noncollusive fashion.

Let us begin, then, by specifying the country's objectives. The country's welfare will be represented in a reduced-form way: the country is better off in any given period, the larger the trade deficit it is allowed to run. Also, there is a loss if the country has had sanctions imposed against it in retaliation for a default. The size of this loss presumably depends on the microeconomic factors discussed in the previous section, but in our analysis all of this is simply summarized by a fixed cost levied on the country. Thus the country's utility function will be written as

$$U = V_1(T_1) + \rho V_2(T_2) - \phi_1 K_1 - \phi_2 K_2 \qquad (3.1)$$
$$V' < 0, V_1'' < 0, V_2' < 0, V_2'' < 0, 0 < \rho < 1$$

where

T_1 = trade balance in dollars in the first period

T_2 = trade balance in dollars in the second period

K_1 = loss from sanctions imposed in the first period

K_2 = loss from sanctions imposed in the second period

ϕ_1 = dummy variable, 0 if no sanctions in the first period, 1 if sanctions are imposed

ϕ_2 = dummy variable, 0 if no sanctions in the second period, 1 if sanctions are imposed.

We assume one crucial piece of uncertainty: the cost of default in the second period, K_2, is not known when first-period decisions are made. It becomes known, however, at the beginning of the second period. This assumption is the proxy for all the actual uncertainty about export growth, terms of trade, political outcomes, and so forth. In this chapter, it is assumed that the debtor and creditors are equally uncertain about the cost of default. Thus, complications arising from asymmetric information are ruled out.

The country is assumed to be able to finance trade imbalances only by borrowing. Initially, the country has an inherited stock of debt, with required debt service D_1 in the first period, D_2 in the second. Its options are illustrated in figure 3-2. If the country defaults on its debt at the beginning, it is constrained to have balanced trade in both periods and incurs the penalty cost of default in both periods. If the country does not default at the beginning, it can borrow in the first period. Its first-period trade balance is therefore

$$T_1 = (1 - \phi_1)(D_1 - L) \qquad (3.2)$$

where L is new borrowing; the first-period trade balance may be either positive or negative. In the second period, the country again has the option of either defaulting or repaying; its second-period trade balance is thus

$$T_2 = (1 - \phi_2)[L(1 + r) + D_2] \qquad (3.3)$$

where r is the interest rate in its first-period borrowing.

Lenders are assumed to be competitive and risk-neutral. Let $\bar{r}$ be the interest rate they receive on safe loans, not subject to default risk, and let P be the probability of default perceived by lenders. Then competition will lead to zero expected profits:

$$\Pi = L[(1 + r)(1 - P) - (1 + \bar{r})] = 0. \qquad (3.4)$$

This equation will implicitly define a supply function of credit to the country.

This is evidently about as simple and compact a model of the problem of international debt

Figure 3-2. A Debtor Country's Options

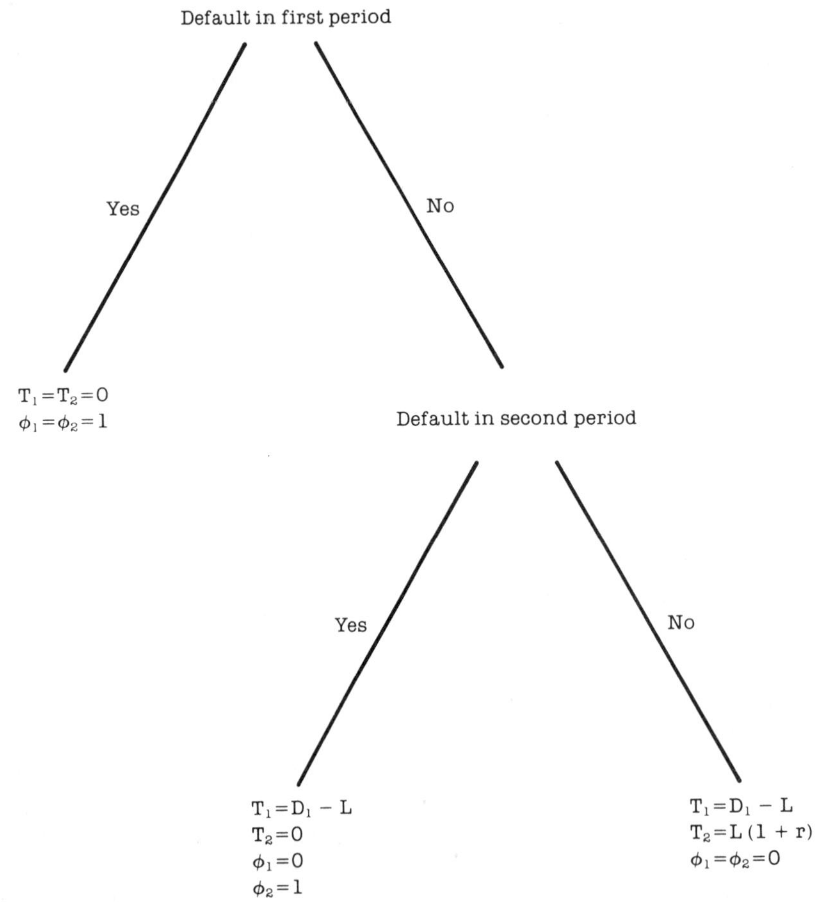

and default as one can imagine. Yet is already rich enough to illustrate the determination of equilibrium lending and the interest rate, the possibility of a liquidity crisis, and the case for rescheduling.

Determination of Lending and the Interest Rate

This model must be solved backwards. First, we ask what happens in the second period, contingent on decisions made in the first. Then we ask how lenders and the borrower will behave in the first period in view of their expectations about how their current actions will affect later outcomes.

Let us then consider the second period. If the country has already defaulted in the first period, it has no decisions to make—it simply runs balanced trade and incurs the penalty cost K_2. If the country did not default in the first period, it has only one available choice, to default or not to default. It is immediately apparent that it will be in the country's interest to default if, and only if,

$$V_2[D_2 + L(1 + r)] < -K_2.$$

Thus, if $f(K_2)$ is the density function of the cost of sanctions in the second period, we will have a probability of default

$$P = \int_0^{-V_2[D_2 + L(1+r)]} f(K_2)dK_2. \tag{3.5}$$

This probability of default is increasing in both the amount borrowed in the first period and the interest rate:

$$\partial P/\partial L = -V_2'(1 + r)f(K_2^*) > 0 \tag{3.6}$$

$$\partial P/\partial r = -V_2' Lf(K_2^*) > 0 \tag{3.7}$$

where K_2^* is the critical cost of sanctions needed to deter default,

$$K_2^* = -V_2[D_2 + L(1 + r)]. \tag{3.8}$$

Also, we can write the country's expected second-period utility as a function of L and r:

$$EU_2 = V_2[D_2 + L(1 + r)] \int_{K_2^*}^{\infty} f(K_2)dK_2 - \int_0^{K_2^*} f(K_2)K_2dK_2. \tag{3.9}$$

This second-period utility is decreasing in both L and r:

$$\partial EU_2/\partial L = V_2'(1 + r)(1 - P) < 0 \tag{3.10}$$

$$\partial EU_2/\partial r = V_2' L(1 - P) < 0. \tag{3.11}$$

Now we turn to the first period. The country has two decisions to make: whether or not to default and, if it does not default, how much to borrow. Both decisions are contingent on the terms offered by lenders. Thus we need to start by defining the debtor's preferences in terms of r and L.

If the country does not immediately default, its first-period utility will simply be

$$U_1 = V_1(D_1 - L). \tag{3.12}$$

Thus, its expected utility overall will be

$$EU = U_1 + \rho EU_2. \tag{3.13}$$

Since the interest rate does not enter into U_1,

$$\partial EU/\partial r = \rho LV_2'(1 - P) < 0, \tag{3.14}$$

that is, the interest rate has an unambiguously negative effect. The volume of loans has a positive effect in the first period, a negative effect in the second; for a credit-constrained country, however, we can assume that, locally at least,

$$\partial EU/\partial L = V_1' + \rho(1 + r)V_2'(1 - P) > 0. \tag{3.15}$$

This means that we can draw an indifference map for the debtor country in r, L space with EU increasing as we move southeast—something we have already done in figure 3-1. This map, however, is drawn on the assumption that the country does not immediately default. The option of immediate default allows the country to assure itself of some reservation level of expected utility U^{min}; if it cannot achieve that level given the supply schedule of lenders, the country will immediately default.

Let us turn, then, to the lenders. Their behavior is described by equation (3.4); the key element is the dependence of their required interest rate on the probability of second-period default, which in turn depends both on the level of lending and the interest rate. The resulting supply schedule is shown as $\Pi = 0$ in figure 3-1. It must always be upward-sloping near $L = 0$, but may, as it is drawn, bend backwards at higher rates. The interpretation of backward bending is that an increase in the interest rate raises the probability of default so much that it lowers the expected return.

We can now solve for equilibrium lending and the interest rate. The country will first find the best combination of r and L available to it given the supply schedule $\Pi = 0$. This is indicated by point E in figure 3-1. However, there is still the question of whether the country does better by servicing its debt than defaulting. On the one hand, if the reservation utility U^{min} corresponds to a curve like I^aI^a, the country will choose point E. If, on the other hand, an immediate default yields an expected utility corresponding to a curve like I^cI^c, the country will choose an immediate default.

When will this happen? A necessary (but certainly not sufficient) condition for default is that at point E we have $D_1 > L$, debt service exceeding new lending. In other words, the country must be forced to run a trade surplus—or, equivalently, to run a current account deficit less than its interest payments. The reason for this is apparent from figure 3-2 and equation (3.1): if $L > D_1$, the country can run a trade deficit in the first period and, at worst, will default in the second. Since immediate default would involve balanced trade in the first period and two periods' worth of sanctions, it is clearly inferior.

What this says is that there is a "liquidity" element to a first-period default. The decision to default depends crucially on the existence of an inherited stock of debt, which gives rise to debt service in excess of the supply of new lending. This immediately suggests that it may be in the interest of existing creditors—the owners of the inherited debt—to postpone the servicing of that debt to avert immediate default. Our next task is to show that this is in fact the case and to use the model to shed some light on the problems that are likely to arise.

Rescheduling and Involuntary Lending

The loan supply schedule $\Pi = 0$ was derived on the assumption of competitive behavior on the part of lenders; that is, along $\Pi = 0$, each loan taken in isolation earns an expected rate of return equal to $\bar{r}$. But we have seen that competitive behavior by lenders can lead to a level of lending so low that the debtor is led to default. What we will now show is that there is scope for collusive behavior on the part of creditors to lend more as a defensive measure, so that the value of existing debt is sustained.

Let us suppose that the creditors of a country that would otherwise default either reschedule debt service or make available additional lending out of which the country can pay its debt service. These are equivalent in cash flow terms (though perhaps not, in a deeper sense, in terms of the expectations they create; see the discussion later in the chapter). Thus, we will focus on new lending. If the creditors lend enough to avert a first-period default, they will succeed in collecting their first-period debt service and will have at least some chance of getting their second-period debt service. The gain will therefore be

$$D_1(1 + \bar{r}) + (1 - P)D_2$$

against which must be set any expected losses on the additional lending.

It is therefore in the interest of the creditors to lend, even at an expected loss, if the lending averts default and the expected loss does not exceed this gain. In other words, a perfectly collusive set of creditors would offer lending as long as $\Pi \geqslant \Pi_{min}$, where

$$\Pi_{min} = -D_1(1 + \bar{r}) - (1 - P)D_2. \tag{3.16}$$

Will collusive creditors be willing to lend enough to forestall a first-period default? The answer is that it will always be in the interest of creditors to lend enough to avert default. To see this, recall that if $L = D_1$, the country will never default; while from (3.4), the expected profit on new loans equal to first-period debt service D_1 is

$$D_1[(1 + r)(1 - P) - (1 + \bar{r}] > \Pi_{min}.$$

The intuition behind this result is again simple. As long as new lending does not exceed debt service, creditors cannot be worse off than they would be if the country were to default. Any prospect of repayment will make them better off.

Figure 3-3 summarizes the implications of this discussion. A debt crisis arises when the minimal utility that a debtor will accept, U^{min}, cannot be achieved with any point on the competitive loan supply schedule $\Pi = 0$. What we have seen, however, is that collusive creditors will be willing to offer low enough interest rates and high enough lending to avert default—that is, the schedule $\Pi = \Pi_{min}$ lies at least partly outside $U = U^{min}$. We know, therefore, that there is some set of arrangements between the creditors and debtor which all prefer to default. This set is indicated by the contract curve AB in figure 3-3. Point A is a "minimal" rescheduling: it gives the debtor just enough not to provoke default. Point B is a "maximal" rescheduling, which is just short of making creditors unwilling to remain in.

Note that for any point in AB the risk of default is enough to make any loan unprofitable when viewed in isolation:

$$(1 + r)(1 - P) < 1 + \bar{r}.$$

Figure 3-3. Rescheduling and the Bargaining Problem

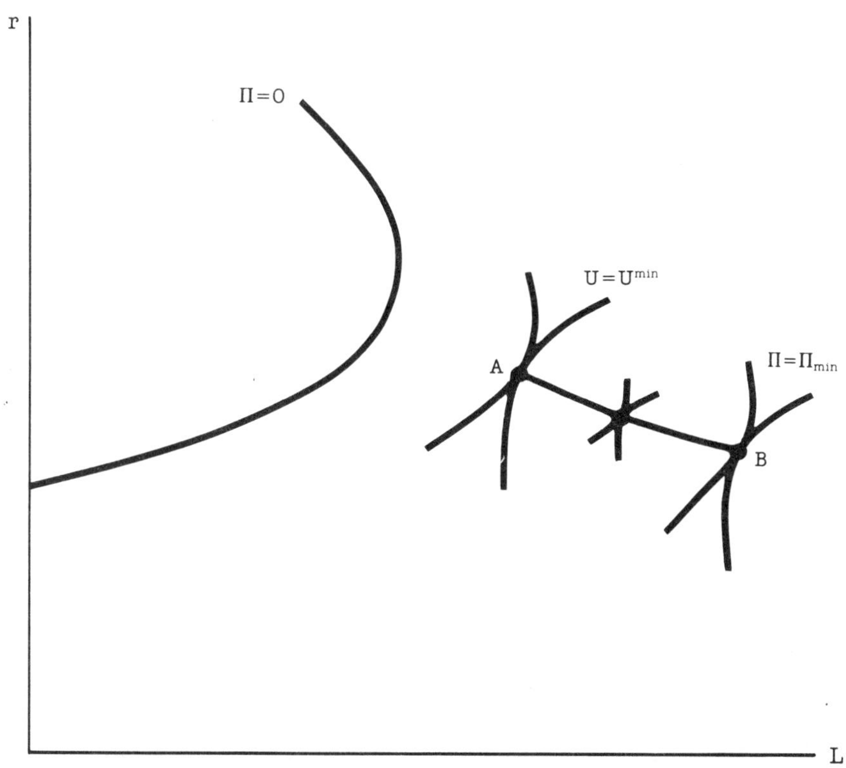

Thus, if creditors are to avert default, they cannot rely on voluntary lending by parties with no stake in whether or not the country pays its existing debt. Lending to reach the desired level must be involuntary or "defensive" in character, carried out either by existing creditors or by non-profit-maximizing third parties.

Note also that the incentive to lend here does not depend on a factual judgment that the problem is one of illiquidity rather than insolvency. Instead, the essential point is that lending has an option value in averting immediate default and preserving the possibility of future repayment.

Will Involuntary Lending Work?

The discussion so far suggests a strong incentive for debtor and creditors to work out a program of temporary financial relief—rescheduling of debt service or involuntary lending—which prevents a loss of lender confidence from provoking an immediate default. Unfortunately, there is no guarantee that such a program will in fact be worked out. Left to themselves, creditors and debtors could fail to reach agreement. It is precisely this possibility which provides the case for an official role in debt negotiation.

The first reason a program of temporary involuntary lending might fail is that it involves a conflict of interest between debtor and creditors. This is made clear in figure 3-3 by the distinction between the minimal rescheduling A and the maximal rescheduling B. In an effort to force an outcome more favorable to itself, each side may attempt to commit itself to a higher minimum. Thus a debtor country's government could try to make some favorable outcome a political commitment, so that a failure to achieve this carries a heavy domestic cost.

In an analogous fashion, major creditors might stake their credibility with smaller banks on holding new lending within some limit. The problem is that, as both sides attempt to establish strong bargaining positions, they may end up with mutually inconsistent minimum demands, which might prevent an agreement that would have been mutually beneficial.

A second problem arises if creditors are not perfectly collusive. There is obviously an incentive in the process of involuntary lending for individual creditors to act as free riders, relying on others to lend enough to avert default. If too many creditors do this, those who do not free ride may not find it worth their while to take up the slack. One way to represent this in our formal analysis is to imagine that there is a collusive "core" group of creditors—perhaps the money center banks—who own a share λ of the initial claims on the country, and that only these creditors will actually lend. The collusive core will find it worthwhile to maintain lending if $\Pi > \lambda \, \Pi_{min}$. But if λ is small, there is no guarantee that the schedule $\Pi = \lambda\Pi_{min}$ includes points that the debtor prefers to immediate default.

This concept of a collusive core and competitive fringe suggests an important further point—that the seriousness of the free-rider problem depends in part on the maturity structure of the inherited debt. The incentive for a country to default immediately rests on a comparison of current debt service with new lending. The incentive for cooperating creditors to lend, however, depends on a comparison of the expected losses on new lending with the whole value of the existing debt. Thus, for a given total indebtedness, the risk of immediate default will depend a good deal on how short the debt is. The greater the extent to which potential free riders are locked in, the less is the burden on others to lend to avert default. Although we will not in this chapter address how the level of "inherited" debt is determined, this analysis does suggest an externality in the choice of maturities ex ante. Individual lenders, who might have the opportunity to free ride in a crisis, have an incentive to lend at short term, giving themselves a better chance to get out if a crisis takes place. Since short-term lending increases the chance that the country and its creditors will not be able to reach agreement on rescheduling, however, lending at short term actually leaves creditors collectively worse off.

Summary

This section has presented a simple, stylized model of international debt in a context where a loss of confidence by lenders can provoke debt repudiation by a borrower. Although the model is far from realistic, it will serve as a useful guide for our analysis of alternative debt strategies. The most important implications of the model are the following:

- A debt crisis represents something qualitatively different from normal borrowing and lending. A crisis occurs when the volume and terms of loans that would be supplied by competitive lenders are insufficient to induce a country not to default. The country cannot attract funds simply by offering a high interest rate, since potential lenders perceive that the high interest rate itself creates an increased incentive for future default.
- Although lending to a country suffering a debt crisis is not profitable for a new lender, it is nonetheless in the collective interest of a country's existing creditors to relend a country enough of its debt service to avert immediate default. Thus, defensive lending represents a rational response.
- Although it is in the interest of creditors to lend, there is no guarantee that creditors and debtors will in fact reach an arrangement that avoids default. The attempts of creditors and debtors to commit themselves to desired outcomes for bargaining purposes can lead to an impasse. Furthermore, creditors may attempt to act as free riders and thus fail to act in their own collective interest. The free-rider problem will be more serious, the shorter is the maturity of the existing debt.

Our next step is to use these implications to analyze the basic policy question: what is the appropriate strategy of creditor-country governments and international organizations for dealing with debt crises?

ALTERNATIVE STRATEGIES FOR THE DEBT PROBLEM

Until the summer of 1982, the official position of the U.S. government was that the United States and other interested parties, such as the IMF and the World Bank, should minimize their involvement in international capital movements. Under pressure of events, this position was abandoned, but there is still an influential body of opinion that sees any sort of official debt strategy as counterproductive (see, for example, Vaubel 1983). On the other side, and probably even more influential, are calls for deeper official involvement, typically the creation of some kind of new international organization to take over developing-country debt.

This section discusses four general strategies for dealing with the debt problem. There is no clear dividing line between the strategies. Instead, they are meant to be points on a continuum, from no official involvement to complete "socialization" of the debt. The four strategies are:

- Laissez-faire. Governments could simply wash their hands of the debt problem, leaving it as an affair to be settled between countries and their creditors.
- The current strategy. The current strategy is a mix of forced lending by creditors, supplementary lending from official sources, and an effort by the IMF to use conditionality to solve the problem of bargaining between creditors and debtors.
- Longer-term restructuring. The current strategy, which requires repeated negotiations to get successive increments of involuntary lending, would be replaced by one big negotiation for each country. This negotiation would establish a schedule of payments that would (if all went well) avert default and also avoid the need to return to the bargaining table.
- Official buyout. In this strategy envisaged by such proposals as Kenen (1983) and Rohatyn (1983), creditors would exchange their claims on countries—at a discount—

for claims on a new official institution. This institution, as the new creditor, could then carry out a restructuring similar to that envisaged in the preceding case.

Laissez-faire

The case for not having a debt strategy—for letting creditors and debtors work it out (or not, as the case may be) on their own—rests on two arguments. The first is a distributional argument: the benefits of official intervention go to irresponsible banks and their irresponsible clients. Second, by bailing these groups out, the official intervenor helps create the expectation that this will happen again, thereby encouraging irresponsible behavior in the future.

These objections to any activist policy carry some weight. They are convincing, however, only if one believes either that creditors and debtors will reach an accommodation without an official role or that there is no accommodation to be made, that is, that the debt should simply be written off. What the above model suggests, however, is that there is room for a mutually beneficial bargain between debtor and creditors and that this bargain may fail to be struck without outside help. The argument for not having a debt strategy is that this is a private matter and is best left to the private sector. The main conclusion of our theoretical exercise, however, is that new lending to problem debtors has the characteristics of a public good, and there is, therefore, a valid reason for public involvement.

The Current Strategy

The current debt strategy involves creditor country governments and the IMF in two central ways. First, official bodies have attempted to resolve the problems that might otherwise have caused creditors and debtors to fail to reach an accommodation. The danger that the players may establish incompatible bargaining commitments is partly defused by having the IMF, through its imposition of conditionality, serve as mediator. Moreover, the free-rider problem is reduced as the Federal Reserve and other monetary authorities exert pressure on banks to go along with rescheduling and new loans.

Second, official lending from the IMF and a variety of other sources, together with rescheduling of debt service on official claims, is a major part of the financial packages (see the breakdown in figure 3-4). This involvement helps both to give the IMF a more credible role as mediator and to mitigate further the free-rider problem.

Some critics of the debt strategy—most notably the *Wall Street Journal*—view this whole process as one of throwing good money after bad. Our theoretical analysis makes a point that should in any case be obvious—lending to a problem debtor to avoid immediate default is always worthwhile as long as the new lending is less than the debt service. If this is true, creditors are getting something from their client, more than they would get in the event of a default. The resource transfer is running from debtor to creditor, and the fact that nominal exposure of the creditors is growing is not relevant. For the three major Latin American debtors, the resource transfer has swung dramatically toward the creditors: in 1983, the net inflow of capital covered less than 40 percent of interest payments. Thus, for creditors as a group, the debt strategy has been a pretty good bargain even in the short run, while preserving the possibility of a return to normal servicing of the debt in the longer run.

The legitimately controversial question concerns the role of official lending. It has been charged that IMF and other official loans in effect represent foreign aid to the debtors and a "bailout" for the banks. The replies to this have been, first, that these are interest-bearing loans, not aid; second, that, since banks remain the main providers of finance, this action is not a "bailout," but a "bailin," in which official lending induces private lenders to take on more, rather than less, of the burden.

Figure 3-4. Sources and Uses of Foreign Exchange: Three Major Latin American Debtors

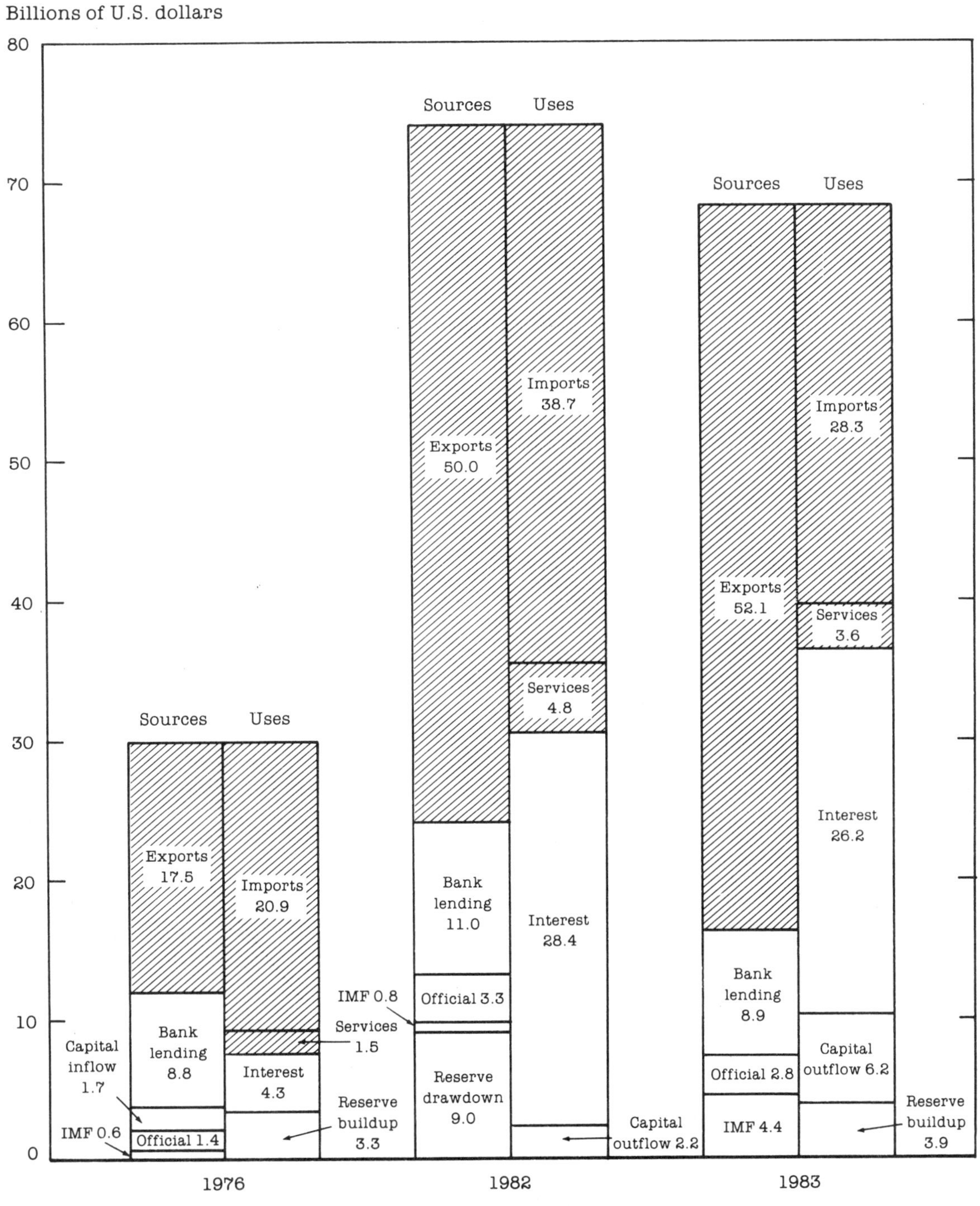

Source: Council of Economic Advisers (1984), chart 2-6.

In the light of our model, this official defense of the role of IMF and other lending appears to be quite untrue. Official lending to problem debtors does contain an element of foreign aid, and it does provide a bailout for banks. It is understandable that, for political purposes, this cannot be stated quite so bluntly, but the question is not whether it is happening but whether it is worth doing.

In what sense is there a foreign aid component to offical lending to problem debtors? As I have argued, the essential feature of a debt crisis is that the probability of default is high enough to make lending viewed in isolation unprofitable. This is what defines a crisis in the first place. Therefore, even if official lending to problem debtors receives market interest, it is nonetheless lending with an expected return below the cost of funds and represents, in effect, a subsidy to the borrower. The subsidy component is completely analogous to the subsidy component in domestic loan guarantees, something that has long been recognized.

It is also misleading to argue that, because IMF lending is associated with lending by banks, it represents a bailin, not a bailout. As we have seen, it is in the collective interest of creditors to lend enough to avert default. Official lending removes some of this burden. It is not useful to point out that new lending by creditors is positive, because zero lending is not the right reference point. The right comparison is with what banks would have had to lend in the absence of the official loans. If the situation is viewed in this light, it is clear that official lending does indeed reduce the burden on creditors. Thus, the charge of bailout in fact has some justification.

The right question, however, is not whether the official lending is costly, or whether it helps banks, but whether it is worth doing. Here, the probable answer is yes. Although this is impossible to prove, it seems hard to believe that creditors and major debtors could have reached agreements that avoided default without substantial official participation in the financial packages. The official lending has served two main purposes. First, the effectiveness of the IMF as a mediator depends in part on the credibility that comes from being a major source of funds. Second, official financing has helped to make up for the free-rider problem by preventing the burden on core creditors from becoming so large as to make them unwilling to participate.

For both of these reasons, therefore, official lending has probably been crucial to the avoidance of default. This represents a real social gain, not simply a transfer to banks and debtor countries—although such a transfer does exist.

Aside from distributional issues, what are the flaws in the current strategy? The most serious flaw appears to be the short horizon covered by negotiations. For the most part, countries have been arranging financial packages that take them only through a year or so. At that point, it is necessary to gather the creditors again and put together another round of involuntary lending. The problem is that at each round there is a risk that agreement will not be reached. The current strategy can thus be faulted for settling too little at each negotiation.

Debt Restructuring

The natural response to the problem of excessively frequent renegotiations of financing would be for debtors and creditors to enter into a longer-term financial arrangement. One might ask why government intervention is necessary to achieve this, since it is in the mutual interest of debtors and creditors. Here, the observation in our theoretical model—that there is an externality in the choice of lending maturity—becomes relevant. It is in the collective interest of creditors to establish a rescheduling of debt service that does not ensure a new crisis a year or eighteen months later. But it is also in the interest of each individual lender to keep the country on a short leash. The current debt strategy recognizes the conflict between the individual and collective interests of creditors with regard to the current flow of lending. Yet it has not tackled the conceptually similar problem of an agreement to lengthen the time between renegotiations.

An extension of the current debt strategy, therefore, would be to establish longer-term financial arrangements that attempt to reschedule the burden of debt service over a long enough period so that the need for additional rounds of rescheduling would be reduced or eliminated.

The major disadvantage of this kind of plan would be a loss of flexibility. The negotiations involved in putting together a financing package for, say, four years would be more difficult than those involved in shorter-term packages. If it then turned out to be desirable to revise the package—an issue discussed in the next section—such a revision might be problematic. In effect, the IMF and the Federal Reserve might turn out to have used up their mediating capital. At the same time, it seems at least equally problematic to expect that the IMF and other concerned agencies will continue achieving the kinds of compromises on which we have so far relied.

In sum, there is a good case to be made for engaging in longer-term debt restructurings than those we have seen so far. (This is my own preferred debt strategy.) Some of the principles that should guide debt restructurings are developed in the next section. We still need to consider one more alternative, however: having a new international institution buy out the existing creditors.

Debt Buyout

The debt reform proposals of Kenen (1983) and Rohatyn (1983) envisage a trading of assets between the creditors of developing countries and an official institution, which we will refer to as the "debt institution" (DI). Creditors receive claims on the DI (which is a global version of New York's Municipal Assistance Commission, or "Big MAC"). The DI in return acquires their claims on developing nations. The advantages gained by this procedure are not spelled out too explicitly in the proposals, but our analysis suggests that a single creditor would be free of the problems of collective action that can prevent creditors from acting in their joint self-interest.

Creating a DI would present important technical problems: it would be difficult to define which countries and which debt would be eligible. Also, there would be a very difficult transition period between the time when such a plan was announced and its implementation.

A more basic objection to any debt buyout, however, has been stated by Cline (1983)—a debt buyout would remove the incentive for creditors to continue lending. This poses several problems. Since debtor nations are currently borrowing to cover part of their interest, the DI would either have to offer highly concessional rates or engage in lending itself. This, in turn, means that the buyout would have to be at a heavy discount, substantial government aid would have to be provided, or some kind of arrangement would have to be made to give the DI the ability to lend. The problem is not insurmountable. Official sources could provide the lending or guarantee borrowing by the debt institution. There is an alternative that would be more politically feasible: a commitment of creditors to involuntary lending could be made a condition for debt buyout. One wonders how attractive such a conditional buyout would be to the creditors, however.

Even if an arrangement is made that permits the debt institution to relend part of its interest receipts, there remains a loss of flexibility. Should it become desirable to lend more, the original creditors would be off the hook and have no incentive to participate.

It should also be noted that, while a DI would have the advantage of eliminating the problems of collective action, this very advantage could create problems in its bargaining position. In the discussion of the costs of default, I suggested one factor that might make credible the threat of sanctions against a defaulting nation. This is the possibility that uncoordinated actions by creditors will close down much of a country's trade, even when these actions are not in the creditors' collective interest. Once developing-country debt has been consolidated in the hands of a DI, this threat disappears. Thus, the DI will in fact have a weaker bargaining position than unconsolidated creditors, so that forming a DI will tend to lead to an outcome further from A and closer to B (see figure 3-3). This may be a desirable outcome in a global sense, but someone has to pay for it. One scenario would be that, when swapping assets with the DI, creditors would have to take a larger discount than their own evaluation of the appropriate discount in the absence of a DI. The other would have official sources making up the difference.

Consolidating developing-nation debt in a DI would thus have one advantage—an end to the free-rider issue—and two serious disadvantages—the removal of the incentive for continued bank lending and the weakening of the collective creditor bargaining position. Because of these disadvantages, claims on debtor countries would probably be worth less in expected value when consolidated in a DI than in their present form. This obstacle to a debt buyout can be overcome only by an injection of official money.

Summary

In this section I have considered four possible strategies for dealing with the international debt problem. The first, a hands-off strategy, was rejected on the grounds that debt crises create a strong incentive for official involvement, because continued lending to problem debtors takes on the character of a public good. This provides a justification for an official role at least as large as in the current debt strategy—even though, contrary to official positions, the current strategy does contain an element of foreign aid and is to some extent a bailout of the banks.

Is there scope for even greater official involvement? The answer suggested is that there is justification for an official role in promoting a longer-term restructuring of debt than has been done so far. The further step of consolidating debt under an official intermediary institution, however, appears to be counterproductive.

GUIDELINES FOR DEBT RESTRUCTURING

In the last section, it was suggested that the debt of developing countries should be restructured in a way that reduces the need for frequent negotiations to assure delivery of the next round of financing. The concluding section of the chapter will expand on this suggestion by outlining some further considerations for a discussion of debt restructuring. These considerations do not constitute an explicit proposal. Instead, they are meant to serve as guidelines for devising detailed schemes.

I begin by examining the question of the purpose of a debt restructuring—is it meant to be a final settlement or is it aimed at lasting only until there is an eventual resumption of voluntary lending? Following that is an analysis of the two key features of a debt resumption, the maturity structure and the interest rate.

The Purpose of Debt Restructuring: Ramp or Bridge?

The appropriate characteristics of debt restructuring depend a great deal on the role restructuring is expected to play. Calls for a global debt institution and an associated restructuring generally seem to come on the assumption that normal access of debtors to capital markets will not resume for the foreseeable future. The implication is that the debtors will have to service their debt out of trade surpluses indefinitely. If that is the case, the debt service is a ramp down to an eventual payoff of debt, and the slope of the ramp must not be too steep: debtors cannot be expected to run too large a surplus, or they will opt out by defaulting.

Currently, major debtors are running large trade surpluses—larger, one can presume, than they would be willing to run on an indefinite basis—yet are still forced to borrow to cover part of their interest. A debt restructuring that is viewed as a once-and-for-all financing plan would therefore have not only to stretch maturities but also substantially reduce the interest rate. In other words, the present value of debt service would have to be written down sharply. A rough order of magnitude can be found in the Economic Report of the President (Council of Economic Advisers 1984). It states that, in 1983, the three major Latin American debtors ran a current account deficit of $9.1 billion, with interest payments of $26.2 billion. Let us suppose that the debt were to be converted into consols, with no repayment of principal at all, and that the Latin debtors could be relied on to continue running the trade surplus of 1983 forever. It would still be necessary, in order to eliminate the current account deficit, to reduce the interest rate by more than a third, which implies an equiproportional capital loss. Leaving some room for principal payment and providing some relief to debtors would require even sharper reductions in the interest rate.

An alternative view, however, is that debt restructuring is not a way of arranging an ultimate repayment of debt but a bridge to a future when voluntary lending resumes. In this case, there is no reason the restructuring need imply an actual reduction in indebtedness. Instead, it could well involve growing debt, as long as the growth is sufficiently slower than the expected growth in measures of the country's debt-servicing capacity, such as exports. A large reduction in the present value of the debt might not be necessary.

As this chapter has repeatedly stressed, the problem of the solvency of major debtors is not a simple factual issue. The real question is how to behave in the face of uncertainty. On one side, we could plan on the working assumption of a favorable outcome and take the risk of not being able to handle the consequences satisfactorily if the assumption is not borne out. On the other side, we could write down the debt in advance to anticipate a possible unfavorable outcome; here the risk is that the write-down could turn out to have been unnecessary.

The choice between these approaches is therefore not a simple matter of facts, but of weighing probabilities and costs. This chapter will not attempt a new analysis of the question. It will simply note that both back-of-the-envelope calculations (Council of Economic Advisers for 1984, chap. 2) and more elaborate simulation exercises (Cline 1983, World Financial Markets 1983) indicate that moderately optimistic assumptions about OECD recovery, interest rates, and so on point to a gradual improvement of key debt indicators. Thus, in what follows, debt restructuring will be viewed as a bridge to a future period of normalcy rather than a way to ramp down countries' debt.

Elements of Restructuring: Maturity

The traditional approach to relieving the liquidity problems of debtors is a rescheduling of principal payments. A restructuring of debt to carry the debtors through the next several years would involve the same objective, a stretching-out of payments. However, as we have just seen, unless there is a large write-down of the debt, a rescheduling of principal will not be enough. Even converting the debt into consols would not be sufficient. What is needed is a way to reschedule some interest as well as principal or, what is equivalent, to allow for growth in the debt.

Rescheduling of interest is not a practice that will be welcomed by bankers or their regulators. Committing oneself to increase exposure in a country over time does not sound like sound banking practice. However, the reality is that the banks are already committed to do this. Once a country is in a debt crisis, its lenders are collectively trapped, with no choice except somehow to reduce the burden of debt service. In this situation, the distinction between interest and principal is of no more than symbolic significance. The important distinction is between forced lending that is less than debt service (and that is therefore still associated with a net resource transfer out of a country) and lending that exceeds debt service. In the current context, however, it is clear that any debt restructuring will fall well short of reversing the direction of resource transfer.

If explicit rescheduling of interest is considered undesirable, there are alternative ways to achieve the same end. Three possibilities are:

- Lending commitments. Creditors could simply commit themselves in advance to lend debtor countries a certain fraction of their debt service for an extended period, such as four or five years. In its implications for actual cash flow, this is identical to a rescheduling of interest, but it might be less offensive to standard practice.
- Indexed loans. Economists and even bankers are by now familiar with the proposition that, in an inflationary environment, the usual distinction between principal and interest is misleading. Thus, there might be acceptance for a conversion of developing-country debts into loans whose interest and principal components are both indexed to grow with some objective measure of world prices, such as the U.S. wholesale price index. In fact, even the distinction between real interest and real repayment of principal is not very useful in a situation where there is no voluntary lending. Indexing may, however, afford a way to make growing nominal exposure seem less unsound.
- Exchange participation. One of the proponents of debt restructuring, Bailey (1983), has proposed converting at least some of the debt of developing nations into proportional claims on these countries' foreign exchange earnings. Since these earnings can be expected to grow in real terms and, therefore, faster than the inflation rate, creditors should be willing to swap conventional claims for the proposed Exchange Participation Notes at a price that would allow a considerable reduction in debt service.

An informal calculation may make the point. Suppose that creditors believe that debtor-country nominal exports will grow steadily at 7 percent a year and that the current rate of interest is 12 percent. If an Exchange Participation Note represents a credible promise, then creditors should be willing to exchange their claims for notes providing current payments equal to only 5 percent of the value of the debt. This would be a sufficient reduction in debt service to eliminate the need for additional involuntary lending.

The problem with this scheme is that those who have discussed it do not find credible the promise that a country will honor a mortgage on its export earnings (see Cline 1983; Guttentag and Herring 1983). It is not entirely clear why this should be so—why is a promise to pay a fixed sum necessarily more credible than a promise to pay 15 percent of one's income? So far, however, the sentiment does seem to be that a financial arrangement this unorthodox would not be enforceable.

The main point is that de facto creditors are rescheduling interest and will continue to do so for some time to come. We should not be afraid of explicit arrangements formalizing the process.

The Level of Interest Rates

The other major variable in debt restructuring is the level of interest rates charged to the debtors. There is an analogue here to the problem of principal versus interest, something that is important in normal situations but loses its usual significance when a debtor is in a crisis situation. For interest rates, the distinction that becomes irrelevant in a crisis is the one between lending at market rates and lending at concessional terms.

The point has already been made that, when a debt crisis has occurred and voluntary lending has ceased, the involuntary lending then taking place is, in effect, already at concessional terms from the lenders' point of view. In other words, the risk of default outweighs any interest premium being charged. If this were not the case, voluntary lending would not have ceased. This means that the appropriate interest rate on involuntary lending may easily be either more than the market rate, reflecting a high probability of default, or less, reflecting the rational desire of creditors to reduce that probability. (See again figure 3-3. On the one hand, it is perfectly possible for even the "minimal" rescheduling at A to involve an interest rate below the riskless rate $\bar{r}$. On the other hand, even the "maximal" rescheduling at B could involve an interest rate above $\bar{r}$.)

The implication is that there is nothing sacred about charging market rates on debt restructuring. Because of the severity of the adjustment burden on debtors, charging rates somewhat below the market is probably in creditors' self-interest. It would not, in fact, be any less reasonable a way to defend their existing claims than their current policy of defensive lending.

In addition to the question of the level of interest rates, there is a question of the adjustment of rates to market conditions. Most of the Latin American debt is on a floating rate, indexed to the London interbank offered rate (LIBOR). During normal times, this indexation protects lenders from being caught between a rising cost of funds and a fixed rate on loans. In the current situation, however, this de jure indexation is not operative de facto. If LIBOR were to rise to 20 percent, the interest paid on Latin American debt would not actually rise accordingly. Countries would demand—and their creditors would have to grant—a reduction in rates. Further, negotiating this reduction in rates would reopen the issues of burden sharing and conditionality and run the risk of a breakdown of agreement. Therefore, lending at a floating rate, like lending at a short maturity, is a strategy that appears to reduce risk for an individual bank while actually increasing it in the aggregate.

What makes this worse is that there is an effective cap on floating-rate loans to problem debtors but no effective floor. In other words, if LIBOR were to fall to 5 percent, the rate on indexed loans would fall correspondingly. Faced with this one-way stickiness of rates, creditors are in the opposite position from that of banks lending to home buyers: they should prefer fixed-rate loans to flexible-rate, even at lower rates. The problem is that the advantages would come from an aggregate shift to fixed-rate loans; no individual lender in isolation has an incentive to do so.

Summary

The central message of this section is that we should recognize that problem debtors and their creditors are not in a normal market situation. In the current regime of involuntary lending, many traditional views about what is sound banking are no longer valid. Lending at short maturity increases risk rather than reduces it. Rescheduling of interest as well as principal is in effect happening, and it may be good banking practice to make this explicit. Market interest rates are not of much use as norms, and lending at concessional terms may be in creditors' self-interest. An attempt by creditors to protect themselves against interest rate uncertainty actually increases their risks.

CONCLUSIONS

This chapter began with two purposes. The first was to set out a framework for thinking about the international debt problem. The second was to assess alternative strategies for coping with this problem.

What has been suggested here is that the right way to think about the debt problem is in terms of a model in which the eventual solvency of debtors is uncertain. The probability of default is high enough to preclude voluntary lending, but it is still in the interest of creditors to lend enough to avert immediate default. It was shown (to some extent, with a simple model and, further, in a less formal discussion) that, once one has entered a regime of defensive or involuntary lending, there are a variety of conflicts between the individual and collective interests of creditors. These conflicts create a justification for official intervention to influence not only the volume of lending but also interest rates and maturity structure. In addition, the IMF and possibly other agencies have a useful role to play as mediators between debtors and creditors.

The implication for debt strategy is that active official intervention in the restructuring of debt is needed both as a way of overcoming creditors' problems of collective action and as a way of defusing the potential for an impasse in the bargaining between debtors and creditors. Official intervention should probably do even more than it has so far, by encouraging longer-term restructuring of debt as a way of reducing the frequency with which new financing must be negotiated. However, the widely circulated proposals for the consolidation of developing-country debt into a new official institution are not well conceived and would prove counterproductive.

These conclusions are based on abstract arguments rather than experience. But experience with debt crises like the present ones is fortunately not available, and many lessons learned in more normal times may have to be unlearned if we are to cope with the difficult world the debt crisis has created.

REFERENCES

Bailey, Norman. 1983. "A safety net for foreign lending." Business Week (January 10):17.

Cline, William. 1983. International debt and the stability of the world economy. Washington, D.C.: Institute for International Economics.

Council of Economic Advisers. 1984. Economic report of the President. Washington, D.C.: Government Printing Office.

Eaton, Jonathan, and Mark Gersovitz. 1981. "Debt with potential repudiation: Theoretical and empirical analysis." Review of Economic Studies 48 (no. 152):289–309.

Guttentag, Jack M., and Richard J. Herring. 1983. "The current crisis in international banking." Brookings Discussion Papers in International Economics, no. 8. Washington, D.C.: Brookings Institution.

Kenen, Peter B. 1983. "A bailout plan for the banks." New York Times (March 6):F3.

Rohatyn, Felix. 1983. "A plan for stretching out global debt." Business Week (February 28):15–16.

Sachs, Jeffrey. 1983. "Theoretical issues in international borrowing." NBER Working Paper no. 1189. Cambridge, Mass.: National Bureau of Economic Research. August.

Vaubel, Roland. 1983. "The moral hazard of IMF lending." World Economy 6, no. 3 (September):291–305.

World Financial Markets. 1983. August.

4

The Developing-Country Debt Problem

Mario Henrique Simonsen

In 1974 commercial banks were highly praised for solving the financial puzzle of the 1970s, namely, how to recycle the surpluses of the Organization of Petroleum Exporting Countries (OPEC) to the oil-importing countries. This prompt response, in contrast to the sluggish increase in international official lending, prevented a major world crisis in which the main victims would have been middle-income countries with restricted access to OPEC capital. The action of commercial banks also started a period in which unprecedented current account deficits were financed by competitive credit markets at floating interest rates. Project loans, conveying external savings to investment programs in developing countries, were used as the basic vehicle for recycling. Since money is fungible and since lenders were not prepared to be repaid in borrowers' local currencies, however, the central part of the story was competitive balance of payments finance, not project finance. Loan maturities were never matched to external account projections of debtor countries, since commercial banks believed that short-term loans were safer than long-term ones, an obvious fallacy of composition as far as balance of payments finance is concerned. Hence, the system was based on periodic debt rollover.

Banks surely knew that sovereign risks were superimposed on the commercial ones, and never overlooked the possibility that a few countries might face balance of payments troubles because of improper economic management. But since debtor countries followed independent economic policies, the chances of a global debt crisis were minimized on the basis of the law of large numbers. The implicit assumption was that the covariance of returns across countries was low and hence would not distort the large-numbers behavior and suddenly transform a large set of good debts into bad ones. That adverse covariance problems could occur was known from the experience of the 1930s, when a debt crisis emerged as a result of a dramatic decline in world trade and economic activity. The possibility that this phenomenon would show up again in the early 1980s was discounted by the belief that economic theory had progressed enough to exorcize the Kondratiev cycles.

In fact, competitive recycling would hardly break down as long as the rate of growth of exports of debtor countries exceeded international interest rates. In this case, indeed, indicators of a reduced debt/export ratio and improved credit standing could be achieved even with a more than complete debt service rollover. Historical evidence after the Second World War suggested that rates of growth of international trade tended to exceed interest rates. Non-oil-exporting developing countries, in particular, expanded the dollar value of their exports at average annual rates of 10.3 percent between 1963 and 1973 and 21.1 percent between 1973 and 1980, more than fulfilling the rollover test. Hence, until 1980 few doubts were cast on the viability of competitive recycling.

The unorthodox blend of tight monetary and loose fiscal policy in the United States since 1981 was unanticipated. In a world of floating exchange rates and interest rates this policy turn pushed the international debt problem into the covariance trap. A crisis emerged as a result of the abrupt escalation of the debt/export ratios and a series of events including the loan defaults of Poland, the Falklands war, and, as a coup de grace, the Mexican moratorium in late 1982. The latter spilled over to a general breakdown of confidence in developing-country debts and led to a hurried retreat of commercial banks from new lending to such nations. Since competitive recycling was based on rollover, debtor countries soon became illiquid and had to apply for widespread rescheduling arrangements.

A lesson from this crisis is that balance of payments finance involves too many externalities to be efficiently carried on by competitive credit markets. The externalities originate in the peculiar nature of collateral in the context of sovereign loans. Some tangible collateral does exist. The external assets of debtor countries may be seized in case of default, but in the present world they stand as nothing but a symbolic proportion of outstanding external debts. Creditors have a much stronger trump card, the price that each country is prepared to pay to maintain access to foreign credit markets by transferring abroad a certain proportion of its export revenues. This is not only an intangible, but also a reflexive collateral, in the sense that its value depends on the behavior of lenders. If lenders decide to cut the access of a debtor nation to the international financial markets, that nation loses most incentives to honor its external obligations. What creditors can get repaid from an illiquid debtor is therefore contingent on whether conflicts are decided by cooperation or by confrontation. This provides, incidentally, a strong argument against competitive pricing of developing-country debts in secondary markets. Pure competition is a noncooperative game that could transform the debt problem into an international financial collapse.

This threatening scenario was actually displayed after the Mexican moratorium. A disruption was prevented by the timely intervention of the International Monetary Fund (IMF) and the major central banks, which tried to persuade commercial banks to act collectively and to cooperate with illiquid developing countries. The emerging rescheduling mechanisms, under the leadership of the IMF, may be characterized as cooperative recycling, combining the Bretton Woods concept of the central lender with the lending capability of commercial banks. The presumption has been that debtor developing countries face a liquidity problem, not a solvency problem, although this idea has been challenged by economists and politicians in both debtor and creditor countries.

The present paper discusses whether developing debtor countries are appropriately viewed as illiquid or insolvent. While the appropriate diagnosis may vary from case to case, some important general principles are presented. Most important in the case of sovereign risk, there is no clear distinction between illiquidity and insolvency. This may look like a disquieting conclusion, but it also conveys a hopeful message: solvency can be insured by international cooperation, appropriate economic policies, and adequate restructuring of the international lending system.

DEBT DYNAMICS

The dynamics of foreign indebtedness can be described by the differential equation:

$$\dot{D} = iD + G \tag{4.1}$$

where D indicates the country's net foreign debt (total external indebtedness—public, private, short and long term—minus foreign reserves), $\dot{D}$ its derivative with respect to time (following the usual convention on dots), and i the average nominal interest rate. G stands for the resource gap (+) or surplus (−), here defined as the noninterest current account external deficit, minus direct investment into the country, plus gross capital exports from the country. This is a debt-related definition: direct investment from abroad reduces the gap (or adds to the surplus) because foreign equity capital is not included in the country's external liabilities. G and D are measured in current dollars, and for the sake of simplicity all the country's foreign debt is taken as dollar denominated. Since the concern here is the debt problem, negative values of D will be excluded from the time span of this analysis. With G and i treated as piecewise continuous functions of time, equation (4.1) is solved by the cumbersome expression:

$$D(t) = \int_{-\infty}^{t} G(\tau)e^{\int_{\tau}^{t} i d\lambda} d\tau,$$

which says that the present net external debt at time t equals the continuously compounded sum of the past resource gaps.

Equation (4.1) is nothing but a balance of payments tautology that splits the net foreign debt increase into two components, the interest payments iD and the nonhereditary part G. Its importance stems from the fact that, except for complicated interest rate renegotiations or write-downs, economic policies in debtor countries can affect the debt paths only through action on the resource gap or surplus. If one takes the interest rate as a constant and treats G as a well-behaved decreasing function of time, which crosses the zero mark at time T_0, as in the upper part of figure 4-1, one is led to the famous three phases of the debt cycle. Phase I is that of positive resource gaps, when debt grows faster than interest rates. In phase II the country scores resource surpluses, but these are not strong enough to offset interest payments. Hence, debt continues to expand although at rates of growth below the interest rate. Finally, in phase III the resource surpluses acquire the necessary momentum to overcome the interest payments, and the nominal debt declines until it is paid off, as in the lower part of figure 4-1.

Table 4-1 shows how the Brazilian foreign debt has expanded between 1971 and 1982. It displays a typical movement from the early stages of phase I, when debt increases are dominated by positive resource gaps, to the later stages of the same phase when debt grows mostly because of interest accumulation. In 1983 Brazil moved to phase II of the cycle. With regard to the analytical assumptions implicit in figure 4-1, empirical evidence indicates that the interest rate cannot be treated as a constant. Nor is the resource gap a steadily declining function of time. When i and G follow more complicated time paths, debt dynamics do not necessarily follow the three phases described above. Doubts may be cast as to whether phase III will ever be reached and come to an end.

An important question is: how long can a developing country remain in phase I of the debt cycle? The answer depends on a key variable of debt dynamics, the difference between the rate of growth of the country's exports and the interest rate on its outstanding debt. When X indicates the dollar value of the country's annual exports of goods and services, $x = \dot{X}/X$ its rate of growth, and $z = D/X$ the debt/export ratio, equation (4.1) can be rewritten so as to emphasize the key variable $(i - x)$:[1]

$$\dot{z} = (i - x)z + g \tag{4.2}$$

where $g = G/X$ stands for the resource gap as a proportion of exports. The above equation yields a well-known stability condition: if the rate of growth of exports exceeds the interest rate, a permanently positive resource gap can be reconciled with a limited debt/export ratio. In fact, if z is to be kept unchanged over time, $\dot{z} = 0$, and equation (4.2) implies a sustainable (steady-state) resource gap equal to:

$$g = (x - i)z, \tag{4.3}$$

which is positive for $x > i$. In this case, resource gaps can be sustained indefinitely without pushing the country into relative overindebtedness.

If the interest rate exceeds the rate of growth of exports, resource gaps cannot be sustained indefinitely, as this implies that the debt/export ratio would grow without limit. In this case, sustained resource gaps are to be considered as evidence that debtor countries are postponing the indispensable adjustment policies.

To sum up, whether sustained positive gaps are acceptable depends on the sign of the $x - i$ difference. The breakdown of competitive recycling can be explained by the sudden and unan-

Figure 4-1. Phases of the Debt Cycle

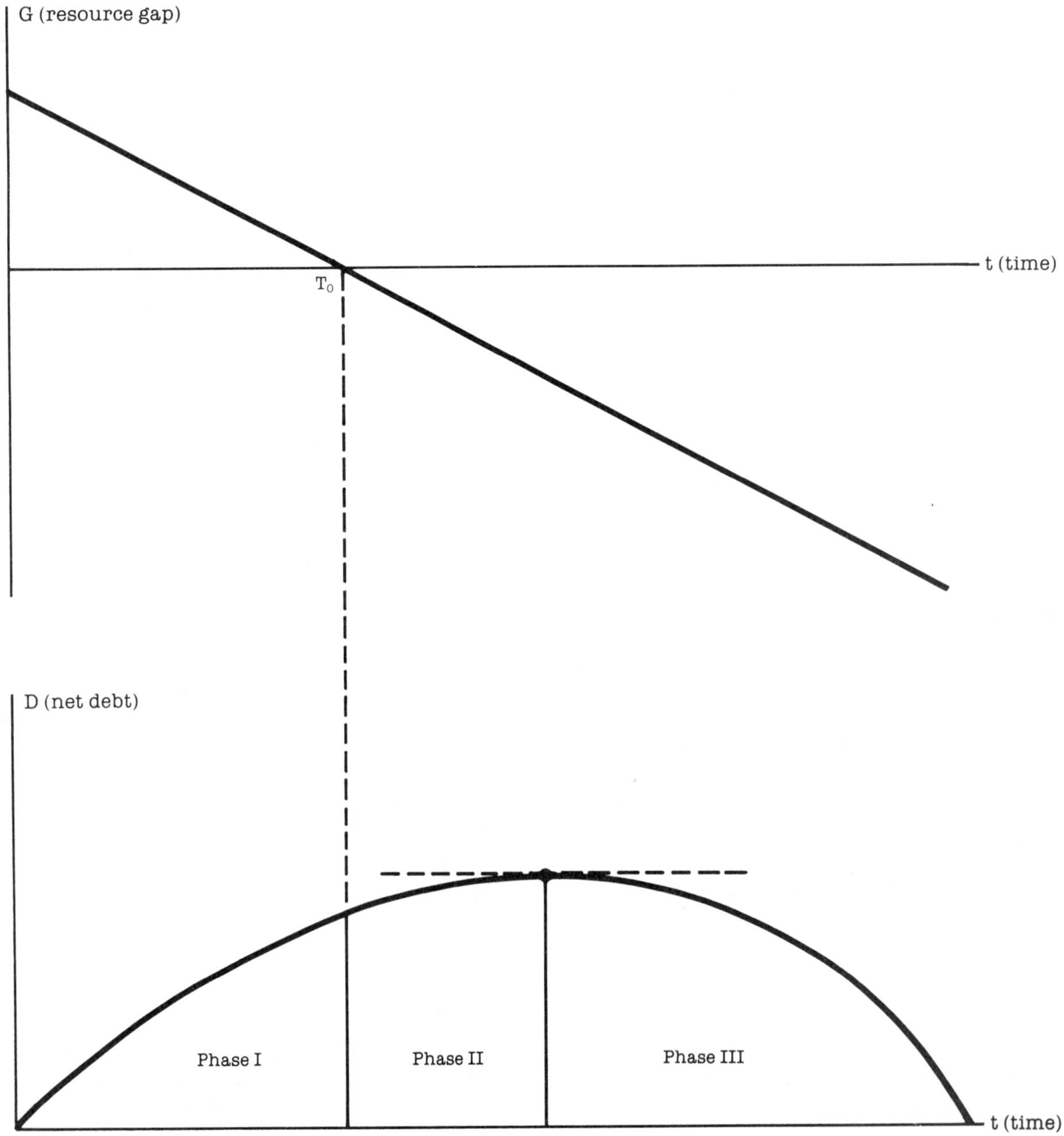

ticipated change of that sign. During the 1970s, when debtor countries were expanding their exports far more rapidly than the interest rates, resource gaps were considered a natural element in the balance of payments of the non-oil-exporting developing countries. In a few cases there was some question as to the size of the gaps, but not as to their sign. With the unanticipated events of the early 1980s—the explosion of international interest rates, world recession, dollar appreciation, and shrinking trade—conventional wisdom concerning resource gaps moved to the opposite pole. In the interim period, debt/export ratios rose substantially, entering in some cases a dangerous zone. A typical example is that of Brazil, where the ratio leaped from 2.6 in 1980 to 3.8 in 1982.

Table 4-1. Brazil's Net Foreign Debt
(millions of U.S. dollars)

Year	Net initial debt D_0	Current account deficit C	Direct investment minus capital exports I	Debt increase $\Delta D = C - I$	Interest payments J	Resource gap $G = \Delta D - J$	End of year net foreign debt $D_1 = D_0 + \Delta D$	Average rate (percent) $i = J/D_0$
1971	4,109	1,307	168	1,139	302	837	5,248	7.4
1972	5,248	1,489	318	1,171	359	812	6,419	6.8
1973	6,419	1,688	940	748	514	234	7,167	8.0
1974	7,167	7,122	887	6,235	652	5,583	13,402	9.1
1975	13,402	6,700	892	5,808	1,498	4,310	19,210	11.2
1976	19,210	6,107	959	5,058	1,810	3,248	24,268	9.4
1977	24,268	4,037	810	3,227	2,103	1,124	27,495	8.7
1978	27,495	6,990	2,047	4,943	2,696	2,247	32,438	9.8
1979	32,438	10,742	2,212	8,530	4,185	4,345	40,968	12.9
1980	40,968	12,807	1,532	11,275	6,311	4,964	52,243	15.4
1981	52,243	11,734	2,326	9,408	9,161	247	61,651	17.5
1982	61,651	16,279	2,542	13,358	11,358	2,379	75,388	18.4

Source: Banco Central do Brasil.

The steep increase in the debt/export ratios and the change of expectations as to the $x - i$ differential transformed what had been accepted as the normal debt dynamics of the developing countries into evidence of overindebtedness. Since no debtor country can uphold a resource gap without its creditors' consent, developing countries were forced to move to phase II of the debt cycle and are now being urged to reach phase III as quickly as possible. This is to say that debtors must sustain a resource surplus $G = -hX$, where $h = -g$ is a positive ratio that transforms equation (4.2) into:

$$\dot{z} = (i - x)z - h. \tag{4.4}$$

Since h is the proportion of exports that the country will set aside to service its external debt, the above equation sheds some light on the Norman Bailey rescheduling proposal: developing-country debt should be replaced by exchange participation notes entitling the holder to a specific participation in the country's export earnings. Although highly impractical from the banking point of view, the proposal emphasizes that foreign debts are to be repaid from part of the export proceeds and not by the sale of assets or natural resources. As such, it provides some useful solvency tests.

A weak solvency test merely requires the debt to be paid off over a finite time horizon. It is automatically fulfilled for any positive h if $x - i \geq 0$; that is, if the interest rate does not exceed the rate of growth of exports. This explains the attractiveness of a situation in which interest rates remain consistently below the rates of growth of international trade. In such situations, debt-servicing problems will ultimately solve themselves. Debtor countries have only to acknowledge two points: (1) exchange rate management should keep the country's exports in line with the expansion of international trade; and (2) the costs of sustaining a certain surplus/export ratio, even for long periods of time, are substantially lower than those of extended moratoriums. Creditors are merely required to understand the dynamics of the debt cycle. If the inequality $x - i \geq 0$ holds, external debts can be paid off in no more than $T = z_0/h$ years, where z stands for the initial debt/export ratio.[2] Countries such as Brazil and Argentina, where z_0 is close to 4, could repay all their external debts in no longer than sixteen years if they were willing to set aside 25 percent of their export revenues to service foreign liabilities. But even if the sustainable surplus/export ratio was only a modest 10 percent, the debt would still be fully repaid within a forty-year time horizon.

If exports expand at a rate below the interest rate, however, a minimum critical effort $h > (i - x)z$ is needed to prevent the debt/export ratio from exploding. This is to say that, if the interest rate exceeds by six percentage points the rate of growth of exports, countries such as Brazil and Argentina would not even meet the weak solvency test unless they were willing to sustain a surplus/export ratio above 24 percent.

Taking h and $x - i$ as constants, equation (4.4) is solved by:

$$z = \frac{h}{i-x}(1 - e^{(i-x)t}) + z_0 e^{(i-x)t}. \tag{4.5}$$

Assuming $h > (i - x)z_0$, as required by the weak solvency test, the number of years to pay off the debt (that is, to reduce z to zero) is given by:[3]

$$T = \frac{\log_e (1 + (x-i)z_0/h}{x-i}, \tag{4.6}$$

which is a decreasing function of both h/z_0 and $x - i$, as indicated in table 4-2.

The trouble with the weak solvency test is that it says nothing about the extension of phase II of the debt cycle. It requires only a consistently declining debt/export ratio, but when exports are growing this does not necessarily imply a declining dollar debt. When solvency is questioned because of uncertainties about the future paths of h and $x - i$, this is a stressful stage of the debt cycle. In spite of their efforts to adjust the balance of payments, debtor countries are not able to meet even the interest payments without additional borrowing. A <u>stronger solvency criterion</u> requires, therefore, that the country be able to reach phase III of the debt cycle in a given period, say, five years.

Since equation (4.1) is equivalent to:

$$\frac{\dot{D}}{D} = i - \frac{h}{z}, \tag{4.7}$$

a country can reach the last phase of the debt cycle only when $h = zi$. If exports are growing, this is a much more stringent condition than the inequality $h > z(i - x)$ of the weak solvency test. Taking $z = h/i$ and $t = 5$ in equation (4.5), the strong solvency test requires that, relative to the initial debt-export ratio z_0, the resource surplus ratio be held at the level:

$$\frac{h}{z_0} = \frac{i(x-i)}{xe^{5(x-i)} - i}. \tag{4.8}$$

Numerical results are indicated in table 4-3. The required adjustment effort h, besides being proportional to the initial debt/export ratio z_0, decreases with the $x - i$ differential and, for a given $x - i$, is an increasing function of the interest rate. That is to say, developing-country debt problems are made more acute by a rise in i, even if $x - i$ remains unchanged.

Table 4-2. Number of Years Required to Pay off the Debt

$x - i$ (percent a year)	h/z_0 percent				
	2	4	6	8	10
−6	∞	∞	∞	23.1	15.3
−4	∞	∞	27.5	17.3	12.8
−2	∞	34.7	20.3	14.4	11.2
0	50.0	25.0	16.7	12.5	10.0
2	34.7	20.3	14.4	11.2	9.1
4	27.5	17.3	12.8	10.1	8.4
6	23.1	15.3	11.6	9.3	7.8

Table 4-3. Strong Solvency Test: Required Resource Surplus as a Percentage of Initial Debt (h/z_0 percent)

x − i (percent a year)	i (percent a year) 7	9	11	13	15
−6	6.7	8.0	9.0	10.0	10.8
−4	6.2	7.3	8.4	9.2	10.0
−2	5.7	6.8	7.7	8.5	9.3
0	5.2	6.2	7.1	7.9	8.6
2	4.7	5.7	6.5	7.3	7.9
4	4.4	5.2	6.0	6.7	7.3
6	4.0	4.8	5.5	6.2	6.7

Whether developing countries with high debt/export ratios will be prepared to achieve the required resource surplus is a questionable point. Fortunately, only a temporary sacrifice is required: once phase III is reached, the surplus/export ratio may be reduced. Also, since adjustment programs are subject to IMF approval, debtor countries may face an all-or-nothing choice. Yet, assuming $z_0 = 4$, the required h implied by table 4-3 ranges from a relatively mild 16 percent in the southwest corner of table 4-3 (where $h/z_0 = 4.0$) to a virtually intolerable 43.2 percent in the northeast corner (where $h/z_0 = 10.8$).

Assuming that a country is able to sustain for five years the surplus/export ratio required by the strong solvency test, an important question still remains: how much will the external debt increase before phase II comes to an end? The answer is provided by the expression:[4]

$$\frac{D_{max}}{D_0} = \frac{(x-i)e^{5x}}{xe^{5(x-i)}-i}. \tag{4.9}$$

Numerical results are shown in table 4-4.

An alternative exercise assumes that the debtor country is prepared to sustain a surplus/export ratio $h = 6.25z_0$ percent (which, for $z_0 = 4$, leads to $h = 25$ percent, as in the Bailey [1983] proposal) until the end of phase II of the debt cycle. The number of years required to reach phase II and the interim debt expansion are both increasing functions of the interest rate and decreasing functions of the x − i differential, as indicated in tables 4-5 and 4-6. Results in the northeastern region of the tables are clearly unmanageable because of both the extension of phase II and the disproportionate debt growth before phase III is reached.

Although based on simple balance of payments tautologies, the foregoing analysis leads to some important conclusions. First, with regard to developing-country indebtedness, there is no clear borderline between illiquidity and insolvency. A number of solvency tests can be developed using the criterion that a country is solvent if and only if its external debt can be paid off. All these tests conclude that solvency depends on the attainable resource surplus/debt ratio (h/z_0) and on the x − i differential. Moreover, for a given x − i, the lower the interest rate, the shorter

Table 4-4. Strong Solvency Test: Debt Peak/Initial Debt (D_{max}/D_0)

x − i (percent a year)	i (percent a year) 7	9	11	13	15
−6	1.008	1.029	1.056	1.090	1.129
−4	1.023	1.047	1.077	1.114	1.157
−2	1.037	1.065	1.098	1.138	1.183
0	1.051	1.082	1.118	1.161	1.210
2	1.065	1.098	1.138	1.183	1.235
4	1.077	1.114	1.157	1.205	1.260
6	1.090	1.129	1.175	1.227	1.285

Table 4-5. Number of Years in Phase II: Resource Surplus = 6.25 Percent of Initial Debt

x − i (percent a year)	i (percent a year)				
	7	9	11	13	15
−6	21.2	35.3	40.5	43.3	45.1
−4	4.3	10.8	14.2	16.3	17.8
−2	2.5	6.7	9.2	10.9	12.1
0	1.7	4.9	6.9	8.3	9.3
2	1.3	3.8	5.5	6.7	7.6
4	1.1	3.2	4.6	5.7	6.5
6	0.9	2.7	4.0	4.9	5.6

Table 4-6. Debt Peak/Initial Debt: Resource Surplus = 6.25 Percent of Initial Debt

x − i (percent a year)	i (percent a year)				
	7	9	11	13	15
−6	1.104	2.005	4.306	9.982	24.206
−4	1.018	1.194	1.540	2.094	2.948
−2	1.010	1.111	1.306	1.600	2.016
0	1.007	1.078	1.215	1.416	1.690
2	1.005	1.060	1.166	1.319	1.523
4	1.004	1.049	1.135	1.259	1.421
6	1.003	1.041	1.114	1.218	1.353

will be the strained phase II of the debt cycle. Since neither h nor x nor i can be predicted accurately, however, the best one can do is to attribute subjective probabilities to the alternative scenarios.

Second, since macroeconomic policies in both debtor and creditor countries affect h, x, and i, actions to increase the solvency probabilities can be undertaken. A set of policy suggestions will be presented in the concluding section of this paper.

THE TRANSFER PARADOX

The most dramatic consequence of the debt crisis was the perverse change of sign in the international flow of funds. Developing countries, in spite of their traditional standing as capital importers, are now being forced to transfer abroad a sizable proportion of their export revenues. (Latin America in 1983 raised its surplus/export ratio to 27.4 percent.) Net resource transfers benefit mainly the United States, whose huge external gaps have no parallel in contemporary economic history.

The optimistic diagnosis explains this reverse flow of funds as a temporary deviation from normal trends. The fact that developing countries are natural capital importers does not mean that they should live with uninterrupted positive resource gaps. Debt/export ratios expanded too swiftly in the past few years, and a temporary run of resource surpluses is now required to restore various indicators of credit standing. Once this has been achieved, developing countries will find the necessary financial support to return to phase I of the debt cycle. As for the positive resource gaps of the United States, they simply reflect an overvaluation of the dollar that sooner or later will be corrected in the exchange markets.

This optimistic view of the transfer paradox, which perhaps enjoys more popularity in international financial circles than in debtor developing nations, relies on three assumptions. First, real interest rates are bound to decline to their 0–4 percent postwar average. Second, world economic growth will be robust enough to allow debtor countries to expand their exports at rates above the interest rates. (Without these conditions, future resource gaps will become unsustainable.) Third, the international financial system will transfer net resources to developing countries once their indicators of creditworthiness, such as interest/export ratios, are brought down to appropriate levels.

All these hypotheses, of course, can be questioned. The idea that real interest rates should be confined within a relatively narrow range, such as 0–4 percent a year, finds no support in economic theory. Surely, interest rates would decline if the United States decided to change its present policy mix, which is based on monetarism and supply-side economics. But there are no indications that this change is about to occur. The combination of tight monetary policy and loose fiscal policy in the leading world economy may have been unfavorable to developing countries, but, at least until now, it looks like a success from the perspective of the United States. Real interest rates are abnormally high before taxes, but not once the effect of income taxes is taken into consideration. Market forces determine the after-tax interest rates, the relevant ones for domestic savers and investors. But interest rates before tax are the ones that burden the balance of payments of the debtor countries and that are high enough to challenge their solvency. In a word, the way income tax laws operate, treating interest as taxable income of lenders and as a deductible expense of domestic borrowers, creates a perverse fiscal transfer from debtor to creditor countries. There is nothing new in this fact; but fiscal transfers are now extremely painful for debtor developing countries.

The assumption that sooner or later exchange markets will force a dollar depreciation can also be challenged. Although prospective current account deficits of the United States may seem absurd, currencies do not necessarily depreciate because of anticipated current account disequilibria. Throughout the 1970s international capital markets provided abundant finance to affect developing-country resource gaps. There is no reason why, during the 1980s, they should not do the same for the United States.

A disquieting thought is that, at least so far, there is no evidence that the optimistic diagnosis is likely to prevail. As previously noted, Latin American countries raised their average surplus/export ratio to 27.5 percent in 1983, transferring abroad $29.5 billion. The required adjustment policies involved substantial social costs, an increase in unemployment, and a 5.9 percent decline in the real per capita income of the region. Since adjustment was achieved through import cuts and not through export growth, however, the debt/export ratio of the region continued to rise, from 3.3 to 3.5, according to estimates of the United Nations Economic Commission for Latin America (ECLA). Hence, in 1983 Latin American countries were not even able to meet the weak solvency test. Part of this adverse outcome can be attributed to linkage effects: import cuts in one country in the region implied export losses for others. But even if, by canceling intraregional trade and debts, statistics described Latin America as a consolidated block, the 1983 situation would still look rather unimpressive for long-term solvency.

This leads to a challenging political question: how stable is a world that, although repudiating colonialism, requests debtor developing countries to transfer abroad 25–30 percent of their export revenues? The obvious condition for stability is that debtor nations be convinced that keeping such transfers is preferable to a confrontation with the world financial community, in terms of the present value of domestic welfare losses. This stability condition would easily be satisfied if developing countries endorsed the optimistic explanation for the transfer paradox discussed above. Political leaders in the main debtor countries suspect, however, that this "temporary" deviation from normal trends could last twenty or thirty years. Many of them even question whether sustained resource surpluses in the range of 25–30 percent of exports will lead to the eventual payoff of the external debts. This, of course, creates a serious potential for confrontation.

What may prevent a disruption is that the best choice for debtor countries may be neither immediate confrontation nor indefinite cooperation, but temporary cooperation followed by ever postponed confrontation. At least in the short run, debtor nations may find it in their interest to sustain substantial resource surpluses, even if they look at the optimistic diagnosis for the transfer paradox as mere wishful thinking. The reason is that not only can the world financial community force the debtor nations to eliminate their resource gaps, but it can also impose a once-for-all resource surplus by cutting off commercial credits.

A debtor country can play tough with its creditors by suspending the payment of both principal and interest. In modern economic diplomacy this need not lead to debt repudiation or even an extended moratorium. The debtor nation simply announces that it would be to honor its commitments but that, unfortunately, its central bank cannot print dollars. In this case, creditors would probably react by cutting the commercial credit facilities, thereby forcing the country to pay most of its imports on a cash basis. Since export receipts lag behind shipments, the debtor country has, in effect, a resource surplus imposed on it worth perhaps four or six months of imports. This is a much more stringent effort than what is required by a typical IMF adjustment program. When the country is illiquid, the loss of trade credit leads to a highly painful and inefficient balance of payments adjustment through import rationing. Perhaps this explains why the proposal of creating a debtors' cartel has found little appeal up to now: it could jeopardize the access of the participating countries to commercial credits. It also explains why illiquid debtor nations had no success in their temporary attempts to depart from IMF conditionality.

In the medium term, however, debtor countries may take the necessary steps to survive a sudden cut in commercial credits. A substantial accumulation of reserves may be out of the question, since lenders are likely to try to keep borrowers on a short leash. The same objective can be obtained, however, through import substitution policies, increased bilateral trade between debtor countries, and the accumulation of inventories of basic imports. Some of these steps, of course, require sacrifices larger than those to sustain the internationally agreed resource surpluses. But they may be preferable to the prospect of transferring abroad 25–30 percent of the export revenues on a long-term basis.

Summing up, the risks of a debtor-creditor international confrontation could be minimized in 1984, but not necessarily in the intermediate run. The proper dimensions of the confrontation should be made explicit. They would hardly take the form of debt repudiation, an ideological move that naturally triggers a number of international reprisals. Instead, developing debtor countries are likely to choose the much more polite "limited ability to pay" approach. In practice, this would mean that they would be willing to sustain a surplus/export ratio high enough to prevent international retaliation, but too low to ensure full debt servicing at market interest rates. A debtors' cartel might eventually blossom and try to achieve what politicians in the debtor countries aim for: a broad debt rescheduling with adequate grace periods, appropriate amortization terms, and fair interest rates.

How can the confrontation be avoided? A happy ending can be achieved only if the surplus/export ratios that debtor nations are willing to sustain are large enough for the country to meet the solvency tests discussed above. As explained in the preceding section, the required surplus/export ratio h is a decreasing function of the rate of growth of exports and an increasing function of the interest rate i. Now, as in Marshallian analysis, x and i affect the supply of h in the opposite directions.

For a developing country, the willingness to transfer resources abroad depends both on the resulting social costs and on the lack of political resentment. High real interest rates undermine adjustment policies because of their effect on the latter. They are interpreted by a number of debtor countries as nothing but colonialism with modern economic weapons. Political leaders often argue that developing nations were caught by the trap of floating interest rates. They were encouraged to borrow with the prospect of low real interest rates and are now forced to repay the debt at rates beyond any usury ceiling.

The social costs of sustained resource surpluses depend on how the surpluses are achieved.

In the most favorable case, they may be the effortless result of an improvement in the terms of trade, as occurred with the OPEC countries after the first oil shock. There is little hope that the developing-country debt problem can be solved through this easy method, however, even if a robust OECD recovery among members of the Organisation for Economic Co-operation and Development (OECD) could bring some help. Resource surpluses achieved by export-led economic growth, on the other hand, would be politically acceptable. Of course, for a country with no weakness in aggregate demand, transferring abroad H billion dollars means giving up the same amount of domestic expenditures. It implies a sizable contraction of real incomes and consumption outlays if domestic savings must be raised to sustain investment levels. But, in a growing economy with low unemployment rates, social tensions are easy to dissipate. The unfavorable scenario is that of scoring resource surpluses at the cost of import compression and prolonged recession. Unfortunately, this was the experience in 1983 for most debtor countries.

THE COMPETITIVE PRICING TRAP

The dogmatic assumption that competitive markets can solve all the world problems has led to a curious proposal: secondary markets for developing-country debt should be established so that the risks of insolvency would be appropriately priced. This proposal, defended by some conservative economists, dismisses the IMF and the coordinated rescue packages, leaving the solution to the wisdom of market forces. Banks would be forced to disclose the "true" value of their assets and write off the losses they have incurred because of imprudent lending. Developing countries could get additional balance of payments finance provided they were prepared to pay market interest rates. In the case of overindebted nations, these rates would be high enough to deter excessive new borrowing and to encourage the adoption of required external adjustment policies even in the absence of IMF conditionality. The free market approach could cause some bankruptcies, but these should be accepted as the deserved punishment for irresponsible lenders and borrowers.

In spite of its naive attractiveness, the proposal contains a major flaw: it overlooks the central reason a developing country may be willing to run a resource surplus over a period of time, which is the expectation of continued access to foreign credit markets. If this access is cut because the country is unable fully to service its debt, the country is likely to react by reducing its resource surplus to zero. Hence, what a country can raise in financial markets depends on whether occasional conflicts are solved by cooperation or will lead to retaliation. Chances of retaliation are much greater in a competitive environment than under cooperative arrangements, since competition excludes the formation of coalitions.

The conclusion is that the free market approach would underprice developing-country debts instead of expressing anything like their "true values." As a result, the interest rates would be pushed even higher than those that would be set by a single monopolistic lender. In many cases this might transform illiquidity into insolvency.

A simple example illustrates the point under discussion. Let us assume that all the external debt D of a certain country falls due on the same day t_0. The country is totally illiquid: to honor its outstanding commitments, it must raise in the foreign financial markets an amount not less than D. The value of the country's foreign assets that can be attached in case of default ($\underline{d}$) is no more than a small percentage of D.

The prospect of resource surpluses, besides involving elements of uncertainty, depends on whether conflicts lead to cooperation or to confrontation. If the hypothesis of calling the country in default is ruled out, the possible resource transfer paths are described by the stochastic process H(t). The corresponding present values are indicated by the random variable H, with mathematical expectation E(H). Since the country attributes a positive value to its access to foreign credit markets, all the possible realizations of H are assumed to be greater than $\underline{d}$.

Now let us assume that default is declared whenever the expected present value of the country's future resource surpluses falls below its foreign debt. In such an event, the country is assumed to react by reducing to zero its resource surplus. Possible resource transfer curves are now described by the stochastic process $H'(t)$, whose realizations are such that $H'(t,w) \leq H(t,\omega)$. Hence, $E(H') \leq E(H)$. To complete the model we assume that participants in the financial market are risk-neutral with rational expectations.

If $D < E(H')$ the country is obviously solvent at day t_0 and can raise the necessary funds to service its debt. If $E(H) < D$ the country can meet only part of its contractual obligations. Now let us take the challenging intermediate case where $E(H') < D < E(H)$. Here, the country is solvent at day t_0 if its problems are to be solved by cooperation, but insolvent if conflicts lead to retaliation. In the latter case, $E(H') = 0$ since the country will react by reducing its resource surplus to zero once it is called in default.

What is the solution to this game? The answer depends on whether cooperative or competitive action is taken. The cooperative solution is the one that would emerge if balance of payments finance were provided by a single monopolistic lender. In this case, since all possible realizations of H are greater than $\underline{d}$, the central lender would rule out the strategy of calling the debtor in default. In other words, since there is little collateral against sovereign risk, the creditor would be better-off receiving only part of the contractual payments rather than pushing the debtor into a disruptive confrontation. Once this course of action is made clear, financial markets would provide the country with the necessary funds $E(H)$ not only to repay the debt D, but also to build up a reserve level $E(H) - D$.

Now let us turn to competitive markets, which follow the rules of noncooperative games. In this case, any creditor would have the choice between two strategies: playing tough, that is, advising the debtor country that it would be called in default whenever its contractual obligations were not met; and playing easy, which means taking no action against a country unable (or perhaps unwilling) fully to service its debt. Competition encourages the first choice, since easy players may simply carry the cost of bailing out the tough ones.

To be specific, let us assume that the country can raise in the financial markets a total sum $G < D$; that is, it can service only part of its external liabilities. Let α_k be the share of the kth creditor in the country's total debt. Creditors are assumed to be atomized enough so that $\alpha_k D < \underline{d}$; that is, the collateral on sovereign risk, although too small to match the country's total debt, covers the exposure of any individual creditor. (This atomization hypothesis avoids mixed strategy solutions for the noncooperative game described below.)

The rules of the game are assumed to be the following: if the total share β of the tough creditors is such that $\beta D < G$, the debtor country will pay βD to those creditors and divide the remaining $G - \beta D$ among the easy players in proportion to their exposures. If $G < \beta D$ the country will respond by reducing its resource surplus to zero, leaving the collateral $\underline{d}$ to be shared among the tough lenders.

Which is the best strategy for the kth lender? With α indicating the aggregate debt-share of its tough competitors, the kth player faces the following payoff table:

$$\text{Tough strategy: } \alpha_k D, \text{ if } (\alpha + \alpha_k)D < G; \ \frac{\alpha_k}{\alpha + \alpha_k}\underline{d}, \text{ if } (\alpha + \alpha_k)D > G$$

$$\text{Soft strategy: } \min \alpha_k(G - \alpha D; 0)$$

Elementary calculations show that, since $\alpha_k D < \underline{d}$, playing tough is preferable to playing easy for any feasible α ($0 \leq \alpha \leq 1 - \alpha_k$). The situation is similar to the two-prisoners dilemma. Individual rationality, here opposed to collective rationality, leads every actor to play tough and eventually to retaliate. Financial markets, anticipating this result, would make $E(H') = 0$. As a consequence, the country would be unable to raise one single dollar to service its debt.

This example obviously describes an extreme case. All the country's foreign debt matures on the same day t_0, when irreversible decisions have to be made, leaving no room for the signaling strategies of iterative games. In spite of its blunt simplicity, however, the example conveys an important message: no serious argument supports the view that competitive financial markets are an efficient structure for providing balance of payments finance. After all, balance of payments are managed by governments, which should not be thought of as atomistic competitive actors. Moreover, the efficiency of competitive markets cannot be accepted as a universal axiom, but only as a theorem that can be proved under specific circumstances where there is no conflict between individual and collective rationality. General equilibrium theory shows that this theorem does not hold when individual optimization leads to externalities or when the problem is to supply an adequate amount of public goods. There is no a priori reason that it should hold for balance of payments finance.

THE RISE AND FALL OF COMPETITIVE RECYCLING

As indicated in the preceding section, efficient balance of payments finance should follow the rules of bilateral monopoly, not those of free competition. In fact, except under purely floating exchange rates, balances of payments are subject to noncompetitive interventions by central banks. Moreover, since there is virtually no collateral on sovereign risk, subtle instruments are required to approach issues of moral hazard: as far as external debts are concerned, there is no clear-cut line between ability to pay and willingness to pay.

The Bretton Woods agreement endorsed the bilateral monopoly approach to balance of payments finance, less because of game-theory considerations than because of the collapse of private international lending during the 1930s. Official lending and direct investment covered most current account deficits until the mid-1960s. Then, with the emergence of the Eurodollar markets, commercial banks provided an increasing share of the supply of international credit.

Competitive recycling flourished because commercial banks, in contrast to official credit agencies, provided a timely response to the challenge of the first oil shock, namely, how to channel the OPEC surpluses to the oil-importing countries. This prompt action avoided an international economic collapse, in which the greatest victims would have been the developing countries unable to attract funds from the major oil exporters. But it also set in motion a system of balance of payments finance that departed considerably from the Bretton Woods concept of a central lender.

Under the bilateral monopoly approach, the central lender would first realize that, since there is virtually no collateral against sovereign risk, a country's external debt should not exceed the pecuniary value of its access to international credit. In other words, foreign debts should be limited to a point at which the social costs of extended moratoriums would exceed those of normal servicing of the external obligations.

Second, the central lender would finance extended resource gaps only if borrowers used the external savings to invest in export promotion and import substitution programs that facilitate eventual repayment of the debt. Loan maturities would be consistent with balance of payments projections, and grace periods would be extended until the expected end of phase II of the debt cycle.

Third, the central lender would monitor the economic policies of each debtor country with a set of conditionality tests. These would be intended to prevent exchange rate overvaluations, to keep inflation under control, to promote wage-price flexibility, and to create the basic conditions for sustained economic growth. Of course, financial assistance could be cut if the conditionality tests were not met.

Fourth, if unanticipated factors pushed some borrower to a point of overindebtedness, the central lender would call for appropriate adjustment policies, possibly including several periods of resource surpluses. If necessary, however, the central lender would not be opposed to refinancing part of the interest payments falling due. In fact, since there is no difference between losing one dollar today and losing this dollar plus interest at some future date, any creditor is better-off receiving part of the interest payments than forcing the game to a stalemate. (Of course, this would not be the case if collateral existed.)

How do these rules compare with the competitive recycling of the 1970s? First, during the 1970s, risks of foreign exchange crises appeared to be minimal, and banks almost took for granted that their loans would be repaid with each country's foreign exchange reserves. These reserves, in turn, would be borrowed from other banks. Moreover, information was scarce on total foreign debts, since official statistics usually omitted both the private sector indebtedness and short-term external liabilities. The full disclosure of the total figures in late 1982 revealed a nightmare for the world financial community. Even Brazil, which had acquired a reputation for comprehensive foreign debt statistics, had accumulated an unrecorded short-term indebtedness close to $10 billion.

Second, in a competitive environment, loan maturities could hardly be reconciled with balance of payments projections. The rollover assumption, therefore, was inherent to the system. Incidentally, a number of countries voluntarily chose to finance their foreign current account deficits with cheaper (but also poisoning) short-term credits. In some cases, such as Brazil and Mexico, foreign branches of developing-country commercial banks used their access to money market facilities to provide balance of payments finance.

Third, although external credits were usually directed toward sound investment programs, competition obscured an obvious fact: money is fungible. A set of good projects does not exclude the possibility of overall economic mismanagement. In fact, some countries used their access to foreign credit markets to promote exchange rate overvaluations that ruined both their balances of payments and their local industries. Commercial banks are perhaps to blame for not retreating when such unorthodox economic policies were implemented. A possible excuse is that some of these policies were defended by respected economists. (The Chilean model, for instance, was hailed for a time as the golden offspring of the Chicago School.) Moreover, there was no way to reconcile competitive recycling with economic policy conditionality.

Fourth, once confidence was disrupted, banks moved to the opposite extreme. In a word, competitive credit markets overreacted to changes in expectations. As previously noted, a single central lender would not object, when necessary, to refinancing part of the interest liabilities of a troubled debtor. However, the rescue packages orchestrated in 1982 and 1983 to provide additional loans to countries already in phase II of the debt cycle met resistance, especially from regional banks. There were two reasons.

On the one hand, although rescheduling of the principal is a common banking practice, interest capitalization triggers the classification of the loan as nonperforming, at least in the United States. The rationale is that commercial risks should be matched by adequate collateral. If a borrower cannot even meet his interest obligations, he is either illiquid or insolvent. In the first case, additional loans can be supplied with the protection of increased collateral. In the second, the best course of action is to declare the borrower in default and attach the collateral. Of course, the logic of this disappears when sovereign risk is involved. In the absence of significant collateral, there is no substantial difference between additional lending to countries in phase II of the debt cycle and partial interest rescheduling.

On the other hand, cross-default clauses in syndicated loans, whereby all the participants agree to call the borrower in default if one participant does so, create a conflict between individual and collective rationality. Because of such clauses, debtor nations cannot discriminate against a group of noncooperative financial institutions so as to exclude them from normal debt servicing. Hence, what an individual creditor can get back from an illiquid country depends on what the whole financial community decides to lend to that country, a total that is only slightly affected by its own contribution. As in the case of voluntary financing of public goods, self-interest leads to retreat.

A simple theoretical model explains the point. Suppose an illiquid country must pay, in year t_0, J million dollars of interest on its outstanding external debt and is able to generate a resource surplus equal to H million dollars. The country is in phase II of its debt cycle, which is to say that $0<H<J$. If L stands for the additional lending to the country, in millions of dollars, creditors will get paid back an amount equal to min $\{J; H+L\}$ and the country will accumulate arrears totaling $J-H-L$. (Negative arrears are to be understood as reserves.) Arrears cost the lenders $a\ (J-H-L)$ million dollars, where $0 < a < 1$, because of the loss of their credit standing. Reserves in the debtor country are assumed to increase their profits by a symmetrical amount. Creditors want to maximize their net payback minus the cost of arrears.

Let us first take the case where balance of payments finance is provided by a single central lender. The objective function to be maximized,[5]

$$f(L) = \min\{J; H + L\} - a(J - H - L) - L,$$

is shown in figure 4-2. Here, $df/dL = a > 0$ for $L < J - H$, and $df/dL = a - 1 < 0$ for $L > J - H$. The optimizing behavior of the creditor leaves the debtor on a short leash (that is, with no positive reserves), but refinances all the interest liabilities that cannot be covered by the country's resource surplus, making $L = J - H$.

Now let us assume that balance of payments finance is supplied by a competitive credit market, where α_k stands for the share of the kth bank in the country's total external debt. We shall assume that no individual share exceeds 50 percent, that is, $0 < \alpha_k < 1/2\ L_k$ and $L = \Sigma\ L_k$ indicate, respectively, the additional lending to the country by the kth creditor and by the whole financial community.

Figure 4-2. Net Payback Minus Cost of Arrears, f(L): Single Central Lender

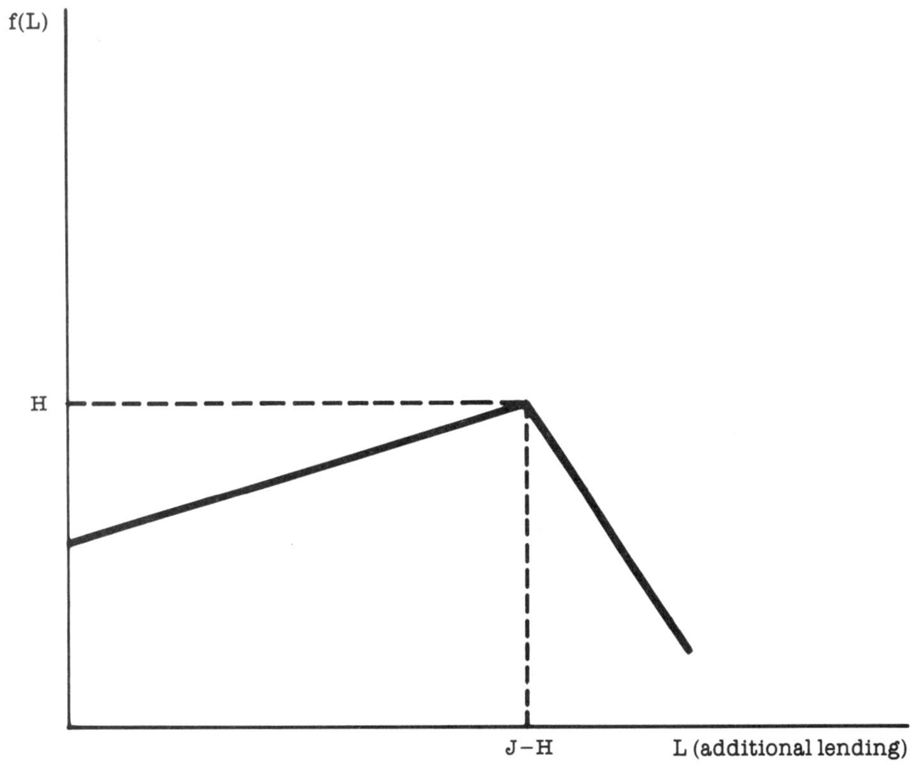

Because of cross-default clauses in syndicated loans, the country is assumed to distribute its payments and arrears in proportion to each creditor's exposure. Hence, the net payoff to the kth bank is given by $\alpha_k \min \{J; H + L\} - L_k$, and the corresponding amount of arrears by $\alpha_k (J - H - L)$. Accordingly, the objective function to be maximized by the kth creditor is

$$g_k(L_k) = \alpha_k [\min \{J; H + L\} - a(J - H - L)] - L_k.$$

The optimizing behavior depends on each creditor's estimates of how his actions influence those of his competitors. The classic noncooperative case is the Cournot equilibrium, in which each actor assumes that his individual choices do not affect the decisions of the other participants. Here $\partial L/\partial L_k = 1$, which is to say that

$$\frac{\partial g_k}{\partial L_k} = \begin{cases} (1 + a)\alpha_k - 1, \text{ for } L < J - H \\ a\alpha_k - 1, \text{ for } L > J - H \end{cases}$$

In any case, $g_k(L_k)$ is a decreasing function of the additional lending L_k by the kth creditor, as in figure 4-3. Taking for granted that the principal has already been rescheduled—that is, that $L_k \geqslant 0$—individual rationality leads to $L_k = 0$ and $g_k(L_k) = g_k(0) = \alpha_k [H - a(J - H]$. All banks refuse to participate in the new loan to the country and, as a consequence, each of them incurs a loss that cooperative action could have prevented, making $L_k = \alpha_k (J - H)$, namely:

$$g_k[\alpha_k (J - H)] - g_k (0) = a\alpha_k (J - H).$$

The above analysis provides the rationale for the equitable burden-sharing principle: under a fair cooperative arrangement each bank should participate in additional loans to the country in proportion to its individual exposure.

Cournot equilibriums assume a noncooperative behavior that is likely to prevail only in highly atomized markets. They can explain neither the emergence of successful cartels such as OPEC, nor the effectiveness of the rescue packages orchestrated by the IMF since late 1982. The foregoing analysis nevertheless leads to some important reflections.

Figure 4-3. Net Payback Minus Cost of Arrears, $f_k(L_k)$: Individual Competitive Lender

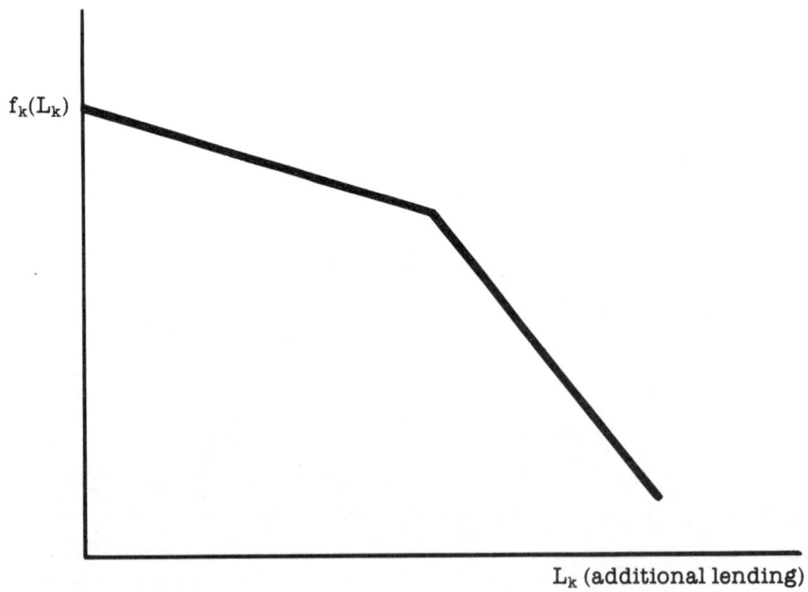

First, the competitive recycling experiment deeply involved a selected number of large banks. Because they were highly exposed in illiquid developing countries, they promptly cooperated with the IMF and the major central banks after the Mexicam moratorium in 1982, thus preventing a disintegration of the international financial system. Had the balances of payments of developing countries been financed by bond markets, as in the early part of the century, a collapse would have been almost inevitable.

Second, although a certain group of large banks is likely to accept cooperative arrangements for a number of years, there is no reason the smaller banks should be willing to sacrifice individual advantage for collective rationality. The Cournot motivation, whereby each bank tries to be bailed out by its competitors, is too strong to be ignored, at least in the case of the regional banks. So far, the damage caused by free riders has been substantially limited through moral suasion by the IMF, the major central banks, and the major commercial banks. The fact that, in January 1984, more than 600 banks agreed to join the $6.5 billion additional lending facility to Brazil shows how effective these cooperative efforts can be in the short run. A discouraging fact, however, is that the $6.5 billion is intended merely to clear the Brazilian arrears and enable the country to meet its interest payments in 1984. According to the IMF projections, a new jumbo loan will be needed for 1985, probably of a smaller size, but still involving several billion dollars.

Debt dynamics tells us that, at least in the next few years, additional loans to countries in phase II of the debt cycle should become routine operations and not be looked upon as extraordinary rescue packages. Whether the present recycling system can rely solely on moral suasion to insure that collective rationality prevails over self-interest is highly questionable, since coalitions among hundreds of participants are hard to sustain. As previously noted, there are strong similarities between additional lending to illiquid countries and the provision of public goods. Nobody can take seriously the idea that public goods should be systematically financed by voluntary contributions. In the same vein, a solution must be found to offset the sovereign risk externality, whereby what a bank gets paid depends, in effect, on what its competitors decide to lend to the country.

The easiest way to cope with the problem would be to accept partial interest capitalization as a normal practice in the early stages of debt-restructuring arrangements. Capitalized interest on loans to debtor-country central banks, in percentages determined by IMF-supported adjustment programs and endorsed by each creditor-country central bank, should be treated by national regulatory authorities as an acceptable rescheduling practice. It should not cause such loans to be classified as nonperforming. Under this procedure the quality of banks' assets would be the same as it is under the current rescue packages to illiquid countries, while debt renegotiations would become much easier.

WITCH HUNTING

Who is to be held responsible for the debt crisis—commercial banks that behaved as imprudent lenders, or debtor developing countries that misused the borrowed external funds? This is the fashionable debate in witch-hunting circles, where every crisis provides an unique opportunity to practice their favorite sport.

The debate reflects nothing but poor logic, since it does not even meet elementary probability tests. Until late 1982, commercial banks never behaved as a collective, but rather as independent decision units. Similarly, debtor countries never coordinated their individual economic policies. The chances of widespread crises being precipitated by the errors of a large number of independent actors are minute. A plausible explanation for the debt crisis must rely on either some external factor or the inadequacy of the recycling system, or both. Hence, the witch-hunting investigation might well be left aside, were it not for the insistent charges by conservative-populist politicians and by poorly informed observers.

As shown in preceding sections, competitive credit markets do not provide an efficient framework for balance of payments finance. Creating appropriate institutions to meet such demands is a task for governments and not for free enterprise. Private banks are not to be held responsible for the flaws of competitive recycling. They were simply playing by the rules of the game. The responsibility lies with policymakers of the world's major financial centers who, failing to realize that efficiency of competitive markets is not to be taken as a universal axiom, reduced to a low profile the IMF and the official lending agencies. William Cline (1983, p. 94), for example, notes that

> as was widely recognized in the mid-1970s and again in 1979–1980, bank lending played a socially valuable role in facilitating the financial recycling of OPEC surpluses to nonoil developing countries in the process of adjustment. Official lending responded only sluggishly, especially to requests from middle-income countries, so that it was primarily bank lending that met the sharply increased need for financing. Moreover, as was repeatedly pointed out at the time, if this lending had not been forthcoming, developing countries would have been forced to cut back their imports from industrial countries, causing an even sharper world recession after the first oil shock.

As to debtor countries, a widespread criticism is that they wasted the borrowed funds on projects with low or even negative rates of return. The charge reflects, once again, the confusion between commercial and sovereign risks. Were it the case, Brazilian and Mexican borrowers would be facing problems with debt servicing in cruzeiros or pesos. If developing countries shared the United States' seigniorage—that is, if they could pay off their foreign liabilities with their domestic currencies—the international debt problem would never have emerged. As previously remarked, project finance was nothing but a veil. The central story was that of balance of payments finance.

Surely, a number of developing countries are to blame for lack of monetary and fiscal discipline. But the adverse effects of expansionary policies on the balance of payments can be prevented if the real exchange rates are kept at appropriate levels. This was the case of Argentina in 1976–78, when substantial current account surpluses were scored in spite of expansionary demand policies that kept the annual inflation rate around 150 percent. Along the same line, the Brazilian crawling peg has been consistently managed so as to avoid a real appreciation of the cruzeiro since 1968, except for an unfortunate intermission in 1980. In Chile, moreover, emergence of external debt problems coincided with a period of tight orthodox controls on aggregate demand.

To sum up, what leads to the disorderly growth of external debt is not the lack of monetary and fiscal discipline, but the inappropriate management of exchange rates. It can be argued, however, that expansionary policies yield the political temptation to overvalue the real exchange rate and thus transfer part of the resulting inflation to the rest of the world. This appears to be the central reason that IMF-supported adjustment programs involve stringent demand controls. (An intriguing question is how an IMF program would deal with the current U.S. fiscal deficit.) Especially in the late 1970s, a number of developing countries damaged their external current account positions with exchange rate overvaluations. In some cases where free capital mobility prevailed (as in Argentina and Mexico), external debts expanded far more rapidly than warranted by current account deficits because of heavy capital flight.

Curiously, two of the most disastrous overvaluation experiments, those of Argentina and Chile, were inspired by a prestigious textbook model, that of a small economy with fixed or predetermined exchange rates.[6] The model, which enjoyed widespread acceptance in academic circles, assumes that wage-price flexibility leads to full employment equilibrium and that the supply of foreign capital to the country is infinitely elastic at a given dollar interest rate (LIBOR)[7] plus a risk premium. The latter plus the predetermined exchange rate devaluation determines the domestic nominal interest rate. Money supply becomes endogenous, with open-market operations offset by countervailing changes in the country's external reserves. Fiscal expansion shows up in the form of additional resource gaps in the balance of payments. Hence, fiscal restraint is the appropriate remedy for current account deficits.

The attractiveness of the model is that it yields an easy anti-inflationary prescription: pre-announce the rate of the exchange rate depreciation and limit the expansion of net domestic credit so as to maintain an adequate level of external reserves. As shown in the appendix to this chapter, even if nominal wages respond to price increases with some lag, the differential between domestic and external inflation rates may converge to the predetermined exchange rate devaluation.

The trouble with the model is that it relies on widespread confidence in the predetermination of exchange rates. If the current account deteriorates because of external shocks, adjustment lags, worsened terms of trade, or improper fiscal policies, however, confidence is likely to be undermined. In this case, insistence on the predetermination rule leads to continuous appreciation of the real exchange rate and to an inevitable policy change.

A practical credibility test is provided by domestic interest rate behavior. If economic agents actually believe in the exchange rate rule, the difference between domestic and international nominal interest rates should approach the predetermined exchange rate devaluation. None of the above-mentioned experiments met this credibility test. With regard to external debt, the most unfortunate case was that of Argentina in 1979–80, when free capital exports were coupled with the so-called tablita, which officially set the dollar/peso daily rates for the next twelve months. The confidence gap was pushed to its extreme point in 1980, when the exchange devaluation was limited to 23 percent, while the peso interest rates remained around 120 percent a year. In the absence of capital controls, international hot money was attracted to the country by the prospect of a 5 percent a month dollar yield. Oddly enough, local authorities accepted this huge differential as the "risk premium of Argentina." As one could expect, the exchange rate rule brought a temporary decline in inflation rates. As a result of the peso overvaluation, however, imports leaped from \$3.5 billion in 1978 to \$9.4 billion in 1980, and in spite of improved terms of trade the external current account moved from a \$1.9 billion surplus in 1978 to a \$4.8 billion deficit in 1980. Since the interest differential attracted a substantial inflow of short-term capital, the country's reserves were kept at high levels, in spite of the increased current account deficits and massive long-term capital outflows. Sooner or later the exchange rate rule was bound to collapse. It did in March 1981, when the new administration of General Viola buried the tablita with a strong peso devaluation.

Chile advanced one step beyond the tablita. In the second quarter of 1979 the exchange rate was pegged at 39 pesos per dollar and kept there for the next three years. In contrast to Argentina, Chile controlled capital exports and succeeded in eliminating the public sector deficit. Protectionism was dramatically reduced. By 1981 the domestic inflation rate was comparable to that of the United States. Because of adjustment lags and wage-price rigidities, tradable goods become extremely cheap compared with the domestic ones. As a consequence, imports increased from \$2.9 billion in 1978 to \$6.6 billion in 1981, expanding the current deficit from \$1.1 billion to \$4.8 billion. Domestic interest rates clearly indicated the lack of confidence in the exchange rate rule. Adverse expectations combined with monetary and fiscal restraint eventually led to dismal recession, and unemployment rates escalated to 20–25 percent. In contrast to other Latin American countries, exchange rate overvaluation in Chile was caused not by the lack of political will to fight inflation, but by blind dogmatism.

Whether or not inspired by fashionable economic models, exchange rate overvaluation was the cause of wasteful growth in indebtedness in some developing countries, especially when capital controls were absent. Had the IMF played a major role in the recycling process after 1974, most of these destabilizing experiments could have been avoided. That these experiments did occur cannot be attributed exclusively to irresponsible economic management in debtor nations. A more serious analytical problem confounded policymakers: the collapse of the Bretton Woods systems and the huge OPEC surpluses after the two oil shocks blurred the concept of an equilibrium exchange rate as a function of current account performance. Once this concept was replaced by that of free market determination of exchange rates, overvaluation could be signaled only by an immediate loss of reserves. But the expansion of international liquidity in the late 1970s postponed any such signaling. Total reserves continued to increase in the group of non-oil-exporting developing countries. This was enough to dispel the idea that debtor developing nations were systematically mismanaging their exchange rates.

To sum up, neither the errors of the lenders nor those of the borrowers can explain the global debt crisis that emerged in late 1982. The central cause has already been indicated in the discussion on debt dynamics: the sudden and unanticipated change of sign in the difference between the growth rate of developing-country exports and international interest rates. From 1974 through 1980 a typical interest rate on developing-country loans, LIBOR plus 1.5 percent a year spread, averaged 10.7 percent. Meanwhile, exports of non-oil-exporting developing countries were expanding at 21.1 percent, overfulfilling the weak solvency test. In 1981–82 the interest rate soared to 16.3 percent a year, while the annual rate of growth of exports declined to 1 percent, challenging any solvency criterion. Even if balance of payments finance had been provided by a single central lender, such a change would have required drastic adjustment policies. Under competitive recycling, the result could be nothing but a crisis.

Witch hunters may argue that rational markets should have anticipated a world recession in the early 1980s, since inflation in OECD countries was escalating to intolerable levels. The inevitable outcome was contractionary policies, which led to a combination of higher international interest rates and lower rates of growth in non-oil developing-country exports. In fact, lenders and borrowers were probably prepared to face a normal adjustment shock, like the one of 1975. What rational economic agents could never foresee was the policy mix of the United States, where tight money was accompanied by loose fiscal policy, which led to an unprecedented rise in real interest rates and the value of the dollar. Expectations are based on historical experience rather than the possibility of unorthodox policy experiments.

POLICY SUGGESTIONS

In late 1982, timely intervention by the IMF and major central banks prevented an international financial collapse. The presumption was that the developing-country debt problem should be treated as an illiquidity crisis and not as a solvency problem. Even if this diagnosis is questionable and may vary from country to country, the optimistic view should be endorsed for two reasons. First, since there is no clearcut line between balance of payments insolvency and illiquidity, adequate handling of the problem combined with appropriate policy steps can actually promote solvency at market terms. Second, as long as a debtor country places a greater value on its access to external credit markets than on the tangible collateral against its loans, creditors have no collective interest in declaring bankruptcy of the debtor.

Since collateral against balance of payments loans is mostly intangible, a functional concept of solvency is required. In the following discussion it will be defined as "sustained cooperation between creditors and debtor countries leading to declining debt-export ratios for as long as is necessary to restore creditworthiness." This concept discards rescheduling proposals (of the Rohatyn style) at nonmarket interest rates. While stretched maturities and even lower spreads are a natural outcome of rescheduling arrangements, there is no reason that creditors should accept any systematic interest rate relief. First, lenders would be better-off by capitalizing into principal any part of the interest obligations that borrowers were temporarily unable to meet. Second, with regard to sovereign risk, there is a cloudy zone between ability to pay and willingness to pay. This is the origin of a serious moral hazard: once interest relief is granted to a debtor country, other indebted nations would demand the same treatment. This would have the effect of transforming good debts into bad ones.

Proposals of the Bailey style, which link the transfer of resources abroad to a certain percentage of exports, although attractive from the point of view of debt dynamics, are inconvenient for two basic reasons. First, they do not rely on existing capital market instruments. Second, they might push debtor countries into autarky and a preference for import substitution over export growth.

How long will the presence of a central coordinator be necessary to sustain the cooperation between creditors and debtor countries? This is a controversial question, but the IMF should be prepared to play this role for an extended period. Developing nations may face a long phase of credit rationing. In the interim, IMF-supported adjustment programs should set balance of payment targets for debtor countries, indicating the amount of principal and interest to be refinanced by their creditors. To play this role, the IMF will need the cooperation of the major central banks and should adjust its conditionality criteria to recognize new exchange rate regimes and the evolving structure of the debt problem.

An initial objection must be dispelled. A frequent criticism is that moral suasion by the IMF and major central banks in the recent rescue packages to Brazil, Mexico, and other developing countries was imprudent, since the prestige of such institutions may be severely hurt if a debtor country eventually becomes insolvent. The charge reflects, once again, the confusion between commercial and sovereign risks. The rationale for the moral suasion effort is that creditors are better-off receiving partial interest payment and refinancing the rest rather than pushing the borrower into a confrontation.

An appropriate international lending system should respond promptly to the IMF-supported adjustment programs. The response has been reasonably automatic in the case of rescheduling principal, but highly bureaucratic in terms of the so-called new money facilities. As previously explained, the asymmetric response is due to two factors: (a) bank regulations, especially in the United States, fail to recognize that additional balance of payments finance to countries in phase II of the debt cycle is equivalent to partial interest capitalization; and (b) financial externalities, inherent in competitive credit markets, cause individual rationality to conflict with collective maximizing behavior, thereby encouraging free riders.

Modifying bank regulations to allow interest capitalization could of course make life too easy for both debtors and creditors and lead to snowballing debts. What regulating authorities should realize is that every instance of partial interest capitalization should not automatically trigger the classification of loans as nonperforming. Additional loans to debtor-country central banks, which are conditional on IMF-supported adjustment programs and duly endorsed by the monetary authorities of the creditor nations, may be essential. Obviously, regulators must defend the health of the banking system; minimum capital requirements as a proportion of both total assets and sovereign exposures are probably the easiest and most effective method of doing this. It should be recognized, however, that the now fashionable rescue packages providing additional loans to illiquid debtor countries do not make banks' assets any better than if interest capitalization were accepted as a normal rescheduling practice under the above-mentioned principles.

This new approach allowing interest capitalization would improve rescheduling arrangements in two ways. First, it would place maturity stretching and temporary increases in bank exposures at the same operational level. Second, it would ease the implementation of the principle equitable burden sharing, since what a bank got paid would no longer depend on what its competitors decided to lend to the debtor country. Of course, moral suasion would still be required to solve the free rider problem, since any individual creditor could oppose not only interest capitalization but also rescheduling of principal. Contingency planning, in fact, should recognize that a coalition of several hundred participants may be impossible to sustain, and that the collective may be able to retain only its core members, the large international commercial banks.

A realistic approach to the problem should blend moral suasion with a substantial increase in official lending to developing countries. Additional official lending is necessary not only to compensate for the retreat of some small private participants (which, incidentally, should never have been involved in balance of payments finance), but also to improve the equilibrium of the international financial system. This does not necessarily imply an additional burden to creditor-country taxpayers, since official credit agencies can use their access to private capital markets. Of course, an idea to be discarded in the upcoming years is that of evaluation of country risk by official agencies. It would lead to still tighter credit rationing of middle-income countries, those who have already been most severely struck by the debt crisis.

To keep debtor developing countries cooperating with the international financial community, a basic question must be addressed: under what conditions will rational policymakers in debtor nations prefer cooperation to retaliation? While precise rupture points are difficult to locate, a general principle remains valid: a growing economy with expanding exports would hardly seek confrontation with its creditors. Continuing to service the debt if it causes prolonged recession is, however, politically unpalatable.

This basic principle suggests a revision of the nature and scope of IMF conditionality. Present criteria have been designed to deal with short-term deviations from equilibrium, where the role of the IMF is only to prime the pump, while market forces accomplish the rest. Unfortunately, the developing-country debt problem may last a decade or even more.

So far, IMF conditionality has concentrated on two points, adequate exchange rate management and demand discipline. The latter is to be achieved through fiscal restraint and limited expansion of net domestic credit. The underlying macroeconomic model assumes that wage-price flexibility leads to full employment equilibrium and that private savings and investment are not affected by budgetary cuts. Hence, any reduction in the public sector deficit leads to an equal improvement in the external current account. Inflation is to be fought through monetary policy so that the political temptation of exchange rate overvaluation does not arise.

Although monetary and fiscal restraints combined with adequate exchange rate management are necessary to reconcile external adjustment with relative price stability, they may not be enough. At present, IMF conditionality is biased toward recession because it overlooks wage-price rigidities. A complicating factor is that some required adjustment policies, including exchange rate devaluations, indirect tax increases, and reductions in subsidies, imply a temporary acceleration of inflation. Wage-price stickiness combined with contractionary aggregate demand policies can lead, under such conditions, to dismal stagflation. A typical example is provided by Brazil, where widespread lagged indexation schemes create highly adverse inflation-output tradeoffs in the short run. In 1983 when the IMF program was implemented, the annual inflation rate leaped from 100 percent to over 200 percent, while real output declined 3.3 percent. Perhaps this can be regarded as a temporary impact of stabilization policies, but inflation was still running at explosive rates in early 1984.

The IMF should consider a prolonged economic slowdown as disturbing as galloping inflation. Especially in developing countries, it leads to social tensions and to political instability. It also yields a false balance of payments test, since the current account improvement that accompanies an economic downturn may be undermined by future recovery. Not only is a relatively quick recovery necessary for political reasons, but sustained export-led growth in the long run is essential for meeting the solvency conditions described earlier in this chapter.

To play its role as coordinator of the developing-country debt rescheduling programs, the

IMF should considerably enlarge its horizons. Strict conditionality, in terms of precise short-term targets, should be limited to three points: balance of payments behavior, real exchange rate levels, and reduction of protectionist measures that could harm other debtor countries' adjustment policies. In addition, the IMF should require from each country a comprehensive economic plan to fight inflation, to promote wage-price flexibility, to strengthen domestic saving, to generate export-led growth, and to encourage the substitution of risk capital for external indebtedness.

Insuring cooperation between creditors and debtors is a necessary but not a sufficient condition for international solvency. The effectiveness of cooperation must be proved to some degree by declining debt-export rations.

A change in the U.S. policy mix (including a substantial cut in the public sector deficit and a once-for-all increase in real liquidity) accompanied by a robust OECD recovery may be essential. The favorable debt dynamics of the 1970s, with exports of the debtor developing countries growing at rates above the international interest rates, could then be resumed. With the help of the resource surpluses of the debtor developing countries, debt-export ratios and other indicators of credit standing would quickly improve, thereby dissipating the clouds of insolvency risks.

There is no perfect substitute for this improved world scenario. Because it cannot be taken for granted, however, contingency plans can help.

First, worldwide income-tax-free bonds could be issued to provide funds for debtor developing-country finance. The rationale for this proposal was explained in the earlier discussion on the transfer paradox. Ideally, all international lending should be conveyed through such income-tax-free capital market instruments. In the short run, however, this may be too radical a proposal. A more moderate suggestion is that such bonds would be issued only by the IMF, the World Bank, and perhaps by some other official lending agencies. The outstanding amounts could be controlled so as to keep the average interest rates paid by debtor developing countries at solvency levels. An alternative proposal, which would yield practically the same result, would be additional capital contributions from creditor countries to official lending agencies in order to compensate for the fiscal transfer caused by the income-tax effects on international interest rates.

Second, refraining from protectionist actions against the exports of debtor countries that are being supported by IMF adjustment programs would be helpful. This would involve an agreement between the main creditor nations and two international institutions, the IMF and the General Agreement on Tariffs and Trade (GATT). The logic of this proposal is crystal clear. Since the trade balances of debtor countries are under strict IMF targets, any export loss must be offset by an equal cutback in imports from creditor nations. Hence, protectionism in creditor countries is self-defeating: it forces equal reprisals by debtor countries, not necessarily for political reasons, but for the immediate balance of payments.

It has been widely publicized that the Latin American recession in 1983 cost the United States almost half a million jobs. It should be stressed that part of this loss could have been avoided by a preferential treatment of Latin American exports. In the absence of balance of payments constraints, protectionism may allow a country to increase employment at the expense of the rest of the world. When a group of countries must meet rigid trade surplus targets, however, protectionist action against their exports is nothing but a boomerang.

A last policy suggestion is an allocation of SDRs[8] to offset the decline of international reserves in the past three years. This would be no more than a marginal help to developing countries. Its impact on world aggregate demand would be minimal, given the rules that limit the use of the SDRs, but it could provide the basis for a more efficient working of multilateral trade. This objective cannot be achieved when debtor countries are kept on the short leash of virtually zero reserves. The SDR allocation would also strengthen the prestige of the IMF and signal renewed political will regarding international financial cooperation.

APPENDIX. WAGE-PRICE FLEXIBILITY AND EXTERNAL ADJUSTMENT

The following macroeconomic model stresses the importance of wage-price flexibility for balance of payments adjustment and analyzes the effects of exchange rate predetermination. The supply side of the model is specified by the equations:

$$p_t = w_t \tag{4.10}$$

$$q_t = (1 - \alpha)p_t + \alpha\,(e_t + p_t^*) \tag{4.11}$$

$$\pi_t = q_t - q_{t-1} \tag{4.12}$$

$$\theta_t = e_t + p_t^* - p_t \tag{4.13}$$

$$w_t - w_{t-1} = (1 - \beta)E_{t-1}\pi_t + \beta\pi_{t-1} + \gamma y_{t-1} \tag{4.14}$$

Equation (4.10) is a markup rule, where p and w stand for the logs of the implicit GNP deflator and the nominal wage index respectively. Equation (4.11) defines q, the log of the consumer price index; e and p^* indicate the nominal exchange rate and the price of the imported goods in logs. Equations (4.12) and (4.13) define the inflation rate and the real exchange rate. Finally, equation (4.14) expresses the rate of increase of nominal wages as a function of expected and past inflation rates and the log of the deviation of real output from full employment equilibrium y_t. E_{t-1} is the conditional expectation operator; β and $1 - \beta$ indicate the proportions of backward-looking and forward-looking responses of nominal wages to price increases; γ is the degree of wage responsiveness to output fluctuations.

Equations (4.10) to (4.14) lead to the Phillips relation:

$$\gamma y_{t-1} = (1 - \beta)\,(1 - E_{t-1})\pi_t + \beta(\pi_t - \pi_{t-1}) - \alpha(\theta_t - \theta_{t-1}). \tag{4.15}$$

In the absence of shocks and of unanticipated policy changes, rational expectations are equivalent to perfect foresight. In this case,

$$\gamma y_{t-1} = \beta(\pi_t - \pi_{t-1}) - \alpha(\theta_t - \theta_{t-1}). \tag{4.16}$$

Adjustment programs usually require a real exchange rate devaluation, that is, an increase in θ. They also attempt to reduce the inflation rate π. As indicated by equation (4.16), the first impact of a real exchange rate devaluation in a full-employment economy (where $y_{t-1} = 0$) is an acceleration of the inflation rate. The temporary output losses required to reduce the inflation rate are inversely proportional to the wage flexibility parameter γ. In the extreme rigidity pole, where $\gamma = 0$, a real exchange rate devaluation pushes the inflation rate to a permanently higher figure. If wages are absolutely flexible ($\gamma = \infty$), inflation can be cured without recession. Since prolonged recession undermines the political will to fight inflation and to adjust the real exchange rate, IMF conditionality should pay more attention to wage-price flexibility.

To analyze the effects of exchange rate predetermination, we shall assume that the supply of foreign capital to the country is infinitely elastic at a given interest rate. Hence, the nominal domestic interest rate is expressed by

$$\begin{aligned} i_t &= r^* + E_{t-1}[(e_{t+1} - e_t) + (p_{t+1}^* - p_t^*)] \\ &= i_t^* - E_{t-1}(p_{t+1} - p_t) + E_{t-1}[(e_{t+1} - e_t) + p_{t+1}^* - p_t^*] \end{aligned}$$

where r^* stands for the external real interest rate, with

$$i_t = r^* + E_{t-1}\,\omega_{t+1}.$$

So

$$\omega_t = (e_t + p_t^*) - (e_{t-1} + p_{t-1}^*) \tag{4.17}$$

indicating the imported inflation rate, the real domestic interest rate is given by

$$r_t = i_t - E_{t-1}\,\pi_t = r^* + E_{t-1}\,(\omega_{t+1} - \pi_{t+1}). \tag{4.18}$$

Equations (4.11) to (4.13) and (4.17) yield

$$(1-\alpha)\,(\theta_t - \theta_{t-1}) = \omega_t - \pi_t, \tag{4.19}$$

indicating that the real exchange rate appreciates if and only if the actual inflation rate exceeds its imported component.

Since the nominal exchange rate is determined by the central bank, and since the supply of external capital is infinitely elastic at a given interest rate, the money supply is endogenous. The demand side of the model is therefore described by the IS equation:

$$y_t = a\theta_t - br_t + c$$

or equivalently:

$$y_t = a(\theta_t - \theta_L) + b\,E_{t-1}\,(\pi_{t+1} - \omega_{t+1}) \tag{4.20}$$

where θ_L stands for the full employment equilibrium real exchange rate.

Let us now discuss anti-inflationary policies based on exchange rate predetermination. We shall assume that until period 0, the economy stands at full employment ($y = 0$) with a constant inflation rate $\pi_t = \pi_O = \omega_t$. At the end of period 0 the central bank announces that the exchange rate policy will make $\omega_t = \omega < \pi_O$. To simplify the analysis, ω will be taken as a constant.

Let us first assume that the exchange rate rule is not questioned by economic agents; this is, that $E_{t-1}\,\omega_{t+1} = \omega$ for $t \geqslant 0$. Since $y_O = 0$, equations (4.15) and (4.19) determine the real exchange rate and the inflation rate in period 1:

$$\theta_1 = \theta_L - \frac{\beta(\pi_O - \omega)}{(1-\alpha)\,\beta + \alpha} \tag{4.21a}$$

$$\pi_1 = \omega + \frac{(1-\alpha)\,\beta\,(\pi_O - \omega)}{(1-\alpha)\,\beta + \alpha} \tag{4.21b}$$

Immediate adjustment to the new exchange rate rule is prevented by the backward-looking response of nominal wages to price increase ($\beta > 0$). The real exchange rate appreciates in period 1, and inflation falls between its initial rate π_O and the target rate ω.

As can be derived from equations (4.15), (4.19), and (4.20), for $t > 2$, θ and π follow the first-order system of difference equations:

$$\begin{bmatrix} \theta_{t+1} - \theta_L \\ \pi_{t+1} - \omega \end{bmatrix} = M \begin{bmatrix} \theta_t - \theta_L \\ \pi_t - \omega \end{bmatrix}. \tag{4.22}$$

M indicates the matrix:

$$M = d^{-1} \begin{bmatrix} d - \dfrac{\gamma\alpha}{1-\alpha} & -\dfrac{\beta}{1-\alpha} \\ \gamma a & \beta \end{bmatrix} \tag{4.23}$$

where $d = \alpha/(1-\alpha) - \gamma b$.

θ_t and π_t converge to the equilibrium values θ_L and ω if and only if the absolute values of the characteristic roots of M are less than one; that is,

$$\gamma < \min\left\{\frac{\alpha}{b(1-\alpha)}\,;\,\frac{4\beta\,(1-\alpha) + 2\alpha}{a + 2b\,(1-\alpha)}\right\}.$$

The fact that the system is unstable for values of γ exceeding the above limit challenges the effectiveness of anti-inflationary policies based on exchange rate predetermination. Even in the convergence case, the adjustment lags indicated on equations (4.21a) and (4.21b) may undermine the confidence in the exchange rate rule.

Lack of confidence, making $E_{t-1}\,\omega_t = \omega + \rho > \omega$, still aggravates the adjustment process, introducing an unanticipated real exchange rate overvaluation, expressed by

$$(I - E_{t-1})\,\theta_t = -\rho.$$

The result can be a further erosion of confidence, which leads to the breakdown of the exchange rate predetermination rule.

NOTES

1. To prove the equivalence between equation (4.1) and (4.2) it is enough to remark that $\dot{D}/D = \dot{z}/z + \dot{X}/X$. One should note that i and x are instantaneous rates. For instance, a 10 percent a year annually capitalized interest rate corresponds to $i = \log 1.1 = 9.53$ percent.

2. In fact, if $x - i \geq 0$, equation (4.4) yields $\dot{z} \leq -h$. Hence, $z(T) < z_0 - hT = 0$.

3. Equations (4.5) and (4.6) assume $x \neq i$; for $x = i$, $z = z_0 - ht$, and $T = z_0/h$.

4. To derive equation (4.9), note that

$$\frac{D_{max}}{D_0} = \frac{D_\delta}{D_0} = \frac{z_\delta X}{z_0 X_0} = \frac{h}{i z_0} e^{\delta x}$$

and use equation (4.8).

5. Min {J; H + L} − L is the net payoff to the lender.

6. Brazil ran a similar exercise in 1980. It was less disastrous because its life was shorter and it had been preceded by a 30 percent maxidevaluation of the currency in December 1979.

7. London interbank offered rate.

8. The SDR is a unit of account in the Special Drawing Rights, a weighted basket of currencies, created by the IMF.

REFERENCES

Bailey, Norman A. 1983. "The safety net for foreign lending." Business Week (January 10): 17.

CEPAL (Comisión Económica para América Latina/Economic Commission for Latin America [ECLA]). 1984. "A Economia da América Latina em 1983." [The Latin American Economy in 1983]. Annual report. Processed.

Cline, William R. 1983. International debt and the stability of the world economy. Washington, D.C.: Institute for International Economics.

Domar, Evsey D. 1975. Essays in the theory of economic growth. Oxford: Oxford University Press.

Dornbusch, Rudiger, and Stanley Fischer. 1980. Macroeconomics. 2d ed. New York: McGraw-Hill.

Simonsen, Mario H. 1983. Dinâmica macroeconômica. São Paulo: McGraw-Hill do Brasil.

———. 1979. "Pagamenti internazionali e indebitamento estero." Revista di Política Económica (January).

Soros, George. 1984. The international debt problem: Solution. New York: Soros Fund Management Co. Processed.

Part II

Commercial Bank Behavior and the Financial System

5

Commercial Bank Lending to Developing Countries: From Overlending to Underlending to Structural Reform

Jack M. Guttentag and Richard Herring

Most explanations of the current debt-servicing problems of developing countries emphasize two features: imprudent borrowing and bad luck. Imprudent borrowing applies to countries that borrowed to finance domestic policies that would not have been sustainable even in a more congenial international economic setting. The original policy initiatives varied widely among countries—from programs that resulted in excessively ambitious infrastructure investments and misconceived import substitution strategies to unaffordable subsidies and excessive military expenditures. In each case, however, the policy initiatives ultimately led to an overvalued exchange rate that was supported through external borrowing.

Bad luck exacerbated the situation for imprudent borrowers and caused problems for countries that might otherwise have had no difficulties servicing their debts. Because of uncontrollable circumstances, policymakers in borrowing countries were confronted with a series of adverse shocks to their capacity to service external debt. Stagnant demand in the major industrial countries led to a sharp drop in the demand for commodities and in commodity prices. An abrupt rise in real interest rates on financial instruments denominated in dollars increased the cost of refinancing maturing debt and of servicing outstanding debt that had been contracted on a floating-rate basis. The accompanying appreciation of the dollar contributed to the worsening financial position of many borrowers who had contracted debt denominated in dollars and who were reliant on export prices that depended on a weighted average of the exchange rates of leading industrial countries.

This deterioration of the world economy, in conjunction with the debt-servicing difficulties of borrowers that had mismanaged their economies, led to a reassessment of the riskiness in lending to developing countries. At first, banks and country borrowers responded by reducing the maturity of debt, but this was only a short-term expedient and, in fact, exacerbated the problem because it made countries more vulnerable to a crisis of confidence and a run by creditors. The run erupted in the fall of 1982 as Mexico, Brazil, and Argentina could no longer roll over their outstanding indebtedness. The result was the debt crisis in which we are still immersed.

In summary, the conventional story about the debt crisis places some emphasis on imprudent borrowing (or endogenous factors in the borrowing country), but most of the emphasis is placed on the deterioration in the world economy (or factors that are exogenous to the borrowing countries). We agreed that both aspects are important. Policy decisions in borrowing countries help to explain why some countries have more serious difficulties than others, and conditions in the world economy explain the timing of the crisis. But we believe that this conventional story is incomplete. Imprudent borrowing is usually impossible without imprudent lending.[1] In several instances, commercial banks continued to lend in support of unsound economic policies long after the residents of the borrowing country had demonstrably lost confidence in

The authors are grateful to Robert Heller, Richard Mattione, and Gordon Smith for comments on an earlier draft. Research for this paper was supported in part by an experimental grant for studies in international economic policy that was awarded to the Brookings Institution by the National Science Foundation.

their government's policies. The consequence was a substantial amount of bank lending that was used to finance capital flight from the borrowing country.

A fuller evaluation of the problem must include an examination of bank decisionmaking. Why did managers of major commercial banks permit their institutions to become so vulnerable to cyclical fluctuations in the international economy and economic mismanagement on the part of a handful of borrowers? And why did the supervisory authorities permit it to happen?

In looking to the future, we are concerned with another important aspect of the debt crisis that has not been fully appreciated. The financial instruments that have been used to transfer funds to developing countries predispose the system to crisis. The types of loan contracts that provide each lender with maximum security, when aggregated over all lenders, create an extremely fragile financial structure. Neither exhortation nor regulation can affect this, but a change in the modus operandi of official international agencies could. The innovations required to improve the financial instruments used in private financial transactions would also provide the means for stabilizing the demand for funds by developing country borrowers. These innovations are described in detail in this chapter.

In the section "Why Banks Became Heavily Exposed," we examine why, despite the dangers of heavy concentrations of exposure to country risk banks nonetheless permitted these exposures to become so large.[2] We will develop three hypotheses: (1) that banks were subject to disaster myopia; (2) that banks underestimated risks because of inadequate information and erroneous inferences from existing information; and (3) that banks took a calculated gamble based on the expectation of official support in the event of adverse outcomes. "The Behavior of Bank Supervisors and Regulators" considers why the bank regulatory authorities were so ineffectual in constraining growing concentrations of country exposure in individual banks. "Changes in the Behavior of Banks and Regulators Since the Crisis" examines the response of the banks and regulators to the crisis and speculates on the consequences for future flows of bank lending to developing countries. A discussion of "Financial Innovations to Enhance Credit Flows to Developing Countries" follows, and the chapter ends with a "Concluding Comment."

WHY BANKS BECAME HEAVILY EXPOSED

Table 5-1 shows that, by mid-1981, major U.S. banks had accumulated claims equal to 10 percent or more of their capital on each of six developing countries. Although concentrations were heaviest in the nine largest U.S. banks, the pattern was similar among the next largest fifteen. Even the smaller reporting banks developed heavy concentrations of exposure. These data specifically pertain to U.S. banks, because no other banks are forced to disclose information in such detail. But information leaked in renegotiations with Mexico and Brazil (under which banks were "urged" to increase their loans by a percentage of initial outstandings) indicates that some major international banks headquartered in other countries were exposed almost as heavily (see Morgan Guaranty 1982).[3]

To investigate why banks became so heavily exposed, we have modeled the loan concentration decision. We assume that banks maximize the expected value of profits, subject to the constraint that the perceived risk of bankruptcy not exceed some probability γ.[4]

Let L_j = the magnitude of the loan to the jth borrower

r_j = 1 plus the expected return on the loan to the jth borrower

R_j = 1 plus the contractual interest rate on the loan to the jth borrower

P_j = the probability that a zero return will be realized on the loan to the jth borrower

Table 5-1. Concentrations of Exposure Relative to Capital, June 1981 (percent)

Country	Nine U.S. money center banks	Next fifteen largest banks	Other banks reporting (143)
Mexico	50.2	41.0	24.3
Brazil	45.5	33.1	15.0
Argentina	20.6	14.4	5.2
Korea, Rep. of	18.8	17.5	7.2
Philippines	13.6	7.8	2.2
Chile	12.2	9.5	5.8

Note: The numerator is the sum of cross-border, nonlocal currency claims on residents of the countries listed, adjusted for external guarantees. The denominator is the total capital of the relevant group of banks, including equity, subordinated debentures, and provisions for loan losses.

Source: Federal Financial Institutions Examination Council, Statistical Release, no. E. 16 (126), December 6, 1982.

$1 - p_j$ = the probability that R_j will be realized

i = 1 plus the risk-free rate or opportunity cost of funds

σ_j^2 = the variance of the expected return on the loan to the jth borrower

σ_p^2 = the variance of the expected return on the bank's portfolio of loans

M = the bank's minimum acceptable value of assets

A = the value of the bank's portfolio of assets at the end of period

V = the shadow price of the risk constraint.

We can express this constraint as

$$\Pr(A \leqslant M) \leqslant \gamma.$$

By making use of Tchebysheff's inequality, we can rewrite this constraint as

$$\gamma[E(A) - M]^2 - \sigma_p^2 \geqslant 0$$

and form the Lagrangian expression:

$$G(L_j, V) = \sum_{j=1}^{n} L_j(r_j - i) + V\,(\gamma[E(A) - M]^2 - \sigma_p^2).$$

For expositional convenience, we have solved this general expression for a two-asset case in which the risk constraint is binding ($V > 0$). L_1 is the amount the bank will choose to lend to country 1 given L_2, which represents the other assets in the bank's portfolio:

$$L_1 = \left(\frac{1 + 2V\gamma[E(A) - M]}{\sigma_1^2 2V}\right)(r_1 - i) - \frac{L_2\sigma_{12}}{\sigma_1^2}.$$

The concentration of loans to country 1—the amount lent relative to capital—will be greater the higher is the expected return relative to the opportunity cost of funds and the lower is the perceived covariance of returns with the rest of the portfolio. Differentiation of the first-order conditions (see the appendix) establishes that the desired concentration increases as the promised return increases ($\partial L_1/\partial R_1 > 0$); declines as the expected probability of a default increases ($\partial L_1/\partial p_1 < 0$ for $p_1 < 0.5$); and declines as the perceived correlation with the rest of the portfolio increases ($\partial L_1/\partial p_{12} < 0$ for $p_{12} > 0$).

We do not know the values of these determinants of concentration. However, we do know that banks that funded themselves at the London interbank bid rate and earned only the contractual spread over the London interbank offered rate (LIBOR) specified in most syndicated loan agreements must have perceived the default probabilities and return covariances as extremely low because the gross returns were so low. At spreads of 50–100 basis points that several of the leading borrowers paid during part of the last decade, the gross, pretax return on capital for a bank with a 5 percent capital ratio is only 20 to 30 percent,[5] a return substantially less than the equity markets seemed to demand from banks.

For the largest banks—those that played an active role in managing syndicated loans and those with offices in the major borrowing countries—the expected returns included not only the promised return on the loans, but also front-end fees (which were sometimes as high as 1.5 percent of the amount lent) and collateral business. Moreover, the very largest banks were generally able to fund themselves at 0.125 to 0.25 percent below the London interbank bid rate. It is conceivable, therefore, that the larger banks perceived the risks to be higher than did the smaller banks. It is more plausible, however, that risk perceptions were much the same and that the larger banks saw the additional gross income as partly a return on their greater investment in foreign infrastructure and international relationships, and partly as excess return. Many large banks viewed international banking as more profitable than domestic banking (see Group of Thirty 1982).

Disaster Myopia

One explanation of why risks and covariances were perceived to be so low is that banks are subject to disaster myopia. The assessment of country risk is a formidable task because the statistical record is meager and of questionable relevance. In the postwar era, the repayment record on country loans was relatively good in comparison with other types of lending. Unlike car loans, mortgages, and many categories of commercial and industrial lending, events that cause losses on country loans are infrequent and the process that generates unfavorable outcomes is not well understood. Moreover, structural changes in the world economy since the last major episode of country defaults in the 1930s—such as the creation of official international financial institutions—suggested that earlier experience might be of little relevance in assessing future probabilities of default.

Since the probability of a country default could not be based on an objective relative frequency distribution, it was necessarily founded on subjective perceptions. Specialists in cognitive psychology and decision sciences have investigated how decisionmakers formulate such perceptions when confronted with low-probability, high-loss hazards. We will argue that several of the insights from this literature—in particular, the availability heuristic, threshold heuristic, and cognitive dissonance—apply to the behavior of banks with regard to country risk.

The availability heuristic is a psychological mechanism by which people evaluate the likelihood of an event. In the terminology of Tversky and Kahneman (1982, p. 164), the availability heuristic is employed whenever a person "estimates frequency or probability by the ease with which instances or associations can be brought to mind." Frequent events are usually easier to recall than infrequent events. But ease of recall is also affected by such factors as the emotional intensity of an experience or the time elapsed since the last occurrence, and these factors can lead to an "availability bias." This bias is easily illustrated by the common experience of driving more cautiously after witnessing an automobile accident, as if in response to a sharp increase in the subjective probability of an accident. Normal, less cautious driving habits usually return as the image of the accident recedes from memory.

Tversky and Kahneman report results of ten controlled experiments performed with 1,500 subjects which demonstrated that, even when probabilities could be objectively determined, people tended to employ the availability heuristic. They argue that their results are equally applicable to very infrequent events where probability judgments cannot be based on a tally of relative frequencies.

We hypothesize that banks were subject to the availability bias in assessing the subjective probability of default by developing countries. As the period since the last major incidence of country defaults lengthened, the ease with which decisionmakers could imagine such an event declined and, thus, so did the subjective probability. This bias was heightened as the generation of managers who lived through the last episode of country defaults was replaced by successive generations; the latter had neither direct experience with the episode nor even indirect experience through personal contact with managers who had.

It is plausible that, at some point, the subjective probability of a wave of country defaults became so low that it was treated as if it were zero. This is an application of the threshold heuristic—an implicit decision rule through which decisionmakers allocate their scarcest resource—managerial attention. The threshold heuristic is necessary to perform even the simplest task. Any decision is vulnerable to a large number of low probability hazards which, if given even cursory attention, would result in complete paralysis. This heuristic becomes an impediment to effective decisionmaking, however, when it leads to the neglect of those few potentially costly hazards that might have been identified and avoided.

The availability heuristic, in combination with the threshold heuristic, can lead to disaster myopia—a tendency to neglect low-probability hazards that may produce large losses. These heuristics, drawn from the descriptive approach to decisionmaking under uncertainty, are at variance with the conventional assumptions of rational expectations that characterize the normative approach to decisionmaking. The rational expectations theory is that market discipline will ensure that decisionmakers form expectations correctly. Those who make systematic errors will incur losses and go out of business. But this hypothesis has little force with regard to expectations concerning low-probability hazards. These hazards occur so infrequently that they may be disregarded with impunity for long periods.

Indeed, under such conditions, competition may drive prudent decisionmakers from the market. A bank that attempts to charge an appropriate default premium for low-probability hazards is likely to lose business to banks that are willing to disregard the hazard.

Tendencies toward disaster myopia are exacerbated by the incentive systems within banks. Evaluations of performance usually cover short periods and use current income that is not adjusted for risk or the front loading of revenue streams. Concern for the future consequences of current lending decisions is further undercut by high job mobility among lending officers. Low-frequency events are especially likely to be disregarded if the lending officer will not be personally identified with the outcome.

Once disaster myopia has culminated in high concentrations of country exposure, decisionmakers may be confronted with new information which implies that country defaults were more plausible than originally estimated. In such cases, decisionmakers may experience cognitive dissonance. This is a psychological mechanism designed to protect the decisionmaker's self-esteem when information arises that casts doubt on the wisdom of past decisions. Such information may be ignored, rejected, or accommodated by changes in other beliefs that justify the past decisions.

Cognitive dissonance is a fundamental proposition in social psychology and has been verified in a number of experiments. It seems as applicable to bankers as to, for example, university professors or international civil servants.[6] Cognitive dissonance may have been a factor in several recent cases, in which bank lending actually increased just before the development of debt-servicing difficulties.[7]

In summary, the hypothesis of disaster myopia suggests that banks assumed heavy concentrations of exposure to country risk because the probability of default was perceived to be negligible. The availability heuristic may have led to a decline in the subjective probability of defaults; the threshold heuristic may have contributed to the effective disregard of default probabilities that were believed to have been very low; and cognitive dissonance may have impeded the response to evidence that the probability of a default was rising.

Miscalculation Because of Inadequate Information and Analysis

Banks may also have underestimated the risk of heavy concentrations of country-loan exposure because of inadequate information and incomplete analysis.

Inadequacies of essential statistical data. Although information on debt service obligations is a critical component of the capacity to repay, banks routinely lend to countries without adequate data on external debt.[8] It is possible, for example, that Mexico might not have been permitted to become so overextended if individual banks had been aware of the amounts their competitors were lending contemporaneously, particularly during the six months before the August 1982 crisis when Mexico borrowed $7 billion.

Similarly, information on international reserves, the balance of payments, and domestic economic activity is available only after a substantial lag, although such information is essential to assessing the effectiveness of a country's economic management.

In the absence of reliable data and objective procedures for estimating the probability of a country default, banks appeared to evaluate the appropriateness of concentrations of country exposure by comparing their exposures with those of peers. This practice was aided and abetted in some countries by the bank supervisors, who were similarly at sea regarding what constituted prudent levels of exposure (see "The Behavior of Bank Supervisors and Regulators"). In the United States, for example, bank examination procedures tend to focus on outliers among a group of otherwise comparable financial institutions. Exposures that conform to the average are less likely to be criticized. Moreover, the Country Exposure Lending Surveys (CELS) that were introduced by the federal regulatory agencies in 1978 provide a ready means for banks to perform peer group analysis on their own. The CELS provide exposure data disaggregated over several different categories such as country residence of borrower, maturity, and peer groups of banks. The practice in many banks of keeping the bank's own country exposures in line with those of peer institutions can lead to false confidence in imprudent exposures, although it may increase the probability of government assistance in the event of a crisis (see below).

Inadequate analysis of covariances. Banks seem to have had particular difficulty in evaluating the covariances among country loans. The experience with the oil shock of 1974 was generally interpreted by bankers as an indication that systematic risks—even in the event of such an extraordinary external shock—were not high. (After all, banks could achieve some diversification against an oil shock by loans to oil-exporting Mexico and oil-importing Brazil.) This view was supported by some economists who argued that the returns on developing-country loans were not likely to be highly correlated because exogenous events would have differing impacts on countries, depending on their specific trade and economic structures and also on policy responses.[9] There appears to have been little serious attention to two systematic linkages created by the loan policies of the banks themselves: all major borrowers were vulnerable to a sharp rise in real interest rates, and all were vulnerable to funding risk when confidence in them evaporated.

The practice of pricing syndicated country loans on a floating-rate basis transferred interest rate risk from bank lenders to country borrowers. As the volume of floating-rate claims on developing countries grew, countries that were not otherwise linked became vulnerable to the same shock, a sustained increase in real interest rates.[10]

In addition, the practice of keeping loan maturities short exposed country borrowers to funding risk. As short-term debt mounted, borrowing countries that were not otherwise alike became similarly vulnerable to a collapse of confidence. Although the initial shock had very different impacts on different countries, lenders created linkages by assuming that problems in one country would be followed by problems in other countries in the same region.

The short-leash fallacy. The strategy of keeping loan maturities short was subject to another analytical pitfall. Some banks apparently assumed that, even if debt problems arose, their own exposure could be reduced before such problems materialized. For example, in its 1981 annual report (p. 26) Citicorp makes the argument that "country risk from foreign currency lending is reduced as the length of the obligation decreases, since shorter maturities permit adjustments in exposure as balance of payments or political conditions change."

This seemingly plausible strategy is subject to a fallacy of composition. When a country has a current account deficit, a bank can reduce its exposure only if some other lender is willing to increase its exposure, or if the country is willing to reduce its stock of foreign assets. If a lender wants to reduce its exposure because it has lost confidence in the country, which is the contingency the short-leash strategy is designed to offset, it is quite probable that other lenders will lack confidence also. With all lenders on the run, it is very unlikely that the country will care to liquidate assets so that some lenders can be repaid. The short-leash strategy is illogical in principle and has not worked in practice.

Misemphasis on accounting values. Confusion of accounting values with true economic values may also have contributed to lenders' willingness to accept large concentrations of exposure. This analytical error is apparent in the assertion that country lending is safe because no major borrowing country has "gone out of business" (Wriston 1982), or the assertion that banks increase profits by rescheduling country loans. Both of these assertions neglect the fact that country loans should be valued as a stream of risky cash flows. The fact that countries continue to exist (even when governments do not) is no guarantee that debt service payments will be made on schedule, and the fact that rescheduled debt service payments are higher is no assurance that such payments will be made.

Since the schedule of debt service payments is uncertain, it should be adjusted for risk. One convenient approach would summarize the present value of a loan to country 1, $PV(L_1)$, as follows:

$$PV(L_1) = \sum_{i=1}^{N} [E(C_t) - A_t]/D_t$$

where $E(C_t)$ is the expected value of the scheduled cash flows, C_t, in period t; A_t is the amount the bank would be willing to pay to be certain of the cash flow in period t, and therefore the difference $E(C_t) - A_t$ is the certainty-equivalent cash flow; and D_t is the risk-free discount factor—the future value in period t of one dollar invested at the risk-free rate.

In terms of this valuation model, it is clear that banks suffer an economic loss (although, under present practices, usually not an accounting loss) when borrowing countries experience debt-servicing difficulties. The present value of claims on a particular borrower is likely to be lowest when a debt crisis erupts and even debt service payments for the near term are in doubt. Once claims are successfully rescheduled, the present value will rise. This will occur because the shift in government policies and the rescheduling of debt service payments to correspond more closely to the borrower's anticipated cash flows will increase the probability that the borrower will be able to meet the payments. But the economic value of the loan will remain below the original level because the borrower's failure to honor past promises may well lead to a larger certainty-adjustment factor. This effect is likely to be larger the longer the grace period and the longer the extension of maturities, because long-term cash flows are more vulnerable to a greater number of unfavorable events than are those in the near term.

In short, the miscalculation hypothesis asserts that banks may have underestimated the risk of lending to developing countries. Poor information and faulty analysis may have caused banks to misassess not only the true financial condition of major borrowers, but also the likelihood that they would get into trouble. Inadequate analysis clearly led banks to be too complacent both about their ability to reduce their exposures and about the impact of loan restructurings on the true economic value of loans.

Implicit Government Guarantees

The third hypothesis is that banks allowed exposures to become very high because they believed that national government or official international institutions would protect them from the full impact of any adverse outcomes. There are two possible explanations for this.

First, deposit insurance may have played a role. To the extent that bank depositors relied on explicit or implied government guarantees, they paid relatively little regard to the portfolio choices of individual banks. Since supervision of the international activities of banks was relatively weak, the consequence may have been that expected returns to banks on heavy concentrations of country exposure were higher than they would have been if depositors had incentives to monitor bank exposures and charge banks default premiums. Moreover, the existence of lender-of-last-resort facilities may have led some banks to be complacent about the risk of a liquidity crisis sparked by the debt-servicing difficulties of a major borrower.

Second, banks may have relied on official international support for debtor countries to protect them from the full impact of debt-servicing problems. The principal supports are the various facilities of the International Monetary Fund (IMF) for adjustment assistance. Such support involves both financial assistance to debtor countries (which, on occasion during the 1970s, appears to have been used to repay bank debt), and the design and supervision of stabilization programs to restore debt service capacity. Banks may also have felt that international economic coordinating bodies such as the Bank for International Settlements (BIS) and the Organisation for Economic Co-operation and Development (OECD) would prevent problems in individual countries from spilling over to become systemwide problems.

In a sense, bank behavior increased the likelihood that, in the event of trouble, government assistance would be forthcoming. By herding—that is, keeping concentrations of exposure roughly in line with competitors—banks made sure that any problem that occurred would be a banking system problem, not just the problem of an individual bank. If all of the major banks get into trouble as a result of the payment difficulties of a major borrowing country or countries, the threat of a banking crisis may induce governments to extend more aid to such countries than they would otherwise.

In summary, the hypothesis concerning government guarantees asserts that banks may have accepted heavy concentrations of exposure because of explicit or implicit guarantees from governments. Insurance on bank deposits at least partially insulates banks from the funding consequences of their portfolio choices. The expectation of official assistance for countries experiencing balance of payments difficulties may have caused banks to take a relaxed view of the consequences of country defaults. Also, the practice of herding may have seemed to offer protection against the possibility that an individual bank would be permitted to go under because of heavy concentrations of loans to a troubled borrower.

We have developed three hypotheses—disaster myopia, miscalculations, and government guarantees—that explain why commercial banks might have allowed their concentrations of country exposure to grow so large. The hypotheses are not mutually exclusive. On the contrary, they tend to be mutually reinforcing. For example, inadequate information and deficient analytical techniques made it very unlikely that the banks were ever forced to confront their disaster myopia, while implicit assumptions about government support would have soothed any residual anxieties.

THE BEHAVIOR OF BANK SUPERVISORS AND REGULATORS

Why did the supervisory authorities permit banks to accumulate such heavy concentrations of exposure to developing countries? Several of the hypotheses that we applied to bank behavior may apply with equal force to the behavior of the bank supervisors. Supervisors may also have been subject to disaster myopia. Cognitive dissonance undoubtedly made it difficult for them to respond effectively when signs of trouble emerged. Moreover, the same informational gaps and analytical inadequacies that impeded bank decisionmaking also hampered the supervisors.

In addition, these officials experienced difficulty in developing an appropriate response to mounting concentrations of country exposure. In the United States, the issue first arose with the question of whether legal lending limits should be applied to country exposures. There was profound ambivalence surrounding the propriety of such constraint. On the one hand, policymakers were very uneasy about increasing concentrations of exposure; on the other, they were equally uneasy about impeding the flow of bank lending to any country that did not have hostile relations with the United States. Policymakers wished to avoid the diplomatic problems involved in restricting the access of some countries to U.S. bank lending. In addition, there was concern over the logical basis for applying a quantitative limit. (Should governments be treated like corporations? Should small, less developed countries be treated like large industrial countries?) Moreover, supervisors were extremely reluctant to override the business judgments of bankers. There was even some concern that country limits might shift flows of lending from sound borrowers to riskier ones.

Instead of quantitative restrictions, the U.S. regulators devised a new supervisory approach that emphasized an appraisal of each bank's internal risk management system and drew concentrations of country exposure to the attention of the bank's directors. The approach attempted to avoid assessing the creditworthiness of individual countries and emphasized instead the diversification of country exposure. Subsequently, the Cooke Committee (the Basel Committee of bank supervisors from the Group of Ten countries, Switzerland, and Luxembourg) adopted similar principles for the supervision of country-risk exposure (see Committee on Banking Regulations and Supervisory Practices 1982). Calling concentrations of exposure to the attention of bank directors may be all that is necessary if such concentrations are the result of inattention or misunderstanding. But when high exposures result from the types of internal and external pressures discussed in this chapter, such measures are likely to be of limited effectiveness. In any event, the new supervisory approach did not reverse the trend toward greater concentrations of exposure.

CHANGES IN THE BEHAVIOR OF BANKS AND REGULATORS SINCE THE CRISIS

Following the events of 1982–83, banks have become strongly averse to holding heavy concentrations of claims on developing countries. This reluctance is likely to continue for some time.

One reason is that, over the next few years, default probabilities will undoubtedly be overestimated rather than underestimated. Instances of payment difficulties are all too available to decisionmakers and thus are likely to lead to high subjective probabilities of default. Moreover, the incentive structure within banks will probably reinforce this tendency. Risk analysts may well be in the ascendancy relative to aggressive, growth-minded lending officers.

Another reason is that many of the traditional rationales for accepting heavy concentrations of exposure have been discredited. Peer analysis will offer little comfort when peer institutions are obviously under pressure. The strategy of keeping maturities short, furthermore, has been proven to be of negligible protection against debt-servicing problems. When the threat of debt-servicing problems has arisen, withdrawal of short-term credits has been difficult, while, after a crisis, short-term debt has often been treated like medium- and long-term debt in the rescheduling process. Recent events have also demonstrated extensive linkages among major borrowing countries. Vulnerability to high real interest rates and a contagious loss of confidence are now well understood, with the consequence that perceived covariances are likely to be much higher than before the debt crisis. Finally, the depressed prices of bank stocks are powerful reminders that what ultimately matters is the economic value of country loans, not their accounting value.

There is a third factor in the reluctance of banks to hold heavy concentrations of claims on developing countries. The implicit guarantees that banks may have anticipated have not been very effective thus far. It has proven to be extremely difficult to mobilize official support for major debtors, especially in the United States. Political opposition to any policies that could be interpreted even remotely as a "bailout" of the banks has been intense. The IMF, furthermore, not only has prevented its funds from being used to service bank debts, it has also required new amounts of bank funds as a precondition for any financial assistance. IMF programs have also been difficult to negotiate and implement when several major trade partners are attempting to carry out stabilization policies at the same time. Also, the international agencies for coordinating economic policies were ineffectual in preventing problems in one country from spilling over and becoming systemwide problems.

As perceived risks have risen—both the subjective probability of a default and portfolio covariances—desired concentrations have fallen. The upshot is that banks now believe themselves to be substantially overexposed to the major borrowing countries. This has been aggravated by the current policy of coercing the existing lenders into making pro rata contributions to troubled borrowers as a condition of IMF assistance. Although some banks have swapped loans among themselves to even out exposures, this has had little impact on the banks' perceptions that they are heavily overexposed.

In the absence of offsetting developments, the result is bound to be a curtailment in the voluntary supply of loans and higher default premiums. Indeed, spreads will reflect not only higher default premiums but, until country exposures can be worked down, a concentration premium to compensate for overexposure.

The crisis has also had its impact on bank regulators. They suddenly found themselves under intense political pressure to "crack down" on the banks at the same time they were attempting to encourage banks to make new loans in support of IMF stabilization programs. It is inconsistent to urge banks to lend to country Z and simultaneously force them to write down the value of outstanding claims on Z or place a binding limit on permissible concentrations of claims on Z.

The International Lending Supervision Act of 1983, Title IX of the act of Congress which authorized the eighth IMF quota increase, directs the federal banking agencies to strengthen the supervision of international lending.[11] The agencies are required to improve existing procedures for the evaluation of country risk. Country-risk exposure is to be explicitly taken into account in determining a bank's capital adequacy, and the regulators are to establish uniform systems for arriving at such an evaluation.

Special reserves are to be established against outstanding claims on countries experiencing debt-servicing difficulties. This measure is to be taken whenever there is a "protracted inability of public or private borrowers in a foreign country to make payments on their external indebtedness" or when "no definite prospects exist for the orderly restoration of debt service." Earnings are to be reduced in order to create the new reserves, which cannot be counted as part of the bank's capital for purposes of determining capital adequacy. Although this provision might have been implemented in such a way as to impede support of IMF stabilization programs by U.S. commercial banks, in fact, it will not apply to claims on any country that seems likely to negotiate and adhere to an IMF program.

Banks will be required to amortize front-end fees on international loans in excess of administrative costs over the life of the loans. This is intended to discourage lenders from taking a short-term view of the impact of international lending on current earnings.

Disclosure of concentrations of international loans is to be increased. Banks must disclose detailed information by country on all exposures exceeding 1 percent of total assets or 20 percent of primary capital. In addition, when individual country exposures exceed 0.75 percent of assets or 15 percent of primary capital, the countries must be identified and the combined exposures reported. These disclosure requirements have already been implemented for publicly owned bank holding companies that are subject to the jurisdiction of the Securities and Exchange Commission (SEC).

Finally, the U.S. banking agencies are instructed to consult with the banking supervisory authorities of other countries in order to coordinate and improve the supervision of international lending. It is not clear whether this simply endorses U.S. participation in the Cooke Committee process or points toward something more formal.

These supervisory changes will certainly not encourage the flow of lending to developing countries, but it is questionable whether they will constrain lending very much. Higher capital/asset ratios do cause banks to scale down participation in markets that yield a very low average return on assets such as interbank placements and some syndicated lending to sovereign borrowers. But regulatory pressures to improve capital positions of the major banks arose independently from, and well before, the debt crisis in response to more general concerns about the soundness of the financial system. It is not clear that taking country exposures into account in the evaluation of capital adequacy will raise required capital/asset ratios still more.

The measure to set aside special reserves against impaired foreign assets may reduce reported earnings in some cases. But the measure may well be applied in such a guarded fashion, and to such clear instances of financial distress in the borrowing country, that the equity markets will have adjusted stock prices long before special reserves have affected reported earnings. If the banks have now learned that it is economic rather than accounting values that are significant, the special reserves will not be pertinent unless they force a cut in dividends—an unlikely scenario (see Guttentag and Herring 1983d, p. 32).

Improved disclosure is designed to lead to greater market discipline over foreign loan decisions.[12] For the major banks that are already overexposed, such discipline is redundant. For some others that might have contemplated additional international lending, however, disclosure may have a chilling effect, particularly in an era when there is widespread anxiety about the creditworthiness of developing countries.

The prospects for a resumption of large-scale flows of bank lending to developing countries may be damaged less by the tightened regulatory procedures than by the atmosphere in which they were legislated. A much more punitive approach than that embodied in the International Lending Supervision Act of 1983 nearly prevailed. During the congressional debate, it became clear that a large, diverse coalition of interests opposes the involvement of U.S. banks in foreign lending. This political fact is likely to have an inhibiting influence as major U.S. banks plan how and where they grow over the next decade. They may place a relatively low priority on lending to developing countries.

Even if banks were not starting from a position in which they perceived themselves to be overexposed to developing countries, the pace of lending would probably fall well below that of the 1970s. Quite apart from the increase in the perceived risk of default and domestic political risks, the expected returns from foreign lending are less attractive than new domestic opportunities. The outlook for the U.S. economy seems relatively favorable, and deregulation is opening new domestic markets to banks. It seems inevitable that growth in bank portfolios will have a domestic bias over the next decade.

If these observations are correct and if their implications of reduced supplies of and higher interest rates on loans to developing countries are unacceptable, new approaches to development finance are needed.

FINANCIAL INNOVATIONS TO ENHANCE CREDIT FLOWS TO DEVELOPING COUNTRIES

Our investigation of financial innovations begins from the premise that flows of official aid will not be increased substantially. Thus, we focus on market mechanisms in which official agencies play a facilitating role, but major reliance is placed on the response of the private sector. We have tried to identify some changes in financial instruments and institutions that will benefit both lenders and borrowers.

The model of bank-lending behavior that we developed in "Why Banks Became Heavily Exposed" can be inverted to derive an expression for the risk premium ($R_1 - i$) on loans to a particular country ($j = 1$):

$$R_1 - i = i \cdot \frac{p_1}{(1 - p_1)} + \frac{L_2 \cdot 2V}{(1 - p_1 (2V\gamma[e(A) - M] + 1)} \cdot \sigma_{12}$$
$$+ \frac{\sigma_1^2 \cdot 2V}{(1 - p_1)(2V\gamma[E(A) - M] + 1)} \cdot L_1.$$

The risk premium depends on, among other things, the perceived probability of a default (p_1), the anticipated covariance of returns (σ_{12}), and the bank's existing exposure to the country (L_1). This third component we term the concentration premium.

Innovations that reduce default probabilities will reduce the risk premium. Similarly, innovations that improve the marketability of country loans and thereby lower existing concentrations of exposure will reduce the concentration premium.

We consider two types of financial innovations. One involves modification of the characteristics of loan contracts between borrowers and lenders. These modifications are directed toward improving the match between debt service obligations and debt service capacity. Better matching should reduce default probabilities and risk premiums.

The second type of financial innovation involves the development of a conduit agency to pool country loans and to issue new claims against these pools. This innovation will (1) provide new incentives (or eliminate existing disincentives) to create the better instruments discussed in the preceding paragraph; (2) convert country loans into marketable certificates, thereby encouraging wider ownership and reduced concentration, which should reduce concentration premiums; and (3) provide a means for imposing market discipline on country borrowers before the onset of a crisis, which should also reduce risk premiums.

Changes in the Design of Primary Instruments to Improve Cash-Flow Matching

Loan instruments minimize default risk if the obligation for contractual repayment is matched as closely as possible to the repayment capacity of the borrower.[13] We will call this "cash-flow matching." Existing types of loan contracts between banks and developing countries are deficient in this regard. Most syndicated loans carry interest rates that float at a fixed margin over a money market rate such as LIBOR, with interest payments due frequently—in most cases, every three to six months. Usually, loan contracts give the borrower the right to choose the period of interest adjustment up to six months, and the transaction is priced by using the deposit rate covering the same period. For example, if the borrower selects three months, the loan will be priced by adding the specified margin over the three-month deposit rate. At the end of the three-month period, the borrower pays the interest and selects a new adjustment period.

This procedure allows the bank to match funds exactly if it so desires. It also results in the greatest possible amount of interest payment volatility since the payment is tied to the rate prevailing on a single day. Scheduled principal reductions follow a variety of patterns but they do not vary with interest payments. Thus, even when the amortization schedule reflects the borrower's capacity to repay, the total payment burden may not. If there is instability in world interest rates, the standard bank loan contract leaves countries exposed to substantial instability in total debt service requirements.

Furthermore, loan contracts make no provision for fluctuations in a country's debt-servicing capacity associated with exogenous shocks, such as a world economic recession or an abrupt change in the terms of trade. If interest rates rise at the same time that the world economy deteriorates, as happened in 1981–82, borrowing countries may find that their debt service obligations increase even as their capacity to pay declines.

This disregard for cash-flow matching on loans to developing countries should be compared with the careful attention to cash-flow matching that typically occurs in the design of residential mortgages in the United States. Instrument design in the residential mortgage market is directed, in large part, toward assuring that the repayment obligations assumed by the borrower, including all prior debt obligations, are within the borrower's current and projected payment capacity.

Why is cash-flow matching emphasized in the design of residential mortgage instruments and virtually neglected in the structuring of bank loans to developing countries? First, a residential mortgage lender has complete information on the existing indebtedness of the borrower, and the residential mortgage is likely to be a major proportion of the borrower's total indebtedness. Thus, the residential mortgage lender has the necessary information and the capacity to achieve the degree of cash-flow matching that may be desired. In contrast, the bank that lends to a developing country does not usually have the data on existing indebtedness necessary for the determination of a cash-flow match. Moreover, the new loan is unlikely to be large enough in relation to the borrower's total indebtedness to have much impact on the cash-flow match of the borrower's debt service obligations in the aggregate.

Second, residential mortgages are collateralized. Collateral protects the mortgage lender from having his claim on the borrower subordinated or diminished in value by subsequent indebtedness incurred by the borrower. It also lessens the moral hazard associated with lengthening repayment periods in response to shocks to the borrower's ability to repay.[14] In contrast, country loans are seldom collateralized and, consequently, bank lenders are very vulnerable to moral hazard.

Individual bank lenders are deterred from structuring loan instruments that improve cash-flow matching because, in so doing, they may lose repayment priority to other lenders. Such options as deferring interest or principal (or both) should the borrower encounter specified conditions of adversity will jeopardize the priority of the lender's claim unless all other lenders can be persuaded to grant the borrower the same options. Cooperative action of this sort is difficult to attain in a competitive loan market, however. The same point applies when banks join forces in a syndicate. The standard syndicated loan agreement carefully safeguards each lender's right to equal treatment in the repayment queue, while the terms offered borrowers exclude repayment options that could cause the syndicate to lose priority to subsequent syndicates.

Indeed, concern about repayment priorities has a perverse effect. As a borrower's economic prospects decline or as the debt service burden rises (or, especially, as the two coincide), the cash-flow requirements arising from new loans tend to become more, rather than less, onerous. This was evident in the case of Mexico, when loan maturities progressively shortened preceding the August 1982 crisis.

A rational borrowing country could itself take the initiative in pressing for instruments better adapted to its needs. In practice, however, governments usually have such short planning horizons that they are reluctant to incur additional current costs for greater long-term stability.

Any realistic proposal for better instruments must come to grips with the factors that have impeded market adaptation. We will return to this problem later, but first we will examine some options for improving the cash-flow match of primary instruments.

In a discussion of instrument modifications, it is useful to distinguish those that would reduce default risk, regardless of the overall cash-flow pattern on existing debt, from those that would have to be adjusted to existing cash-flow patterns in order to be beneficial. In the latter category are instruments designed to deal with long-term trends in payment burdens. Considerable attention has been paid to the so-called tilt problem that arises when nominal interest rates incorporate a significant expected inflation premium. The inflation premium compensates the lender for the decline in the real value of the principal and interest payments, with the consequence that amortization in real terms is accelerated and the real payment burden declines over time. To compensate for this tilt in the real payment burden, many types of residential mortgages have been designed to generate rising nominal payments. It is not clear that such instruments would improve the cash-flow match for developing countries. New borrowing and, consequently, the aggregate nominal payment may rise so rapidly that the aggregate real payment burden would increase over time, even though the real payment burden of each individual loan would decline.

Without detailed projections of future cash flows, it is not possible to infer how new instruments should be designed from the standpoint of long-term trends in payment burdens. Instead, the appropriate conclusion is one regarding the policy for designing instruments: payment patterns on new loans should be designed with reference to explicit projections of the borrower's expected cash flows.

We now consider instrument modifications that would reduce default risk at the margin, regardless of the overall cash-flow pattern of existing debt. First, we discuss instruments designed to deal with instability in the borrower's required payments and, second, instruments designed to deal with instability in the borrower's capacity to service the debt.

Variability in interest-rate payments has been a major problem because, under current arrangements, changes in short-term market interest rates are reflected quickly in the interest payments required. To some extent, the division of exposure to interest rate risk is a zero-sum game between the borrower and lender. Nonetheless, it may be in the collective interests of the lenders to reduce the borrower's exposure to interest rate risk if by so doing the risk that the borrower will default can be sufficiently diminished. As an illustration, we have sketched below three modifications in the primary loan instrument that would reduce shocks to the borrower's required interest payments without significantly increasing the interest rate exposure of the lenders. There is thus a presumption that such modifications could enhance the welfare of both borrowers and lenders. Moreover, such modifications would provide benefits at the margin regardless of the borrower's existing debt service commitments. The magnitude of benefits would, of course, depend on the relative weight of the modified instrument in the total stock of debt.

Instrument modifications that would reduce the borrower's exposure to interest rate risk include:

- Permitting interest accruals by adjusting the interest rate more frequently than interest payments are made. For example, the interest rate could be adjusted quarterly but paid annually.

- Permitting long averaging periods for the interest rate index. For example, instead of tying the loan rate to the LIBOR rate that occurs at noon on the last day of the rate adjustment period, the base rate could be the average of daily LIBOR rates over the previous six months. (Prepayment penalties would deter the borrower from refinancing when interest rates decline.)
- Capping interest payments. For example, the interest rate used to calculate the payment during the period might be constrained within a band plus or minus 0.5 percent of the interest rate used to calculate the previous interest payment. The principal would be adjusted to reflect changes in the market interest rate greater than the band.

Many other variations are possible. Indeed, it is relatively easy to identify useful modifications; the difficulty is in overcoming disincentives that prevent individual lenders from adopting them (see below).

It is also possible to design instruments to deal with instability in the borrower's debt service capacity. For this objective to be accomplished, debt service payments must be tied to factors that are positively correlated with the country's foreign exchange earnings. Lessard (1982a, b) has evaluated a number of instruments designed for this purpose, including commodity-price-indexed securities, world-trade-indexed securities, and quasi-equity investments in specific projects or sectors of the developing-country borrower. Lessard identifies the conditions under which positive-sum benefits could accrue to borrowers and investors through adoption of these instruments, subject to the important condition that moral hazard could somehow be overcome. The substantial capital losses sustained by holders of oil-linked Mexican bonds when Mexico adopted exchange controls in 1983 underscore these hazards. Because of moral hazard, primary instrument modifications for dealing with instability in the borrower's capacity to repay will probably be even more difficult to implement than will modifications for handling instability in debt service requirements. But implementation may be facilitated through institutional innovation, the subject to which we now turn.

Transforming Primary Instruments through a Conduit

Adoption of modifications in primary instruments could be greatly eased by the actions of a conduit that would buy primary instruments, pool them, and sell participation interests in the pool. The conduit role could be performed by one of the existing international financial agencies such as the IMF or the World Bank or by a new entity created specifically for the purpose. The Federal Home Loan Mortgage Corporation, a quasi-government agency in the United States, has developed an efficient secondary market in conventional home mortgages by performing a conduit function. This model has been followed with minor adjustments by some strictly private conduit firms.

The conduit we envisage would perform the following functions:

- It would buy loans from those who originate them now (commercial banks) or from others who might enter the business. The existence of a secondary market eliminates the need to hold new loans until maturity and thereby encourages the development of specialists in loan origination.
- It would establish the legal and accounting procedures necessary to place a number of purchased loans to a given country in a given currency in a closed-end pool and would issue certificates representing undivided participation interests in the pool. It would also establish the form of the certificates, including rate, denomination, maturity, principal repayment schedule, mode of sale, custody and delivery of documents, and other details of the transaction.
- It would establish eligibility requirements covering the characteristics of the loans it buys. These requirements would be determined by the preferences of the investors to

whom participation interests are sold,[15] and by public policy objectives that will be discussed below.

- It would establish eligibility requirements for borrowers, in much the same way as any prudent lender. These requirements would be formalized for use by the originating lenders and would provide information on total indebtedness, including maturity structure and other central features of a country's financial status. Unless the conduit provides extensive guarantees to investors, this information on borrowers would have to be provided to investors.
- It would establish servicing obligations, including warranties or coinsurance by loan sellers, to assure their interest in originating good loans and in maintaining proper surveillance over old ones.
- It would establish a marketing system for selling the certificates. This could range from self-administered auctions to over-the-counter sales through branches of cooperating banks to large underwritings by major investment banking houses.
- It would make a market for its certificates or arrange for others to do so. (Dealer firms make a secondary market for participation certificates of the Federal Home Loan Mortgage Corporation.)
- It would perform cash-flow transformations of primary securities to meet investor demands. The duration of the certificates issued by the conduit need not be the same as the duration of the primary securities. For example, the conduit might buy ten $10 million, five-year claims on a country, each requiring straight-line amortization (20 percent of principal repaid each year). It could then issue five certificates of $20 million each, with holders of the first certificate receiving all principal repayments at the end of year 1, holders of the second, all principal repayments at the end of year 2, and so on. If the duration of certificates is carefully tailored to fit the preferences of individual investors, the conduit may substantially reduce the yield it is required to pay on its certificates.[16]
- It would provide some guarantees to the certificate holders. These guarantees might range from reimbursement for losses in the event of misfeasance by the servicing agent to guaranteeing absolutely the timely payment of interest and principal. More extensive guarantees increase the attractiveness of the certificates, which, in turn, increases the conduit's leverage in setting loan and borrower eligibility requirements. We will return to this subject at the conclusion of this section.

A chief benefit of the instrument transformation accomplished by the conduit is that the certificates issued by the conduit are much more marketable than the primary instruments it purchases. The process of pooling similar types of primary loan instruments creates a large volume of homogeneous instruments in which it is efficient for dealers to make markets.[17] (For example, dealers may make a market in $100 million of claims against a pool of 100 loans of $1 million each, where they would not make a market in the individual loans.) Guarantees offered by the conduit, as well as standardized documentation, increase homogeneity between certificates issued against different pools; this increases the marketability of all the certificates issued by the conduit.[18]

Recently, there has been considerable resale activity in country loans by banks with differing concentrations of exposure or different views on the riskiness of claims against particular countries.[19] Even some restructured loans have been negotiated. Transactions have included outright sales and swaps, which sometimes involve side payments. Such activity, however, does not constitute a well-organized secondary market. Each transaction is negotiated ad hoc between heavily exposed lenders. One investment bank has formed a joint venture to bring sellers of restructured foreign debt together with buyers. Its managing director has said, "We do not see this activity as constituting a market, but rather as a series of transactions that must be dealt with on a case by case basis" (Brown 1984).

The volume of subparticipations, in which the seller retains title to the loan and the borrower may not be aware of the transaction, has also grown; but a subparticipation is basically a relationship transaction in which deals are arranged directly between banks that do other types of business with each other. The bank buying a subparticipation depends mainly on the selling bank's concern for its reputation not to "dump" questionable loans. In the event of a loan restructuring, the legal status of the buyer may be tenuous, and the documentation defining the rights and duties of buyer and seller varies from case to case (see also Grant 1982).

One impediment to increasing the volume of transactions in primary instruments is that heavy information costs make it difficult to attract buyers that do not already hold country loans. The primary loan instruments are very heterogeneous, and the buyer may be faced with the possibility that the seller is dumping the loans he least desires for reasons known only to the seller. Buyers can protect themselves against this only by investigating the situation carefully, by relying on a long-term relationship with the seller, or by depending on the seller's concern for his reputation.

In contrast to the rudimentary secondary market activity in country loans that currently prevails, the certificates issued by the conduit would be traded in a well-organized market. Moreover, the certificates would attract a much broader range of lenders because information costs would be lower and the conduit would provide safeguards against the dumping of inferior loans by the originator. Indeed, as the volume of activity increased, it is likely that issues of certificates would be rated by independent agencies; thus, information costs would be lowered still further. As ownership of claims on developing countries is spread across a larger number of lenders through the activity of the conduit, the heavy concentration of claims held by a relatively small number of large banks would be reduced. Borrowing countries would benefit directly from the consequent reduction in concentration premiums, or relaxation of supply constraints, or both.

The development of a well-functioning secondary market will have other direct, short-run benefits for lenders and borrowers: lenders will accept a somewhat lower return if claims are marketable, and the cost of funds to borrowers will decrease or the supply will increase (or both will be concurrent). In our view, however, the most important benefit is long term in nature. An efficient secondary market generates reliable data on the market value of country loans. These data can provide an effective means of disciplining the behavior of both borrowers and lenders. Greater market discipline may help to avoid cycles in which overexpansion of debt is followed by excessive contraction and may thereby reduce the probability of default. Thus, greater market discipline may lower default premiums and reduce the average cost of funds to developing countries.[20]

Market discipline on lenders is most effective if loans are periodically marked to market, although shareholders are likely to take account of these data on the market value of loans even if bank supervisors and accountants do not.[21] In a recent paper (Guttentag and Herring 1984) we have argued that mark-to-market accounting would encourage banks to exercise greater prudence in lending. In particular, banks will have a strong incentive to monitor closely the economic policies of borrowing countries, since new loans in support of unsustainable policies will cause a decline in the market value of outstanding loans.

Information on the market values of country loans will also have a stabilizing effect on the demand for loans. The market will exercise continuous surveillance over the policies of borrowing countries. Adoption of imprudent policies will lead to a decline in the market value of outstanding loans. It would constitute tangible and public evidence of the market's lack of confidence in the borrowing country's policies and would reduce the supply of new loans to sustain such policies. This would place the proponents of imprudent policies on the defensive and strengthen the opposition favoring prudent economic management.

In addition to establishing an efficient secondary market, the conduit would take direct measures to improve the stability of financial flows to developing countries. Through its purchasing policies, it would provide incentives to originate primary instruments that improve the cash-flow matching of debt service payments and debt service capacity. Moreover, through the requirements for loan eligibility the conduit would discourage the use of other primary instruments that worsen cash-flow matching. It would further strengthen prudent borrowing behavior by requiring borrowing countries to report detailed information on projected debt-servicing requirements and capacity to service debt.

The ability of the conduit to influence the volume and composition of a country's borrowing depends on the conduit's market "clout"—what it can offer the borrower to induce it to accept the conduit's conditions. Given the volume of borrowing, the conduit's clout will depend on the difference between the borrower's average interest cost with and without the conduit's services. The differences will be positive because the certificates are more marketable than the primary instruments, and wider placement of certificates will reduce the concentration premium. Also, improved cash-flow matching, increased market discipline, and the borrower's compliance with the conduit's information requirements and other conditions will reduce the probability of default. These benefits will develop only over time, however, and in the short run the conduit will need to offer some guarantees on its certificates to place them with investors. This would require some sort of government support of the conduit's liabilities. We believe that some of the official funds currently allocated to assistance for balance of payments adjustment could be more productively allocated to support conduit operations.[22]

CONCLUDING COMMENT

We have argued that the wave of overlending that ended with the Mexican debt crisis in August 1982 is likely to be followed by an era of excessive caution in bank lending. If this assessment is plausible, and if excessive caution has unacceptable consequences for economic growth and development, it is important to consider policies that will facilitate the flow of lending to developing countries. The proposal to establish a conduit is not designed to deal with the current problems of countries immersed in a debt crisis. (We have proposed policies to manage the current crisis in a separate paper [Guttentag and Herring 1984].) Rather, the conduit is designed to improve the normal functioning of the market for loans to developing countries and prevent debt crises from occurring.

We see the conduit as supplementing the IMF by shifting the emphasis of adjustment policy. The current modus operandi of the IMF is to provide assistance and impose conditions ex post after a balance of payments crisis has occurred. We believe that resources could be more efficiently employed ex ante, in support of conduit operations that would promote prudent borrowing and prevent crises from occurring. As in other situations, a pence of prevention may be worth a pound of cure.

APPENDIX

In this appendix[23] we explicitly solve for the bank's desired stock of loans to country 1. We show how the demand will vary with respect to the contract rate, the default premium, and the perceived covariance between the expected returns on the loan to country 1 and the rest of the portfolio. All symbols are defined in the text.

The bank's objective is to maximize expected profits subject to the constraint that the risk that the value of the bank's assets fall below some specified minimum not exceed γ. This is equivalent to solving the Lagrangian expression

$$\underset{L_1,V}{\text{Max}}\ G(L_1, V) = L_1(r_1 - i) + L_2(r_2 - i) + [\gamma[L_1(r_1 - i) + L_2(r_2 - i) - M]^2\sigma_p^2].$$

The first-order conditions for an optimum are:

$$(5.1) \qquad \frac{\partial G}{\partial L_1} = (r_1 - i) + 2V[\gamma[E(A) - M](r_1 - i) - (L_1\sigma_1^2 + L_2\sigma_{12})] \geq 0$$

$$(5.2) \qquad \frac{\partial G}{\partial V} = \gamma[E(A) - M]^2 - \sigma_p^2 \geq 0$$

when the risk constraint is binding and $L_1 > 0$, $V > 0$, and the first-order conditions (5.1) and (5.2) are equalities. The risk constraint can be solved for the change in demand for L_1 with respect to a change in the contract rate.

$$L_1(r_1 - i) + L_2(r_2 - i) - M = \frac{(L_1^2\sigma_1^2 + L_2^2\sigma_2^2 + 2L_1L_2\sigma_1\sigma_2\rho_{12})^{1/2}}{\gamma^{1/2}}.$$

By definition

$$r_1 = (1 - p_1)R_1 \quad \text{and} \quad \sigma_1^2 = R_1^2p_1(1 - p_1).$$

Substituting for r_1 we get:

$$(5.3) \qquad L_1((1 - p_1)R_1 - i) + L_2(r_2 - i) - M = \frac{(L_1^2\sigma_1^2 + L_2^2\sigma_2^2 + 2L_1L_2\sigma_1\sigma_2\rho_{12})^{1/2}}{\gamma^{1/2}}$$

$$\frac{\partial L_1}{\partial R_1}[(1 - p_1)R_1 - i] + (1 - p_1)L_1 = \frac{(2L_1\sigma_1^2 + 2L_2\,\sigma_1\sigma_2\rho_{12})}{2\gamma^{1/2}\sigma_p}\frac{\partial L_1}{\partial R_1}.$$

Simplifying we obtain

$$(5.4) \qquad \frac{\partial L_1}{\partial R_1} = \frac{(1 - p_1)L_1}{\left[\dfrac{\sigma_1^2L_1 + \sigma_1\sigma_2\rho_{12}L_2}{\gamma^{1/2}\sigma_p} - (r_1 - i)\right]}.$$

The numerator will be positive so long as the probability of default is less than 1. The sign of the denominator can be established by noting that when $r_1 - i > 0$ and $V > 0$, the expression in brackets in (5.1) must be negative. Thus:

$$\frac{\gamma\sigma_p(r_1 - i)}{\gamma^{1/2}} < (L_1\sigma_1^2 + L_2\sigma_{12})$$

and

$$\frac{\sigma_1^2L_1 + \sigma_1\sigma_2\rho_{12}L_2}{\gamma^{1/2}\sigma_p} > r_1 - i$$

where $\sigma_{12} = \sigma_1\sigma_2\rho_{12}$. Consequently, the denominator of (5.4) is positive and $\dfrac{\partial L_1}{\partial R_1} > 0$.

To establish the impact of a change in the probability of default holding σ_2 and ρ_{12} constant, partially differentiate L_1 with respect to p_1 in (5.3).

$$\frac{\partial L}{\partial p_1}(r_1 - i) - R_1L_1 = \frac{2[\sigma_1^2L_1 + \sigma_1\sigma_2\rho_{12}L_2]}{2\gamma^{1/2}\sigma_{p_1}}\frac{\partial L_1}{\partial p_1} + \frac{[2L_1^2\sigma_1 + 2L_1L_2\sigma_2\rho_{12}]}{2\gamma^{1/2}\sigma_p}\frac{\partial \sigma_1}{\partial p_1}$$

$$\frac{\partial L_1}{\partial p_1}\left[(r_1 - i) - \left(\frac{\sigma_1^2 L_1 + \sigma_{12} L_2}{\gamma^{1/2}\sigma_p}\right)\right] = L_1\left[R_1 + \left(\frac{\sigma_1^2 L_1 + \sigma_{12} L_2}{\gamma^{1/2}\sigma_p\sigma_1}\right)\frac{\partial \sigma_1}{\partial p_1}\right]$$

$$(5.5) \qquad \frac{\partial L_1}{\partial p_1} = \frac{L_1\left[R_1 + \left(\frac{\sigma_1^2 L_1 + \sigma_{12} L_2}{\gamma^{1/2}\sigma_1\sigma_p}\right)\frac{\partial \sigma_1}{\partial p_1}\right]}{\left[(r_1 - i) - \frac{\sigma_1^2 L_1 + \sigma_{12} L_2}{\gamma^{1/2}\sigma_p}\right]}$$

$$\frac{\partial \sigma_1}{\partial p_1} = 1/2\,\frac{R_1[1 - 2p_1]}{[p_1(1 - p_1)]^{1/2}} > 0 \quad \text{so long as } p_1 < 0.5$$

$\sigma_{12} = \sigma_1\sigma_2\rho_{12}$ and thus $\sigma_{12} > 0$ so long as $\rho_{12} > 0$. If $p_1 < 0.5$ and $\rho_{12} > 0$, the numerator of (5.5) is positive. The denominator of (5.5) is negative since it is the negative of the denominator of (5.4). Thus, $\frac{\partial L_1}{\partial p_1} < 0$.

To ascertain the impact of a change in the correlation between the expected return on the loan to country 1 and the rest of the portfolio holding p_1 constant, partially differentiate L_1 with respect to ρ_{12} in (5.3).

$$\frac{\partial L_1}{\partial \rho_{12}}(r_1 - i) = \left(\frac{L_1\sigma_1^2 + L_2\sigma_{12}}{\gamma^{1/2}\sigma_p}\right)\frac{\partial L_1}{\partial \rho_{12}} + \frac{L_1 L_2\sigma_1\sigma_2}{\gamma^{1/2}\sigma_p}$$

$$\frac{\partial L_1}{\partial \rho_{12}} = \frac{(L_1 L_2\sigma_1\sigma_2/\gamma^{1/2}\sigma_p)}{\left[(r_1 - i) - \left(\frac{L_1\sigma_1^2 + L_2\sigma_{12}}{\gamma^{1/2}\sigma_p}\right)\right]}.$$

The numerator is positive and the denominator is negative, just as in (5.5). Thus, $\frac{\partial L_1}{\partial \rho_{12}} < 0$.

NOTES

1. The qualifier is appropriate because Kahn (1984) has recently developed a model in which imprudent borrowing can take place without imprudent lending. In Kahn's model, creditors correctly anticipate the probability of a default and charge an appropriate default premium. Because residents of the debtor country make their borrowing decisions independently, however, they do not properly take into account the deadweight costs imposed on the economy by a default.

2. For a detailed analysis of these dangers, see Guttentag and Herring (1983b).

3. U.S. bank claims on all developing countries were about 35 percent of the total at the end of 1981, and the share of U.S. banks in total bank claims on Mexico, Argentina, and Brazil was 38 percent, 34 percent, and 32 percent, respectively.

4. This approach to modeling the diversification decision was introduced by Roy (1952). For an application to bank decision making, see Blackwell (1976).

5. This return is calculated from the relationship $r = S \cdot A/E + i$ where r is the pretax rate of return to shareholders; S, the present value-equivalent spread (the contractual spread adjusted to reflect front-end fees and commitment fees); A/E, the asset-equity ratio; and i, the interbank rate. The pretax returns in the text are based on $S = 50$ or 100, $A/E = 20$, and $i = 0.10$.

6. Akerlof and Dickens (1982) have recently made an application of the concept of cognitive dissonance to economic decisions.

7. A recent International Monetary Fund (IMF) report (Brau et al., 1983, p. 5) notes, "Of the non-oil developing countries that either have restructured or were in the process of restructuring their bank debt between 1978 and the third quarter of 1983, all experienced a period of very rapid increase in international bank loans prior to the development of debt service difficulties." Although some of this increase in outstanding exposure was attributable to borrowers having drawn on previously established commitments, a considerable amount of the increase was from new, short-

term lending just before the crisis. The Country Exposure Lending Survey for U.S. banks indicates that, from December 1981 to June 1982 (the period just before the crisis erupted), interbank loans, which are usually not subject to prior commitments, increased to all of the major Latin American debtors. Moreover, commitments increased to Brazil (by 50 percent) and to Venezuela (by 5 percent), and declined only slightly to Mexico (−3 percent).

8. The recent efforts by the bank supervisory authorities, coordinated by the Bank for International Settlements, have substantially improved the historical information base regarding commercial bank indebtedness. The reporting delays, however, are still a critical problem. Thus, the recent IMF attempt to forecast bank lending is especially useful.

9. See Goodman (1981) for a statistical analysis which concluded that loans to developing countries presented substantial scope for diversification.

10. See Guttentag and Herring (1980) for an analysis of this risk. Note that the reliance on instruments denominated in dollars created a similar, though less serious, linkage.

11. The Act is very much like the Joint Memorandum which the three agencies submitted to Congress during the spring of 1983.

12. See Guttentag and Herring (1983c) for an analysis of the formulation of disclosure policy with an application to country exposures.

13. In preparing this section, we benefited from reading two unpublished papers by Donald Lessard (1982a, b).

14. For a discussion of how concern about moral hazard results in unduly short maturities on loans to developing countries, see Guttentag and Herring (1983a).

15. Investors will be indifferent to those characteristics of the loans in the pool that bear on risk only if the certificates issued against the pool carry full insurance by a completely credible insurer. For further discussion of this and other aspects of conduit operations, see Guttentag (1980 and 1982).

16. The Federal Home Loan Mortgage Corporation and other conduits have performed such transformations on residential mortgages with considerable success.

17. The optimum degree of instrument homogeneity in a given pool depends on a number of factors (such as the extent of pool insurance) which cannot be pursued here. The issue is discussed in Guttentag (1982).

18. The smaller are individual pools, the more important are guarantees in creating marketability.

19. In addition, several new instruments have evolved to enhance the marketability of medium-term claims on borrowers, such as floating-rate notes, revolving underwriting facility notes, and prime underwriting facility strips. These new instruments have generally not been available to most developing countries. For a recent review of these instruments, see Grant (1983).

20. This greater discipline on borrowers is not without potential cost. Markets may sometimes send *false* signals regarding a country's condition or prospects or (as suggested to us in correspondence by Gordon Smith) *biased* signals, in the sense that the market does not take account of the social value of additional lending to a country experiencing temporary difficulty. False signals should not be a problem because, in principle, a conduit with superior information can make additional profit by ignoring them. The appropriate remedy for biased signals is adequate line-of-credit arrangements.

21. Currently, the absence of mark-to-market accounting rules appears to be a serious impediment to sales of country loans. Banks are reluctant to sell some of their claims on a country at a discount because questions might be raised about the value of the remaining claims on their balance sheet. This provides a major incentive for swaps.

22. See Guttentag and Herring (1983d) for a proposal that would increase the effectiveness of the IMF in mobilizing financial support for stabilization programs, without requiring that the IMF use its own financial resources.

23. We are grateful to P. Vankudre for his assistance on the appendix.

REFERENCES

Akerlof, George, and William T. Dickens. 1982. "The economic consequences of cognitive dissonance." *American Economic Review* (June): 307–19.

Blackwell, Norman R. 1976. "An investigation of the theory of credit rationing." Ph.D. diss., University of Pennsylvania, Department of Finance.

Brau, E., and R. W. Williams, with P. M. Keller and M. Nowak. 1983. "Recent multilateral debt restructurings with official and bank creditors." *Occasional Paper 25*. Washington, D.C.: International Monetary Fund, December.

Brown, Christopher R. 1984. "Selling restructured sovereign debt." *International Financial Law Review* (March): 9.

Citicorp. 1981. *1981 Citicorp annual report*. New York.

Committee on Banking Regulations and Supervisory Practices. 1982. "Management of bank international lending: Country risk analysis and country exposure measurement and control." Basel, March. Processed.

Goodman, Laurie S. 1981. "Bank lending to non-OPEC LDCs: Are risks diversifiable?" Federal Reserve Bank of New York Quarterly Review (Summer): 10–20.

Grant, Charles. 1982. "A boom in brokering out loans." Euromoney (November): 37–41.

———. 1983. "The liquefaction of the Euromarkets." Euromoney (October): 132–42.

Group of Thirty. 1982. How bankers see the world financial market. A Survey by the Office of the Group of Thirty. New York.

Guttentag, Jack M. 1980. "The conventional passthrough market: Trickle or flood?" In Savings and loan asset management under deregulation. Proceedings of the Sixth Annual Conference of the Federal Home Loan Bank of San Francisco, December 8–9.

———. 1982. Mortgage passthroughs: Structure and policy. Washington, D.C.: Mortgage Insurance Companies of America, June.

Guttentag, Jack M., and Richard Herring. 1980. "Financial disorder and Eurocurrency markets." In Bank structure and competition. Federal Reserve Bank of Chicago, May 1–2.

———. 1983a. "What happens when countries cannot pay their bank loans? The renegotiation process." Journal of Comparative Business and Capital Market Law 5:209–31.

———. 1983b. "Uncertainty and insolvency exposure by international banks." Brookings Discussion Papers in International Economics no. 4. Washington, D.C. June.

———. 1983c. "Disclosure policy and international banking." Brookings Discussion Papers in International Economics no. 7. Washington, D.C. December.

———. 1984. "The current crisis in international lending." Studies in International Economics no. 2. Washington, D.C.: Brookings Institution.

Kahn, Robert B. 1984. "External borrowing and the commons nature of foreign exchange." Unpublished Working Paper. MIT, Department of Economics.

Lessard, Donald. 1982a. "Measures to increase the effectiveness of private international finance for developing countries." Working Paper. MIT, April.

———. 1982b. "Appropriate non-concessional industrial financing for developing countries." Working Paper for the First UNIDO Consultation Meeting on Industrial Financing, October.

Morgan Guaranty Trust Company. 1982. World Financial Markets (October).

Roy, A. D. 1952. "Safety first and the holding of assets." Econometrica 20, no. 3 (July): 431–49.

Tversky, Amos, and Daniel Kahneman. 1982. "Availability: A heuristic for judging frequency and probability." In Judgment under uncertainty: Heuristics and biases, edited by Daniel Kahneman, Paul Slovic, and Amos Tversky. Cambridge and New York: Cambridge University Press.

Wriston, Walter. 1982. "Banking against disaster." New York Times (September 14): A27.

6

Debt and the Efficiency and Stability of the International Financial System

Alexander K. Swoboda

Several analyses of the current debt problem have focused on the role played by a few key economic variables in restoring creditworthiness to currently distressed countries. In perhaps the best-known study, William Cline (1983) argues that, if oil prices remain stable, if real interest rates decline slightly, and if growth in the Organisation for Economic Co-operation and Development (OECD) countries reaches 3 percent a year on average for the period 1984–86, the debt problem will be basically manageable. The added proviso is that an adequate flow of financial resources to the developing countries be achieved over the same period. This type of analysis skirts almost entirely the fact that the international financial system may well have become significantly more fragile over the past twenty years, not so much because of the aggregate amount of debt extant or the magnitude of required capital flows, but because of the form the debt has taken and specific institutional changes in the international financial system.

The present chapter deals mainly with such long-run issues of capital market structure. Its central argument is that several features of the current system of resource transfer from lenders to borrowers, particularly to heavily indebted developing countries, have rendered the system increasingly unstable, inefficient, or both. Moreover, policies to stabilize the system in the short run may further increase inefficiency and work at the expense of stability and the proper transfer of resources in the long run.

The ultimate aim of this analysis is to contribute to a better understanding of the requirements for restoring efficiency and stability to the international financial system.

The argument proceeds in three main parts. The first summarizes the characteristics of the evolution of international lending to developing countries in the guise of a number of stylized facts that are most relevant to financial stability. This discussion is kept quite brief, as those facts are documented adequately elsewhere (see, for instance, Swoboda 1982, 1983; World Bank 1984; and International Monetary Fund 1983). The second section examines the problems and distortions, actual or potential, that are entailed by these developments. The third deals with prospects and policy implications; it focuses on how to achieve stability while restoring efficiency. Existing proposals for institutional change are reviewed in the light of this double criterion. An attempt is then made to delineate an appropriate institutional mix—that is, to delineate, in broad terms, the respective role of national governments, international institutions, and markets in achieving a stable international lending system.

The focus of the chapter is such that a number of important, and obviously related, issues cannot be examined. In particular, short shrift is given to the transition ("how-do-we-get-from-here-to-there") problem which is obviously crucial in practice. In addition, little is said about the required macroeconomic policy framework of either industrialized or developing countries. Moreover, issues relating to the optimum volume of borrowing and lending or to optimum debt management in macroeconomic terms are hardly mentioned.

The author has benefited greatly from comments by D. Bock, N. Hope, and C. Michalopoulos. He is also indebted to Gordon Smith for his useful editorial comments.

Table 6-1. Indicators of International Banking and Lending Growth
(average annual rates of growth)

Period	Eurocurrency: Total assets (1)	Eurocurrency: Claims on nonbanks (2)	Eurocurrency: Market net size (3)	Deposit banks: Foreign assets[a] (4)	Deposit banks: Foreign liabilities[a] (5)	World money[a] (6)
1966–80	29.4	35.4	28.4	28.4	27.2	11.5
1966–73	37.4	45.6	33.6	31.6	30.0	10.2
1973–80	21.9	25.8	23.4	25.2	24.4	12.9

Sources: Columns 1–3, BIS Annual Reports; columns 4–6, International Monetary Fund (IMF), International Financial Statistics.

a. Columns 4, 5, and 6 refer to IMF "world" aggregates (all countries).

STYLIZED FACTS

The growth of private, particularly bank, lending to developing countries is part of the general evolution of international financial markets in the postwar period. Banks have played a leading role in the expansion of international lending since well before the first oil shock (as table 6-1 documents). The share of bank relative to bond financing has increased substantially in international lending. Thus, the share of bond financing in net new bank and bond financing has declined from roughly 31 percent to roughly 19 percent from the three-year period 1975–77 to the three-year period 1978–80.[1]

The major role of private financial markets and banks in development finance is a more recent phenomenon. In 1973, some 38 percent of disbursed public, or publicly guaranteed, external debt of all developing countries was owed to private creditors; by 1982, that percentage had risen to 55 percent (see World Bank 1984 for the basis of these and the following figures). For major borrowers, the corresponding figures are 41 percent and 62 percent, respectively; for Latin America and the Caribbean, they are 58 percent and 77 percent. The share of financial market (increasingly bank) credits vis-à-vis supplier credits underwent a similar increase: from 65 percent to 91 percent for all developing countries over the same period. This increase in the share of private as compared with official credit, and in bank as contrasted to other private credit, took place in the context of a very rapid increase in the total outstanding debt of developing countries. Total medium- and long-term (MLT) debt of all developing countries grew at 21 percent a year on average from 1973 to 1980, at a 19 percent average annual rate from 1973 to 1983. The debt of a number of large borrowers (such as Mexico) grew even more rapidly.

A similar pattern emerges from an examination of flows. Table 6-2 shows the percentage share of official development assistance (ODA), direct investment, and commercial loans in oil-importing developing countries; the sum of these capital flows equals the current account minus the change in reserves plus short-term borrowing. Two features of table 6-2 are worth singling

Table 6-2. Composition of the Capital Inflows of Oil-Importing Developing Countries
(percent)

Capital inflow	Low income 1970	Low income 1980	Middle income 1970	Middle income 1980
ODA	81	86	21	20
Private direct investment	7	3	22	11
Commercial loans	12	11	57	69

Source: World Bank, World Development Report 1981 (New York: Oxford University Press, 1981).

out. First, the difference between low- and middle-income oil-importing countries is striking: ODA plays the predominant role for the first group, commercial loans for the second. In addition, total net capital flows in real terms increased by less than 60 percent for the first group but by more than 150 percent for the second over the ten-year period. Second, for the middle-income countries, the growth of commercial loans is at the expense of private direct investment.[2] However, a similar breakdown for 1982 and especially 1983 would show, were it available, a significant drop in the proportion of commercial loans, not because of a rise in ODA or direct investment, but because of the fall in bank lending to developing countries.

That fall is part of a general decrease in net resource transfers to the developing nations in the last two years. According to the 1983–84 edition of World Debt Tables, net transfers on MLT debt (disbursements minus principal repayments and interest) to all developing countries declined from $32.8 billion in 1978 to $24.8 billion in 1980. They rose to $30.4 billion in 1981, to decline abruptly to $6.6 billion in 1982, and precipitously to a net outward transfer of $11 billion in 1983. Thus, famine succeeded feast. It was not evenly spread, however. Hardest hit were the major borrowers (and, among them, especially the Latin American ones), who had already experienced a negative transfer of $6.6 billion in 1982 and for whom the net outward transfer was estimated at $21 billion for 1983. The situation of low-income Africa is also very difficult: net MLT transfers remain positive but have fallen by almost half from their very low 1981 level. Regional differences reflect, to some extent, the regional character of the debt problem. This may be an appropriate place to caution against overgeneralizations. For instance, doubtful bank loans tend to be concentrated in Latin America and Eastern Europe; a significant part of doubtful export credits are concentrated in Africa, which are predominantly the problem of export-financing agencies rather than of the banks.

So far, we have sketched three stylized facts that have characterized international lending: the increasing role of private credit in the balance of payments financing of middle-income developing countries; the declining share of direct investment and of bonds in that financing; and the recent decline in private (mainly bank) capital flows toward developing countries. The last decline is particularly abrupt for Latin American countries. This indicates that, although aggregate lending flows may be relatively stable (recently, however, these have also declined substantially), lending to individual countries or regions is much less stable when debt-servicing difficulties arise.

A fourth stylized fact characterizing international lending to developing countries is the increasing share of indebtedness that is being incurred by governments (or is subject to government guarantees) and, within the latter, the increasing share that is being incurred to financial institutions.[3] For all developing nations, the share of private nonguaranteed debt in total MLT debt decreased from 23 percent in 1973 to 19 percent in 1982. For Latin America and the Caribbean, the decline was from 37 percent to 27 percent. The decline will be accelerating as a result of 1983 reschedulings which have transformed private into public liabilities. The increasingly preponderant role of banks in MLT private lending to governments or under government guarantees is illustrated in table 6-3, which also strikingly illustrates the decline in bonds and suppliers' credits in government external finance of developing countries.

A fifth characteristic is the heavy exposure of banks and, perhaps, overconcentration of that exposure on a few countries, regions, and banks. This is difficult to document if only because "heavy" exposure and "overexposure" are subjective and relative concepts. As evidenced by debt to banks or financial markets relative to gross national product (GNP), a number of countries appear more heavily indebted than others; Venezuela, Mexico, and Argentina are examples. Furthermore, some large countries appear to be more indebted than some small ones, but this is far from a universal rule. There are also different patterns of concentration among banks in different industrial countries: the exposure to Latin America relative to Eastern Europe is much higher for U.S. banks than for European banks. Finally, large banks tend to be much more

Table 6-3. MLT Public Borrowing from Foreign Private Creditors (percent)

Public borrowing	1970	1976	1982
Debt outstanding at year end (billions of U.S. dollars)	15.8	71.1	229.0
Financial institutions	32	68	83
Variable interest rates	10	69	80
Fixed interest rates	90	31	20
Bonds	20	9	7
Suppliers' credits	42	20	9
Other	7	3	...

... Negligible.
Source: World Bank, World Debt Tables, 1983–84 Edition (Washington, D.C., 1984), p. xxiii.

exposed than smaller banks. For instance, the exposure of the nine largest U.S. banks to Eastern Europe and nonoil developing nations relative to capital was roughly 235 percent in 1982; that of all other banks roughly 99 percent (calculated from Cline 1982, table 5). The notion of overexposure and overconcentration also derives from the analogy with the limits on the proportion of capital that banks are allowed to lend to any single borrower—the 10 percent, or now 15 percent, rule applicable to U.S. banks. With three exceptions (out of a possible total of eighteen), exposure of the nine major U.S. banks to Brazil and Mexico, taken singly, exceeded 50 percent of capital at the end of 1982. In contrast to domestic lending, of course, exposure to individual borrowers in a foreign country should be aggregated when that country experiences debt-servicing difficulties.

Sixth, there are a number of institutional characteristics of lending to developing countries that are worth noting. Among these, the spread of the syndicated loan technique and of variable interest rate loans (see table 6-3) figure prominently. Together with a decrease in maturity and in the proportion of loans at concessional terms, rising interest rates have combined with floating-rate lending to exacerbate the liquidity problems of borrowing countries. Finally, "involuntary" lending has become the rule rather than the exception. To quote from the World Debt Tables, "only about half the new publicized Eurocredits in the first three quarters of 1983 represented 'spontaneous' lending, as more than $13 billion (47.5 percent) went to 10 developing countries as part of their debt restructurings" (World Bank 1984, xi–xiii). One might add that a number of other credits were extended, essentially in the hope of avoiding restructurings.

PROBLEMS AND DISTORTIONS IN THE CURRENT SYSTEM

The stylized facts sketched in the preceding section, together with current international debt and financial difficulties, partly reflect general problems and distortions to which international lending, notably to developing countries, is subject. Some of the problems could arise in a domestic context also; others only where sovereign lending is involved. At a very general level, the problems arise from two main sources: uncertainty and imperfect information, on the one hand; an inadequate institutional, regulatory, and legal framework, on the other hand.[4] These problems are so closely interconnected that any classification scheme is, of necessity, somewhat arbitrary. One method is to begin with the economics of lending under certainty and perfect competition, then proceed to the problems that arise when uncertainty and imperfect information are introduced, and finally determine what additional features are introduced by international rather than domestic lending. Such is the procedure followed in this section. It also identifies a number of "problems" to which capital and loan markets—and, in particular, international lending to developing countries—are subject. Although the approach is generally enumerative and analytical, an attempt will be made to suggest the relevance of each problem to current international debt difficulties and to the design of a more stable and efficient international financial system.

Consider, then, the determination of the volume of loans and of the lending rate in a competitive world of lenders and borrowers under certainty. Each borrower would face a horizontal supply curve of loans up to a maximum amount, beyond which, given the known present value of all his future income streams, he would become insolvent. He would borrow (in each period) that amount which maximizes utility intertemporally; on the production side, this implies borrowing enough to equate the marginal product of capital to the marginal cost of capital (the borrowing rate plus the rate of depreciation of capital). The rate of interest adjusts to clear the credit market in the aggregate. The international analogue is a world in which capital flows from where its return is low to where it is high, to equate the marginal product of capital worldwide, thus maximizing world potential output in the process. One crucial assumption of the model, beyond certainty, is that defaults never occur; that is, that borrowers never exercise the option to default. Implicitly, the cost of default is assumed to be always higher than its benefits. This may be a tenable assumption in the domestic context, where assets are at least partly recoverable and where the legal framework prohibits debt repudiation by a solvent borrower; it is less tenable in an international context.

If endogenous default (repudiation) is set aside for the moment, matters become more complex when uncertainty—and risk—are introduced. Yet these would be relatively trivial concerns in a world of perfect information (the objective joint probability distributions of returns on existing projects are known and identified with specific borrowers) and in the absence of risk-changing (producing) behavior on the part of borrowers. In that environment, interest differentials among projects or borrowers are attributable to risk premiums that correctly price unsystematic, country- or borrower-specific risk. Actual credit markets, however, are not characterized by perfect information; nor are borrowers unable to affect the riskiness of the projects in which they engage. Asymmetric information raises, in the literature's jargon, problems of adverse selection—or the "lemon" problem. Risk-modifying behavior is at the root of the moral hazard, or incentive problem.

Adverse Selection

Consider a world in which borrowers can be classified into groups, each undertaking projects of different riskiness. These groups are observationally indistinguishable from the lenders' point of view, although they know of the existence of the various risk groups. The lenders' expected return will be a function of both the interest rate they charge and of the probability that all or part of the loan will be repaid, in other words, of the loan's riskiness. The problem is that, as the rate of interest is raised, members of the lower-risk project groups may be discouraged from borrowing, leaving the lender (banks) with a loan portfolio of high risk and lower expected return. The interest rate acts as a screening device, and it is often rational for the lender to charge a lower interest rate and to ration credit because of the adverse selection effects of a higher interest rate.

A number of devices, available to both borrowers and lenders, can mitigate the effects of adverse selection. In order to identify riskiness of individual borrowers, lenders can try to find screening devices other than interest rates or collateral requirements, for instance, information gathering through credit-rating agencies or departments. High-quality borrowers can attempt to signal their creditworthiness to lenders by building a reputation for prompt payment, for example. For the signal to be believable, higher-quality borrowers must be able to send it at lower cost to themselves than lower-quality borrowers could.[5] International lending is likely to be replete with adverse selection problems. Credit rating as a screening device is unreliable;

signaling is particularly difficult. Credit rationing and discrimination against low-risk, high-quality borrowers are likely. However, these problems would probably not be much more severe in the international than in the domestic context were it not for some of the specific international problems identified below (see, in particular, the points relating to endogenous default decisions, sovereign versus commercial lending, and domestic versus international credit markets).

Moral Hazard

Moral hazard occurs when risk-modifying behavior is possible in an uncertain world. In the present context, moral hazard creates incentives for borrowers to behave in a perverse way when interest rates rise, specifically, by undertaking riskier projects. In the words of Stiglitz and Weiss (1981, p. 393), "Higher interest rates induce firms to undertake projects with lower probabilities of success but higher payoffs when successful." As a result, the expected return to the lender may well decrease. One response by lenders is to monitor the behavior of borrowers and to specify the actions that the borrower may undertake ex ante. Perfect monitoring, however, is impossible in a world of costly and imperfect information; partial monitoring is achieved through such devices as bond covenants, strictly specified loan contracts, and lender representation on boards of directors.

Borrowers might precommit themselves to specific projects. Sachs (1983) has shown that such precommitment can be advantageous to the borrower as it allows lenders to impose less strict credit ceilings or lower the loan rates, or both, as compared with the situation where monitoring is not possible. The problem, as always, is that there are, in a multiperiod world, incentives for the borrower to renege on the commitment after the loan has been granted. Effective and credible precommitments are not easy to design; signaling is again relevant. Inefficiencies arise when monitoring is not perfect. In the insurance context, it becomes impossible to price insurance ex ante as a function of future loss-prevention activity. Partial remedies would entail making the insured bear part of the loss through "deductible" clauses or through "coinsurance," or pricing insurance according to actual past loss-prevention activities (Hirshleifer and Riley, 1979).

The credit market counterpart is that low- and high-risk borrowers are charged the same rate, which penalizes the low-risk borrowers and subsidizes "imprudent" behavior. Partial solutions would be to require higher equity participation by borrowers or to give ex post concessions on loan terms that reward prudent behavior. Moral hazard problems in domestic lending are, of course, magnified in an international context. Monitoring is very difficult; credible precommitment even more so. Sovereign borrowing by governments or their agencies adds yet another dimension to the difficulties of monitoring borrower behavior. Although individual loans may be tied nominally to specific projects, loan proceeds are in practice often assimilated into general government revenue. Loans that are destined to finance specific projects may have low monetary returns, even if their social returns are high. The servicing of those loans is therefore predicated on future general revenues, that is, on the government's ability to tax. Furthermore, any attempt at monitoring will meet with accusations of political interference. In this context, banks' insistence that countries submit to International Monetary Fund (IMF) programs can be as an indirect attempt at monitoring in the form of conditionality. In a similar (albeit exceptional) way, the more favorable conditions allowed on debt renewal after Mexico's implementation of a stabilization program can be interpreted as pricing loans (insurance) in accordance with actual prudent behavior (actual loss-prevention behavior).

Endogenous Default Decision

We have not yet considered the possibility that a borrower, although solvent, may decide to default. So far, when defaults occurred, they were the result of bankruptcy brought about by realizations of project returns that fell below mean expected returns. It is true that the presence of adverse selection and moral hazard may result in higher bankruptcy rates than would otherwise be the case; however, the decision to default has not been treated as endogenous in preceding sections. Following Eaton and Gersovitz (1981), one might call repudiation a borrower's decision to default on debt even though he is solvent. It is only natural that prominence should have been given to the decision to repudiate debt as an endogenous economic decision in the context of international rather than domestic lending. In domestic credit markets, debt repudiation is prohibited by law, and the assets of the borrower are recoverable by the lender (although at a cost). In other words, it is fairly safe to assume that, for domestic borrowers, the cost of repudiation (though not necessarily of bankruptcy) exceeds its benefit. This assumption cannot be made as a matter of course about international lending, even if costs have, with very few exceptions, exceeded benefits so far on the basis of revealed preference.

The possibility of endogenous default introduces an additional dimension of moral hazard in international lending. A growing literature seeks to determine the costs of, and incentives toward, default when repudiation is possible. In a broad sense, the benefit to the repudiator is the present value of future interest and amortization payments; the costs include attachment of those assets that are recoverable, exclusion from borrowing in the future, disruption of international trade relations, not to mention loss of foreign political goodwill and of reputation. How severe those costs are in terms of future loss of utility from consumption will depend partly on the characteristics of the borrowing country's economy. This type of analysis may lead to empirically based models for explaining and predicting repudiations, or, at the least, to debt reschedulings (Saunders 1983). Its relevance here is different—the reaction of the lender is of the essence. Prudent lenders will ration credit in order to keep the borrower's benefits from repudiation below its expected costs. This may be inefficient, compared with the situation where the borrower can renounce the default option, because loan volume will be below, or loan costs above (or both), what they could otherwise have been. Moreover, adverse selection may well set in. The end result may again be incorrect pricing of risk and discrimination against high-quality borrowers, that is, overlending to the wrong borrowers and underlending to the right ones. As Sachs (1983) has shown, it would be desirable for borrowers in those circumstances to precommit their policies in a way that reduces the likelihood of repudiation or, if this were not possible, to prefer higher penalties for debt repudiation as a means of reassuring lenders and thus easing credit conditions.

Although borrowers may not actually default, they may threaten to default to obtain better terms on new loans or concessions on old ones, for instance, in a rescheduling negotiation. The higher the fraction of a lender's capital at stake in loans to any single borrower, the higher that borrower's bargaining power should he threaten to default. Hence, here is an incentive for borrowers to concentrate their indebtedness on one or a few lenders (see Swoboda 1982 and de Grauwe and Fratianni 1984). In terms of bargaining power, concentrated exposure is to the advantage of borrowers, diversification to that of lenders. The problem is that, when exposure is concentrated, reschedulings may take place when none is really needed; when exposure is diversified, however, it is difficult to arrange for reschedulings on concessional terms, even when needed or when in the collective interests of both borrowers and lenders (more about this appears below).

Collective Action

One response to problems of adverse selection, moral hazard, and endogenous default is collective action on the part of lenders, in this case, the banks. Sachs (1983) views the syndication technique as one instance of collective action that helps diversify risk among lenders. To de Grauwe and Fratianni (1984), collective action by banks, either through syndications or other means, can be analyzed in terms of the theory of clubs. Collective action may help the monitoring and screening of borrowers by spreading information costs or allowing for information pooling (the creation of formal or informal credit-rating agencies at the international level). It also can raise the cost of default to borrowers by giving credibility to sanctions that are collective rather than individual. This contributes to reducing both moral hazard problems and the frequency of defaults. In addition, banks acting collectively may be able to exercise some degree of conditionality on borrowers, while they are unlikely to be able to do so when acting individually.

Collective action, however, requires that the cohesion of the club be maintained. Symptoms of failure in this regard are the so-called free-rider and panic problems. The free-rider problem manifests itself in periods of both feast and famine. It is particularly acute when club participants are of unequal size. Suppose that one bank incurs costs in gathering information on a borrower and subsequently decides to lend to that borrower on the basis of that information. Other banks can then follow the leader at low cost. In the words of de Grauwe and Fratianni (1984, p. 19), "the actions of the 'free riding' banks have devalued the claims of the first bank on the borrowing country." Free riding can be viewed here as a type of informational externality; its consequence is that an informational equilibrium may not exist or that it involve socially insufficient information gathering (Hirshleifer and Riley 1979). The problem in this form is unlikely to be very serious in practice. Leading banks can and do internalize the benefits from information gathering by tying this activity to that of lead manager of the loan, with front-end fees serving as compensation for their leading activities. It is true that the smaller banks have tended to follow the larger ones, but the origins and nature of this form of free riding, I will argue further below, are probably not to be sought in the externality at stake here.

Free riding is a more serious problem once loans go sour. The incentives to leave the club are strong for banks that do not have a large stake (relative to their capital) in a syndicated loan when the issue of rescheduling or new lending to a troubled borrower comes up.[6] They will attempt to shift the higher risk or lower return on new or rescheduled loans to those banks that have a larger stake, forcing the latter to increase their exposure and the riskiness of their portfolios. In this respect, cross-default clauses are a double-edged sword. On the one hand, they reinforce the incentive to keep the club together; on the other hand, by threatening to call a default, lenders that have a minor interest can force the other members to allow them to leave the club and to repurchase their membership fee on terms advantageous to the exiting members. One consequence is that rescheduling at concessional terms to avoid a default may be difficult to achieve, lest the free-riding banks leave the syndicate.

Another collective action problem, Sachs (1983) argues, is that, although syndicated lending may help spread risk, that very spreading of risk may lead to panics in the event of temporary liquidity difficulties encountered by a borrowing country. The essence of the argument goes as follows. Suppose that there are many lenders. The risk premium required by each bank is a function of the ratio of loans to capital. A temporary liquidity problem arises that requires the borrower to incur additional debt if he is to avoid default. If an individual lender believes other banks will not lend new money, the risk premium required by the single bank could be large enough to force the country into default, and the bank will then not lend. In other words, while it may be rational and efficient for the banks to lend the required amount collectively, it may not be rational for a single bank to do so. The expectation that other banks may stop lending becomes self-fulfilling and a panic ensues. The result of that panic is to turn a temporary liquidity problem into a solvency crisis.

The international financial system has responded in a variety of ways to these problems of collective action. There has been a shortening of maturities, larger banks have taken on a policing role and a larger share of syndicated loans, and the IMF has acted as an organizing agent for the banks.[7] "Involuntary lending" is one name for the last two practices. These methods, however, constitute emergency measures to cope with crisis situations rather than optimal long-run responses. They lead to further concentration of exposure, on the one hand, and to serious moral hazard problems where the IMF is concerned, on the other hand. The optimal response might instead be precommitment by club members to actions such as reschedulings contingent on future states of the world. Such precommitments are a way of avoiding free riding on the up side as well as on the down side by raising the expected cost of club membership.

Contagion Effects

Casual observation indicates that debt problems tend to spread across both borrowers and lenders. Banks tend to contract lending simultaneously and to resume in unison. Moreover, the debt difficulties of one country seem to contaminate the creditworthiness of its neighbors. One example is the spreading of the 1982 Mexican crisis to affect the borrowing power of most of its Latin American neighbors. A model of contagion in crisis situations has been provided by Guttentag and Herring (1982). The basic idea is that the risk premium that banks require over their cost of funds (inclusive of a "normal" markup) when lending to developing countries is a function of two types of risks. The first is the systematic risk that attaches to sovereign lending in general (the risk that derives from the possibility of a catastrophe or generalized default); the second, the risk of default, or debt-servicing delay, specific to loans to a particular country. In ordinary times, only the second of these two types of risk is perceived to exist. In times of crisis, systematic risk increases abruptly, risk premiums to all sovereign borrowers rise, and the range of spreads narrows. A change in the perception of the likelihood of catastrophe may thus result in a general liquidity crisis, where credit rationing and withdrawal from lending by banks may turn illiquid borrowers into insolvent ones.

The actual importance of contagion effects is difficult to appraise. Such effects might have been present in two cases: the period following the 1974 bank failures (Herstatt and Franklin National, in particular) and the period following the Mexican crisis of 1982. However, the general rise in risk premiums remained relatively moderate, and the range of spreads did not uniformly narrow. On the contrary, spreads among groups of banks widened in the first case (tiering in the interbank market); and the second case seemed to represent a regional, Latin American, rather than general, case of contagion. One might thus interpret at least the first of these two cases as a rational and differentiated market reaction to overcommitment of certain groups of banks in the interbank market. This is not to deny that contagion effects may represent an important potential danger in international financial markets.

Sovereign versus Commercial Lending

The literature on developing-country debt has tended to focus on two related aspects of the difference between sovereign and commercial lending. First, when repayment difficulties arise in sovereign lending, recoverability of the borrower's current assets by the lender is extremely difficult and becomes almost impossible when the debtor is a government or one of its agencies. Irrecoverability of assets is partly a consequence of the absence of a legal and enforcement system that would be common to both lender and borrower. This contributes to making the default or repudiation decision endogenous, as discussed above. An additional element is thus added to usual commercial, and transfer, risk.[8] Second, as Kharas (1981a, b), among others, has emphasized, borrowing by a government implies that debt-servicing capacity will depend not only on the country's growth prospects but also on the government's ability and willingness to tax and to generate a fiscal surplus. Willingness alone is, of course, not enough to guarantee ability.

Three other aspects of sovereign borrowing that are relevant to the stability and efficiency of international lending and that may not have received sufficient attention in the literature may be mentioned here. First, ownership of the assets ultimately financed by the government's borrowing may not be vested in the government's hands, exacerbating the recoverability problem not only for foreign lenders but also for the borrowing government.

Second, private borrowing in developing nations is often put at a disadvantage relative to government, or government guaranteed, borrowing. For instance, private borrowing often is pushed to the end of the queue when servicing difficulties arise; it thus carries a higher transfer risk than government borrowing. This discrimination against private borrowing may contribute to the prominence of syndicated lending to governments over the issue of private debt in different forms (such as bond finance).[9] Since it is unlikely that government investment decisions and project selection will obey as strict profitability criteria as will those of private investment, the riskiness of sovereign lending may increase with the proportion of borrowing that is done by governments and their agencies or borrowing that bears government guarantees.[10]

A third aspect is that sovereign borrowing by governments makes it all but impossible to tie loans to specific projects. This has two major undesirable consequences. First, debt-servicing difficulties tend to affect all loans to a country simultaneously. Failure of one project can lead to debt-servicing problems in all other projects since there is no way of making an individual loan bear the risk on an individual project.[11] A second, and related, consequence is that it becomes very difficult simultaneously to recognize actual losses on past loans and to engage in new lending. In other words, new loans have to bear the burden of capital losses on past projects financed by old loans. When a firm experiences difficulties in domestic lending, the firm can obtain new loans at reasonable terms after a restructuring has shared past losses between the creditors and the debtor. Furthermore, loans that are not extended to the firm in difficulty can be transferred to firms that have more worthwhile projects. In international sovereign lending, once a country's debt-servicing problems lead to a write-down of its liabilities in the books of lending banks, new loans are unlikely to be forthcoming to any entity or project except at significantly harder terms. The new projects, which may offer a perfectly acceptable risk-return tradeoff at normal interest rates, may well not be worthwhile at these harder terms.

Regulation, Expected Bailouts, and Moral Hazard

Much of what precedes, and a good deal of the literature, deals with general credit market issues and abstracts from special characteristics of banks as both lenders and borrowers. Banks are regulated financial intermediaries whose fate is intimately linked to that of the domestic and international monetary systems. Regulation of banks in fact derives from recognition of their special role in the monetary system. In particular, the social costs of bank failures are usually considered to be higher than the private costs to bank owners or depositors. Two ways of dealing with this perceived externality are most usual: the provision of deposit insurance, which limits the costs of bank failure to depositors and limits the likelihood of generalized runs on the banks, and the provision of lender-of-last-resort facilities by national monetary authorities to prevent the liquidity or solvency problems of single banks from spreading to the banking and monetary system as a whole. The price banks have to pay for these services is submission to regulations lest the insurance thus provided lead them to engage in imprudent behavior—the moral hazard problem once more.

The arguments in this section are that the special character of banks as regulated and "insured" intermediaries goes a long way toward explaining some of the characteristics of recent international lending; that this character is at the root of a number of serious distortions; and that it has contributed to the instability of international lending flows, notably to developing countries. Deposit insurance and lender-of-last-resort services give rise to the perception that banks, at least large banks, will not be allowed to fail.[12]

My guess is that, at least for a good part of the 1970s and again very recently, there has been such a perception that banks, or their largest debtors, would not be allowed to fail.[13] As a consequence, depositors have been willing to lend to banks, and investors have been willing to acquire bank stocks even though they themselves would not have been willing to acquire the assets held by banks directly. Banks, in turn, have been willing to acquire assets at rates of return lower than the riskiness of these assets (or of their contribution to the risk of the banks' overall portfolio) would have justified, had the implicit guarantee mentioned above not been available.

One reason for this hypothesis is that international bank lending has kept growing until recently in spite of the increase in perceived country risk, a narrowing of spreads, and diminishing capital/asset or capital/deposit ratios.[14] Why, if spreads are inadequate, as banks often claim, have they not increased their margins or refused to lend? In addition, why have banks not issued additional capital or refused to engage in unprofitable activities? On the basis of observed behavior, neither the market nor the industry believed until recently that banking was in serious trouble—or, if it was, that it would not be rescued.

The perception that banks will not be allowed to fail has several distortive effects. By enabling banks to obtain funds at lower cost than they otherwise could and to invest in assets that are riskier than those their stockholders would choose to hold directly, it confers a distorted advantage to bank over direct finance and it biases international bank portfolios toward higher risk (and return). In addition, large lenders and borrowers have the advantage at the expense of smaller ones. One may hesitate to let a large entity fail, but afford to let a small one do so (compare New York versus Yonkers, or Chrysler versus Studebaker). An untoward consequence of implicit guarantees to large borrowers and lenders is that they create incentives for brinkmanship. Banks can raise the probability of a bailout by concentrating their lending on one large borrower (who then cannot be allowed to fail since the banks' stake is too high) or by following one large bank that has a large stake in one country. Borrowers have a similar incentive to incur very large liabilities to one or a few banks which cannot be allowed to fail.

Thus, the expectation of bailouts partly explains four features of recent international lending and the distortions they entail. First, it helps explain why bank loans rather than other forms of finance have come to play such an important role in development financing. This biases the pattern of risk sharing among borrowers and lenders away from equity participation by lenders. Inefficient pricing of risk is one consequence.

Second, it contributes to the herd instinct that motivates small banks to follow large ones. There is free riding here, not because the informational advantages of large banks can be appropriated by small banks, but because the latter can appropriate the guarantee extended to large banks.

Third, to the extent that there is a belief that large final borrowers tend to be rescued while smaller ones may not, smaller borrowers, who may be more creditworthy than the large ones, may be discriminated against. The cost is a lower return to capital and higher risk; world potential output diminishes.

Fourth, inappropriate pricing of "intrinsic" risk results in profit margins for the banks that are too small to build up adequate provisions should implicit or explicit guarantees be lowered. If the market perceptions of implicit guarantees change, an abrupt withdrawal from loans to heavily indebted countries ensues. Matters are not helped if the authorities guarantee that large banks will not be allowed to fail even if default by the borrowing countries occurs. In that case, there will be a strong incentive for the smaller banks, who have lost their guarantee, to withdraw. A policy of leaving the cost of lender-of-last-resort facilities somewhat undefined is often espoused by monetary authorities lest moral hazard set in. Such a policy is clearly counterproductive insofar as it tends to create instability in international lending. Changing expectations as to the likelihood of bailouts may thus contribute to a feast and famine syndrome in lending to developing countries.

In sum, implicit guarantees distort resource allocation basically because the authorities provide insurance at too low a price (see Kareken 1977). Furthermore, the fact that the guarantees are implicit creates uncertainty as to their credibility and tends to be destabilizing for capital flows. Thus, the conferring of implicit guarantees may have led to (or reinforced) overlending and overexposure to a number of countries; emerging doubts as to the reliability of the guarantees may have prompted abrupt withdrawals. The policy issue this argument raises is straightforward. Removing implicit or explicit guarantees to banks requires a perception that (even large) banks could conceivably be allowed to fail. The dilemma is how to implement such a policy without actually precipitating important bank failures, without destabilizing the international financial system as a whole, and without preventing capital from flowing efficiently to developing nations.

Liquidity, Solvency, and Loss Sharing

It is often argued that liquidity problems call for responses different from those for solvency problems. Although distinctions can be drawn on the basis of whether a borrower's net worth remains positive or becomes negative, these distinctions are difficult to make in practice—and can be questionable even in theory. Assume for the moment that the distinction can be made.[16] Illiquidity would call for temporary loans to tide the borrower over; refinancing or a rescheduling at market terms is in order.

Insolvency requires that the burden of losses be shared between borrowers and lenders. Outright repudiation is one way of sharing the loss; the lenders bear all the loss in the present unless they can recover some of the borrower's assets; the borrower bears the cost of sanctions in the future. Note that sanctions play no useful role in sharing actual losses; they only add some future losses, often to lenders as well as to the borrower. The purpose of sanctions is, of course, different: it is to increase the expected cost of future defaults by the same or other borrowers and thus to diminish their likelihood. At the other extreme, a solvency problem can be dealt with, or rather papered over in the present, by a rescheduling at market or even penalty rates. The effect is to make the borrower appear to bear the cost. In fact, the lender bears it; he has only postponed the day of reckoning to the future. The intermediate and sensible way of dealing with a solvency problem is for lender and borrower to share the losses so that both would be better off than if default were actually to occur. One way of achieving this result is a rescheduling at concessional terms.

Unfortunately, the present institutional framework biases the actual response toward one of the extreme solutions rather than toward the more efficient middle course for several reasons.[17]

First, a borrower's difficulties may well be due to a mixture of liquidity and solvency problems (themselves due to incorrect macroeconomic policies). This is particularly true for a sovereign borrower where insolvency of some projects creates liquidity problems for solvent ones or vice versa. Moreover, net worth today depends on projected future income growth, which is not only difficult to estimate, but also depends on the policy measures undertaken by the borrower—yet another instance of moral hazard. In general, the problem is to estimate what portion of the sovereign debt of major borrowers is to be considered "insolvent." Estimates, mostly intuitive, differ sharply. Thus, Cline (1983) argues that the problem is essentially one of illiquidity, provided his most likely scenario of world macroeconomic development over the next few years materializes. In contrast, Sjaastad (1983) and de Grauwe and Fratianni (1984) are examples of the more pessimistic view that a substantial portion of outstanding developing-country debt is bad debt.[18] (Intuitively, I would side with this second strand of opinion, while recognizing that the question, as posed, is essentially unanswerable. It is hard to believe that any one of the large borrowers would not ultimately be solvent and able to reimburse its present debt and accrued interest were it to devote all its resources from here to eternity to the task. But in that case the incentive to repudiate might become overwhelming.)

There are incentives for both borrowers and lenders to treat debt-servicing difficulties as if they arose from liquidity rather than solvency problems. For the lenders, recognizing that there is a solvency problem entails writing off old loans which, if they can only be rescheduled, can be kept on the balance sheet at book value. The absence of gradual write-off provisions or of a secondary market that would allow market-pricing of the risk of (partial) default on old loans does not help. It also makes the pricing of new loans inefficient and provides an incentive for the borrowers to aquiesce in rescheduling at market or penalty rates. Banks that carry loans at book value (even though they know these loans are basically nonperforming) may still be willing to extend new loans to borrowers to postpone default. They could not do so, under most present supervisory rules, if old loans were classified as nonperforming. This situation provides borrowers with the incentive to continue pretending their problem is one of liquidity since doing otherwise would shut them entirely out of new loans.

One basic problem is, again, that there is no good way of distinguishing between old and new loans or of identifying various loans to sovereign borrowers with a specific project. In addition, disputes as to the true nature of the problem relate directly to who bears the burden of the losses that have been incurred. It is in the interest of lending countries to identify the problem as one of illiquidity of the borrower. In that case, the taxpayer in the indebted country should (and will) pay. If the problem is identified as one of (partial) insolvency, the costs will have to be shared by the lending countries. This gives rise to a new bargaining situation, which ultimately will decide whether the depositors, the stockholders, and the managers of the banks will pay or whether it will be the lending country's taxpayers.

Domestic versus International Credit Markets

Most, if not all, of the problems mentioned above are potentially or actually present, in one guise or another, in domestic as well as in international credit markets. In domestic markets, however, procedures have gradually evolved over time to deal with their impact on efficiency, stability, and equity. Credit-rating agencies help screen borrowers, covenants serve to monitor disclosure behavior, legal criteria distinguish between ordinary and fraudulent bankruptcy, safeguards against panics exist, and the fiscal system helps redistribute the cost of capital losses in an equitable fashion. Few enforceable procedures for sharing gains and losses—be they legal, market, or political—are available or customary in international lending in an age when gunboat diplomacy is somewhat out of fashion. The problems, however, have to be coped with and have been resolved in a variety of ways. The solutions in the international context, I have argued, have often been less than optimal. Before a discussion of the prerequisites of a more stable and efficient international financial system, capable of dealing appropriately with the various issues listed so far, it might be useful to attempt a rough estimate of the relative importance of these problems.

Relative Importance of Structural Problems

A quantitative appraisal cannot be attempted here and would be, in any event, extremely difficult if only because of the speculative nature of the arguments presented above. They offer both competing and complementary hypotheses about trends in behavior, and their empirical implications are sometimes observationally equivalent. Hence, any appraisal will be highly personal. The question is which problems are most relevant to the proper functioning of international capital markets in the long run. In other words, if the overall debt/wealth ratio is sustainable, what are the most important problems that need to be solved if an optimal structure of the debt is to be achieved in the long run and if reemergence of current problems is to be avoided?

With this perspective, the most important problems concern inefficiencies introduced by:

- The threat of endogenous default and the difficulties of renouncing this option credibly; the consequences are a higher risk premium than necessary, credit rationing, and concentration of exposure
- The nature of sovereign borrowing, by governments, their agencies, or under government guarantees, which entails the crowding out of private borrowers and makes it difficult to separate risk on new and old loans and to tie lending or investment to specific projects
- Moral hazard in relation to the behavior of lenders, particularly intermediaries; the untoward consequences here are biases against smaller borrowers and lending by nonbanks, and toward overexposure by banks
- The absence of appropriate risk-sharing devices among borrowers, lenders, and others which tends to remove the process of risk transfers and sharing from the market and makes it exceedingly difficult to recognize bad loans.

In other words, there are several ways in which the problems of the current system have distorted the instruments used to transfer claims internationally and the behavior of lenders and intermediaries, of borrowers, and of the authorities.

With respect to instruments, there are a number of serious problems. First, several factors have made for an exaggerated share of bank lending in total capital flows to developing countries. Second, bank loans do not allow for risk sharing except when default occurs or is threatened. Third, the absence of a well-developed secondary market for bank loans makes their pricing difficult. Fourth, markets for other instruments, especially those incorporating more of an equity element, have not developed to a considerable extent. The reasons for these trends are to be sought in the regulatory framework, in problems of the enforceability and the definition of property rights internationally, in the preponderance of government borrowing, and in the behavior of borrowing governments.

The behavior of lenders and intermediaries has, again, been influenced by incentives for bank finance rather than for other forms. Moreover, distortions in the pricing of risk have encouraged imprudent lending, overexposure, and a resistance to recognizing past losses. Borrowers, in turn, have had some incentives to behave imprudently. Overexposure has reinforced their bargaining position, and the absence of a well-developed secondary market in their debt has removed one important incentive for good macroeconomic behavior on their part. Furthermore, the attitude of borrowers toward direct investment and borrowing by their own private sector has often been basically counterproductive to the efficient functioning of the world capital market.

Achieving long-run stability and efficiency in international lending requires that these distortions be removed.

ACHIEVING LONG-RUN STABILITY AND EFFICIENCY IN INTERNATIONAL LENDING

The rash of debt-servicing difficulties of 1982–83 did not result in any major default, no large bank collapsed, nor did panic lead to the collapse of the international financial system. The incipient crisis was handled through a combination of emergency measures by central banks, international institutions, and commercial banks, not to mention violent downward adjustment in imports and growth by the borrowers. Reschedulings and heavy reliance on involuntary or coerced lending were the two main measures used to avoid a collapse of gross lending to the developing countries and the defaults this would have triggered. The short-run success of the operation, however, carries with it the danger of complacency. Crisis management is not an adequate response to the longer-run structural problems of the international financial system.

On the contrary, the measures that were adopted may help embed instability and inefficiency into the system. Coerced lending is a prime example; it tends to increase the overexposure of the banks that are already committed and to discourage new lenders. It also is a potentially unstable solution should the incentives to run outweigh the strength of coercion.

If long-run stability and efficiency in international credit markets are to be achieved, some prerequisites must be met. The concern of this section is to delineate these requirements in the light of the preceding analysis. Looking beyond the short run, I give, with one or two exceptions, short shrift to transition problems that may be all-important in practice. The analysis is carried out on the premise that doing nothing is not desirable, since the problems identified above would only become worse. The starting point is to ask what should be achieved. I then suggest some means for implementing these goals and proceed to evaluate various proposals for reform in the light of the analysis. Finally, some suggestions are made for improving the structure of markets in sovereign debt, and the division of responsibilities among different institutions is considered briefly.

Prerequisites for Efficient International Lending

The ultimate function of international lending is to maximize potential world output and growth by bringing about an efficient allocation of resources. To achieve this aim, the international financial system must, first, allow capital to flow from where its return is low to where it is high. But it must do more than that in an uncertain world where information is less than perfect. The following four criteria appear particularly important:

- Risks should be priced properly. In particular, individual risks should be dissociated from each other, priced individually, and actively traded (efficiently transferable) among as large a number of agents of different ilk and degree of risk aversion as possible, in order to maximize gains from risk diversification.
- The social and private cost of risk should be equated, which requires the correction of "externalities" rooted in indivisibilities and in informational and institutional imperfections, notably imperfections inducing moral hazard.
- A stable and clear regulatory framework that provides definitions of the rights and obligations of borrowers, lenders, and intermediaries is required. The role of such a framework is to foster efficiency, in particular, by reducing the cost of information processing, and to help resolve equity issues (especially by specifying accepted procedures for distributing capital gains and losses). In addition, regulations should not magnify instability when shocks occur, as interest ceilings or inadequate provisioning and write-off rules tend to do.
- Finally, comparative advantage should be used as a guide to the proper functional distribution of roles among institutions such as governments, supervisory authorities, international organizations, and markets.

These principles are very broad; nevertheless, they are particularly relevant in several areas.

The first of these is the need to break down indivisibilities in risk that arise from sovereign borrowing.[19] The second and related need is to devise a mechanism that allows flexibility in the pricing and trading of risks. Creation of a secondary market for loans may be the best approach to this problem. Third, that part of risk that cannot be diversified away should be borne (and shared) by the borrower and lender, not shifted to some third party. This is particularly important if overlending and overborrowing are to be avoided. In other words, it is important to put risk back where it belongs. Market incentives are the best way to achieve this aim; they should not be distorted by expected bailouts of borrowers, lenders, or commercial banks. In general, market solutions to what are essentially market problems should be encouraged.

A further implication is that, where losses have occurred, they should be recognized, and some agreed mechanism for sharing them should be found. In particular, the only choice should not be between total or zero loss; partial losses should be recognized for what they are and not be considered irretrievable for international lending. Difficulties in recognizing partial losses arise both from the form of the dominant financing instrument of developing countries, bank loans, and from the absence of alternative subordinated instruments. The double consequences of excessive reliance on bank loans are rigid (book) valuation of old loans and a flight from new loans whenever the perceived value of the old loans falls significantly below book value. A secondary market would help value old loans more correctly. At the same time, a procedure for rescheduling old loans at concessional terms should be found. Again, this is difficult, if only because the procedure should not encourage partial defaults when none is needed.

A solution to these problems is difficult enough in a basically sound and stable financial system. It is particularly difficult when, as is now the case, there has been an accumulation of "bad" debt and overexposure as a result of previous distortions. The phasing-in problem cannot be ignored, lest the medicine kill the patient along with the disease.

Before more specific recommendations are developed, it may be well to review very briefly the main proposals that have been made to deal with the "debt crisis."

Proposals for Reform: Marginal and Radical

Proposals to deal with the debt problem range from marginal changes in regulation to comprehensive plans for assistance to both debtors and the banks that include the creation of new lending or subsidizing agencies. The proposals are usually related to specific problems, and whether they are of the marginal or radical variety depends in large measure on whether their proponents consider the problem to be one of temporary illiquidity or of fundamental insolvency. Most of the proposals are directed at specific, current problems rather than at structural reform.

Three concerns appear to dominate the proposals. The first is to reduce the overexposure of banks and to safeguard the stability of the international financial (or banking) system. Proposals with this objective range from relatively minor changes in the regulatory framework, to strengthening the provision of lender-of-last resort facilities, to the taking over of the banks' "bad" assets, at varying degrees of discount, by official national or international bodies. The second concern is to ensure a continued flow of lending to the developing countries. Here suggestions range from the provision of insurance on new loans by existing or new bodies to maintaining the present system of involuntary lending. The latter is to be achieved by reinforcing policing procedures on free riders (by the banks, governments, or the IMF), by *avoiding* any reform that may threaten the book value of existing bank loans, and by carrying reschedulings at or above market rates of interest. The third concern is to provide debt service relief to borrowers suffering from long-run structural problems. Depending on the specific proposal, the debt relief is to be provided by banks, central bank governments, and existing or new international institutions and usually involves the creation of new financial instruments to be exchanged for existing ones.

This piecemeal approach has a potential drawback that is immediately apparent: proposals for solving one of the three problems are likely to make the other two worse. Indeed, this is one of the main criticisms that has been leveled at various plans by Guttentag and Herring (1983b) and Cline (1983). Since Cline presents a fairly exhaustive listing and summary of proposed measures, only a few comments need be offered here.

Proposals to safeguard stability. Proposals for safeguarding the stability of the international banking system, short of outright subsidies, fall into two main categories: regulation by national monetary or supervisory authorities and provision of lender-of-last-resort facilities. The former has received particular attention in the United States where discussion has focused on the proposals contained in the Joint Memorandum of the Federal Bank Regulatory Agencies. The proposed regulation attempts to avoid overexposure of banks and to avoid imprudent lending. More specifically, it includes accounting rules that determine the appropriate amount of provisioning and valuation of assets according to a new classification system (debt service impaired, reservable, loss), rules covering disclosure of country exposure, and measures relating required capital/asset ratios to country exposure concentration. The Joint Memorandum rejects country limits as an additional measure, although such limits are advocated by others.[20]

Official proposals for bank regulation have been criticized on the ground that they do not contain a mechanism to maintain new lending to developing countries. This is somewhat unfair since bank regulation is not a panacea and since provisioning and valuation rules contained in the proposals are mild precisely for fear of forcing too sharp a downward revision in the book value of loans to countries in debt service difficulty. Few current loans should fall in the reservable category; thus, there should be no regulatory obstacle to the extension of new loans (the continuation of involuntary lending). In fact, probably the real defect of the proposed legislation is that it does little to correct existing overexposure of banks or to prevent such overexposure from occurring in the future.

The second regulatory safeguard that has been advocated is provision of lender-of-last-resort facilities at an international level. There is some concern that national facilities may not be adequate to cover international banks and their activities. There are two problems: existing agreements among monetary authorities (essentially the Basle Concordats) leave loopholes and do not resolve all conflicts of jurisdiction; and such agreements concern supervisory and not lenders-of-last-resort functions. Although progress is being made on the first of these matters, there is little likelihood that it will be on the second. Lenders of last resort will remain national for the moment. The greatest contribution that could be made here is a clear statement by individual monetary authorities of what they are willing to do, under what circumstances, at what cost, and for whom. The "policy" of maintaining uncertainty on the available extent of lender-of-last-resort facilities, supposedly to reduce moral hazard and imprudent behavior, is destabilizing, inefficient, and ineffective. It is destabilizing since uncertainty as to the provision of the facilities encourages the runs that the policy is designed to avoid; it is inefficient because it adds to risk with no clear benefit and raises information costs; it is ineffective since it may not reduce imprudent behavior if the banks believe that the authorities will provide the facility in the end. Reducing imprudent behavior requires a clear statement of its cost at the outset.[21]

Proposals to ensure continued lending. A second category of proposals is designed to deal with the continuation of new lending to the developing countries. Those that fall short of outright subsidies have not been numerous. For the most part, they boil down to maintaining the present system of involuntary lending, in the hope that lending will again become voluntary when the worst of the present situation is over. Rescheduling at or above market rates has been advocated to give an incentive to banks not to cut their losses and run, while lengthening the maturity structure of developing-country debt. Another suggestion is to encourage collective action by the banks in their own self-interest, perhaps with the help of the newly created Institute of International Finance. Most of the proposals envisage a greater role for the IMF in the banks' new lending. The IMF's involvement can take several forms: sharing of new lending among the banks involved in a rescheduling; making IMF programs conditional on new bank lending; more simply, letting the banks ride the coattails of IMF conditionality, a substitute for monitoring by the banks themselves; or sharing information with the banks and even acting as a rating agency. For obvious reasons, these are uncomfortable roles for the IMF to play, and the IMF should refuse to play them except in short-run emergencies. Another proposal is for the IMF to borrow resources in the market to finance its adjustment programs. The double problem here is that such lending may then substitute for lending that would have been taking place through the market, and the IMF's own credit rating may become damaged in the process.

Other proposals to maintain new lending imply a substantial subsidy element. One popular form is the issuance of guarantees or the provision of insurance to private lenders by various bodies, in particular export credit agencies. This is basically a form of debt relief (although applied to new lending rather than to old loans).

Debt relief. As Guttentag and Herring (1983b) have pointed out, debt relief plans can be classified according to who receives assistance (the banks, debtors, or both), who provides the aid (central banks, the IMF, the World Bank, or some new entity), and the type of financial instrument being created (debt, equity, and so on). For instance, the Kenen (and, in part, the Rohatyn) plan offers assistance to the banks (by enabling them to liquefy frozen assets albeit at a discount) but mainly to the debtors (who are forgiven some interest and get longer maturities). The provider of the assistance is a new institution, the International Debt Discount Corporation, that is, the taxpayer; and the new instrument is a long-term bond issued by the corporation. In contrast, the Aliber proposal has the U.S. government providing relief to the banks through purchases of bank-subordinated debt with warrants attached. Most of the plans have the agency providing the debt relief issue long-term bonds. The proposal by Bailey is original in this respect; it proposes the issuance of Exchange Participation Notes that are a claim on a fraction of the borrowing country's export receipts and thus are a hybrid instrument with a significant "equity" content.

All these plans can and have been criticized (see chapter 3 by Krugman in this volume). Thus, Cline (1983) has charged that they mostly prejudge the illiquidity versus insolvency issue in favor of the latter and thus contribute to turning good debt into bad. Most important to Cline, these plans "would eliminate the incentive for new involuntary lending" by transferring old loans to some agency and would thus precipitate the very crisis they are designed to avoid. In addition, he argues, they are likely to have a dire effect on bank capital, they provide incentives for debtors to disrupt debt service to obtain relief, and they unrealistically require a very substantial commitment of public capital. That last point is also a criticism made by Guttentag and Herring (1983b), who likewise share Cline's concern about the plans' effect on the supply of new loans. In addition, they worry that interest forgiveness constitutes a form of foreign aid unrelated to efficiency, equity, or national security interests. Fundamentally, they argue, these plans do little to reduce the excessive concentration of exposure among banks and may even worsen it. Furthermore, they do not impose discipline on lenders and borrowers; they may worsen either depending on whether the debtor or creditor is the recipient of the relief.

These critics have their own plan. They are poles apart but each offers the advantage of consistency. Cline's is a "balanced strategy" based on the conviction that the debt problem is basically one of illiquidity and thus can be coped with in the long run when the macroeconomic and trade environments will have improved. Continuation of involuntary lending is of the essence in the short run while marginal regulatory and other improvements are being put in place. Contingency planning should, however, take place for cases in which specific countries prove to be the victim of more structural, long-run problems. But the approach should be applied case by case.

Guttentag and Herring are less sanguine of long-term prospects and propose a comprehensive plan capable of providing some relief and of cushioning bank balance sheets if no improvement in the situation of debtors occurs and large losses have to be taken. The plan also attempts to keep money flowing to developing countries in the short run and pursues two long-run structural objectives: (1) to discourage imprudent borrowing and lending by providing a continual control mechanism that is in place before a crisis occurs; and (2) to reduce, not aggravate, concentrations of country risk exposure relative to bank capital.

The Guttentag-Herring plan is a fairly detailed six-part proposal, and only its main features can be summarized here. The first three parts are designed, respectively, to insure new lending, to enable servicing of old loans, and to cushion the impact of debt-servicing difficulties on bank balance sheets. They are, according to the authors, aimed at short-run problems in contrast to their next three proposals which aim at long-run reform. The goal of the latter proposals is mainly to reduce bank overexposure and to force discipline on borrowers and lenders. The first suggestion is that, under certain circumstances and with IMF approval, debtor countries be allowed to issue new marketable consol certificates with prior claim; this last provision should enable them to obtain new loans. Second, old government debt could also be transformed into consol certificates, but without prior claim, at specified terms and under specific debt-servicing difficulties. Third, an administrative rule could be proposed concerning the book value of old debt in the banks' balance sheet: for every month that interest is delinquent, the value of the loan would be written down by 1 percent. This should cushion the impact of bad debt on the banks' balance sheet. The fourth could require that all cross-border loans be periodically marked to market. This would constrain imprudent behavior of lenders by recognizing explicitly the riskiness of loans and of borrowers and by providing "tangible and public evidence of the market's lack of confidence in the borrowing country's policies." A mark-to-market rule needs market values, and the fifth proposal is to create a secondary market in country loans. Guttentag and Herring propose the creation of a "conduit" organization that would make a market in country loans, as the Federal Home Loan Mortgage Corporation makes a market in conventional home mortgages (see their discussion in chapter 5). Finally, country exposure data on individual banks should be disclosed to enable bank creditors and shareholders to monitor more effectively the country risks assumed by banks.

The detail of Guttentag and Herring's plan (1983b) can be debated and criticized, especially with respect to the prior claim of new debt or the trigger mechanisms envisaged. The spirit of the plan, however, is correct, as I indicate in the preceding section. The emphasis on letting borrowers and lenders assume risk through mark-to-market rules and the creation of a secondary market are particularly welcome. In brief, the proposals are in the same spirit as some of the more modest (and general) suggestions that follow.

Some Suggestions for Improving the Structure of Markets in Sovereign Debt

With few exceptions (notably Guttentag and Herring 1983b), the proposals reviewed in the preceding section put emphasis on the solution of short-run problems without paying much attention to their consequences for the structure of international financial markets in the long term. The main requirements for a sounder long-run structure were reviewed above. The suggestions that follow are proposed in that spirit. They should be considered as broad strategic targets rather than as specific proposals. They also should be considered as supplements to, rather than substitutes for, the more sensible short-run measures that have been proposed. They fall into six categories.

Encouraging markets in a diversity of instruments. At the moment, there exist very few instruments for the international financing of either the governments or firms of developing countries. This is partly a consequence of the predominance of bank loans, partly a consequence of the preponderant role of government and country (transfer) risk in international lending risk. I have argued above that the most unfortunate result is that risks in individual projects, firms, or industries of developing countries cannot be traded among wealth owners, at least internationally.

Therefore, the suggestion is that markets in a diversity of instruments with different risk characteristics be actively encouraged. The gains could be quite substantial. The general case for international risk transfers through instruments other than debt has been made by Lessard (1982), who also provides some rough estimates of gains from transferring risks associated with copper-price fluctuations for countries specializing in that commodity's production (see

Lessard 1977). Fostering markets in new instruments of course requires that the characteristics of the instruments be specified in such terms as covenants, prior claims, and sinking funds and that governments in the borrowing countries establish a reputation for fair treatment of such instruments. Some equity component in international flows of capital is highly desirable. Whether this is achieved by the issue of convertible bonds, indexation clauses that tie interest payments to the price of a specific commodity, or outright equity issues is not of prime importance. I would trust capital markets to invent such instruments if the legal and political framework is supportive. It may be that multilateral organizations could play a useful role in buying such instruments and possibly making a market in them.

One may well ask why such new instruments have not been introduced and markets for them been developed so far (although there recently have been some beginnings in that direction). One very partial answer is the bias toward bank loans for reasons noted above. Perhaps a more important response is that government authorities in developing countries have often been hostile to various forms of private direct investment and have generally mistrusted market mechanisms. Prerequisites for the development of such markets are, therefore, more positive policies on the part of borrowing countries.

Encouraging secondary markets in debt instruments. In general, it would seem important to have active markets in the debt instruments of developing countries, both because this would allow risk transfers and because markets are needed to establish a price for risk and a more economic basis for asset valuation than original book value (see chapter 5). In the long run at least, an active secondary market in the country loans of banks should be encouraged. This could have several advantages.

First, the overexposure of some of the large banks cannot be reduced without contracting new lending flows unless another party is able and willing to acquire the assets of the large banks. Even the reshuffling of bank loans on specific countries among the large banks could improve diversification and reduce the extent of overexposure.[22] To allow for the possibility of portfolio reallocation is all the more important when the single borrower's limit of 15 percent of capital suddenly bites as the result of a government taking over private debt obligations.

There is a second advantage to an active secondary market in the country loans of banks. Fluctuations in the price of sovereign loans fulfill at least three functions. They allow asset values to reflect the market's estimate of the risk return tradeoff on the assets. At the moment, country loans tend to be worth all or nothing to the banks. If interest remains current (and no default is thus called), market value would be a better indicator of the asset's worth to the holder. Another function of fluctuations in loan prices is to induce prudent behavior on the part of lenders. A bank will be far less inclined to lend imprudently if it has to carry the loans at market value (on the assumption that a mark-to-market rule is applied to bank balance sheets). This knowledge automatically removes at least part of the implicit guarantees which, it is argued above, have such a negative influence on the behavior of banks. (I agree with Guttentag and Herring that fuller disclosure is important here because it enables the banks' creditors and equity holders to monitor bank behavior.)

Finally, fluctuations in the price of existing bank loans (or other securities) serve to induce prudent behavior on the part of borrowers. Banks have been complaining that they cannot exercise conditionality on sovereign borrowers. Although an individual bank cannot do so, the market can. A fall in the price of claims on a particular country immediately raises the cost of new borrowing. This is a powerful inducement to the country to service its debt regularly and promptly. It is also an incentive to adopt policies that have a favorable impact on its borrowing costs and to offer credible precommitments on such policies. Furthermore, a country could buy back its own debt if it proved advantageous and thus could send signals of its capacity to maintain creditworthiness.[23]

Although market valuation of country loans is a useful long-run reform, its introduction in the short run may pose two main problems. If a large discount on the debt of major borrowers should appear, bank balance sheets may be so badly affected that they pose solvency problems for the banks. A device for cushioning the impact on bank balance sheets, such as the rule of 1 percent a month suggested by Guttentag and Herring (1983b), would be required. Second, the current portfolio position of banks is probably one of severe disequilibrium. One indication is that much of the lending is "involuntary." The lumping together of all loans to a sovereign debtor in the presence of the 15 percent rule is, as mentioned above, another. Thus, there is the danger that the excess supply in the loans of particular countries would drive their price down brutally in the short run should constraints on portfolio allocations be suddenly removed. To avoid such an effect, a rule or agreement might be instituted to limit the percentage of their country loans that individual banks can sell per period. That rule could be gradually phased out.[24]

There is a related but more general issue that is raised by Mario Simonsen (see chapter 4) who argues that market prices for the loans of countries facing debt-servicing problems would be biased signals for individual lending. The markets would not internalize the "public good" aspect of loans to a country in trouble and would thus discount the country's obligations too heavily. This may indeed be a serious problem once countries have gotten into trouble, and it does reinforce the importance of solving the transition issue. After transition problems are solved, however, it is not the role of markets to internalize the "public good" aspect of lending referred to above. Rather, it should be up to public national or international agencies to provide incentives for further loans to countries in trouble if they deem that this is in the public good. Furthermore, pricing of loans in secondary markets does promote prudent behavior on the part of borrowing countries and provides the incentives needed to stay, or get, out of trouble. It thus removes the moral hazard element involved in ex post rescue operations or forced lending, undertaken for the "public good."

Debt relief. In some cases, debt relief may need to be given to debtor countries, both to avoid total default on old loans and to allow renewed productive investment and growth. There is no good suggestion for solving this problem that would not create some moral hazard. The least harmful solution might be to give such relief within the framework of rescheduling negotiations and on a case-by-case basis. This is the forum where the two parties to the loan contract meet directly, and it is the "imprudent" lenders that should bear the cost of the relief, at least in the first instance.

The process of rescheduling may well be improved in a number of ways. Among these, the inclusion of debt coming due over several years has received much attention recently; this is important if longer-run consolidation of debt is to be achieved. In addition, the transformation of at least some of the debt into "equity" type instruments is worth encouraging since it would also contribute to the process of risk transfer advocated above.

Reducing moral hazard produced by lenders' governments. The production or perpetuation of moral hazard through the provision of insurance at too low a price should be avoided. We have already seen what this implies in terms of provision of lender-of-last-resort facilities. I have also argued that such facilities should be made available to small and large banks on an equal basis in order to avoid inequities and instabilities.

Moral hazard is produced by authorities in a variety of other ways. A relevant example is the encouragement of bank lending for foreign policy reasons. This creates a moral claim for the lenders which they may attempt to extend to other categories of loans. It would be far better to use explicit cost incentives or guarantees on specific loans that are deemed in the national interest. The problem is to distinguish between old guarantees and new. It may well be that, in a number of cases, old guarantees, whether explicit or implicit, should be honored on equity grounds even if new ones are denied.

IMF not a lender of last resort. A similar point applies to the IMF role in recent involuntary lending. Moral suasion by the IMF may well have been (and in some cases may still be) the only, or least damaging, way of avoiding a crisis brought about by panic among the lenders. It is not the role of the IMF, however, to act as a lender of last resort to the banks. Nor should it produce moral hazard by inducing the banks to believe they have a claim on its good offices, especially when, as might frequently have been the case, the IMF rendered a service to the banks for which it could have charged them a fee. The service was to act as an organizer of the banks' collective action in their own best interest.

The proper division of functions among banks, markets, and authorities. This brings me to the last point: what is the proper division of functions among the banks, markets, and authorities to ensure stability of the international financial system and the efficient transfer of capital from surplus to deficit regions?[25] In this context, there have been proposals for the IMF to supplement (or cooperate with) banks in the recycling process, for banks and governments to cooperate in creating various safety net designs, for the creation of some supranational supervisory authority (at least for the close harmonization of supervisory tasks), and for the creation of a lender of last resort at the international level. I remain highly skeptical of such proposals. What appears both more practical and more desirable is to ensure a clear and appropriate division of tasks among these bodies.

The problem is reminiscent of the assignment problem in international macroeconomics: there are a number of targets that need to be matched with an equal number of instruments in an efficient and stabilizing manner. The targets here are a speed of international adjustment compatible with noninflationary growth of the world economy, an efficient long-run transfer of resources from surplus to deficit areas and from rich to poor, and a sound international banking and financial system.

The IMF seems to be in the best position to contribute to an adequate adjustment mechanism by restricting its dealings to member governments and monetary authorities and by judiciously exercising conditionality. Accomplishing this in a noninflationary fashion requires monetary restraint on the part of major countries in a world in which international reserves play a diminished role with exchange rate flexibility. These reserves are neither centrally created nor related to an outside asset such as gold but are, instead, in large portion composed of major national currencies. Such monetary restraint should also help insure that banks will refrain from inappropriate short-term lending for balance of payments purposes. The transfer of longer-term resources from surplus to deficit regions can be left safely to private markets, including banks, in response to economic incentives, as long as the latter are not distorted for political or other reasons. The transfer of resources from rich to poor on concessional terms should be the explicit purview of governments and aid agencies.

Insuring the soundness of the international financial and banking system while avoiding a confidence crisis is perhaps the most difficult task. In principle, a clear regulatory framework that puts the risk clearly where it belongs, namely, with the banks, would by itself provide sufficient incentives for soundness in international lending. Some suggestions to this effect have been made above. But what if a crisis occurred nonetheless?

This is where a lender of last resort may be useful. However, it would be unwise to think that such a lender could be found at an international level. Nor is such an international lender of last resort necessarily needed. National lenders of last resort may suffice—and in any event will have to. For this to be the case, jurisdictional problems will have to be solved, national central banks whose financial intermediaries have large foreign exchange liability positions will have to keep adequate foreign exchange reserves, and penalties for having to borrow at the lender of last resort will have to be sufficiently high not to encourage imprudent behavior on the part of the private sector.

Summary of proposals. These suggestions, or proposals, can be summarized briefly. The first suggestion is that markets in instruments other than straight debt (bank loans or bonds) be actively encouraged. The second is that secondary markets for straight debt, in particular bank loans, be fostered. Third, debt relief should be given where needed; this is most appropriately done within the context of reschedulings and on a case-by-case basis. Fourth, clear rules on available lender-of-last-resort facilities should be stated and national governments should refrain from offering implicit guarantees to their financial institutions. Fifth, involuntary lending should be phased out as rapidly as possible and the IMF role should be confined to dealing with its member governments. Sixth, an appropriate division of labor among markets, governments, and international institutions would leave the markets to allocate private capital among countries. It would also put the risk of capital transactions on lenders and borrowers and should emphasize that concessional lending or aid is a direct and urgent task of governments and multilateral agencies created for the purpose.

These are necessary conditions for a properly functioning international capital market that would transfer resources efficiently from surplus to deficit regions, notably toward the developing countries. These conditions, however, are by no means sufficient. To belabor the obvious, a number of other conditions are just as important, if not more so. They include, first, stable macroeconomic policies on the part of industrial countries; in this context, control of the aggregate budget deficits of rich countries is needed if only to avoid crowding out the current account deficits of poorer ones. Second, there must be sensible macro- and microeconomic policies on the part of the developing countries to maximize potential growth, to make for productive investment of borrowed resources, and to create a climate favorable to the transfer of such resources. Finally, the reduction of protectionism and the encouragement of liberal trade policies are essential if debtors are to be able to earn foreign exchange and resources are to be transferred in real terms among countries.

NOTES

1. For a more detailed discussion of the internationalization and growth of banking in the postwar period, see Swoboda (1982).

2. In 1970, net capital inflows were larger than the current account deficit allowing for reserve accumulation, whereas, in 1980, the deficit was financed by a large reserve reduction in addition to capital inflows.

3. This, of course, reflects the increased role played by banks in capital flows to developing nations.

4. The issues analyzed in this section have been the object of a growing literature in recent times. For an excellent survey of the general issues involved, see Hirshleifer and Riley (1979). For a well-known application to domestic credit markets, see Stiglitz and Weiss (1981). A useful survey of some of the international issues involved is Saunders (1983). An excellent synthetic analysis is contained in Sachs (1983). Important but more specific contributions are Eaton and Gersovitz (1981a, b) and Guttentag and Herring (1982). The paragraphs that follow draw freely on that literature; my approach differs in a number of respects, however, notably in the emphasis on the role of implicit guarantees and the extension of moral hazard issues to intermediaries (the banks), in addition to original lenders and borrowers. For a useful survey of the debt capacity literature, see McDonald (1982); for some historical background material, see Sachs (1982).

5. One standard example is the role of education as a signaling device in labor markets. If more productive workers can acquire education at lower cost than unproductive ones, education can serve as a valid signaling-screening device in worker selection.

6. The larger banks will, of course, try to raise the cost of leaving to the smaller ones through various devices, including use of correspondent relationships, recourse to IMF goading, and so on. An alternative would be to reduce the incentive to leave by extracting better terms from borrowers.

7. De Grauwe and Fratianni (1984) argue that the first of these responses is counterproductive, the other two

productive. Even the last two may be less than optimal, however. The recent creation of the Institute of International Finance can also be seen as a response of the banks to the collective action problem.

8. We will not discuss transfer risk specifically here.

9. One complaint often heard is that bondholders have had very little to say in reschedulings and that other claimants have unfairly taken precedence in negotiations.

10. There may also be a tendency for governments to overborrow, for at least two reasons. First, governments may well tend to overestimate the social return of their investment projects. Second, as Kharas (1981a) and Sachs (1983) show, when tax rates are constrained, it is optimal for a country not to invest until the marginal product of capital equals the marginal cost of capital. If the country nevertheless brings these two rates into equality, it overborrows relative to the optimum.

11. Gordon Smith has pointed out to me that failure of a project or group of projects would matter in this context only if its failure seriously affected the government's ability to tax and effectuate transfers, as might happen with the failure of heavy investments in, for example, the export of oil or copper. It is also true, however, that anything that affects the government's ability to tax and effectuate transfers may lead to problems of debt service payments on projects that are perfectly sound and profitable on their own.

12. An earlier development of this argument can be found in Swoboda (1982). I have since found the riskier portfolio point made briefly by John Kareken (1977, p. 507) in a comment on a paper by Robert Solomon. The riskier portfolios are, in a sense, not riskier to the bank because of the implicit guarantees it receives from monetary authorities.

13. The remainder of this paragraph and the next two are based on Swoboda (1983).

14. The decrease in spreads is partly misleading since it is compensated by various front-end fees. Furthermore, floating-rate loans have taken part of the interest risk out of bank financing. But the counterpart is an increase in default risk in a period of rising real interest rates, and some interest rate risk remains since loan rates are adjusted only at discrete intervals.

15. This is not to argue that all of the increase in bank lending to developing nations is to be attributed to the role of implicit guarantees. Ample liquidity in industrial countries, falling rates of return on domestic loans, and increased competition are just as important.

16. Of course, whether a country does experience such problems depends in good measure on its past, especially its macroeconomic policies. Whether it is insolvent depends on its future policies. This issue is ignored here but will be taken up briefly below.

17. Some of the reasons have already been mentioned earlier. See, in particular, the section "Sovereign versus Commercial Lending."

18. To discuss the proportion of outstanding developing-country debt that is "bad" or "doubtful" in general terms can be highly misleading. Distinctions should at least be drawn between debt owed to banks or to the IMF or other multilateral agencies, and debt guaranteed or insured by export-financing agencies. The discussion here concerns only the first category, which is probably most important, at least for the Latin American debtor countries. In contrast, a large portion of the debt of African countries guaranteed or insured by export-financing agencies can be considered as bad, as can some developing-country debt to the IMF.

19. This can never be accomplished fully, since transfer risk is always potentially present in sovereign borrowing. Better micro- and macroeconomic policies by borrowing governments and a higher share of "equity" financing, however, should help.

20. For discussion and contrasting appraisals of the Joint Memorandum, see Cline (1983) and Guttentag and Herring (1983b).

21. For a recent analysis of the lender-of-last-resort function in an international context that makes most of these points clearly, see Guttentag and Herring (1983a). For a survey and analysis of supervisory practices, see Dale (1982).

22. Some reshuffling is already taking place and a secondary market—so far very thin and specialized—is beginning to emerge.

23. An added advantage to pricing loans in the secondary market is that it disciplines the regulators by providing them with a more "objective" yardstick for the valuation of bank assets.

24. Again, one may ask why more of a secondary market in bank loans has not emerged spontaneously. The answer is partly that it is beginning to emerge, but also that both the form that bank loans have taken so far and the incentives against marking the value of loans to market have hindered its appearance.

25. The remainder of this subsection is taken almost verbatim from Swoboda (1983).

REFERENCES

Cline, William R. 1983. International debt and the stability of the world economy. Policy Analyses in International Economics. Washington, D.C.: Institute for International Economics.

Dale, Richard. 1982. Bank supervision around the world. New York: Group of Thirty.

Eaton, Jonathan, and Mark Gersovitz. 1981a. Poor-country borrowing in private financial markets and the repudiation issue. Princeton Studies in International Finance no. 47, June. Princeton N.J.: International Finance Section, Princeton Unviersity.

———. 1981b. "Debt with potential repudiation: Theoretical and empirical analysis." Review of Economic Studies 48 (April).

de Grauwe, Paul, and Michele Fratianni. 1984. "The political economy of international lending." International Economics Research Paper no. 42. Catholic University of Louvain. January. Processed.

Guttentag, John M., and Richard J. Herring. 1982. "Credit rationing and financial disorder." University of Pennsylvania, Wharton School Working Paper, December. Processed.

———. 1983a. The lender-of-last-resort function in an international context. Princeton Essays in International Finance no. 151, May. Princeton, N.J.: International Finance Section, Princeton University.

———. 1983b. "The current crisis in international banking." Brookings Discussion Papers in International Economics no. 8, December. Washington, D.C.: Brookings Institution. Processed.

Hirshleifer, Jack, and John C. Riley. 1979. "The analytics of uncertainty and information—An expository survey." Journal of Economic Literature 17 (December).

International Monetary Fund. 1983. "Recent multilateral debt restructurings with official and bank creditors." Occasional Paper 25 (December). Washington, D.C.

Kareken, John H. 1977. "Comment on Robert Solomon, 'A perspective on the debt of developing countries.'" Brookings Papers on Economic Activity, 2.

Kharas, Homi. 1981a. "Constrained optimal borrowing by less developed countries." Domestic Finance Study no. 75. Washington, D.C.: World Bank, Development Policy Staff Public and Private Finance Division, August. Processed.

———. 1981b. "On structural change and debt servicing capacity." Domestic Finance Study no. 74. Washington, D.C.: World Bank, Development Policy Staff, Public and Private Finance Division, August. Processed.

Lessard, Donald R. 1977. "Risk efficient external financing strategies for commodity producing countries." Cambridge, Mass.: MIT, November. Processed.

———. 1982. "Appropriate non-concessional industrial financing for developing countries." Cambridge, Mass.: MIT, July. Processed.

McDonald, Donogh C. 1982. "Debt capacity and developing country borrowing: A survey of the literature." IMF Staff Papers 29 (August).

Sachs, Jeffrey D. 1982. "LDC debt in the 1980s: Risk and reforms." In Crises in the Economic and Financial Structure, edited by Paul Wachtel. Lexington, Mass.: D.C. Heath.

———. 1983. "Theoretical issues in international borrowing." Cambridge, Mass.: Harvard University, Economics Department, August. Processed.

Sachs, Jeffrey D., and Daniel Cohen. 1982. "LDC borrowing with default risk." NBER Working Paper no. 925. Cambridge, Mass.: National Bureau of Economic Research.

Saunders, Anthony. 1983. "The determinants of country risk: A selective survey of the literature." Washington, D.C.: International Monetary Fund. Processed.

Sjaastad, Larry A. 1983. "The international debt quagmire: To whom do we owe it?" World Economy 6 (September).

Stiglitz, Joseph E., and Andrew Weiss. 1981. "Credit rationing in markets with imperfect information." American Economic Review 71 (June).

Swoboda, Alexander K. 1982. "International banking: Current issues in perspective." Journal of Banking and Finance 6 (September).

———. 1983. "Stabilizing a fragile international financial system." In International lending in a fragile world economy, edited by Donald Fair and Raymond Bertrand. The Hague: Martinus Nijhoff.

World Bank. 1984. World debt tables, 1983–84 edition. Washington, D.C.

Part III

An Econometric Approach to Creditworthiness

7

Is There Life after Debt? An Econometric Analysis of the Creditworthiness of Developing Countries

Daniel McFadden, Richard Eckaus, Gershon Feder, Vassilis Hajivassiliou, and Stephen O'Connell

The rapid growth in the international debt of developing nations and the increasing number of debt reschedulings because of repayment difficulties have generated widespread concern about international financial instability and its impact on world trade and the economies of both developing and developed countries. Difficulties in repayments of international debt are not a modern phenomenon; they have a history that dates back well into the nineteenth century. It is not even true that the contemporary history of debt difficulties began in the late 1970s. Throughout much of its life the activities of the International Monetary Fund (IMF) have involved implicit or explicit assistance to countries experiencing difficulties with their international debt.

THE PROBLEM

The magnitude of repayment problems has reached an unprecedented level, however, and has increasingly involved commercial banks. Figure 7-1 shows the growth of international debt in relation to GDP for the ninety-three developing countries in this study. The frequency of repayment problems, defined broadly to include arrears on long-term debt, higher-tranche IMF conditionality, or reschedulings, is shown in figure 7-2.[1] Of the ninety-three countries, 82 percent encountered repayment problems during at least one year in the 1970–82 period. The amount of debt rescheduled in the past five years is shown in table 7-1.

The main focus of this study is an econometric analysis of the precursors of repayment problems and estimation of crisis probabilities. As background, it will be useful to summarize some important features of international debt. The proximate sources of debt difficulties are current account deficits, which must be financed by foreign exchange inflows. Table 7-2 shows that non-oil-exporting developing countries had persistent, growing current account deficits during the 1973–83 period. This table also shows the sources of finance of the current deficits. Negative entries indicate asset adjustments that use foreign exchange and require additional financing.

One notable feature of table 7-2 is the net accumulation of foreign exchange reserves amounting to $73.7 billion over the period. Since one would expect repayment difficulties to be associated with exhaustion of available reserves, some explanation is required to reconcile the patterns

Gershon Feder is at the World Bank; the remaining authors are at the Department of Economics, MIT. This research was supported by the MIT Center for Energy Policy Research, with additional support from the World Bank. All opinions expressed in this paper are solely those of the authors. We are indebted to Rudiger Dornbusch, Donald Lessard, and Jeffrey Sachs for useful discussion.

Figure 7-1. The Ratio of Growth of International Debt to GDP
(93 developing countries)

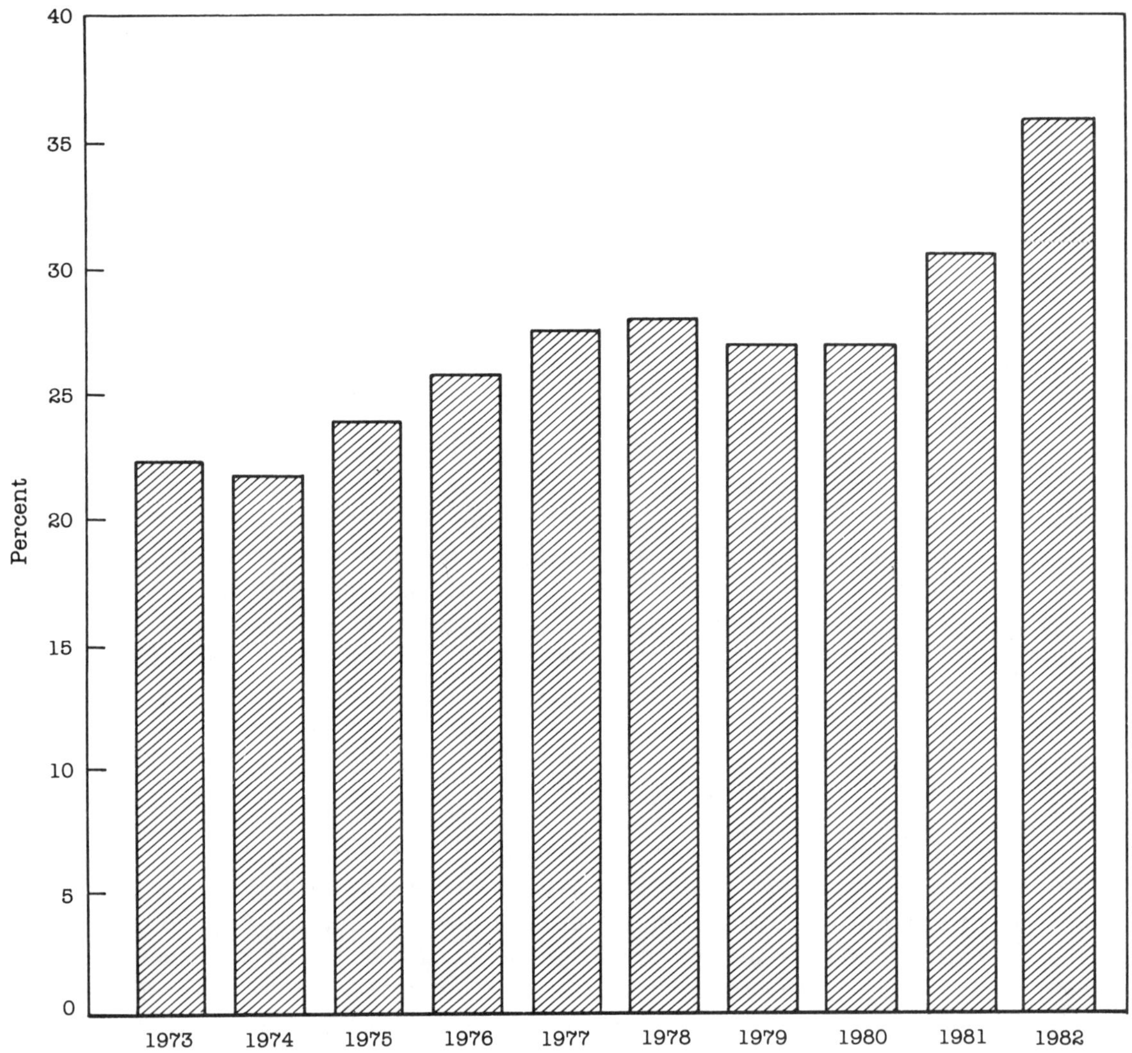

in table 7-2 and figure 7-2. One possibility is aggregation over countries with strong reserve and payment positions and countries with opposite characteristics. There are in fact large variations across countries in reserve holdings. A second possibility is that the buildup of reserves is a transactions demand to meet the requirements for disbursing and servicing the international debt. In particular, countries may hold reserves to attract credit or to meet lenders' requirements. The ratio of reserves to international debt actually declined slightly (from 0.43 to 0.37) between 1970 and 1981. The reserve buildup might also be due to increased precautionary demand in the face of increased volatility of international markets, to the reporting of temporary reserve positions, or even to the reporting of some capital outflows as reserves. In any case, it is clear that reported reserve accumulation has been a significant component of the demand for foreign exchange by developing countries.

Of the sources of finance, non-debt-creating flows (official transfers, direct investments, SDR allocations, and gold sales) have been an important component, amounting to 40.5 percent of the current account deficits between 1973 and 1983. Long-term official borrowing has averaged 28.4 percent in this period.

Figure 7-2. Repayment Problems and Crises
(77 to 90 reporting countries)

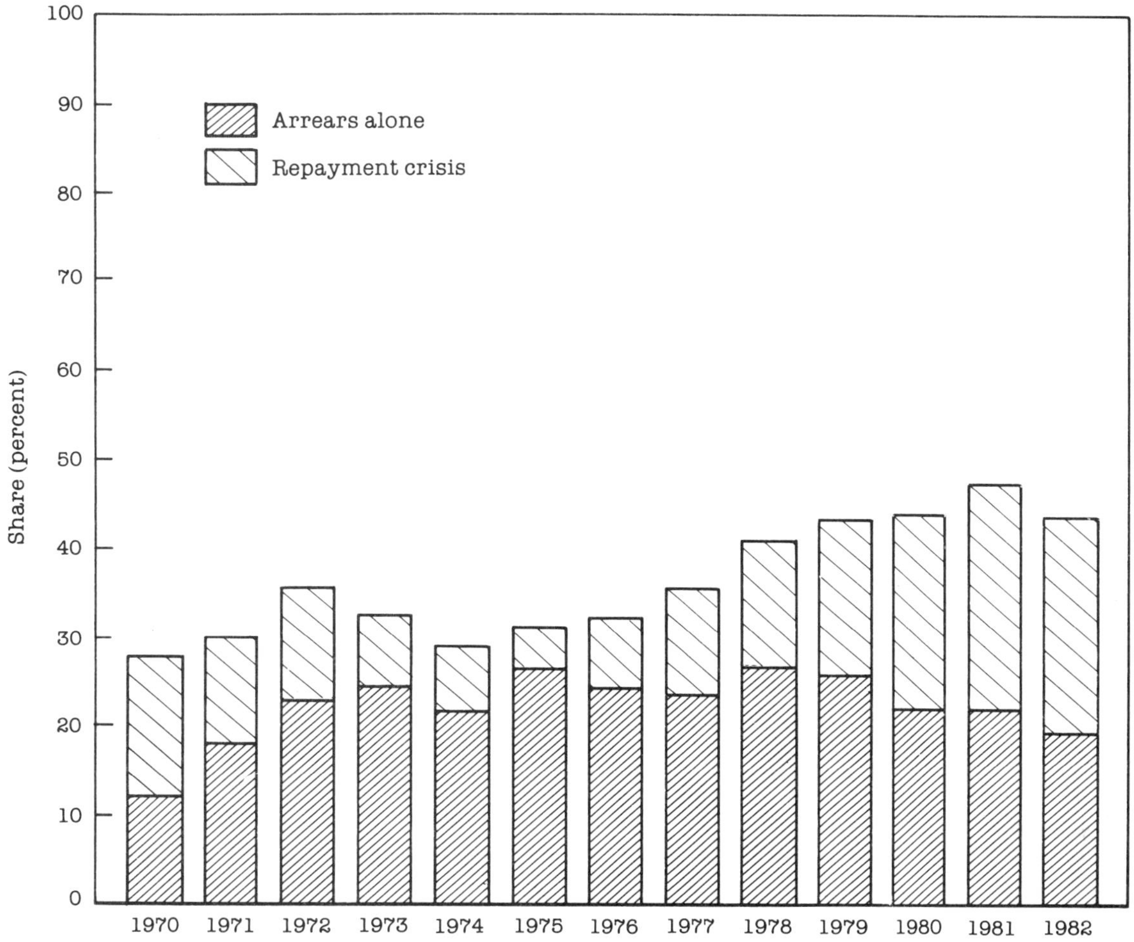

Long-term and short-term borrowing from private financial institutions averaged 39.3 percent and 18.5 percent, respectively. While the IMF plays a significant role as a source of international credit ratings and as an enforcer of credit terms, it is not itself an important source of finance. The line for other exceptional finance in table 7-2 shows errors and omissions, which in many developing countries are believed to reflect capital outflows that escape reporting. The concatenation of crises in 1982 and 1983 may have been accompanied, even precipitated, by relatively large-scale capital flight.

Some characteristics of the supply of international credit to the non-oil-exporting developing countries are summarized in table 7-3. The average annual growth rate of total debt from 1973 to 1982 was 19 percent in current dollars and 10 percent in constant dollars. For the middle-income oil importers the ratio of debt to GNP rose from 1.4 percent in 1970 to 3.1 percent in 1981. In spite of the public focus on the growth of syndicated medium- and long-term loans by commercial banks, the growth of short-term loans was faster in all but two of the ten years since 1973. Even so, by 1982 short-term debt was still slightly less than 20 percent of total debt. The growth rates were uneven over the period, with medium- and long-term debt showing a declining rate of growth and the growth pattern of short-term debt rather more choppy. The relative growth in short-term debt suggests a growing vulnerability of developing countries to

Table 7-1. Incidence of Reschedulings

	Official multilateral debt reschedulings[a]		Bank debt reschedulings[b]	
Year	Number	Amount (millions of U.S. dollars)	Number	Amount (millions of U.S. dollars)
1975	1	230		
1976	1	270		
1977	3	249		
1978	3	1,783	2	449[c]
1979	4	2,987	2	2,847[d]
1980	3	3,072	5	1,243
1981	7	1,079	6	1,656[e]
1982	6	529	6	4,867
1983	9	4,219[f]	20	59,288[g]

a. Seven countries have rescheduled debt more than once.
b. Signed or agreed in principle, excluding two nonmembers of the IMF.
c. Peru rescheduled twice in the year.
d. Turkey rescheduled twice in the year.
e. Excluding two Polish reschedulings (April and November) with a combined total of $4.6 billion.
f. Through August 1983.
g. Excluding a Polish rescheduling for an amount of $1.0 billion.

Source: IMF, Recent Multilateral Debt Restructurings with Official and Bank Creditors (Washington, D.C., 1983), pp. 16, 22.

the potential unwillingness of creditors to extend short-term lines of credit. It may be surprising that the growth of lending by international institutions has been slightly faster than that by private sources, with government lending advancing at a distinctly slower pace. Private debt was not a rapidly growing component of the total, rising from 46.7 percent of total debt in 1973 to 49 percent in 1982. Lending by both international institutions and private suppliers accelerated after the increase in oil prices in the early 1970s and slowed down after that. Debt service payments grew faster than total debt from 1973 to 1982 primarily because of rising interest rates. The striking increases in the level of debt service that took place in 1978 and 1979 also reflect the end of grace periods and maturation of loans negotiated in the 1973–75 period.

What are the fundamental causes of the persistent current account deficits of developing countries since 1970 and what difficulties have they faced in financing these deficits? Table 7-4 lists factors related to repayment problems. These factors are not mutually exclusive and may themselves be manifestations of more fundamental causes. Some are associated with the precipitation of a crisis, others with increased susceptibility to repayment problems.

Factors 1–4 reflect developments in the world economy that are largely beyond the control of developing countries and their creditors, although contractionary policies in industrialized countries must bear most of the responsibility for drops in the exports of developing countries. Increased volatility of trade, factor 4, exacerbates debt problems because more smoothing of consumption and long-term capital investments is required.

Factors 5–10 reflect the characteristics and behavior of developing countries. Factors 6–8 are facets of their macroeconomic and development policies. Pegging exchange rates at unsustainable levels or borrowing to finance current consumption can lead to a "day of reckoning." These policies also signal to creditors a lack of the economic control necessary to generate the foreign exchange inflows for debt service. If the developing country has undertaken investment programs that because of poor management or changing world conditions cannot repay their financing costs, added pressure is placed on the economy. In extreme cases the specter of insolvency may arise. In other cases, the development plan may be sound but have a long payoff

(Text continues p. 186.)

Table 7-2. Current Account Financing: Non-oil-exporting Developing Countries, 1973–83 (billions of U.S. dollars; numbers in parentheses are percentages)

Item	1973	1974	1975	1976	1977	1978	1979	1980	1981	1982	1983
Current account deficit	11.3	37.0	46.3	32.6	28.9	41.3	61.0	89.0	107.7	86.8	67.8
Use of reserves	−10.4	−2.7	1.6	−13.0	−12.5	−17.4	−12.6	−4.5	−2.1	7.1	−7.2
	(−92.0)	(−7.3)	(2.8)	(−39.9)	(−43.3)	(−42.1)	(−20.7)	(−5.1)	(−1.9)	(8.2)	(−10.6)
Non-debt-creating flows	10.3	14.6	11.8	12.6	14.4	17.9	23.9	24.1	28.0	25.1	24.2
	(91.2)	(39.5)	(25.5)	(38.7)	(49.8)	(43.3)	(39.2)	(27.1)	(26.0)	(28.9)	(35.7)
Long-term official borrowing, net	4.9	6.8	11.7	10.5	11.4	13.8	13.3	17.6	23.0	19.5	23.8
	(43.4)	(18.4)	(25.3)	(32.2)	(39.4)	(33.4)	(21.8)	(19.8)	(21.4)	(22.5)	(35.1)
Long-term private financial borrowing	6.5	10.3	14.2	15.3	9.4	19.5	21.7	28.4	35.7	18.5	39.1
	(67.5)	(27.8)	(30.7)	(46.9)	(32.5)	(47.2)	(35.6)	(31.9)	(33.1)	(21.3)	(57.7)
Long-term, other borrowing	0.3	1.0	1.3	2.2	3.8	3.9	1.5	1.2	4.0	3.7	1.1
	(2.7)	(2.7)	(2.8)	(6.7)	(13.2)	(9.4)	(2.5)	(1.3)	(3.7)	(4.3)	(1.6)
IMF credit	0.1	1.5	2.1	3.2	...	...	0.2	1.2	5.6	6.3	13.5
	(0.9)	(4.1)	(4.5)	(9.8)	(0.0)	(0.0)	(0.3)	(1.3)	(5.2)	(7.3)	(19.9)
Borrowing from monetary authorities	0.1	0.1	0.3	1.4	0.4	0.3	0.2	0.6	0.3	4.4	−2.7
	(0.9)	(0.3)	(0.6)	(4.3)	(1.4)	(0.7)	(0.3)	(0.7)	(0.3)	(5.1)	(−4.0)
Arrears	...	...	...	...	1.5	0.4	0.8	1.1	2.4	7.1	−5.0
	(0.0)	(0.0)	(0.0)	(0.0)	(5.2)	(1.0)	(1.3)	(1.2)	(2.2)	(8.2)	(−7.4)
Other short-term borrowing	3.3	8.3	8.9	5.8	2.7	4.9	14.6	20.8	10.1	−11.5	−16.5
	(29.2)	(22.4)	(19.2)	(17.8)	(9.3)	(11.9)	(23.9)	(23.4)	(9.4)	(13.2)	(24.3)
Other exceptional financing	−3.8	−2.9	−5.6	−5.9	−3.3	−2.8	−1.4	−4.5	−3.7		
	(−33.6)	(−7.8)	(−12.1)	(−18.1)	(−11.4)	(−6.8)	(−2.3)	(−5.1)	(−3.4)		

... Negligible.

Source: IMF, World Economic Outlook (Washington, D.C., May 1983), table 25.

Table 7-3. External Debt of Non-oil-exporting Developing Countries, 1973–82 (billions of U.S. dollars; numbers in parentheses are percentages)

External debt	1973	Growth	1974	Growth	1975	Growth	1976	Growth	1977	Growth	1978	Growth
Total debt outstanding	130.1	(23.5)	160.8	(18.7)	190.8	(19.5)	228.0	(22.2)	278.5	(20.8)	336.3	(16.3)
Maturity												
Short-term	18.4	(23.4)	22.7	(20.3)	27.3	(21.6)	33.2	(28.0)	(42.5)	(16.9)	49.7	(14.3)
	(14.1)		(14.1)		(14.3)		(14.5)		(15.3)		(14.8)	
Medium- and long-term	111.8	(23.5)	138.1	(18.4)	163.5	(19.2)	194.9	(21.0)	235.9	(21.5)	286.6	(16.7)
	(85.9)		(85.9)		(85.7)		(85.5)		(84.7)		(85.2)	
Creditor												
Government	37.3	(16.4)	43.4	(15.9)	50.3	(15.1)	57.9	(16.8)	67.6	(17.0)	79.1	(12.6)
	(28.6)		(27.0)		(26.4)		(25.4)		(24.3)		(23.5)	
International institutions	13.7	(21.2)	16.6	(22.3)	20.3	(22.2)	24.8	(25.0)	31.0	(23.9)	38.4	(18.8)
	(10.5)		(10.3)		(10.6)		(10.9)		(11.1)		(11.4)	
Private	60.8	(28.1)	77.9	(22.1)	95.1	(20.7)	114.8	(19.6)	137.3	(23.2)	169.1	(18.1)
	(46.7)		(48.4)		(49.8)		(50.3)		(49.3)		(50.3)	
Debt service payments	17.9	(23.5)	22.1	(13.6)	25.1	(10.8)	27.8	(24.8)	34.7	(45.0)	50.3	(29.2)
Interest	6.9	(34.8)	4.3	(12.9)	10.5	(3.8)	10.9	(24.8)	13.6	(42.6)	19.4	(44.3)
	(38.3)		(41.9)		(41.8)		(39.4)		(39.2)		(38.6)	
Principal	11.1	(15.3)	12.8	(14.1)	14.6	(15.1)	16.8	(15.6)	21.1	(46.4)	30.9	(19.4)
	(61.7)		(58.1)		(58.2)		(60.6)		(60.8)		(61.4)	

Source: IMF, Recent Multilateral Debt Restructurings with Official and Bank Creditors (Washington, D.C., December 1983), table 1, p. 4.

Table 7-3 (continued)

External debt	1979	Growth	1980	Growth	1981	Growth	1982	Average annual, rate of growth, 1973–82
Total debt outstanding	391.1	(19.6)	467.6	17.8	550.8	11.5	614.2	(18.8)
Maturity								
Short-term	56.8	(46.3)	83.1	(19.4)	99.2	(12.8)	111.9	(22.2)
	(14.5)		(17.8)		(18.0)		(18.2)	
Medium- and long-term	334.4	(15.0)	384.4	(17.5)	451.6	(11.2)	502.3	(18.2)
	(85.5)		(82.2)		(82.0)		(81.8)	
Creditor								
Government	89.1	(14.1)	101.7	(11.5)	113.4	(10.8)	125.7	(14.5)
	(22.8)		(21.8)		(20.6)		(20.5)	
International institutions	45.6	(16.7)	53.2	(17.7)	62.7	(13.2)	71.0	(20.1)
	(11.7)		(11.4)		(11.4)		(11.6)	
Private	199.7	(14.9)	229.5	(20.2)	275.8	(9.1)	300.8	(19.4)
	(51.1)		(49.1)		(50.1)		(49.0)	
Debt service payments	65.0	(17.2)	76.2	(22.2)	93.1	(12.8)	105.0	(21.7)
Interest	28.0	(44.3)	40.4	(33.7)	54.0	(6.3)	57.4	(26.5)
	(43.1)		(53.0)		(58.0)		(54.7)	
Principal	36.9	(−3.0)	35.8	(9.2)	39.1	(21.7)	47.6	(17.6)
	(56.9)		47.0)		(42.0)		(45.3)	

Table 7-4. Potential Factors Related to Repayment Problems

Factors in the world economy

1. Price increases in noncompressible imports, notably energy prices
2. Price decreases for major export commodities of developing countries
3. Export demand slumps because of recessions in industrialized countries and competition in world markets
4. Increased volatility in trade

Factors in debtor countries

5. Shocks to the productive capacity of developing countries from weather, social unrest, and other noneconomic factors
6. Poor economic management (unsustainable debt financing of consumption or government operations, severe domestic inflation, unemployment, or price distortions)
7. Investment programs whose returns are inadequate to repay their financing costs
8. Unsustainable growth targets and development plans
9. Speculation and capital flight
10. The potential threat of default on sovereign debt and the use of this threat to extract concessions from creditors

Factors affecting the supply of credit

11. Increased interest payments because of higher interest rates in industrialized countries
12. Increased amortization because of the decline in maturities and a larger proportion of short-term debt
13. "Crowding out" of developing countries' credit by competition from industrialized nations and oil exporters
14. Increased susceptibility to market imperfections because of reduced share of official long-term lending for capital projects, limited capacity of official institutions to guarantee debt, and large rollovers required on short-term debt
15. Erratic behavior of creditors induced by institutional rules on exposure, distortions in incentives of loan managers, and panics

period. Hence short-term shocks may create liquidity problems. For example, oil price increases in 1973 and 1979 widened current account deficits of oil importers and led most industrialized nations to deflate their economics. The developing economies on the whole, however, attempted to maintain their growth and development plans.

Capital flight, factor 9, is associated with the precipitation of repayment crises in circumstances where other factors have led to pressure on the current account. Capital flight is fueled by political instability, attempts to regulate capital markets, and anticipation of policy reversals caused by conflicting or unrealistic macroeconomic objectives. The potential threat of default, factor 10, enters the strategy of the developing country in bargaining with creditors. As described by Eaton and Gersovitz (1980) and Sachs and Cohen (1982), the country may balance the costs of default (the attachment of foreign assets and the elimination of most trade and trade credits for a significant period) against the benefits of repudiation. Short of actual repudiation, it may use this threat to extract concessions from creditors. On the other side, creditors have a strong incentive to grant such concessions rather than write off loans. Since the benefits of repudiation rise relative to cost as the total debt rises, one would expect suppliers of new credit to become more reluctant as debt grows. Strategically, a developing country might benefit from a precommitment not to repudiate. There are, however, not many ways for sovereign nations to do this.

Factors 11–15 reflect the characteristics and behavior of suppliers of credit. Increased debt service because of rising interest rates or accelerated amortization schedules puts pressure on the current account. Falling maturities on long-term debt and an increasing share of short-term debt presumably reflect a diminished supply of new credit, imposition of more conditionality, or shifts away from traditional suppliers of long-term credit toward less-preferred sources. In a perfectly competitive capital market, if borrowers in industrialized and oil-exporting countries were to "crowd out" the credit demand of developing countries, this would illustrate the proposition that international interest rates adjust to clear the market. A more direct form of crowding out can occur in markets that have rationing in response to the threat of repudiation, since increased demand from low-risk borrowers may widen the credit demand gaps for developing countries, even at higher interest rates.

Capital market imperfections may also increase countries' susceptibility to crises. Both the declining importance of official long-term lending for capital projects and the limited capacity of official institutions to guarantee debt will increase the vulnerability of developing countries to suppliers who are hypersensitive to short-term expectations regarding the riskiness of their loan portfolios. If the demand for credit by industrialized countries and oil exporters becomes more volatile (because of macroeconomic instability or oil demand shocks), the resulting volatility of debt service costs and the potential liquidity problems of developing countries are increased. This causes their creditworthiness to decline, which results in increased risk premiums and stricter exposure ceilings.

The problem of market imperfections may be exacerbated by some of the institutional features of lenders. Legal and customary rules limiting exposure of leading banks, combined with the restrictions on competition implicit in loan conditions, may inhibit the supply of credit to heavy borrowers even when solvency is not seriously in question. The limited accountability of loan officers, the distortion of incentives by official guarantees, and the signals provided by lead banks can all introduce a divergence between the assessment of a developing country's true creditworthiness, made on the basis of complete information, and the short-run market assessment.

Is it possible to allocate responsibility for debt problems among the factors listed in Table 7-4 by an econometric analysis of panel data on a number of developing countries? Since neither causality nor mutual exclusiveness between factors is claimed, the question must be refined. A full attribution of causality would require a microeconometric analysis of the information flows and decision processes of different agents, among other things. A few distinguishing characteristics deserve note, however. Unless factors in the world economy are completely "sterilized" by developing-country economic policy, there should be a positive relationship between adverse movements in terms of trade and repayment problems. If imperfections in the supply of credit are unimportant, a mean-preserving increase in volatility of terms of trade should not affect fundamental solvency and should be uncorrelated with repayment problems. If supply factors such as crowding out are important, then the repayment problems of a developing country should be related to world conditions as well as to its own characteristics. It does not appear possible, however, to separate factors such as high international interest rates from the effects of developing countries' accommodations to balance of payments pressure. Some indicators of characteristics of developing countries, such as indices of management quality, can be tested for effect. Tests of the importance of capital flight are limited by the unavailability of accurate data. There is some hope of measuring the benefits and costs of default to debtors and creditors and then, on the basis of the implied bargaining game, classifying countries at each date in terms of their attractiveness to new suppliers. Sorting out these factors is not the primary focus of this study. Since the detection and management of debt crises depends on which factors dominate, however, careful testing of these effects should be of high priority in future research.

Before beginning an econometric analysis of repayment problems, one must ask whether it is reasonable to expect a macroeconomic pattern that is stable over countries and over time. Case studies make clear that the circumstances of different developing countries vary considerably, and the apparent origins of repayment problems are quite heterogeneous. However, the proximate "cause" of repayment difficulties, inadequate foreign exchange inflows to finance current account deficits, is the same for everyone. It might be expected that difficulties arising from a variety of sources would all be mediated through the macroeconomic variables affecting the balance of payments accounts. With modest uniformities in macroeconomic behavior, one might then expect stable macroeconomic leading indicators of debt crises.

The empirical literature on creditworthiness does suggest the presence of some systematic relationships between macroeconomic variables and the occurrence of debt crises. Discriminant analyses of reschedulings by Frank and Cline (1971), Grinols (1976), and Sargen (1977), and logit analyses by Feder and Just (1977), Mayo and Barrett (1977), Feder, Just, and Ross (1981),

Table 7-5. Significant Macroeconomic Correlates of Repayment Crises in Developing Countries

	Study[a]					
Variable	Frank-Cline (1971)	Grinols (1976)	Feder-Just-Ross (1981)	Sargen (1977)	Saini-Bates (1978)	Cline (1983)
Debt service/exports	+		+	+		+
Principal service/debt	−					−
Imports/reserves	+		+			+
Debt/GDP		+				
Debt/exports		+		+		+
Debt service/reserves		+				
GNP per capita			−[b]			
Foreign exchange inflows/debt service			−			
(Current account)^2/ exports						−[c]
Exports/GNP			−			
Rate of domestic inflation				+		
Growth rate of money supply					+	
Growth rate of reserves					−	−[d]
Growth rate of GNP per capita						−
Total borrowing/total imports						−

a. Variables with significant effects are indicated by sign of effect. Note that these studies differ in countries and time periods considered and in details in definitions of both dependent and independent variables.

b. Defined relative to U.S. GNP per capita.

c. This variable is multiplied by the sign of the current account surplus.

d. Cline reports significant positive and negative signs on this variable.

and Cline (1983) have identified a number of macroeconomic correlates of debt crises, summarized in table 7-5. There are questions as to whether these studies identify leading rather than coincident indicators of repayment problems and whether the statistical assumptions underlying reported standard errors are justified.[2] Nevertheless, the reported effects generally coincide with the expectations of macroeconomic theory: an increased debt burden or depleted reserves are associated, as are domestic monetary variables, with problems that tend to indicate debt financing of government operations, lax macroeconomic management, or pursuit of ambitious development plans without adequate domestic saving. The significance of income may reflect both the ability to pay and the presence of a government infrastructure adequate to control trade and exchange activities. The strong positive effect of openness of the economy, measured by the ratio of exports to GNP, is noteworthy—an open economy is more vulnerable to problems generated by productivity or export price fluctuations, but it also has more at stake in maintaining trade relationships and is more susceptible to international market pressures that discipline domestic policy.

How stable are these macroeconomic correlations across countries and across time? Feder, Just, and Ross (1981) find significant area dummies. Saini and Bate (1978) find significant shifts in several variables (such as imports/reserves, and rate of inflation) between the 1960s and the 1970s. These results suggest that there may be significant country and time effects which are not readily captured in an econometric analysis and which place an upper bound on the precision of econometric ratings of creditworthiness.

Repayment problems, as they have been defined here, appear as arrears on principal or interest, higher-tranche IMF arrangements, or rescheduling requests. Of these, arrears are likely

Table 7-6. Repayment Problems

Year t-1		Year t								Row total
		R	A	I	RA	RI	AI	RAI	ϕ	
	R	0	0	1	0	0	0	0	2	3
	A	0	171	0	4	1	8	5	44	233
	I	0	1	38	0	7	4	0	31	81
	RA	1	4	0	1	0	0	3	0	9
	RI	0	0	2	0	1	1	0	3	7
	AI	0	7	2	1	0	7	3	2	22
	RAI	0	4	1	1	2	2	2	0	12
	ϕ	3	52	33	0	3	4	0	564	659
Column total		5	239	80	8	14	26	14	646	1,032
Total all years		5	253	90	9	15	26	15	712	1,125

Legend: R = Rescheduling, A = Arrears on long-term debt (arrears on principal exceeding 1 percent, or arrears on interest exceeding 0.1 percent of debt outstanding and disbursed), I = IMF higher-tranche support, ϕ = None. Combinations of letters indicate combinations of forms.

Note: Data for ninety-three countries, 1970–82, excluding eighty-four missing observations.

to be the first symptom, or even a deliberate signal, of difficulties. Reschedulings or IMF arrangements come later as part of the resolution of problems after their presence is generally recognized. We date IMF arrangements and reschedulings at time of initial public request rather than time of final agreement. Nevertheless, there may be protracted negotiations before requests are announced.

Table 7-6 gives the distribution of repayment problems for ninety-three countries between 1970 and 1982 and shows the pattern of transitions between forms. Repayment problems occur in 36.7 percent of the country-years observed. Arrears are the most common problem, present in 73.4 percent of the years where any form of problem occurs. Furthermore, arrears are a strong one-year-ahead indicator of future problems: 83.3 percent of countries with arrears in year t have a problem in year t + 1, while this is true for only 20.6 percent of countries without arrears in t.

Because of institutional rules, credit suppliers are believed to be more averse to arrears on interest than to arrears on principal. If so, foreign exchange available for debt service should be applied first to interest, and interest arrears should be uncommon. Table 7-7 gives the structure of arrears and indicates that, to the contrary, arrears on interest are common.

Table 7-7. Structure of Arrears on Long-term Debt

	All arrears		Significant arrears[a]	
Arrears	Number	Percent	Number	Percent
On interest only	49	14.0	95	30.2
On principal only	78	8.9	30	9.5
On both	431	77.1	190	60.3
Total	558	100.0	315	100.0

Note: Data for ninety-three countries, 1970–82, excluding seventy-six missing observations.

a. Arrears on principal less than 1 percent, and arrears on interest less than 0.1 percent of debt outstanding and disbursed are deemed to be cosmetic.

AN ECONOMETRIC MODEL FOR DEBT REPAYMENT PROBLEMS

An initial question in an analysis of international debt is: what constitutes a repayment crisis? To anticipate and manage problems of developing countries, it is desirable to identify circumstances in which the foreign exchange inflows required by trade conditions and domestic policy responses cannot be met through ordinary rollovers or new loans, and the result is therefore arrears on interest or principal due, higher-tranche IMF support, or reschedulings. Within this broad definition of a repayment problem, the cases leading to IMF higher-tranche arrangements or reschedulings have more severe implications for developing countries' macroeconomic policies and will be termed "crises." We will concentrate on the problem of quantifying the probability of the onset of a repayment problem and the probability that this problem will become a crisis.

Additional questions are how international reserves and arrears behave when a developing country is in an ongoing crisis and how the conditions of IMF support or the rescheduling agreement restrict debtor and creditor behavior. In particular, there appears to be considerable variation among countries in their attitudes toward arrears versus IMF arrangements. Some countries appear anxious to avoid arrears and agree readily to IMF conditions, whereas others accept IMF policies only as a last resort in connection with a formal rescheduling of debt. In this study, we will classify either IMF arrangements or reschedulings as crises. The question of how attitudes toward IMF support interact with domestic macroeconomic policy will be left for future study.

Another question that poses conceptual and measurement problems is the duration of a crisis. The resolution of a repayment problem under IMF conditionality may take one to three years; within such an arrangement multiple reschedulings may be anticipated as additional debt becomes due. In some cases countries have satisfied initial IMF conditions and avoided further reschedulings, while in other cases events have led to new difficulties and unanticipated reschedulings within a period of IMF conditionality. This suggests that ideally crises should not be defined on a calendar-year basis and that crisis duration will be difficult to model. The issues of macroeconomic response to ongoing crises and the duration of crises are left as topics for future research.

In this section we develop an econometric model of the onset of a repayment problem characterized by arrears on long-term debt, and of a crisis in which IMF support or a rescheduling is requested. Although the details are not formalized here, our approach is based on the idea that the developing country has some intertemporal welfare function of macroeconomic variables. It will set policy to maximize this function, balancing the benefits of consumption and investment financed by current account deficits against the costs of financing these deficits. If the quotas or penalties associated with arrears or reschedulings are not too severe, the country may be unwilling to adopt domestic policy measures such as deflation or exchange controls in order to avoid a repayment problem or crisis.

A developing country has in each period a demand function for new foreign loans that may be the result of intertemporal optimization subject to macroeconomic constraints and behavior. The specification of this demand is discussed in appendix A.

Lenders have a new loan supply function that depends on their assessment of creditworthiness. We assume that demand and supply are <u>not</u> fully equilibrated by adjustments in the interest rate spread. This assumption is justified first by the observation that spreads play the double role of indicating scarcity and signaling creditworthiness. It is disadvantageous to both countries and banks to allow spreads to rise to market-clearing levels if this signals a degree of risk unacceptable to other country creditors or to bank depositors. Furthermore, the increased probability of repudiation of debt at high spreads may restrict supply to such a degree that no spread will clear the market. Explicit models of this phenomenon have been developed by Cooper and Sachs (1984).

If new loan supply exceeds demand, the observed transactions lie on the demand curve and the country experiences no repayment problems. If demand exceeds supply, the country first borrows the quantity supplied voluntarily by the market and, second, may go into arrears on debt service, a form of involuntary lending. Beyond some arrears limit, either borrowers or lenders find it less costly to request a rescheduling or restructuring of debt than to tolerate further arrears.

In summary, the model has three regimes, determined by the level of excess demand for new foreign loans. If excess demand is negative, there is no repayment problem and observed loans lie on the demand curve. If excess demand is positive but less than the limit on arrears, then observed loans lie on the supply curve and the level of arrears equals the gap between demand and supply. Finally, if excess demand exceeds the arrears limit, then a rescheduling or IMF arrangement is requested, and observed new loans, rollovers, and arrears are an outcome of the rescheduling negotiations.

The econometric model is completed by specifying the functional forms of demand, supply, and the arrears limit, the variables entering these functions, and the distribution of unobservables. This model permits an estimation of new loan demand and supply and the limit on arrears. A limited-information version using qualitative data yields estimates of the probabilities of repayment problems and of reschedulings. General background on econometric models of these types can be found in Maddala (1983), McFadden (1984), and Hajivassiliou (1983). The model formulation used in this study extends the very interesting switching regression analysis of debt problems by Eaton and Gersovitz (1981) and Shishido (1984). Appendix B gives the details of the econometric specification.

EMPIRICAL RESULTS

We have analyzed data for ninety-three developing countries over the period 1970–82. The starting date is the first period in which debt data are systematically available, the ending date the last year in which arrears data are available. The primary data sources were the IMF International Financial Statistics for most macroeconomic and trade variables, and the World Bank for debt and arrears. Reschedulings and IMF arrangements were assembled from IMF annual reports and Euromoney surveys and validated by comparison with World Bank records. In the panel of countries, some years are omitted because of missing observations. The data and construction of variables are discussed further in appendix C.

We first investigate the robustness of the Feder, Just, and Ross (1981) model of repayment problems when applied to the larger sample used in this study. The dependent variable is defined to be a rescheduling or restructuring of debt, IMF higher-tranche support, arrears on principal exceeding 1 percent of debt outstanding and disbursed, or arrears on interest exceeding 0.1 percent of debt. This is a somewhat broader definition of repayment problems than was employed by Feder, Just, and Ross. Other differences from the original study are use of probit rather than logit, which should affect only the scale of coefficients, and the lagging of all explanatory variables by one year to reduce the problem of simultaneity.

Table 7-8 reports maximum likelihood estimates of this model using 687 observations from ninety-three countries in the years 1971–82. All explanatory variables are lagged one year. Nondebt inflows are capital account items in the balance of payments—primarily foreign direct investment—that do not entail debt obligations. Model 1 parallels the original Feder, Just, and Ross specification. The pattern of a decreasing probability of repayment problems with a decreasing debt service due/exports ratio or increasing ratios of nondebt inflows/debt service due, services/imports, or GNP/population is the same as found by Feder, Just, and Ross. The earlier study found an increase in the exports/GNP ratio lowered the probability of problems; we obtain the same sign, but the effect is insignificant.

The inclusion of the lagged dependent variable in model 2 shows strong apparent state depend-

Table 7-8. Probit and One-factor Models of Repayment Problems

Variable (lagged one year)	Model 1	Model 2	Model 3	Model 4
Constant	0.00377	−0.0733	0.299	0.127
	(0.26)	(4.28)	(1.49)	(0.64)
Debt service due/exports	1.159	0.693	1.527	0.835
	(3.28)	(1.72)	(3.71)	(1.75)
Nondebt inflows/debt service due · 1,000	−1.221	−4.929	−4.600	−4.301
	(2.18)	(0.90)	(0.72)	(0.68)
Reserves/imports	−1.243	−1.097	−2.234	−1.369
	(4.81)	(3.86)	(6.11)	(4.00)
Exports/GDP	−0.171	−0.038	0.194	−0.068
	(0.57)	(0.11)	(0.49)	(0.16)
Real GNP/population · 1,000	−0.296	−0.162	−0.220	−0.174
	(3.23)	(1.55)	(1.42)	(1.32)
Repayment problem dummy		1.638		0.745
	—	(13.68)	—	(10.79)
Standard deviation of country effect			0.823	0.371
	—	—	(10.51)	(3.92)
Log likelihood	−401.823	−299.620	−352.385	−297.001

— Variable excluded from estimation.

Note: Absolute values of t-statistics are given in parentheses.

ence. Except for the reserves/imports ratio, the effect of the lagged dependent variable is to lower substantially the significance of the other variables in the model.

To investigate the apparent state dependence found in models 1 and 2, we consider models that introduce a random country effect with the same variables. This "one-factor" specification is discussed in appendix B. Maximum likelihood estimates of this model, without and with a lagged dependent variable, are given in models 3 and 4 in table 7-8. This model has a unit standard deviation of the period-by-period disturbance; hence in model 3, 40.4 percent of the variance underlying repayment problems is due to a persistent country effect.[3] We conclude from model 4 that there are both true state dependence and country effects. These two effects plus the reserves/imports ratio and a marginally significant debt service due/exports ratio are the major determinants of the probability of repayment problems.

Next consider the model described in the preceding section and in equation (7.7) in appendix B. The probability of repayment problems should be increasing in state economic variables that increase demand for new foreign credit, as outlined in appendix A, and decreasing in variables that increase lender confidence and increase the supply of new loans. To capture demand effects, we enter variables related to debt service due (including accumulated arrears), reserves, imports, income, and terms of trade. Lender effects are entered in the models reported here by using conventional measures of creditworthiness such as the ratios of imports to GNP and debt to exports, GNP per capita, and the growth rate of GDP. To adjust for country scale, we normalize demand variables by exports or by GDP.

Table 7-9 gives models for the same definition of repayment problems as table 7-8. The fitted models are logit rather than probit forms. Except for a scale factor, this should have almost no effect on coefficients. The explanatory variables are lagged one year. To reflect the expectations associated with capital flight, we include a variable that is zero for country observations when there are flexible exchange rates and, for observations associated with pegged rates, equals the rate of growth of the real exchange rate (= domestic inflation rate − growth of nominal local currency/dollar exchange rate − U.S. inflation rate). Model 5 for the full sample shows the increasing probability of problems when reserves, GNP per capita, or the growth rate of GDP fall, or when imports, debt, or debt service due rise. The effect of movements in the real exchange rate is of expected sign, but not significant. The table includes the percentage of

Table 7-9. Probabilities of Significant Arrears, Reschedulings, or IMF Support

Variable (lagged one year)	Model 5 all 1971–82	Model 6 Nonpoor 1971–82	Model 7 all 1971–75	Model 8 all 1976–82	Model 9 all 1971–82
(Total reserves − gold)/GDP	−2.196	0.059	3.271	−6.418	−2.181
	(2.16)	(0.07)	(2.43)	(4.73)	(2.15)
Imports/GDP	1.512	0.924	−2.067	3.193	1.298
	(3.11)	(1.61)	(1.85)	(5.02)	(2.31)
Debt/exports	0.523	1.11	0.613	0.519	0.320
	(4.10)	(4.35)	(2.51)	(3.33)	(2.13)
Debt service due/exports	1.437	−0.577	−0.377	2.306	0.948
	(2.14)	(0.61)	(0.25)	(2.88)	(1.23)
Real GNP per capita/1,000	−0.500	−0.712	−0.237	−0.677	−0.265
	(3.04)	(3.30)	(0.91)	(2.95)	(1.37)
Real growth GDP	−5.673	−6.695	−6.863	−4.355	−2.425
	(3.43)	(3.15)	(2.39)	(2.04)	(1.28)
Real exchange rate change	0.839	0.083	0.162	1.383	0.770
if pegged rate	(1.58)	(0.11)	(0.18)	(2.13)	(1.38)
Constant	−1.242	−1.351	−0.629	−1.614	−2.253
	(5.12)	(3.70)	(1.44)	(4.97)	(7.38)
Repayment problem	—	—	—	—	2.746
indicator					(13.11)
Sample size	728	479	273	455	728
Log likelihood	−415.4	−251.5	−149.8	−249.8	−312.8
Percent correct	72.25	77.24	73.99	72.31	82.55
Percent (no/yes)	29.60	27.27	27.27	31.15	23.53
Percent (yes/no)	17.36	22.17	25.90	26.43	14.49

— Variable excluded from estimation.
Note: Absolute values of t-statistics are given in parentheses.

country-years that would be classified correctly using the criterion of maximum probability. Also given are the percentages of cases classified into one category by the maximum probability criterion that are in fact misclassified. For example, percent (no/yes) = 29.6 means that this percentage of countries predicted to have repayment problems, in fact, do not.

Model 6 excludes countries with per capita GNP below $500 per year in 1981. The effects of reserves and debt service due are insignificant for this group. These variables are associated with short-run liquidity problems of generating the foreign exchange flows to cover current account deficits. The observed pattern suggests that poor countries are liquidity-constrained, whereas nonpoor countries are affected by longer-run creditworthiness factors.

Models 7 and 8 break the observations into two periods, 1971–75 and 1976–82. There are substantial differences in coefficients between the periods. The effect of reserves strongly reverses sign, reducing the probability of problems in the latter period. Open economies with a high ratio of imports to GDP have fewer problems in the earlier period but more problems in the later period. Debt service due and movement in the real exchange rate become significant only in the latter period. A likelihood ratio test for equality of coefficients in the two periods yields a chi-square statistic of 31.6 with 8 degrees of freedom, leading to rejection at the 0.05 percent level. We conclude that the coefficients of this model are definitely not stable over time.

Model 9 adds an indicator of lagged repayment problems. There is again an apparently strong state dependence. The coefficients of other variables are not strongly affected, although debt service due, GNP per capita, and the growth rate of GDP lose significance. A test of stability of the coefficients of model 9 between the 1971–75 and 1976–82 periods rejects stability at the 5 percent level, but not the 1 percent level.

Table 7-10 contains alternatives to the table 7-9 models, which examine several hypotheses about repayment problems. Model 10 incorporates the cumulative counts of years of reschedulings or IMF support since 1970 and should capture some of the country and long-term state

Table 7-10. Alternative Models of Repayment Problems

Variables (lagged one year)	Model 10	Model 11	Model 12	Model 13
(Total reserves − gold)/GDP	−1.725	−2.315	−4.829	−3.973
	(1.78)	(2.26)	(4.25)	(3.38)
Imports/GDP	1.422	1.977	1.684	2.205
	(2.93)	(3.26)	(2.89)	(4.05)
Debt/exports	0.499	0.418	0.322	0.553
	(3.89)	(3.29)	(2.32)	(3.91)
Debt service due/exports	0.810	1.610	0.641	1.493
	(1.18)	(2.41)	(0.84)	(2.05)
GNP/population · 1,000	−0.485	−0.494	−0.269	−0.477
	(2.92)	(2.92)	(1.48)	(2.59)
Real growth GDP	−5.585	−5.323	−0.571	−5.616
	(3.32)	(2.93)	(0.32)	(3.01)
Real exchange rate change if pegged	0.846	—	—	—
	(1.68)			
Cumulative reschedule since 1970	0.298	—	—	—
	(1.90)			
Cumulative IMF support since 1970	0.134	—	—	—
	(2.06)			
Index of outward orientation	—	−0.193	—	—
		(0.88)		
Rescheduling indicator	—	—	1.095	—
			(1.61)	
IMF support indicator	—	—	1.735	—
			(6.66)	
Arrears on interest indicator	—	—	1.693	—
			(6.18)	
Arrears on principal indicator	—	—	3.559	—
			(7.28)	
Growth rate of real GDP in industrial countries	—	—	—	0.038
				(0.69)
Real Eurodollar interest rate	—	—	—	−0.003
				(0.39)
Growth rate of real Third World debt	—	—	—	−0.455
				(0.14)
Constant	−1.326	−1.133	−2.040	−1.471
	(5.39)	(3.83)	(7.04)	(3.15)
Sample size	728	688	822	597
Log likelihood	−409.1	−386.9	−344.1	−366.0
Percent correctly predicted	74.31	73.84	81.51	73.20

— Variable excluded from estimation.
Note: Absolute values of t-statistics are given in parentheses.

effects. Both historical variables are found to be significant. Model 11 adds an index of the outward orientation of the economy suggested by Balassa (1984). The regression

$$\log(\text{EXPPOP}) = -1.918 + 1.148^* \log(\text{GNPPOP}) - 0.251^* \log(\text{POP}) - 0.0038^* \text{SFM},$$

where EXPPOP = exports per capita, GNPPOP = GNP per capita, POP = population, and SFM = share of fuel and minerals in exports, is fitted to a 1976 cross-section of sixty-four countries ($R^2 = 0.89$) and the index is defined as

$$\text{Outwardness index} = \frac{\text{Actual 1976 exports per capita}}{\text{Predicted 1976 exports per capita}}.$$

This index is assumed constant over the period of observation, 1971–82. Balassa (1984) has argued that outward-oriented countries are less likely to experience repayment problems, the main reasons being the ability of growing exports to generate the exchange flows necessary to service debt and the lack of exchange controls that make capital flight profitable. We find no significant effect of outward orientation beyond its impact through the variables in model 5.

Model 12 explores the relative impact of indicators of different types of previous problems. Reschedulings, IMF support, and significant arrears on interest are found to have comparable coefficients, although the first of these is insignificant. Significant arrears on principal are found to have a stronger effect. Model 13 tests the effect of world variables that may be related to the supply of credit: the real growth rate of GDP in industrialized countries, which reflects a level of investment in those countries that could crowd out lending to developing countries; the real Eurodollar interest rate, which reflects the tightness of credit markets; and the growth rate of real debt outstanding to developing countries, excluding arrears. None of these world variables is significant.

In the full model described in the preceding section, level data on new loans and arrears are used to identify separately the demand and supply of new loans and the limit on arrears. This model is fitted to 822 country-year observations, of which 45.3 percent involve no repayment problem, 39.4 percent involve arrears without IMF support or rescheduling, and 15.3 percent involve either a rescheduling or IMF standby authority or extended fund facilities. The econometric specification is given in appendix B. New loans and arrears are expressed in ratios to exports. As shown in table 7-11, demand for new loans is strongly increasing with respect to debt service due exports and imports GDP, and decreasing with respect to real GNP per capita. Supply of new loans decreases when there are past repayment problems; it is found to increase with the debt/exports ratio. This may reflect historic lending based on judgments of the export potential or strategic position of countries, rather than current judgments of creditworthiness. Also, this sign might occur if lenders have an incentive for institutional reasons to roll over problem loans rather than declare them in default.

Supply is insignificantly increasing in the ratio of principal due/exports, with a coefficient that is significantly less than 1. This suggests that lenders are reluctant to roll over principal due, and as a result there is considerable pressure on liquidity when principal payments are high.

A significant positive correlation is found between the unobserved factors entering demand and supply. The standard deviation of demand is substantially larger than that for supply—an indication that most shocks underlying repayment problems come from the demand side.

The limit on arrears has a mean of the form $1/B = e^{z\gamma}$, where B is defined as in appendix B, z is the vector of variables influencing this limit, and γ is the associated vector of coefficients given in the last column of the table. The limit falls in the presence of previous repayment problems and rises with debt service due, which suggests that lenders may judge arrears as a percentage of payments due.

POLICY IMPLICATIONS

The model of repayment problems estimated in the last section can be used to describe international credit histories and simulate the effects of alternatives to actual events and policies. By itself, the model is limited to one-period-ahead forecasts. When coupled with a macroeconomic model that provides forecasts of standard macroeconomic ratios, however, the system can provide multiyear forecasts. The accuracy of such forecasts will be limited by the macroeconomic model and by the presence of time and country effects on repayment behavior. Furthermore, this system cannot anticipate the political upheavals, wars, and natural disasters that sometimes precipitate repayment crises. Subject to these caveats, the system should be useful for analyzing the impact of alternative policies for a few years ahead.

Table 7-11. The Full Model of New Loan Demand and Supply

Variable (lagged one year)	New loan demand	New loan supply	Limit on arrears
Constant	−0.347	0.438	0.219
	(3.223)	(6.99)	(0.57)
Debt service due/exports	6.524	—	1.845
	(25.27)		(2.39)
Real GNP per capita	−0.391	0.020	−0.081
	(5.26)	(0.49)	(0.38)
Growth rate of real GNP	0.096	0.06	0.078
	(0.120)	(1.17)	(0.04)
Imports/GDP	0.949	—	—
	(4.89)		
Reserves/imports	—	0.077	—
		(0.89)	
Exports/GDP	—	−0.041	−0.306
		(0.369)	(0.33)
Debt/exports	—	0.088	0.156
		(2.64)	(1.17)
Indicator for rescheduling or IMF support	—	−0.145	−1.330
		(1.93)	(6.08)
Indicator for arrears	—	−0.306	—
		(6.48)	
Interest due/exports	—	0.455	—
		(0.505)	
Principal due/exports	—	0.215	—
		(1.13)	
Standard deviation	1.276	0.468	
	(8.90)	(20.28)	
Correlation	0.279		
	(4.79)		

— Variable excluded from estimation.
Note: Absolute values of t-statistics are given in parentheses.

The first simulation exercise is a calculation of probabilities of repayment problems for eight selected countries through 1985. A simple and mechanical first-order vector autoregression is applied to the pooled panel data on the explanatory variables. The VAR coefficients are given in table 7-12. Note that while VAR methods are often fairly reliable for short-term forecasting, this system does not enforce macroeconomic consistency conditions. We have not tested the forecasting accuracy of the VAR.

Table 7-13 gives the calculated probabilities of repayment problems from model 5 for Argentina, Brazil, Chile, Republic of Korea, Mexico, Peru, the Philippines, and Venezuela. On average, the annual probabilities of repayment problems in these eight countries are similar to the 0.37 probability in the entire panel of countries. Argentina, Brazil, Chile, and Peru show generally upward trends, while the remaining countries fluctuate without clear trends. All the countries have elevated probabilities during the period 1979–83, particularly Argentina, Brazil, Chile, Mexico, and Peru. The forecast years 1984–85 have probabilities declining slowly from the earlier peaks but remaining quite high for the South American countries. Several countries had elevated probabilities earlier in the period: Argentina in 1977, Brazil in 1976 and 1979, Chile in 1976, Korea in 1972, and Peru in 1978.

To assess the importance of oil price shocks from the Organization of Petroleum Exporting Countries (OPEC) and the worldwide recession in 1981–83 in repayment problems, we have constructed two counterfactual alternatives to the base scenario. An OPEC scenario assumes no OPEC price increases, so real fuel import prices are fixed at 1971 levels. Laspeyres import price indices are constructed with the use of 1970 import shares and the base and alternative

Table 7-12. Vector Autoregressions for Macroeconomic Ratios

Lagged variables	Dependent variables							
	RESIMP	IMPGDP	DBTEXP	DSDEXP	GNPPC	GRGDP	EXPGDP	RER
RESIMP	0.875*	0.034*	−0.139*	−0.030*	0.035*	0.040*	−0.002	0.061*
IMPGDP	−0.055	0.923*	0.280*	−0.046	−0.026	−0.011	0.065*	−0.006
DBTEXP	−0.001	0.002	0.873*	0.016*	−0.001	−0.001	0.001	−0.022*
DSDEXP	0.053	0.023	−0.242*	0.805*	0.019	0.015	0.006	0.082
GNPPC	0.011	−0.009*	−0.031	0.009	1.016*	−0.004	0.006*	0.082
GRGDP	0.126	0.001	−0.046	0.032	0.083*	0.101*	−0.032	0.060
EXPGDP	0.050	0.118*	−0.518*	0.024	0.091*	0.038	0.950*	−0.030
RER	—	—	—	—	—	—	—	0.126*
Constant	0.017	−0.007	0.333*	0.031*	−0.027*	0.025*	−0.008	0.031
R^2	0.772	0.958	0.851	0.794	0.993	0.059	0.959	0.036
Number of observations	789	770	790	789	813	813	770	712

* Significant at 5 percent level.
— Variable excluded from estimation.
Legend:
RESIMP Reserves/imports
IMPGDP Imports/GDP
DBTEXP Debt outstanding and disbursed/exports
DSDEXP Debt service due (including arrears)/exports
GNPPC GNP per capita
GRGDP Growth rate of GDP
EXPGDP Exports/GDP
RER Rate of change of real exchange rate

world fuel price series, and the relative price index is used to deflate base scenario imports. Substitution of the import mix away from fuels in the face of rising relative fuel prices will cause this calculation to overstate the reduction in real dollar imports associated with the elimination of OPEC price increases. The assumption is made for this scenario that the import reduction translates dollar for dollar into a reduction in new foreign borrowing, with a proportionate reduction in debt service due. Other macroeconomic variables, GDP, reserves, and exports are assumed to remain at base scenario levels.

A growth scenario begins from the OPEC scenario and adds the assumption of no worldwide recession or sharp increase in real interest rates. Specifically, real GDP for a country is assumed to grow after 1981 at the same rate as in the 1971–81 decade, with imports, exports, and reserves keeping pace so that ratios in these variables remain at base levels. Nominal Eurodollar

Table 7-13. Estimated Probabilities of Repayment Problems

Year	Argentina	Brazil	Chile	Korea	Mexico	Peru	Philippines	Venezuela
1972	0.20	0.28	0.38	0.47	0.28	0.26	0.39	0.12
1973	0.10	0.30	0.44	0.46	0.21	0.31	0.42	0.11
1974	0.15	0.22	0.32	0.26	0.23	0.35	0.29	0.09
1975	0.11	0.47	0.16	0.38	0.28	0.31	0.33	0.06
1976	0.07	0.58	0.51	0.35	0.34	0.46	0.32	0.05
1977	0.40	0.52	0.48	0.22	0.37	0.50	0.36	0.06
1978	0.09	0.61	0.35	0.24	0.43	0.56	0.37	0.09
1979	0.35	0.78	0.57	0.25	0.48	0.52	0.46	0.14
1980	0.23	0.77	0.47	0.34	0.44	0.40	0.45	0.15
1981	0.27	0.61	0.44	0.50	0.30	0.42	0.36	0.17
1982	0.25	0.79	0.65	0.34	0.29	0.57	0.42	0.16
1983	0.96	0.61	0.95	0.43	0.86	0.70	0.54	0.24
1984	0.57	0.53	0.66	0.37	0.43	0.51	0.44	0.15
1985	0.50	0.47	0.57	0.35	0.38	0.47	0.43	0.15

Source: From table 7-9, model 5.

interest rates are assumed beginning in 1981 to be reduced by 5 percent, yielding roughly zero real interest rates.

Figures 7-3 to 7-8 graph the probabilities of repayment problems for six oil-importing countries in the base, OPEC, and growth scenarios. Also indicated are years in which repayment problems (reschedulings, IMF support, or significant arrears) occur. Figure 7-3 for Argentina shows relatively little impact from energy costs, but a major effect of recession. The model does not clearly detect the start of a repayment problem in 1975, but easily identifies the 1983 crisis.

Figure 7-4 for Brazil shows a major impact from energy costs. Its probabilities are relatively high over the entire period, peaking at the time of a crisis in 1982 and declining thereafter. Figure 7-5 for Chile also shows a substantial energy price effect and in addition a major recession impact in 1983. The probabilities for Chile are initially high, drop sharply in 1974–75, but then return to fairly high levels and rise dramatically beginning in 1982.

Figure 7-6 for Korea shows moderate probabilities throughout the period, but with an increase from 1979–81 during which repayment problems occur. Most of Korea's problems can be attributed to energy prices. Figure 7-7 for Peru shows elevated probabilities in 1976–79, at a time when problems did occur, and a sharp rise in probabilities in 1982–83. Energy prices account for a significant proportion of Peru's risk, with an additional recession effect in 1983. Figure 7-8 for the Philippines shows moderately high probabilities, with relatively little fluctuation at the time of repayment problems in the mid-1970s. Again energy prices are a major contribution to risk.

Figure 7-3. Argentina: Probability of Repayment Problems

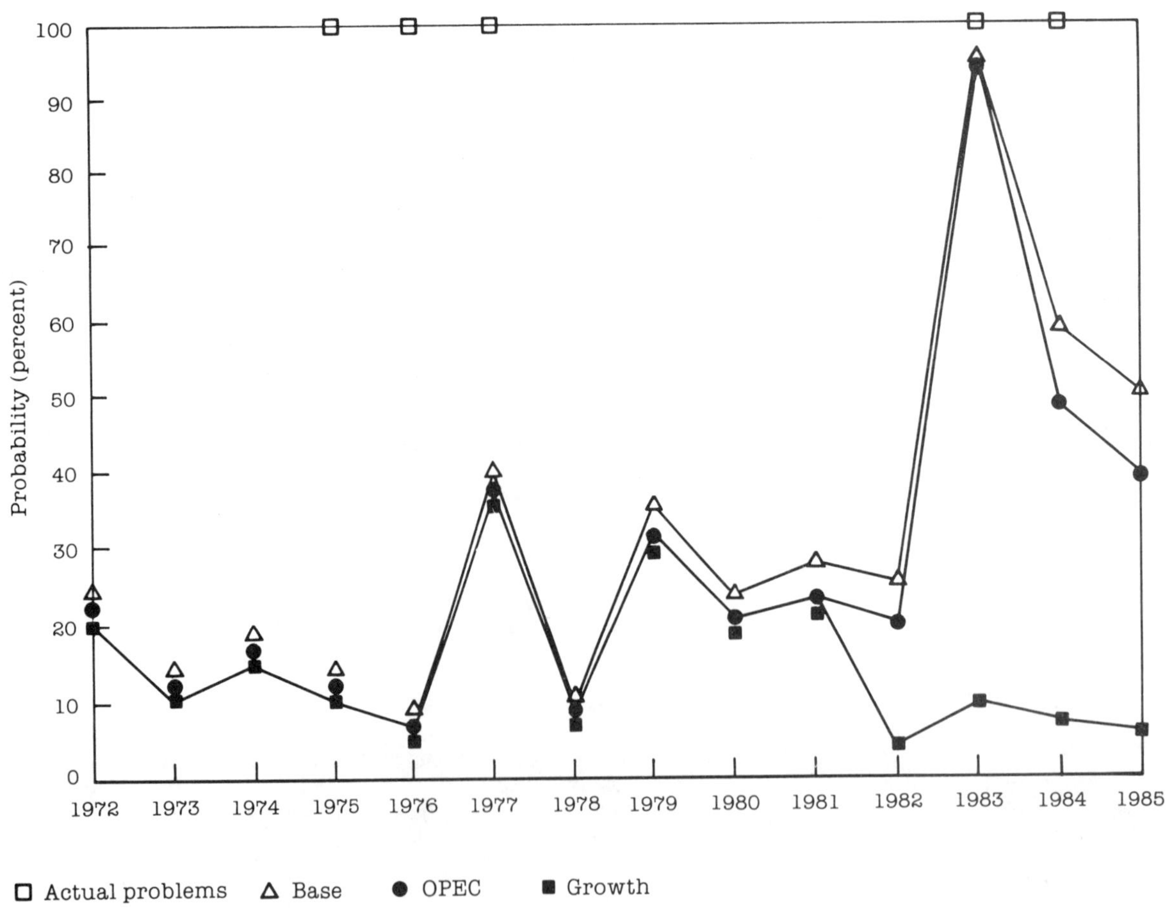

Figure 7-4. Brazil: Probability of Repayment Problems

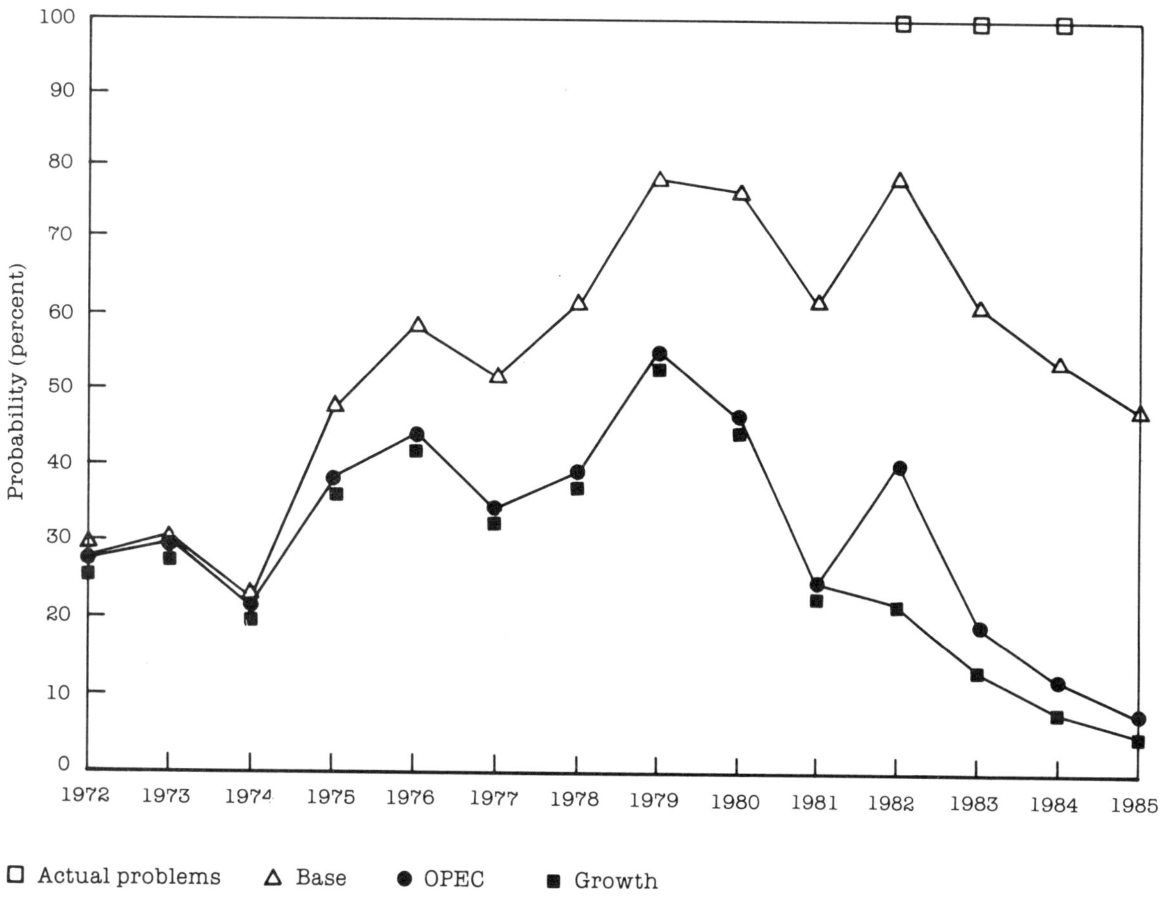

The conclusion of these scenarios is that for most oil importers, increases in real fuel prices have substantially increased the probability of repayment problems. Substitution away from high-cost energy and lax macroeconomic management in the absence of pressures from energy import costs would reduce the gap in probabilities indicated by the scenarios, but it would not alter the conclusion that energy price increases have been a major source of international credit risk. The effects of worldwide recession have been dramatic for some countries and a major factor in Argentina, Brazil, and Chile in the 1982–83 period. With these exceptions, the recession appears to have increased debt risks only moderately.

Figure 7-5. Chile: Probability of Repayment Problems

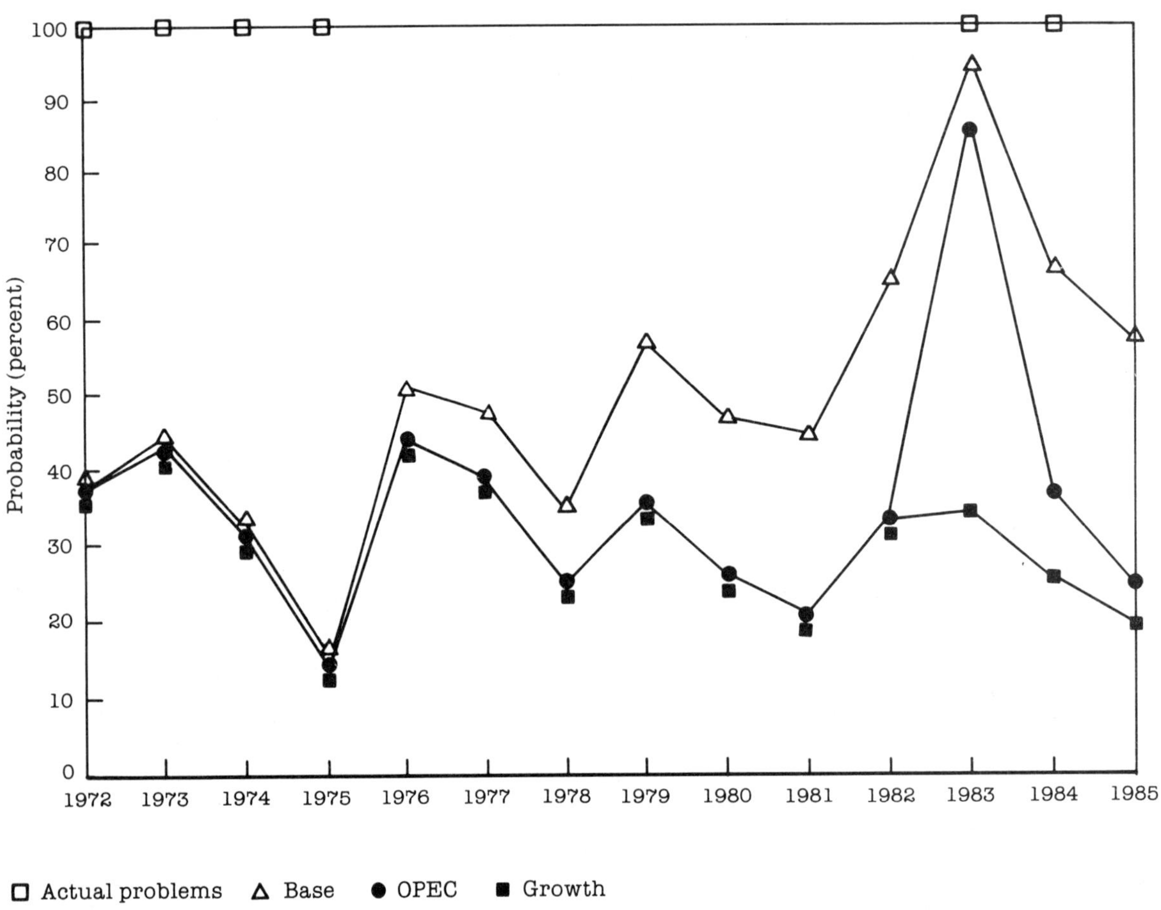

Figure 7-6. Korea: Probability of Repayment Problems

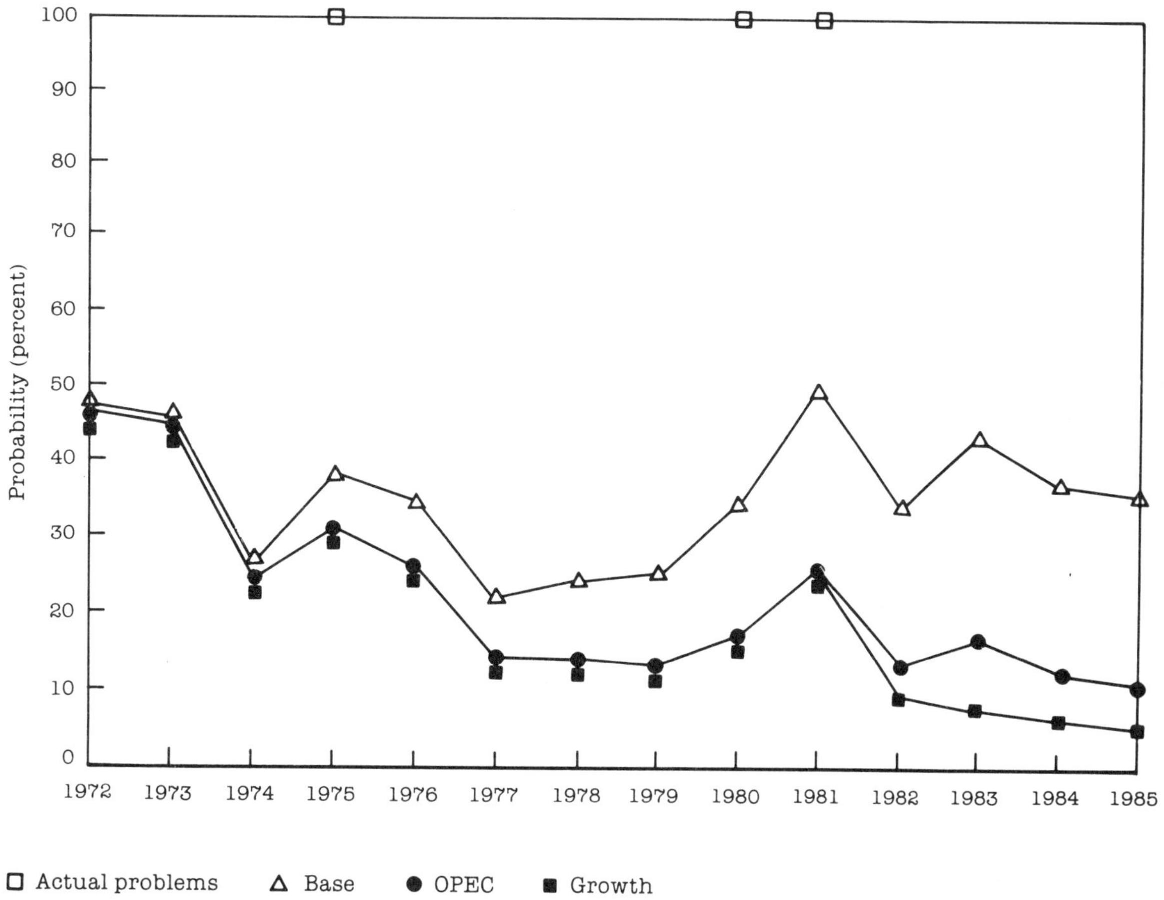

Figure 7-7. Peru: Probability of Repayment Problems

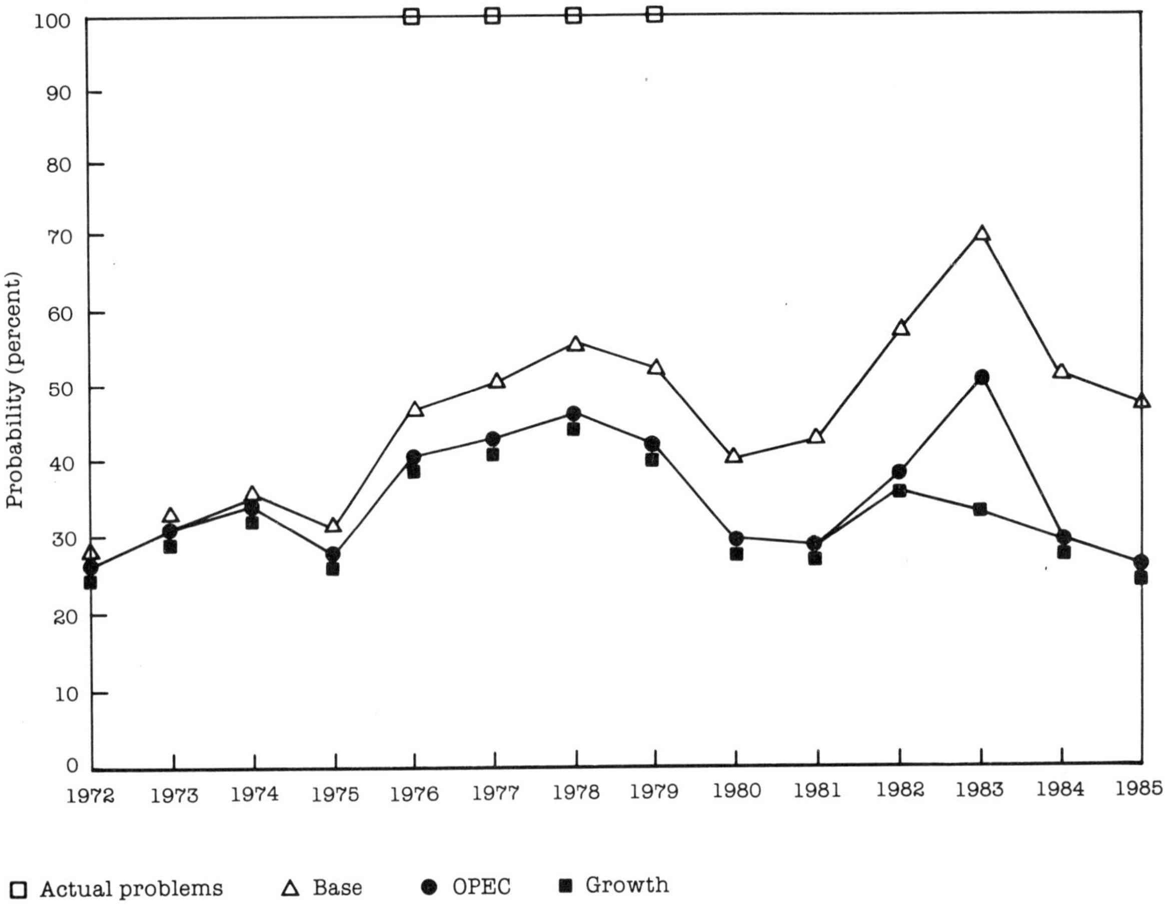

Figure 7-8. Philippines: Probability of Repayment Problems

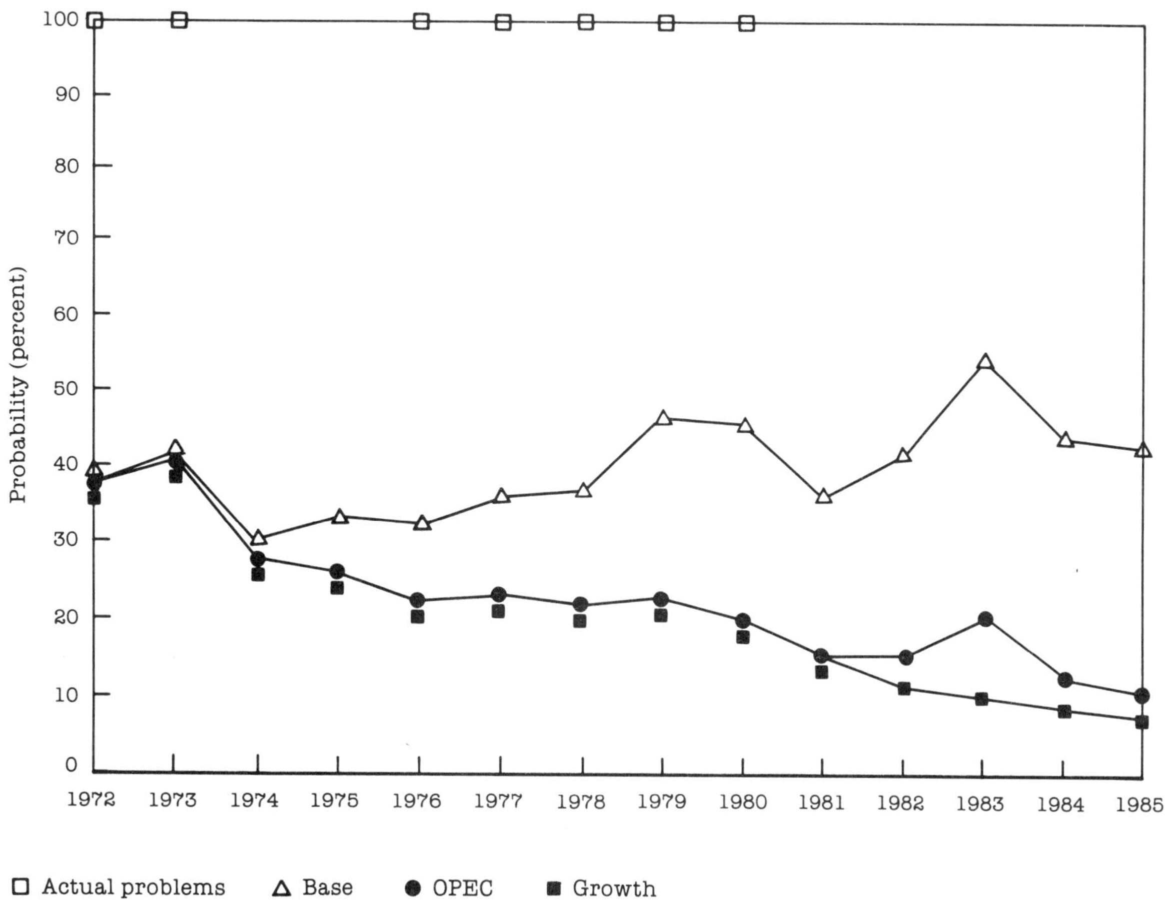

APPENDIX A. NATIONAL ACCOUNTS AND NEW FOREIGN LOAN DEMAND

The current account surplus (CA) satisfies the income identity

$$CA = X - M - ILF - OTP, \tag{7.1}$$

where X = exports, M = imports, ILF = interest paid on loans from foreigners, and OTP = other net factor payments and transfers to foreigners, and all quantities are denominated in dollars. The balance of payments identity relates CA to financial flows,

$$CA = \Delta NIR + \Delta BF - \Delta LF - FDI, \tag{7.2}$$

where NIR = net international reserves, BF = foreign bonds held domestically, LF = loans from foreigners, FDI = foreign direct investment, and $\Delta NIR = NIR - NIR_{-1}$ denotes a net addition to stock.

Let N = new foreign loans and PLF = payments of foreign loan principal due. Then $\Delta LF = N - PLF$ and the identities can be combined to yield an expression for new loan transactions:

$$N = PLF + ILF + \Delta NIR + \Delta BF - FDI + OTP - X + M. \tag{7.3}$$

Interest and principal payments on foreign loans sum to debt service paid (ILF + PLP = DSP). Debt service paid can also be written as debt service due (including past arrears outstanding) less current arrears, DSP = DSD − A. Substituting these definitions in (7.3) yields

$$N + A = DSD + \Delta NIR + \Delta BF - FDI + OTP - X + M. \tag{7.4}$$

This identity must hold for ex post observed new loans and arrears, and it also constrains the ex ante macroeconomic plans of a country maximizing intertemporal welfare. Viewed as an ex ante constraint, (7.4) contains the terms DSD, FDI, OTP, and X that are essentially predetermined, the terms ΔNIR and M that are instruments or targets of policy, and the term ΔBF, arising primarily from capital flight, which is driven by expectations of movements in the terms of trade. To protect its credit reputation, a country always prefers rollovers to arrears. Then the one-period-ahead ex ante demand for new loans satisfies

$$N^D = DSD^e + \Delta NIR^e + \Delta BF^e - FDI^e + OTP^e - X^e + M^e, \tag{7.5}$$

where N^D = demand for new foreign loans, and the superscript e denotes expectations. Defining these expectations as functions of the historical state of the country and the characteristics of announced macroeconomic policy completes the specification of new loan demand.

APPENDIX B. ECONOMETRIC MODELS FOR REPAYMENT PROBLEMS

Let N^D denote demand for new foreign loans, N^S denote supply, and L^* denote a limit on arrears which triggers a rescheduling. Define "desired" arrears to equal excess demand for loans, $A^* = N^D - N^S$. Then observed new debt (N), observed arrears (A), and an indicator $\delta = 1$ if rescheduling and $\delta = -1$ otherwise, are given by the following three regimes:

1. Excess supply: $A^* \leqslant 0$, $N = N^D$, $A = 0$, $\delta = -1$.
2. Moderate excess demand: $0 < A^* \leqslant L^*$, $N = N^S$, $A = N^D - N^S$, $\delta = -1$.
3. Large excess demand: $A^* > L$, $\delta = 1$.

Econometric models are obtained by specifying the distribution of components of N^D, N^S, and L^* not observed by the analyst, and the functional form and dependence of the systematic components on observed variables. Write

$$\begin{bmatrix} N^D \\ N^S \\ L^* \end{bmatrix} = \begin{bmatrix} D \\ S \\ L \end{bmatrix} + \begin{bmatrix} \varepsilon_D \\ \varepsilon_S \\ \varepsilon_L \end{bmatrix}, \tag{7.6}$$

where D, S, L are systematic components depending on the observed state of the country, and ε_D, ε_S, ε_L are random components. The probability of a repayment problem is

$$\text{Prob}\,(A^* > 0) = \text{Prob}\,(\varepsilon_S - \varepsilon_D < D - S), \tag{7.7}$$

and the probability of a rescheduling is

$$\text{Prob}\,(A^* > L^*) = \text{Prob}\,(\varepsilon_S + \varepsilon_L - \varepsilon_D < D - S - L). \tag{7.8}$$

Approximating the distributions of the random variables in (7.7) or (7.8) by logistics or normals yields logit or probit models of repayment problems or of reschedulings. The systematic parts of these models depend on <u>excess</u> demand D − S and do not permit separate identification of demand and supply.

A full model using level data on N and A that has a specification practical for estimation can be derived starting from the assumption that ε_D and ε_S are jointly normally distributed,

$$\begin{bmatrix} \varepsilon_D \\ \varepsilon_S \end{bmatrix} \sim N\left(\begin{bmatrix} 0 \\ 0 \end{bmatrix}, \begin{bmatrix} \sigma_D^2 & \rho\sigma_D\sigma_S \\ \rho\sigma_D\sigma_S & \sigma_S^2 \end{bmatrix}\right), \tag{7.9}$$

and $L^* = L + \varepsilon_L$ is independently distributed as a generalized exponential,

$$\text{Prob}\,(L^* \leqslant \ell) = 1 - e^{-B\ell - C}, \tag{7.10}$$

with B and C nonnegative functions of observables. This is a relatively flexible statistical specification; however, the specific combination of normals and exponential is chosen to yield tractable estimation forms.

The joint normal distribution (7.9) yields, after some manipulation, the conditional distributions

$$(A^*|N^D) \sim N[D\rho\sigma_S/\sigma_D - S + (\sigma_D - \rho\sigma_S)N^D/\sigma_D, \sigma_S^2(1 - \rho^2)] \tag{7.11}$$

$$(N^S|A^*) \sim N\left[S + (A^* + S - D)\sigma_S(\rho\sigma_D - \sigma_S)/\sigma^2, \frac{\sigma_D^2\sigma_S^2}{\sigma^2} \cdot (1 - \rho^2)\right] \tag{7.12}$$

and the marginal distribution $A^* \sim N(D - S, \sigma^2)$, where $\sigma^2 = \sigma_D^2 - 2\rho\sigma_D\sigma_S + \sigma_S^2$.

The probability of regime 1 observations $A = 0, N = N^D, \delta = -1$ is

$$\begin{aligned} P(A = 0, \delta = -1, N = N^D) &= P(A^* \leq 0|N^D = N)P(N^D = N) \\ &= \Phi\left(\frac{S - D\rho\sigma_S/\sigma_D - (\sigma_D - \rho\sigma_S)N/\sigma_D}{\sigma_S\sqrt{1 - \rho^2}}\right)\frac{1}{\sigma_D}\phi\left(\frac{N - D}{\sigma_D}\right), \end{aligned} \tag{7.13}$$

where ϕ and Φ are the standard normal density and cumulative distribution function, respectively. The probability of no repayment problem implied by this specification is a probit model

$$P(A = 0, \delta = -1) = \Phi\left(\frac{S - D}{\sigma}\right). \tag{7.14}$$

The probability of regime 2 observations $A > 0, N = N^S, \delta = -1$ is

$$\begin{aligned} P(A > 0, \delta = -1, N = N^S) &= P(N^S = N|A)P(L^* > A|A)P(A) \\ &= \frac{1}{\sigma_S\sigma_D\sqrt{1 - \rho^2}}\phi\left(\frac{N - S - (A + S - D)\sigma_S(\rho\sigma_D - \sigma_S)/\sigma^2}{\sigma_S\sigma_D\sqrt{1 - \rho^2}/\sigma}\right)e^{-BA-C}\frac{1}{\sigma}\phi\left(\frac{A - D + S}{\sigma}\right). \end{aligned} \tag{7.15}$$

The probability of the regime 3 observation $\delta = 1$ is

$$\begin{aligned} P(\delta = 1) = P(L^* < A^*) &= \int_0^\infty P(L^* < A^*|A^*)P(A^*)dA^* \\ &= \int_0^\infty (1 - e^{-BA^*-C})\frac{1}{\sigma}\phi\left(\frac{A^* - D + S}{\sigma}\right)dA^* \\ &= \Phi\left(\frac{D - S}{\sigma}\right) - \int_{\frac{S-D}{\sigma}}^\infty e^{-B\sigma t - C - B(D-S)}\phi(t)dt \\ &= \Phi\left(\frac{D - S}{\sigma}\right) - \Phi\left(\frac{D - S}{\sigma} - B\sigma\right)e^{-C+B(S-D)+B^2\sigma^2/2}. \end{aligned} \tag{7.16}$$

Note that this binary probability is more complex than the simple logit or probit approximation to the probability of a rescheduling suggested in (7.8).

The models above permit dependence of outcomes on the state of the country in the previous period, through specification of the functions D, S, B, and C. However, they do not incorporate the possibility of persistent unobserved country effects. Binary probit models of repayment problems or reschedulings can be generalized in a tractable way to incorporate random country effects. Define an indicator $\lambda = 1$ for a repayment problem ($A^* > 0$) and $\lambda = -1$ otherwise. Suppose country i is observed in a sequence of periods $t = 1, \ldots, T$, and let $(\lambda_{i1}, \ldots, \lambda_{iT})$ denote the observed history of problems. Desired arrears in period t can be written $A_{it}^* = D_{it} - S_{it} + \nu_i - \eta_{it}$, where ν_i is a random country effect and η_{it} is a random disturbance varying across countries and periods. Assume ν and η are independently normal with zero means and constant variances, and assume ν is independent across countries and η is independent across periods and countries. This is termed a "one-factor" model for A*.

Given these assumptions,

$$\text{(7.17)} \qquad P(A^*_{it} > 0|\nu_i) = P(\eta_{it} < D_{it} - S_{it} + \nu_i) = \Phi\left(\frac{D_{it} - S_{it} + \nu_i}{\sigma_\eta}\right),$$

where σ^2_η is the variance of η. Then

$$\text{(7.18)} \quad P(\lambda_{i1}, \ldots, \lambda_{iT}) = \int_{-\infty}^{+\infty} \frac{1}{\sigma_\nu} \phi\left(\frac{\nu}{\sigma_\nu}\right) \Phi\left(\lambda_{i1} \frac{D_{i1} - S_{i1} + \nu}{\sigma_\eta}\right) \ldots \Phi\left(\lambda_{iT} \frac{D_{iT} - S_{iT} + \nu}{\sigma_\eta}\right) d\nu.$$

This probability can be computed tractably by Gaussian quadrature. When the variance σ^2_ν is zero, this model reduces to the independent probit model of repayment problems. Reschedulings can be analyzed by an analogous one-factor model generalizing (7.8).

In principle, a one-factor structure could be added to the full model, with a persistent random country effect entering new loan demand; we leave this generalization for future research.

APPENDIX C. DATA DEFINITIONS AND SOURCES

The following abbreviations are used for data sources:

ARR	World Bank confidential data file on arrears
BOP	World Bank, World Tables, economic data sheet 2, balance of payments (computer tape)
ERP	(U.S.) Council of Economic Advisers, Economic Report of the President
IFS	IMF, International Financial Statistics (computer tape)
UNITS	United Nations, Yearbook of International Trade Statistics
WDT	World Bank, World Debt Tables (computer tape)
WT	World Bank, World Tables, economic data sheet 1 (computer tape)

IFM data were generally used when both IMF and World Bank data were available for the same variable. All conversions between dollar and local currency values were done with the use of the period average exchange rate from IFS. Table 7-14 gives means and standard deviations for the variables.

Dependent Variables

Reschedulings. The dummy variable for reschedulings was constructed from (unpublished) IMF sources and from our own country-by-country investigations. Reschedulings include Paris Club renegotiations, commercial bank renegotiations, and aid consortia renegotiations. We followed the Feder, Just, and Ross (1981) procedure of shifting the date of rescheduling if the key economic developments precipitating the rescheduling occurred in a different year. This resulted in the reclassification of roughly 40 percent of the reschedulings in the data. A small number of aid-motivated reschedulings (for instance, India in 1974–76) were excluded.

Presence of IMF support. Dummy variables for the presence of an IMF standby agreement (second or higher tranche) and use of the IMF Extended Fund Facility were obtained directly from the IMF.

Net new loans/exports. Net new loans are given by end-of-period debt minus end-of-previous period debt, using total disbursed public or publicly guaranteed medium- and long-term debt

Table 7-14. Mean and Standard Deviation of Variables

Variable	Mean	Standard deviation
Reserves/debt	0.104	0.156
Reserves/imports	0.290	0.259
Imports/GDP	0.351	0.245
Exports/GDP	0.292	0.225
Debt/GDP	1.094	1.091
Debt service due/exports	0.160	0.186
Nondebt inflows/debt service due	4.647	16.44
Real GNP per capita	0.689	0.640
Real GNP growth	0.051	0.058
Departure from PPP	0.035	0.166
Real growth of total Third World debt	0.103	0.033
Real Eurodollar rate	−0.079	0.083
Industrial country GDP growth (percent)	3.492	1.673
Outwardness index	1.11	0.562
Cumulative payments problems (reschedulings or IMF)	0.182	0.595
Net new loans/exports	0.148	0.546
Arrears/exports	0.041	0.178
Import price deflator	148.9	36.6

plus total disbursed private medium- and long-term debt. Both variables were taken from WDT, in U.S. dollars. When private debt was not reported, we set it at zero. The debt figures are normalized by exports of goods and nonfactor services, obtained from WT in local currency values and converted using the period average exchange rate from IFS.

Arrears. Data on beginning-of-period stocks of arrears on interest and principal in U.S. dollars were obtained from confidential files at the World Bank. Arrears on principal of smaller than 1 percent of outstanding debt were set at zero, as were interest arrears of less than 0.1 percent of debt.

Independent Variables

Exports/GDP. For exports, see above. Gross domestic product was taken from IFS, in local currency units.

Debt service/exports. Debt service is interest and amortization due in the current period, including outstanding arrears. Arrears outstanding at the end of the period were added to debt service actually paid during the period (from WDT). Note that although current debt service due is predetermined, the entire ratio is lagged. This was done because end-of-1982 arrears were not available.

Debt/exports. For end-of-period debt and current exports, see above.

Reserves/imports. Total reserves minus gold were taken from IFS, in U.S. dollars; imports of goods and nonfactor services, in local currency units, were taken from WT and converted.

GNP per capita. Gross national product in U.S. dollars was taken from WT and converted to real 1972 dollars using the U.S. GNP deflator from ERP.

Growth rate of GNP. The growth of real GNP was calculated from the WT real GNP data.

Deviation from PPP · QFIXER. As an indicator of real exchange rate movements, we compute the difference between the rate of domestic consumer price inflation and the sum of exchange rate depreciation and the growth rate of the U.S. GNP deflator. This variable was interacted with a dummy variable (QFIXER) indicating a fixed exchange rate regime. The dummy was taken from the annual IMF publication *Exchange Arrangements and Exchange Restrictions*.

Imports/GDP. See above.

Outwardness index. See explanation in text.

Real Eurodollar rate. The end-of-year six-month Eurodollar deposit rate (i^*) from Morgan Guaranty (World Financial Markets) was adjusted using domestic consumer price inflation (Π) and the rate of depreciation of the exchange rate (e) to yield r^*, the real six-month Eurodollar rate:

$$(1 + r^*) = \frac{(1 + i^*)(1 + e)}{(1 + \Pi)}.$$

The consumer price index and period average exchange rate were taken from IFS.

Growth in total LDC debt. The growth in disbursed medium- and long-term debt for all developing countries together was taken from WDT.

Growth in industrial country GDP. GDP growth for industrial countries was taken from the IMF International Financial Statistics Yearbook, 1983.

Import price deflator. A Laspeyres import price deflator was constructed for each developing country as follows:

$$P = \frac{\sum_{j=1}^{3} \Theta_{j72} P_{jt}}{\sum_{j=1}^{3} \Theta_{j72} P_{j72}}$$

where P_{jt} is the real dollar price (nominal divided by the U.S. GNP deflator) of the jth import category and Θ_{j72} is the 1972 import value share for the jth category. The three categories are: (1) food and raw materials, (2) fuel, and (3) manufactures. The value shares are from UNITS [the food and beverage category was used for (1)]; the prices are also from UNITS with the exception of (3), for which we used the index of dollar unit values for industrial countries' manufacturing exports to developing countries from the World Bank, Commodity Price Trends, 1982–83.

Cumulative payments problems. As an indicator of previous debt problems, we constructed an index of the number of years since 1970 in which a rescheduling occurred. A similar variable was constructed covering IMF agreements.

Non-debt inflows/debt service due. Nondebt inflows include foreign direct investment and net private official transfers (from IFS).

NOTES

1. Arrears on principal below 1 percent of disbursed debt and arrears on interest below 0.1 percent of disbursed debt are treated as cosmetic and are not counted as repayment problems.
2. Cline (1983) attempts to address the potential simultaneity problem by entering most variables lagged one period.
3. $0.404 = (0.823)^2/[1 + (0.823)^2]$.

REFERENCES

Aliber, R. 1980. A conceptual approach to the analysis of external debt of the developing countries. World Bank Staff Working Paper no. 421. Washington, D.C. (October).

Balassa, Bela. 1984. "The problem of the debt in developing countries." Washington, D.C.: World Bank. Processed.

Butler, J. S., and R. Moffit. 1982. "A computationally efficient quadrature procedure for the one-factor multinomial probit model." Econometrica 50 (no. 3):761–64.

Cline, W. R. 1983. International Debt and the Stability of the World Economy. Washington, D.C.: Institute for International Economics.

Cooper, R. N., and J. D. Sachs. 1984. "Borrowing abroad: The debtor's perspective." Harvard University. Processed.

Council of Economic Advisers. 1984. Economic report of the President. Washington, D.C.: Government Printing Office.

Eaton, J., and M. Gersovitz. 1980. "LDC participation in international financial markets: Debt and reserves." Journal of Development Economics 7:3–21.

———. 1981. "Debt with potential repudiation: Theoretical and empirical analysis." Review of Economic Studies 48 (February):289–309.

Feder, G., and R. E. Just. 1977. "A study of debt-servicing capacity applying logit analysis." Journal of Development Economics 4:25–38.

Feder, G., R. Just, and K. Ross. 1981. "Projecting debt-servicing capacity of developing countries." Journal of Financial and Quantitative Analysis 16 (no. 5):651–69.

Federal Reserve System. Federal Reserve Bulletin. Washington, D.C. Various issues.

Frank, C., and W. Cline. 1971. "Measurement of debt-servicing capacity." Journal of International Economics 1:327–44.

Glick, R. 1983. "Multiperiod models of foreign borrowing: An analytic review of the literature." New York University Graduate School of Business (February). Processed.

Grinols, E. 1976. "International debt rescheduling and discrimination using financial variables." U.S. Treasury Department. Unpublished manuscript.

Hajivassiliou, V. A. 1983. "Estimating and testing an aggregative disequilibrium model of the U.S. labor market." MIT. Processed.

Heckman, J. 1981. Statistical models for discrete panel data." In Structural analysis of discrete data with econometric applications, edited by C. Manski and D. McFadden. Cambridge, Mass.: MIT Press.

International Monetary Fund. Exchange arrangements and exchange restrictions: Annual report. Washington, D.C. Various issues.

———. 1983. World economic outlook. Washington, D.C.

———. 1983. Recent multilateral debt restructurings with official and bank creditors. IMF Occasional Paper no. 25. Washington, D.C.

Maddala, G. 1983. Limited dependent and qualitative variables in econometrics. Cambridge, Eng.: Cambridge University Press.

Mayo, A., and A. Barrett. 1977. "An early warning model for assessing developing country risk." In Proceedings of a symposium on developing countries' debt, edited by S. Goodman. Washington, D.C.: Export-Import Bank.

McFadden, D. 1976. "A comment on discriminant versus logit analysis." Annals of Economic and Social Measurement 5 (no. 4):511–23.

———. 1981. "Econometric models of probabilistic choice." In Structural analysis of discrete data with econometric applications, edited by C. Manski and D. McFadden. Cambridge, Mass.: MIT Press.

———. 1982. "Qualitative response models." In Advances in econometrics, edited by W. Hildebrand. New York: Cambridge University Press.

———. 1984. "Econometric analysis of quantitative response models." In Handbook of econometrics. Vol. 2. Edited by A. Griliches and M. D. Intriligator. New York: Elsevier North-Holland.

Morgan Guaranty Trust Company of New York. World Financial Markets. New York. Various issues.

Sachs, J., and D. Cohen. 1982. LDC borrowing with default risk. National Bureau of Economic Research Working Paper no. 925 (July). Cambridge, Mass.

Saini, K., and P. Bates. 1978. Statistical techniques for determining debt-servicing capacity for developing countries: Analytical review of the literature and further empirical results. Federal Reserve Bank of New York Research Paper no. 7818 (September). New York.

Sargen, N. 1977. "Use of economic indicators and country risk appraisal." Economic Review of the Federal Reserve Bank of San Francisco (Fall):19–35.

Shishido, H. 1984. Econometric analysis of international credit rationing: A disequilibrium approach. Washington, D.C.: World Bank. Processed.

United Nations. 1983. Yearbook of international trade statistics, 1981. Vol. 1. New York.

World Bank. 1983. Commodity price trends, 1982–83 ed. Washington, D.C.

———. 1984. World debt tables: External debt of developing countries, 1983–84 ed. Washington, D.C.

———. 1984. World tables. 3d ed. Baltimore, Md.: Johns Hopkins University Press.

———. 1983. World development report, 1983. New York: Oxford University Press.

PART IV

Country Experiences: Lessons and Issues

8

External Debt, Budget Deficits, and Disequilibrium Exchange Rates

Rudiger Dornbusch

This chapter explores the role of disequilibrium exchange rates and budget deficits in promoting external indebtedness and the current debt crisis. Oil, U.S. interest rates, and the 1981–82 world recession are often isolated as the chief causes of the world debt crisis. But these factors have only made much more apparent and unsustainable an underlying disequilibrium in which exchange rate overvaluation and budget deficits were perpetuated by continuing and excessive recourse to the world capital market.

Because the details of the disequilibrium differ quite a bit between countries, I will look at three different episodes: Argentina, Chile, and Brazil. In one case capital flight played a key role in the growth in debt; in the other cases the level and composition of spending assumed primary importance. These determinants are investigated for the period 1978–82, which was chosen because it coincided with major changes in the world economy and with disequilibrium real exchange rate policies in several countries.

I will start by laying out a framework and some facts concerning the debt accumulation.

SOME FACTS AND A FRAMEWORK

Latin American debt problems are not new, and only a year after the Mexican and Brazilian problems became apparent the literature abounded with references to episodes of overlending in the 1930s and before. Here is a typical quotation from 1937:

> The history of investment in South America throughout the last century has been one of confidence followed by disillusionment, of borrowing cycles followed by widespread defaults, and of a series of alternating repudiations and recognitions of external debts. Willingness to maintain service payments has certainly been less high than in the British Empire, and excesses were inevitable under the conditions which existed while the United States was investing such huge sums in these countries.... The ability of the most credit-worthy governments to avoid default must necessarily be impaired if any considerable part of the nominal value of loans has not, in fact, been put to the use for which it was intended. (Royal Institute of International Affairs 1937, p. 266.)

After the wholesale default on external debt in the 1930s there was a long gap during which current account imbalances were financed by a reduction in reserves (accumulated during the war), by direct capital inflows, by official aid, and by borrowing through international institutions.[1] Table 8-1 shows external debt data for benchmark years for several countries. The data problems, even for the very recent years, are overwhelming. But even so, the table conveys a notion of the very rapid growth of external indebtedness in the 1970s.

An earlier version of this paper was presented at the ISPE Seminar on public economics at the University of Santa Cruz, February 1984. I am indebted to Domingo Cavallo, Eliana Cardoso, John Cuddington, and Stanley Fischer for helpful comments.

Table 8-1. Gross External Public or Publicly Guaranteed Debt
(billions of U.S. dollars, end of year)

Country	1945	1956	1960	1970	1975	1983
Argentina	0.9	0.7	1.5	5.0	7.9	38.5
Brazil	0.4	1.5	1.8	5.5	22.2	93.7
Chile	0.4	0.3	0.6	3.2	5.3	18.7
U.S. price level (1970 = 100)	41	68	75	100	137	235

Note: The data for 1945, 1956, and 1960 include only debt in excess of one-year maturity. The price level reported in the last row is the U.S. GNP deflator. The unit value index in dollars for world trade would show a somewhat larger cumulative increase.
Sources: United Nations (1964) and Morgan Guaranty.

Table 8-2. Prime Rate, World Growth, and Price Inflation in World Trade
(average annual pecentage rate)

Period	Prime rate	Inflation rate in world trade	World growth
1970–73	6.7	12.4	4.7
1979–82	15.5	4.4	1.1

Sources: International Financial Statistics (International Monetary Fund [IMF]) and Council of Economic Advisers, Economic Report of the President (Washington, D.C.: Government Printing Office, 1984).

From the supply side the conventional explanation for the lending burst is the oil shock, which made petro dollars available for financial intermediation by commercial banks. This is brought out by the fact that from 1970 to 1983 the share of bank lending in total debt increased from only 25 percent to nearly 75 percent. On the demand side the reasons for the debt buildup are much less clear-cut. Oil, interest rates, and the world recession are often cited and are certainly a good part of the story in some countries.

Table 8-2 and figure 8-1 show the important differences in the world macroeconomic setting for the debtors in the early 1970s and in the 1978–82 period. The earlier period is clearly a debtors' paradise with high growth, sharp real commodity price increases, and low nominal interest rates coupled with high inflation. The 1978–82 period is just the reverse and to that extent must account for some of the debt problems. To be more precise, I will show that the degree and particular kind of openness—unrestricted capital flows, free trade in goods, both or neither—influence the way in which households and firms respond to exchange rate misalignment and commercial and fiscal policy.

A Framework

The balance of payments accounts provide a link between the increase in gross external debt and the portfolio and spending decisions of the economy.

The increase in gross external debt corresponds to the sum of three items identified from the balance of payments accounts:

(8.1) Increase in gross external debt = current account deficit
− direct and long-term portfolio capital inflows
+ official reverse increases
+ other private capital outflows.

With respect to capital account transactions I make a distinction between direct investment and long-term portfolio capital flows on the one hand and, on the other, the short-term flows, which for simplicity can be thought of as "hot money" on the way in and as "capital flight" on the way out. Equation (8.1) then shows that an increase in gross external debt can have three

Figure 8-1. Industrial Production and Real Material Prices
(1975–77=100)

Source: International Financial Statistics.

broad sources: current account deficits not financed by long-term capital inflows, borrowing to finance an official reserve build-up, or private capital flight.

The accounting identity in (8.1) immediately draws attention to the fact that the debt buildup does not correspond one-for-one to a resource transfer from lending countries to the borrowers. Part of the increased gross debt merely reflects capital flight and thus no change in aggregate net foreign assets. Another part reflects the capitalization through increased borrowing of the inflation component in nominal interest payments. The resource transfer is limited to the inflation-adjusted current account.[2]

The various components in (8.1) for Argentina, Brazil, and Chile in 1978–82 need to be identified empirically. Table 8-3 shows estimates of the components of the gross debt increase. Balance of payments and external debt data from different sources are used to try and piece together the "proximate sources" of the increase in gross external debt. The difference in data sources and the precariousness of debt and balance of payments data imply that these estimates cannot be very precise. Despite these limitations, the data give a good idea of the difference in patterns between countries.

In the case of Argentina the current account deficit is financed largely by direct investment and portfolio capital inflows. The increase in debt therefore corresponds to a large extent to the financing of capital flight—the central bank borrows abroad and sells foreign exchange to private residents, who use the proceeds to acquire foreign assets. The breakdown is of course not entirely precise because the current account certainly underestimates military imports.

Table 8-3. Components of the Increase in Gross External Debt, 1978–82 (billions of U.S. dollars)

Country	Increase in gross external debt	Current account			Direct and portfolio capital inflow	Residual[a] (reserve gains + capital outflows)
		Total	Trade	Interest		
Argentina	26.8	−10.6	6.8	−9.3	7.2	23.4
Brazil	48.8	−58.4	−4.7	−33.7	11.5	1.9
Chile	11.5	−11.4	−3.9	−5.1	1.3	1.4

a. This column is calculated as the part of debt increase not accounted for by the current account deficit or the net capital (direct and portfolio) outflows. Interest payments are not adjusted for inflation.

Sources: Morgan Guaranty, Data Resources, Inc., and the International Monetary Fund (IMF).

For Argentina it has been suggested that the underestimate may be as much as $7 billion. Underinvoicing of exports, overinvoicing of imports, and underestimates of tourism and smuggling further distort the data.

The table makes it clear that the Argentinian case is primarily one of increased debt to finance capital flight, not current account imbalances. Thus the government incurs external debts and uses the proceeds to finance private capital outflows or private acquisition of foreign assets. The increase in gross external debt misrepresents the net foreign asset position of the country, since increased public debts are matched for the most part by larger private foreign assets. But inasmuch as the latter are removed from the control and disposition of the authorities, there is nevertheless a "debt problem."

In the case of Brazil and Chile the residual item in the last column accounts for very little. The increased debt reflects current account deficits, not capital flight. In both cases direct investment and portfolio capital flows finance only part of the current account deficits, and hence external debt increases by the difference. Both countries, unlike Argentina, have a cumulative trade deficit and, of course, deficits on service account. In both cases interest payments account for half or more of the increase in debt. To explain the large cumulative account balances and the capital flight I now turn to theoretical considerations. I take as given that the experience in the individual countries was highly unusual and ask in what ways policies created circumstances in which economies indulge in large current account deficits or large-scale capital flight?

THEORY

It is ordinarily thought that large increases in external debt have as their counterpart large cumulative current account deficits. These current account deficits, in turn, reflect either an imbalance between private saving and investment or a public sector budget deficit. More formally, from the national accounts the current account deficit or increase in net external liabilities is:

$$\text{Increase in net foreign liabilities} = \text{Private investment} - \text{Private saving} + \text{Budget deficit.} \quad (8.2)$$

Episodes of current account deficits can, in this sense, be analyzed in terms of the shocks to which the economy is exposed and the impact they exert on saving, investment, and the budget. The channels through which saving, investment, and the budget are affected will be discussed within the framework of standard neoclassical macroeconomics. Transitorily high levels of investment and budget deficits or transitorily low levels of saving will be identified.

Saving

Household saving behavior takes place in the standard multiperiod framework. Saving is governed by wealth, which is the present value of after-tax labor income plus the value of initial assets, and by the real interest rate. The real interest rate is the world nominal rate adjusted for depreciation and the domestic rate of inflation. The latter can differ from that abroad to the extent that traded and nontraded goods or export and import prices change over time or through changes in exchange rate or commercial policy. (On this point see Bruno 1976, Obstfeld 1983, Svensson and Razin 1983, and Dornbusch 1983a.)

There are several channels through which events in the economy can lead to a reduction in saving:

- An increase in wealth because of perceived higher future incomes or an increase in the future rental on domestic real capital. Since by assumption the gains in output occur only in the future, but consumers are forward looking, the anticipations lead to higher current spending and thus to dissaving.
- The effect of expected future income gains on current spending is reinforced if these anticipated gains come together with the removal of borrowing constraints and increases in wealth that make it possible to spend at the level of normal income.
- Dissaving may be the counterpart of intertemporal resource allocation by the household in response to intertemporal relative price and hence real interest rate movements. With high intertemporal substitutability, consumption occurs in periods when interest rates are low and inflation is high.

Purchases of consumer durables are an important reason for variations in measured saving. Anticipated intertemporal variations in the real price of durables (and, even more strongly, in the availability of durables) affect the timing of purchases. They lead to purchases in periods when the real price is low. This effect is more strongly at work the higher the rate of price increase on durables relative to interest and the rate of physical depreciation. The confidence in a strong resale market and hence increased liquidity of durables reinforces the tendency for intertemporal substitution of purchases, as does a reduction in credit constraints. (See Mishkin 1976 and Deaton and Muellbauer 1980, chap. 14.)

In the context of an open economy, a transitory real appreciation (or an overvaluation) of the exchange rate would therefore lead one to predict dissaving. Consumers would concentrate purchases of imported durables in those periods, and current account deficits would tend to be large.

A critical question is to what extent private saving behavior is affected by government budget deficits. In other words, do households, in response to deficits, build up assets in anticipation of future taxes on their own incomes and those of their heirs? It is assumed that these effects are limited to taxes borne directly by the current generation and do not extend further. Thus deficits are by and large not offset by increased current and future saving. Effects on saving result only from directly anticipated taxation or from a reduction in the value of assets that reflects future taxes on the income from those assets.

Investment

Investment is affected through three channels. The concern here is with the link between exchange rates and investment. Inventory investment is influenced by the cost of carrying inventories relative to the return on the goods being carried. Business fixed investment is influenced by changes in the desired capital stock and by changes in the adjustment costs associated with capital formation. A formal model is sketched in the appendix, but the focus here is simply on the main ideas.

An anticipated depreciation implies capital gains on imported goods, specifically on materials and consumer or producer durables. Firms would, other things being equal, purchase importables before an anticipated depreciation and hold them to collect capital gains. But that tendency is dampened by three factors: first, there will after a point be increasing marginal costs of carrying inventories; second, there is uncertainty about the future price; and third, carrying inventories involves an alternative cost in terms of nominal interest forgone. The optimal inventory for risk-averse firms, given these considerations, will depend on the mean and variance of the expected real return on inventories, on inflation relative to interest rates, and on the marginal carrying cost. Reduced variance and increased anticipated depreciation that is not reflected in interest rates will raise inventory investment and hence imports of materials or of producer and consumer goods.

To discuss business fixed investment, it is useful to think of a standard neoclassical theory based on adjustment costs. Real exchange rates here play a role because they determine the desired capital stock by influencing the user cost of capital or by affecting the adjustment cost. Real exchange rates affect adjustment costs because investment has import content, specifically in the form of imported machinery.

What are the effects of a transitory real appreciation? While the real exchange rate is overvalued, the real price of imported goods is low and, for that reason, investment is high. During the period of overvaluation, capital is being accumulated because the overvaluation in fact constitutes an investment subsidy for those investment activities that have import content. Once the real depreciation occurs, the accumulation of capital is reversed.

A second channel through which overvaluation influences investment is via the desired stock of capital. Suppose investment has significant import content and that capital is used in the production of tradables. A transitory overvaluation and anticipated real depreciation now exerts opposing effects on investment. The low real price of tradables depresses the stock demand for capital, but the investment subsidy implicit in overvaluation tends to promote investment. The net result depends on how significant the subsidy is as a determinant of investment. When import content is important the net result will still be a transitory investment boom and hence an import boom in investment goods.

Once again the anticipated real depreciation that has been assumed is not fully matched by higher interest rates. To the extent that nominal interest rates rise in anticipation of depreciation, this raises the user cost and therefore reduces any impact on investment.

There are thus strong links between the time path of the real price of imports and the purchases of imported investment goods. Anticipation of real depreciation must produce an import bulge.

The Budget

The government, in principle, obeys the intertemporal budget constraint. The budget constraint states that the present value of tax revenues (including the inflation tax) must equal the initial debt plus the present value of outlays. Subject to political constraints on the rate of cut in outlays or the rate of increase in taxes, the government would practice tax smoothing as suggested in Barro (1983). A permanent loss in revenues would be immediately and fully offset through increased tax rates or reduced outlays, leaving debt unchanged. Transitory shocks to revenue or to outlays would be substantially met by debt finance. The increase in debt is in turn amortized over the long term by a small increase in taxes and a small cut in outlays.

An increase in interest rates reduces the present value of the excess of taxes over outlays and hence requires an adjustment in the path of taxes and expenditures. Once again, if the shock is transitory, debt finance will bridge the gap in the short term while small changes in taxes and outlays ensure intertemporal solvency of the government. If the increase in interest rates is permanent, then immediate adjustment of tax rates relative to outlays occurs and debt remains unchanged.

The tightness of the debt finance model must be relaxed to allow for three practical considerations. First, there are constraints on the rates at which politicians can or will change taxes and outlays. Second, it may take time to identify disturbances as transitory or permanent, since all disturbances are initially assumed to be transitory, particularly when they are adverse. Third, debt default, both internal and external, is a way of ensuring the intertemporal budget constraint, although such a "policy" would of course be reflected in the interest rate required by holders of the public debt.[3]

The government budget problem is made more specific by the introduction of specific standard of living constraints. Such constraints imply that in the presence of adverse shocks to the real income of the favored group, additional outlays are required to support the standard of living. If tax adjustments or reductions in the standard of living can occur only over time, there is a built-in link between (adverse) economic shocks and the budget. Adverse shocks therefore invariably involve an early stage of deficit finance, even if they are persistent.

A failure to smooth taxes and outlays as well as benefits in the case of a permanent disturbance does need justification. Why might taxpayers prefer to see low tax rates now and pay for those low rates by higher future rates that will yield equal present-value tax collection? Why would those who receive government benefits desire a front-loaded flow of benefits rather than a steady stream of equal present value? The tax-smoothing model rejects such behavior as irrational and predicts that a government following noxious policies along these patterns would be thrown out of office for failing to maximize voters' welfare. But the moment the private sector discounts at a rate in excess of the market rate of interest the future is systematically undervalued and biased toward debt finance. The argument is reinforced when liquidity constraints lead part of the population to discount at exceptionally high rates.

There is, of course, an interdependence between the model of debt finance and the private sector's optimal intertemporal allocation of resources and portfolio choice. The more the government chooses debt finance, postponing required tax increases, the more the private sector can adjust to the future increased taxes or debt default by holding nontaxable assets (dollars and washing machines). This raises the cost to the government of delaying adjustment, but does not eliminate altogether the tendency toward short-run deficit finance.

In concluding on the issue of the budget, it is worth noting two important linkages between the exchange rate and government outlays. First, to the extent that there is an external public debt, a real depreciation raises the real value of debt service in terms of domestic output and hence is likely to increase the budget deficit. There is thus a potential tradeoff between international competitiveness and a balanced budget.

The second link between exchange rates and the budget arises in cases of exchange rate guarantees. If the government has guaranteed a given exchange rate sometime in the past but has since found it necessary to depreciate, the resulting exchange rate subsidy will cause the budget to deteriorate. Where exchange rate guarantees and external debt exist and it is difficult to adjust taxes, there is thus a tendency to seek overvaluation as one of the ways to minimize debt finance.

In this review of the various channels through which the current account is affected by transitory and permanent disturbances, the point is that anticipated real depreciation acts in a most forceful way to generate current deficits in the external balance. In addition, through the budget, current and transitory shocks to receipts and outlays tend to be translated into deficit finance and hence into external deficits. The next section discusses how these considerations help explain the current accounts and external debt accumulation of Chile and Brazil.

APPLICATION TO CHILE AND BRAZIL

In Chile and Brazil external debt increases are the counterpart of current account deficits. They represent levels of spending and resource absorption in excess of current income. But the details of the process differ. In Chile overvaluation is the key, while in Brazil the budget deficit assumes a central role.

Chile

Following hyperinflation in the early 1970s, Chile experienced economic stabilization and a reform of fiscal and commercial policy in 1973–77. The budget deficit was moved from more than 10 percent of GNP in the early 1970s to actual surpluses in 1979–80. Tariffs were reduced from average nominal rates near 100 percent, with individual rates widely dispersed, to a uniform rate of only 10 percent by 1978. Inflation was reduced from over 500 percent a year to practically zero, and, to top it off, growth in 1977–81 averaged 8 percent a year.

Today the country's performance bears little resemblance to that performance: output has declined since 1981 by 10 percent, and unemployment stands at 30 percent. Exchange rate policy and excessive recourse to external debt finance are at the center of the explanation.

In an effort to speed up the process of disinflation the Chilean authorities decided in early 1979 to experiment with the "law of one price." The exchange rate was fixed at 39 pesos to the U.S. dollar, in the hope that the pegging would directly cut down the rate of inflation and also break inflationary expectations. At the time, however, Chilean inflation was still more than 30 percent, far above the rate in the United States. Moreover, formal indexing arrangements linked wage increases to past inflation. As Corbo (1983) has documented, the combination of inflation and indexation led over time to growing overvaluation as wages were pushed up relative to the prices of importables and the world prices of exportables. The growth in real wages for those employed of course implied a sharp gain in the standard of living. The loss in employment in response to overvaluation was slow to build up, and thus the period 1977–80 offered a spectacle of yet another "miracle."

The Chilean boom conditions in the early stage of overvaluation lend support to the notion that in the short run real depreciation is deflationary. Here the real appreciation, by raising real wages, has expansionary effects on aggregate demand before the employment effects and bankruptcy start making their inroads. This point has been emphasized by Diaz Alejandro (1963) and more recently by Calvo (1982) in the Argentinian context.

Table 8-4 shows the ratio of consumption and of gross fixed investment to GDP (in constant 1977 prices), as well as the budget deficit ratio. It is clear that 1980–82 is the period to focus on, since consumption sharply rises as does the investment ratio and the budget deficit. Investment and saving behavior mirror the sharp deterioration in the current account.

We now focus on the mechanism through which consumption and investment spending increased so sharply in 1980–81. Figure 8-2 shows the real exchange rate — import prices relative to the prices of nontradables — for the period. The real appreciation, on this measure,

Table 8-4. Consumption, Fixed Investment, and the Budget Deficit in Chile (percent of GDP)

Item	1960–69	1970–79	1978	1979	1980	1981	1982
Investment	20.2	15.7	16.5	19.6	23.9	23.9	9.6
Consumption	79.7	75.8	72.4	71.1	70.5	76.2	76.1
Budget deficit	2.9	6.8	0.8	−1.7	−3.1	−1.6	2.4
Current account deficit	n.a.	n.a.	7.7	5.7	7.2	14.6	9.4

Sources: Banco Central de Chile and *International Financial Statistics*.

Figure 8-2. The Chilean Real Exchange Rate
(1972:II = 100)

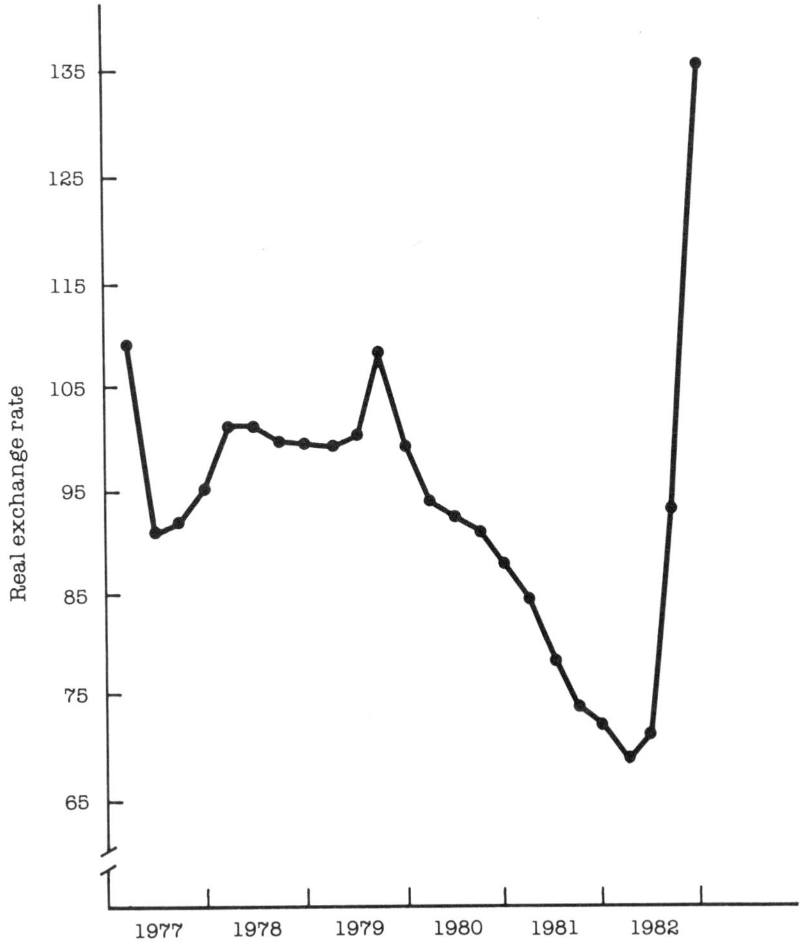

Source: Corbo and de Melo (1983).

amounted to 25 percent by early 1982. Table 8-5 shows some of the implications. Imports of all goods increased very sharply over the period, peaking in 1981. As an example, the growth of imports of automobiles was immense both as a percentage of total imports and as a fraction of the existing stock. After peaking in 1981, imports fell off sharply.

Table 8-6 shows the same pattern in more detail and reports the quantity indexes for different groups of imports. In each case there is a sharp peak in 1981 and a decline in 1982–83. The pattern is significantly more pronounced for capital goods than for intermediates, even though in the latter category automobile parts and pieces and intermediate industrial goods, unlike primary commodities, show very high growth rates.[4]

The pattern of strongly growing imports through 1981 reflects in part the very strong performance of the Chilean economy. In addition, the increase in asset prices that took place in 1977–81 implied increased wealth and hence the allocation of part of the gain in wealth to increase consumption. Harberger (1983a) in particular has emphasized this point.

In addition to the impact of growth and wealth on consumption and investment, there appears to be a strong real exchange rate effect on the composition and level of spending. By 1981 the

Table 8-5. Chile: Imports and the Real Exchange rate

Item	1978	1979	1980	1981	1982
Imports (billions of U.S. dollars)	3.00	4.22	5.82	6.78	3.83
Trade balance (billions of U.S. dollars)	−0.52	−0.32	−0.45	−2.41	0.29
Real exchange rate (1978 = 100)	100	100.6	90.7	76.9	92.0
Automobiles (1,000s)					
Stock	335.8	386.0	458.7	573.8	n.a.
Imports	11.4	33.6	51.6	79.5	30.3
Production	17.1	16.5	25.2	20.6	7.9

n.a. Not available.
Sources: Banco Central de Chile and Corbo and de Melo (1983).

Table 8-6. Import Quantity Indexes for Chile
(January–June of each period)

Imports	1980	1981	1982	1983
Total	100	133	92	68
Consumption goods	100	175	125	75
Automobiles	100	226	90	38
Electric domestic	100	156	68	n.a.
Capital goods	100	134	90	38
Machinery	100	128	119	52
Transport equipment	100	140	53	20
Breeding stock	100	328	85	50
Intermediate goods	100	117	81	76

n.a. Not available.
Source: Banco Central de Chile.

sustainability of the increasingly overvalued exchange rate was becoming an open question. Although the government had sworn to sustain the exchange rate, the growing problems of competing export and import firms and growing unemployment made it more and more plausible that either depreciation or a return to protection, or both, would take place. In these circumstances it is clear that a sharp increase in purchases of importables could be expected. Tables 8-3, 8-4, and 8-5 clearly bear that out. (See, too, in figure 8-3 the trade balance for 1981, which shows an all-time high deficit.) They also show that once the overvaluation came to an end in June 1982, the import boom collapsed.

The real exchange rate directly affects saving and investment and hence the current account. But it also works through a separate channel. Overvaluation, once the short-run expansionary effects have passed, leads to a change in the composition of spending. Demand for domestic goods declines and demand for importables rises. The shift implies a reduction in domestic output and employment. The fall in income reduces saving of the private sector and it also leads to an increased budget deficit. Accordingly, the indirect effects cause the external balance to deteriorate.

The steep decline in world copper prices in 1981–82 further reinforced the effect of declining income on the external balance. If the decline is perceived as transitory, it leads to dissaving both by households and by the public sector and hence enlarges the external deficit and borrowing. Although the copper price decline is often cited as an explanation for the external deficit and debt accumulation, the explanation cannot be extended too far. Even in 1982 the dollar value of copper exports exceeded the 1978 level by a large margin.[5]

One further factor, which is particularly evident in the Brazilian case, is the effect of increased interest rates in the world market. For a debtor country this implies a deterioration in the intertemporal terms of trade and hence an adverse real income effect. It is estimated that the direct contribution to the deficit of higher interest rates in the world market is $3.2 billion.

Figure 8-3. Chile: Ratio of Trade Surplus to Exports

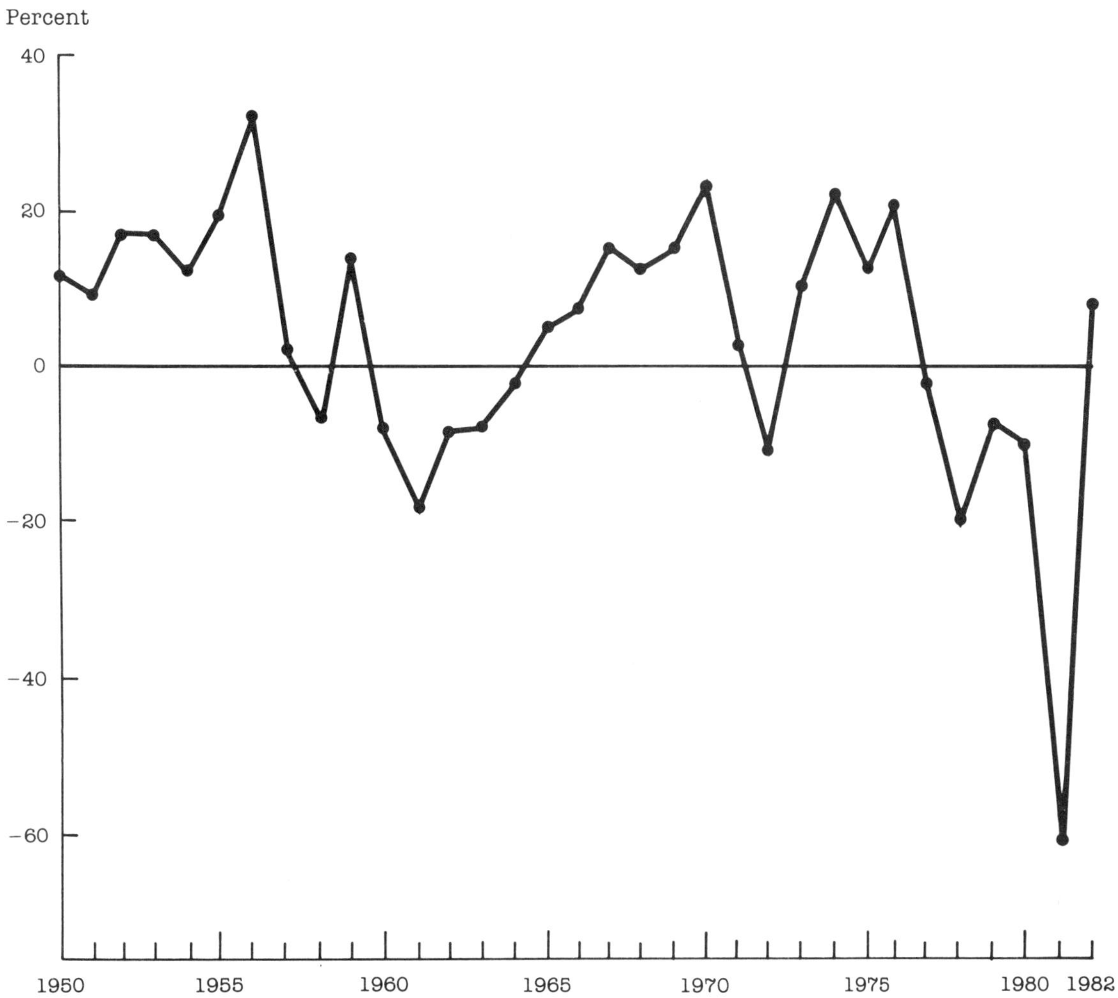

To a large extent the increase in Chile's external debt is the counterpart of a domestic accumulation of consumer and producer capital. This invites the question whether any lack of optimality is involved in what happened in 1978–82. If so, where does the "debt problem" reside? Did consumers and firms benefit from the disequilibrium exchange rate, and if so, at whose expense? Furthermore, assuming that the debt ultimately must be serviced, is there a welfare loss from disequilibrium exchange rate policy, aside from the implications for financial stability and economic activity?

The welfare economics of disequilibrium exchange rates appear quite straightforward. Suppose that the government borrows in the first period in the world market and uses the proceeds to finance a transitory consumption or investment subsidy on importables. In later periods taxes are collected to discharge the external debt. This represents the public finance aspects of the overvaluation policy and neglects all macroeconomic side effects. It is shown in the appendix that a subsidy of this kind will have net adverse welfare effects. This is all the more the case when the macroeconomic effects are taken into account.

The actual story is somewhat more complicated because the private capital market must be considered. Consumers and firms perceive a net subsidy only to the extent that market interest rates do not reflect the anticipated depreciation. Since the government itself did not, in fact, lend at negative expected real interest rates, it must be concluded that interest rates which do not fully reflect anticipated depreciation imply disagreement in the capital market about the likely timing and magnitude of depreciation. Those anticipating large and certain depreciation borrow and import; those anticipating small and unlikely depreciation are the lenders. But the government comes back into the act when a policy of bailing out troubled banks serves as a safety net and, in effect, makes the whole operation almost exactly like the pure finance scheme laid out above.

Brazil

The deterioration of the Brazilian external indebtedness is largely attributable to failure to adjust the budget to the combined external shocks of higher world interest rates and increased real oil prices. Higher interest rates and increased oil prices were almost automatically reflected in larger deficits through two channels: government subsidies that maintained a low domestic price of oil and government external borrowing through state enterprises to finance the increased debt service. Domestic adjustment through tight money served to raise interest rates and stop growth, but its primary purpose was to stimulate external borrowing to finance the current account. Failure to depreciate the real exchange rate meant that the economy stagnated despite growing external deficits and debt.

Table 8-7 shows the external shocks. The terms of trade, as a consequence of higher oil prices and the world recession, deteriorated vastly. In addition, interest rates (including spreads) nearly doubled. The combined effect immediately implied a very significant deterioration in the external balance unless drastic domestic adjustment policies were pursued. Table 8-7 indicates the cumulative actual increase in debt between 1978 and 1982 as well as a calculation of the effect of higher oil prices and interest rates.

The latter calculation cumulates the difference between the cost of servicing the 1978 debt level at actual rates rather than at the 1978 LIBOR (London interbank offered rates) and also the difference between the actual and the 1978 level of oil import expenditures. The sum, cumulated at actual interest rates, is reported in the last row. It measures approximately the increase in debt "due to external shocks." It turns out to amount, cumulatively, almost exactly to the actual increase in external debt. The calculation supports the notion that the debt problem is due to the shocks, but it leaves open the question of the macroeconomic channels through which the shocks are translated into external deficits and debt accumulation. The budget deficit is an essential channel.

Table 8-8 shows the budget deficit as a fraction of GDP as well as the growth rate of real output. Budget data are not available before 1980. After that time, data are available for both

Table 8-7. External Shock to the Brazilian Economy

Item	1978	1979	1980	1981	1982
LIBOR	8.9	12.1	14.2	16.8	13.2
Terms of trade (1977 = 100)	76	79	65	55	54
Oil price (U.S. dollars, 1977 = 100)	101	127	238	275	260
Actual debt increase (cumulative, billions of U.S. dollars)		7.4	16.7	27.1	35.2
Oil and interest effect[a] (cumulative, billions of U.S. dollars)		3.6	11.7	23.5	34.8

a. For method see text.
Sources: IMF, Data Resources, Inc., and Conjunctura (Fundação Getulio Vargas).

Table 8-8. The Brazilian Public Sector Deficit and Growth
(percent of GDP)

Item	1978	1979	1980	1981	1982
Public sector deficit	n.a.	n.a.	7.5	12.7	15.8
Operational	n.a.	n.a.	n.a.	6.0	6.8
Monetary correction	n.a.	n.a.	n.a.	6.7	9.0
Real diesel price (1973 = 100)	139	154	158	190	188
GDP growth	4.8	6.7	7.9	−1.9	1.4

n.a. Not available.
Sources: IMF, Data Resources, Inc., *Gazeta Mercantil*, and Lauro Ramos.

the operational budget and the separate category, the inflation-indexation component of interest payments (or "monetary correction").

The link between the budget and current account deficits stems in large part from extensive subsidies. The government subsidizes diesel oil because the supply of merchandise to the country's interior is dependent on road transport. While the real price of oil in the 1963–82 period increased sixfold in the world market, the domestic price did not even double. Subsidies were also applied to a range of other goods, especially food products: agricultural subsidies at fixed nominal rates implied real interest rates of −60 percent and even more.

Since the budget deficit absorbed the external shocks, there was no automatic private adjustment in response to increased world interest rates and increased real oil prices. Nor did the increased budget deficit lead to offsetting domestic saving in the anticipation of future taxes. Thus the external shocks translated fully and automatically into the current account. The increased interest costs were financed by increased external borrowing through state enterprises, as was the increased budget deficit stemming from higher real oil prices.

Imputing the increased external debt entirely to the oil and interest rate shocks may overstate a good case. Clearly there were other elements at work in the external accounts. For example, increased oil prices led to increased import spending in oil-producing countries, and Brazil was able to secure a significant share of these new trade flows, thus dampening the impact of oil on the external balance. Another favorable influence on the current account stemmed from overvaluation in other countries of Latin America. On the other side, Brazil's mispricing of tourist allowances led to a frivolous waste of foreign exchange. But these qualifications do not change the basic message that failure to adjust to the oil and interest rate shocks is the basic reason for Brazil's increased foreign debt.

Brazil is certainly not a case where the increased external deficit reflected an increase in investment. In 1965–77 investment as a fraction of GDP averaged 21.7 percent. In the period 1978–81 it averaged only 20.5 percent. The increased deficit thus reflects consumption and the budget, not an investment boom. In fact, the increasing monetary tightness that was pursued in order to raise interest rates and thus attract capital flows cut into investment.

The poor external performance of the country was not due entirely to a failure to adjust the budget for increased costs of debt and subsidized programs. A good part of the poor performance stems from a systematic overvaluation of the exchange rate. Figure 8-4 shows the real rate of exchange measured by noncoffee export prices relative to the domestic price level. The exchange rate policy of the post-1968 period had been to maintain a purchasing power parity relative to the U.S. wholesale price index. But that policy of course implied that there was no adjustment for increased real oil prices and interest rates, nor for the vagaries of the dollar in terms of other major currencies.

The balance of payments consequences of the external shocks were contained by increasing domestic oil production and by correcting domestic growth, thereby sharply reducing non-oil imports. At the same time, the exchange rate overvaluation of Argentina and the growth in oil-

Figure 8-4. Brazilian Export Profitability

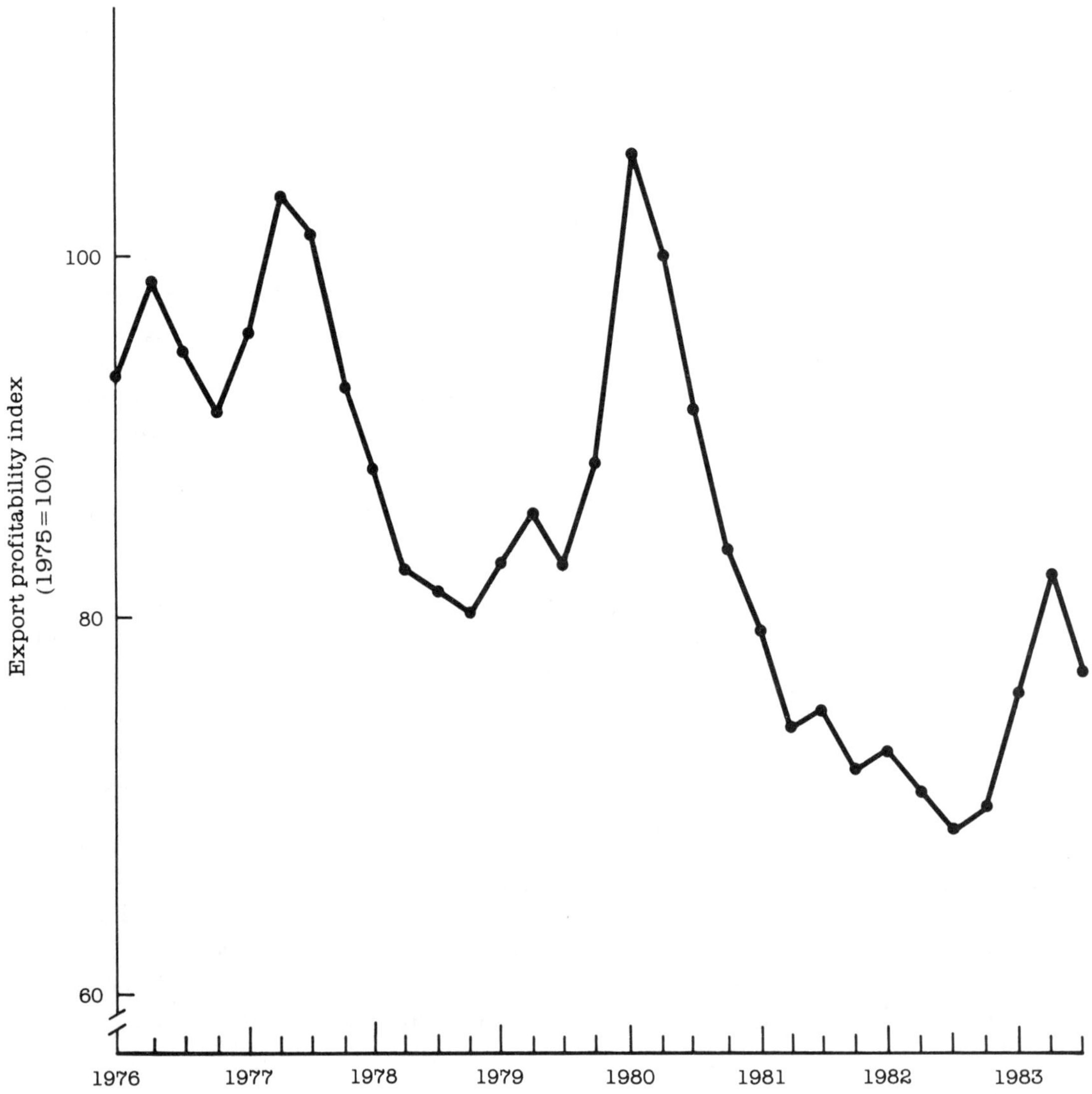

Note: Export profitability is measured by the price of noncoffee exports relative to the domestic price level.

exporting countries' imports from Brazil led to a temporary export boom. In 1979–81 export revenue grew at an average annual rate of 23 percent. The strong export growth and the poor experience with the late 1979 maxi-devaluation—inflation and no persistence of the real depreciation because of preannounced depreciation below the full, accelerated indexation—misled policymakers into maintaining a constant real exchange rate. Failure to seek a large real depreciation as the long-run adjustment to the deterioration in the external sector thus ultimately led to the 1982 debt crisis and the catastrophic collapse of activity.

Unlike in Chile and in Argentina, there was no capital flight or flight into imported durables in Brazil. In part this is a consequence of the fact that the country is closed both on trade and on capital account. Imports are severely restricted, and thus a Chilean-style flight into imported durables is inconceivable. The only capital flight, aside from under- and overinvoicing, took place through the black market or through special accounts in the central bank where exchange rate guarantees are offered to capital importers. But on neither account does the capital flight lead to increased external indebtedness. In one case it is reflected in the increased premium in the black market. In the other case firms and banks have borrowed abroad in dollars and wish to repay their loans prior to maturity can liquidate their dollar debts by making a deposit in the central bank, with the central bank carrying the loan and the exchange rate risk to maturity. Hence capital flight takes the form of paying off dollar loans by making deposits in the central bank. There is no impact on foreign exchange reserves. The only effects are a monetary contraction and, should a devaluation take place prior to maturity, a future increase in the budget deficit as the central bank purchases foreign exchange to service the debt. (See Dornbusch and Moura da Silva 1983.)

In 1973–75 developing countries were generally applauded for sustaining growth in the face of world recession by running external deficits financed in the world capital market. Brazil followed that pattern at the time and again in the 1978–82 period. The experience raises the question of how a country should decide between financing and adjustment in the face of transitory shocks, such as interest rate increases, or more permanent shocks, such as increased real oil prices. Moreover, in the presence of long-term domestic energy projects—such as Brazil's alcohol program and oil production—is it sensible to sustain growth even if debt in the interim rises to a higher long-run level?

The Brazilian experience makes it particularly clear that we are only now starting to think of sensible models of the optimal level of external debt. So far models tell us mainly that debt trajectories are unsustainable if the trend growth rate of exports, say, falls short of the rate of interest. Brazil's case suggests that the automatic capitalization of transitory interest rate shocks or terms of trade shocks runs into risks if rolling over is not automatic. In such a model the joint probability of adverse shocks and credit rationing, and their persistence, may lead to a pattern exactly the opposite of the one in 1973–75. Debt should be retired through a deflationary strategy before the costly credit rationing occurs, or aggressive export promotion and import substitution measures should accompany the continued borrowing. The Brazilian philosophy, "debt does not get paid, debt gets rolled" is then misleading.

ARGENTINA: CAPITAL FLIGHT

In the case of Argentina external debt accumulation financed primarily capital flight, not current account inbalances. Unlike Chile, Argentina had severe political instability, continuing high protection, but completely unrestricted capital flows. For these reasons, the purchase of external assets rather than imported durables was the obvious way to escape from instability and expected depreciation. Moreover, again unlike in Chile, there was clearly no sharp increase in investment. Thus the trade deterioration in 1979–80 is not a significant part of the debt story. Nor does the $1 billion deterioration in the travel account explain much of the increased debt. The large outflow of short-term capital indicated in table 8-9 is more central to the explanation of the debt buildup. Of course, the trade data do not include all military imports—as much as $7 billion are missing according to one estimate—and to that extent too much of the debt increase may be apportioned to the capital account transactions.

Figure 8-5 shows the Argentinian real exchange rate, which is central to an explanation of the capital flows. Under Finance Minister Martinez de Hoz the exchange rate was used systematically to stabilize inflation. Initially, until December 1978, the rate was managed by the central bank's allowing deliberate real appreciation. From December 1978 until March 1981 the rate followed a preannounced tablita. In 1980 the continued prefixing of the exchange rate became doubtful. Overvaluation was apparent, and the coming change in the presidency led to the fear of depreciation and instability. With no limitations on private capital outflows there was a

Table 8-9. Argentina: Trade, Capital Flows, and Debt

Item	1978	1979	1980	1981	1982
Trade balance	2.9	1.8	−1.4	0.7	2.7
Current account	1.9	−0.5	−4.8	−4.7	−2.5
Increase in debt	2.8	6.5	8.0	8.5	0.9
Long-term capital and direct investment	0.4	0.5	0.9	2.0	3.3
Short-term capital and errors and omissions	−1.3	1.5	−2.4	−8.5	−4.9

Source: International Financial Statistics.

Figure 8-5. The Argentinian Real Exchange Rate

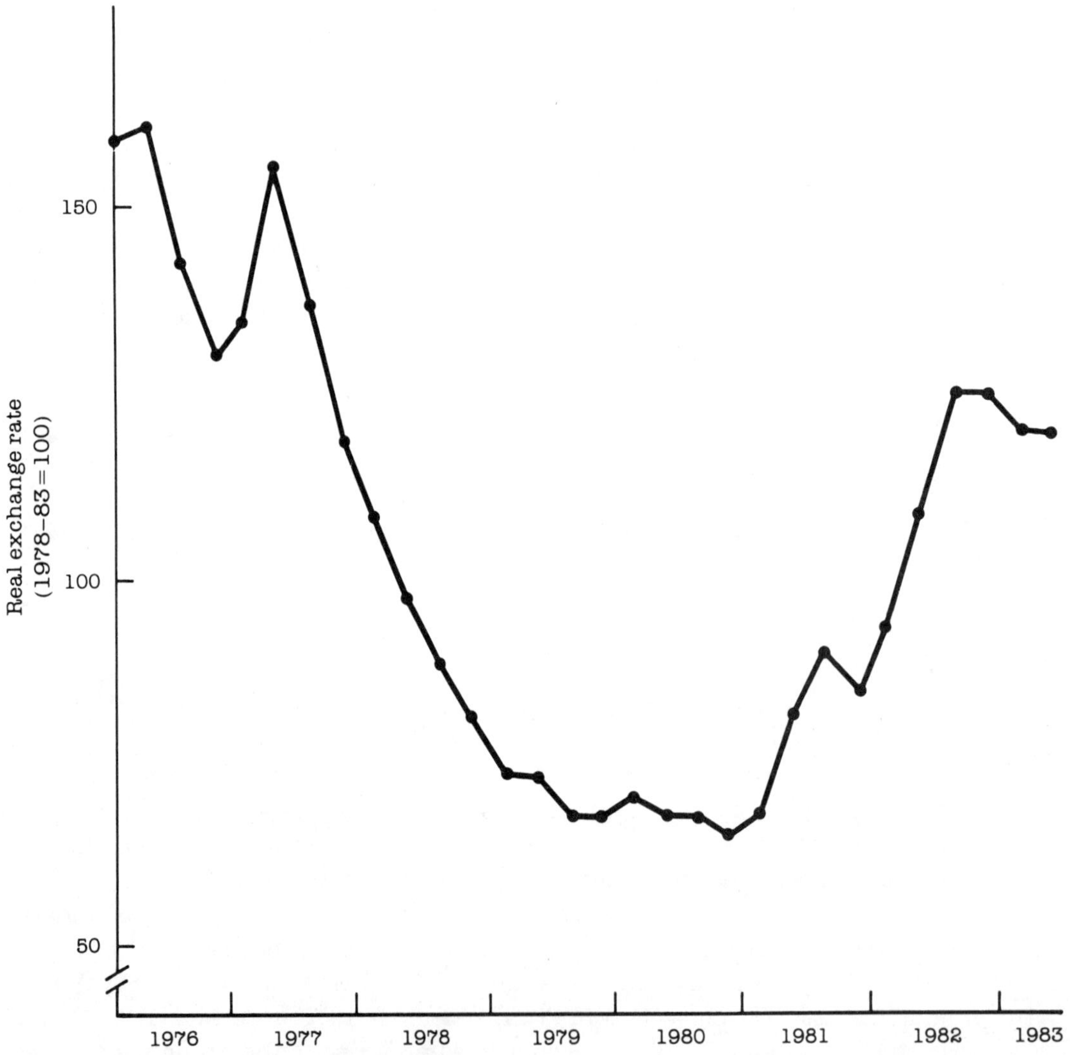

Note: Ratio of import prices to domestic prices.

Table 8-10. Argentinian Financial Instability

Item	1978	1979	1980	1981	1982
Real exchange rate (1978–83 = 100)	92	68	66	78	109
Inflation (December to December)	176	160	101	105	165
Real interest (passive rate)	−15.6	−9.5	−4.4	6.6	−26.2
Budget deficit (percent of GDP)	10.1	9.0	11.3	16.4	17.2
Excluding debt service	1.8	2.4	7.2	8.2	5.3

Sources: Cavallo (1983), Data Resources, Inc., International Financial Statistics, and Indicadores de Coyuntura.

massive shift into foreign assets. The flight into foreign assets included purchases of foreign currency, bank deposits, and securities as well as real estate, especially in the United States and Brazil.

The source of capital flight was the combination of currency overvaluation, the threat of devaluation, and ongoing and increasing domestic financial instability. The domestic instability derives from an inability to bring fiscal deficits under control and stop the inflationary process in a decisive way. In fact, in 1980–81 the deficit deteriorated significantly, even when debt service is excluded, as shown in table 8-10. By 1982 the Malvinas war, and the resulting inability to tap the world capital market further, combined with domestic exchange control to end the episode.

The most interesting aspect of the Argentinian public external indebtedness is that it appears to be matched, one-for-one or better, by increased private holdings of external assets. But because the authorities have no access to these assets, there is nevertheless an acute debt problem. In the aftermath of these disturbances, the question remains whether any significant portion of the capital would return following the implementation of an effective stabilization program. Experience indicates that this is not likely to be the case.

CONCLUSION

The popular view of growing developing-country debts is that they reflect unsound budgetary policies or unsustainable growth programs. Sachs (1981), by contrast, has argued that current account imbalances of the 1970s on average reflect high productive investment that fully justifies external borrowing. Bankers who have poured money into these countries certainly favor the view that they have supported productive investment, thus making it plausible that debts should be serviced. The present review of the debt experience of Argentina, Brazil, and Chile reveals a much more mixed story. Only in Chile does investment play any significant part in the current account deterioration. Imports of consumer goods play at least as significant a role. The burst in imports and the resulting current deterioration is due primarily to currency overvaluation.

In Argentina and Brazil increased investment plays absolutely no role in the debt increase. In the case of Brazil the budget deficit and the lack of an adjustment of the public sector to external shocks are behind the debt growth. The failure to adjust the real exchange rate in this case explains the long-term debt difficulties. In the case of Argentina, currency overvaluation in conjunction with prospects of political instability and international capital mobility explain the increased debt. Here the current account plays a small role, and capital flight is behind the rapid increase in debt.

The episodes in no way suggest that investment is unimportant in the context of current account imbalances. But whether it does play a significant role depend in part on whether trade and capital flows are unrestricted and in part on the prospects for economic stability. When trade is relatively unhampered and prospects are bright, investment may be central. In other cases public sector dissaving or capital flight are more plausible sources of external imbalance.

There are important differences in the three episodes studied. The countries differ, in the 1978–82 period, in their financial and political stability and in their openness. Argentina was the most unstable and the most open on capital account. Capital flight, therefore, was the obvious response to political uncertainty, exchange rate instability, and deteriorating expected returns on domestic assets. While some trade liberalization accompanied the overvaluation, flight into importables, other than tourism, was still minor.

Chile was at the other extreme, with domestic political stability and, at least initially, a budget surplus. The complete liberalization of trade, together with overvaluation and the initial prosperity of households and firms, led to an incredible import boom that made up for years of high tariff walls. But because there was no expectation of a financial collapse, currency reform, wealth taxes, and so forth, capital outflows never came into play in a major way.

Brazil shared Argentina's financial instability; the budget deficit was vast and any attempt at stabilization took the form of tight money, which, in the context of indexation, aggravated the condition of the financial system by causing debt to grow more rapidly, the tax base to shrink, and firms to go bankrupt. The 1979 change in the economic team signaled a drift toward fiscal irresponsibility, but even so the Chilean- or Argentinian-style flight into foreign assets or goods was impossible because the economy was firmly closed. Financial instability could be sustained only by raising interest rates to force items into the world capital market, renewing loans, and taking fresh credit, thus financing the budget and current account deficit. With the economy closed to trade flows and with high interest rates, these policies continued until the external borrowing constraints of 1982 emerged. Because there had been no timely policy of real depreciation, the country was unprepared to absorb the drying up of external credit except through a severe and lasting depression.

The experiences of the three countries studied here are by no means unique. During the 1978–82 period most Latin American countries came into financial difficulties, as did other countries around the world. This raises the interesting question of the reason for the worldwide debt problem. An obvious reason is that the world recession, dollar appreciation, and unanticipatedly sharp increase in U.S. interest rates, simultaneously converted into problem cases countries that were to differing degrees in financial difficulties. But it must also be recognized that there was a common element in the policies and events: it was not only Brazil, Argentina, and Chile that had overvalued exchange rates, import sprees, or capital flight financed by external borrowing. The same occurred in 1981–83 in one form or another in Mexico, Venezuela, and Israel, to name only a few. Indeed, it may even be occurring in the United States right now.

APPENDIX

Investment

Significant changes in investment can come about through two channels. The first is a transitory increase in investment as a result of an increased desired capital stock; the other is a change in the timing of investment in response to intertemporal relative price variations. A standard investment model isolates these effects.

The desired capital stock k depends on the required rate of return net of capital depreciation, $i + d - \dot{Q}/Q$, and on the real price of capital (Q/P) as can be derived from the standard arbitrage condition:

$$Pf'(k)/Q = i + d - \dot{Q}/Q \tag{8.3}$$

or

$$k = g[(i + d - \dot{Q}/Q)Q/P)];\ g' < 0. \tag{8.4}$$

On the investment side we assume adjustment costs and also that imports as well as domestic output are inputs in the production of investment. We assume a proportional import requirement and an increasing marginal domestic input requirement. The solution to the investment problem then is a rate of investment that depends positively on the real price of capital in terms of imports, Q/Pm.[6]

$$I = h(Q/P,v); \qquad v = Pm/P \tag{8.5}$$

where v is the real exchange rate or the real price of domestic goods in terms of importables. The investment model is completed by the capital accumulation equation:

$$\dot{k} = h(Q/P,v) - \delta k \tag{8.6}$$

where δ denotes the rate of physical depreciation.

The rational expectations equilibrium, given a constant real exchange rate and interest rate, can be visualized in terms of the conventional phase diagram. The equilibrium capital stock and the real price of capital follow a saddle path to the steady state.

Consider now the anticipation of an increase in the real cost of imports which acts as a temporary investment stimulus. This is shown in figure 8-6. Starting from an initial equilibrium at point E, there is an expectation that the real exchange rate will depreciate or the real price of imports in terms of domestic goods will rise in the future. There is an immediate jump in the real price of assets, and that higher real price promotes a transitory investment boom. Once the real depreciation does take place (point E″) the real price of capital keeps rising, but

Figure 8-6. The Investment Effects of an Anticipated Real Depreciation

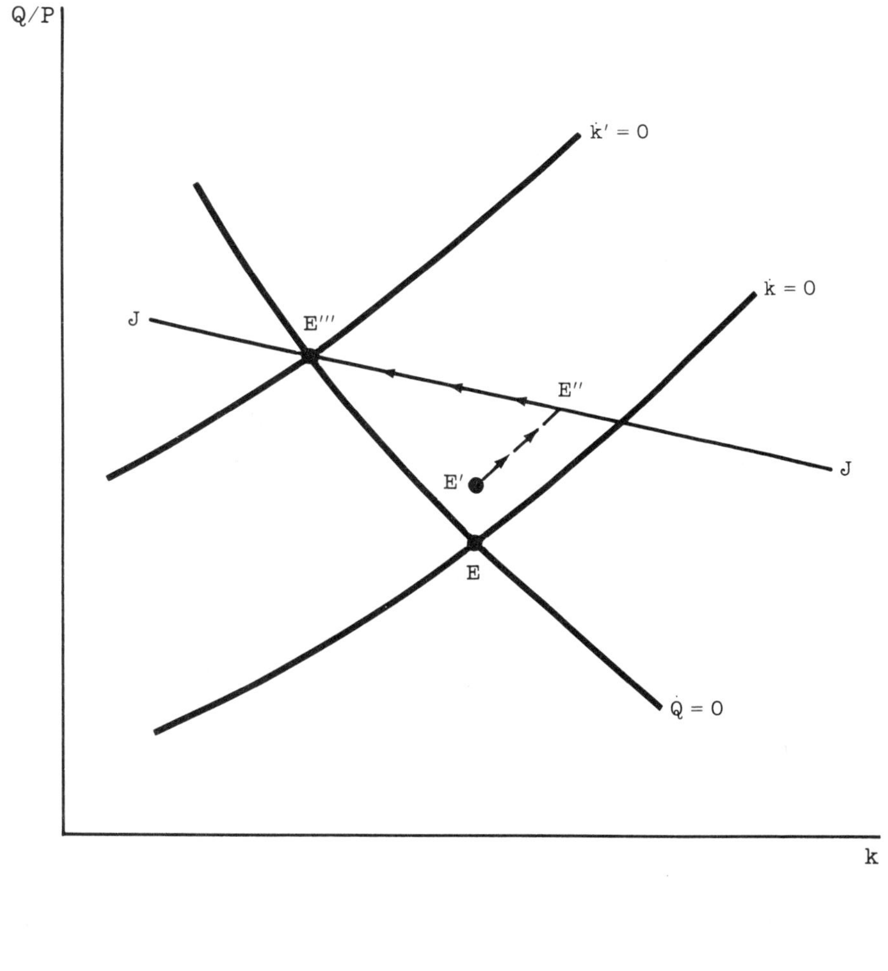

now disinvestment takes place. With an anticipated real depreciation, therefore, investment and hence investment goods imports are expected to be high. The obverse analysis, of course, applies to a transitory decline in the real price of imports.

The exposition so far assumed that capital is used to produce domestic goods but has itself import content. There is another case in which anticipated real depreciation has a significant impact on investment. In this case capital is used to produce tradables and investment has an import content. A real depreciation must in the long run raise the real price of capital, but the capital stock may rise or fall. However, with the anticipated increase in the real price of tradables, there will be an investment boom and hence a boom of investment goods imports.

Consumer Durables

Consider a much simplified model of consumer choice focusing on durables. We neglect time preference, depreciation, and resale as well as nondurables. The consumer's welfare depends on the services from durables in two periods, the second denoted by a prime:

(8.7) $$U = V(S) + V(S').$$

Services are given by the cumulative stock

(8.8) $$S = D, S' = D + D'$$

Figure 8-7. Consumer Durables and Disequilibrium Exchange Rates

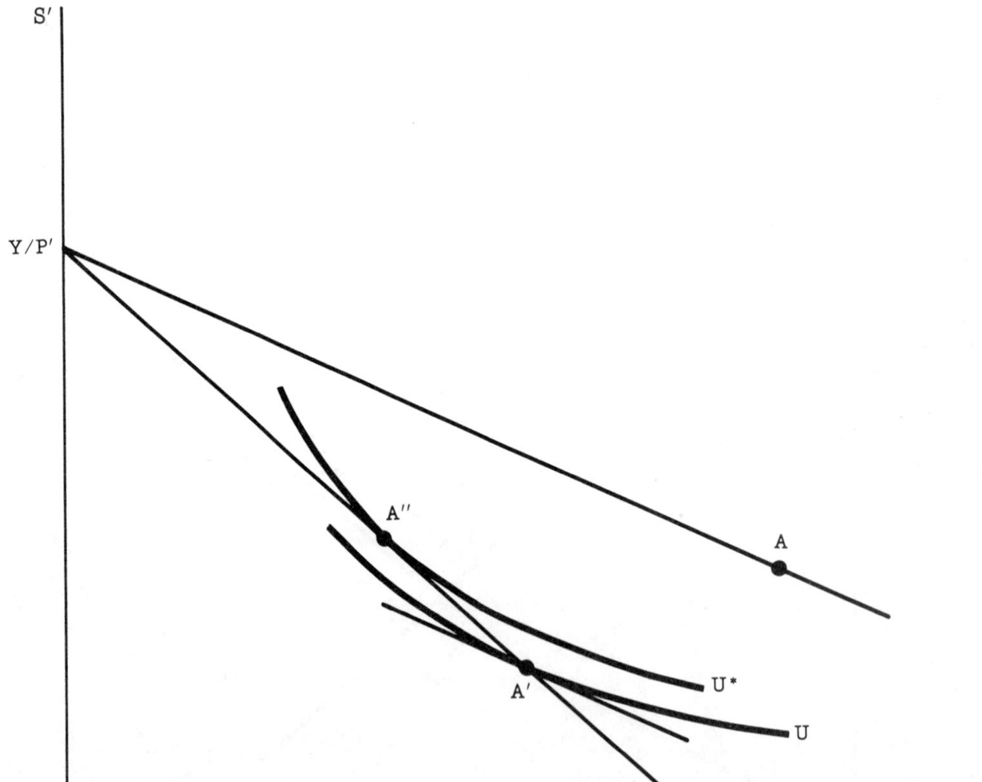

where D denotes durable purchases and a prime denotes the second period. The budget constraint is:

$$Y - T = PD + P'D' \tag{8.9}$$

where $Y - T$ denotes the present value of income net of taxes and P' is the discounted second period price. We assume $P < P^* < P'$ where P^* is the equilibrium real price under a correctly valued real exchange rate while P is the price consumers actually face.

For the aggregate economy, tax payments are $T = (P^* - P)D$, but the individual household takes taxes as unrelated to purchases. The individual faces the budget line obtained by adding D to both sides of (8.9) to obtain:

$$S' = (Y - T)/P' + (1\text{-}D/D')S. \tag{8.9a}$$

Figure 8-7 shows the consumer equilibrium. The consumer views the budget line as having a slope $dS'/dS = 1 - P/P'$, which is flatter than the slope of the social budget line $dS'/dS = 1 - P^*/P'$. Consumer equilibrium, including the subsidy distortion owing to overvaluation, is at point A′ on indifference curve U, with excessive purchases of durables in the first period and a level of welfare lower than at A″ on indifference curve U*. It is apparent that the larger the subsidy, the further the equilibrium lies to the southeast of A″, thus causing welfare to deteriorate further.

If the consumer does not take into account future taxes, the consumption point A would be chosen in the first period, leading to second period distress once the taxes are collected. This consideration is of interest because it helps explain the collapse of durable purchases after 1981.

NOTES

1. For a discussion see Sachs (1982a), United Nations (1964), and the annual reports of the Foreign Bond Holders Protective Council.

2. Let A/P^* be net real foreign assets measured in terms of world prices. Then the change in real net foreign assets is:

$$\Delta(A/P^*) = \Delta A/P^* - \frac{A}{P^*}\frac{\Delta P^*}{P^*} = CA/P^* - \frac{A}{P^*}\frac{\Delta P^*}{P^*},$$

which is the inflation-adjusted current account.

3. Wealth taxes or levies as a way of responding to shocks have been insufficiently considered in the recent deficit finance literature, though not, of course, in the interwar writings.

4. In interpreting these numbers it is necessary to bear in mind that from 1980 to 1981 industrial production was approximately flat while from 1981 to 1982 it declined by around 20 percent. GDP growth in 1981 was 5.7 percent, −14.3 percent in 1982, and −0.5 percent in 1983.

5. The dollar value of copper exports and the real price of copper (1980 = 100) show the following pattern:

	1978	1979	1980	1981	1982
Exports (billions of U.S. dollars)	1.27	1.9	2.15	1.72	1.73
Real price (1980 = 100)	81	102	100	82	73

The real price of copper here is measured in terms of the unit value of industrial countries' exports.

6. Suppose firms in the investment business maximize the value of profits $Z = QI - aPmI - Pb(I)$ with $b', b'' > 0$. The coefficient a denotes the constant unit import content of investment. The first order condition is $b'(I) = (Q/P - av)$ or $I = h(Q/P, v)$ with $v = Pm/P$.

REFERENCES

Barro, R. 1974. "Are government bonds net wealth?" Journal of Political Economy (December).

———. 1983. Macroeconomics. New York: John Wiley & Sons.

Blanchard. O. 1983a. "Debts, deficits and finite horizons." Unpublished manuscript, MIT.

———. 1983b. "Debt and the current account deficit in Brazil." In Financial policies and the world capital market: The problem of Latin American countries, edited by Pedro Armella and Rudiger Dornbusch. Chicago: University of Chicago Press.

Borenzstein, E. 1984. "Fiscal policy and foreign debt." Unpublished manuscript, MIT.

Bruno, M. 1976. "The two-sector open economy and the real exchange rate." American Economic Review 66:566–77.

Calvo, G. 1982. "Real exchange rate with fixed parities." Unpublished manuscript, Columbia University.

Cardoso, E. 1983. "Stabilization in Latin America: Popular models and unhappy experience." Unpublished manuscript, Boston University.

Cavallo, D. 1983. "Deficit fiscal, endeudamiento del gobierno y tasa de inflacion: Argentina 1940–1982." Estudios (April/June).

Cavallo, D., and Y. Mundlak. 1983. "Real exchange rate, trade policies and sectoral growth—The case of Argentina (1946–82)." Unpublished manuscript, Hebrew University.

Cline, W. 1983a. International debt and the stability of the world economy. Washington, D.C.: Institute for International Economics.

———. 1983b. "International financial rescue: Viability and options." Unpublished manuscript, Washington D.C., Institute for International Economics.

Corbo, V. 1983. "An overview of macroeconomic developments in the last twenty years." Pontifica Universidad Catolica de Chile.

Corbo, V., and J. de Melo. 1983. "Liberalization and stabilization in Chile: 1974–82." Unpublished manuscript, Washington D.C.: World Bank, Development Research Department.

Corbo, V., and R. Matte. 1983. "Flujos de capitales y el rol de la politica montearia: el case de Chile." Unpublished manuscript, Pontifica Universidad Catolica de Chile.

Dagnino Pastore, J. 1983. "Progress and prospects of the Latin American adjustment program." Unpublished manuscript, Buenos Aires.

———. 1984. "The anti-inflationary experiment, Argentina 1979–81: An assessment." In Liberalization and stabilization: Recent experience in the Southern Cone, edited by N. Barletta, M. Blejer, and L. Landau. Washington, D.C.: World Bank.

Deaton, A., and J. Muellbauer. 1980. Economics and consumer behavior. New York: Cambridge University Press.

Diaz Alejandro, C. 1963. "A note on the impact of devaluation and the redistributive effect." Journal of Political Economy (June).

———. 1981. "Southern Cone stabilization policies." In Economic stabilization in developing countries, edited by W. Cline and S. Weintrab. Washington D.C.: Brookings.

———. 1983a. "Studies of the 1930s to the 1980s." In Financial policies and the world capital market: The problem of Latin American countries, edited by Pedro Armella and Rudiger Dornbusch. Chicago: University of Chicago Press.

———. 1983b. "The Brazilian debt crisis." Brookings Papers on Economic Activity 2.

Dooley, M., et al. 1983. "An analysis of external debt positions of eight developing countries through 1990." Unpublished manuscript, Board of Governors of the Federal Reserve.

Dornbusch, R. 1982. "Stabilization policy in LDCs: What lessons have we learned?" World Development (September).

———. 1983a. "Real interest rates, home goods and optimal external borrowing." Journal of Political Economy (February).

———. 1983b. "Discussion." In Prospects for adjustment, edited by J. Williamson. Washington D.C.: Institute for International Economics (June).

———. 1984. "Argentina since Martinez de Hoz." Unpublished manuscript, MIT.

Dornbusch, R., and A. Moura da Silva. 1984. "Dollar deposits in Brazil: The 432 effect." Revista Brasilera de Economia (March).

Dornbusch, R., and S. Fischer. 1984. "The world debt problem." Unpublished manuscript, MIT.

Edwards, S. 1983. "Stabilization with liberalization: An evaluation of ten years of Chile's experience with free market policies: 1973–83." Unpublished manuscript, University of California, Los Angeles.

Enders, T., and R. Mattione. 1983. "Latin America: The crisis of debt and growth." Unpublished manuscript, Brookings.

Fernandez, R. 1983. "The expectations management approach to stabilization: Argentina 1976–81." Unpublished manuscript, CEMA.

French-Davis, R. 1983. "Deuda externa y apertura financeira en Chile." Collection Estudios Cieplan 11 (December).

Harberger, A. 1983a. "Welfare consequences of capital inflows." Unpublished manuscript, University of Chicago.

———. 1983b. "A primer on Chile." Unpublished manuscript, University of Chicago.

Hause, J. 1966. "The welfare cost of disequilibrium exchange rates." Journal of Political Economy (October).

Johnson, H. G. 1966. "The welfare cost of exchange rate stabilization." Journal of Political Economy (October).

Martin, R., and M. Selowski. 1984. "Energy prices, substitution and optimal borrowing in the shortrun." Journal of Development Economics.

Mishkin, F. 1976. "Liquidity, consumer durable expenditure and monetary policy." American Economic Review (September).

Murphy, R. 1983. "Tariffs, real exchange rates and fiscal policy: An intertemporal analysis." Unpublished manuscript, MIT.

———. 1984. "Essays on macroeconomic adjustment in open economies." Unpublished manuscript, MIT.

Obstfeld, M. 1983. "Intertemporal price speculation and the optimal current-account deficit." Journal of International Money and Finance 2:135–45.

Rodriguez, C. 1982. "The Argentine stabilization plan of December 20th." World Development (September).

———. 1982a. "Politicas de estabilizacion en la economia Argentina 1978–82." Unpublished manuscript, CEMA.

Royal Institute of International Affairs. 1937. The problem of international investment. London: Frank Cass & Co.

Sachs, J. 1981. "The current account in the macroeconomic adjustment process in the 1970s." Brookings Papers on Economic Activity 1.

———. 1982a. "LDC debt in the 1980s: Risk and reform." In Crises in economic and financial structure, edited by P. Wachtel. Lexington, Mass.: Lexington Books.

———. 1982b. "The Current account in the macroeconomic adjustment process." Scandinavian Journal of Economics 84 (2):147–59.

Simonsen, M. 1983a. "Brazil: External adjustment and economic perspectives." Unpublished manuscript, Fundacao Getulio Vargas.

Svensson, Lars E. O., and Assaf Razin. 1983. "The terms of trade and the current account: The Harberger-Laursen-Metzler effect." Journal of Political Economy 91, 1(February):97–125.

United Nations. 1964. El financiamento externo de America Latina. New York.

9

Lessons for Debtor Country Managers and Policymakers

Arnold C. Harberger

A discussion of this length should not try to make too many points, but sometimes this rule is difficult to follow. The main point of this chapter is that countries should begin to worry when capital inflows reach unsustainable rates. However, several important qualifications will necessarily come into focus as I review the experience of specific countries. I hope these secondary points will not detract from the central idea.

I begin by summarizing my views (see Harberger 1983) on the welfare consequences of capital inflows, particularly two arguments favoring some type of control over inflows of capital. The first has to do with the fact that developing countries typically face an upward-rising supply curve of capital funds. Therefore the marginal cost to the country of additional borrowing exceeds the average cost. This is a genuine negative externality that in principle justifies a tax on foreign borrowing (that is, each additional foreign loan tends to increase the country risk premium to be paid as other foreign loans are renewed or new ones made). On the basis of a rather rough judgmental analysis, I suggested in my previous work that the "optimal" tax on foreign borrowing might be of the same order of magnitude as the premium over the London interbank offered rate (LIBOR) on loans to a country.[1]

The second argument for controlling the rate of capital inflow is macroeconomic. It is based on a simple macroeconomic model containing home goods and tradables. Simulations made with this model, using what I judged to be plausible parameters, have demonstrated that a smoother rate of inflow of capital would, in general, produce a smoother time path of real output (and also of prices, if a fixed exchange rate is assumed). One of the critical variables in the picture is the real exchange rate, which, under the assumptions made, is clearly very responsive to capital inflows (and outflows).

My earlier analysis led me to conclude that, other things being equal, countries have good reasons to prefer a steady (and, it is hoped, sustainable) rate of capital inflow, especially in view of the fact that paths of capital inflow that rise very substantially above the sustainable level necessarily have to be cut back, probably sharply, at some point in time. If k is the debt limit imposed on a country by the international financial community (expressed as a ratio of foreign debt to gross domestic product [GDP]), and if g is the rate of growth of GDP, then a country can stay at that debt limit by incurring, each year, new debt equal to the fraction gk of GDP. This is what I regard as the sustainable level of net increment to debt. When a country starts out with very little debt, it is not unreasonable to contemplate a somewhat faster rate of new indebtedness for a time, but prudence dictates that even in this case the rate should not greatly exceed the sustainable level, if it is assumed that the shocks entailed in sharp reductions of capital inflows are something to avoid.

This discussion is primarily concerned with the specific experiences of several countries, the point being that high rates of capital inflow drive the real exchange rate down (that is, cause it to be highly appreciated), a situation that then has to be sharply reversed when the rate of capital inflow is curtailed. The model referred to above provides the theoretical basis for expecting that this type of association between capital movements (as, so to speak, the independent variable) and the real exchange rate (as the dependent variable) will indeed occur.

But two important qualifications have to be made at the outset. First, when a country incurs foreign debt for the exclusive purpose of buying additional tradable goods, this should in principle not affect the real exchange rate. It is the use of foreign loans for the purpose of buying nontradables that creates pressure on the real exchange rate. Typically, a foreign loan will be used to finance some expenditure on tradables and some on nontradables; here, it is the part spent on nontradables that produces real exchange rate effects. Unfortunately, the fraction of foreign loans spent on nontradables is not constant—it varies dramatically from loan to loan and from borrower to borrower within a country. It also varies from one time period to another, a fact that creates tremendous problems for those who seek to establish strong econometric relationships connecting, say, net international borrowing to the real exchange rate.

A second and related qualification concerns payments for financial services. If the money being newly lent (as a net addition to debt) is just matched by international interest payments, then, too, there is no "transfer problem" and no effect on the real exchange rate.

The second of these two qualifications can easily be handled simply by subtracting interest payments from the net increment of debt. For the purposes of this discussion, the concept of net transfers (gross loan receipts minus total debt service payments) used in the World Bank's *World Debt Tables* neatly deals with this second qualification. It does not, however, cope with the first qualification. Nonetheless, this concept will be used in the empirical reporting that follows. Since I have no way of breaking down the net transfers into the parts spent on tradables and nontradables, I will simply work with net transfers, acknowledging that ideally we would want them multiplied by an unknown and temporally variable ratio—the proportion spent on nontradables.

Of interest here are the cases of Chile, Argentina, Mexico, Venezuela, and Indonesia, which are examined in differing degrees of detail. In the late 1970s and early 1980s, the first four had rates of capital inflow that were far above the sustainable level. In all four cases the inflow was subsequently sharply reduced.

Chile, until the very end of the 1970s, had held the rate of capital inflow in check by means of banking regulations. Had this policy been continued, I believe the entire crisis there could have been averted. Under the regulations, of course, the international banking community felt frustrated; it saw Chile as a banker's paradise with real interest rates in the range of 3 to 4 percent a month. When the restrictions were relaxed, the major international banks vied with each other to reach the Chilean market. When later they discovered that the Chilean banking system was not as sound as they had believed, they sharply reduced the flow of foreign funds to Chile.

Most of my discussion on Chile centers on the thesis that it was the abrupt turnaround of capital flows that caused the current Chilean crisis. The fixing of the exchange rate in 1979, which most people believe to have been the cause, contributed little if anything to the problem. The internal source of difficulty in Chile was a proliferation of bad loans within the banking system. The rolling over of these loans, capitalizing interest along the way, created what I call a "false" demand for credit, which, when added to the demand that would normally be viable, allowed real interest rates to reach unprecedented (and, to many, incredible) levels.

In Argentina the cause of the massive capital inflow was quite different. The country had, by early 1979, not solved its fiscal deficit problem. The financing of the deficit through money creation carried with it inflation of upwards of 6 percent a month. At this point the Argentine government sought to use exchange rate policy to help break inflationary expectations. It set a future time path (called a *tablita*) of daily devaluations of the peso. At the time, the economic authorities had in mind bringing about fiscal reforms so as to yield an ever declining deficit; such reforms would have been totally compatible with the steady slowing of the devaluation rate.

The tragedy is that the authorities got their tablita, but not their fiscal reform. The result was that during 1980, for example, peso interest rates of 6 to 7 percent a month combined with devaluation rates of 1.5 to 2 percent a month. In the presence of totally free capital movements (which were decreed very early by the Videla-Martínez de Hoz economic team), it thus became possible for foreign capital to earn 4.5 to 5 percent a month in dollars. The capital inflow induced by this incentive was huge and caused a tremendous, indeed unprecedented, appreciation of the peso. But as prospects dimmed that the government could stick to the tablita, investors began to withdraw their funds, and Argentines began to speculate against the peso by shipping their funds overseas. As the situation deteriorated, something close to a panic developed. Capital inflow turned into capital outflow, and the real exchange rate had to be sharply depreciated. (As in Chile, serious problems existed within the banking system of Argentina; these undoubtedly also played a role in precipitating the dramatic turnaround of capital flow that took place.)

Venezuela, Mexico, and Indonesia are all major exporters of oil. To the extent that oil prices boom and that the extra revenues are repatriated and spent on nontradable goods, the effects on the real exchange rate are virtually identical to what happens when capital inflows rapidly increase. A flexible exchange rate naturally appreciates under these circumstances; under a fixed exchange rate, the inflows cause the money supply to expand and the level of internal costs and the prices of nontradables to rise, while the prices of tradables other than oil remain fixed. In both cases the real exchange rate appreciates (that is, foreign currency becomes cheaper), and exports (other than oil in the case of an oil boom) are put into a price-cost squeeze, with the most vulnerable of them being crowded out.

Both analysis and experience lead to the conclusion that the most prudent way to deal with an oil boom is to start by spending only part of the increased flow of foreign exchange, and that if a country desires to spend the full flow, it should work up gradually to this point. This principle was agreed to by officials of all three countries, but only in Indonesia was it followed. Both Mexico and Venezuela, by way of contrast, not only moved rapidly to spend the full increment of funds, but moved quickly to the point where they were spending more than this increment. In effect, they mortgaged the future flow of increased oil revenues in order to go on a binge of project (and other) public spending right away. Of course, future oil flows can be mortgaged only once, and both Mexico and Venezuela soon found that there was no way to continue their previous rate of borrowing.

Among the major developing-country oil exporters, Indonesia seems to have done the best job of managing the 1979 oil price boom. It has been able to do this in large measure because the economic team in government had great experience and authority, and was able to resist the numerous political and social pressures that can quickly operate to convert an oil price boom into a public spending and borrowing binge.

POLICY DIAGNOSES FOR SPECIFIC COUNTRIES

In undertaking the diagnoses that follow, I have considered that the lessons to be drawn concerned policies that in one way or another helped lead up to a country's debt problem. At the very least, these policies dealt with matters that impinged in one way or another on capital movements. Thus, policy relating to the size of a country's fiscal deficit comes into the picture, but the specific design of its income tax or of its tariff structure does not. Readers should approach what follows in this spirit.

Chile

Chile is the country whose economy I have studied most closely.[2] Its economy was in a chaotic state at the time of the military coup in September 1973: inflation was approaching 1,000 percent a year, and the banking system in a single year acquired government obligations equal in value to about 40 percent of a year's GDP and to more than six times the initial M_2. Black markets were rampant; economic inefficiency was to be found everywhere.

The Chilean government did little to control inflation until well into 1975, when it instituted a major program of expenditure reductions that effectively eliminated the fiscal deficit. It had earlier introduced an important structural reform of the tax system and had embarked on a major trade liberalization program that ended up producing, by mid-1979, an essentially uniform 10 percent tariff. Inflation was reduced gradually, falling below 100 percent only in 1977, and below 30 percent only in 1981. Controls were reduced, simplified, or eliminated, and public sector prices rationalized. Chile's rationalization of its economic policies was much more thoroughgoing than that carried out by Argentina, and on the whole has been highly praised by technical experts. Without a doubt the Chilean policy package worked well for quite a while. After a sharp fall of 12.9 percent in 1975 (about a third of which might reasonably be attributed to the fiscal tightening that took place then), GDP growth averaged close to 8 percent a year for the next five years, and even in 1981, when trouble began brewing, GDP grew by 5.7 percent. That, however, was followed by a precipitous fall of 14.3 percent in 1982.

Most businessmen, journalists, and economists are of the opinion that what went wrong in Chile all stems from the fixing of the exchange rate in July 1979 at 39 pesos to the dollar. They imply, and sometimes directly assert that, say, a flexible exchange rate regime or a crawling peg would have solved the entire problem. They point to the fact that, after the fixing of the exchange rate, the Chilean consumer price index (CPI) rose 21 percent while the wholesale price index (WPI) rose 30 percent in the last half of 1979. The indexes then went on to rise by 31 percent (CPI) and 28 percent (WPI) in 1980. If that is not evidence of an overvalued exchange rate, they ask, what *is*?

My answer is that this is, perhaps, evidence of a falling real exchange rate. But it is certainly not a sign that a devaluation is called for. To me, the following are among the signs that indicate a devaluation is called for:

- Prices of tradables are sharply "too low" relative to nontradables.
- Recession takes place in the manufacturing sector, as the most output-responsive tradables sector.
- Wages are out of line on the high side.
- The country has been losing international reserves.

In Chile's case, none of these tests is adequately met until somewhere around the middle of 1981.

The relative price of tradables. For Chile, the price of tradables relative to nontradables can be measured in two ways. First, the national accounts are already broken down into these two components, though only on an annual basis. Their respective deflators are the relevant price indices. According to this indicator, the relative price of tradables went from 100 in 1979 to 99 in 1980. Then it fell to 87 in 1981 and to 77 in 1982.

A second way of gauging this relationship is to take the ratio of the wholesale price index (which is heavily weighted with tradables) to the consumer price index (which contains both tradables and nontradables). Though the movements of the WPI/CPI ratio will not be of the same magnitude as those of the tradables/nontradables price ratio, the directions of movement and the relative magnitudes of movements among periods should be similar. Most important, this ratio can be calculated month by month. The WPI/CPI ratio actually rose by 3 percent between 1979 and 1980; then, like the ratio of the deflators of tradables and nontradables, it fell in the two subsequent years, by 10 percent in 1981 and by an additional 3 percent in 1982. But more interesting is the comparison among key months. The WPI/CPI ratio, starting from index 100 in July of 1979, fell to 82 in May 1982, the month before the devaluation. However, by April of 1981 it had fallen only to 94—a weak signal indeed. Most of the adjustment came between May 1981 and May 1982.[3]

Industrial production. The industrial production index of the National Statistical Institute (INE) stood at 107.7 in June 1979; it peaked at 125.0 in October 1980, again at 122.8 in March 1981, and yet again at 121.2 in July 1981. Then—two years after the fixing of the exchange rate—began the precipitous fall, that carried the index to an average of 86.4 in 1982 (Banco Central de Chile 1983a, p. 75).

The industrial production index of the Industrial Development Society (SOFOFA) stood at 105.6 in June 1979. Its successive peaks were 116.4 in September 1980 and 118.3 in July 1981. Once again, the index fell sharply between the second half of 1981, when it averaged 109.4, and the first half of 1982, when it averaged 89 (Banco Central de Chile 1983a, p. 77).

Thus, both indexes of industrial production fail to give the signal corresponding to an excessively appreciated exchange rate until more than two years after the official parity was set at 39 pesos to the dollar. Added evidence in the same direction is that the share of manufacturing in the gross domestic product actually rose slightly (from 21.2 percent in 1979 to 21.4 percent in 1980 and 22.0 in 1981) before falling to 19.6 percent in 1982. Recall also, in interpreting these percentages, that 1980 and 1981 were years of quite successful growth, whereas 1982 witnessed a calamitous fall in real GDP (Banco Central de Chile 1983b, p. 2418).

Real wages. Real wages began moving seriously out of line in August 1981. That year the share of labor in total GDP was almost precisely equal to its 1977 value of 0.394, and in 1980 it was equal to its 1978 value of 0.385. There is no sign of its being out of line before 1982, for which the relevant data were not available at the time of writing. A close approximation may be made, however, by comparing movements in real wage rates with those of real GDP. INE's index of real wages and salaries (deflated by the recalculated CPI) rose by 8.7 percent in 1980 over 1979 and by 8.88 percent in 1981 over 1980 (Banco Central de Chile 1983a, p. 151). This compares with the real growth rates of GDP—of 7.8 and 5.7 percent, respectively—in these years. The differences do not appear to signal any serious disequilibrium (recall, too, that the INE index is based on a sample, and does not represent the entire work force). In 1982, however, INE's real wages index fell by 0.23 percent, while GDP fell by 14.3 percent. Obviuosly, a disequilibrium situation was developing here.

From the movements of industrial production and unemployment, we can presume that most of the drop in GDP occurred early in 1982. We can then inquire into the time path by which the disequilibrium was produced. Here there can be little doubt that the disequilibrium arose before the devaluation of the peso and that the devaluation helped to correct it. From January through May 1982, real wages averaged more than 10 percent above those of a year earlier, despite unemployment of 19.1 percent in the second quarter (according to INE). Later in the year, real wages fell sharply, so that from September through December they averaged some 12 percent below their levels of a year earilier.

The upward wage adjustment of August 1981 appears to be the point at which wages began to be significantly out of line with movements in GNP. Real wages in May-July averaged about 7 percent above those of a year earlier; this figure jumped to 14.8 percent in August and 15.8 percent in September. Real wages kept going up in absolute terms through the year, reaching their annual peak in December (by which time unemployment had already grown to 13.5

percent). They reached their overall peak in May 1982—the month before the first devaluation. Only starting in June did they begin to erode, presumably as a consequence of the devaluation process itself. By this time, unemployment was well over 20 percent.

We thus have a picture of real wages moving grossly out of line on the high side—as we expect them to be when a devaluation is called for—starting in about August of 1981, and of disequilibrium growing rapidly up to the June devaluation (Banco Central de Chile 1983a, pp. 153, 201).

International reserves. Chile's international reserves did not peak until 1981. They stood at a little over $1 billion at the end of 1978, and by December 1979 they had risen to $2.3 billion. Their growth continued steadily through 1980 and into 1981, when they stood above $4 billion for seven months (including August and September), and were above $3.9 billion in each of the first ten months. They began eroding steadily (though slowly) in the last quarter of 1981, and in the months immediately before the June devaluation their level was a little over $3.4 billion.

In my opinion, the loss of reserves was not the principal factor behind the decision to devalue the peso in June of 1982. The problem lay in the unbearably high rate of unemployment and in the associated depression of industrial production. Nonetheless, the steady drain of reserves after September 1981 was indeed a signal that the exchange rate was not in line. It, together with the other three signals already discussed, was definitely calling for a devaluation of the real exchange rate at this time.

Those who argue that Chile's great error was the fixing of the rate of 39 in July 1979 might well be asked where they consider a free rate would have gone over the same period. The presumption is that if the fixed rate of 39 led to a rise in reserves, a "cleanly" floating rate (under which the central bank would neither buy nor sell reserves) would have led to an even more highly appreciated exchange rate.[4]

The sharp reversal of capital flow. Some relevant data on what I believe was the source of pressure on Chile's real exchange rate are presented in table 9-1. Line a shows the inflow of capital from abroad. In general, a capital inflow will tend to cause the real exchange rate to appreciate. (Actually, as noted at the outset of this discussion, this is true only to the extent that the immediate users spend the borrowed funds on nontradables; one of the serious problems in analysis of this type is that we possess no accurate breakdown of the patterns in which foreign borrowings were allocated to purchase tradable and nontradable goods—a fact that makes time series analysis potentially treacherous.)

Two main forces operate to offset the capital market pressure on the real exchange rate. First, payments of interest and other charges on preexisting debt represent a flow of funds in the

Table 9-1. Capital Market Pressure on Chile's Real Exchange Rate, 1978–82

Item	1978	1979	1980	1981	1982
a. Inflow of capital	1,946	2,247	3,165	4,769	1,304
b. Payments for financial services	489	675	930	1,428	2,050
c. Accumulation of reserves	712	1,047	1,244	70	−1,165
d. Net pressure on the real exchange rate [(a) − (b) − (c)]	745	525	991	3,271	419
e. Relative index of exchange rate pressure [(d) ÷ GDP]	0.050	0.025	0.036	10.0	1.7

Source: Banco Central de Chile (1983a, p. 237). Chilean GDP data converted to U.S. dollars at average exchange rates from International Monetary Fund (IMF), International Financial Statistics (Washington, D.C., 1983).

other direction. If this flow were exactly to match the inflow of capital, there would be no pressure on the real exchange rate. Likewise, if, as capital flowed in from abroad, the dollars (or other foreign currencies) were acquired by the central bank and accumulated as international reserves, there would again be no pressure.[5]

These two offsetting forces have been taken into account in table 9-1 by subtracting the relevant magnitudes for each year from the corresponding inflow of capital. The resulting net figure is given in row d,[6] and is expressed as a fraction of GDP in row e. Note that the relative index exchange rate pressure oscillated between 2.5 and 5 percent of GDP through 1980. Then in 1981 it leaped to 10 percent—surely an unsustainable figure.[7] But recall that 1981 was a good year, not a bad one. The high rates of inflow of capital meant that total spending exceeded the total value of production by 10 percent. Many activities were booming, though some were already feeling the exchange rate squeeze. Industrial production was nearly at a peak level, GDP was at an all-time high, and according to a University of Chile survey (Banco Central de Chile 1983a, b) in June 1981 unemployment dipped below double digits for the first time since 1974.

I believe that had the rate of capital inflow tailed off slowly, Chile would have avoided a serious crisis. But obviously this was not the case. Between 1981 and 1982, the index of exchange rate pressure swung from +10.0 to +1.7—a swing equal to more than 8 percent of GDP. Moreover, these figures refer to the ex post results; also present in the picture was a 14 percent fall in real GDP between 1981 and 1982—without doubt, a fall precipitated mainly by the very pressures we are analyzing.

Figure 9-1 illustrates my perception of what happened. In 1981, Chile was in equilibrium with a low real exchange rate. At this rate, demand for tradables exceeded the local supply by 10 percent of GDP. Then the crisis hit; the supply of funds from abroad fell sharply and the economy had to adjust. Unfortunately, for reasons given below, much of the adjustment came through a fall in income. This is reflected in figure 9-1 by a shift to the left in the demand curve for tradables. In the new situation, the excess demand for tradables is much smaller (and would have been a large excess supply had not more than a billion dollars of reserves been spent), and the real exchange rate is somewhat higher.

Obviously, the situation would have been much better had the upward adjustment of the real exchange rate been even sharper. If the upward adjustment had been all the way to e*, perhaps the decline in income could have been avoided. But do not think that an upward adjustment to e* would have been easy. The authorities do not control the real rate of exchange; their instrument of policy is the nominal rate. Nonetheless, there can be no doubt that, had there been greater flexibility in the Chilean economy in late 1981, the heavy cost of the crisis—in terms of high unemployment, lost output, bankruptcies, and so on—could have been significantly reduced.

Copper prices. Movements of copper prices added to the upward pressure on the real exchange rate. The relative price of copper (that is, the London Metal Exchange price deflated by the U.S. wholesale price index) stood at an average of 83 in 1979, dropped slightly to 80 in 1980, then fell precipitously to 59 in 1981 and 49 in 1982 (indexes with 1978 = 100, Banco Central de Chile 1983b). The interesting aspect of this story, however, is how well the Chilean economy absorbed the 1981 shock. The reason is to be found in the degree to which the Chilean economy as such is insulated from the copper industry. To a degree, this industry is geographically isolated from the rest of the economy, but, more important, its direct contacts with the private economy are through its wages bill, which tends to fluctuate relatively little in response to copper price movements. It is the government (through CODELCO, its copper company) that absorbs the brunt of fluctuations in copper prices. I have not been able to ascertain exactly how the cut in copper prices influenced spending—or, more particularly, to determine how

Figure 9-1. Demand for and Supply of Tradables (T) (including nonfinancial services) as Functions of Their Relative Price Level (P_t/P_n)

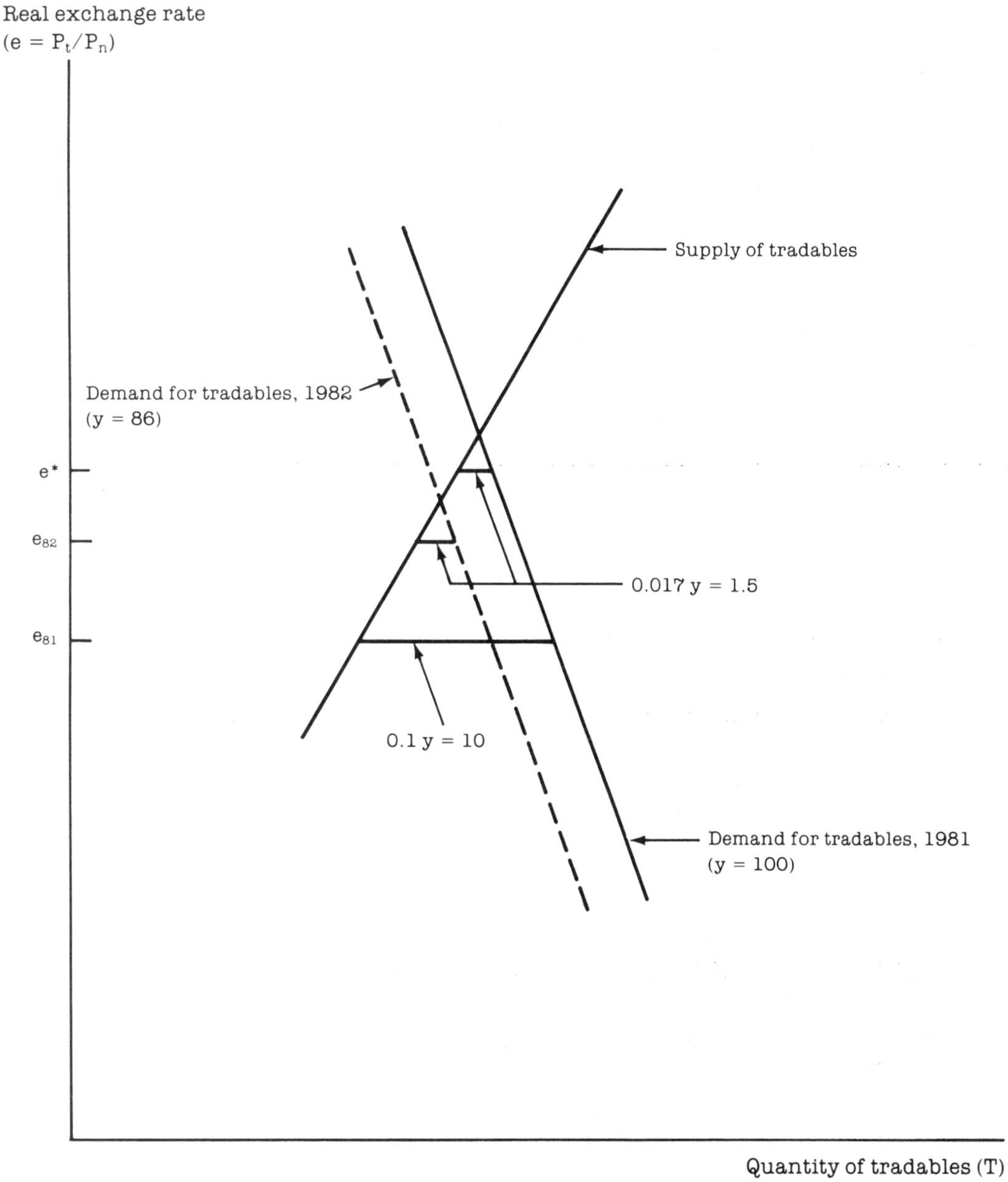

Note: P_t = nominal price level of tradables; P_n = nominal price level of nontradables; T = quantity of tradables; y = index of real income.

Chile managed to prosper up to mid-1981 in spite of the copper price collapse. Whatever the answer to this puzzle, there can be no doubt that the massive drop in copper prices has to be taken as an important additional factor pressing for a substantial real devaluation of the peso.

Chile's labor law. The real exchange rate has many guises—among them (1) the nominal exchange rate multiplied by a foreign price index and divided by a domestic one; (2) the internal (that is, within the country) price level of tradable goods deflated by the internal price level of nontradables; and (3) the ratio of the nominal exchange rate to an index of wages. If the foreign price index is the foreign price level of goods traded (with Chile) and the domestic price level is the price level of nontradables, (2) can be seen to revert to (1). Meanwhile, (3) can be seen to approximate (2) given that the nominal exchange rate is the predominant local variable in determining the internal prices of world-marketed goods, and that the wage level is the principal component of the price of services, which in turn make up most of the nontradables.

The adjustment called for by the shutting down of the capital inflow can thus be seen to entail either a reduction in wages (if the nominal exchange rate remained fixed) or a rise in the nominal exchange rate (if wages remained fixed). Neither of these alternatives was possible under the labor law that was in force in Chile, which had been written when the Chilean economy was at the height of its late 1970s boom. This law mandated essentially that every new labor contract must provide at a minimum a full cost-of-living adjustment from the date of the previous contract. For practical purposes, it made reductions in real wages illegal in any covered activity.

Nothing could bring about the required adjustment while this labor law was in effect. Yet something obviously had to be done. Indeed, as mentioned earlier, the whole problem was exacerbated by the sharp upward wage adjustment that occurred in August 1981, just as the crisis was brewing. According to reliable reports, the preferred alternative of the economic team in early 1982 was a decreed reduction of 15–20 percent in all wages and salaries (perhaps with some exceptions at the lowest levels), which, it was hoped, would help to maintain the exchange rate at 39. The reports go on to say that this proposal was taken seriously and discussed at the highest levels of government. The final decision, however, was to devalue the peso. Yet even for the devaluation to work, the labor law would have had to be modified. A modification was finally made—it provided that the real wages pacted in new labor contracts could fall below their previous level, but not below a floor equal to their level at the moment the labor law had taken effect. This left an ample margin for downward real wage adjustment, and Chile's experience since the June 1982 devaluation attests that a serious modification (devaluation) of the real exchange rate was indeed made possible.

The monetary effects of devaluation. A devaluation from 39 to 46 pesos to the dollar was declared in June 1982. This devaluation was "calibrated" to approximate what would have happened if Chile, rather than pegging to the dollar in July 1979, had pegged the peso to a basket of major currencies (roughly on a trade-weighted basis). Although I believe (in retrospect) that the policy of pegging to a basket would have been better for Chile than that of pegging to the dollar, and that with such a policy Chile might have averted a major crisis, the failure of the attempt (ex post, in June 1982) to replicate this scenario is quite clear. The new peg (which was to follow local inflation in a crawling peg fashion) did not last more than two months. It was replaced by a short period of a free float, in which the upward pressure on the exchange rate proved severe, and was finally followed by the reinstitution of serious exchange controls, with a parallel market alongside the official one.

From June 1982 to June 1983 the real exchange rate rose by some 50 percent, as the nominal official rate doubled (from 39 to 78), while consumer prices rose by about a third (with U.S. prices increasing only modestly). The immediate objective of an increased real exchange rate (which, in my view, was an absolute necessity, given the circumstances of the capital market)

Table 9-2. Real Money Balances and International Reserves, 1982–83

Date	Real money holdings (M_2) (billions of 1978 pesos)	International reserves (millions of U.S. dollars)
June 1982	150.1	3,369
August 1982	147.9	2,947
December 1982	132.0	2,577
March 1983	116.0	1,578
May 1983	107.1	1,518

Source: Banco Central de Chile (1983b, pp. 1323, 1378).

was thus achieved, but the intended reduction of unemployment was substantially frustrated. In fact, postdevaluation unemployment exceeded the second quarter level of 19.1 percent, and reached 23.9 percent in the third and 21.9 percent in the fourth quarter of 1982 and 21.7 percent and 19.5 percent in the first and second quarters, respectively, of 1983.

These monetary effects entailed a reduction in desired holdings of peso cash balances combined with a large loss of dollar reserves. The fall in real M_2 (see table 9-2) signified a reduction in the banking system's capacity to grant credits to domestic borrowers; the loss of reserves worked in the other direction. The net result was that real domestic credit fell only slightly during the period between the June devaluation and May 1983. However, in January 1983, there was a spate of bank failures, which was accompanied by a major bailout operation by the Central Bank. As a consequence, the banking system was far less able to grant what I call "good" credits in May 1983 than in June 1982.

The banking system. It is now becoming clear that the condition of the Chilean banking system played a prominent role in determining the course of economic events after 1974. At the time of the military coup in September 1973, hundreds of Chilean corporations were in government hands, nearly all of them generating substantial losses. Those that had been simply "intervened" by the government (that is, not expropriated) were returned to their owners, but those that had been officially expropriated were (with a few exceptions like the major copper mines) sold at auction to the highest bidder.

Regardless of the category to which they belonged, the firms were in a weak financial position at the time they passed back from government to private hands. The deep recession of 1975 can only have made things worse. While I know of no study that explicitly traces the economic fate of the enterprises in question, there can be little doubt that a significant fraction of them must have reached the borderline of technical bankruptcy at some point during the 1975 recession.

The Chilean banks probably began to accumulate a stock of bad loans starting at that relatively early point. Rather than write off these loans as bad debts, the typical practice appears to have been to roll them over, and to let interest accumulate along the way. The apparent reason for this practice was that, upon recognizing a bad loan as such, a bank would have to reduce its capital and surplus so as to reflect the loss. This, in turn, would reduce all sorts of legal limits—on lending, on deposits, and on borrowing from abroad—all of which were typically expressed as multiples of capital and surplus.

As time went on and the volume of bad loans held by the banking system grew, the supply of credit available for "genuine" loans was progressively squeezed. This superimposition of what in effect was a "false" demand for credit on top of a true or good demand is probably the main reason that Chilean interest rates remained so high throughout most of the 1975–82 period. The high interest rates—which hovered much of the time around 3 or 4 percent a month in real terms—were in turn partly responsible for putting in peril the financial situation of yet other companies, which may have begun the period in a relatively healthy condition but simply could not withstand the steady drain on their resources that the high interest rates entailed.

The beginning of the present banking crisis in Chile probably dates back to May 1981, when the major private sector sugar company, the Viña del Mar Sugar Refining Company (CRAV), went bankrupt. It was not the failure as such that caused the problem, but rather the laxity of banking practices, which was revealed as the evidence unfolded. (Several banks had made their loans to CRAV essentially without collateral, "on the signature only" of its distinguished director, Don Jorge Ross.)

From July to September 1981, the financial system appeared to be surmounting the crisis. Interest rates, which had risen sharply in the wake of the CRAV failure, began to drift downward, and calm seemed to have been restored in the Chilean financial community. However, new rumblings appeared in October, and by November 1981 eight financial institutions were "intervened" by the central bank. These eight included four banks (of which the largest was the Banco Español) and four financieras (which together accounted for about half the assets of the entire financiera system).

The decision of the government was finally to bail out these institutions fully—in the sense of guaranteeing the payment of their obligations both to their depositors and to their other creditors. In doing so, the government followed a precedent set several years earlier when the Banco Osorno had failed in an isolated occurrence. Most qualified observers think that it was a mistake to bail out failing institutions so fully—especially since there is essentially a complete continuum of possibilities: bailout of principal but no interest, bailout of principal plus part of the interest, bailout of 90 percent of principal but no interest, and so on.

The precedent set by these earlier bailout operations served as the ostensible justification for the international private banking community to insist on a complete bailout of almost the entire Chilean banking system when the crisis wave hit once again in January 1983. The end result of a lengthy process of negotiations was that the government extended its own guarantee to all outstanding foreign debts of the Chilean banking system.

The consequence of the progressive bailouts of Chile's banks is a wad of bad or dubious paper in the portfolio of the Central Bank. This paper, as long as it exists, limits the capacity of the banking system to make loans to viable enterprises. To the extent that bank credit serves as a productive input (or lubricant) in the economic process, the constricted amount of resources available for credits to truly viable enterprises will limit the pace of Chile's recovery.

In effect, there is no plausible way that the policymakers can make real M_2 go up—indeed, the weakening of confidence in the wake of the devaluation crisis has made it fall significantly. International reserves have already fallen to only a little more than a third of their earlier peak. The policymakers do not want to lose more and have agreed not to do so, but even if the existing reserves were to be "used," they are not large enough to finance a very big dose of stimulatory credit expansion. Thus, we can pretty well rule out any major expansion of credit in real terms.

A current view (April 1984). The story of the Chilean economy in 1981–83 is grim, and the outlook for the future is somber. It will probably take until 1986 for the 1981 level of real output to be regained and for the unemployment rate in the greater Santiago labor market to drop back to the 10–12 percent range within which it oscillated during the late 1970s. There seems to be no policy capable of eliciting a quicker recovery; rather, the scenario of recovering to 1981 levels within two years is itself optimistic.

Key danger signals would be further efforts on the part of the public to flee from the currency and further substantial reductions in real money holdings. Such reductions would have as their counterpart a further squeezing of the amount of "good" credit (in real terms) available to the system.

Hopeful signs at the moment are

- The unemployment rate, though high, is significantly below its earlier peak of 23.9 percent and is declining. The most recent (October-December 1983) figures show national unemployment at 14.4 percent, that in greater Santiago at 16.5 percent.
- Preliminary figures show quarterly GDP rising. Having reached its trough in the fourth quarter of 1982 and the first quarter of 1983, it is by now back to or above its level of the first quarter of 1982.
- Up to this writing, at least, Chile has shown the policy restraint necessary to ensure that the nominal devaluation of the peso also entails a significant real devaluation. This has given a new stimulus to tradable goods production (particularly of nonmineral exports).
- Quotations in the parallel market, which earlier had reached levels in excess of 130 pesos per dollar, have in recent months ranged between 90 and 100 (compared with an official rate of around 85).
- In spite of a number of government retreats from the liberal, noninterventionist policy system that prevailed between, say, 1975 and 1982, the basic structure of economic policy in Chile is sounder than that in most other Latin American countries. Chile still has a basically uniform tariff (now at a 20 percent rate), a sound tax system, expenditure restraint on the part of government (which has kept public sector deficits down to manageable—that is, noninflationary—proportions), and a reasonably "economic" pricing policy of public sector enterprises. These attributes of the policy structure should give Chile a certain edge over other countries in the struggle (universal these days among the Latin American countries) for economic recovery.

A personal assessment: what went wrong? It should be clear by now that I do not consider the fixing of the exchange rate at 39 pesos to the dollar to be the critical error lying behind Chile's current troubles. I hope that I have demonstrated that the Chilean economy performed quite satisfactorily while (under the fixed rate system) internal prices were rising—a movement many people take as evidence that the fixed exchange rate policy was wrong. During this period (up to mid-1981), there were none of the signals that typically reveal an overvalued exchange rate. All these signals, however, began to appear beginning roughly at the midpoint of 1981.

The timing is right, with respect to these signals, to support the hypothesis that the need for a real devaluation arose because of the sharp turnaround in the rate of capital inflow into Chile. This turnaround was the result of a number of forces.

First, the international banking community had for several years made Chile its "darling." Bankers came from all over the world to try to thrust new credits on Chile. The inflow of capital was kept within bounds largely because of the regulations of the central bank—regulations governing the amount and maturity of the borrowings by Chilean banks from abroad, the interest rates that foreign lenders could receive from Chile, the length of time that foreign money had to stay in Chile before repatriation, and so on. These regulations, in turn, were gradually being moderated. It was probably the relaxation of restrictions mandated in early 1980 that permitted what in retrospect was, to my mind, a significantly excessive inflow of capital in 1981. Some share of the blame, then, rests with those who propounded the relaxation of regulations, without maintaining vigilance against "excessive" capital inflows. But we must be careful here. There were few voices on the Chilean scene (including my own) warning against excessive capital inflows.[8]

Some share of the blame also rests with the international bankers, whose zeal seems to have exceeded their prudence in Chile, where there was a special element of riskiness in the portfolios of most banks, probably as early as 1975. The "false demand" for credit stimulated by the continual rollovers of essentially bad (or at least dubious) loans was surely a main cause of high real interest rates in Chile. The force of these interest rates was temporarily moderated (for Chilean borrowers) by the price rises between July of 1979 and, say, December of 1980, but as the economy moved into 1981 this force reasserted itself. From the point of view of the international bankers, real interest rates in Chile were high throughout the period—for they thought in terms of dollars. They probably viewed Chilean nominal interest rates of 3 and 4 percent a month as virtually guaranteeing that Chilean bankers (who were the borrowers that the international bankers faced) would easily be able to pay their debts. So eager were the international bankers that Chilean banks for a time received rates as low as LIBOR plus 0.625 percent and LIBOR plus 0.75 percent on their loans from abroad. These foreign bankers simply did not do their homework well; they did not look behind the facade and at the reality of the portfolios of Chilean banks.

Some part of the blame must also fall on the Superintendency of Banks in Chile, which was charged with seeing to it that the local banks followed prudent practices. Somehow it does not appear to have discovered, until too late, that many (probably most) Chilean banks were courting excessive risks.

Chilean bankers, obviously, must take a share of the blame. They were hopeful that economic prosperity would carry weak and failing firms out of their troubles. But many of them also were reluctant to swallow bad loans (and thus reduce their capital and surplus) simply because this would greatly limit their capacity to lend to others (at high real interest rates).

Those whose actions led up to the failure of CRAV also enter the picture because, in a sense, it was their mistake that helped precipitate the crisis. In my view, it was the unbusinesslike nature of the mistake—CRAV's speculatively buying sugar futures at prices that were perhaps four or five times the sustainable long-run equilibrium price—that brings them into my list of the blameworthy. Had their mistake been more excusable, I would simply have said that, with a weak banking structure, some other event would have triggered greater vigilance by international lenders and brought about a denouement similar to what in fact occurred.

Finally, we come to the policymakers. I think that the biggest mistake of the policymakers ultimately lay in overlooking the need to keep the banking system under a stricter discipline. This could have been achieved in two ways. On the one hand, a hands-off policy, allowing the Banco Osorno to go under, would have signaled clearly that the government was not about to bail out the system. This would have induced much more prudent behavior on the part of Chilean banks with respect to their dubious loans, and much more caution on the part of foreign banks, in place of the zeal with which they tried to press loans upon Chile.

The second way of enforcing a stricter discipline upon the banks would have been for the authorities to take more seriously their role in superintending the Superintendency of Banks. I think that until recently the regulation of banks received too little attention in discussions of economic policy, in courses on the subject, in the professional literature, and elsewhere. Few who have witnessed the banking disasters in Chile, Mexico, and Argentina (not to mention the problems of other countries and the major multinational banks) can doubt that the supervision of banks is indeed a most serious and important responsibility of economic policymakers. This responsibility ultimately rests with the government as such, and not only with the persons and organisms (such as the Superintendency of Banks) specifically charged with the function.

Whichever way might have been chosen—letting Banco Osorno fail without bailout (or with a more limited rescue operation) or more rigorously supervising banking operations in general—the Chilean economy would have been much better off. Indeed, there would have been no incompatibility between an incomplete bailout of Banco Osorno, on the one hand, and a more rigorous vigilance over banking operations in general, on the other. This is the most important mistake that I lay at the doorstep of the authorities. (I also admit categorically that in 1976–79, when the good decisions were there to be made, I did not perceive these matters to be of the same importance that I now attribute to them.) Also of some weight were what I consider the significant misjudgment of letting capital flow in too rapidly, especially in 1981, and the delay in modifying the labor law so as to permit the real exchange rate to rise, once the signals pointed clearly to the need for such an adjustment.

The policy messages are clear:

- The Chilean regulations placing various (and potentially flexible) restrictions on the inflow of capital were distinctly a good thing. The failure of policy lay in permitting the great inflow of capital that started in 1978 (see table 9-1) and then went up drastically in 1980 and 1981. Had there been less inflow, less adjustment would have been necessary, and the magnitude of the problem that "began" in mid-1981 would have been greatly reduced.
- Chile could well have avoided the problem that started in mid-1981 had the banks been better regulated. If they had been better regulated, the international banks would not have been disillusioned and there probably would not have been such a sharp reduction in the inflow of capital between 1981 and 1982. The pressure would have not have been so great.
- One aspect of banking policy concerns bailouts of failing banks. Chile's 100 percent bailout of depositors and creditors (though happily not of shareholders) in such banks gave bad signals both at home and abroad. It invited the remaining Chilean banks to continue with imprudent practices, and it led the international banks to take excessive risks. With bailouts of less than 100 percent, the size of the problem would have been doubly diminished. Less international capital would have come to Chile in the first place, and the international bankers would have been more content to keep up the flow.
- Even if none of the above steps had been taken, Chile still would have surmounted its crisis at much lower cost if its labor law had been modified in a timely way, at least early enough to prevent the unwise wage boost of August 1981, but failing that, as soon thereafter as possible. Waiting until unemployment had reached some 19 percent before facing this problem was a great mistake.
- When the devaluation was finally undertaken in June 1982, it was folly to link it to a face-saving formula that was almost certain to be too little. Much stronger measures came later; if the initial devaluation had been more tenable, it might have stuck. A too small devaluation and the sequential exchange rate experiments that followed precipitated capital flight and a huge loss of reserves.

Argentina

The overall economic policy in Argentina was quite good from 1976 through 1980 (the era of Martínez de Hoz as finance minister). Serious efforts were made to rationalize a genuinely chaotic policy structure inherited from the preceding government. Some fiscal reforms were made, the deficits of public enterprises were greatly reduced, and a somewhat gradual program of trade liberalization was set in motion. The government deficit was reduced to about 3 percent of GDP, most of it financed by expansion of bank credit. It appears to have been the policy of the government to allocate about 20 percent of domestic credit to the government and 80 percent to the private sector (that is, it did not attempt to squeeze private sector credit so as to offset new advances to the government; it simply allowed the inflation to work itself out). This is not a bad policy, especially for high-inflation countries, for, after all, it is not advisable to squeeze private sector credit down to zero in the name of sterilizing advances to the government.

Starting from the situation just described, the Argentines could easily have worked the rate of inflation down, over a period of years, as they further reduced their fiscal deficits. That is, I

Table 9-3. Argentine Exchange Rates, 1976–82

Item	1976	1977	1978	1979	1980	1981	1982
Market exchange rate[a]	0.275	0.060	0.100	0.162	0.199	0.725	4.855
Consumer prices	2.5	7.0	19.2	49.8	100	204	541
GDP deflator	3.0	7.7	19.9	49.9	100	206	n.a.
Wholesale prices	3.7	9.3	22.9	57.0	100	210	746
CPI real exchange rate[b] (1975 = 100)	0.74	0.83	0.63	0.45	0.35	0.45	1.07
WPI real exchange rate[b] (1975 = 100)	0.87	0.82	0.71	0.53	0.48	0.60	1.01
GDP (1980 prices)	25.3	26.9	26.0	27.9	28.2	26.5	25.0

n.a. Not available.

a. The nominal exchange rate is the peso price of the U.S. dollar.

b. Real exchange rates are defined as the nominal peso price of the U.S. dollar, divided by an Argentine price index and multiplied by the corresponding U.S. price index.

see no major mistake in what has just been described, especially in view of the fact that when Martínez de Hoz took over, inflation was roaring upwards at the rate of 30 percent a month!

What, then, went wrong in Argentina? In my view it was the setting of Argentina's tabular exchange rate (tablita) at too low a rate of devaluation, given the fiscal deficit, combined with the complete opening of the capital market early in the Martínez de Hoz regime.

I date the start of the trouble at the time the first tablita was set, around December 1978. Internal inflation was then going on at the rate of about 25–30 percent per quarter; M_2 had grown by more than 200 percent in 1978 and would continue to do almost that in 1979 (see table 9-3). Consonant with this were interest rates on time deposits (even as short as seven days) ranging upwards of 6 and 7 percent a month. Trouble arose when the exchange rate was set on a path starting at 15 percent a quarter, and slowing to 3 percent a month by late 1979, to 2 percent a month by mid-1980, and to about 1.5 percent a month through late 1980.

What with the huge peso interest rates in 1979 and the promise of a much lower rate of devaluation, nearly $5 billion of net capital flowed in, almost all of which ended up as an addition to the reserves of the central bank. The influx continued into 1980, but only at about half the rate, and there is strong evidence that probably as early as the second quarter of 1980 the by now well-known flight of capital from Argentina was getting started. (Other short-term capital, not indicated elsewhere, had a value of −$1.5 billion in the second and −$1.2 billion in the fourth quarter of 1980, according to International Financial Statistics.)

The arbitrage possibilities that were opened up by this system became evident when it is considered that in late 1979 one could bring in foreign funds (from whatever source), convert them to pesos, deposit them at 6.5 or 7 percent in a bank (or lend them directly at even higher rates), and in the process lose only about 3 percent a month on the exchange rate. In late 1980 the bank interest rate was about 6 percent and the exchange loss only 1.5 percent a month. But by then, as already indicated, the "smart money" was leaving the country. And rightly so, for the whole system broke down in early 1981. The reserve loss over the whole of 1980 was $2.7 billion; that of the first quarter of 1981 was $3.0 billion.

The tragedy is that the debacle could so easily have been avoided. Had the rate of devaluation in the tablita been set close to the ongoing rate of inflation, and had it been reduced only slowly (as the fiscal deficits that at bottom were fueling the inflation were brought under control), the magnificent opportunities for arbitrage outlined above would simply not have existed. The huge inflow of funds would not have appeared, and there would have been no cause for speculating against the peso in late 1980 and January 1981.

How did the authorities make so important a mistake? Three related and nonconflicting reasons come to mind. First, there can be no doubt that the Argentines were impressed by the success of the tabular system in Chile during 1978. What had been a 92 percent rate of inflation in 1977 was brought down to 40 percent within a year. Moreover, Argentina's own inflation seemed stuck at about 175 percent during 1977 and 1978. One of the main justifications of a tabular system is that it permits the introduction of a true numeraire in an otherwise rudderless situation. This is particularly true if the country is using a crawling peg exchange rate system (which to my mind is the only sensible alternative at very high inflation rates). So the Argentines had good reason to want to try a tablita as a way of getting their own inflation rate unstuck.

Second, at the time the tablita was set in place, the nominal exchange rate had been rising at a rate much lower that the rate of inflation. The devaluations projected in the tablita were thus not inconsistent with the recent movements of the exchange rate. But they were inconsistent with the rate of inflation being generated by the fiscal deficit and with the resulting high peso interest rates. Speculators act quite differently if they have a table of changing exchange rates, preprogrammed and known in advance, than if they see the rate move 30 percent one quarter, then 10 percent in another, then 15 percent in a third.

Third, there is the fiscal deficit itself. One can make sense out of the whole picture by assuming, as I have been told by reliable witnesses, that the authorities had a plan for reducing the deficit, and that the stages of the tablita were in fact thought to be compatible with the projected deficits. On this interpretation, the real trouble would have come about when the Finance Ministry and the central bank failed to "sell" their package of reforms to the rest of the government. I am inclined to believe that this was the case, because it gives a plausible explanation of why the set of policies discussed above was chosen in the first place and why it broke down.

Nonetheless, a plausible reason is not an excuse. It is too risky to engrave in stone, as it were, something like a tablita and to use it as a threatening element in attempts to persuade a government of the urgency of adopting a particular tax package. At the very least, according to this interpretation, when the tax package failed, a new tablita, compatible with the actual—not the desired—fiscal setup, should have been immediately adopted. But still far preferable would have been not to have run so grave a risk at all, to have proceeded more cautiously, introducing successive tablitas with lower devaluation rates only when the fiscal situation justified such a move.

Many people criticize Argentina for having completely opened the capital market too soon, and they claim that it should have waited until the trade liberalization was more or less complete. My own arguments for maintaining some degree of control over capital movements are different ones (see the opening section of this chapter). Things went quite well for Argentina up until late 1980, when the capital flight that precipitated the devaluation crisis of early 1981 really got under way. The capital inflows of 1979 and 1980 appear to have helped push the real exchange rate down to unprecedented levels of 0.45 in 1979 and 0.35 in 1980 (all but one observation on the CPI real exchange rate from 1963 to 1975 lie between 0.75 and 1.01). But even this did not inhibit the ongoing prosperity, as GNP grew quite well, at least in 1979.

The agony, it seems, comes not when capital is coming in in large quantities, even though the real exchange rate goes down, but when a sharp reduction in the rate of inflow takes place, and the real exchange rate has to be adjusted upward.

In the Chilean case, the great inflow was caused by a too sharp relaxation of restrictions, and the sharp reduction occurred largely because of the altered policies of the international banking community. In Argentina, the great inflow was caused by a combination of policies that created an incredible arbitrage opportunity, where the country was in effect paying 3 to 4 percent a month in dollars in order to get large quantities of incremental reserves. The outflow was caused when people rightly realized that the scheme could not work indefinitely; it was private speculation, then, that triggered the crisis in the Argentina case. In both cases the real exchange rate fell to unprecedentedly low levels, which was not a particularly painful part of the process. The painful part came when changes in capital flows required a sharp upward adjustment of the real exchange rate.

Recall, too, that in the case of Argentina the process of capital movements was complicated by the fact that some capital inflows were being offset by capital flight. This is not a phenomenon that I have studied, but I am told that the total amount of flight capital may be as high as $20 billion. Surely the essentially completely free movement of capital into and out of Argentina made this capital flight easier. In my opinion, however, we should not understate human ingenuity when it comes to capital flight. It is easier for a country the size of Argentina to control the inflow than the outflow of capital. Having said that, I think that the conditions were just about ideal for capital flight in 1979 and 1980—for anybody willing to forgo the gains available in the Buenos Aires market. Not only was it simple and straightforward to take funds out of Argentina, but the peso was at its highest real value ever, relative to the dollar. It is the combination of policies discussed above that produced this situation.

Venezuela, Mexico, and Indonesia

This section concerns a particular issue of policy—how to deal with an oil bonanza or a similar boom in the price of a principal export good. Although I do not really "know" the economies of Venezuela, Mexico, and Indonesia, I have worked briefly on this issue in all three. At the time of the 1973–74 oil boom I was spending a few days working with the Fondo de Inversiones of Venezuela, which had the main responsibility for deciding what to do with the proceeds of the oil boom. There was actually no serious controversy in those meetings as to the appropriate economic principles to apply:

- Oil in the ground represents national wealth.
- When it is extracted and sold, the proceeds should be treated as wealth; this means they should be invested, not consumed.
- The most prudent way of investing them is to treat them as endowments or pension funds are treated. This suggests they should be distributed in a diversified portfolio of investments in the capital markets of the world, where they will earn a certain average real rate of return.
- These funds should be repatriated slowly over time, as worthy investment projects are found. From this point of view, a worthy investment project is one with a strong expectation of yielding more than the average real rate of return of the portfolio being held abroad.

Despite the strong agreement among the "experts" that these were the proper principles, it is widely understood that they were rather quickly violated. Apparently many projects of low and even negative yield were undertaken, and some of the funds were used for current purposes. The result was that Venezuela's foreign debt was only slightly down in 1975 compared with 1973, and by 1977 had multiplied to nearly three times that of 1973.

Sometimes in the later 1970s I had occasion to work in the presidency of the Republic of Mexico for a few days, discussing exactly the same problem—what to do with Mexico's oil proceeds—and quickly reaching a virtual consensus that the principles listed above represented the most sensible strategy. Moreover, with the experience of Venezuela already in the background, there was a strong determination among the Mexican authorities present that Mexico should not go down the same road as Venezuela had.

The story of the second oil crisis is told in table 9-4. Venezuela's external debt increased 175 percent during 1977–82, while its GDP increased 3 percent. Mexico's debt increased 142 percent, while its GDP went up 41 percent. Despite the rise in GDP, Mexico ended up in a tumultuous

Table 9-4. Basic Data for Indonesia, Venezuela, and Mexico, 1977–82

Year	Indonesia	Venezuela	Mexico
Total public and publicly guaranteed debt (Debt outstanding disbursed)			
1977	11.7	4.4	20.8
1978	13.1	6.9	25.6
1979	13.2	9.8	29.2
1980	14.9	10.9	33.6
1981	15.7	11.4	42.7
1982	18.4	12.1	50.4
Growth of debt 1977–82 (percent)	57	175	142
Growth of real GDP, 1977–82 (percent)	40	3	41
Real exchange rate (1975 = 100) (Nominal rate × U.S. GDP deflator ÷ country's GDP deflator)			
1977	0.86	0.98	1.28
1978	0.89	0.99	1.19
1979	1.02	0.88	1.08
1980	0.87	0.78	0.94
1981	0.88	0.76	0.85
1982	0.90	0.78	1.28

Source: World Bank (1983a), and IMF, International Financial Statistics, various issues.

financial and exchange rate crisis. In contrast, Indonesia's debt grew only 57 percent, while GDP grew 40 percent over the same period.

The real exchange rate history of the three countries, given in the bottom panel of the table, also carries messages of interest. The Mexican real exchange rate fell from 1.28 to 0.85 before the devaluation crisis of 1982 restored it to its 1977 level. In the case of Venezuela, there was a simple erosion of the real exchange rate by about 20 percent. In Indonesia, the real exchange rate ended higher than it began and overall suffered far less fluctuation.

How can we interpret these events? What happened, both in Venezuela (actually two different times) and in Mexico, to erode the determination to follow a prudent policy with respect to the use of oil proceeds? My interpretation is this. One of the perennial problems of central bankers, finance ministers, and to an extent governments in general is the parade of supplicants for favors of one kind or another. This is probably truer in smaller countries than in, say, the United States or Germany. In any case, the supplicants may want special treatment (tariffs, import prohibitions, tax exemption, subsidized credit, and the like), they may want a change in general policy (tax reduction, credit expansion, lower interest rates), or they may simply be advocates of some particular public sector projects.

When times are really tough, it is relatively easy for a finance minister or a central banker to say no. This, I believe, was how the team of Antonio Ortiz Mena (as finance minister) and Rodrigo Gomez (as president of the Banco de Mexico) carried Mexico to a 5 percent real growth rate over a period of something like fifteen years, without any help from oil. When someone came asking, they could respond, "We simply have no funds for things like what you want." But what could even they have said, in 1979, to a state governor asking for money for a pet project? The idea that there are no funds is absurd in the presence of an oil bonanza. So the job of those who need to impose economic and financial discipline on an economy is made much more difficult by an oil bonanza. They must say no to many powerful and important people—and the parade of solicitants continues, day after day. There is no time or resources to investigate the merits of all the pet projects proposed. Under this type of daily pressure, the probability is very high that the authorities in question will sooner or later cave in to some demands. And when this happens, other solicitants, previously rejected, will reappear soliciting again for their projects, a governor saying perhaps, "You have helped Puebla and Sonora; why can't you help Guerrero?" The analogy with the way a dam breaks is too apt to be dismissed.

How, then, did Indonesia escape? I see two reasons. First, Indonesia had been burned once before. After the first oil boom the Indonesian oil company, Pertamina, went on an enormous spending spree, investing in all sorts of projects of diversification, but most notably in a very costly steel project that in the end resulted in a huge scandal. The losses to the country associated with just this project have been estimated at anywhere from $1 billion to $2 billion. In the wake of this scandal, important reorganizations occurred, and the leading government authorities vowed that nothing similar would ever happen again.

The second reason is the leading government authorities themselves. Indonesia's finance minister, Ali Wardhana, has the longest tenure in office (some fifteen years) of any of his counterparts in major countries. Another commanding figure, Professor Wodjojo, has been involved in the planning process for approximately the same time. By leading the very successful economic development of their country over a long period, they have gained not only prestige, but a strong persuasive power and moral force. To me, they are distinct parallels to Gomez and Ortiz Mena in their period in Mexico, and if anybody could have saved Mexico from its present predicament, it is they.

The bottom panel of table 9-4 shows what happened to the real exchange rates of these countries. The two countries that expanded their debt very sharply (Venezuela and Mexico) also suffered sharp declines in their real exchange rates—Mexico's had to be rectified by the devaluation crisis of 1982. Indonesia, however, managed to maintain almost complete stability in the real exchange rate. It did so by what I would call a "precautionary devaluation" in 1978. The ostensible purpose of this was to maintain the exchange rate facing other producers of tradable goods, particularly of other export products.

It is well known that the natural effect of something like an oil boom or a capital inflow is to lower the equilibrium real exchange rate. Is it not folly, then, to try to hold back this tide? The answer is, sometimes yes, sometimes no. There may be other instruments at the disposal of policymakers that can be sensibly used to accommodate a constant real exchange rate, the most natural of which, in the case in point, is a relaxation of import restrictions. Though I am not familiar with the details of the measures taken, this is clearly what was done in Indonesia, as imports grew 10 percent in the year following the devaluation, and another 50 percent the subsequent year.

Real Exchange Rate Policies

When speaking more generally of policies designed to influence (or stabilize) the real exchange rate, one must realize that taking the real exchange rate as a target deprives one of the standard adjustment mechanisms discussed in international trade theory. Both a flexible exchange system and a fixed rate system bring about adjustment through their influence on the real exchange rate, which we will define here as the nominal exchange rate E times the ratio of the two price levels P_1/P_2. A flexible rate policy brings about adjustment predominantly through movements of E; a fixed rate policy works exclusively through P_1/P_2 (except when it is abandoned temporarily for a devaluation). In any case, EP_1/P_2 does move, in response to real disturbances, to bring about a new real equilibrium under both fixed and flexible rate policies. Thus a policy that stabilizes EP_1/P_2 has to seek other ways of adjusting to real disturbances. Most commonly, trade restrictions are altered.

Examples of the successful pursuit of a real exchange rate policy following this approach can be found in Chile and Brazil in the late 1960s. Both attempted to stabilize the real exchange rate at a level that would stimulate nontraditional exports. And both were in the fortuitous situation of starting with lots of restrictions on imports. Thus it was easy—as the new, higher real exchange rate produced more export proceeds—to reduce, relax, or eliminate some of the preexisting restrictions on imports. The policy worked very well in both cases and has much to recommend it as a natural path to trade liberalization.

In a similar way, if a country has reason to make significant imports of capital, and wants to avoid the normal effect of such imports in reducing the real exchange rate, the natural way to do this is to reduce existing import restrictions. This is a policy that I genuinely approve, but I see it as a one-way street. The presence of preexisting restrictions gives rise to the opportunity to avoid a normal adjustment, which, though on the whole good, inevitably contains some negative elements. I would not argue that, once having reduced restrictions to a low level, countries should make a practice of dealing with, say, an outflow of capital, by imposing new restrictions. Rather, let the real exchange rate move!

SUMMARY AND CONCLUSIONS

The main purpose of this chapter has been to explore the relationship between capital flows into and out of a developing country and its real exchange rate. Theoretically, as long as part of a capital inflow is spent on nontradables, the real exchange rate will tend to fall (appreciate); and as long as the funds to finance a capital outflow are raised in part by contracting spending on nontradables, the real exchange will tend to rise (depreciate). In particular, brusque changes in the rate or direction of capital flows can be expected to generate serious pressures on the real exchange rate—upward if inflows are sharply cut, downward when much new capital floods in.

Empirically, we saw that when new capital flooded into Chile, Argentina, and Mexico it caused a sharp fall in the real exchange rate (in each case for a different reason). When the capital flows were sharply curtailed in each of these economies, great pressure built up to bring them to a new equilibrium at a much higher real exchange rate.

Certain subordinate themes were taken up in the discussion of specific countries. It was strongly argued that the widely held view blaming most of Chile's problems on the fixing of the exchange rate in July of 1979 is simply incorrect. Far more important was the failure to modify, about mid-1981 or a bit later, a wage law that practically precluded reductions in real wages. This was the main factor causing the huge buildup of unemployment between, say, June 1982 and June 1983. Other difficulties originated with Chile's banking system. Here flaws can be found on all sides: the early full bailout of a single failing bank (Banco Osorno) gave wrong signals both to domestic bankers and foreign lenders; even before these signals but certainly after them, domestic bankers were imprudent in maintaining large amounts of bad and dubious loans in their portfolios; the Superintendency of Banks did not pursue its regulatory functions very rigorously and did not spot the trouble; higher government authorities did not suspect (and hence did not check on) this laxity on the part of the superintendency.

A third source of Chile's problem was the abrupt relaxation, most importantly around mid-1980, of banking regulations that until then had kept capital inflows within moderate and relatively sustainable levels. The changes in these regulations opened the floodgates to foreign portfolio investment. International banks fought with each other to supply more loans to the Chilean financial market in 1980 and 1981, only to change their minds between 1981 and 1982. Their turnabout was probably the factor most directly precipitating Chile's crisis.

In the case of Argentina, the subordinate theme concerns the need for compatibility between monetary, fiscal, and exchange rate policy. The adoption of a tabular exchange rate system (the tablita) in early 1979 was not itself a great mistake. The mistake was in setting the pre-fixed rate of devaluation at a level that was incompatible with the ongoing rate of internal monetary expansion and price inflation. The consequence was a massive inflow of essentially speculative capital, followed by a sharp reverse flow—almost large enough to create financial panic—when it appeared that the government could no longer hold the line.

The final subsidiary point stems from a comparison of the ways in which Mexico and Venezuela, on the one hand, and Indonesia, on the other, confronted the oil price boom of 1979. It concerns economics less than other things—the nature of political pressures, the frailty of many governments in confronting them, the factors that contribute to resisting them. The underlying point is that an oil boom (when the oil industry is government-owned) invalidates most of the usual excuses by which governments turn down those who press for expenditures of various kinds. This leads many governments—not just those of Mexico and Venezuela but those of most other developing-country oil producers—to cave in before the pressures, even to the point of borrowing heavily against future revenues. To resist these pressures requires not only great courage and determination on the part of the ministers and other leaders involved; it also requires a great moral authority that commands widespread respect throughout the society. Indonesia was fortunate in having an economic team that met these conditions; the Indonesian nation and people were the beneficiaries.

NOTES

1. The argument can be sketched as follows. Suppose the actual risk-inclusive supply curve of funds facing a country is $i = r_o + \lambda(D/y) + \mu(D/y)^2$, where r_o is LIBOR, i is actual interest paid, D is country debt, Y is GDP, and $\lambda > 0$, $\mu \geqslant 0$. Total cost is then $i(D/y) = r_o(D/y) + \lambda(D/y)^2 + \mu(D/y)^3$, and marginal cost is the derivative of this with respect to (D/y). Taking the derivative of the right-hand side of the above equation, we obtain $MC = r_o + 2\lambda(D/y) + 3\mu(D/y)^2$. But since $i = r_o + \lambda(D/y) + \mu(D/y)^2$, this can also be written $MC = i + \lambda(D/y) + 2\mu(D/y)^2$. If the risk premium is a linear function of (D/y)—that is, if $\mu = 0$—then the excess of MC over i will be precisely the amount by which i exceeds r_o. That is, the externality associated with rising risk is precisely the premium over LIBOR. Where the relevant curve is concave upward (that is, $\mu > 0$), the externality is greater than this. This assumes the borrowing country perceives i as the true cost of its debt, that is, that it gains no fillip of utility when the prospect of default increases. The underlying model of my 1983 paper was based on a quasi-monopsony power being generated by differing perceptions of risk by borrowers and lenders, the lenders' perception always being greater than that of the borrowers. The case presented here is a simple but, in my view, broadly plausible illustration of how such differential perceptions work to confer quasi-monopsony power. For more on differential perceptions, see Harberger (1980, p. 336).

2. Some of the material in this section is drawn from Harberger (1984).

3. I conducted a survey of price movements in Chile during 1979 for a business client. It was done by first classifying the 300-odd elements in the price index for greater Santiago into tradables and nontradables. Then each of the tradables was matched with a foreign price, chosen, for example, from the International Monetary Fund's quotations of commodity prices, from publications of the U.S. Commerce Department or the Federal Reserve System, and the like. The criterion was that the foreign price had to be available on a monthly basis. When the Chilean data on tradables were replaced by the foreign prices times the exchange rate, and then inserted with appropriate weights into the Chilean CPI, the end result was virtually identical to the 39 percent inflation reported in the Chilean index. Thus, even though the Chilean price index rose by 39 percent from December 1978 to December 1979 while U.S. consumer prices rose by less than 14 percent in the same period, the careful introduction of the relevant foreign prices (translated by the exchange rate) into the Chilean CPI reveals no contradiction—no violation of the "law of one price." A cursory followup study done in 1980 suggested that the Chilean prices of tradables rose somewhat more than the law of one price would dictate, but the differences could plausibly be explained by a widening of retail margins, both because of Chile's growing prosperity and because of rising real wages.

4. This, of course, assumes that under a freely floating rate capital movements would have been similar to what they were under the pegged rate—but we can only speculate about that.

5. This statement must be qualified. It is certainly true that when the central bank borrows abroad to build up reserves, the effect is zero pressure on the real exchange rate. It is just like private citizens borrowing abroad to build up foreign balances or an electric company borrowing abroad to buy Siemens generators. In all these cases the real exchange would be unaffected. However, when the central bank acquires reserves, it may do so by printing money. This would not tend to affect the real exchange rate if the nominal rate were freely floating, but could have a transitional effect tending to a temporary appreciation of the real exchange rate if the nominal rate were fixed. With respect to comparative statics and the forces determining the real equilibrium of the economy, the procedure followed in table 9-1 is correct. If, in an attempt to take into account the transitional effect just referred to, we redefine the meaning of

exchange rate pressure as simply (a)–(b), and the relative index as (a)–(b) expressed as a fraction of GDP, the relative index, starting in 1978, now becomes 0.907, 0.075, 0.081, 0.102, –0.031. If this series is used, the main message of the table—that there was a drastic change in pressure between 1981 and 1982—is actually strengthened. Now the swing in relative pressure amounts to over 13 percent of GDP.

6. Row d is, of course, equal to the balance of trade including nonfinancial services. I consciously give it a new label here, so as to emphasize its connection with the capital account and its importance as a determinant of the real exchange rate.

7. If g is the country's GDP growth rate and k is the equilibrium ratio of net foreign debt to GDP, the ratio will stay constant if net capital inflows are the fraction gk of GDP. A value of 0.8 to 1.0 is surely high for k, and a rate of 0.06 is surely optimistic for g. This leads to the judgment that the sustainable rate of net capital inflow is probably no higher than 0.05 or 0.06. Note, too, that gk refers to net capital inflows, which is line a of table 9-1 divided by GDP. This rate reached some 15 percent of GDP in 1981, up from 10 percent in 1980.

8. A policy dilemma confronted the Chilean authorities at the time. Real interest rates were very high through most of 1981; the "needs" of the Chilean capital market were great. Why not, then, add to the supply of funds through larger capital inflows from abroad? Those who thought this way favored liberalizing regulations governing inflows. But when capital floods in in sustainable amounts, it helps to create a situation in which a real exchange rate adjustment is going to be required. Those who felt that the costs of such an adjustment exceeded the benefits of a somewhat quicker arrival of foreign funds tended to argue for a more cautious approach to liberalizing the regulations governing inflows. (An added issue was the extent to which a preferred set of borrowers profited from their easier access to foreign credits.)

REFERENCES

Banco Central de Chile. 1983a. Indicadores económicos y sociales 1960–82. Santiago.

———. 1983b. Boletín Mensual.

Harberger, Arnold C. 1980. "Vignettes on the world capital market." American Economic Review 70 (May): 331–37.

———. 1983. "Welfare consequences of capital inflows." Washington, D.C.: World Bank, October. Processed.

———. 1984. "La crisis de la devaluación Chilena de 1982." Cuadernos de Economía. Forthcoming.

International Monetary Fund (IMF). International Financial Statistics. Washington, D.C. (monthly).

World Bank. 1983. World debt tables. Washington, D.C.

10

The Foreign Debt of Mexico

Leopoldo Solís and Ernesto Zedillo

During most of the first half of the century, Mexico was absent from international capital markets. From the start of the Mexican Revolution (1910) to the signing of the Suárez-Lamont Agreement (1942), the country was unable to fulfill its old foreign debt obligations and failed many times to reach a rescheduling agreement with its creditors. It was during the 1950s and the 1960s that the country's international credit was reconstructed. Throughout this period, foreign financing came mainly from official sources, and its macroeconomic significance was, if not negligible, relatively modest. A true turning point occurred in 1973: the net flow of the foreign public debt, which had averaged a bit more than $200 million a year throughout the previous two decades, increased to more than $1.6 billion in 1973 alone, and from then on kept growing rapidly.

Thus, the stock of the foreign public debt, which was $6.8 billion at the end of 1972, reached almost $21 billion by the end of the Echeverría administration (1976) and soared to $58 billion by the time President López Portillo left office (1982). The country's total external debt (including that of commercial banks and of private sector firms) had reached $27.3 billion by late 1976 and stood at $84.1 billion six years later.

Although the entire period since 1973 constitutes in many, but not all, respects a somewhat homogeneous chapter in Mexico's history as a foreign debtor, this chapter will focus on the López Portillo administration (1977–82), the process of adjustment under way since December of 1982, and the perspectives of the Mexican foreign debt problem for the rest of the present decade. This work can be taken as a sequel to previous studies that have analyzed with considerable detail what occurred up to late 1976 (Solís 1981 and Zedillo 1981).

BACKGROUND

Mexico's economic prospects were rather dismal in early 1977. A few months earlier, the twenty-two-year era of fixed parity had been terminated, thus marking the beginning of what appeared to be a profound financial crisis. As the new administration took office in December of 1976, the prevailing economic situation was characterized by falling industrial production; the highest inflation rate in many decades; a public sector deficit that had climbed from 2.5 percent of gross domestic product (GDP) during the 1950s and 1960s to 10 percent of GDP; an exchange rate floating around a nominal value more than two times higher than it had been a few weeks earlier; shrinking and frightened sources of external credit; and, as is usual in this type of setting, an economic policy blueprint sanctioned by an International Monetary Fund (IMF) stand-by agreement.

These considerations are those of the authors and should not be attributed to their employer. José Ochoa and Héctor Pérez provided useful research assistance.

Adjustment during 1977, if not traumatic, was fairly substantial. The public sector's deficit as a percentage of GDP fell by more than 3 percentage points. Total real investment decreased almost 7 percent from a level already depressed, and the current account deficit was reduced 60 percent. Not surprisingly, GDP growth registered its lowest rate in more than two decades. But the early fears about the country's ability to continue borrowing in international capital markets proved unwarranted. Without much trouble, the public sector was able to raise the funds targeted in the IMF program. Actually, this achievement was not very surprising. Shortly after taking office, the new administration started to speak rather openly about the country's oil reserves, acknowledging that they were much higher than previously thought. Thus, proven hydrocarbon reserves, which stood at 6.4 billion barrels at the end of 1975, increased to 11.2 billion by the end of 1976 and to 16 billion by late 1977.

By late 1977, expectations about Mexico's economic prospects were very encouraging and contrasted sharply with those of the previous year. Although several other circumstances—such as the reconciliation of the public and private sectors, and the early successes of the economic adjustment program—contributed, the announcements about oil reserves and plans to export crude were undoubtedly the main "animal spirits" that led to the speedy recovery of the economy in 1978. This recovery marked the beginning of a four-year period of unprecedented prosperity that, paradoxically enough, preceded the worst economic crisis in half a century of Mexican economic history.

The rough figures of table 10-1 speak for themselves. During 1978–81 GDP growth averaged 8.4 percent. Unlike what had happened in the previous administration, not only did public investment soar but private investment as well. Thus aggregate fixed investment, which had been less than 20 percent of GDP in 1977, reached almost 26 percent of the same variable in 1981. By any measure, the labor market became, indeed, a supplier's market. Furthermore, the bet on oil was a winning one. Proven reserves consistently kept growing and their exploitation evolved rapidly. Crude exports, which had been only 200 thousand barrels a day in 1977, surpassed the million-barrel-a-day mark by late 1980. The timing to tap the oil wealth seemed even more fortunate: crude prices more than doubled between late 1975 and late 1980.

For a while, the rough indicators of external debt were very positive. The stock of foreign public debt grew rather conservatively during 1977–80 (see table 10-2). The net flow of the aggregate averaged only $3.2 billion—far less than the average of more than $4 billion registered in the last three years of Echeverría's term. Other components of the country's external debt grew more rapidly. The private sector's foreign debt—including both firms' and banks'—which had amounted to $6.8 billion at the end of 1977, reached almost $17 billion by late 1980. However, the total external debt, when measured against the size of the economy, consistently decreased through 1980. As shown by figures in table 10-2, the ratio of total debt to GDP fell from 35.8 percent in 1977 to 31.3 percent in 1980.[1] When the net flow of the total external debt is assessed against total fixed investment and current account income, however, it begins to take on importance right after 1978, as shown in table 10-3. This fact should not be all that surprising if the evolution of Mexico's current account deficit (see table 10-4) is taken into account.

In any case, the public foreign debt, which had been the bankers' headache in 1976, evolved very reasonably through 1980. Its net flow, with respect to several relevant macroeconomic aggregates after the initial adjustment of 1977, was kept in rather modest proportions during two-thirds of the López Portillo administration: the net flow averaged 2.5, 7.5, and 35.1 percent, respectively, of GDP, public expenditure, and the public sector deficit during 1978–80.

The relative adjustment in the size of the foreign public debt during that period, together with the expectations created by the new oil wealth, should help explain the tremendous upgrading of Mexico's credit in international capital markets. Fierce competition among foreign lenders to grant new loans to the Mexican government and to public enterprises was common during

Table 10-1. Some Basic Indicators of the Mexican Economy

Year	GDP real growth (percent)	Inflation (percent)		Investment						Exchange Rate		Oil	
				Public		Private		Total					
		Average	December to December	Change[a]	GDP[b]	Change[a]	GDP[b]	Change[a]	GDP[b]	Nominal[c]	Real (index)[d]	Reserves[e]	Production[f]
Average 1973–76	6.7	16.3	16.4	16.2	8.9	6.1	11.7	9.0	20.6	14.4	90.7	7,175.8	513.9
1976	4.2	15.8	17.1	−6.9	7.9	5.6	13.1	0.4	21.0	19.9	99.3	11,160.0	578.4
1977	3.4	27.2	27.4	−6.0	8.9	−7.3	10.7	−6.7	19.5	22.7	102.8	16,001.6	981.1
1978	8.2	17.5	16.2	20.9	10.0	10.5	11.1	15.2	21.1	22.7	99.1	40,194.0	1,212.6
1979	9.2	18.2	20.0	27.8	11.0	22.4	12.4	20.2	23.4	22.8	93.9	45,803.6	1,471.0
1980	8.3	26.3	29.8	12.4	10.1	17.1	13.3	14.9	23.4	23.3	84.1	60,126.3	1,936.0
1981	7.9	28.0	28.7	15.8	10.8	13.9	14.1	14.7	24.9	26.2	76.9	72,008.4	2,313.0
1982	−0.5	58.9	98.9	−14.2	9.3	−17.3	11.7	−15.9	21.0	96.5	145.3	72,008.4	2,748.2
1983	−4.7	101.9	80.8	−28.6	7.0	−22.6	9.5	−25.3	16.5	143.9	115.7	n.a.	n.a.

n.a. Not available.

a. Percentage change in real investment.

b. Investment as percentage of GDP.

c. Nominal exchange rate at the closing of December of each year; for 1982 and 1983 it is the controlled rates. In pesos per U.S. dollar.

d. Real exchange rate index calculated as described in appendix A to this chapter. Value of index at the closing of December of each year. Base value is the average of 1978.

e. In millions of barrels; includes oil and natural gas.

f. Daily production in thousands of barrels.

Sources: Banco de México, Indicadores Económicos, Subdirección de Investigación Económica, various issues. Banco de México, Indices de Precios, Subdirección de Investigación Económica, various issues. Secretaría de Programación y Presupuesto, Sistema de Cuentas Nacionales de México, various issues. PEMEX, El Sector Petrolero Mexicano, 1979–1982: Estadísticas Seleccionadas, Gerencia de Análisis y Evaluación del Mercado Internacional, Coordinación de Comercio Internacional (1983).

Table 10-2. Recent Evolution of Total External Debt

	Stock of foreign debt[a]				Foreign debt as percentage of GDP[b]	
Year	Public	Private	Commercial banks	Total	Public	Total
1976	20,846.4	4,900.0	1,600.0	27,333.7	24.9	32.6
1977	23,833.7	5,000.0	1,800.0	30,633.7	27.8	35.8
1978	26,422.5	5,200.0	2,000.0	33,622.5	25.7	32.7
1979	29,757.2	7,900.0	2,600.0	40,257.2	23.2	31.4
1980	33,872.7	11,800.0	5,100.0	50,772.7	20.9	31.3
1981	52,156.0	14,900.0	7,000.0	74,056.0	27.6	39.1
1982	58,145.6	18,000.0	8,000.0	84,145.6	29.8	43.1
1983	62,632.4	17,500.0	7,500.0	87,632.4	36.2	50.7

a. Millions of U.S. dollars; end-of-year value. These figures include only liabilities with financial institutions. Figures for 1983 are preliminary.

b. This variable was converted into dollars by means of an "equilibrium" exchange rate calculated as described in appendix A to this chapter.

Sources: Banco de México, *Indicadores Económicos*, Subdirección de Investigación Económica, various issues. Secretaría de Hacienda y Crédito Público, *México: Economic and Financial Statistics*, December 1983.

the booming years. In a matter of hours and days, important credit lines could be arranged. Putting together Eurocredit syndications was not a difficult task at all; there was always an excess demand to subscribe them. Undoubtedly, the difficulty of many foreign lenders in placing new loans in the public sector was not unrelated to the ease with which the Mexican private sector was able to finance itself abroad during the same period.

Needless to say, Mexican negotiators took full advantage of the bullishness of the market to improve the maturity profile and cost of the country's debt (see Zedillo 1981, pp. 58–89). What had been a very expensive debt in 1976, with maturities heavily concentrated in the medium term, became a nicely scheduled one two years later, carrying very low spreads and comparable to those paid by prime customers in Western industrialized countries. The national oil company (Petróleos Mexicanos, PEMEX) was of paramount importance in improving the cost and profile of the debt, and its "financial glamour" was fully utilized for this purpose. PEMEX's participation in gross borrowings by the Mexican public sector increased from 14.5 percent in 1977 to almost 40 percent by 1979.

Until 1980 foreign borrowing continued to be relatively cheap. The implicit nominal interest rate obtained from the relevant balance of payments figures—which are possibly underestimated—averaged 10 percent during 1977–80. The average real rate, based on price-of-imports inflation, was negative (−5 percent) for the same period.

The whole foreign debt scenario changed dramatically in just one year. By the end of 1981 the country's total external debt had surpassed the $74 billion mark—a nominal increase of 46 percent over the previous year. Not only had the level of the debt changed significantly, but also its maturity profile and its cost.

Why it happened is, of course, the relevant question. A detailed analysis will be required to discern the external and internal factors underlying the evolution of the debt outlined above. For the sake of didactics, the analysis is divided into two parts. First, the growth of the debt between 1978 and 1981 is broken down into several components. The main concern of this "accounting" exercise is to isolate the external shocks that might have influenced the debt's behavior. Second—to the extent that the results of the first exercise point more to internal than to external factors in explaining the growth of debt—a more detailed description is provided of domestic economic policy and its outcome during these years.

Table 10-3. Flows of External Debt

Year	Net flows[a]		Interest payments[a]		Net flow of total external debt as percentage[b] of		Net flow of foreign public debt as percentage[b] of			Interest payments on external debt as percentage of	
	Total external debt	Foreign public debt	Total external debt	Foreign public debt	Total fixed investment	Current account income	GDP	Public expenditure	Public sector deficit	Merchandise exports	Current account income
Average											
1973–76	4,770.0	3,506.4	1,195.2	874.9	33.6	69.0	5.1	16.4	58.0	41.1	17.3
1977	3,287.3	2,987.3	1,973.9	1,542.3	19.5	35.8	3.5	11.3	51.8	42.5	21.5
1978	2,988.8	2,588.8	2,571.6	2,023.1	13.8	25.6	2.5	7.8	37.8	42.4	22.1
1979	6,634.7	3,334.7	3,709.3	2,888.4	22.1	40.8	2.6	7.8	35.3	42.1	22.8
1980	10,515.5	4,115.5	5,476.7	3,957.6	26.9	42.2	2.5	7.1	32.3	36.2	22.0
1981	23,283.3	18,283.3	8,287.8	5,476.0	48.0	75.6	9.7	22.8	66.0	43.2	27.2
1982	10,089.6	5,989.6	11,264.0	8,400.4	23.2	32.8	3.1	6.4	17.4	51.8	35.4
1983	3,486.8	4,486.8	9,861.4	7,346.2	22.4	12.3	2.5	6.1	29.2	46.1	34.9

a. Millions of U.S. dollars.

b. All comparisons between a dollar and a peso variable were made by means of an "equilibrium exchange rate" calculated as described in appendix A.

Sources: Banco de México, Indicadores Económicos, Subdirección de Investigación Económica, various issues. Secretaría de Programación y Presupuesto, Sistema de Cuentas Nacionales de México, various issues.

Table 10-4. Balance of Payments
(millions of U.S. dollars)

Year	Current account	Net flow of total external debt	Direct foreign investment	Loans abroad	Special drawing rights	Other capital flows and errors and omissions	Change in reserves[a]
1977	−1,596.4	3,300.0	326.0	−64.9	—	−1,307.6	657.1
1978	−2,693.0	2,988.8	364.5	−15.8	—	−210.4	434.1
1979	−4,870.5	6,634.7	742.6	17.6	70.0	−2,175.5	418.9
1980	−7,223.3	10,515.5	1,244.5	10.8	73.5	−3,470.1	1,150.9
1981	−12,544.3	23,283.3	1,188.7	−359.7	69.6	−10,625.4	1,012.2
1982	−4,878.5	10,089.6	708.7	−117.3	—	−10,468.7	−4,666.2
1983	5,454.7	3,486.8	373.8	−250.5	—	−5,895.2	3,260.6

a. Positive sign indicates an increase in net reserves; 1983 figures are strictly preliminary.
Source: Banco de México, Indicadores Económicos, Subdirección de Investigación Económica, various issues.

SOURCES OF GROWTH OF EXTERNAL DEBT, 1979–81

Methodology

The methodology consists in using a very simple accounting framework so that the 1979–81 increases in the debt, which were higher than might have been expected back in 1978, can be decomposed into several components. Some of these components reflect external shocks, while the rest can be attributed to internal factors. This methodology is basically the one used by Balassa (1979). The results reported here are comparable to a similar work on an earlier period of the Mexican economy (Zedillo 1981), which used the same methodology.

The accounting framework can be explained in very simple terms. Take the following balance of payments identity:

$$NF_t = P_t^m M_t - P_t^x X_t + r_t D_{t-1} - FI_t - OF_t + \Delta R_t \tag{10.1}$$

where

- NF_t = Net flow of total external debt in current dollars
- M_t = A column vector whose components are the different expense items of the current account, excluding interest payments on the external debt, expressed in real terms
- P_t^m = A row vector of import prices
- X_t = A column vector whose components are the different export items of the current account, expressed in real terms
- P_t^x = A row vector of export prices
- r_t = Nominal interest rate on the external debt
- D_t = Total external debt in current dollars ($D_t = D_{t-1} + NF_t$)
- FI_t = Net flow of direct foreign investment in current dollars
- OF_t = Other flows through the capital account in current dollars
- ΔR_t = Changes in international reserves in current dollars

Next, introduce values for the same variables assuming that trends expected in the base year prevailed. More specifically, trend values for the components of X_t will refer to what would have been observed if the expected trend of foreign demand had proven right, and the country had maintained its share unchanged in the corresponding market.[2] Trend values of the M_t's are calculated under the assumption that the income elasticity of import demand and the rate of growth of the economy behaved as warranted by their past trend.[3] Trend values of prices and of all other right-hand variables are based on "best" guesses—either statistical or judgmental—that might reasonably have been made in the base year.

An overbar is used to denominate trend prices and a T for trend values of all the other variables. Thus the trend value of NF is:

$$NF_t^T = \bar{P}_t^m M_t^T - \bar{P}_t^x X_t^T + r_t^T D_{t-1}^T - FI_t^T - OF_t^T + \Delta R_t^T. \tag{10.2}$$

Next, hypothetical values for the real exports and real imports are introduced. In the case of exports, hypothetical values refer to what would have been observed if the country had kept its share in the relevant world markets unchanged, irrespective of fluctuations in foreign demand.[4] In turn, hypothetical imports are derived from the rate of growth actually observed in the country, under the assumption that the income elasticity of import demand remained equal to its trend value.[5] Assume that hypothetical prices equal actual prices. An H is used for hypothetical values.

By subtracting (10.2) from (10.1) and assuming

$$FI_t = FI_t^T, OF_t^T = 0, \Delta R_T = \Delta R_t^T,$$

equation (10.3) can be obtained after some rearrangement and simplification (define the sum vector as $\bar{1} = [1, 1, \ldots, 1]$):

(10.3)

Row
1. $NF_t - NF_t^T$
2. $= \bar{1}(X_t^T - X_t^H)$
3. $+ (P_t^x - \bar{1})(X_t^T - X_t^H)$
4. $+ (P_t^m - \bar{P}_t^m)M_t^T - (P_t^x - \bar{P}_t^x)X_t^T$
5. $- (P_t^x - \bar{P}_t^x)(X_t - X_t^H)$
6. $- (P_t^m - \bar{P}_t^m)(M_t^H - M_t)$
7. $- (P_t^m - \bar{P}_t^m)(M_t^T - M_t^H)$
8. $+ (r_t - r_t^T)D_{t-1}^T$
9. $- \bar{1}(X_t - X_t^H)$
10. $- (\bar{P}_t^x - \bar{1})(X_t - X_t^H)$
11. $- \bar{1}(M_t^H - M_t)$
12. $- (\bar{P}_t^m - \bar{1})(M_t^H - M_t)$
13. $- \bar{1}(M_t^T - M_t^H)$
14. $- (\bar{P}_t^m - \bar{1})(M_t^T - M_t^H)$
15. $+ r_t(D_{t-1} - D_{t-1}^T)$
16. $+ OF_t$

This equation provides a framework for measuring the relative contributions of external and internal factors to the deviations of indebtedness from trend ($NF_t - NF_t^T$).

The term in row 2, the difference between trend and hypothetical exports, accounts for the effect of changes in foreign demand on the country's real exports. It is named the export volume effect.[6] Its meaning will be better understood if it is recalled that the trend values are those that would have prevailed, other things being equal, had the original expectations proven right. Hypothetical values are the ones that would have been observed had the country kept its share constant in world markets, notwithstanding their expansions or contractions. The difference between trend and hypothetical values therefore measures the constant-price effects of changes in foreign demand conditions. Thus it becomes a measure of a "pure" external shock. To obtain the effects of reduced foreign demand in current prices, it is necessary to add a price-increase component. This is shown in row 3.

The two terms in row 4 constitute the pure terms of trade effects. Two things should be noted here. First, they are measured with respect to the trend values of imports and exports. If they were measured with respect to actual values, deviations over trend in the trade gap could easily distort the assessment of the terms of trade effects.[7] Second, changes in actual prices are measured against trend prices, since trend international inflation (which is somewhat expected) should not be considered a "shock."

The term in row 8 shows the effect of variations (with respect to trend values) in the interest rate paid on the external debt. This effect constitutes a pure external shock.

All terms from rows 9 to 16 are the result either of policy reactions to external shocks or of internal shocks that further complicated the debt situation. Admittedly, this approach does not permit a clear-cut separation of the two phenomena. In each term, they could be interacting in opposite directions, with policy reactions reducing the need for additional foreign indebtedness and internal shocks increasing it.

The terms in row 9 account for the export promotion effect, which is the difference between actual and hypothetical real exports, with a negative sign. If actual values were to exceed hypothetical values, it would imply that the country's export performance proved to be better than was warranted by foreign demand conditions. In this case—according to the methodology followed—a policy reaction identified as an export promotion effect would exist. If, on the contrary, actual exports fell short of hypothetical values, it would imply that an internal shock had caused a contraction of the country's world-market shares. Rows 5 and 10 show the impact of inflation on the export promotion effect. This impact is divided into shock and trend components. The former, which arise when foreign prices deviate from their trend values, should also be considered as external shocks.

The import substitution effect is accounted for in row 11. Recall that hypothetical imports are defined by the actual rate of GDP growth. If, for example, hypothetical values exceed the actual values, it will be taken as the result of a reduction in the elasticity of imports with respect to their trend value. The opposite would suggest the presence of an internal shock that increased such elasticity. Rows 6 and 12 contain the price components of the import substitution effect. As in the case of the export promotion effect, there is an external shock; it is shown in row 6.

The term in row 13—the difference between trend and hypothetical imports—quantifies the effect on imports of deviations in GDP growth with respect to its trend value. This is clear when the only difference between the trend and hypothetical imports is that the former are calculated for the trend value of GDP growth, and the latter for its actual value. A GDP growth rate below its trend value would imply, other things being equal, a reduction in the requirements for foreign financing. As in the above cases, the import effects of reducing growth are adjusted by the impact of international inflation. Row 7 accounts for this external shock.

To sum up, terms 2 to 8 of equation (10.3) constitute the debt-inducing effects of external shocks. All the other terms should be associated with internal phenomena; they are the result of either policy reactions to external shocks or of internal shocks that further complicated the debt situation. The two types of internal phenomena cannot be disentangled.

Application of Methodology

This exercise takes 1978 as base period for several reasons. First, the Mexican economy was roughly in "equilibrium," having observed a good rate of GDP growth, while registering a relatively low current account deficit. Variables such as the real exchange rate also seemed to be around their long-run equilibrium levels (as argued in appendix A), and it was also a year of declining inflation. Second, GDP growth in countries of the Organisation for Economic Cooperation and Development (OECD) was, on average, quite satisfactory, and the world economy in general had already recovered from the effects of the first oil shock.

The period of analysis is restricted to 1979–81. To keep the intuitive appeal of concepts such as trend and hypothetical exports, it is necessary to apply the method to a shorter period. Since 1982 was already a year of heavy (albeit ex post) adjustment, it is advisable to analyze it separately.

As is usual in this type of work, the selection of variables such as price indexes and proxies of world demand is a very cumbersome and, to a large degree, arbitrary job. The measurements reported should therefore not be accepted as exact quantifications. They merely suggest orders of magnitudes of interesting phenomena that are not quantified in official statistics.

The items contained in the X_t's are the following:

- Exports of non-oil primary products
- Exports of manufactured products
- Exports of oil and derivatives
- Tourism
- Border transactions.[8]

The M_t's include the following:

- Imports of current (consumption and intermediate) goods
- Imports of capital goods
- Tourism (travel expenses of Mexicans abroad)
- Border transactions.

For all the other items in the current account, except interest payments, it is assumed that the actual trend and hypothetical values are all the same. This assumption allows us to exclude them from the analysis and simplifies data requirements and calculations. All sources of relevant data may be found in appendix B.

Results

The numerical results obtained from the application of the above methodology are presented in very detailed fashion in table 10-5 and summarized in table 10-6. The figures in table 10-5 are in the order suggested by equation (10.3).

A first striking result refers to the additional external debt ($NF_t - NF_t$), which is shown in row 1. It amounted to \$4.4 billion in 1979 and kept growing in each of the following two years to reach an impressive value of \$19.1 billion in 1981. Consequently, during 1979–81 the country's external debt grew somewhat more than \$31 billion over and above what seemed to be warranted back in 1978; almost two-thirds of this additional growth, however, occurred in 1981.

The debt's growth is accounted for in the following rows of table 10-5. From equation (10.3) it is clear that effects with a positive sign contributed toward increasing the additional debt, whereas those with a negative sign helped reduce it.

Table 10-5. Sources of Growth of External Debt, 1979–81

Row	Item	1979	1980	1981
1.	Additional external debt[a]	4,381.9	7,833.1	19,104.2
2.	Export volume effects[b]	32.2	993.0	1,094.8
	Non-oil primary products	15.3	286.8	240.8
	Manufactures	36.3	105.7	55.6
	Non-oil merchandise exports	51.6	392.5	296.4
	Oil and derivatives	−21.8	527.9	786.8
	Total merchandise exports	29.8	920.4	1,083.2
	Tourism	−22.6	−10.5	−19.6
	Border transactions	25.0	83.1	31.2
3.	Effects of international inflation on export volume effects[a]	−5.2	783.2	1,290.4
	Non-oil primary products	2.0	30.1	81.4
	Manufactures	2.7	17.8	12.3
	Non-oil merchandise exports	4.7	47.9	93.7
	Oil and derivatives	−9.9	735.3	1,196.7
4.	Pure terms of trade effects[a]	465.5	734.9	1,199.1
	Current goods	44.1	211.6	618.9
	Capital goods	1,138.2	2,710.4	3,010.7
	Total merchandise imports	1,182.3	2,922.0	3,629.6
	Tourism expenses	7.5	37.5	64.3
	Border transaction expenses	84.5	225.9	304.9
	Total "imports"	1,274.3	3,185.4	3,998.8
	Non-oil primary products	38.4	386.1	331.6
	Manufactures	−66.0	−184.9	−190.3
	Non-oil merchandise exports	−27.6	201.2	141.3
	Oil and derivatives	−781.2	−2,651.7	−2,940.9
	Total merchandise exports	−808.8	−2,450.5	−2,799.6
5.	Shock of inflation on export promotion effects[a]	−290.6	−3,484.6	−5,806.0
	Non-oil primary products	3.2	76.8	7.6
	Manufactures	1.7	28.0	46.0
	Non-oil merchandise exports	4.9	104.8	53.6
	Oil and derivatives	−295.5	−3,589.4	−5,859.6
6.	Shock of inflation on import substitution effects[a]	72.2	919.1	1,618.4
	Current goods	15.6	96.1	333.6
	Capital goods	41.2	724.5	1,004.3
	Total merchandise imports	56.8	820.6	1,337.9
	Tourism expenses	0.3	9.8	34.7
	Border transactions expenses	15.1	88.7	245.8
7.	Shock of inflation on import effects of deviations in GDP growth[a]	39.9	168.2	287.7
	Current goods	2.2	17.7	67.7
	Capital goods	36.4	143.8	207.2
	Total merchandise imports	38.6	161.5	274.9
	Tourism expenses	0.3	2.2	5.0
	Border transactions expenses	1.0	4.5	7.8
8.	Effect of interest rate on variations in trend debt[a]	1,136.4	2,134.5	3,415.8
	Total external shocks[a]	1,450.4	2,248.3	3,100.2

(Table continues p. 268.)

Table 10-5 (continued)

Row	Item	1979	1980	1981
9.	Export promotion effects[b]	−815.0	−2,660.9	−3,562.2
	Non-oil primary products	−145.2	−353.7	−41.5
	Manufactures	66.2	424.1	718.2
	Non-oil merchandise exports	−79.0	70.4	676.7
	Oil and derivatives	−744.3	−2,813.0	−4,372.8
	Total merchandise exports	−823.3	−2,742.6	−3,696.1
	Tourism	1.7	96.3	221.1
	Border transactions	6.6	−14.6	−87.2
10.	Impact of inflation on export promotion effects[a]	−59.7	−370.8	−617.5
	Non-oil primary	−21.8	−113.9	−21.6
	Manufactures	3.3	43.3	113.5
	Non-oil merchandise exports	−18.5	−70.6	91.9
	Oil and derivatives	−42.4	−329.1	−791.5
	Total merchandise exports	−60.9	−399.7	−699.6
	Tourism	0.3	33.3	124.0
	Border transactions	0.9	−4.4	−41.9
11.	Import substitution effects[b]	1,386.8	4,015.6	6,214.2
	Current goods	823.0	1,232.4	1,710.8
	Capital goods	236.8	1,926.9	2,649.9
	Total merchandise imports	1,059.8	3,159.3	4,360.7
	Tourism expenses	25.7	168.6	390.1
	Border transactions expenses	301.3	687.7	1,463.4
12.	Impact of inflation on import substitution effects[a]	93.0	434.6	1,077.3
	Current goods	64.2	199.7	432.8
	Capital goods	6.9	113.7	235.8
	Total merchandise imports	71.1	313.4	668.6
	Tourism expenses	2.0	27.7	99.9
	Border transactions expenses	19.9	93.5	308.8
13.	Effects on imports of deviations in GDP growth[b]	366.8	683.4	996.2
	Current goods	116.4	227.5	347.1
	Capital goods	209.2	382.5	546.7
	Total merchandise imports	325.6	610.0	893.8
	Tourism expenses	20.9	38.7	56.1
	Border transactions expenses	20.3	34.7	46.3
14.	Impact of inflation on import effects of deviations in GDP growth[a]	18.1	70.5	160.7
	Current goods	9.1	36.9	87.8
	Capital goods	6.1	22.6	48.7
	Total merchandise imports	15.2	59.5	136.5
	Tourism expenses	1.6	6.3	14.4
	Border transactions expenses	1.3	4.7	9.8
15.	Effect of debt stock on interest payments[a]	0.0	596.1	2,017.4
16.	Other capital flows[a]	2,175.5	3,470.1	10,625.4
	Impact of inflation on income from tourism and border transactions[a]	−234.0	−653.8	−907.5
	Internal shocks[a]	2,931.5	5,584.8	16,004.0

a. Millions of current U.S. dollars.
b. Millions of 1978 U.S. dollars.
Source: Appendix B.

Table 10-6. Summary of Sources of Growth of Exernal Debt, 1979–81
(percent of additional external debt)

Row	Item	1979	1980	1981
1.	Additional external debt	100.0	100.0	100.0
2.	Export volume effects	0.7	12.7	5.6
3.	Effects of international inflation on export volume effects	−0.2	10.0	6.8
4.	Pure terms of trade effects	10.6	9.4	6.3
5.	Shock of inflation on export promotion effects	−6.6	−44.7	−30.3
6.	Shock of inflation on import substitution effects	1.6	11.7	8.5
7.	Shock of inflation on import effect of deviations in GDP growth	0.9	2.1	1.5
8.	Effect of interest rate on variations in trend debt	25.9	27.2	17.8
	Total external shocks	33.1	28.7	16.2
9.	Export promotion effects	−18.6	−34.0	−18.6
10.	Impact of inflation on export promotion effects	−1.4	−4.7	−3.2
11.	Import substitution effects	31.6	51.3	32.6
12.	Impact of inflation on import substitution effects	2.2	5.5	5.6
13.	Effects on imports of deviations in GDP growth	8.4	8.7	5.2
14.	Impact of inflation on import effects of deviations in GDP growth	0.4	0.9	0.8
15.	Effect of debt stock on interest payments	0.0	7.6	10.6
16.	Other capital flows	49.7	44.3	55.7
	Impact of inflation on income from tourism and border transactions	−5.4	−8.3	−4.9
	Internal shocks	66.9	71.3	83.8

External Shocks

The first external shock to consider is the effect of changes in foreign demand for the country's exports.[9] As should be expected from the overall world trade performance during those years, Mexico's export markets did contract over the period of analysis. Other things being equal, this phenomenon would have meant an additional indebtedness of almost $4.2 billion (the sum of rows 2 and 3), mainly accounted for by the reduction in world markets for primary products, including crude.[10] This shock alone explains almost 23 percent and 12.5 percent of the additional debt of 1980 and 1981, respectively. The pure terms of trade effects, as defined above, were also consistently adverse throughout the three-year period, totaling $2.4 billion. The surge in the price of oil, applied to the trend value of exports of this product, were not sufficient to offset the effect of higher-than-expected prices on trend imports. As shown in table 10-5, this effect was especially sizable in the case of capital goods imports. But the effects of these two shocks were more than offset by the impact of oil price inflation on the volume of crude that Mexico was able to sell beyond what seemed warranted by external demand (see row 5 of table 10-5). This effect—other things being equal—had a debt-reducing impact of $3.6 billion in 1980, and of $5.8 billion in 1981.

Clearly, the most significant adverse external shock was caused by the sharp rise in the interest rate on the external debt. On average, almost one-fourth of the additional indebtedness of 1979–81 is explained by the interest rate shock (row 8).

Netting out the impact of all external shocks, the Mexican debt picture was not overwhelmingly complicated by foreign conditions. The overall effect of external shocks averaged less than

30 percent of the higher-than-trend indebtedness of the study period. Furthermore, and quite contrary to the official posture of the time, this analysis shows that external conditions had a declining relative importance in explaining the additional debt incurred during 1979–81.

Internal Shocks

It is clear from the above that factors other than external shocks caused the debt "explosion." The methodology distinguishes four main categories of phenomena of an internal nature: the country's export performance (rows 9 and 10); increases in the propensity to import beyond what past trends would have warranted (negative import substitution, rows 11 and 12); GDP growth over and above its trend value (rows 13 and 14); and other capital flows, mainly capital flight (row 16).

Of all these internal phenomena, the only one that did not have a debt-inducing impact was the export promotion effect. This is explained by the fast increase in the country's oil exports during the period. The volume of crude exports increased 200 percent, whereas world demand fell 25 percent. Since all the other export items (except non-oil primary products) had a rather disappointing performance, debt grew faster than otherwise would have happened, especially in the case of exports of manufactures and tourism services. As a whole, the export-promotion effects, including "trend" inflation, caused a nominal reduction in the debt's growth of a bit more than $8 billion.

The story is quite different in the case of all the other effects. Especially striking are the results for the import substitution effects, which are shown in rows 11 and 12 to account for almost a third of the additional debt in 1979–81 and more than half of it in 1980. Never before had Mexico's absorption of foreign goods been as dynamic as it was during this period. Average real growth in imports of merchandise was more than three times the average real GDP growth over the same span of time (in the 1950s and 1960s this "elasticity" was around one). Admittedly, the most vigorous impulse in imports growth came from the capital goods item—a fact explained by the rapid rise in gross fixed investment. But current imports, both merchandise and services, were also important. The economy's growth was pushed beyond its trend path before investment projects were fully mature, and this push caused additional debt to be incurred at that time. Trend GDP growth has been around 6.5 percent for the past thirty years. Even allowing for the bonus growth induced by the expansion of the oil sector, it is clear that actual GDP was on a track well above the one of potential output. This phenomenon explains the effects of rows 13 and 14, which account for $2.5 billion of additional indebtedness. A similar impact came from the interest payments paid on the stock of external debt that accumulated in excess of its trend value (row 15).

The most impressive internal shock leading to fast growth in the external debt was, however, other capital flows. Since this variable includes errors and omissions of the balance of payments, it covers other important phenomena such as smuggling which strictly speaking are different from capital flows. Still, it can be argued that smuggling is, after all, mainly a consequence of an ill-conceived trade policy and an overvalued exchange rate—both of which are clearly associated with internal policy decisions. Nevertheless, any guess as to the size of smuggling (say, 10 percent of nominal merchandise imports in each year) leaves an impressive value to be explained purely in terms of capital flight.

It could also be claimed that capital flight is not necessarily the result of internal conditions, and that external factors should also play a role in explaining portfolio adjustments leading to capital outflows as large as the ones that occurred in Mexico. It will be argued later that any external shock that might have triggered a flight from the peso could easily have been counterbalanced by a more active and opportune use of domestic economic policy instruments. Altogether, the other capital-flows items of row 16 account for more than 50 percent of the additional indebtedness accumulated throughout the three-year period. By far the largest impact of other capital flows took place in 1981 when they accounted for $10.6 billion of the additional debt.

To sum up, between the end of 1978 and the close of 1981, the total external debt grew by $40.4 billion. An optimistic but prudent observer of both internal and external factors would have foreseen in 1978, an increase of around $9.0 billion (notice that during 1977–78, when oil exports were still modest, the average net flow of the total external debt was $3.0 billion). But the imaginary analyst would have proved to be terribly wrong, for the external world and internal developments in Mexico over the next three years were quite unexpected, and so was the evolution of the foreign debt. As the above counterfactual exercise has shown, however, by an overwhelming margin, his miscalculations on the way domestic economic policy would be conducted proved to be much more damaging to his foreign debt forecasts than what happened in the external environment.

INTERNAL SHOCKS DURING THE LÓPEZ PORTILLO ADMINISTRATION

Although the country's indebtedness increased sharply in 1981, the internal phenomena underlying it started to develop a few years earlier.

Despite the traumatic events of the mid-1970s, which were too recent to be forgotten, the public-expenditure-led-growth model was revived by 1980 and promoted as vigorously as it had been during the peak Echeverría years. What was supposed to be a three-year program to correct fiscal disequilibrium was overridden after one year. The public sector's overall deficit (the financial deficit of table 10-7) as a proportion of GDP could not be lowered beyond the initial adjustment of 1977.

Although the emphasis on public expenditure to achieve high GDP growth was obvious a year after the López Portillo government took office, nobody seemed to worry, for it was claimed that the failed model was being revived on a basis quite different from the one used in the previous administration. First, it was said that the new oil wealth would finance Mexico's development in a noninflationary way, and that taking advantage of such wealth required the expansion of public investment. Second, it was affirmed that the government was going to

Table 10-7. Public Finance
(percent of GDP)

	Public expenditure				Public income			Financial deficit		
Year	Total	Without interest payments[a]	Without PEMEX	PEMEX expenditure	Total	Oil sector	Non-oil sector	Total	External	Internal
1976	33.6	30.3	30.2	3.5	23.8	3.9	19.9	9.9	3.8	6.1
1977	30.9	29.0	27.2	3.7	24.2	4.3	19.8	6.7	3.1	3.7
1978	32.2	30.2	27.5	4.7	25.5	5.0	20.4	6.7	4.0	2.7
1979	33.6	31.4	28.3	5.3	26.2	6.1	20.1	7.4	4.5	2.9
1980	35.6	33.5	30.4	5.2	27.8	8.0	19.7	7.9	4.9	2.9
1981	42.4	40.0	35.0	7.5	27.7	8.0	19.7	14.7	6.2	8.5
1982	48.9	40.8	41.3	7.6	31.0	12.4	18.6	17.9	14.1	3.8
1983	42.6	29.3	35.6	6.1	33.9	16.2	17.7	8.7	−3.0	11.8

a. Paid by the public sector on its internal and foreign debts.

Note: Some sums may not check because of rounding errors.

Sources: Secretaría de Hacienda y Crédito Público, Estadísticas Hacendarias del Sector Público (Dirección General de Informática y Evaluación Hacendaria, 1983); and Secretaría de Hacienda y Crédito Público, Estadísticas de Finanzas Públicas (Dirección General de Informátion y Evaluación Hacendaria, 1984).

activate other policy instruments left practically untouched earlier. In this respect, there were some encouraging signs at the beginning. A financial reform restructured the banking system and modernized the instruments of monetary control, making interest rate policy more flexible and attentive to real yields and to developments in foreign financial markets. On the fiscal side, an in-depth reform was announced with the introduction of the value added tax. With respect to industrial and commercial policy, there were some early but inconclusive attempts to rationalize the whole structure of relative prices by eliminating quantitative restrictions on imports and simplifying fiscal incentives for industrial activities. Third, this time the public sector was not going to be alone in enhancing the country's stock of capital; private investment was to be encouraged so that a more balanced pattern of growth evolved.

As mentioned before, this strategy produced very impressive results for investment and GDP growth, as well as job creation, for four years. At the same time, however, some fundamental disequilibriums in the Mexican economy had taken on renewed force and reached tremendous and unprecedented proportions.

External shocks have been analyzed in the previous section. It will suffice, with the help of table 10-4, to recall that the early adjustment in the current account deficit of 1977–78 had petered out by 1979, when the deficit reached $4.9 billion. This occurred even though the value of oil exports had increased almost four times in only a few years, and non-oil exports had also been growing very dynamically. By 1979 the Mexican economy was importing more than $12 billion worth of merchandise—a fairly high figure if assessed against any macroeconomic variable. But imports increased further to almost $20.0 billion the following year. As a consequence—and even though oil exports had almost reached the $10.0 billion level—the current account deficit exceeded $7.2 billion. This seemed inconceivable for an oil-endowed developing country, even if due account is taken of international inflation and its impact on import prices and interest rates. The current account deficit reached that level in a year when oil revenues had increased two and a half times; observers of the Mexican economy should have been startled. To the comfort of international bankers, Mexico became the "champion of absorption"—not only of its own oil revenues, but of foreign resources as well.

External disequilibrium was just the tip of the iceberg. The most notable evidence of disarray in the Mexican economy was the unchecked expansion in aggregate demand, led by the growth in public expenditure. Table 10-7 tells the story of the public finances during the López Portillo years. Public expenditure as a proportion of GDP had peaked at 33.6 percent during the previous administration. In spite of the early rhetoric about reducing public expenditure, this proportion was reached again in 1979 and was surpassed by two percentage points in 1980. The need for increasing PEMEX investment was not the sole cause; non-PEMEX public expenditure as a share of GDP was consistently augmented from 1977 on. Although public income from the oil sector almost doubled as a proportion of GDP between 1977 and 1980, the overall deficit was never reduced to the level contemplated at the beginning of the administration.

What happened was just the opposite; there was a turn for the worse after 1978. The monetary impact of the public sector deficits is better assessed by looking at a concept that in Mexican public finances is called the "internal" deficit.[11] As shown in table 10-7, the deterioration of this factor was more acute than that of the overall financial deficit. The government's retreat from early intentions of increasing the relative size of fiscal and public enterprise revenues explains as much of this imbalance as does the overflow of all categories of public expenditure. Considering the size of the public sector disequilibrium and the expansion in domestic credit thus induced, it is not surprising that the annual average growth of the money supply was more than 30 percent during 1977–81.

The impact of the fiscal deficit on domestic market disequilibrium was reinforced by the rapid expansion of private demand, both in consumption and investment. In spite of the rather precipitate and unplanned opening of the economy to foreign imports, the strong demand pull was bound to have a significant effect on domestic inflation. As shown by the figures of table 10-1, inflation was lowered only temporarily to the levels of 1975–76 and promptly took off again in 1979. But for more than four years—and well into 1981—the exchange rate was kept practically fixed. Obviously this situation had to lead to a growing overvaluation of the Mexican peso, as shown by the index of the real exchange rate of table 10-1. Considering the overheating of the economy and the exchange rate policy followed at the time, it is not at all surprising that the external sector disequilibrium worsened to the degree it did, despite increased oil revenues. Those phenomena explain the negative import substitution effect and the effects on imports of deviations over trend value in GDP growth that were analyzed in the previous section.

The economic imbalance of 1980 should have sufficed to alert policymakers of the risks ahead. At that point, far less than an overall adjustment was needed. A mild cleanup of public finances to stop the worsening trend of the fiscal deficit, plus some adjustments—especially in exchange rate policy, with possibly a more active crawl—would have done the trick. Admittedly, the budget approved for fiscal 1981 explicitly incorporated the objective of not allowing the overall deficit to increase further in nominal terms. Unfortunately, this was just a formality. In practice, even a timid gradualistic approach on fiscal matters and exchange rate policy sounded like heresy—an insult to the rationale of the time. The most popular members of the cabinet were those who produced the grandest projects and programs, overriding the budget approved by Congress. As happened in the Echeverría years, the president himself authorized the out-of-budget items that were requested.

The momentum of the public-expenditure-led-growth model proved to be overwhelming. The warning voices of the more prudent members of the cabinet failed to provoke any change of course. This explains why the 1981 budget overlooked not only internal bottlenecks but also conditions abroad. Perhaps the most dramatic example of this miscalculation is provided by the projections on the value of crude exports for 1981. The budget assumed that Mexico could export a volume 75 percent higher at a price of 10 percent higher than in 1980, although oil prices were already above $30 a barrel and the world economy had started to enter a deep recession.

The official scenario still had some credibility during the first half of 1981. The beginning of the debacle took place in June when it became clear that PEMEX had to lower its crude prices in order to continue receiving orders from abroad. This was too hard to swallow. Instead of facing market signals—as had been done two years previously when oil prices started their upward swing—the Secretariat of National Properties and Industry (SEPAFIN) designed a "new" marketing strategy whereby buyers unwilling to pay the Mexican prices would be bumped from PEMEX's customer list (New York Times 1981). The result was that a good percentage of Mexican oil exports remained on the international crude market for several weeks. Although wealthy Mexicans had started to read the basic economic statistics in a less complacent way, the possibility of a sharp devaluation of the peso still looked somewhat academic just before the oil affair. Such a possibility became an open threat by mid-June, however, and led to a tremendous capital flight and to "dollarization" of deposits in the Mexican banking system.

The seriousness of the situation demanded bold actions that again were either postponed or not taken. Although there was official admission that the peso was under heavy attack, little was done beyond rhetoric to face what was becoming a financial crisis. The domestic currency continued to be devalued daily at an annual rate of only 9 percent. An across-the-board cut of 4 percent in public expenditure was decreed, but with respect to a level that was already higher than budgeted. As it turned out, not even this timid adjustment was made. By late July, the targeted overall deficit had been revised upward to 540 billion pesos (from less than 415 billion pesos in the original budget). When the year was over, however, the deficit reached 865 billion pesos. This was not caused by a relative fall in public income, as was officially argued at the time, since the ratio of public income to GDP remained unchanged. The underlying cause was the tremendous increase in public expenditure. As can be verified in table 10-7, it expanded from 35.6 percent of GDP in 1980 to 42.4 percent by 1981. As a consequence, the overall deficit reached almost 15 percent of GDP (it had been 10 percent in the "worst" Echeverría year). One does not have to be in the monetarist camp to realize that such an imbalance inevitably produces a profound disequilibrium in the money market, which sooner or later has to be settled by adjustment in either prices or the balance of payments, or both.

The balance of payments effect was the dominant one in the Mexican economy during 1981. The current account deficit soared to $12.5 billion (see table 10-6) with the import bill reaching $25.1 billion. Although oil exports did not reach the level officially forecast, they did reach a value of $14.6 billion—47.5 percent more than in the previous year. Equally impressive was the drain via capital account. It was shown above that officially computed capital outflows, plus errors and omissions, had a value of $10.6 billion. Even conceding that as much as one-fourth of this amount was unrelated to the capital account (because of smuggling, for example), there remains a negative balance of almost $8 billion that has to be explained in terms of capital flight.

Right after the oil problem, however, far from sinking into a financial crisis that would have forced an immediate adjustment, the Mexican economy, with its fundamental disequilibriums, continued to grow. How was it able to do this? The answer can be found in the availability of foreign financing. As said before, Mexico's total external debt grew more than $23 billion in 1981 alone. Of course, most of this new debt was contracted by the public sector. The net flow of the foreign public debt was $18.3 billion. In addition, all of the increase in the external debt of commercial banks (around $2.0 billion) was re-lent to the public sector. Undoubtedly, in 1981, foreign financing became the slack variable that forestalled the necessary adjustment.

Needless to say, such external borrowing had to bring about profound and adverse consequences. Immediately, there was a sharp deterioration in lending conditions to Mexico. At the close of 1980 the short-term foreign public debt was only $1.5 billion. A year later, it had jumped to $10.8 billion, not counting the amounts obtained through Mexican commercial banks. The enviable spreads of a few months earlier were being displaced by new ones that were considerably higher (as described in Castro 1983).

It will take the talent of a top specialist on highly competitive but imperfect markets to understand why international bankers did not stop lending to Mexico before they did. One possible, yet unexplored, explanation is that they did not realize individually the aggregate implications of their actions. Some may have believed the official story that Mexico was merely experiencing a temporary cash-flow problem, and therefore yielded to the temptation of recycling (short-term and profitably) the then abundant petrodollars. Others, traditionally involved in Mexico, may simply have followed the inertia of past years. What seems to be clear, however, is that very few knew how fast Mexico's debt was growing during the second half of 1981. It is highly suggestive that the balance of payments statistics released in February 1982 reported a net increase in the foreign public debt of $14.5 billion for 1981—almost $4 billion less than the actual figure (Banco de Mexico 1982).

Despite some final and very costly resistance, it was announced that the peso was being devalued—initially 40 percent—on the night of February 17; a few days later a rather orthodox overall stabilization package was announced. For a few days it seemed possible that the Mexican economy could pass from a booming situation to an orderly adjustment. The initial adjustment program, however, was soon overridden by measures that were clearly inconsistent with it. For example, the program called for a maximum emergency wage increase of 10 percent, but a few weeks after the devaluation, the government decreed wage increases of up to 30 percent. The program also called for immediate increases in the prices charged for services and goods produced by public enterprises; several months had to pass, however, before the first significant raise was announced. Rather, an "emergency" plan to support productive firms was implemented. By providing fiscal relief and granting outright subsidies, this plan partially undid the adjustment sought by the devaluation and constituted another clear signal that it would take a while before public finances could indeed be improved. Pressures to finish projects already started made it very difficult to control the nominal expansion in public expenditure.

Meanwhile, clashes between the government and private sector spokesmen—reminiscent of the ones that had occurred six years previously—became more frequent and fiery. It was not surprising that by early April 1982 there were signs that the capital flight had resumed. Another major devaluation was avoided for several months, only at the expense of exhausting foreign exchange reserves and using the last "voluntary" foreign credit available to Mexico. Renewing short-term credits obtained during 1981 became increasingly difficult; renewal periods became shorter and shorter while spreads climbed higher and higher.

To alleviate an impressive piling up of short-term credits inherited from 1981, three important medium-term syndications were arranged during the first semester of 1982. The first, placed by PEMEX in February, raised $2.0 billion. Nacional Financiera, S.A. (NAFINSA), a state development bank, was the borrowing agency in the second, which took place in March. It provided $1.2 billion. The last syndication consisted of a "jumbo" loan of $2.5 billion, with the Mexican federal government as debtor, and was arranged during May and June.

In many ways, this credit was a turning point. As the facility was being put together, it became clear that the market's perception was that Mexico's creditworthiness was completely deteriorating. Even though the pricing of the loan was very attractive compared with previous deals, it took an enormous effort on the part of Mexican negotiators to gather the necessary commitments (see Castro 1983). To their dismay, only 75 banks accepted out of 650 that had been invited to subscribe. Considering the enormous difficulties that had to be faced before signing the loan on June 30, it became clear that the only debt-management expedient left was to continue rolling over short-term credits—at any price and at any maturity. This, of course, could not last.

The peso continued to be under heavy speculation during July. Too late, it was decided to implement some of the measures in the Economic Adjustment Program that had not yet been put into effect. Accordingly, at the beginning of August 1982, it was announced that the prices of some basic products were being raised. After this announcement was made, pressure on the central bank's reserves became unbearable. On August 6, 1982, a new two-tier foreign exchange system was set up. Speculation continued, and just one week later dollar-denominated deposits in the Mexican banking system were made payable only in domestic currency. Banks were also ordered to suspend temporarily foreign exchange transactions. In the face of these events, which scared away foreign creditors, it became clear that normal credit conditions could not be expected for a long time.

At that moment, the financial authorities could have either waited for foreign creditors to make public the country's insolvency or confronted the facts and declared unilaterally that the country was not able to keep up with payments on principal. Wisely, the second approach was followed. On August 20, Secretary of Finance Jesús Silva-Herzog met with representatives of a large number of creditor banks and requested a three-month moratorium on payments of principal, as well as the formation of an advisory group of creditors to negotiate the restructuring of the foreign public debt. A few days earlier, the Mexican government had obtained important financial backing in the form of credits from the U.S. Commodity Credit Corporation and the U.S. Treasury Department. Negotiations with the Bank for International Settlements to obtain a dollar credit for $1.85 billion from several of its members were initiated in the last days of August. Early that month, formal talks had begun with an IMF mission about a standby agreement.

The realism displayed in August was comforting to Mexico's creditors only for a while. On September 1, President López Portillo announced that private banks were being nationalized and that blanket foreign exchange controls were being instituted. The international banking community must have panicked at the possibility of such a radical approach to the management of the foreign debt problem—a possibility that, indeed, was very feasible for a few weeks. Fortunately for all concerned, this did not happen.

EVENTS OF 1983

When President López Portillo left office December 1, 1982, the Mexican economy was experiencing a crisis even more profound than the one six years earlier—something inconceivable for a country that had earned $47 billion in oil revenues and had gone through a rapid process of capital formation during the previous five years. By the end of 1982 real GDP had fallen 0.5 percent; inflation had reached almost 100 percent (according to the growth of the consumer price index from December to December); the monetary authorities had lost control of the foreign exchange market, where the average official exchange rate was less than half the black market rate;[12] capital flight continued practically unchecked, in spite of the supposedly comprehensive foreign exchange controls; the public sector's financial deficit had reached 17.9 percent of GDP during the year; the domestic financial system was shrinking; and, for practical purposes, there was a moratorium on foreign debt obligations.

In fact, during the last four months of 1982, the country complied only with payments of interest and a minor percentage of payments on the principal of foreign public debt. All payments on private foreign debt had been suspended. The country's overall external debt picture was dismal. The public sector already had arrears of $8.1 billion in payments of principal and $14.3 billion was to come due in 1984 and 1985. The private sector's situation was relatively worse. It owed $18.0 billion to foreign financial institutions, two-thirds of which had repayment periods that went no further than 1984. It also declared $4.0 billion in liabilities outstanding with foreign suppliers (not included in the debt figures of tables 10-2 and 10-3) when a registry at the Secretariat of Commerce was opened.

On general economic policy, the new administration opted for drastic adjustment; it had no alternative. At the core of the stabilization program were efforts to correct the public finance disequilibrium and reduce the deficit to 8.5 percent of GDP in 1983. In addition to important across-the-board real cuts in public expenditure, stiff actions were taken immediately on the income side. They included significant increases in both the value added tax and income tax rates for upper brackets, as well as major revisions in the prices charged by public enterprises (for gasoline, electricity, and so on). At the same time, important changes were made to rectify the exchange rate and financial policies. The blanket system of exchange controls was replaced by a rather standard system of dual exchange rates, consisting of a controlled market (including all merchandise exports, the majority of merchandise imports, and all flows related to foreign debt) and a "free" market (for remaining transactions). Initially the exchange rate for the free market was set fairly close to the rate prevailing on the black market, thus leading to a significant reduction in the volume of black market transactions. The controlled market called for an opening rate that overshot the purchasing power parity equilibrium value. A daily "crawl" in this rate also followed. In the financial sphere, domestic interest rates were increased and monetary targeting was strictly tied to the prescribed reduction in the fiscal deficit.

A number of the above measures were contained in the letter of intention that was submitted to the IMF Board of Directors in November 1982 and ratified as soon as the new administration took over. The agreement reached with the technical mission of the IMF called for a net flow from private foreign banks to the public sector in 1983 of $5.0 billion. To the creditors' surprise, the IMF managing director let it be known that he would "not recommend the approval of the IMF Agreement to the Executive Board of the IMF without assurances from both official sources and commercial banks that adequate external financing was in place for the success of the Mexican Adjustment Program and the IMF Agreement, and that the principles of a realistic restructuring scheme of the Mexican debt would be favorably considered by the community."[13] The telex from which the foregoing quotation was taken contained the principles of the strategy followed by the Mexican government to deal with both the borrowing of net resources and the restructuring of the foreign public debt in 1983.

To obtain the additional financing required for 1983 an unprecedented number of banks were asked to subscribe a mammoth loan of $5.0 billion. Each creditor's relative participation in the deal was defined on the basis of its exposure in the country as of August 1982. The implication is that every bank with assets in Mexico was requested—and somehow subtly forced—to underwrite the facility. This element of "fairness" explains, to a great extent, the enthusiastic response of the largest banks in raising the needed resources. Attractive pricing also helped to close the deal. Creditors were offered, at their option, a spread of 2.5 over LIBOR or 2.125 over prime. The maturity requested—only six years, including a three-year grace period—was not hard on lenders either. Attractive commitment and facility fees were offered as well. With the assistance of the advisory group and of top officials from the IMF and several central banks—including the U.S. Federal Reserve—the credit was granted almost on time, with an impressive total of 526 banks participating.

With regard to the restructuring of the foreign public debt, the target was to reschedule all payments falling due between August 23, 1982, and December 31, 1984, with the exception of payments on "excluded" debt. The latter comprised credits granted or guaranteed by official entities—either government or multilateral—and other minor categories. Consequently, the rescheduling was applied primarily to debt owed to private financial institutions. Mexican negotiators asked for a principal repayment period of eight years, including a four-year grace period. In exchange, creditors were to be paid, at their own election, a rate of LIBOR plus 1.875 or prime plus 1.75. They were also offered a 1 percent restructuring fee. This rescheduling effort was also quite successful. Only a year after the original request was made, the first set of restructuring contracts was signed. By the end of 1983 twenty-seven restructuring agreements between Mexican public sector entities and their foreign creditors had been concluded, representing liabilities of $23 billion dollars.

The problem of the private sector's foreign debt proved to be as challenging as that of the public sector. Arrears in interest that had accrued during the last four months of 1982 and early 1983 (almost $0.9 billion) were addressed first. Debtor firms were asked to constitute—through a peso payment, and at the controlled rate of exchange—dollar-denominated deposits in favor of their foreign creditors. These deposits earned a commercial rate (typically LIBOR plus 1.0) and were transferred by the central bank in several installments for complete liquidation by the end of 1983.

It was clear, however, that an overall renegotiation of private sector debt was unavoidable. From the start, two important decisions were made by the Mexican financial authorities. First, the government was not going to assume private sector debt—that is, foreign lenders would have to retain the commercial risk involved in their credits, and debt renegotiations would have to take place individually between lenders and borrowers. Second, debtors would receive no subsidy to settle their foreign obligations. (See Zedillo 1983 for a description of this mechanism.)

To encourage the restructuring process, it was decided to offer coverage for exchange risk on principal and interest payments that were rescheduled according to the guidelines issued by the financial authorities. Firms were able to trade their dollar obligations for peso-denominated liabilities as long as the former could be restructured as long-term debt. Accordingly, firms were able to transfer the foreign exchange risk of their liabilities to the public sector. This mechanism was also successful, and by the time the deadline rolled around (late October 1983), private liabilities for almost $12 billion had been covered by the facility. Almost 100 percent of that amount corresponded to obligations renegotiated to mature in eight or more years, including a four-year grace period. Nearly 300 different financial institutions and 200 foreign suppliers participated.

The private foreign debt that did not come under the above program was settled or restructured through other mechanisms. More than $800 million of debt owed to foreign suppliers was repaid through two other programs made public by the central bank on February 28 and August 3, 1983. These programs allowed firms—through a peso payment—to make dollar-denominated deposits which could be used to pay foreign suppliers. Well ahead of schedule, the central bank made these deposits transferable, thus settling the respective obligations. Another segment of private foreign debt involving some $2 billion was already long-term and covered for exchange risks by virtue of another system of foreign currency swaps offered by the Banco de México since 1977. Loans guaranteed by agencies of foreign governments are to be settled through bilateral agreements that are in the process of negotiation. The remaining debt was largely that of firms in excellent financial condition whose liabilities are automatically rolled over and whose prospects are good for exporting, thus automatically granting them coverage against fluctuations in the exchange rate.

The process of restructuring the country's foreign debt was greatly facilitated by the way the economy adjusted during 1983.[14] The target of reducing the public sector's overall financial deficit to 8.5 percent of GDP was almost achieved (see table 10-7). But even more striking was the adjustment in the balance of payments: the trade surplus amounted to $13.7 billion, while that of the current account was $5.6 billion.

Admittedly, a good part of the balance of payments adjustment was brought about by the drastic reduction (47 percent) in imports. During 1983 the nominal value of merchandise imports was less than that registered five years earlier. In any case, the current account adjustment permitted a very satisfactory recovery of international reserves and an important liquidation of private foreign debt—especially that owed to foreign suppliers. It is estimated (see tables 10-2 and 10-4) that the total foreign debt grew at most by $3.5 billion during 1983—a nominal increase that, as argued below, implies a reduction in real terms.

Apart from some pressures during February and March because of uncertain ties in the international oil market, the foreign exchange market was rather calm during 1983. The controlled rate kept crawling at a decreasing percentage rate (13 centavos a day) throughout the year; the overadjusted free rate was virtually fixed until September, when it also began to depreciate at a daily rate of 13 centavos.

As can be expected following this kind of adjustment, real economic activity fell significantly in 1983. Gross fixed investment and GDP fell in real terms by 25.3 percent and 4.7 percent respectively, the sharpest contractions in such variables since the early 1930s. As is also usual in the early stages of most stabilization programs, the least impressive achievement was obtained on the inflation front: the consumer price index rose 81 percent (December to December).

The economic adjustment paid off in terms of improved creditworthiness. In December of 1983 a general agreement reached with the advisory group defined the conditions for new lending of $3.8 billion to the Mexican government during 1984. Lending banks were again asked to participate on the basis of their pro-rata exposure to Mexico in August 1982. This time, however, conditions were softened significantly, with creditors being offered, at their option, 1.5 percent over LIBOR or 1.125 percent over prime. Instead of the six-year maturity obtained in the previous deal, the new credit carried a ten-year term, including a five-and-a-half-year grace period. Commitment and facility fees were also reduced. Another encouraging fact was the relatively quiet way in which a $4.5 billion PEMEX acceptance facility was renewed for two more years in mid-1983.

As this chapter is being written (mid-1984), one can almost say that the debt crisis of 1982 has been overcome. Fears that Mexico would provoke an international financial hecatomb began to fade as the problems of other debtor countries came into focus.

PROSPECTS

Needless to say, the fact that a major crash was avoided does not imply that the future of Mexican foreign debt is all that clear and bright. Actually, there are many hindrances, both internal and external, on the road ahead. The most important question, of course, is whether the Mexican economy is truly on the right track to correct its basic imbalances. This correction is a necessary condition for restoring economic growth. Even if it is assumed that the stabilization program now in effect is technically correct, the question remains whether the government will be able to stick to it—resisting social and political pressures—until its most positive results become evident and are reflected in an improvement of the population's standard of living. And even if it is granted that present economic policy has a good chance of being successful, the foreign debt picture for the coming years remains uncertain in many other respects.

The first concern is with the amortization profile of the country's external debt in the coming years (see table 10-8). During 1985 alone, \$11.7 billion of the outstanding debt will come due; another \$38 billion will be payable over the following three years (1986–88). It is fair to say, however, that such a profile has nothing to do with the way the country will pay off its external debt. Under no macroeconomic scenario would it be possible to generate the current account surpluses needed to comply with such a repayment schedule. Nor would payment be required by creditors, because gross borrowings would be at least as high as amortizations falling due, if international capital markets return to normalcy. The rolling over of external debts was, in general, the standard procedure until 1982. This expedient is not feasible for the near future in view of current market conditions. For this reason, representatives of the Mexican government and the commercial bank advisory group sat at the negotiating table during the summer of 1984 to discuss a rescheduling package of almost \$49 billion. A preliminary agreement was reached in early September by which the debt to be rescheduled would have a total repayment period of fourteen years computed from 1985. Repayment would start in 1986, but with rather minor amounts. This program, if accepted by all creditors, would imply—apart from a prepay-

Table 10-8. Amortization Profile of the Foreign Debt
(millions of U.S. dollars)

Year	Public sector[a]	Private sector	Total
1985	10,558	1,171	11,729
1986	9,004	1,205	10,209
1987	12,738	986	13,724
1988	10,991	3,073	14,064
1989	9,312	2,893	12,205
1990	7,245	2,714	9,959
After	6,857	4,047	10,904
Total[b]	66,705	16,089	83,132

a. Excludes all debt owed by Mexican commercial banks and liabilities with the International Monetary Fund.
b. Outstanding projected to December 1984.
Source: Secretaría de Hacienda y Crédito Público (1984).

ment of up to \$1.5 billion corresponding to the \$5.0 billion jumbo loan—total amortization payments to commercial banks of \$4.7 billion during 1985–89. Current contracts would have implied amortizations for \$45 billion during the same period.

Even if it is assumed that all nominal payments of principal on public and private debts falling due in the next six years are effectively postponed, the impact of the debt's future evolution on economic growth is uncertain. Rescheduling of coming maturities unaccompanied by new lending would still mean a net real outflow of resources, as occurred in 1983 and will occur again in 1984. During these two years the net flow of external savings was positive in nominal terms. When international inflation is considered, however, the real debt fell on average 3.0 percent a year.

The postwar scenario of rapid growth, not only for Mexico but also for many other developing countries, has had the essential feature of a positive real net flow of external credit. Furthermore, historically this credit has been granted at very low real rates of interest. In view of this, it is of interest to pose the following questions: What is the probable impact on GDP growth of alternative scenarios concerning the future evolution of the real external debt? How sensitive to alternative real interest trajectories are these probable impacts? How do some traditional indicators of debt burden behave under such alternative scenarios?

To shed some light on the above questions, the simplest kind of growth-cum-debt model would seem appropriate.[15] Admittedly, richness in the analysis, especially of structural and monetary phenomena, is lost by relying on this kind of apparatus, but it focuses attention on the main issues.

Let

Y_t = Gross domestic product

σ = The reciprocal of the incremental capital-output ratio

K_t = Capital stock

δ = Depreciation rate of capital stock

I_t = Gross fixed investment

C_t = Total consumption

S_t = Domestic savings (gross)

s = Domestic savings rate

d_t = Net flow of the foreign debt

M_t = Imports of goods and nonfactor services

x_t = Exports of goods and nonfactor services

r_t = Real interest rate on the foreign debt

D_t = Total foreign debt ($d_t = D_t - D_{t-1}$)

Assuming a fixed-coefficient technology (or a well-behaved neoclassical production function in a scenario of fixed real wages), output is given by

$$Y_t = \sigma K_t. \tag{10.4}$$

Given that

$$Y_t - Y_{t-1} = \sigma(K_t - K_{t-1}) \tag{10.5}$$

and

$$(10.6) \qquad K_t - K_{t-1} = I_t - \delta K_{t-1},$$

equation (10.4) becomes

$$(10.7) \qquad Y_t = \sigma I_t + (1 - \delta) Y_{t-1}.$$

Consider now the following basic identities:[16]

$$(10.8) \qquad C_t + I_t + X_t - M_t = Y_t = C_t + S_t + r_t D_{t-1}$$

and

$$(10.9) \qquad d_t = M_t - X_t + r_t D_{t-1}.$$

Consequently,

$$(10.10) \qquad I_t = S_t + d_t.$$

Given the savings function

$$(10.11) \qquad S_t = s(Y_t - r_t D_{t-1})$$

and using (10.7), investment can be expressed as

$$(10.12) \qquad I_t = \left[\frac{s(1-\delta)}{1-s\sigma}\right] Y_{t-1} - \left(\frac{s}{1-s\sigma}\right) r_t D_{t-1} + \left(\frac{1}{1-s\sigma}\right) d_t.$$

For given structural parameters (δ, σ, s) and initial conditions, the trajectory of Y_t can be obtained from equations (10.7) and (10.12) under alternative scenarios for d_t and r_t. The balance of payments consistency of the results can be checked by means of equation (10.9) for alternative scenarios of export performance. It is then straightforward to obtain a few of the relevant indicators of debt burden.

To simulate equations (10.7) and (10.12), the value of the structural parameters and s were assumed to be equal to their observed average values during 1961–81, as calculated from the Mexican national accounts (σ = 0.40; s = 0.20). Relying on estimates for other countries, δ was given a value of 3 percent.

The equations were simulated for the period 1985–90; consequently, the initial conditions refer to 1984. These conditions are D_{84} = \$90.6 billion, which is the expected nominal value of the total stock of foreign debt by year's end,[17] and Y_{84} = 180.0, which is the estimated value of GDP expressed in billions of dollars. This was obtained by taking a forecast of the 1984 nominal value of GDP in pesos and dividing it by the projected equilibrium exchange rate for 1984 according to the method described in appendix A. It is assumed that the peso real rate of exchange is kept constant throughout the period of forecast. As posed, the model yields results expressed in constant "1984" dollars.

RESULTS

Equations (10.7) and (10.12) were numerically solved for a number of possible paths of D_t and r_t. To simplify the analysis, the following rule was used for D_t:

$$D_t = D_{t-1}(1 + \gamma)$$

where γ is a constant varied in each scenario (γ ranging from −0.05 to 0.07). The real rate of interest (r_t) was also assumed constant, but simulations were run for two possible values (r_t = 0.04 and r_t = 0.08). Tables 10-9 and 10-10 summarize the results of the exercise. They are

Table 10-9. Results of Growth-cum-Debt Model
($r = 0.04, \sigma = 0.4$)

γ	$\bar{g}$	R1	R2	R3
0.07	0.068	0.509	0.130	0.014
0.06	0.066	0.488	0.124	0.009
0.05	0.063	0.467	0.118	0.004
0.04	0.061	0.446	0.113	0.000
0.03	0.059	0.426	0.108	−0.004
0.02	0.057	0.407	0.103	−0.008
0.01	0.055	0.388	0.098	−0.014
0.00	0.053	0.370	0.093	−0.015
−0.01	0.051	0.352	0.088	−0.018
−0.02	0.049	0.334	0.084	−0.020
−0.03	0.047	0.318	0.080	−0.023
−0.04	0.046	0.301	0.076	−0.025
−0.05	0.044	0.285	0.072	−0.027

consistent with an evolution of exports of goods and nonfactor services given by

$$x_t = x_0 (1 + 0.05)^t. \qquad t = 1,\ldots,6$$

For a given value of γ, each row shows the average value of GDP growth during 1985–90, as well as the 1990 value of the following indicators:

$$R1 = \frac{D_t}{Y_t}$$

$$R2 = \frac{r_t D_{t-1}}{X_t}$$

$$R3 = \frac{(D_t - D_{t-1}) - (r_t D_{t-1})}{Y_t}.$$

On the basis of current GDP and balance of payments forecasts, it is estimated that R1 = 0.5, R2 = 0.2, and R3 = −0.05 for 1984. Notice that R3 measures the real net transfer of resources as a proportion of GDP.

Considering first the low-interest-rate scenario (table 10-9), it can be seen that zero real growth in the external debt would be consistent with an average rate of GDP growth of 5.3 percent during 1985–90. The debt/GDP ratio (R1) would be lowered to 37 percent by 1990, which is still high by historical standards (it averaged 33 percent during 1976–80). The debt

Table 10-10. Results of Growth-cum-Debt Model
($r = 0.08, \sigma = 0.4$)

γ	$\bar{g}$	R1	R2	R3
0.07	0.066	0.514	0.260	−0.005
0.06	0.064	0.492	0.248	−0.009
0.05	0.062	0.471	0.237	−0.013
0.04	0.059	0.451	0.226	−0.017
0.03	0.057	0.430	0.215	−0.021
0.02	0.055	0.411	0.205	−0.024
0.01	0.053	0.392	0.195	−0.027
0.00	0.051	0.373	0.186	−0.030
−0.01	0.049	0.355	0.177	−0.032
−0.02	0.048	0.337	0.168	−0.034
−0.03	0.046	0.320	0.159	−0.036
−0.04	0.044	0.304	0.151	−0.038
−0.05	0.043	0.288	0.144	−0.039

service ratio R2 in 1990 would be less than half of its 1984 value, and the net transfer would continue to be negative, although only 1.5 percent of GDP. According to this framework, a systematic fall in the real foreign debt, such as the one observed during the past two years (around 3 percent), would allow a GDP growth of at most 4.7 percent. A rate of economic growth as high as the historical one (around 6.5 percent) is consistent with a real increase in the foreign debt of around 6 percent a year.

In the context of this model, a doubling of the real interest rate, from 4 to 8 percent, does not prove very costly in terms of GDP growth. Only one-fifth of a percentage point is lost from such an increase in the interest rate. The result is logical to the extent that the effects on GDP of a rise in the interest rate are divided between consumption and savings. (Admittedly, a model in which there is an effective foreign exchange constraint on investment could yield a very different result from the one reported here.) A higher interest rate is much more damaging in terms of the servicing ratios, which prove to be much higher under this scenario.

At first sight, the above results may look encouraging. A few caveats are in order, however. A zero rate of real growth of the Mexican debt still means a net nominal borrowing effort of between $4.5 billion and $6.0 billion (depending on international inflation) for a year as close as 1985. That does not seem very easy to reach, considering the rescheduling effort that lies ahead. Achieving trend growth (the minimum needed to avoid a continuous deterioration in the unemployment situation) would put such a requirement between $9.0 billion and $11.0 billion. This framework is optimistic in several other respects. For example, by taking $\sigma = 0.4$, a fairly productive economy is assumed. In the two peak years of the previous two administrations (1974–75 and 1980–81), as public expenditure exploded, σ dropped to 0.3. If the incremental capital/output ratio (ICOR) were equal to 3.3, zero real growth in the debt would imply average GDP real growth of only 3.0 percent. Furthermore, the rate of real export growth (5 percent a year) used in the exercise is not at all conservative, considering the depressed outlook for the international oil market. Most of the effort will have to come from exports of manufactures, and fierce competition from other developing countries and U.S. protectionism will not help much in this respect.

Capital flight—which, it is hoped, will subside if sound domestic economic policy is applied—may also change the growth outlook dramatically. As proven in 1981, portfolio adjustments of that kind can swallow as much as 40 percent of the net flow of the foreign debt.

Admittedly, the foregoing scenarios could be significantly altered if another important structural parameter—the domestic savings rate—is increased. This can only occur slowly, over time, however. Furthermore, the outcome in this case depends critically on the availability of export markets to absorb the unconsumed domestic product made available when the savings rate is increased.

To sum up, faith in Mexico's long-run solvency as a foreign debtor seems to be warranted as long as a delicate balance is maintained among several phenomena. These phenomena are the success of the current stabilization program, an orderly rescheduling of maturities that fall due in the coming years, a return to normality in international capital markets so that a modest increase in the real stock of debt proves feasible, and an expansion of international trade—if not a spectacular one at least one better than that of the past few years.

All these are necessary conditions. The failure of any one of them could convert a manageable debt problem into a disastrous experience for all parties involved.

APPENDIX A

Using the formulation suggested by Lipschitz (1979), an index of the real exchange rate (IRR) was computed with the following formula:

$$IRR = \prod_{i=1}^{n} (e_i P_i/P)^{w_i}.$$

where e_i is an index of the domestic currency price of foreign currency; P_i, an index of the price level in country i; P, an index of the domestic price level; and w_i the weight of country i in the index

$$\left(\sum_{i=1}^{n} w_i = 1.0\right).$$

The wholesale price index of each country was used (n = 21); w_i was determined according to each country's participation in Mexico's total merchandise trade; the base year is 1978 and was chosen for several—albeit arbitrary—reasons. First, it was a year of high economic growth. Second, merchandise imports—excluding those by the oil sector—grew 15 percent in real terms, not a very high income elasticity. Third, non-oil merchandise exports grew 8 percent in real terms; other exports such as tourism also grew dynamically. Fourth, the "errors and omissions" item of the balance of payments was negligible, which suggests that capital flight and smuggling were insignificant. In short, even though 1978 was a year of rapid growth, the external sector was very much in equilibrium. The fact that it is a rather recent year is convenient too. All relevant data were obtained from the International Financial Statistics of the IMF.

According to the above methodology, during 1972–83 the equilibrium exchange rate (pesos per U.S. dollar; average value for the year) was as follows:

1972	13.845
1973	13.788
1974	14.152
1975	14.049
1976	16.356
1977	21.592
1978	22.753
1979	23.963
1980	26.383
1981	32.758
1982	50.566
1983	100.800

APPENDIX B

Table 10-11. Actual Exports
(millions of U.S. dollars)

	Current prices				1978 prices		
Exports	1978	1979	1980	1981	1979	1980	1981
Non-oil primary products	1,714.5	2,116.5	2,039.8	2,158.2	1,876.3	1,846.0	1,613.0
Manufactures	2,485.4	2,726.2	2,652.8	2,688.2	2,536.0	2,271.2	2,199.8
Non-oil merchandise exports	4,199.9	4,842.7	4,692.6	4,846.4	4,412.3	4,117.2	3,812.8
Oil and derivatives	1,863.2	3,975.0	10,441.3	14,573.3	2,733.8	4,363.3	5,780.8
Total merchandise exports	6,063.1	8,817.7	15,133.9	19,419.7	7,146.2	8,480.5	9,593.6
Tourism	1,121.0	1,443.3	1,671.2	1,759.6	1,138.2	1,027.8	908.4
Border transactions	2,363.7	2,919.2	3,722.1	4,770.1	2,463.5	2,565.2	2,836.0
Total	9,547.8	13,180.2	20,527.2	25,949.4	10,747.9	12,073.5	13,338.0

Note: Export items whose actual and trend values were assumed to be equal are not included in this and the following tables.

Source: Banco de México, Indicadores Económicos, Subdirección de Investigación Económica, various issues. Constant price figures calculated with the use of the indexes in table 10-12.

Table 10-12. Export Price Indexes
(1978 = 100.0)

Exports	Actual 1979	Actual 1980	Actual 1981	Trend 1979	Trend 1980	Trend 1981
Non-oil primary products[a]	112.8	110.5	133.8	115.0	132.2	152.1
Manufactures[b]	107.5	116.8	122.2	105.0	110.2	115.8
Non-oil merchandise exports[c]	109.8	114.0	127.1	109.0	118.7	129.5
Oil and derivatives[d]	145.4	239.3	252.1	105.7	111.7	118.1
Total merchandise exports[c]	123.4	178.5	202.4	108.0	116.5	125.9
Tourism[e]	126.8	162.6	193.7	116.0	134.6	156.1
Border transactions[f]	118.5	145.1	168.2	114.0	130.0	148.1
Total[c]	122.6	170.0	194.6	110.4	121.9	134.7

a. Constructed with quantum and value data of a large sample of products. Data from Banco de México, Indicadores de Comercio Exterior, Subdirección de Investigación Económica, various issues.

b. The item "consumer goods (non-food), except automotive" of the U.S. general imports unit-value indexes was used as a proxy for this variable. Data from U.S. Department of Commerce, Highlights of U.S. Exports and Import Trade (FT990), various issues.

c. Implicit.

d. Constructed from data in Petróleo Mexicanos, El Sector Petrolero Mexicano, 1977–1982: Estadísticas Seleccionadas, July 1983.

e. The item "Hotels, Restaurants, etc." of the National Consumer Price Index, adjusted by variations in the exchange rate. From Banco de México, Indicadores Económicos, Subdirección de Investigación Económica, various issues.

f. Consumer price index of a border city adjusted by variations in the exchange rate; from the same source as note e.

Note: Trend values are calculated from average rate of growth of actual indexes during 1976–78.

Table 10-13. Trend and Hypothetical Exports in 1978 Prices
(millions of U.S. dollars)

Exports	Trend[a] 1979	Trend[a] 1980	Trend[a] 1981	Hypothetical[b] 1979	Hypothetical[b] 1980	Hypothetical[b] 1981
Non-oil primary products	1,746.5	1,779.0	1,812.2	1,731.1	1,492.2	1,571.5
Manufactures	2,638.5	2,801.0	2,973.6	2,602.2	2,695.4	2,918.0
Non-oil merchandise exports	4,385.0	4,580.1	4,785.8	4,333.3	4,187.6	4,489.5
Oil and derivatives	1,967.7	2,078.1	2,194.7	1,989.5	1,550.2	1,407.9
Total merchandise exports	6,352.7	6,658.2	6,980.5	6,322.9	5,737.8	5,897.4
Tourism	1,117.3	1,113.6	1,109.9	1,139.9	1,124.1	1,129.5
Border transactions	2,495.1	2,633.7	2,780.1	2,470.1	2,550.6	2,748.8
Total	9,965.1	10,405.5	10,870.5	9,932.9	9,412.5	9,775.7

a. Let $\bar{g}^{x,i}$ be the trend rate of growth in "world" exports for item i; then

$$X_t^{T,i} = X_0^i(1 + \bar{g}^{x,i})^t. \qquad t = 1,2,3$$

b. Let g be the actual rate of growth in "world" exports of item i during year ℓ; then

$$X_t^{H,i} = X_0^i \prod_{\ell=1}^{t} (1 + g_\ell^{x,i})^t. \qquad t = 1,2,3$$

Note: U.S. imports of each merchandise category were used as a proxy of world exports; relevant data from U.S. Department of Commerce, Highlights of U.S. Export and Import Trade (FT990), various issues. Travel expenses abroad of U.S. citizens were used as a proxy of world market of tourism exports; these data were obtained from the table of U.S. International Transactions published in U.S. Department of Commerce, Survey of Current Business, various issues. The latter figures were deflated by consumer prices of industrial countries as reported in IMF, International Financial Statistics, various issues. The sum of U.S. real imports of manufactures and travel expenses was used as the relevant proxy for border transactions. Trend growth of each item was calculated as the average rate of growth during 1973–78.

Table 10-14. Actual Imports
(millions of U.S. dollars)

Imports	Current prices 1978	Current prices 1979	Current prices 1980	Current prices 1981	1978 prices 1979	1978 prices 1980	1978 prices 1981
Capital goods	1,981.6	3,573.9	5,174.0	7,575.4	3,257.9	4,172.6	5,231.6
Current goods	5,935.9	8,405.8	13,658.3	16,354.2	6,987.4	9,518.0	11,140.5
Total merchandise imports	7,917.5	11,979.7	18,832.3	23,929.6	10,254.3	13,690.6	16,372.1
Tourism	519.0	683.5	1,043.6	1,571.1	625.9	854.0	1,168.1
Border transactions	1,631.8	2,245.7	3,129.5	4,584.3	2,012.3	2,473.9	3,324.4
Total	10,068.3	14,908.9	23,005.4	30,085.0	12,883.4	17,018.5	20,864.6

Note: Import items whose actual and trend values were assumed to be equal are not included in this and the following tables.

Source: Banco de México, Indicadores Económicos, Subdirección de Investigación Económica, various issues. Constant price figures calculated with the use of the indexes in table 10-16.

Table 10-15. Import Price Indexes
(1978 = 100.0)

Imports	Actual 1979	Actual 1980	Actual 1981	Trend 1979	Trend 1980	Trend 1981
Capital goods[a]	109.7	124.0	144.8	107.8	116.2	125.3
Current goods[b]	120.3	143.5	146.8	102.9	105.9	108.9
Total merchandise imports[c]	116.9	137.6	146.2	104.2	108.7	113.6
Tourism[d]	109.2	122.2	134.5	107.9	116.4	125.6
Border transactions[e]	111.6	126.5	137.9	106.6	113.6	121.1
Total[c]	115.7	135.2	144.2	104.7	109.8	115.2

a. The item "capital goods except automotive" of the U.S. domestic exports unit-value indexes was used as a proxy for this variable. Data from U.S. Department of Commerce, Highlights of U.S. Export and Import Trade (FT990), various issues.

b. The item "consumer goods (non-food), except automotive" of the U.S. domestic exports unit-value indexes was used as a proxy for this variable. Data from same source as note a.

c. Consumer price inflation in industrialized countries was used to construct this index. Data from IMF, International Financial Statistics, various issues.

d. Consumer price inflation in the United States was used to construct this index. Data from same source as note c.

Note: Trend prices obtained from average rate of growth of actual price indexes during 1976–78.

Table 10-16. Trend and Hypothetical Imports in 1978 Prices
(millions of U.S. dollars)

Imports	Trend[a] 1979	Trend[a] 1980	Trend[a] 1981	Hypothetical[b] 1979	Hypothetical[b] 1980	Hypothetical[b] 1981
Capital goods	2,318.5	2,712.6	3,173.8	2,434.9	2,940.1	3,520.8
Current goods	6,541.4	7,208.6	7,943.9	6,750.6	7,591.1	8,490.6
Total merchandise imports	8,859.8	9,921.2	11,117.6	9,185.5	10,531.2	12,011.4
Tourism	579.3	646.7	721.9	600.2	685.4	778.0
Border transactions	1,690.6	1,751.5	1,814.7	1,710.9	1,786.2	1,861.0
Total	11,129.8	12,319.4	13,654.2	11,496.6	13,002.8	14,650.4

a. Let E_j^m be the trend income elasticity for item j of imports and $\bar{g}$ the trend rate of growth of GDP; then

$$M_t^{T,j} = M_0^j (1 + E_j^m \bar{g})^t. \qquad t = 1,2,3$$

Notice that the income elasticity is simply defined

$$E_j = (\Delta M_t^j / M_{t-1}^j)/(\Delta GDP/GDP_{t-1}).$$

The fact that the trend value of this variable has to be estimated for a period in which the real exchange rate was roughly constant allows us to consider such trend income elasticity without explicitly introducing a price elasticity.

(Notes to table continue p. 287.)

Table 10-16 (continued)

Furthermore, deviations in the actual income elasticity from its trend value should indicate that other variables, such as the real exchange rate, have changed too.

b. Let g be the actual rate of GDP growth during year ℓ; then

$$M_t^{H,J} = M_0^J \prod_{\ell=1}^{t} (1 + E_J^M g_\ell).$$

Note: The trend income elasticities were 2.5 for capital goods, 1.5 for current goods, 1.71 for tourism, and 0.53 for border transactions. They were obtained by a simple logarithmic regression on GDP for the 1960–78 period (the observations for 1974–76 were dropped). Trend growth of GDP was obtained by regressing its natural log on time for 1960–78. Trend growth thus obtained was 6.5 percent a year; this value was increased by 0.3 to allow for the impact of the oil sector's increased output on trend GDP.

NOTES

1. Comparing debt figures—which are measured in dollars—with variables that are calculated in domestic currency has to be done with some care. The usual procedure is to convert peso-denominated figures into dollars by means of the observed exchange rate. This method yields a very distorted picture when the period of analysis has been characterized by high inflation rates and an insufficiently adjusted exchange rate. Another distortion in such comparisons may arise for periods following a significant devaluation in the exchange rate. In order to smooth out—if not avoid altogether—these difficulties, all ratios in this chapter involving a peso-denominated variable and a dollar one have been calculated with an "equilibrium exchange rate" derived from a purchasing power parity (PPP) method that is explained in appendix A.

2. Let $\bar{g}_t^{x,i}$ be trend or expected rate of growth in world exports for item i; then

$$X_t^{T,i} = X_0^i(1 + \bar{g}^{x,i})^t. \qquad t = 1,2,3$$

3. Let E_j^m be the trend income elasticity for item j of imports and $\bar{g}$ the trend rate of growth of GDP; then

$$M_t^{T,J} = M_0^j(1 + E_j^m\bar{g})^t. \qquad t = 1,2,3$$

Notice that the income elasticity is simply defined as $E_j = (\Delta M_t^j/M_{t-1}^j)/(\Delta GDP/GDP_{t-1})$. Since the trend value of this variable has to be estimated for a period in which the real exchange rate was roughly constant, we can consider such "trend" income elasticity without explicitly introducing a price elasticity. Furthermore, deviations in the actual income elasticity from its trend value should indicate that other variables, such as the real exchange rate, have changed too.

4. Let $g_t^{x,i}$ be the actual rate of growth in world exports of item i during year ℓ; then

$$X_t^{H,i} = X_0^i \prod_{\ell=1}^{t} (1 + g_\ell^{x,i}). \qquad t = 1,2,3$$

5. Let g be the actual rate of GDP growth during year ℓ; then

$$M_t^{HJ} = M_0^j \prod_{\ell=1}^{t} (1 + E_j^M g_\ell).$$

6. The terminology is kept as close as possible to that in the original Balassa study.

7. For example, take a two-period case in which $M_0 = X_0$ and $(\Delta Pm)M_1 > (\Delta P_x)X_1$, so that an adverse terms-of-trade effect seemingly took place. This judgment would be erroneous, however, if the bigger import bill were the result of an increase in the price of imports that was smaller than the increase in the price of exports, accompanied by a much bigger increase in real exports.

8. Border transactions refer to the trading of goods and services between cities along the Mexican-U.S. border. The inflation content of all phenomena associated with "exports" of tourism and border transactions are excluded from the external-shock variables, since their relevant price increases are very much determined by internal inflation.

9. Changes in foreign demand reflect the difference between trend and actual world exports (the relevant ones for each item), assuming the country could keep its share in such markets unchanged.

10. This is not to say that Mexican oil exports actually decreased. If they had kept their base-period share in world markets, they would have decreased significantly. They actually increased, however, because the country was able to have an export promotion effect in this particular product.

11. Expenditure on domestic goods and services minus public sector's income denominated in pesos (nonforeign exchange earnings).

12. At the time, there were two official rates (50 and 70 pesos per dollar); the black market rate fluctuated around 140 pesos.

13. Quoted from a telex sent by the secretary of finance of Mexico to the international banking community on December 8, 1982, p. 4.

14. This description of the economic adjustment during 1983 is very superficial. This topic would merit by itself a major piece of research.

15. A preliminary analysis with a two-gap model showed that the foreign exchange constraint will not be binding economic growth during the coming years. Consequently, in the model used here growth is limited only by the availability of total savings.

16. Transfer payments abroad other than interest payments on the foreign debt are ignored because of their relatively small size. Direct foreign investment and accumulation of reserves are also ignored in equation (10.9), under the assumption that they will have similar values throughout the period of analysis. d_t can take care of other capital flows such as capital flight. All variables are expressed in "real" dollars.

17. The official figures in Secretaría de Hacienda y Crédito Público (1984) estimate that the total foreign debt would reach a value of $95.8 billion by the end of 1984. By subtracting from this figure the debt owed to the IMF as well as a rough estimation of net payments during 1983 and 1984 of private debt not registered in the official statistics, the figure of $90.6 billion is obtained.

REFERENCES

Balassa, Bela. 1979. "Policy responses to external shocks in developing countries: Implications for international trade and long-term growth." World Bank, Development Research Department, Washington, D.C. Processed.

Banco de México. 1982. Informe Anual 1981. Mexico City.

———. 1984. Informe Anual 1983. Mexico City.

Castro, E. 1983. "Algunas consideraciones sobre el financiamiento externo de México en los años de 1980–1982." Mexico City. Processed.

Lipschitz, L. 1979. "Exchange rate policy for a small developing country, and the selection of an appropriate standard." IMF Staff Papers 26:423–49.

Secretaría de Hacienda y Crédito Público. 1984. "Mexico: Development financing strategy." Mexico City. Processed.

Solís, Leopoldo. 1981. Economic policy reform in Mexico: A case study for developing countries. New York: Pergamon.

New York Times. 1981. "Mexico, in switch, will lift oil price." June 17.

Zedillo, Ernesto. 1981. "External public indebtedness in Mexico: Recent history and future, oil bounded optimal growth." Ph.D. dissertation, Yale University.

———. 1983. "The program for coverage of exchange risks: A general description and financial aspects." Mexico City. Processed.

———. 1984a. "The Mexican external debt: The last decade." In Politics and economics of Latin American indebtedness, edited by M. Wionczek. Boulder, Colo.: Westview Press.

———. 1984b. "Mexico's recent balance of payments experience and prospects for growth." Mexico City. Processed.

11

Korea's Experience with External Debt Management

Yung Chul Park

The rapid buildup in the external debt of the developing countries since 1973 has created serious economic and political problems that could frustrate the development efforts of these countries and threaten the international financial system. In outstanding debt, the Republic of Korea ranks fourth among Third World borrowers and has witnessed a noticeable deterioration in its debt-servicing capacity. At the same time, it is widely recognized that Korea has successfully adjusted to a series of adverse external developments since 1973. In the process, it has maintained growth momentum while avoiding the financial difficulties other countries now face. The exceptional performance of the Korean economy in recent years supports this assessment.

The purpose of this chapter is to analyze Korea's experience with debt accumulation and management over the past two decades and to identify some of the factors that may explain Korea's successful debt management. This chapter is organized into six sections. The first presents a profile of Korea's external obligations and analyzes several aspects of the outstanding debt pertinent to this discussion. The second section discusses the evolution and causes of Korea's foreign debt accumulation. This is followed by a review of Korea's response to external and internal shocks in the third and fourth sections. The fifth examines questions related to the efficiency and optimality of foreign borrowing. A summary and concluding remarks are found in the final section.

EVOLUTION OF KOREA'S EXTERNAL INDEBTEDNESS, 1960–83: AN OVERVIEW

At the end of 1983, Korea's total foreign debt, including short-term obligations, amounted to $40.1 billion, and it was the fourth largest borrower behind Brazil, Mexico, and Argentina in the Third World.[1]

The total debt rose to 53 percent of nominal dollar gross national product (GNP) in 1983 from about 30 percent five years earlier (see table 11-14 in appendix B to this chapter). Between 1979 and 1983 Korea's external indebtedness doubled, growing on average 22.5 percent a year. Export earnings also rose, but at a much slower rate. As a consequence, Korea's debt service as a proportion of exports climbed markedly.

Much of the increase in external debt has come from the short end of the maturity distribution, thereby raising short-term obligations (maturities less than a year) to over 36 percent of the total in 1983 (see table 11-1). Some concern has been voiced that such a large share of short-term debt could precipitate debt-servicing problems when liquidity is not adequate.

Prior to the 1970s, foreign loans with variable interest rates constituted less than 5 percent of the total. Since 1973, a growing proportion of capital inflows has been contracted at floating interest rates. Between 1977 and 1983, more than 60 percent of new loans were subjected to

The author is indebted to Rudiger Dornbusch for many stimulating discussions and for clarifying some of the arguments made here. Helpful comments and suggestions have been provided by Gordon Smith.

Table 11-1. Profile of Korea's External Debt
(billions of U.S. dollars; percentages in parentheses)

Year	Gross external debt	Net external debt[a]	Short-term debt	Debt with variable interest rates (percent of gross debt)	Average cost of foreign borrowings[e]
1965	0.18	0.05	—		
	(5.89)[b]	(1.66)[b]	—		
1970	2.25	1.57	0.37		2.33
	(28.17)	(19.66)	(16.61)[c]		
1973	4.26	2.76	0.70		4.39
	(31.55)	(20.44)	(16.46)		
1975	8.46	6.75	2.41		6.18
	(40.57)	(32.37)	(28.49)		
1977	12.65	7.60	3.72		4.65
	(33.80)	(20.31)	(29.37)		
1979	20.50	14.20	6.60	56.90[d]	7.01
	(32.87)	(22.77)	(32.20)		
1980	27.37	19.90	10.61	61.50	9.24
	(44.72)	(32.51)	(38.78)		
1981	32.49	24.30	11.76	63.2	10.28
	(48.35)	(36.17)	(36.20)		
1982	37.31	28.00	14.22	65.30	9.37
	(52.70)	(39.55)	(38.10)		
1983	40.10	30.80	14.50	65.60	7.37
	(53.39)	(41.01)	(36.16)		

a. Gross debt minus external assets, which include foreign exchange reserves, exports on credit, "A" account loans from the head offices of foreign banks to foreign branches of Korean banks, and others.
b. As percentage of nominal dollar GNP.
c. As percentage of gross external debt.
d. Data provided by the Bank of Korea.
e. Actual interest payments divided by the debt for the end of the previous year (percent).
Source: Economic Planning Board, Korean Economic Indicators (1983); and data provided by the Bank of Korea.

variable interest rates. The persistence of high interest rates has raised Korea's average interest cost to over 10 percent in recent years from less than 5 percent in the early 1970s. Coupled with an increasingly large share of foreign debt with flexible interest rates, these high interest rates have added to Korea's debt-servicing burden. Because of Korea's close trade relations with both the United States and Japan, these two countries have been the two major lenders, accounting for about 45 percent of the total debt at the end of June 1983. Multilateral sources accounted for 21.7 percent, the European Community for 17.1 percent, and others for 16.5 percent.

The buildup in external debt in Korea has been closely associated with chronic current account deficits and the need for holding larger reserves to accommodate a growing volume of foreign transactions. As shown in table 11-2, throughout the 1970s the cumulative increases in current account deficits and reserve holdings accounted for practically all of the debt increase. During the 1979–83 period, there was a sharp drop in the use of foreign funds for these purposes. This was related to a large increase in exports on credit financed by foreign loans. Unlike the case in some developing countries, private claims on nonresidents have been virtually nonexistent.

The rapid growth in debt and accompanying debt-service obligations have raised serious questions as to whether Korea has borrowed too much and whether it can manage its burgeoning debt. In some quarters, the very soundness of Korea's rapid growth over the past two decades has been challenged. At the abstract level, one could perhaps obtain a set of conditions that may help determine both the optimality and the sustainability of a given amount of debt. However, application of these criteria to reality encounters many difficulties and often provides little guidance for making practical judgments on issues related to debt-servicing capacity.

Table 11-2. Components of the Increase in Gross External Debt, 1966–83
(billions of U.S. dollars)

Components	1966–70	1973–77	1979–83
1. Increase in gross external debt	2.28	9.00	25.23
2. Current account deficit	1.91	4.52	18.39
Oil payments	0.37	5.71	25.46
Interest payments	0.15	2.24	15.02
3. Reserve accumulation	0.46	3.57	1.97
4. Capital outflows[a]	0.03	0.65	2.14
5. Direct and portfolio capital inflows	−0.12	−0.68	−0.96
6. Others[b]	0.11	0.81	3.81
7. (2) + (3)/(1)	104.00	89.86	80.70

a. Includes exports on credit, overseas investment, import prepayments, and subscriptions to international institutions.

b. Includes errors and omissions, foreign assets of foreign bank branches, and overseas interoffice special account.

Sources: Economic Planning Board, Korean Economic Indicators (1983); Economic Planning Board, Major Statistics of Korean Economy (1983); and data provided by Bank of Korea.

Several indicators purporting to gauge the debt-servicing capacity have been calculated and their changes over time have been extensively analyzed for the Korean economy. In table 11-15 in appendix B the various indicators, for what they are worth, seem to suggest that Korea is not likely to experience any difficulties in servicing its debt. For a debt situation to be sustainable, lenders must also view it as such. Several international lending organizations, including the International Monetary Fund (IMF), have expressed their confidence in Korea's debt-servicing capacity and its management of the economy. More than anything else, Korea's successful adjustment to the external shocks and its exceptional economic performance in recent years have added to the confidence of international lenders in Korea's economic future.

Although Korea's external debt difficulties are by no means serious—and in fact quite mild compared with the predicament faced by other developing economies—several aspects of the structure of its debt and balance of payments other than the large share of short-term debt suggest potential risks. The sheer size of the debt and the surge in the debt/GNP ratio have become a cause for concern and emerged as the most serious debt issue since Korea launched its debt-financed development through export promotion in the early 1960s.[2] To reduce the growth of external obligations, the Korean government plans to raise domestic savings to 28.6 percent of GNP by 1986 from the 24 percent level in 1983, and to sustain the real growth of export earnings at over 10 percent for the remaining three years of the fifth five-year development plan (see Government of Korea 1984). Judging from the past savings record and the unfavorable trade environment, these targets may be overly ambitious.

Korea's vulnerability to any deterioration in the climate for lending to developing countries is widely recognized. Notwithstanding its exceptional economic performance, Korea's access to international financial markets could be severely limited if any neighboring countries default on their debt service. Economists have also called attention to the danger associated with the high degree of rigidity in Korea's external payments. The sum of debt service and imports for such essentials as oil, grains, and raw materials for exports may total up to 80 percent of commodity exports.

In recent years Korea's current account imbalances have been dominated by the deficit of the public sector (see table 11-16 in appendix B), mainly because of the huge deficit run by government corporations. By definition, the current account deficit is the sum of the private and public deficit, that is, the excess of investment over savings. In 1982 the private sector produced a small surplus. Since government corporations are relatively unresponsive to demand management policies and government efforts at export promotion or import substitution, one could argue that it is more difficult than before to reduce the size of the current account deficit.[3]

EVOLUTION AND CAUSES OF KOREA'S FOREIGN DEBT ACCUMULATION

As can be observed in table 11-14 in appendix B, there were three periods of rapid buildup in Korea's foreign debt. Between 1965 and 1969 debt increased more than tenfold to $1.8 billion. The second upsurge took place during the first oil crisis. In 1974–75 the outstanding debt more than doubled. The third buildup occurred during the second oil crisis, 1979–80, when gross debt mounted by 38 and 33.5 percent in successive years.

Looking over the evolution of Korea's external debt, one could suggest a number of factors responsible for its rapid accumulation. Some of these factors were external shocks over which Korea had no control. In the 1970s three external factors—oil price increases, high interest rates, and the worldwide recession—accounted for a large part of the accumulation. The promotion of investment in heavy and chemical industries that began in the early 1970s also contributed to the debt increase and the subsequent debt-service burden because it caused a significant distortion in the allocation of resources. The debt explosion in the latter part of the 1960s was entirely in response to a policy reform. This section examines some of the structural reasons for the debt growth. It will be followed by a review of the policy responses and adjustment to both internally and externally generated shocks.

Debt-financed Development Strategy

One of the major causes of Korea's debt accumulation is closely associated with some of the characteristics of its long-term growth strategy, in particular, the way in which the five-year development plans have been formulated and executed. The formulation of a five-year development plan begins with a reasonable target rate of growth. Within the framework of the Harrod-Domar model with a given capital output ratio, the target rate of growth determines the required investment. The marginal propensity to save is assumed to be exogenous, though changing over time. If the domestic savings expected to be available during the plan period cannot meet the required investment, then the shortfall is made up by foreign capital inflows, which are assumed to be available.

In actual planning, Korean planners have relied on an increasingly sophisticated input-output model with many constraints. However, the fundamental philosophy underlying the planning has not changed: whenever necessary, the planners have always been prepared to borrow abroad to achieve a target rate of growth. A heavy reliance on foreign savings was regarded as unavoidable in the early stages of development, though certainly not desirable in the long run. Rapid growth through the promotion of exports would, it was argued, gradually raise the propensity to save and hence reduce Korea's dependence on foreign savings. The growth of domestic savings as a percentage of GNP during the latter part of the 1960s was impressive, but not sufficient to support fully the investment required to sustain the rapid growth planned by the authorities.

By the early 1970s, Korea's exceptional growth performance had been recognized and thus helped establish the nation's creditworthiness in international financial markets. Although Korea's debt-service ratio reached a 20 percent level in the early 1970s, Korea did not have any serious problems in lining up additional loans. The availability of foreign loans, more than anything else, appears to have encouraged the Korean authorities to pursue an expansionary demand policy during the first oil crisis to maintain a high rate of growth. The planners were not prepared to sacrifice growth and employment in favor of a response to the balance of payments problems such a policy could bring about.

During the latter half of the 1970s the planners once again demonstrated their readiness to incur large debts to promote investment in heavy and chemical industries. From the past record of domestic savings, it was clear that the huge investment program in capital-intensive industries would aggravate a current account situation that was fragile at best. Again the planners were not overly concerned about the adverse balance of payments consequences. Investment promotion caused a sharp increase in the ratio of investment to GNP—to over 30 percent from a historical average of 23 percent in 1978—and maintained it at that high level for the next five years. This, of course, was accompanied by an equally large increase in the current account deficits (see table 11-17 in appendix B).

In a development planning framework in which an investment target is given and foreign borrowing is the residual, movements in the current account deficits will be determined largely by fluctuations in domestic savings. The Korean data support this proposition. From 1966 to 1977, fixed investment as a proportion of GNP remained relatively stable and certainly more stable than the domestic savings GNP ratio (see table 11-17 in appendix B). During this period, the average investment ratio was 23.8 percent, with a standard deviation of 2.02. Domestic savings as a proportion of GNP fluctuated between 11.4 and 25.1 percent, with a mean of 18.1 percent and a standard deviation of 4.3 percent. As can be seen in table 11-17 in appendix B, the sharp deterioration of the current account for the 1974–75 period was clearly the result of a downward shift in savings. The subsequent improvement followed an upward shift in the savings ratio.

The large current account deficits in 1978 and 1979 were clearly due to an investment shift, which was in turn the consequence of a large increase in investment in capital-intensive industries. What is striking is that the investment ratio remained at about the 30 percent level for the next four years. As a result, the increase in the current account deficit over 1980-81 was caused by a sharp decline in the savings ratio.

The preceding argument should not be interpreted as implying that the availability of foreign capital has made Korean authorities complacent about mobilizing domestic savings. It is true that the savings target has not been as vigorously pursued as the export target, but it would be unfair to say that the Korean government has not been trying. Korea's domestic savings rate, which was 22.4 percent of GNP on average during 1979–83, is one of the highest among developing countries, and there is no evidence of a reduction in domestic savings following the influx of foreign capital.

High Import Intensity of Exports

It was in general expected that export expansion would raise domestic savings as it promoted the growth of output and employment and that it would also narrow the foreign exchange gap. Export expansion throughout the period has been phenomenal, but part of that expansion has been spurious because most exporters have used large quantities of imported intermediate goods in their production processes. In fact, the growth of imported raw materials and intermediate goods used directly and indirectly in export production has been faster than export growth itself. Krueger (1979, p. 137) shows that the direct import content of manufactured exports rose even more rapidly than exports until 1970.

Input-output data show that the increase in the direct and indirect import intensity of exports has risen markedly during the 1980s (see table 11-3). In 1970, the import intensity was 0.26. Five years later it rose to 0.36. After a small drop in 1978, it went up again to 0.38. The figure for 1980 is somewhat biased in that it reflects in part a sharp deterioration in the terms of trade. The 1978 figure is not subject to such a bias because by then export prices had fully recovered relative to import prices after the first oil crisis.

Why has the import intensity of exports been so high and, in fact, even rising in Korea? There are several reasons for this, all related to the characteristics of the export incentive system in Korea. Exporters have had literally unlimited access to imported inputs and have paid neither tariffs nor indirect taxes on them. (The tariff exemption system was changed to a drawback system in 1975.) During the 1960s and early 1970s, wastage allowances were granted on

Table 11-3. Import Inducement Ratio

Demand component	1970	1973	1975	1978	1980	Japan (1975)
Consumption	0.13	0.17	0.19	0.17	0.23	0.11
Investment	0.39	0.45	0.48	0.48	0.42	0.12
Exports	0.26[a]	0.35	0.36	0.36	0.38	0.17
Total demand	0.20	0.26	0.29	0.28	0.3	0.12

a. One minus the import inducement ratio may be defined as the value added share of exports.

Note: Import inducement ratio is defined as the direct and indirect increase in imports per unit increase in a final demand component.

Source: Bank of Korea, Summary Analysis of 1980 Input-Output Tables (December 1982).

imported duty-free raw materials over and above the actual requirements of export production, although they have since been pared down to the actual requirements. These incentive features, combined with the fact that the exchange rate was overvalued throughout the 1970s, have increased the attractiveness of imported intermediate goods in comparison with what would have been most efficient. According to a recent study, Korea's nominal exchange rate (vis-à-vis the U.S. dollar) was overvalued by as much as 16 percent on average during the latter part of the 1970s in terms of a real effective exchange rate against a basket of currencies of Korea's major trading partners (Cha, Park, and Park 1983, p. 58).

The export financing system, which supplies subsidized short-term credit tied to export volume, is biased in favor of short-term investment which can produce exports soon after plant operations begin. Financial incentives also encourage a relatively capital-intensive production technology in export production (see Park 1983). Because of these incentive features it has been more profitable to export goods that require mostly assembly of imported parts and components than to develop and export these intermediate inputs themselves. Largely because of this investment bias, exporters have neglected the development of skill and technology, manpower training, and new export products. During the latter part of the 1970s, it was not uncommon in some industries, such as machinery, to import capital goods to acquire technology that was otherwise unavailable.

Since 1965, export incentives have been extended to domestic producers of intermediate goods used in export production. Many of these import substitution activities were not profitable, however, because of the limited domestic market. The incentive system definitely favored exports over import substitution, and positive import substitution was in response to economic development rather than a result of deliberate protectionist policies. The limited degree of import substitution may be inferred from the contribution of import substitution to output growth. According to Kim and Roemer (1979) and Kim (1979), the contribution of import substitution to GDP growth during 1963–73 was about 16 percent, or less than half that of export expansion.

Beginning in the early 1970s, Korean planners launched a massive investment program to restructure industries. The new development strategy was designed primarily to promote both import substitution and export promotion in heavy and chemical industries. As will be discussed later, the import substitution efforts increased the imports of capital goods and intermediate goods, thus contributing to a growing current account imbalance.

Preference of Debt Financing over Foreign Direct Investment

Foreign direct investment has played a minor role in Korean development and has been much less important than in other developing countries. As shown in table 11-18 in appendix B, foreign direct investment accounted for less than 5 percent of total foreign capital inflows between 1955 and 1980, except for the 1972–76 period when the share rose to 10 percent. A greater reliance on foreign direct investment as a source of capital financing and a channel for technology transfer could have alleviated Korea's foreign debt burden.

There are several reasons for the insignificance of foreign direct investment. Korea lacks one of the most important inducements for foreign investment—natural resources. This disadvantage has been further compounded by Korea's national security problems. During the 1960s, the Korean government preferred foreign loans so as to minimize Japanese ownership and control of Korean businesses. Even in the 1970s, feelings toward foreign direct investment were adverse, especially toward Japanese investors. Having demonstrated its ability to penetrate world export markets and its growth potential in the 1960s, Korea has since had relatively easier access to foreign loans on favorable terms and has not until recently had to solicit direct investment for foreign capital financing.

Until the mid-1970s, Korean exports came mostly from labor-intensive industries and did not require sophisticated technology to sustain their rapid expansion. The standardized products such as textiles, clothing, footwear, and simple electronics that constituted the bulk of Korea's exports do not require sophisticated marketing through an overseas network and servicing. For these products, the entire marketing effort from design to sales has often been carried out by the foreign importers. For these reasons, Korean planners and businesses did not seek foreign partners to gain marketing expertise.

Perhaps the most important reason overseas borrowing has been emphasized more than direct foreign investment is that foreign debt financing has been much more attractive than equity financing. As shown in table 11-4, throughout the 1970s the real interest rate on foreign loans was consistently negative, largely because of an overvalued exchange rate in an inflationary environment. In the case of foreign direct investment, however, the implicit subsidies associated with the negative real interest rate are repatriated in the form of investment earnings.

Interest Rate Differential between Home and International Financial Markets

From 1965 to 1979, the real interest rates Korean borrowers paid on foreign loans were mostly negative, except for those years when large currency devaluations were undertaken (see table 11-4). During the 1966-70 period, the foreign rate of interest (London interbank offered

Table 11-4. Cost of Foreign Capital
(annual average; percent)

Item	1966–70	1971–75	1976–80	1981–83
1. Domestic bank lending rate[a]	24.4	17.0	18.0	12.5
Curb market interest rate	54.2	40.1	41.3	30.6
2. Foreign interest rate[b]	6.4	7.9	11.5	11.1
3. Foreign inflation rate (GNP deflator)[c]	4.7	8.3	6.0	4.2
4. Exchange rate depreciation[d]	5.1	7.8	5.5	10.1
5. Domestic inflation rate (GDP deflator)[e]	14.6	19.8	20.7	9.8
6. Real foreign interest rate [(2) − (3)]	1.7	−0.4	5.5	6.9
7. Interest rate differential between home and foreign markets [(1) − (2) − (3)]	12.9	1.3	1.0	−8.7
8. Real private cost of borrowing abroad [(2) + (4) − (5)]	−3.1	−4.1	−3.7	11.4

a. Discounts on bills of Deposit Money Banks (three-year moving averages).
b. Ninety-day LIBOR (London interbank offered rate).
c. Three-year moving averages of Japan and United States.
d. Bank of Korea standard concentration rate (three-year moving averages).
e. Three-year moving averages.
Source: Bank of Korea, Monthly Bulletin, various issues.

rate, LIBOR) adjusted for an exchange rate change was lower than the rate paid on domestic borrowing by as much as fifteen percentage points, depending on how expected exchange rate changes are estimated.[4] Even during 1971–79, the foreign borrowing rate was consistently lower than the domestic rate, though the difference narrowed considerably.[5]

Much of the difference could be explained by the suppression of domestic interest rates and the overvaluation of the exchange rate while inflation was accelerating. In the 1970s, the high rate of inflation, which induced an upward adjustment in the expected rate of inflation, encouraged Korean firms to anticipate negative real interest rates on their foreign borrowing.

The interest rate differential was no doubt one of the powerful incentives to Korean firms to borrow abroad, especially during the latter part of the 1960s. Although the differential fell considerably during the 1970s, it did not have much impact on actual foreign borrowing. Won currency lending by domestic banks was tightly controlled and rationed out to industries and sectors in a rigid manner. The costs of obtaining funds from other sources were at times prohibitively high.

Under these circumstances, Korean firms turned to foreign borrowing as an alternative source of credit. In particular, exporters who were allowed to import intermediate and capital goods for export production borrowed heavily in the form of trade credits—and borrowed much more than they would have if domestic credit had been adequately available. Thus, the combination of low interest rates, tight credit rationing, and the import privileges given to exporters produced a strong demand for foreign loans that was difficult to control.

ADJUSTMENT TO INTERNAL SHOCKS AND DEBT ACCUMULATION

In this and the subsequent section I analyze the Korean government's policy responses and adjustment to both internally and externally generated disturbances. The analysis relies on a framework developed by Sachs (1981) and Dornbusch (chapter 8 in this volume), in which current account surpluses or deficits are treated as the outcome of intertemporal choices of households, firms, and government and hence are largely explained by shifts in investment and saving. In this model it is important to determine whether the disturbances to which the economy is exposed are permanent or transitory, anticipated or unanticipated. Equally important would be to identify the macroeconomic channels through which the disturbances affect investment and saving.

The investment-saving model predicts that an increase in the price of oil that is perceived to be permanent will not affect the current account because it will reduce both real income and consumption by about equal amounts. A transitory increase in export demand will lead to a corresponding increase in saving, whereas a permanent increase simply results in more imports without affecting intertemporal decisions and hence the current account.

In the investment-saving model, exchange rates are important in explaining movements in the current account. Dornbusch (chapter 8) identifies several links between exchange rates on the one hand and saving and investment on the other. An expected real depreciation of exchange rates could cause dissaving since it would induce households to purchase imported durables. A transitory real appreciation—that is, an overvalued exchange rate that it is not reflected in interest rates—will increase inventory investment and thus imports of raw materials and both consumer and producer goods.

Real exchange rates also determine the desired capital stock by influencing the user cost of capital or by affecting the adjustment cost. An overvaluation of the real exchange rate, which is not matched by interest rates, implies an investment subsidy. An anticipated real depreciation therefore leads to a transitory increase in investment with a relatively high import content, because it increases the desired capital stock through its effect on the user cost. The overvaluation also implies lower adjustment costs because of the low relative price of imported goods; hence, during the period of anticipated real depreciation, investment will be high (Dornbusch chapter 8).

Interest Rate Reform and Foreign Loan Guarantees, 1965–70

For more than a decade before the monetary reform of 1965, foreign capital inflows consisted mostly of foreign aid. Private capital flows were very small and as such could not play a significant role in resource allocation. It is partly true that Korea could not have begun to attract significant nonconcessionary private capital until it had established its creditworthiness in international capital markets. More important, however, was the combination of depressed domestic financial markets, an overvalued exchange rate, and political uncertainties, which simply discouraged lending to Korea.

The military government that came to power in 1961 was determined to create an environment more conducive to capital inflows. In 1962, a supplement to the Foreign Capital Inducement Law promulgated a year earlier established procedures for granting repayment guarantees on foreign loans, a step which paved the way for a massive inflow of foreign capital. In September 1965, a monetary reform more than doubled deposit and lending rates at the banking institutions. In 1966, the Foreign Capital Inducement Law was amended to increase the attractiveness of lending and investing in Korea. These changes led to a flood of foreign capital inflows for the next several years. To foreign lenders, the interest rate differentials and the loan guarantee system, which eliminated the risks of default and exchange rate depreciation, provided strong incentives to lend to Korea. Korean borrowers were encouraged by the cost differentials between domestic and foreign interest rates (see table 11-4), and according to Frank, Kim, and Westphal (1975, p. 117), they did not expect the exchange rate to change as much as it did during the late 1960s.

Foreign debt increased from less than $60 million in 1962 to $2.25 billion by the end of 1970. Korean firms were encouraged to invest heavily in light manufacturing industries with export potential because the increased availability of foreign exchange enabled them to import many more capital goods and intermediate goods than previously. The foreign capital inflows therefore sustained a high rate of investment and hence rapid growth for the next six years (see table 11-5). Mainly because of the increased availability of foreign capital, fixed investment jumped to 20.2 percent of GNP in 1966 from an average of less than 14 percent in the early years of the 1960s and climbed further to 25.8 percent in 1969 (see table 11-5).

Exports began to surge, and so did domestic savings, which more than tripled as a proportion of GNP between 1965 and 1969. Perhaps the single most important cause of the increase was the upward adjustment in the real rate of return on financial assets after the monetary reform.[6] The rise in domestic savings was, however, hardly sufficient to finance the steep increase in investment demand. As a result, the current account deficit grew to 8.4 percent of GNP in 1968 and stayed at that level on average for the next four years. Despite the continuing imbalances, capital inflows were large enough to enable the central bank to accumulate foreign reserves at a faster pace than before, and beyond a desirable level.[7]

Beginning in 1969, domestic saving took a nose dive and fell below 15 percent of GNP by 1971 while investment demand continued to be high. The current account deficit/GNP ratio thus remained largely unchanged. It would be reasonable to assume that by the early 1970s the rapid growth of exports, after several years of successful promotion, was expected to be maintained. Such an expectation would result in increases in consumption and imports. Another development responsible for the drop in saving was the downward adjustment in interest rates when the exchange rate was overvalued. The adjustment brought the real interest rates on financial assets below 7 percent, down from 14 percent only four years earlier. Between 1965

Table 11-5. Macroeconomic Developments, 1964–73
(annual average)

Item	1964–65	1966–67	1968–69	1970–71	1972	1973
GNP growth rate (percent)	7.7	9.7	12.5	8.2	5.7	14.1
Gross fixed investment (percent of GNP)	13.1	20.8	25.4	22.2	20.0	23.4
Inventory investment (percent of GNP)	1.4	1.0	2.0	3.0	2.2	2.3
Domestic savings (percent of GNP)	8.1	11.6	17.0	15.2	16.5	22.8
Current account deficits						
Millions of U.S. dollars	8.5	147.7	494.5	735.0	371.2	308.8
Percent of GNP	0.3	3.7	8.4	8.4	3.5	2.3
Commodity exports (millions of U.S. dollars)[a]	147.1	285.3	539.0	951.3	1,624.1	3,225.0
Rate of growth	42.1	35.4	39.5	31.0	52.2	98.6
Grain imports (millions of U.S. dollars)	18.0	59.5	164.5	270.5	259.0	398.0
Buildup in foreign debt (millions of U.S. dollars)	36.0	234.5	577.0	561.0	667.0	671.0
Debt service (including short-term interest) as percent of export earnings	6.8	8.6	13.6	31.3	25.6	18.9
Terms of trade (1980 = 100)	113.3	130.0	135.2	133.3	132.1	125.4
Real exchange rate[b]	459.6	445.0	384.6	369.5	413.2	489.6
Inflation rate (GNP deflator)	18.1	15.1	15.5	14.8	16.1	13.4
M_2 growth rate	33.8	61.7	66.7	24.1	33.8	36.4
Unified budget (percent of GNP)	n.a.	n.a.	n.a.	1.6	4.6	1.6

n.a. Not available.
a. Customs clearance basis.
b. From table 11-20 in appendix B.
Source: Economic Planning Board, Korean Economic Indicators (March 1984); and Bank of Korea, Economic Statistics Yearbook (1983).

and 1970, the real exchange rate appreciated by almost 36 percent. It was not surprising that saving took a dive.

A large buildup in inventory investment, which was as high as 3.6 percent of GNP in 1971, stood out as an important factor in the current account developments during 1969–71. The upsurge in inventory holdings in 1969, mostly in agricultural products, was the consequence of the large increase in grain imports (more than 107 percent) and a bumper rice crop. For the next two years (1971–72) there was a noticeable accumulation of inventories of manufactured final goods, including imported capital goods and imported raw materials. The increase was likely to have been caused by the anticipated devaluation after two years of a sharp real appreciation and a slowdown in export growth.

Controls on foreign borrowing had been in effect since 1962. In practice, however, foreign loan applications for financing investment in priority sectors were generally encouraged, and no strict limits on foreign borrowing were reinforced. As a result of the rapid increase in debt and the accompanying debt-service obligations, the debt-service ratio increased sharply in the late 1960s despite the rapid growth of exports. By 1971, the ratio had shot up to over 30 percent (see table 11-5).

Concerned with the apparent deterioration in Korea's debt-service capacity, the IMF required the Korean government in a standby agreement to issue letters of intent to limit foreign capital movements of one- to three-year loans, while very long-term loans were given liberal treatment (Frank, Kim, and Westphal 1975, p. 122). The effect of the IMF pressure was clearly visible. The growth of total debt slowed to 25 percent in 1970 and 30 percent in the following year. This deceleration brought about a sharp decrease in the growth of imports, particularly capital goods.

In 1970, it looked as though the economy was cooling off. There was an appreciable drop in investment demand, caused mostly by the decline in capital inflows and in part by the tight monetary policy of the preceding three years. The growth of export demand was also declining from its previous very high levels. The reduction in the growth of aggregate demand continued throughout 1971. The need to generate employment called for expansionary measures. An expansionary policy, however, was likely to aggravate the current account deficit, which showed no sign of abatement. Thus the authorities found themselves in a bind, pursuing two conflicting objectives. This classical policy dilemma in the end led to an emergency measure and a substantial exchange rate devaluation.

The high rate of growth of output and exports during 1965–69 had bred an expectation in the business community that the expansion would continue for a considerable period. This optimism in turn led Korean firms to maintain a high rate of investment with funds obtained from both domestic financial institutions and foreign sources, supplemented when necessary by short-term funds from the curb market. The average cost of capital in real terms was relatively low so long as prices kept rising and depreciation of the exchange rate was gradual. However, the major devaluation in 1971, which had been designed mainly to stimulate exports, also caused a sudden jump in the won cost of foreign debt servicing. This created severe short-run financial problems for firms that had borrowed heavily abroad, which was particularly the case for larger firms.

As an increasing number of these firms found themselves unable to meet the principal and interest payments to their foreign creditors, the guaranteeing banks were forced to make good on their commitments. Korea was faced with an impending debt management crisis. The government could have let these debt-ridden firms go bankrupt and weathered the painful consequences, but this alternative was not acceptable. It was feared that the poor performance of the economy and an increasing number of business failures would undermine the nation's credit standing in the international capital markets and would thus hamper the inflow of much needed foreign loans. With this option there would also have been a considerable sacrifice of growth and the risk of generating a high unemployment rate. As a result, a more costly but less painful alternative was chosen: it was simply to bail out these troubled firms and exporters.

The Presidential Emergency Decree announced on August 3, 1972, opened the government's rescue effort. (For detailed discussion see Cole and Park 1983, chap. 5.) The decree had two purposes: to stimulate economic activity by reviving investment demand, which was a short-run objective; and to alleviate the interest burden of business firms by abrogating by fiat the existing informal loan contracts.

Two important features of the decree are pertinent to this discussion:

- All loan agreements between firms with a business license and lenders in the curb market as of August 2, 1972, were nullified and replaced by new ones. The borrowers would have to repay their informal loans over a five-year period after a three-year grace period at a 1.35 percent monthly interest rate. Otherwise the lenders had the option of switching their loans into shares of the borrowing firms.
- There was an overall reduction in the interest rates of banking institutions. The time deposit rate was lowered from 17.4 to 12.6 percent and general loans up to one year from 19 to 15.5 percent.

Beginning in 1968, the nominal exchange rate was allowed to depreciate gradually so as to maintain purchasing power parity (Frank, Kim, and Westphal 1975, p. 67). By June 1971 the exchange rate had depreciated to 326 won per dollar when a devaluation of 13 percent was undertaken. After further gradual devaluation, the won-dollar exchange rate was fixed at 400 in June 1972. As a result of a series of devaluations the real exchange rate depreciated by 10 percent in 1972. In the meantime, the U.S. dollar was subjected to two devaluations. The first devaluation of about 10 percent in early 1972 was the result of the Smithsonian Agreement.

Another devaluation of about 10 percent stemmed from a parity change for the dollar in early 1973 and the subsequent flotation of other major currencies vis-à-vis the dollar. This new currency alignment had the effect of depreciating the won with respect to currencies other than the dollar. As a consequence of these changes, the domestic currency depreciated by 18.5 percent in 1973 and by almost 30 percent over a two-year period.

From the fourth quarter of 1972, in part because of a sharp depreciation of the real exchange rate, exports skyrocketed and in 1973 expanded by 90 percent. The economy grew by 16.5 percent in 1973, which was the highest rate of growth in the nation's history. The sudden spurt in exports was accompanied by an equally impressive rise in domestic savings (a 6.3 percentage point increase in the saving/GNP ratio in 1973). The export growth lifted the economy out of the mild slowdown in 1971 and 1972 and, more important for the present discussion, rescued Korea from its first debt crisis.

Promotion of Capital-intensive Industries, 1975–79

After a decade of promoting the export of labor-intensive manufactures, the Korean authorities began in the early 1970s to promote skill- and technology-intensive industries, which are known in Korea as the heavy and chemical industries.[8] A massive investment program in these industries, financed largely by foreign loans and central bank credit, was put into effect in 1973 and pursued vigorously until 1979. To the dismay of policymakers who conceived of this industrial restructuring, the development strategy ran into a host of financing, engineering, quality, and marketing difficulties. This section analyzes the effects of the industrial restructuring policy on inflation and the balance of payments. Its effect on resource allocation is discussed below.

Much of the investment in the heavy and chemical industries, which was by and large induced by distorted incentives, took place during the 1977–79 period when the economy was already experiencing a high rate of inflation. To support this large increase in investment, the government allocated $4.66 billion of foreign loans to the heavy and chemical industries, which accounted for more than 30 percent of total foreign loans approved and almost 80 percent of the loans absorbed by manufacturing between 1976 and 1980 (see table 11-19 in appendix B). Although the estimates vary, the loan figure represented anywhere from 40 to 50 percent of nominal fixed investment undertaken in these industries during the period. A large part of the foreign loans allocated to the social overhead capital sectors was earmarked for augmenting infrastructure facilities, such as the industrial sites and roads needed to promote these industries. Therefore, the actual infusion of foreign resources into the heavy and chemical industries was much greater than the amount of foreign loans used directly for fixed investment in these industries.

As a result of the large investment, the ratio of fixed investment to GNP shot up to 33 percent in 1979 from a historical average of about 25 percent. Since the domestic savings/GNP ratio did not rise in tandem, the high rate of investment expanded aggregate demand and put pressure on the external balance. To make matters worse, the investment program entailed serious supply-side problems that intensified inflationary pressures emanating from the demand side. During 1977–79, more than 70 percent of manufacturing investment was undertaken in heavy and chemical industries (see the section below, on "Efficiency of Foreign Loan Allocation in the 1970s"). This lopsided allocation of investment resources generated severe sectoral imbalances between the tradable and nontradable sectors and within the tradable sector. The lack of investment in light manufacturing—the traditional export sector—had adverse effects on Korea's export performance, while sluggish investment in the nontradable sector created a supply shortage and rapid price increases.

Since the one-shot devaluation in 1974, the nominal exchange rate had been kept at 480 won per U.S. dollar. Because of the high rate of domestic inflation relative to the rates of inflation in Korea's major trading partners, Japan and the United States, there was an 18 percent real appreciation of the won between 1974 and 1979 (see table 11-20 in appendix B).[9] Other things being equal, such a real appreciation causes a shift of aggregate demand in favor of traded goods, including exportables and importables whose prices in a small open economy are greatly influenced by conditions prevailing in world markets. The real appreciation, on the supply side, induces a shift of domestic resources to the more profitable nontraded goods sector. These demand and supply shifts would in general slow down price increases and would be reflected in a deterioration in the current account.

Despite these market forces operating in the economy, the expected resource shift did not take place. On the contrary, a large share of resources was channeled to the tradable goods, in particular the heavy and chemical sectors, through the government's directed resource allocation. As a consequence, the excess demand for nontradables remained unabated and their prices went up further. To complicate matters further, this forced allocation of resources to heavy and chemical industries did not help meet the domestic demand for tradables. One reason was that a large increase in this demand was for high-quality and processed food products and consumer durables. Since the bulk of investment resources was allocated to the capital goods sector, the excess demand for consumer goods had to be satisfied by imports. Another reason was that Korean firms continued to import machinery and petrochemicals, thereby reducing sales that were expected to go to producers of domestic import substitutes, because of suspected low quality and the difficulty of securing domestic financing for purchases in the domestic market.

Although most of the heavy and chemical industries—shipbuilding, basic metals, and power-generating equipment in particular—were from the beginning developed for export, in the short run they were not able to generate export earnings. As a result, while the tradable goods sector was saddled with huge idle capacity, the import demand for tradables rose sharply. The combined effect of these developments was a widening trade deficit and rampant inflation. From 1975 to 1979, the price of imports increased less than 1 percent a year and export prices about 8 percent, whereas the deflator for social overhead capital and services, which may be used as a proxy for a price index for nontradables, rose by 22 percent a year on average (see table 11-6). The current account deficit rose to 7.2 percent of GNP in 1979 from a small surplus in 1977.

The investment program also produced a cost-push effect. Production inefficiencies and underutilized capacity reduced labor productivity considerably. Despite the decline in productivity, however, nominal wages, and hence unit labor costs, soared. Because skilled workers were in short supply, their wages were bid up by firms in heavy and chemical industries, while high-paying jobs abroad lured many construction workers to the Middle East. Between 1975 and 1979, the unit labor cost index (1975 = 100) more than doubled (see table 11-21 in appendix

Table 11-6. Changes in Sectoral GNP Deflators, 1960–83
(annual averages; percent)

Period	Mining and manufacturing	Social overhead and others	Agriculture, forestry, and fishery	GNP
1960–64	17.3	14.1	28.9	18.7
1965–69	9.2	17.7	9.3	13.4
1970–74	13.1	17.0	21.3	17.7
1975–79	16.7	22.8	22.4	21.0
1980–83	12.5	14.9	7.2	12.9

Source: Bank of Korea, National Income in Korea (1982); and Bank of Korea, Monthly Bulletin (February 1984).

B). This cost-push effect was validated through money expansion and subsequently undermined Korea's international competitiveness. As a result, larger foreign borrowings were needed.

POLICY RESPONSE AND ADJUSTMENT TO EXTERNAL SHOCKS

The First Oil Crisis, 1973–77

The oil price increases of late 1973 and 1974 dealt a severe blow to the Korean economy. Because Korea was entirely dependent on imported oil, the price increase caused a 43.4 percent deterioration in Korea's terms of trade between 1972 and 1975 (see table 11-7). The world recession and trade protectionism then triggered by the oil crisis precipitated a sharp drop in world demand for exports, which suddenly dampened Korea's growth prospects. These adverse developments, coupled with the excessive credit expansion of the previous two years, provoked a steep increase in the rate of inflation and foreign debt for the next several years.

To examine the effect of the external shocks on the current account during the first oil crisis, I have decomposed the current account identity and then estimated its change over time (see appendix A). This exercise is presented in table 11-8. Compared with the 1972–73 base period, the current account deficit as a percentage of nominal potential gross domestic product (GDP) in U.S. dollars was higher (deteriorated) by more than 7 percentage points in 1974 and 5.4 percentage points in the following year. As expected, the deterioration associated with the terms of trade loss was substantial: it amounted to an increase of 5 percentage points in the current account/potential GDP ratio. It was not, however, the only, and certainly not the major, cause. The sum of the expansion of capital goods imports in relation to fixed investment and other imports, excluding oil, relative to GDP (row 6, import replacement, in table 11-8) was the main element producing the imbalance in the current account. This jump, equivalent to a deterioration of 10 percentage points, was larger than the actual increase in the deficit ratio. A similar development took place in 1975.

Table 11-7. Macroeconomic Developments, 1972–77

Item	1972–73 (average)	1974	1975	1976	1977	1978
GNP growth rate (percent)	9.9	7.7	6.9	14.1	12.7	9.7
Gross fixed investment (percent of GNP)	21.7	25.3	25.5	24.1	26.7	30.8
Inventory investment (percent of GNP)	2.3	6.3	4.5	1.5	1.1	0.4
Domestic savings (percent of GNP)	19.7	19.9	19.1	23.9	27.5	28.5
Current account deficits (billions of U.S. dollars)	0.3	2.0	1.9	0.3	−0.0	1.1
Percent of GNP	2.9	10.8	9.1	1.1	0.0	2.1
Commodity exports (billions of U.S. dollars)[a]	2.4	4.5	5.1	7.7	10.0	12.7
Rate of change	72.8	38.3	13.9	51.0	29.9	27.0
Construction service exports (millions of U.S. dollars)	14.7	23.3	39.1	438.0	1,246.1	2,148.4
Oil payments (billions of U.S. dollars)	0.3	1.0	1.3	1.6	1.9	2.2
Raw material imports (billions of U.S. dollars)	1.6	3.0	2.9	3.7	4.7	6.2
Buildup in gross foreign debt (billions of U.S. dollars)	0.7	1.7	2.5	2.1	2.1	2.2
Terms of trade (1980 = 100)	128.8	102.1	92.1	105.1	112.4	117.8
Nominal exchange rate	396.2	406.0	484.0	484.0	484.0	484.0
Real exchange rate	451.4	483.4	484.0	437.6	435.2	447.8
Unit labor cost (1975 = 100)	69.6	87.8	100.0	125.3	151.8	182.2
Inflation rate (GNP deflator, percent)	14.8	29.5	25.7	20.7	15.7	21.9
M_2 growth rate	35.1	24.0	28.2	33.5	39.7	35.0
Unified budget deficit (percent of GNP)	2.9	4.0	4.6	2.9	2.6	2.5

a. Customs clearance basis.

Source: Bank of Korea, National Income in Korea (1982); Bank of Korea, Economic Statistics Yearbook (1984); and Economic Planning Board, Major Statistics of Korean Economy (1983).

Table 11-8. Changes in the Current Account between Each Year and the 1972–73 Base Period
(ratio to potential GDP, percent)

Item	1974[a]	1975	1976	1977
1. Current account imbalances/potential output (actual change)	7.258	5.351	−1.782	−3.476
2. Terms of trade effect	4.893	4.284	1.183	−0.254
Import price	−0.462[b]	−1.573	−6.772	−11.495
Capital goods	−1.816	−1.621	−2.605	−3.048
Oil	3.064	3.302	2.954	2.608
Other	−1.710	−3.255	−7.121	−11.055
Export price	5.355	5.858	7.956	11.242
3. Interest rate effect	0.167	0.458	0.023	0.040
4. Accumulated debt effect	−0.142	0.134	0.210	0.170
5. Import replacement	9.528	7.621	10.727	14.769
Capital goods	3.385	2.150	2.742	1.907
Noncapital goods	6.358	5.312	7.546	12.364
Oil conservation efforts	−0.215	0.159	0.439	0.498
6. Export promotion	−7.883	−7.791	−15.932	−21.667
Construction services	−0.031	−0.098	−1.632	−3.954
7. Aggregate demand adjustment	1.183	1.123	2.532	4.067
Fixed investment	0.680	0.736	1.292	2.463
Domestic output	0.503	0.387	1.241	1.604
8. Total effect [(2)+(3)+(4)+(5)+(6)+(7)]	7.747	5.829	−1.256	−2.874
9. Interaction effects and adding-up errors [(1)−(8)]	−0.489	−0.478	−0.526	−0.602

a. The decomposition factors were calculated by using an average of current year and base period weights.
b. Negative sign indicates a balance of payments improvement.
Note: See appendix A for a description of, and data used for, the decomposition.

I have conducted a counterfactual exercise based on the decomposition analysis presented in table 11-8 to trace changes in the current account in the absence of the external shocks. Table 11-9 shows that even if the oil price had been fixed at the 1973 level, the deficit ratio would have been as high as 8.1 percent in 1974. This confirms my contention that the oil price hike was only part of the current account story. The current account development is examined below by focusing on the effect the external shocks exerted on investment and saving.

It is not clear whether the oil price increases of late 1973 and 1974 were perceived in Korea as temporary or permanent, though they do not appear to have been anticipated. Even if the higher relative oil price was expected to be maintained, it was difficult, if not inconceivable, to adjust consumption fully within a short time to the loss in real income caused by the actions of the Organization of Petroleum Exporting Countries (OPEC). The Korean government had launched an ambitious investment program for the development of heavy and chemical industries less than a year before. The success in export promotion had made Korean businesses more confident than before in penetrating the foreign markets. Under these circumstances, it was perhaps natural that Korean planners chose an adjustment path that required little sacrifice in growth and employment. Such a policy response inevitably forced the economy to incur a large foreign debt and to expand domestic liquidity beyond a desirable level.

To facilitate this protracted adjustment, the Bank of Korea, the central bank, went to international financial markets to secure bank loans to finance the imports needed to sustain the rapid growth Korea had been accustomed to. To mitigate the current account deterioration, heavy taxes were imposed on oil products to minimize their use, the predeposit requirement for imports was raised, more export credit with a lower interest rate was made available, and finally the exchange rate was devalued by almost 22 percent toward the end of 1974. These measures were clearly designed to alleviate the worst effects of the price increases and to maintain overall growth.

Little effort was made to hold down domestic price increases. Bank credit was expanded by

Table 11-9. Counterfactual Analysis
(percent)

Item	1972	1973	1974	1975	1976	1977
1. Actual ratio of current account deficit to potential output	4.61	3.52	11.35	9.43	2.26	0.56
Hypothetical ratio						
2. With oil prices fixed at 1973 level	—	—	8.10	5.68	−1.60	−3.19
(1)−(2)			3.24	3.75	3.85	3.75
3. With interest rates fixed at 1973 level	—	—	11.16	8.92	2.20	0.49
(1)−(3)			0.18	0.51	0.06	0.07
4. With fixed oil prices and interest rates	—	—	7.92	5.17	−1.65	−3.26
(1)−(4)			3.43	4.26	3.91	3.82
5. With 1973 construction service exports	—	—	11.37	9.52	3.68	3.82
(1)−(5)			−0.03	−0.09	−1.42	−3.26
6. With 1973 oil prices, interest rates, and construction service exports	—	—	7.95	5.26	−0.24	−0.01
(5)−(6)			3.40	4.17	2.49	0.57

Note: Based on the decomposition exercise in appendix A.

nearly 50 percent to help finance the needed imports. As a result, wholesale prices rose by 42 percent in 1974. The current account deficit widened to 10.8 percent of GNP in 1974—the highest ever in Korea's history—and almost half this huge deficit was financed by bank borrowing and the depletion of foreign reserve holdings, which fell by 3.5 percent in the course of a year. Because of the heavy foreign borrowing, Korea's external debt more than doubled to $8.5 billion over the 1974–75 period. Nevertheless, debt service as a percentage of current earnings remained virtually unchanged. This was largely due to a strong export performance.

Mostly as a reflection of the short-run difficulty in the adjustment of consumption to a lower real income, and of a high rate of inflation, domestic savings as a fraction of GNP plunged by four percentage points to 19 percent in 1975 from about 23 percent in 1973. In contrast, gross fixed investment displayed a modest rise to 25.3 percent of GNP in 1974 (from 23.4 in 1973). Table 11-7 shows that it had remained at that level until 1978, when the ratio shot up to a 30 percent level.

Much of the increase in fixed investment during the 1973–75 period could be attributed to the new investment program for heavy and chemical industries and the government's determination to sustain rapid growth. Despite the sharp increase in domestic prices caused by the oil crisis, the nominal exchange rate was not adjusted until the end of 1974. The transitory overvaluation was certainly conducive to investment in heavy and chemical industries, which have a high import content.

During 1974–75, inventory investment also contributed to the worsening of the current account. In 1974, inventory investment swelled to 6.3 percent of GNP, the highest in history. About 80 percent of the pile-up consisted of manufactured final goods, including imported capital goods and imported raw materials. Korean exporters did not anticipate, or were not prepared for, a sharp deceleration in export growth to about 40 percent in 1974 from almost 100 percent in the previous year. The increased anticipated real depreciation may explain the bulge in imported raw materials and capital in 1974: the volume of imported raw materials was more than four times the 1973 level. The large accumulation of inventories of imported raw materials and final goods continued in 1975. This time, however, the bulk of inventory investment was the result of an increase in the government's rice imports.

Export earnings began to soar in 1976 with a worldwide recovery and rich construction opportunities for Korea in the Middle East, and the terms of trade also improved. As shown in the decomposition exercise, the entire improvement in the current account during 1976–77 came from the two sources: the terms of trade gain and rapid export growth. In 1976, construction service exports skyrocketed to $438 million from a paltry figure of $39 million in 1975. This expansion was followed by a tripling of the service earnings in 1977. Apparently, the marked increase in export demand was perceived as a transitory phenomenon. A large part of the export earnings was saved, which led to such a dramatic improvement in the current account that a small surplus was recorded in 1977.

The expansionary policy response to the oil price shock seemed to have paid off handsomely in growth and employment. Whle many non-oil-producing countries experienced a negative rate of growth, Korea managed to grow by 7.7 percent and 6.9 percent in 1974 and 1975 respectively. The growth response was, however, not without costs. It seriously undermined the stability of the economy and made it increasingly difficult to implement anti-inflationary policies.

In the light of Korea's response to the first oil shock an important question is to what extent it was appropriate to postpone the required adjustment by resorting to foreign borrowing. Krueger (1979, p. 152) argues that if Korea had been forced to curtail imports abruptly by the unavailability of foreign credit, the resulting dislocations would have prevented the rapid resumption of export growth. Korea's ability to borrow allowed it to weather the oil price increase and gave policymakers the time to alter domestic policy and adapt to a hostile environment. This view is widely shared, and in theory, given real world rigidities, lengthening the adjustment period could reduce the costs of adjustment (Martin and Selowsky 1981).

Citing Taiwan's opposite policy response to the oil shock, many critics have pointed out that debt-financed growth was uncalled for—or at least excessive. They argue that rapid growth would have been resumed even if restrictive policies had been adopted. In retrospect, the critics argue, the expansionary policy made adjustment costs higher than they would otherwise have been, because it added to the inflationary pressures that were building up.[10]

The Second Oil Crisis and High Interest Rates, 1979–83

As noted in the preceding section, after two years of relative price stability, there occurred a steep increase in prices in 1978 as the accelerated pace of the investment program for heavy and chemical industries and the rapid monetary expansion in the 1975–77 period built up strong domestic demand. This situation, combined with a decline in export growth, produced a current account deficit which amounted to 2.1 percent of GNP in 1978. The deficit soared to 8.7 percent of GNP in 1980 before returning gradually to the 1978 level in 1983. Between 1978 and 1983 Korea's foreign debt more than doubled, mostly because of the accumulation of current account deficits.

Already feeling strong inflationary pressures coupled with a slowdown in growth, Korea was struck by a series of external and internal shocks that precipitated an economic downturn and a huge accumulation of foreign debt. As a consequence of the second oil crisis in 1979 that doubled the price of oil within a year, the terms of trade deteriorated by 17 percent between 1978 and 1981 (see table 11-10). The cost of servicing the foreign debt, approximated by the Eurodollar rate (ninety days), rose to more than 18 percent in 1980 from less than 8 percent three years previously. Grain imports expanded by an annual average of 60 percent during 1979–81 because of a poor harvest in 1978 and 1979 and a failure of the rice crop in 1980 (see table 11-10). Export earnings suffered from the deepening world recession and an erosion in Korea's international competitiveness caused by the sharp increase in unit labor costs. While Korea was beset by these problems, it had to confront the social and political problems unleashed by the death of President Park in October 1979. The ensuing political turmoil and uncertainties clouded the business climate and further complicated the management of the economy.

The combined effect of the adverse shocks implied a significant deterioration in the current account in the absence of any domestic adjustment policies. According to the decomposition in

Table 11-10. Macroeconomic Developments, 1978–83

Item	1978	1979	1980	1981	1982	1983
GNP growth rate	9.7	6.5	−5.2	6.2	5.6	9.3
Gross fixed investment (percent of GNP)	30.8	32.8	31.9	28.9	30.3	31.8
Inventory investment (percent of GNP)	0.4	2.9	−0.7	0.3	−3.3	4.2
Domestic savings (percent of GNP)	28.5	28.1	21.9	21.7	22.4	24.5
Current account deficit (billions of U.S. dollars)	1.1	4.2	5.3	4.6	2.6	1.6
As percent of GNP	2.1	6.7	8.7	6.9	3.7	2.2
Commodity exports (billions of U.S. dollars)[a]	12.7	15.1	17.5	21.3	21.9	24.4
Rate of change	27.0	18.4	15.9	21.7	2.8	11.4
Oil payments (billions of U.S. dollars)	2.2	3.1	5.6	6.4	6.1	5.6
Interest payments (billions of U.S. dollars)	1.0	1.5	2.7	3.6	3.8	3.4
Grain imports (billions of U.S. dollars)	0.5	0.9	1.2	2.1	1.0	1.2
Buildup in gross foreign debt (billions of U.S. dollars)	2.2	5.6	6.9	5.1	4.8	2.8
Terms of trade (1980 = 100)	117.8	115.3	100.0	97.9	102.2	103.8
Nominal exchange rate	484.0	484.0	607.4	681.0	731.1	775.8
Real exchange rate	447.8	408.6	452.4	438.7	423.1	445.3
Unit labor cost (1975 = 100)	182.2	202.3	224.3	232.8	254.8	269.6
Inflation rate (GNP deflator)	21.9	21.2	25.6	15.9	7.1	2.9
M_2 growth rate	35.0	24.6	26.9	25.0	27.0	15.2
Unified budget deficit (percent of GNP)	2.5	1.4	3.2	4.6	4.3	3.6

a. Customs clearance basis.

Sources: Bank of Korea, National Income in Korea (1982); Bank of Korea, Economic Statistics Yearbook (1984); and Economic Planning Board, Korea Economic Indicators (March 1984).

table 11-11, the terms of trade loss accounted for much of the deterioration in 1980–81, whereas a drop in export growth was the major cause in 1979. A counterfactual exercise based on the decomposition analysis in table 11-12 shows that in the absence of the external shocks, Korea would have accumulated a significant current account surplus after 1981 with a near balance in 1980. As a first approximation, this result bears out the belief that the buildup in foreign debt during the 1979–83 period was largely due to the adverse external shocks. In what follows, I will identify the macroeconomic channels through which the external shocks were translated into current account imbalances and accumulation of foreign debt. An upward shift in investment combined with a fall-off in domestic savings was the major channel.

Table 11-10 shows a marked shift in gross fixed investment in 1978. The investment/GNP ratio leaped to almost 31 percent from less than 27 percent in 1977. What is striking is that the investment ratio has remained stable on average at the level of 31 percent since then, despite considerable fluctuations in GNP growth. Much of the increase in fixed investment during the 1978–80 period reflected the concentrated investment in heavy and chemical industries. Although the planners, realizing the overinvestment, began to readjust sectoral investment in these industries, they could not postpone or scale down the investment projects they had approved or were committed to. A substantial increase in inventory investment, which was close to 3 percent of GNP, also added to the deficit. As in 1974, an unanticipated slowdown in export expansion and a transitory overvaluation of the exchange rate after four years of pegging explained the bulk of the increase.

In sharp contrast to the investment behavior, domestic savings tumbled down to about 22 percent of GNP, after a sustained rise that began in 1976, and remained at that level before turning up in 1983. Some of the factors responsible for the decline were familiar. As was the case during the first oil crisis, saving was discouraged by a combination of factors: the anticipated real exchange rate depreciation, the negative real domestic interest rates, and the worsening in the terms of trade caused by the oil price and foreign interest rate increase. To make matters worse, even the weather was bad. Beginning in 1978, the volume of the rice crop declined for three consecutive years. In 1980 rice output was almost half the 1978 level, and overall agricultural losses accounted for approximately four percentage points of the negative GNP

Table 11-11. Changes in the Current Account between Each Year and the 1977–78 Base Period
(ratio to potential GDP; percent)

Item	1979[a]	1980	1981	1982	1983
1. Current account imbalances/potential output (actual change)	4.838	6.099	4.398	1.675	0.607
2. Terms of trade effect	−1.581[b]	6.186	8.014	4.860	4.015
Import price	−2.846	6.490	8.666	3.719	3.142
Capital goods	−1.507	−0.645	−0.331	−0.139	0.216
Oil	0.389	3.892	4.472	3.973	3.274
Other	−1.728	3.242	4.524	−0.114	−0.348
Export price	1.265	−0.303	−0.651	1.141	0.873
3. Interest rate effect	0.586	1.308	1.746	1.534	0.945
4. Accumulated debt effect	−0.324	0.082	0.457	0.653	0.886
5. Import replacement	2.143	−0.641	−1.192	−0.724	−0.842
Capital goods	1.003	−0.278	0.644	−0.246	0.061
Noncapital goods	1.666	−0.284	−1.095	0.310	0.271
Oil conservation efforts	−0.526	−0.079	−0.741	−0.788	−1.174
6. Export promotion	5.106	4.309	2.753	2.216	0.123
Construction services	0.789	1.464	1.272	0.986	1.674
7. Aggregate demand adjustment	−1.213	−5.269	−7.538	−7.012	−4.771
Fixed investment	0.228	−1.154	−2.281	−1.778	−0.981
Domestic output	−1.442	−4.114	−5.257	−5.234	−3.790
8. Total effect [(2)+(3)+(4)+(5)+(6)+(7)]	4.715	5.977	4.240	1.527	0.455
9. Interaction effects and adding-up errors [(1)−(8)]	0.123	0.122	0.158	0.148	0.152

a. The decomposition factors were calculated by using an average of current year and base period weights.
b. Negative sign indicates a balance of payments improvement.
Note: See appendix A for a description of, and data used for, the decomposition.

growth. The shortage in rice had to be made up by imports of grain, which increased by 60 percent a year for the 1979–81 period. Grain rose to 8 percent of the total imports in 1981 from less than 4 percent in 1978.

The hostile external environment and the domestic political problems of the Korean government were much more dramatic than during the first oil crisis period. A rise in unemployment would pose a serious threat to an already shaky social stability. Nevertheless, it was evident to policymakers that, unlike in 1974, the growth policy was simply not a viable alternative. The foremost reason was the questionable availability of the external finance needed to lengthen the adjustment period. Indeed, it was rather obvious that any further deterioration in the current account could seriously undermine Korea's credit standing in international financial markets and cripple its ability to borrow.

Most of all, it was inconceivable that exports would grow as fast as they had done during the 1976–77 period. This pessimism of course reflected the rise in trade protectionism and expectations of deepening world recession. Persistently high interest rates and the diminished availability of external finance also raised the cost of borrowing abroad. Given the continuous requirement for external borrowing, the best policy alternative was to pursue stabilization policies with the hope of reducing the size of the current account deficit. To these considerations was added the argument that it would be relatively easier for a caretaker government to implement unpopular stabilization measures.

In January 1980, the caretaker government introduced a policy package clearly intended to improve the current account. It included a 20 percent devaluation of the won vis-à-vis the dollar, an upward adjustment of bank deposit and lending rates by five to six percentage points, and a 60 percent increase in energy prices for end-users. In announcing the stabilization package, the government also reaffirmed its determination to continue with a tight fiscal and monetary policy. By January, however, the economy had already begun to slow down, and in succeeding

Table 11-12. Counterfactual Analysis
(percent)

Item	1977	1978	1979	1980	1981	1982	1983
1. Actual ratio of current account deficit to potential output	0.5	3.16	6.72	7.96	6.33	3.56	2.48
Hypothetical ratio							
2. With oil prices fixed at 1978 level			5.49	3.51	1.67	−0.62	−0.96
(1)−(2)	—	—	(1.23)	(4.45)	(4.66)	(4.18)	(3.44)
3. With interest rates fixed at 1978 level			6.21	6.65	4.42	1.83	1.36
(1)−(3)	—	—	(0.51)	(1.31)	(1.91)	(1.73)	(1.12)
4. With fixed oil prices and interest rates			4.98	2.20	−0.24	−2.35	−2.07
(1)−(4)	—	—	(1.73)	(5.76)	(6.57)	(5.91)	(4.55)
5. With 1978 construction service exports			5.95	6.73	5.65	3.37	1.72
(1)−(5)	—	—	(0.77)	(1.23)	(0.68)	(0.19)	(0.76)
6. With 1978 oil prices, interest rates, and construction service exports			4.21	0.97	−0.91	−2.55	−2.83
(1)−(6)	—	—	(2.50)	(6.99)	(7.24)	(6.11)	(5.31)

Note: Based on the decomposition exercise in appendix A.

months the overall performance of the economy deteriorated further. Concerned with this development, the government eased its restrictive policy during the latter half of the year.

In early 1981, economic recovery remained as elusive as before despite a strong surge in export orders. The government took a further reflationary measure in April and official interest rates were lowered on three occasions during the last two months of 1981. The nominal dollar exchange rate was devalued by about 12 percent, but because of the rapid domestic inflation, the real exchange rate appreciated by 3 percent for the year as a whole. Overall policy during the year may be described as a strategy of muddling through; at best it was moderately expansionary.

The moderately expansionary policy pursued throughout 1981 gave way to an actively reflationary policy in 1982 partly by design, but mostly because a financial scandal that broke out in May of that year required a substantial infusion of fresh credit into the economy. In January the government implemented a number of measures to stimulate investment in housing construction and exports. These measures were followed by a reduction of bank interest rates on both deposits and loans by an average of four percentage points. This adjustment, together with the financial scandal and a proposal that would have imposed greater regulatory oversight on the unofficial financial sector, contributed to a sharp increase in the supply of money. At year's end M_2 had grown by 27 percent and M_1 by almost 46 percent. Nevertheless, the rapid liquidity expansion did not have much impact on either inflation or the current account (see table 11-10). With the expectation of an imminent recovery of the world economy, policymakers placed domestic price stability ahead of all other objectives in 1983. Accordingly, they reversed the policy stance from moderately expansionary to restrictive. In 1983, the expansion of the money supply measured by M_1 was limited to 17 percent for M_1 and 15.2 percent for M_2.

The current account started to improve in 1981, and within three years its deficit as a fraction of GNP declined to the 1978 level. As the preceding discussion shows, domestic stabilization measures were at best a way of muddling through and contributed little to improving the current account during 1982–83. This can be seen from table 11-12 where the current account improvement through the demand adjustment was getting smaller during the period. Instead, the reversal in the current account reflected mostly the increase in saving associated with the sustained improvement of the external environment.

During 1981–83, both the price of oil and foreign interest rates fell, and the terms of trade improved by 6 percent. As a result, oil and interest payments as a percentage of export earnings declined. With the upturn in the advanced economies, Korea's exports have picked up again. With a substantial gain in rice production, grain imports fell by 53 percent in 1982, though they recorded a moderate increase in 1983. All these favorable developments paved the way for 9.3 growth in GNP with a 3 percent annual inflation. They have also contributed to an upward shift in the saving/GNP ratio and a corresponding improvement in the current account.

EFFICIENCY AND OPTIMALITY OF FOREIGN BORROWING IN KOREA

At an abstract theoretical level, it is possible to create a set of conditions that govern the optimality or efficiency of foreign borrowing. Application of these conditions to a fast-growing economy such as Korea's entails a great many problems, and it is not easy to assess the allocative efficiency or optimality of foreign borrowing. The analysis in this section contains more informed speculation than hard facts, because hard facts are difficult to obtain, and when it comes to allocative efficiency, economics does not tell us much. Hence, my conclusions are no more than strong impressions.

Has foreign borrowing been extended beyond or kept below the point which would optimize the long-run growth of GNP in Korea? Although there does not seem to be universally accepted criteria for judging the optimality of foreign borrowing, several pieces of evidence suggest that Korea has not borrowed over and above what may be regarded as an optimal or prudent level.

At a macroeconomic level, Sachs (1981) argues that the buildup in external debt should not pose a problem if it reflects increased investment in the context of rising or stable—but not declining—saving rates. The growth in debt might be a concern if borrowing reflected an attempt to maintain consumption at unsustainable levels. To judge by this criterion, Korea has not borrowed beyond its debt service capacity.[11] As pointed out earlier, the Korean government exercises almost complete control over the allocation of foreign loans between industries and sectors. Because of this strict supervision, the degree of diversion of loans to uses other than designated ones appears to be relatively low (Park 1984). Furthermore, private claims on nonresidents have been practically nonexistent. Although it has displayed considerable fluctuations, domestic saving as a proportion of GNP has been rising in recent years (see table 11–17 in appendix B).

During the first three five-year-plan periods, the actual rates of growth consistently exceeded the target rates set by the planners, and did so during the second five-year plan by as much as three percentage points. Despite the rapid growth in foreign debt, consumption as a percentage of GNP declined during this period. Frank, Kim, and Westphal (1975, p. 107) show that, assuming a gross capital/output ratio of 2.5, about four percentage points of Korea's growth rate could be attributed to foreign savings during the 1960s. Using actual incremental capital/output ratios, the Bank of Korea (1984) has also estimated the contribution of foreign savings to growth. During the 1970s, the estimates show, the contribution declined with the rapid rise in the capital intensity of the economy. Nevertheless, foreign savings during the 1972–82 period accounted for an average of 1.8 percentage points of Korea's actual annual growth. The same study shows that between 1967 and 1982 foreign savings contributed as much as 36 percent of the actual increase in employed workers over the period. These estimates are no more than rough calculations and certainly overstate the actual contribution since they ignore other factors that contribute to employment growth. Nevertheless, they point to the important role foreign capital has played in Korean economic development.

Efficiency of Foreign Loan Allocation in the 1960s

Few firms in Korea can expect to borrow from abroad without payment guarantees issued by the domestic financial institutions controlled by the government. Mainly through the guarantee system, the government regulates access to international capital markets, the sectoral destination of foreign capital, and the type of investment project to be financed by foreign loans. Table 11-19 in appendix B presents a breakdown of the sectoral destination of both commercial and public loans since 1966. As can be seen from this table, except for the 1980–82 period, the social overhead capital sectors received almost as much from both commercial and public sources as did manufacturing. Within manufacturing, heavy and chemical industries have received a growing share of foreign capital inflows. Krueger (1979, p. 199) has little doubt that the social rate of return on capital exceeded the foreign borowing rate so that foreign loans were effectively used during the 1960s.[12] However, there were incentives for excessive borrowing and hence misallocation of resources in the latter part of the 1960s. Between the actual foreign interest rate adjusted for exchange rate depreciation and the domestic financing cost there was a large discrepancy of more than thirteen percentage points in favor of foreign borrowing (see table 11-4).

During the 1966–70 period, the foreign interest rate adjusted for foreign inflation was about 1.5 percent, whereas the real cost of foreign borrowing faced by Korean borrowers was negative and about 3 percent. Since borrowers expected a stable exchange rate (Frank, Kim, and Westphal 1975, p. 117), this expectation understated the true cost of borrowing and induced Korean firms to borrow more than they otherwise would have.

If Korean borrowers had been allowed to borrow up to the level at which the real rate of return to capital equals the cost of borrowing, given the rate differential between the domestic international capital markets, the aggregate level of borrowing would have been too high to be absorbed in an efficient manner.[13] Such a large inflow would have distorted sectoral resource allocation because the negative real interest rates on foreign borrowing would have induced local borrowers to use capital-intensive techniques and to invest in more capital-intensive industries. In addition, there would have been sectoral inefficiencies because some sectors were relatively favored and some were disadvantaged, in contrast to what would have happened had all been free to borrow at the true social cost. In particular, foreign commercial loans were often tied to imports of capital goods. As a result, low-cost foreign loans favored those sectors that were relatively heavy users of imported capital equipment (Frank, Kim, and Westphal 1975, p. 117).

In practice, however, the government approved foreign loans on the basis of investment priority and profitability. This rationing constrained the level of foreign borrowing well below the level that would have been realized in the absence of government control. In most cases, foreign loans financed only a fraction of the total cost of the projects undertaken. The remainder had to be obtained from domestic sources at much higher rates (Krueger 1979, p. 200).

Although excessive foreign borrowing occurred during the latter part of the 1960s because of distorted incentives, Krueger (1979, p. 201) argues that the low cost of foreign borrowing did not constitute a major distortion in resource allocation. The reason was that much of the foreign borrowing was allocated to efficient export-oriented industries which were labor-intensive in their factor uses and enjoyed comparative advantage.

Efficiency of Foreign Loan Allocation in the 1970s

During the 1970s, the real interest rates on foreign borrowing continued to be negative, though the differential between domestic and foreign borrowing costs (row 7 in table 11-4)

Table 11-13. Investment in Manufacturing
(billions of won, 1975 prices)

Investment	1977–81 plan (A)	1977	1978	1979	1977–79 (B)	Achievement (B)/(A) (percent)
Heavy industry	2,893	588	1,024	1,194	2,806	97
Basic metals	731	263	357	331	951	130
Machinery, electronics, and ships	1,145	139	309	379	827	72
Chemical and other	1,017	186	358	484	1,028	101
Light industry	1,621	193	252	304	749	46
Textiles	900	152	140	155	447	50
Other	721	41	112	149	302	42
Total	4,515	781	1,276	1,498	3,555	78

Note: This table is also quoted by Balassa (1980).
Source: Data provided by Economic Planning Board (EPB).

was almost negligible. The low real interest was certainly one of the factors that encouraged Korean firms to use increasingly more capital-intensive techniques and to invest in capital-intensive industries. Using the manufacturing census data, Hong (1979, p. 26) shows that the capital intensity in manufacturing rose steadily between 1966 and 1976: over the decade, the intensity (capital stock per worker) more than doubled. One calculation shows that the capital intensity in 1980 was almost four times higher than in 1968 (Park 1983). As a reflection of this rising trend, the aggregate capital intensity of exports rose rapidly, and by 1975 it had increased to 3.1 from 0.6 in 1960. Although we do not have any recent data, it most likely rose at a faster rate in the latter part of the 1970s.

It is difficult to associate changes in factor intensity with those in the wage/rental ratio, but the subsidies on credit, including foreign loans, could in part be held responsible for the rise. In particular, it was probably true of the rise in the capital intensity of exports since exporters have been by far the most favored borrowers. More important, however, the government has allocated a growing share of domestic and foreign resources through credit rationing to capital-intensive heavy and chemical industries in the process of restructuring the manufacturing sector of the economy.

As presented in table 11-13, the actual amount of investment undertaken in the heavy and chemical industries between 1977 and 1979 was enormous—even larger than the planned level, which was, in retrospect, ambitious to begin with. It was excessive in that much of the investment in these industries turned into idle capacity. To be sure, some industries—iron and steel, shipbuilding, and electronics—have been successful in improving their efficiency and in expanding their export markets. Largely because of the good performance of these industries, the share of heavy industrial exports in total manufactured exports has been rising (see table 11-22 in appendix B). During 1980–82, the share was 45 percent, twice the level of the early 1970s.

However, chemicals (including petroleum and petroleum products), nonferrous metals, and machinery have failed to achieve efficiency in terms of international competitiveness and remain largely high-cost industries with unpromising export prospects.[14] A large part—in some cases as much as 50 percent—of the investment in these inefficient industries has been financed by foreign borrowing. As presented in table 11-22 in appendix B, during 1975–80 the three high-cost industries received more than 40 percent of the total foreign loans allocated to heavy and chemical industries, and 87 percent during 1980–82. Within the policymaking circle in Korea, it is often argued that the three sectors are developed primarily for domestic import substitution in most developing countries, and as such a certain degree of inefficiency is to be expected. In the case of Korea, they have been promoted not only for import substitution, but also for exportation in the future to exploit the economies of scale. This strategy has resulted in higher resource costs than if they were developed only for import substitution.[15]

SUMMARY AND CONCLUDING REMARKS

The purpose of this chapter has been to analyze Korea's experience with foreign debt accumulation and management over the past two decades, 1965–83. Although the debt-servicing capacity is not addressed here, several other studies and some of the conclusions of this study suggest that Korea is not likely to experience any debt-servicing difficulties in the near future. This assessment has been reinforced by the remarkable performance of the economy for the past two years.

In summary, one could make several tentative conclusions which are not necessarily backed by strong evidence or hard facts.

- The accumulation of external debt in Korea has been closely associated with chronic current account deficits and the need for holding larger foreign exchange reserves. Capital account transactions have by and large been accommodating and have financed the current account deficits.[16] Under these circumstances, policy efforts attempting to slow down the growth of external debt have concentrated on eliminating the current account imbalances. Unlike the case in some developing countries, capital flight has never been a serious policy concern in Korea. To be sure, the tight controls imposed on capital movements helped stem the problem. More important, however, was the high rate of return to capital in a rapidly growing economy, which provided strong incentives to invest in domestic industries rather than abroad.

- With a limited number of policy tools of uncertain effectiveness, it has not been possible to achieve simultaneously all three objectives of growth, price stability, and external (current account) balance. Whenever conflicts have risen between the growth target and the management of external debt, Korean planners have not hesitated to sacrifice the objectives of balance of payments and price stability to the extent that foreign finance has been available. Its availability has been not fortuitous, but the result of Korea's exceptional economic performance.

- Rapid growth through the promotion of exports was expected to reduce gradually Korea's dependence on foreign resources. While the growth of exports and output was impressive, the current account remained persistently in deficit throughout the 1970s. Korea experienced a foreign debt crisis—or more properly a balance of payments crisis—during 1970–71 and after the first and second oil crises. In the early 1970s, the thrust of Korea's policy response was to step up export promotion by engineering a substantial depreciation of the real exchange rate (including export subsidies). Each time exports grew rapidly—owing in part to the depreciation but mostly to a worldwide recovery—and rescued Korea from the crisis.

  During the second oil crisis, however, Korea shifted its policy to a more classical prescription. Monetary and fiscal policies were tightened, and the real exchange rate was depreciated to move resources to the tradable goods sector. Once again, exports responded (of course with the help of the world economic recovery) and spared Korea from potentially embarrassing debt-servicing problems.

- From the pattern of policy adjustment to external shocks in the 1970s, one can infer that Korean planners did not have any view of an appropriate level or flow of foreign capital. Since 1979, mounting debt and the debt-service burden in an uncertain international financial environment have made policymakers aware of the magnitude of Korea's debt problem. The revised fifth five-year development plan reflects this growing concern and the determination of the government to reduce the rate of growth of debt. The revised document does not, however, indicate the level of debt the authorities consider optimal, though it is clear that they are trying to eliminate the current account deficit as soon as possible. With the growing debt, the government has been actively encouraging foreign direct investment and since 1982 has begun to relax restrictions on foreign investment and to simplify the processing of proposals for foreign investment projects.

• It is widely recognized that the Korean experience with debt management is a "success case" both in maintaining rapid growth and in avoiding financial difficulties other countries now face. This recognition naturally raises an interesting question as to what aspects of policy management have proved particularly important in maintaining a balance between the desire to sustain a high rate of growth by borrowing abroad and the concern to avoid the pitfalls of a debt crisis if external circumstances change abruptly.[17]

One can easily dismiss the argument that the private sector largely took care of itself while the government was prudent in fiscal management so that budgetary deficits were kept within bounds. As shown in table 11-16 in appendix B, the public sector has been the major source of chronic current account deficits in Korea. Another popular explanation is that an export-led development strategy such as Korea has been pursuing will best achieve sustainable external payments balance without sacrificing growth or imposing import restrictions (Morgan Guaranty 1984, p. 9).

Although there is little doubt that an outward-looking strategy has contributed to rapid output and employment growth in Korea, it is difficult to prove, both theoretically and empirically, how export promotion policies or export growth per se could insulate the economy from the recurrence of balance of payments problems. To be tenable, this argument has to explain why some countries have been able to export whereas other countries at a similar development stage and with a similar factor endowment have not.

More plausible explanations, in my view, should focus on the predominance of the external sector and the role of exports as an engine of growth. Over the past two decades exports, starting from a small base, have grown to more than 42 percent of GNP in 1983. In the process, exports have become a powerful engine of growth and proved responsive to incentives. As a result, a sharp increase in exports either caused by a worldwide economic boom or engineered by providing incentives could easily turn around the situation and pull the economy out of a balance of payments problem. Because of the predominance of the external sector, not to mention the large size of the foreign debt, Korean planners realized that they could not deviate too far from a reasonable balance of payments policy. This constraint also explains in part the decisive policy actions on the part of the Korean government in response to an incipient current account deterioration.

• With the continuing world economic recovery, Korean planners forecast that the current account deficit, which has been declining, will turn into a surplus by 1986. Thereafter, Korea's gross debt will fall as a proportion of GNP. These rosy projections are somewhat dampened by several aspects of the structure of debt and trade that suggest potential risks. One disturbing aspect is the inefficiency of public enterprises that account for a large share of Korea's current account deficits. Another concern is that after the two oil crises adjustment to the external shocks was greatly facilitated by the improvement of the external environment. Except for export promotion and intermittent exchange rate devaluations, the authorities were not able to make other adjustments (import substitution and demand management), but such adjustments might be of greater significance in the future if the trade environment deteriorates.

A third concern is related to the marked increase in the share of capital-intensive producer goods in total exports. In recent years, heavy and chemical industries have constituted more than 50 percent of Korea's manufactured exports. It is expected that the share will continue to rise. As a result of this change in the commodity structure, Korean exports will be subject to more cyclical fluctuations than before. This relative instability will in turn make it more difficult to manage balance of payments problems and foreign debt in the future. Finally, it should be noted that because of its heavy dependence on imported raw materials, Korea is vulnerable to a rise in the prices of commodities and raw materials which will help many Latin American countries. A resurgence in the world demand for these commodities and the subsequent price increases are likely to erode Korea's ability to service its foreign debt.

APPENDIX A

To decompose the current account, we begin with a simplified definition of the current account in U.S. dollars (D_t) for year t.[18]

(11.1) $$D_t = M_{kt} + M_{ot} + M_{jt} + V_t - E_t$$

where

M_{kt} = Dollar value of capital goods imports (CIF)

M_{ot} = Dollar value of oil imports

M_{jt} = Dollar value of noncapital goods imports, including imports of nonfactor services not accounted for in M_{kt}, plus transfers

V_t = Dollar value of factor service payments

E_t = Dollar value of exports of goods and services.

Define the value of imports in 1975 dollars as follows:

(11.2) $$J^*_{kt} = M_{kt}/P_{kt}$$

$$J^*_{ot} = M_{ot}/P_{ot}$$

(11.3) $$J^*_{yt} = M_{jt}/P_{jt}$$

where

J^*_{kt} = Capital goods imports in 1975 dollars

J^*_{ot} = Oil imports in 1975 dollars

J^*_{yt} = Noncapital goods imports in 1975 dollars

P_{kt} = Dollar price index of capital goods imports (1975 = 1.0)

P_{jt} = Dollar price index of noncapital goods imports (1975 = 1.0)

P_{ot} = Dollar price index of oil (1975 = 1.0).

Define the import coefficients as follows:

(11.4) $$J_{kt} = J^*_{kt}/I_t$$

$$J_{ot} = J^*_{ot}/Z_t$$

(11.5) $$J_{yt} = J^*_{yt}/Z_t$$

where I_t is fixed investment in 1975 dollars and Z_t is GDP in 1975 dollars. We also define the following variables:

(11.6) $$X_t = E_t/P_{xt}$$

(11.7) $$r_t = V_t/NF_{t-1}$$

where r_t is the rate of return on foreign capital, P_{xt} is dollar price index of exports (1975 = 1.0), and NF_{t-1} is dollar value of net external capital stock at the end of the previous year.

Substituting equations (11.2) through (11.7) into equation (11.1), we obtain

$$(11.8)\qquad D_t = P_{kt}\cdot J_{kt}\cdot I_t + P_{ot}\cdot J_{ot}\cdot Z_t + P_{jt}\cdot J_{yt}\cdot Z_t + r_t NF_{t-1} - P_{xt}X_t.$$

Potential output in current dollars (Y_t^*) is defined as

$$(11.9)\qquad Y_t^* = P_{yt}Z_t^*$$

where Z_t^* is potential output in 1975 dollars, and P_{yt} the implicit GDP deflator (1975 = 1.0) divided by the won/dollar exchange rate (1975 = 1.0).[19]

Dividing equation (11.8) by (11.9), we obtain

$$(11.10)\qquad \frac{D_t}{Y_t^*} = J_{kt}\left(\frac{P_{kt}}{P_{yt}}\right)\left(\frac{I_t}{Z_t^*}\right) + J_{ot}\left(\frac{P_{ot}}{P_{yt}}\right)\left(\frac{Z_t}{Z_t^*}\right) + J_{yt}\left(\frac{P_{jt}}{P_{yt}}\right)\left(\frac{Z_t}{Z_t^*}\right) + r_t\left(\frac{NF_{t-1}}{Y_t^*}\right) - \left(\frac{P_{xt}}{P_{yt}}\right)\left(\frac{X_t}{Z_t^*}\right).$$

Now estimate the difference between the deficit ratio in year t and the base year denoted by subscript 0. Differentiating equation (11.10) with respect to time and collecting terms, we then have:

$$\Delta\left(\frac{D_t}{Y_t^*}\right) = \left[J_{k_0}\left(\frac{I_0}{Z_0^*}\right)\Delta\left(\frac{P_{kt}}{P_{yt}}\right) + J_{y_0}\left(\frac{Z_0}{Z_0^*}\right)\Delta\left(\frac{P_{jt}}{P_{yt}}\right) + J_{o_0}\left(\frac{Z_0}{Z_0^*}\right)\Delta\left(\frac{P_{ot}}{P_{yt}}\right) - \left(\frac{X_0}{Z_0^*}\right)\Delta\left(\frac{P_{xt}}{P_{yt}}\right)\right]$$

$$+\left(\frac{NF_{t-1}}{Y_0^*}\Delta r_t\right) - \left(\frac{P_{x_0}}{P_{y_0}}\right)\Delta\left(\frac{X_t}{Z_t^*}\right) + \left[\left(\frac{P_{k_0}}{P_{y_0}}\right)\left(\frac{I_0}{Z_0^*}\right)\Delta J_{kt} + \left(\frac{P_{j_0}}{P_{y_0}}\right)\left(\frac{Z_0}{Z_0^*}\right)\Delta J_{yt} + \left(\frac{P_{o_0}}{P_{y_0}}\right)\left(\frac{Z_0}{Z_0^*}\right)\Delta J_{ot}\right]$$

$$(11.11)\qquad +\left[J_{k_0}\left(\frac{P_{k_0}}{P_{y_0}}\right)\Delta\left(\frac{I_t}{Z_t^*}\right) + J_{y_0}\left(\frac{P_{j_0}}{P_{y_0}}\right)\Delta\left(\frac{Z_t}{Z_t^*}\right) + J_{o_0}\left(\frac{P_{o_0}}{P_{y_0}}\right)\Delta\left(\frac{Z_t}{Z_t^*}\right)\right]$$

$$+ r_0\,\Delta\left(\frac{NF_{t-1}}{Y_t^*}\right) + \text{second- and third-order terms.}$$

(a) $\Delta\left(\frac{D_t}{Y_t}\right)$ = Actual change in the ratio of current account imbalances to potential output

(b) $J_{k_0}\left(\frac{Z_0}{Z_0^*}\right)\Delta\left(\frac{P_{kt}}{P_{yt}}\right)$ = Change in the relative price of imported capital goods

(c) $J_{o_0}\left(\frac{Z_0}{Z_0^*}\right)\Delta\left(\frac{P_{ot}}{P_{yt}}\right)$ = Change in the relative price of crude oil

(d) $J_{y_0}\left(\frac{Z_0}{Z_0^*}\right)\Delta\left(\frac{P_{jt}}{P_{yt}}\right)$ = Change in the relative price of other imported goods

(e) $\left(\frac{X_0}{Z_0}\right)\Delta\left(\frac{P_x}{P_y}\right)$ = Relative export price changes

Terms of trade effect = (b) + (c) + (d) − (e)

(f) $\left(\frac{NF_0}{Y_0}\right)\Delta r_t$ = Interest rate effect

(g) $r_0\,\Delta\left(\frac{NF_{t-1}}{Y_t}\right)$ = Accumulated debt effect

(h) $\left(\frac{P_{k_0}}{P_{y_0}}\right)\left(\frac{I_0}{Z_0^*}\right)\Delta J_{kt}$ = Import replacement for capital goods

(i) $\left(\frac{P_{j_0}}{P_{y_0}}\right)\left(\frac{Z_0}{Z_0^*}\right)\Delta J_{yt}$ = Import replacement for noncapital goods

(j) $\left(\frac{P_{o_0}}{P_{y_0}}\right)\left(\frac{Z_0}{Z_0^*}\right)\Delta J_{ot}$ = Oil conservation efforts

Import replacement = (h) + (i) + (j)

(k) $\left(\frac{P_{x_0}}{P_{y_0}}\right)\Delta\left(\frac{X_t}{Z_t^*}\right)$ = Export promotion

(l) $J_{k_0}\left(\frac{P_{k_0}}{P_{y_0}}\right)\Delta\left(\frac{I_t}{Z_t^*}\right)$ = Change in fixed investment

(m) $J_{y_0}\left(\frac{P_{j_0}}{P_{y_0}}\right)\Delta\left(\frac{Z_t}{Z_t^*}\right) + J_{o_0}\left(\frac{P_{o_0}}{P_{y_0}}\right)\Delta\left(\frac{Z_t}{Z_t^*}\right)$

= Change in domestic output

Demand adjustment = (l) + (m).[20]

APPENDIX B

Table 11-14. Korea's External Debt, 1960–83

(millions of U.S. dollars)

Debt	1961	1962	1963	1964	1965	1966	1967	1968	1969	1970
1. Long-term	4	10	52	78	121	285	487	893	1,376	1,702
Percent of row (5)	18.2	17.2	49.5	56.5	68.4	81.0	75.4	74.5	76.4	75.8
Public and private	4	10	52	78	112	276	474	808	1,261	1,594
Public	4	10	33	42	52	114	191	301	446	588
Private	—	—	19	36	60	162	282	506	815	1,006
Bank loans	—	—	—	—	—	—	—	40	70	75
Bonds outstanding	—	—	—	—	—	—	—	—	—	—
IMF facilities	—	—	—	—	9	9	13	45	45	33
2. Medium-term	18	48	53	59	56	62	93	218	230	170
Percent of row (5)	81.8	82.8	50.5	43.5	31.6	17.6	14.4	18.2	12.8	7.6
Trade credits	19	48	53	59	56	62	93	218	230	170
Cash loans	—	—	—	—	—	—	—	—	—	—
3. Short-term[b]	—	—	—	—	—	6	66	89	186	357
Percent of row (5)	—	—	—	—	—	1.7	10.2	7.4	10.3	15.9
Private	—	—	—	—	—	—	60	72	114	193
Banks	—	—	—	—	—	6	6	17	72	164
4. Foreign banks "A" account[c]	—	—	—	—	—	—	—	—	8	16
Percent of row (5)	—	—	—	—	—	—	—	—	0.6	75.8
5. Total foreign debt	22	58	105	138	177	352	646	1,199	1,800	2,245
6. Foreign direct investment	—	1	3	6	17	17	29	44	51	76
7. GNP in nominal U.S. dollars	2,103	2,315	2,718	2,876	3,006	3,671	4,274	5,226	6,625	7,834
8. Foreign debt/GNP [(5)/(7)]	1.0	2.5	6.0	4.8	5.9	9.6	15.1	22.9	27.2	28.7
9. Foreign debt plus direct investment/GNP [(5) + (6)/(7)]	1.0	2.5	6.1	5.0	6.4	10.0	15.8	23.8	27.9	29.6

a. Preliminary figures.

b. Includes trade credit and bank refinance.

c. Foreign currency funds borrowed by the branch offices of foreign banks from their headquarters or other branches for paid-in capital and other operational uses.

Sources: Economic Planning Board, Economic Indicators of Korea (March 1983); and Bank of Korea.

1971	1972	1973	1974	1975	1976	1977	1978	1979	1980	1981	1982	1983[a]
2,332	2,833	3,420	4,545	5,745	7,080	8,583	10,533	13,337	16,137	20,127	22,611	25,000
78.8	78.9	80.3	76.6	68.0	67.2	67.9	70.8	65.1	58.9	61.9	60.6	62.3
2,116	2,670	3,294	3,995	4,999	6,145	7,477	9,399	10,977	12,827	14,349	15,689	16,500
906	1,320	1,688	2,028	2,470	3,114	3,640	4,320	5,270	6,531	7,899	9,374	—
1,210	1,350	1,606	1,967	2,529	3,031	3,837	5,079	5,707	6,296	6,450	6,315	—
153	155	126	399	465	483	602	620	1,980	2,309	4,174	5,322	6,500
—	—	—	19	19	93	163	251	242	288	358	341	600
63	8	—	132	262	359	341	263	138	713	1,246	1,259	1,400
111	116	139	153	302	408	350	483	561	617	602	488	600
3.8	3.2	3.3	2.6	3.6	3.9	2.8	3.2	2.7	2.3	1.9	1.3	1.5
—	114	136	150	285	386	335	480	522	576	564	462	—
—	2	3	3	17	22	15	3	39	41	38	26	—
450	600	612	1,136	2,167	2,681	2,923	2,593	4,651	7,575	8,486	10,307	10,500
15.4	16.7	14.4	19.1	25.6	25.4	23.1	17.4	22.7	20.3	26.1	27.6	26.2
246	397	489	413	1,158	1,499	1,828	1,041	2,251	4,158	4,110	4,020	—
204	203	123	723	1,009	1,182	1,095	1,552	2,400	3,417	4,376	6,287	—
29	40	89	103	242	364	792	1,262	1,951	3,036	3,275	3,908	4,000
1.0	1.1	2.1	1.7	2.9	3.5	6.3	8.5	9.5	11.1	10.1	10.5	10.0
2,922	3,589	4,260	5,937	8,456	10,533	12,648	14,871	20,500	27,365	32,490	37,314	40,100
112	170	325	481	544	646	737	826	953	1,023	1,128	1,228	1,596
9,370	10,570	13,500	18,550	20,850	28,680	37,430	51,960	62,370	61,200	67,190	70,800	74,900
31.2	34.0	31.6	32.0	40.6	36.7	33.8	28.6	32.9	44.7	48.4	52.7	53.5
32.4	35.6	34.0	34.6	43.2	39.0	35.8	30.2	34.4	46.4	50.0	54.4	55.7

Table 11-15. Indicators of Korea's Debt-servicing Capacity (percent)

Year	Total foreign debt/GNP	Debt service/GNP	Debt service ratio (long-term only)	Debt service ratio (including interest on short-term)	Rescheduling probability[a]	Real net interest payments (percent of exports)[b]
1961	1.0	0.0	0.4	0.4	n.a.	n.a
1962	2.5	0.1	0.7	0.8	9.5	n.a.
1963	6.0	0.1	1.0	1.0	18.0	n.a.
1964	4.8	0.2	2.6	2.6	22.3	n.a.
1965	5.9	0.5	5.0	5.0	11.5	n.a.
1966	9.6	0.4	3.0	3.2	7.4	n.a.
1967	15.1	0.8	5.2	5.4	6.7	n.a.
1968	22.9	0.9	5.2	5.4	8.0	n.a.
1969	27.2	1.5	7.8	8.6	9.4	n.a.
1970	28.7	3.3	18.2	18.5	10.9	n.a.
1971	31.2	3.6	19.8	21.0	14.2	n.a.
1972	34.0	3.9	18.4	18.7	9.8	n.a.
1973	31.6	4.5	14.2	14.8	2.0	n.a.
1974	32.0	3.8	12.4	14.4	2.3	−0.8
1975	40.6	4.1	12.0	14.4	2.9	−0.6
1976	36.7	4.0	10.6	12.1	2.0	2.0
1977	33.8	4.2	10.2	11.1	1.3	0.6
1978	28.6	4.6	12.3	13.9	1.3	0.1
1979	32.9	5.1	13.3	16.3	1.2	−1.1
1980	44.7	6.9	13.0	18.5	1.2	−1.6
1981	48.4	8.4	13.8	20.7	1.2	3.0
1982	52.7	8.4	15.9	21.0	1.6	6.9
1983	53.5	7.9	15.4	19.3	n.a.	n.a.

n.a. Not available.

a. Probability figures are from Kim (1983).

b. Data obtained from Dooley, Helkie, Tryon, and Underwood (1983).

Source: Appendix B.

Table 11-16. Sources of Current Account Imbalances in Current Market Prices
(billions of won)

	Private sector				Public sector													
										Private sector (percent)				Public sector (percent)				
Year	Individual (A)	Private corporations (B)	Financial institutions (C)	Subtotal (D=A+B+C)	Government (E)	Government corporations (F)[a]	Subtotal (G)	Statistical errors (H)	Current account deficits and surpluses (I)	A/GNP	B/GNP	C/GNP	D/GNP	E/GNP	F/GNP	G/GNP	H/GNP (percent)	I/GNP (percent)
1963	7.3	−9.5	−3.1	−5.3	7.4	−15.8	−8.4	−4.9	−18.6	1.5	−1.9	−0.6	−1.1	1.5	−3.1	−1.7	−1.0	−3.7
1964	12.4	−7.3	0.4	5.5	12.4	−12.5	−0.1	−11.2	−5.8	1.7	−1.0	0.1	0.8	1.7	−1.7	0.0	−1.6	−0.8
1965	17.6	−31.1	1.0	−12.5	19.7	−11.4	8.3	10.0	5.7	2.2	−3.9	0.1	−1.6	2.4	−1.4	1.0	1.2	0.7
1966	31.3	−69.8	1.7	−36.8	7.7	−12.4	−4.7	13.5	−28.1	3.0	−6.7	0.2	−3.5	0.7	−1.2	−0.5	1.3	−2.7
1967	26.3	−72.5	−0.6	−46.9	21.7	−48.8	−27.1	22.1	−51.9	2.1	−5.7	−0.1	−3.7	1.7	−3.8	−2.1	1.7	−4.1
1968	36.9	−133.1	−5.8	−102.1	21.0	−34.7	−13.7	−6.0	−121.8	2.2	−8.1	−0.4	−6.2	1.3	−2.1	−0.8	−0.4	−7.4
1969	76.4	−139.7	0.0	−63.3	−20.0	−61.3	−81.3	−13.6	−158.2	3.5	−6.5	0.0	−2.9	−0.9	−2.8	−3.7	−0.6	−7.3
1970	34.0	−188.8	−3.8	−158.6	19.7	−58.9	−39.2	4.3	−193.5	1.2	−6.9	−0.1	−5.8	0.7	−2.2	−1.4	0.2	−7.1
1971	57.0	−188.7	−3.4	−135.1	−6.1	−125.5	−131.6	−28.0	−294.7	1.6	−5.6	−0.1	−4.0	−0.2	−3.7	−3.9	−0.8	−8.7
1972	146.5	−39.1	−5.1	102.3	−80.9	−195.2	−276.1	29.2	−144.6	3.5	−0.9	−0.1	2.5	−1.9	−4.7	−6.6	0.7	−3.5
1973	370.9	−238.8	5.1	137.2	−64.6	−104.4	−169.0	−91.4	−123.2	6.9	−4.4	−0.1	2.6	−1.2	−1.9	−3.1	−1.7	−2.3
1974	263.0	−582.4	33.5	−285.9	−183.1	−213.1	−396.2	−138.3	−820.4	3.5	−7.8	0.4	−3.8	−2.4	−2.8	−5.3	−1.8	−10.9
1975	167.7	−394.1	5.8	−220.6	−265.0	−463.2	−728.2	35.5	−913.3	1.7	−3.9	0.1	−2.2	−2.6	−4.6	−7.2	0.4	−9.0
1976	513.8	−438.7	54.3	129.4	162.0	−438.5	−276.5	−4.6	−151.8	3.7	−3.2	0.4	0.9	1.2	−3.2	−2.0	0.0	−1.1
1977	1,063.0	−518.8	108.0	652.2	−175.7	−735.4	−911.1	264.7	6.0	5.9	−2.9	0.6	3.6	−1.0	−4.1	−5.0	1.5	0.0
1978	1,306.9	−1,439.5	172.8	40.2	110.1	−1,015.5	−905.4	339.9	−525.3	5.4	−5.9	0.7	0.2	0.5	−4.2	−3.7	1.4	−2.2
1979	1,286.8	−2,812.0	217.8	−1,307.4	99.9	−1,145.1	−1,045.2	343.4	−2,009.2	4.1	−9.0	0.7	−4.2	0.3	−3.7	−3.3	1.1	−6.4
1980	561.0	−2,737.5	218.1	−1,958.4	−444.4	−1,302.3	−1,746.7	480.8	−3,224.3	1.5	−7.4	0.6	−5.3	−1.2	−3.5	−4.7	1.3	−8.7
1981	521.5	−1,562.4	88.2	−952.7	−562.7	−1,861.4	−2,424.1	358.5	−3,018.4	1.1	−3.4	0.2	−2.1	−1.2	−4.1	−5.3	0.6	−6.6
1982	1,618.6	−578.1	−581.6	458.9	−66.5	−2,287.2	−2,353.7	−59.2	−1,954.0	3.1	−1.1	−1.1	0.9	−0.1	−4.4	−4.5	−0.1	−3.8
1983	1,711.2	−2,105.1	−481.6	−875.5	1,153.4	−1,674.0	−520.6	174.5	−1,221.6	2.9	−3.6	−0.8	−1.5	2.0	−2.9	−0.9	0.3	−2.1

a. Figures for savings and investment of government corporations include nonfinancial operations of the Federation of Agricultural and Fisheries Corporations.

Note: A, B, and C refer to savings minus investment in each sector.

Source: Bank of Korea, Economic Statistics Yearbook, various issues.

Table 11-17. Domestic Savings, Gross Fixed Investment, and Current Account as Percent of GNP, 1965–83
(percent)

Year	Investment/GNP: Gross fixed investment	Investment/GNP: Inventories	Saving/GNP	Current account/GNP
1965	14.8	0.2	7.4	0.3
1966	20.2	1.4	11.8	−2.8
1967	21.4	0.5	11.4	−4.5
1968	25.0	0.9	15.1	−8.4
1969	25.8	3.0	18.8	−8.3
1970	22.9	2.4	15.7	−7.8
1971	21.5	3.6	14.6	−9.0
1972	20.0	2.2	16.5	−3.5
1973	23.4	2.3	22.8	−2.3
1974	25.3	6.3	19.9	−10.9
1975	25.5	4.5	19.1	−9.0
1976	24.1	1.5	23.9	−1.1
1977	26.7	1.1	27.5	0.0
1978	30.8	0.4	28.5	−2.1
1979	32.8	2.9	28.1	−6.7
1980	31.9	−0.7	21.9	−8.7
1981	28.9	0.3	21.7	−6.9
1982	30.3	−3.3	22.4	−3.7
1983	31.8	−4.2	24.5	−2.2

Sources: Economic Planning Board, Korean Economic Indicators (March 1984); and Bank of Korea, Economic Statistics Yearbook (1984).

Table 11-18. Foreign Loans and Investment
(millions of U.S. dollars; arrival basis)

Period	Loans: Public	Loans: Commercial	Direct foreign investment	Total
1959–61	4.4	—	—	4.4
1962–66	115.6	175.6	16.7	307.9
Percent of total	37.5	57.0	5.4	
1967–71	810.8	1,354.7	96.4	2,261.8
Percent of total	35.8	59.9	4.3	
1972–76	2,388.9	3,043.9	556.0	5,988.8
Percent of total	39.9	50.8	9.3	
1977–79	2,529.5	4,793.7	328.8	7,652.0
Percent of total	33.1	62.6	4.3	
1980–83	6,246.5	4,434.1	404.1	11,084.7
Percent of total	56.4	40.0	3.6	

Source: Economic Planning Board, Handbook of Korean Economy (1983).

Table 11-19. Foreign Loans by Destination
(millions of U.S. dollars)

Destination	1966–70	1971–75	1976–80	1981–82
Total	1,693.2	4,523.2	11,810.5	5,734.1
Agriculture, forestry, and fisheries	193.5	588.9	795.8	528.2
Percent of total	11.4	13.0	6.7	9.2
Mining	17.6	...	10.2	13.8
Percent of total	1.0	...	0.1	0.2
Manufacturing	674.1	1,753.0	4,658.7	873.9
Percent of total	39.8	38.8	39.4	15.2
Heavy and chemical	384.1	1,191.1	3,649.4	734.6
Percent of manufacturing	57.0	67.9	78.3	84.1
Light	290.1	561.9	1,009.3	139.3
Percent of manufacturing	43.0	32.1	21.7	15.9
Social overhead	668.8	1,348.7	4,581.9	3,183.9
Percent of total	39.5	29.8	38.8	55.5
Services	110.3	603.9	1,718.3	828.3
Percent of total	6.5	13.4	14.5	14.4
Others	29.9	228.4	38.9	306.0
Percent of total	1.8	5.0	0.3	5.3

... Negligible.

Source: Economic Planning Board, Economic Indicators of Korea (1983).

Table 11-20. Indices of Nominal and Real Exchange Rate

	1962	1963	1964	1965	1966	1967	1968	1969	1970
Nominal exchange rate[a]	372.31 (130.00)	372.31 (130.00)	226.33 (213.85)	181.77 (266.27)	178.38 (271.33)	178.92 (270.51)	174.96 (276.64)	167.81 (288.42)	155.56 (311.13)
Effective nominal exchange rate[b]	410.13	410.78	251.09	202.55	196.32	201.57	198.67	188.94	174.17
Purchasing power parity[c]	310.56	258.86	198.92	185.45	173.42	155.03	141.90	130.55	117.03
Real effective exchange rate (REER)[d]	119.88 (430.73)	143.83 (336.51)	113.78 (425.39)	98.01 (493.80)	102.36 (470.54)	115.41 (419.37)	123.29 (392.56)	128.54 (376.54)	132.92 (364.12)

a. Monthly average.

b. Effective nominal exchange rate is calculated as a weighted average of the won prices of the currencies of Korea's four major trading partners, where the weights are given by each country's trade share.

c. Trade weighted.

Table 11-21. Wages, Productivity, and Unit Labor Cost in Manufacturing

	Nominal wages			Consumer price	Real wages		
Year	Amount (won)	Index (A) (1975 = 100)	Change (percent)	index (1975 = 100)	Amount (won)	Index (1975 = 100)	Change (percent)
1960	2,330	6.1	—	14.1[b]	16,525	43.1	—
1961	2,610	6.8	11.5	15.3[b]	17,059	44.4	3.0
1962	2,780	7.2	5.9	16.3[b]	17,055	44.4	0.0
1963	3,180	8.3	15.3	19.6[b]	16,224	42.3	−4.7
1964	3,880	10.1	21.7	25.5[b]	15,216	39.6	−6.4
1965	4,600	12.0	18.8	27.6	16,667	43.4	9.6
1966	5,420	14.1	17.5	30.7	17,655	46.0	6.0
1967	6,640	17.3	22.7	33.9	19,587	51.0	10.9
1968	8,400	21.9	26.6	37.6	22,340	58.2	14.1
1969	11,270	29.4	34.2	42.3	26,643	69.4	19.2
1970	14,301	37.3	26.9	49.1	29,126	75.9	9.4
1971	16,611	43.3	16.2	55.7	29,822	77.7	2.4
1972	18,923	49.3	13.9	62.2	30,423	79.3	2.0
1973	22,330	58.2	18.0	64.2	34,782	90.6	14.3
1974	30,209	78.7	35.3	79.8	37,856	98.6	8.8
1975	38,378	100.0	27.0	100.0	38,378	100.0	1.4
1976	51,685	134.7	34.7	115.3	44,827	116.8	16.8
1977	69,168	180.2	33.8	127.0	54,463	141.9	21.5
1978	92,907	242.1	34.3	145.3	63,942	166.6	17.4
1979	119,515	311.4	28.6	171.9	69,526	181.2	8.7
1980	146,684	382.2	22.7	221.3	66,283	172.7	−4.7
1981	176,176	459.1	20.1	272.9	64,557	168.2	−2.6
1982	202,117	526.6	14.7	292.8	69,029	179.9	6.9

a. Labor productivity = Output index/labor input index.

b. Consumer price index in Seoul City.

Sources: Economic Planning Board, Monthly Statistics of Korea, various issues; Ministry of Labor, Report on Monthly Labour Survey, various issues; and Office of Labor Affairs, Yearbook of Labour Statistics (1971).

1971	1972	1973	1974	1975	1976	1977	1978	1979	1980	1981	1982
137.97	122.85	121.51	119.22	100.00	100.00	100.00	100.00	100.00	79.68	71.07	66.20
(350.80)	(393.97)	(398.32)	(405.97)	(484.00)	(484.00)	(484.00)	(484.00)	(484.00)	(607.43)	(681.03)	(731.13)
151.04	125.03	116.23	118.40	100.00	101.04	96.58	85.01	86.24	69.97	63.55	63.24
106.87	104.88	122.92	119.08	100.00	90.42	89.92	92.53	84.45	74.48	64.42	57.87
129.10	117.13	98.85	100.12	100.00	110.60	111.21	108.08	118.47	106.98	110.32	114.39
(374.90)	(413.21)	(489.61)	(483.41)	(484.00)	(437.62)	(435.22)	(447.83)	(408.55)	(452.43)	(438.72)	(423.11)

d. REER = $e_k \cdot \Sigma_{i=1}^{4} w_i \cdot WPI_i \cdot e_i/CPI_k$, where e_k = the won/dollar exchange rate, w_i = the trade weight for country i, WPI_i = wholesale price index for country currency/dollar exchange rate, and CPI_k = consumer price index for Korea.

Note: Figures in parentheses are the levels of nominal and real exchange rates.

Source: IMF, International Financial Statistics, various issues.

Labor productivity[a]		Unit labor cost	
Index (B) (1975 = 100)	Change (percent)	(A)/(B) (1975 = 100)	Change (percent)
19.0	—	32.1	—
21.3	12.1	31.9	−0.6
21.8	2.3	33.0	3.4
23.2	6.4	35.8	8.5
25.3	9.1	39.9	11.5
29.7	17.4	40.4	1.3
30.9	4.0	45.6	12.9
36.3	17.5	47.7	4.6
43.6	20.1	50.2	5.2
55.1	26.4	53.4	6.4
62.1	12.7	60.1	12.5
68.0	9.5	63.7	6.0
73.9	8.7	66.7	4.7
80.4	8.8	72.4	8.5
89.6	11.4	87.8	21.3
100.0	11.6	100.0	13.9
107.5	7.5	125.3	25.3
118.7	10.4	151.8	21.1
132.9	12.0	182.2	20.0
153.9	15.8	202.3	11.0
170.4	10.7	224.3	10.9
197.2	15.7	232.8	3.8
206.7	4.8	254.8	9.5

Table 11-22. Foreign Loans Allocation and Export Performance in Heavy and Chemical Industries (millions of U.S. dollars)

Industry	1975–76		1977–78		1979–80		1981–82	
	Foreign loans	Exports	Foreign loans	Exports	Foreign loans	Exports	Foreign loans	Exports
Manufacturing Total	1,224.5	10,968.7	2,268.1	19,958.5	1,743.3	29,443.5	873.9	38,952.9
Heavy and chemical industries[a]	868.6	3,587.4	1,829.8	7,501.0	1,400.7	12,705.2	734.6	19,397.0
Percent of manufacturing	70.9	32.7	80.7	37.6	80.3	43.2	84.1	49.8
Chemicals[b]	268.3	422.1	648.2	697.2	268.5	1,356.2	347.4	1,863.7
Percent of heavy and chemical industries	30.9	11.8	35.4	9.3	19.2	10.7	47.3	9.6
Metal and nonferrous metals	368.4	977.3	870.7	2,136.7	865.7	4,269.9	91.8	6,164.6
Percent of heavy and chemical industries	42.4	27.2	47.6	28.5	61.8	33.6	12.5	31.8
Iron and steel	351.7	600.3	835.5	969.0	778.0	2,572.9	—	3,744.4
Percent of heavy and chemical industries	40.5	16.7	45.7	12.9	55.5	21.7		19.3
Transport equipment	142.6	526.0	142.6	1,798.3	91.4	2,250.6	98.6	5,422.2
Percent of heavy and chemical industries	16.4	14.7	7.8	24.0	6.5	17.7	13.4	28.0
Shipbuilding	36.0	414.5	125.3	1,327.7	41.8	1,132.5	—	4,243.1
Percent of heavy and chemical industries	4.1	11.6	6.8	17.7	3.0	8.9		21.9
General machinery[c]	55.3	414.5	112.4	697.9	165.2	1,233.5	137.9	1,616.0
Percent of heavy and chemical industries	6.4	11.6	6.1	9.3	11.8	9.7	18.8	8.3
Electrical machinery	33.9	1,247.5	55.7	2,170.9	9.6	3,595.0	58.9	4,330.5
Percent of heavy and chemical industries	3.9	34.8	3.0	28.9	0.7	28.3	8.0	22.3
Light industries	355.9	7,381.3	438.3	12,457.5	342.6	16,738.3	139.3	19,555.9
Percent of manufacturing	29.1	67.3	19.3	62.4	19.7	56.8	15.9	50.2

a. Standard International Trade Classification (SITC), 33, 5, 67, 68, 69, 7, and 86.

b. Exports include petroleum and petroleum products (SITC 33).

c. Exports include professional, scientific and controlling instruments, photographic and optical goods, watches and clocks (SITC 86).

Sources: Bank of Korea, Economic Statistics Yearbook, various issues; and data provided by Bank of Korea.

NOTES

1. The official figures do not include the actual or contingent foreign exchange liabilities incurred by overseas construction and trading subsidiaries of Korean companies and by foreign offices of Korean banks. It is not clear whether these liabilities should be included in the official tally. When they are, it is estimated that Korea's external debt amounted to anywhere from $46 billion to $48 billion at the end of 1983.

2. Korea experienced a sharp rise in its debt-service ratio in the 1970–72 period. The major concern at that time, however, was not debt management problems but the growing current account deficits. On this point, see Krueger (1979, p. 148).

3. According to Corden (1977, p. 50), the private sector can take care of itself, so the current account deficit that originates in the private sector's deficit is not a problem and not a matter for public policy concern. Although one may assume that decisions to incur a deficit in the private sector are optimal, one cannot make this assumption about the public sector. The current account deficit caused by the public sector's investment in excess of its savings is a balance of payments problem and may indeed be a matter for policy concern.

4. The foreign interest rate in table 11-4 does not include the spread, fees, and other costs, nor do domestic lending rates account for other hidden costs. The level of the curb market rate indicates that the domestic lending rate was kept below a realistic level, and thus the actual differentials to Korean borrowers were much higher than those shown in table 11-4.

5. The difference could persist so long because of the tight controls on capital inflow and fragmented and disorganized domestic capital markets. I return to this point in the discussion of efficiency and optimality of foreign borrowing in Korea.

6. For a discussion on the effect of monetary reform on saving, see Cole and Park (1983, chap. 7). One could also argue that the increase was in part due to expectations that the export expansion would be transitory.

7. The most difficult problem the Korean authorities faced at that time was the management of domestic liquidity arising from a rapid buildup of reserves and the subsequent increase in the money supply. After considering several alternatives, the authorities decided to accumulate foreign reserves, squeeze the supply of domestic credit, and, in time, reduce the deposit interest rates. To offset the expansion of the money supply as a result of the accumulations of reserves, they attempted to reduce the rate of expansion of domestic credit by raising the reserve requirements of the banking sector. As a result, they were mobilizing domestic financial savings (and real savings also) at a high rate of interest, converting them into foreign reserve assets, and in so doing lending to foreign borrowers at a low interest rate. The liquidity management policies amounted to subsidizing foreign savers at the expense of domestic savers.

8. According to the Bank of Korea's definition, based on Korea Standard Industrial Classification (KSIC), heavy and chemical industries include: 351, industrial chemicals; 353, petroleum products; 369, other nonmetallic mineral products; 371, iron and steel; 372, nonferrous metals; 381, fabricated metal products except machinery and equipment; 382, nonelectric machinery; 383, electrical machinery, apparatus, and appliances; 384, transport equipment; and 385, professional and scientific measuring and controlling equipment, photographic and optical products.

9. Over the years, exchange rate devaluation had become a politically unpopular and increasingly difficult measure to carry out. Because of real wage rigidity, it was argued that devaluation would simply be dissipated into price rises without improving export competitiveness. Understandably, firms oriented to the domestic market always resisted devaluations. In the 1970s, the opposition was joined by exporters who had accumulated large amounts of foreign loan liabilities. Exporters were concerned about possible large losses in their net real foreign asset positions associated with discontinuous and unexpected devaluations. While resisting devaluations, exporters demanded continuous increases in export subsidies—mostly financial—to compensate for the loss in competitiveness resulting from the overvalued currency; and the government acquiesced more often than not. It was therefore not surprising that Nam (1981, p. 194) found the real effective exchange rate inclusive of export subsidies was much more stable than the rate without the subsidies.

10. In 1974, the Taiwan economy grew by 1.1 percent. After moderate growth the following year, the economy picked up and registered 13.5 percent growth in 1976. For the next three years rapid growth was accompanied by stable prices. The annual rate of increase of the wholesale price index was about 3 percent on average, whereas it was almost 11 percent in Korea. This continuing inflation erased much of the gains from the expansionary policy in Korea. In hindsight, the critics may have been right, but one cannot fault policymakers for not having accurately predicted the future. If they had expected a rapid worldwide economic recovery, they might have taken a more conservative policy.

11. This conclusion is also backed by other indicators of debt-servicing capacity.

12. From 1954 to 1971, the real rate of return to capital in manufacturing rose steadily from about 12 to 26 percent. Although these estimates overstate the actual return, they suggest that even after adjusting for risks the rate of return to capital in Korea was far higher than the real borrowing cost. See Hong (1979, pp. 180–81), where the rate of return is defined as the ratio of incremental value added to investment and therefore represents the nonlabor rate of return.

13. The large accumulation of foreign reserves above a prudent level indicates the limited absorptive capacity of Korea during the 1960s.

14. This conclusion is based on a series of studies analyzing the cost of production and the international competitiveness of Korea's capital goods industries published by the Bank of Korea (1983).

15. The cause of excessive investment and the inefficiency of some of the heavy and chemical industries are discussed in detail by Park (1983).

16. Commercial foreign loans, and public loans as well, are often tied to purchases of capital and intermediate goods abroad. Short-term private capital inflows have been essentially a financing item.

17. The author is grateful to Rudiger Dornbusch for raising this question and proposing several explanations.

18. This decomposition of the current account is suggested by Bacha (1983).

19. Potential output data are kindly provided by Sang Woo Nam at the Korea Development Institute.

20. In our estimation of these changes the decomposition factors were calculated by using an average of current year and base period weights. For J_y, for example, we used ½ $(J_{yo} + J_{yt})$.

REFERENCES

Bacha, E. L. 1983. "Foreign debt, balance of payments, and growth prospects of developing countries." Paper prepared for UNCTAD Balance of Payments Adjustment Project. Processed.

Balassa, B. 1980. "Korea during the fifth five-year development plan: An advisory report." Paper prepared for the Government of Korea. Processed.

Bank of Korea. 1982. Summary report of the 1980 input-output table. Research Department. December. (Korean.)

———. 1983. Current state of Korea's industries. Series no. 83-1 to 83-9. (Korean.)

———. 1984. Foreign debt and domestic savings. March. (Korean.)

Cha, T. S., S. Y. Park, and N. K. Park. 1983. A comparative study of export competitiveness in Korea, Japan, and Taiwan. Seoul: Korea Institute of Economics and Technology. (Korean.)

Cole, D. C., and Y. C. Park. 1983. Financial development in Korea, 1945–78. Studies in the Modernization of the Republic of Korea, 1945–75. Cambridge, Mass.: Council on East Asian Studies, Harvard University.

Corden, W. M. 1977. Inflation, exchange rates and the world economy. Chicago: University of Chicago Press.

Dooley, M., W. Helkie, R. Tyron, and J. Underwood. 1983. "An analysis of external positions of eight developing countries through 1990." International Financial Discussion Paper no. 227. Washington, D.C.: Federal Reserve Board (August).

Frank, C., K. S. Kim, and L. Westphal. 1975. Foreign trade regimes and economic development: South Korea. New York: National Bureau of Economic Research.

Government of Korea. 1984. A revision of the fifth five-year development plan. Seoul. April. (Korean.)

Hong, W. T. 1979. Trade distortions and employment growth in Korea. Seoul: Korea Development Institute.

Kim, I. C. 1983. "Models of foreign debt accumulation and Korea's debt management." Korea Development Institute (KDI) Review (Fall). (Korean.)

Kim, K. S. 1979. "The pattern and sources of Korea's industrialization." Seoul: Korea Development Institute. KDI Working Paper.

Kim, K. S., and M. Roemer. 1979. Growth and structural transformation. Studies in the Modernization of the Republic of Korea, 1945–75. Cambridge, Mass.: Council on East Asian Studies, Harvard University.

Krueger, A. 1979. The development role of the foreign sector and aid. Studies in the Modernization of the Republic of Korea, 1945–75. Cambridge, Mass.: Council on East Asian Studies, Harvard University.

Martin, R., and M. Selowsky. 1981. Energy prices, substitution, and optimal borrowing in the short-run. World Bank Staff Working Paper no. 466. Washington, D.C.: July.

Morgan Guaranty Trust Company of New York. 1984. "Korea: Adjustment model for the 1980s?" World Financial Markets (March).

Nam, C. H. 1981. "Trade, industrial policies, and structure of protection in Korea." In Trade and growth of the advanced developing countries in the Pacific Basin, edited by W. T. Hong and L. Krause. Seoul: Korea Development Institute.

Park, Y. C. 1983. "South Korea's experience with industrial adjustment in the 1970s." ILO-ARTEP Working Papers. Bangkok. August.

———. 1984. "Resource allocation and government intervention." Honolulu, Hawaii: East-West Center. February. Processed.

Sachs, J. 1981. "Current account and macroeconomic adjustment in the 1970s." Brookings Papers on Economic Activity no. 1. Washington, D.C.: Brookings Institution.

Afterword

Issues, Institutions, and Reforms

D. J. Wood

While the contributions to this volume differ in many respects, the authors seem to agree that the familiar distinction between solvency and liquidity problems is a lot trickier than is commonly supposed. The distinction is seen as being sensitive not only to the assumptions one makes about the global economy—the rate of OECD growth and the price of oil, for instance—but also to the "rules of the game" that are assumed to apply to international lending and debt restructuring. Krugman and Simonsen argue quite persuasively, in my view, that these rules should continue to provide for cooperative rather than competitive pricing solutions when creditor confidence is abruptly lost. Swoboda, who tries to look beyond the current set of troubles, gives greater weight to strengthening market mechanisms. But all are agreed that the existing rules (or approaches) can be, and should be, improved.

I agree with this assessment and would like to elaborate on a few points. First, there is the question of burden-sharing in the context of debt restructuring. What should guide the level of contribution provided by the debtor country (in the form of a surplus on goods and services), by the commercial creditors (in the form of loans in excess of what would be individually profitable), and by official sources? In the case of some of the major Latin American borrowers, for example, the surplus on goods and services financed about 40 percent of interest payments due in 1983, while the exposure of commercial lenders increased by about 7 percent. Were these contributions about right? How does one decide?

The analytical frameworks suggested by Simonsen and Krugman would seem to require that the increase in the exposure of the commercial banks be somewhat less than the interest due to these banks. Otherwise the banks lose the justification that they are at least getting something back for agreeing to an increase in exposure. But how much less? Even for the large banks that are willing to stay in for the long haul, it is no doubt important that their overall exposure in the heavy debtor countries decline in relation to other assets and to their capital. A growth in exposure of less than 10 percent would be strongly desired by the banks on this ground alone, even if the average interest rate on their claims is much higher than 10 percent. Moreover, the consolidation of private sector and public sector debt in some countries has made sovereign risk exposure grow more rapidly than would otherwise be the case, and this too will give the banks an incentive to widen the gap. Finally, of course, there is the free-rider problem which the papers collected here quite properly highlight.

The proportion of the interest burden that the commercial banks as a group are likely to find acceptable may thus be expected to decline as the average interest rate on outstanding claims rises above the rate of growth of their overall balance sheets. Tight money adds to pressure not only via its impact on the interest rate but also via its impact on the growth in bank assets and capital.

The threat that this poses to successful negotiations will depend, of course, on the contribution made by the debtor country's surplus on goods and services. As several authors have noted here, the willingness of borrowing countries to accept such a surplus, and more particularly to allow this surplus to finance a substantial fraction of the interest payable, will depend on the social and political costs of achieving the surplus as well as on the future gains to the debtor country expected from unimpaired access to trade and capital markets.

The weighing of costs and benefits in this kind of situation is likely to be very much influenced by perceptions of whether the negotiations are handled in a constructive way or in a confrontational way. In contrast to the typical situation in which a debtor country is asked to adjust to impersonal market realities, the adjustment called for in the current wave of debt restructuring is based on a less impersonal and less market-driven estimate: namely, the estimate of what banks as a group will tolerate under the pressure of moral suasion from their authorities. This clearly adds to the risk of the negotiations becoming polarized.

Moreover, as Krugman observes, the risk of the negotiations breaking down is higher the more frequently the issue is joined and the longer nonmarket solutions are required. He calls attention in this regard to the possibility of the free-rider problem intensifying over time, thus causing commercial banks to seek a declining share of the restructuring burden. I myself would give even greater weight to the social and political costs of maintaining a trade surplus for an extended period. Austerity—even very severe austerity—can be justified as a response to crisis. But there must be light at the end of the tunnel.

The pressures implicit in this diagnosis of the negotiating positions of commercial creditors and borrowing countries seem to point to an increasing role for official finance and for official action that fosters collaborative rather than confrontational responses. Unless the trade environment for major debtors improves beyond current expectations, one can expect mounting difficulties in covering interest payments through the combination of increased commercial bank exposure and a surplus on goods and services. Official finance can help keep the pressures from becoming unmanageable.

Under the heading of official finance I would include not only the IMF and the World Bank, but also the regional banks and the export credit agencies. Each of these sources has its own distinct role to play. In the case of the World Bank, its net transfers are small in relation to overall resource flows to the major debtors. This fiscal year, for example, its net disbursements to Brazil and Mexico together are likely to total about $1 billion. This sum could drop to less than half of the current level by fiscal 1987 if new lending is constrained by a shortage of capital; or it could roughly double if the proportion of fast-disbursing loans were to increase sharply even in the context of quite modest growth in the level of new commitments. While neither of these extreme cases is perhaps very likely, a variation of even a few hundred million dollars could be significant at the margin either in alleviating or exacerbating the pressures I have cited. Of course, taking account of potential resource flows from other official sources only reinforces this point.

Krugman's concern with the subsidy implicit in official action is somewhat exaggerated—at least as it applies to the World Bank. It, among others, has traditionally been accorded a preferred creditor status in the event of debt rescheduling. As long as this situation continues, additional financing by the Bank does not substitute for risk that would otherwise be borne by commercial lenders or borrowing countries. There is admittedly a degree of public subsidy implicit in the Bank's use of the callable capital provided by shareholders. This subsidy—which I think is rather different from what Krugman has in mind—benefits only the borrowing country.

The contribution of official sources—whether subsidized or not—is not the only way they help resolve the financing problem. As Simonsen observes, they must also deal with policy aspects which may be critical in maximizing the likelihood of a favorable outcome. His analytical framework concentrates on increasing the rate of growth of exports (X) and decreasing the average interest rate on outstanding debt (I). The theme of increasing X is very much music to the ears in the World Bank. I will, however, defer to Anne Krueger on this topic, since it is a subject I know little about and she knows a great deal. On the theme of decreasing I, the ideas put forward are a very mixed bag.

Capitalizing interest attracts much attention, and it may be administratively convenient since it may permit some banks to sidestep the embarrassment of committing new funds to a troubled borrower and may also finesse arguments over the spread to be charged. But apart from these administrative conveniences—which must, of course, be set against the regulatory problems—this step does not seem to be fundamentally much different from the commitment of new funds and, as such, is unlikely to alter the negotiating positions of either creditors or debtors.

Encouraging risk capital is another frequent theme. Although I certainly agree with the desirability of encouraging this type of financing, it seems important to conceptualize foreign direct investment not as a reduction of I, but rather as a transformation which makes part of I better correlated with debt-servicing capacity. This improved correlation—which is roughly analogous to better management of X − I—is a worthwhile objective. The same objective may also be pursued by more active management of the currency exposures and inflation-rate-based exposures that exist implicitly in the difference between X and I.

The issuance of IMF special drawing rights (SDRs) as an alternative to debt-financed increases in reserves is financially attractive because it can help alleviate pressure on exposure limits. In addition, SDRs are likely to be less expensive than commercial borrowing—at least for the category of countries we are considering. It should be recognized, however, that the reduction in I attributable to an SDR allocation is mainly a reduction in gross interest expenditures (assuming the SDRs are held in reserves) rather than a reduction in net interest payments.

My cautionary comments on these various ideas are not meant to suggest that there is little scope for improvement on the financing side of the debt problem. I therefore conclude with some observations on types of improvements which I think are worth pursuing.

In retrospect it is clear that too much reliance was placed on a single financing instrument, the syndicated bank loan. Swoboda is, in my view, entirely correct in pointing to the need to encourage a diversity of instruments. The small banks that acquired participation in syndicated loans on the basis of an attractive spread and the reputation of the lead manager were not buying what they thought they were buying. Their eventual exit from the business will no doubt come as a relief to them and ought to be welcomed as a contribution to increased soundness of the system.

For the future, creditors that expect liquidity in their claims should not expect it to flow from a shortened maturity profile. It will come instead from contractual arrangements that provide for a takeout (such as a line of credit or a put option) in the event of crisis or from the existence of a well-functioning market for the type of security they acquire.

To this extent, I am entirely in agreement with Swoboda, but I part company with him in his vision of all commercial bank loans becoming much more akin to marketable securities. The core sovereign lending of the major commercial banks ought to remain in the form of loans that are not readily marketable, and the accounting value of those loans ought to be stable unless there is a serious question about the servicing of the loans at remunerative rates of interest. The banks that choose to be in this business ought to recognize that major reductions in their exposure cannot be achieved quickly and may not be achieved at all—except at very high penalties—in the event of a generalized crisis of confidence. The instuments these banks use for the core of their business should reflect this reality. As the architects say, form should follow function.

This is not to say that adjustments in exposure at the margin should not be facilitated. As an alternative to a secondary market in bank loans, consideration could be given to a floating rate instrument with a new final maturity (that is, a consol), along the lines of what was issued by a U.K. bank in April 1984. This would presumably yield a somewhat lower return than an ordinary bank loan because of its greater liquidity to the creditors.

Why try to perpetuate a sizable volume of ordinary bank lending? Why not go the whole way, as Swoboda suggests? The basic reason is that there is little or no prospect of providing adequate liquidity "backstopping" to a market that enhances the bulk of current commercial bank exposure. Without such backstopping, the market would be highly volatile—almost certainly destructively so.

In theory, of course, a country could finance itself entirely with equity instruments or debt of very long maturity. But the main virtue of this theoretical construct is to make clear just how far reality is from that ideal. For the foreseeable future, there is going to be a rollover risk that debtor countries will not be able to manage with their own resources. All creditors know this. Hence the only way to avoid a "run on the bank" in the event of a serious shock is to have a liquidity backstop that is large in relation to what creditors could withdraw (that is, refuse to roll over).

Such a volume of liquidity is not available now—nor is it in prospect. The resources of the IMF can deal with crises that do not involve substantial or prolonged alteration in the willingness of commercial banks to lend. But if the banks' willingness to roll over loans is seriously reduced, the requisite liquidity is just not available. Rather than advocating a structure that requires a volume of liquidity that is quite unlikely to materialize, I would urge development of a more diversified financial structure in which the degree of liquidity accorded commercial creditors varies. The core lending of the major banks will continue to be relatively illiquid, whatever nominal maturity these loans may carry. A modest security market may be feasible to facilitate adjustments in this exposure at the margin. Official support could well be helpful in developing such a market. Liquidity would thus be achieved, albeit in association with the risk of variation in market price. Finally, there ought to be opportunities for investors who demand liquidity and limited market risk, although this too will come at a price—namely, acceptance of lower returns.

The transition from the financing structure of the 1970s to some modified and, one hopes, improved structure is unlikely to be smooth or simple. Just as official institutions have a role to play in building Krugman's "ramp," they ought also to be concerned with shoring up the foundations of the structure on the other side.

Prospects and Proposals

Anne O. Krueger

This volume provides a first-rate diagnosis of the debt issue and an analysis of the ability of current institutional arrangements to cope satisfactorily with potential problems. Each of the chapters covers a multitude of issues pertaining to the debt problem, and each has a number of insights worthy of note. I wish to focus on the proposals for action and attempt to delineate the underlying assumptions that lead the authors to their somewhat different results and, on occasion, lead me to differ with the authors.

There are four fundamental questions to which answers may legitimately differ. The answers will determine one's view of the debt problem and of alternative solutions (ranging from the view that the problem is already largely resolved to the need for new instruments for containing the problem).

The questions are : What is the productivity of a capital inflow to a developing country? What were the causes of the rapid increase in the number of countries with debt-servicing difficulties? What is the prospect for the evolution of the international economy over the next five to ten years? What forms should highly productive capital inflows take (assuming that the answer to the first question is positive)? I propose to address selected aspects of each of these questions in turn.

Turning to the first question, I take the evidence to be overwhelming that, historically, capital flows from highly developed areas to less developed areas have represented an efficient allocation of world resources. Indeed, private capital flows to developing countries emerged in the 1960s and 1970s (before the first oil price increase in 1973) as an efficient response of the international financial market to a profitable opportunity. Although it is possible to interpret the post-1973 increase in lending to developing countries as a one-time and, possibly, unwarranted event, the alternative view has more appeal. That is, the success of some developing countries in raising their living standards and savings rates permitted them to shift from reliance on concessional assistance (which undoubtedly contributed to that success) to greater reliance on private capital markets. Stated in yet another way, the private financial market responded to underlying "real" conditions. On that interpretation, in countries that attain certain minimal preconditions (a literate and somewhat experienced labor force, infrastructural development, and the like) and that gear their domestic macroeconomic policies (especially those affecting the exchange rate and the interest rate) to growth and efficient resource allocation, there will be abundant profitable investment opportunities—far more than can be financed domestically, even with a high domestic savings rate. Under these circumstances, a capital inflow is efficient from the viewpoint of world resource allocation and also from the viewpoint of the individual country.

Private international capital flows, seen in that light, can be regarded as an indication of success with development: only countries that have attained a certain minimum level of development can rely on the private capital market. From that proposition, it follows that the emergence of private commercial debt, which is after all a reflection of cumulative past capital flows, was a phenomenon to be expected and welcomed. Indeed, one would expect and hope that private net capital flows would resume and increase in importance in the decades ahead. If there are high rates of return on additional investment in developing countries and those flows do not materialize, it will be a symptom of market failure.

In recent years, however, an additional question has arisen: what is the level of the world's real interest rate? A major question affecting the future of the entire international economy is the likely level of real interest rates over the next decade. I ignore the nominal rate, largely because rates of price increase can, by definition, be expected to be equal to the difference between the real and the nominal rate. For most developing countries, the net effect of a one percentage point increase in world prices of commodities and the resulting rise in nominal interest rates is an improvement in their debt service ratio. That is, interest payments rise by less than export earnings so that both the debt service ratio and the real value of outstanding debt decline.

Historically, the real rate of interest has stayed in the 3–5 percent range; only in recent years has it been higher. For developing countries, which faced declines of 4–5 percent a year in their export prices, the 14–16 percent nominal interest rates of 1981–83 represented incredible real rates of interest. While no one contemplates a return to real rates of interest in the 15–20 percent range, it surely makes a significant difference whether the real rate of interest at which developing countries can obtain additional capital resources is 3–5 percent or 7–10 percent. Clearly, the size of the warranted capital inflow would be far smaller if the higher rates should prevail. Indeed, the above statements about the desirability and efficiency of capital inflows were predicated on the assumption that real interest rates would remain in the 3–5 percent range. If the world is entering a new era, with real rates of interest at more than double their historical levels, it is arguable whether, and how much, additional net capital flows to developing countries would be economical. Thus, the contribution that private capital flows can make to the growth of developing countries in the future will hinge crucially on the real rate of interest. If real rates remain around 8–10 percent or higher, Simonsen is probably empirically correct in his judgment that countries such as Brazil should not resume net borrowing in excess of their interest obligations. If, however, real rates return to their historical 3–5 percent range, I suspect that all reasonable observers would expect there to be many more profitable uses of capital in countries such as Brazil than can be financed out of domestic savings, even if appropriate incentives are given to savers.

That much said, however, there is another point: while borrowing (or other forms of capital inflow) is economically efficient when the expected rate of return on additional investment exceeds the cost of the resources, all borrowing, or indeed all capital flows, is not necessarily very productive in practice. Individuals can borrow either to enhance their earning capacity (thereby raising their future income levels) or to finance current consumption in excess of current income (thereby reducing future income levels). Countries, too, can accumulate liabilities for either reason. Since there is ample evidence that the rate of return on virtually all investments in a given country is significantly affected by overall macroeconomic policies, the distinction between "productive" and "unproductive" uses of funds is much more difficult in the case of loans to foreign countries than in the case of loans to individuals.

We are now at a point where we can address the second question: the causes of the current difficulties. Any assessment of the borrowing pattern of the developing countries in the 1970s suggests that some countries were resorting to the private international capital market to augment their already healthy savings rates because productive investment opportunities abounded (Korea may well be the most notable case in point). Others borrowed to finance essentially unsustainable consumption patterns, rather than adjust their economies to the post-1973 changes in the international economy (Turkey is one obvious example).

What happened after the second oil price increase? In 1979 many developing countries had much higher levels of outstanding debt relative to their ability to finance it than they had had in 1973 when the first oil price shock occurred; the ensuing recession was considerably longer and more severe than had been anticipated; and real rates of interest rose dramatically. The result was that a number of countries experienced debt-servicing difficulties at about the same time. Under alternative circumstances, some of these countries might have been able to adjust their monetary, fiscal, and exchange rate policies without a debt-servicing crisis. Others would sooner or later have faced debt-servicing difficulties, but these would surely have been spaced over a longer period and seen as individual episodes (as was the Turkish debt rescheduling of January 1980), rather than as part of an international "financial crisis."

From the vantage point of the developing countries (and probably also for an efficient allocation of world resources), it is hoped that net international lending will resume should the real interest rate reach more normal levels in the long run. If it does, and if more and more developing countries attain the necessary minimum level of development to become creditworthy in private markets, debt reschedulings for individual countries may still be necessary from time to time. And, should another unexpectedly prolonged and deep recession occur at some future date, it is likely that debt-servicing difficulties will again be widespread. Thus, in answer to the second question posed, I conclude that the "debt crisis" was in reality a number of individual situations, all of which came to a head with the recession and high real interest rates of the early 1980s. Some would have occurred at later dates in a more buoyant international economy, while others would have been manageable with policy changes but without rescheduling.

We can now turn to the third question: what are the prospects for the international economy? Clearly, the current debt-servicing ratios of some developing countries are too high. As Simonsen has pointed out, the rate at which debt service ratios can move toward more sustainable levels is the difference between the rate of growth of foreign exchange earnings on current account and the rate at which the debt service burden grows. If interest rates are constant, the debt service ratio can fall either because the rate of growth of foreign exchange receipts is high or because countries suppress their imports so much that their current accounts improve despite stagnant export earnings. Most observers agree that the latter has already happened to an extent that is inconsistent with long-run sustainability of debt service obligations, and further compression will likely be accompanied by falling levels of income.

For the developing countries as a group, it is likely that their export earnings will grow at a rate slightly in excess of the rate of growth of OECD trade, since their share has been rising over time. However, the prospects for growth of export earnings hinge crucially on the rate of growth of OECD trade (in terms of value, as well as volume). If growth is sluggish, not only will protectionist tendencies in developed countries be stronger, but sluggish growth itself will make export expansion more difficult for the developing countries. To be more specific, if OECD real growth averages, say, 3.5 percent, a growth rate of world trade of about 5 percent would be quite consistent with past relationships between trade and national incomes. With 5 percent growth of world trade, developing countries could increase their trade at an annual rate of at least 6 percent. If that 6 percent is combined with average increases in commodity prices of about 5 percent a year, it would imply that developing countries could expand their export earnings at about 11–12 percent annually.

Total debt could therefore increase at a rate of 7–8 percent and still be consistent with a gradually falling debt service ratio. For different countries, after an interval of time, more rapid rates of growth of debt could once again be sustained once debt service ratios have been restored. Whether those rates of increase would permit a net transfer of resources to developing countries during the transition period depends crucially on the nominal and real interest rates, a subject which will be addressed below. For present purposes, let us suppose instead that OECD growth averaged 2 percent (a relatively bleak outlook) and world trade grew at only 3 percent annually. Even with the same 5 percent annual increase in the prices of developing countries' exportables, debt could grow only at around 5 percent annually if debt service ratios were to reach sustainable long-term levels. Given prospective rates of interest, that outcome would surely imply negative net transfers of resources over a considerable period. That, in turn, would imply relatively slow expansion of imports in many developing countries, with adverse implications for the ability of developing countries to resume growth.

Finally, there is the question of the optimal composition of capital inflows. This is a complicated question and one that cannot be satisfactorily addressed here. Let me simply make a few points. First, it is clear the composition of inflows shifted during the 1970s. While the focus of this volume is largely on Latin American debt, for another class of debtors (mostly in Africa), with much lower debt service ratios, the ability to service debt seems if anything more questionable than for countries with high debt service ratios. The lesson here seems clear: very low-income countries are not viable candidates for medium- and long-term debt except at highly concessional terms; their development prospects are crucially dependent upon the availability of concessional assistance. (The Simonsen proposal for tax-free World Bank bonds is in reality a proposal for a particular means of obtaining additional concessional assistance.)

A second point has to do with the maturity structure of debt. To the extent that bank lending of five to ten years' maturity financed development projects with twenty- to thirty-year payoff periods, there would have been a problem in matching payments against returns on projects even in a noninflationary environment. With inflation, however, higher nominal interest rates imply the implicit repayment of a higher fraction of the principal of the debt in an earlier period. Suppose, for example, the real rate of interest is 3 percent, reflecting a rate of inflation of 10 percent and a nominal rate of interest of 13. Then 10 percent of the principal is implicitly paid off in the first year of the loan through the inflation premium built into the interest payments.

One lesson of the 1970s is that increased attention will have to be paid to the maturity structure of the debt. Currently, over 70 percent of the principal on the outstanding medium- and long-term public and publicly guaranteed debt of the developing countries is scheduled to be repaid by the end of 1987. Not only is such a schedule infeasible, it is also undesirable on efficiency grounds: the size of the implied shift in current account balances is staggering.

Developing countries may wish to reconsider their earlier preference for borrowing over equity foreign investments. While the latter may have some disadvantages, they imply a very different sharing of risks from that entailed in borrowing or bond financing: when earnings decline (for whatever reason), interest payments on debt nonetheless continue. When equity capital is involved, reduced earnings imply reduced financing obligations.

Given these considerations, what are the implications for alternative proposals for reform of financing? As pointed out by Krugman, there is a clear case for recognizing that annual rescheduling is in no one's interest: it is unrealistic, it creates false expectations, and it drains developing countries of some of their top economic policymaking talent for short-term fire fighting. Rescheduling onto a more satisfactory long-term footing would do much to realign the maturity structure of the debt with the payout period of development projects—itself highly desirable.

In considering proposals which go beyond this, however, one principle seems sufficiently important to repeat: a number of proposals for making the debt-overhang problem manageable would simultaneously reduce the likelihood that net capital inflows to developing countries will resume in due course. Given a better-than-even-money chance that the real interest rate will return to historical levels, and given the contribution that the resumption of positive net capital flows could make to development prospects, it seems patently evident that reform proposals should be evaluated, at least in the beginning, on the basis of whether they would endanger prospects for resuming net lending. Since reforms addressing the overhang would at best ameliorate stressful situations for a year or two, and since the costs of forgoing possible future inflows are substantially greater than that, even for the currently heavily indebted countries, I would conclude that any reform that prejudices new net lending is undesirable. For that reason, I concur with Simonsen and Krugman that "wholesale" reforms of the system are probably unwise.

There are, however, a number of things that could happen, and interesting questions as to why they have not. First, one wonders why bonds or loans have not been indexed so that the repayment period is not affected by inflation under floating-rate debt. Indeed, it is an interesting question why fixed nominal repayment schedules have not been developed, under which outstanding principal would automatically increase at high interest rates. Other ways to make debt more manageable and control the uncertainties of high interest rates are also devisable. Recent experiences of the developing countries suggest that such instruments could benefit them, without significant costs to the lenders.

I conclude by agreeing with Krugman, Simonsen, and Swoboda: the current international financial system, despite its defects, offers enough benefits to all parties that wholesale reform is unwarranted, as it could endanger the future flow of benefits from international capital flows. If the world economy resumes a satisfactory rate of growth quickly, and especially if the real interest rate returns to more normal levels, we may well hear more about the debt problems of developing countries in the years to come as more of them become sufficiently developed to gain access to private capital markets. That would be a symptom of success in development, although problems would go along with that.

There is no denying that a number of developing countries will have some difficult years until their debt service obligations reach more sustainable levels. Whether those years will be merely difficult or instead will be impossible will depend on the international economy. If the reasonably optimistic outlook proves to be correct, growth in heavily indebted developing countries may resume in 1984 and gradually accelerate as their debt service situation improves. Should, however, the growth of world trade be slower and the real rate of interest higher, the "debt crisis" will pale into insignificance when contrasted with the crisis of growth that will be engendered for the developing countries.

The full range of World Bank publications, both free and for sale, is described in the Catalog of Publications; the continuing research program is outlined in Abstracts of Current Studies. Both booklets are updated annually; the most recent edition of each is available without charge from the Publications Sales Unit, Dept. B, The World Bank, 1818 H Streets, N.W., Washington, D.C. 20433, U.S.A.